Philosophical and Sociological Reflections on Labour Law in Times of Crisis

Philosophical and Sociological Reflections on Labour Law in Times of Crisis

Edited by

Eduardo von Adamovich
and Marcel Zernikow

Cambridge
Scholars
Publishing

Philosophical and Sociological Reflections on Labour Law in Times of Crisis

Edited by Eduardo von Adamovich and Marcel Zernikow

This book first published 2022

Cambridge Scholars Publishing

Lady Stephenson Library, Newcastle upon Tyne, NE6 2PA, UK

British Library Cataloguing in Publication Data
A catalogue record for this book is available from the British Library

ISBN (10): 1-5275-8349-X
ISBN (13): 978-1-5275-8349-8

TABLE OF CONTENTS

Part 2. The Essence of Labour Law: On Universal Principles and Diverging Legal Rules

A. ***Regional or Country-Specific Reports***

B. ***Universal Principles***

ACKNOWLEDGEMENT

The University Bretagne Sud (UBS) offered financial support for the publication fees related to proofreading of the present book.

INTRODUCTION

Starting from the assertion that crisis is part of the essence of labour law, this international compendium of essays is written by labour law researchers from different countries, who accepted the challenge of critically reflecting on the same disciplinary branch. Although the global health crisis related to Covid-19 was only in its beginning stages when the call for contributions to the present book was launched, it was clear that this crisis would have further social and economic consequences in all countries. Despite the different ways in which the overwhelming effect manifests in each country, it is certain that this period will scar the juridical sector. This observation also justifies the temptation to reflect on labour law from a global point of view. Given that work guarantees subsistence for a considerable part of the population in different states, labour law has an undeniable societal and economic impact and therefore is necessarily affected by the current crisis.

The connecting point between all of the contributions collected here is that they apply reflections from other disciplines, mainly philosophy, sociology or economy, to demonstrate what characterises labour law as a branch of the discipline. We considered this approach to be relevant before the current crisis, which is susceptible to bringing into question major principles and institutions of labour law. However, it is also true that labour law as such has survived different crises thanks to safeguards which are part of its essence and make it resist. From this point of view, the exercise here was for authors to identify the existing theoretical foundations of labour law in their legal systems by comparing experiences of crises from the present and the past. To summarise the method of this collective book, it is necessarily interdisciplinary. As it assembles contributions from labour lawyers who reflect on their own and/or various other legal systems at the same time, this compendium also has an important multicultural character and might contribute to comparative law.

These reflections essentially lead to the conclusion that labour law has been in constant transformation since its emergence. Starting with a theoretical approach, we seek to establish an overview of the theories which allow us to regard labour law as such. Among theories of the twentieth century, one may find those based on constitutional law and which see an order beyond the state, or even an order anchored in the latter. They were motivated by the fact that the new categories had quickly found their place in the constitutions of Mexico (1917), Russia (1918) and Germany (1919), for example. This theoretical renewal could be retrospectively criticised, insofar as it was interpreted as giving rise to theories which, for some, also addressed authoritarian corporate thought. With the fall of authoritarian regimes and the predominance of a liberal democratic order, labour law was called upon to align with a new theoretical construction which was initially very beneficial, both in Europe and in South America. This context ended, however, in the 1970s or 1980s when the financial crisis led to restrictions on social rights. A new theoretical framework emerged which may still have repercussions today, consisting precisely of making social rights conditional on economic and financial satisfaction. This last model unfortunately led to the flexibilization of labour law and the abolition of social rights which had formerly been based on these same constitutions. Is there not a great risk that idealist constitutionalism in labour law imposes models of society which, in fact, do not exist? From the point of view of natural law, some authors may reflect on the principles which bring them to the conclusion that human dignity, for example, should exist irrespective of any legislative intervention. Does the current crisis, as a fact that defies hitherto almost uncontested legal constructions, not remind us of the need for questioning? To conclude, contributors might argue that labour law's essence is beyond positive law and even the constitutional systems that arose in welfare societies.

To reach a conclusion on the actual questions labour law has to solve nowadays, it may also be of interest to remember the societal circumstances in which labour law took its impetus. Was it not born out of the emergence of the "social question"? In the age of industrialisation, the discovery of mass production, urbanization and technological advances altered realities. These circumstances created fertile ground for discourse on the social role of private law. If these reflections remained partially unheard and could not directly influence positive law, they were nonetheless fundamental to the development of labour law as such. This also explains why labour law was — and still is — doomed to develop outside legislative formalism. Originally established as a set of rules which neither emanated from the state nor directly resulted from private autonomy, labour law can be considered as the result of political struggles between opposing forces: employees on one side, employers on the other. This specificity of labour law is reflected, among other things, in a "panel" of sources ranging from legislative standards to professional practices, including collective autonomy and the productive force of unions. Thus, sources can serve as a starting point for researching the place of labour law within the discipline of law. However, the study should also verify current legal problems. The advantage of the sociological point of view may be that it helps us verify the presuppositions put forward according to current circumstances. Eventually, the sociological point of view will bring us to the conclusion that labour law will be called upon to adapt as realities change.

Given the aforementioned theoretical foundations, it is of the utmost importance to remind ourselves that renewing a branch of a discipline does not necessarily equal devastation. However, the ambition of considering social realities is likely to have caused misunderstandings about the (legal) normativity of labour law. With positivist legalistic thought dominant at the time of its advent, labour law might have constituted a real atavism. Preparing the way for a new understanding, Gustav Radbruch asked the question: What role do laws – in the original sense of the term – play among all types of norms, and according to our absolute vision of the world? In this provocative formulation one may identify the question about the essence of law. This question targets *a fortiori* the emancipatory question if labour law is not part of law. It may even be answered positively by considering that labour law overcomes the abstract idealism of Kelsen's theory. Such a reading suggests an understanding of law that combines the sociological, political and economic forces from which it emerges. This might bring us closer to various theoretical attempts such as the three-dimensional theory of law by the Brazilian philosopher, Miguel Reale. According to the latter, law is expressed in conjunction with fact, value and norm.

More generally, contributors to this book should assume the main task of academics in this legal area, who are constantly in search of new methods to reconcile the protection of workers' social benefits with the dynamics of business, environmental preservation and the struggle for greater equality. However, an ongoing adaptation process needs theoretical frameworks more than ever. This book aims to deliver those by assembling philosophical and sociological foundations of the law as a discipline and labour law in particular.

The first part collects together the theoretical bases from philosophy and sociology which are required for reflecting on labour law. The book then goes on to demonstrate the exhausting effects of global financial and health crises, as well as technological demands, on traditional institutes of legal protection in this area.

By including country and regional reports, the second part aims to draw out how the legal discipline has mobilized institutes and concepts to struggle with the deepening social inequalities resulting from societal transformations. As similar challenges arise – to a different extent – in all jurisdictions, this book also tries to explore new patterns of thinking from a global point of view by illustrating universal principles to deal with these challenges. As emphasised before, the objective of this book is to provide incentives to leave the habitual framework of legal thought.

This brings us to the third part which illustrates recent economic evolutions (fragmentation and flexibility), society (minorities and migration) and technology (online platforms and new kinds of work relationships). In light of these impacts, the question to be answered is: What are the characteristics of contemporary labour law? Examples of these transformations (platform work, robots, etc.) help us to rethink labour law in the new and constant context of crisis. While we have taken the current crisis as a starting point which reveals the necessity for rethinking and developing labour law further, the main concern is broader.

Therefore, the fourth part reminds us that, if we take these facts seriously, we are able to shape the future of work. Although some authors imagine irreversible transformations of this branch of the discipline, others remind us to stick to the ideas that initially underlay the foundation of labour law. While the aforementioned challenges could be considered as new parameters to be taken into account, they should not affect the essence – and thus the existence – of labour law itself.

Part 1.

Theoretical Bases for Reflecting on Labour Law: Lessons from Philosophy and the Sociology of Law

CHAPTER 1

SOME REFLECTIONS ON THE PHILOSOPHY OF LAW AND LABOUR LAW

GIUSEPPE CASALE

Philosophy has questioned the law since the time of the ancient Greeks. Legal philosophy (or the philosophy of law) is a branch of philosophy and, like ethics and political philosophy, is a part of the philosophy of practical reason (Finnis 2014). The aim of the philosophy of law is to investigate the nature of law, exploring its relation to human values, behaviours and political communities. The central task of legal philosophy is to seek a general explanation of the normativity of positive law. The philosophy of law thinks about law, inviting the interpreter to assume the future as a fundamental phenomenon of time (Heidegger 2005).

In general, the four major theories of legal philosophy are natural law, legal positivism, Marxism and realism. However, the philosophy of law becomes interrelated with labour law when we deal with the area of legal philosophy and legal interpretation.

Legal Philosophy and Legal Interpretation

Legal interpretation has always been the subject of great attention in academic debates. While it is considered a central activity of legal practitioners (e.g. judges), it is often overlooked in legal theories by philosophers. However, legal interpretation is not the only tool by which conclusions in the legal field are produced. For example, some authors argue about "a broad meaning of legal interpretation, which concerns all interpretative activities that take place in the legal field of experience" and "a narrow sense of legal interpretation […] which concerns interpretative activity focused on texts" (Villa 2010).

Labour disputes often revolve around problems of interpretation, as exemplified in cases of individual legally binding contracts or collective agreements. That said, the situation becomes even more complex when it is necessary to interpret labour law texts such as statutes or constitutional charters. It is commonly believed that through the activity of legal interpretation, the one who interprets (the court) must seek the intention of the drafter, but identifying such an intention is often very complicated. For example, labour laws are often written by groups of people for whom the subjects have no common intention; or in some texts of labour legislation or constitutional provisions it is possible to identify different types of intention (one general and one specific). Moreover, these labour laws govern future circumstances that have yet to occur and which are often not easily foreseeable (Bix 2012). In this regard, jurisprudence plays a fundamental role in legal interpretation. Jurisprudence, like the other branches of philosophy, can be divided into several categories. Of these, the three main ones are analytic jurisprudence, normative jurisprudence and critical theories of law (Coyle 2013).

Analytical Jurisprudence

Analytical jurisprudence can be defined as "a branch of legal positivism that attempts to provide analytical tools by which the law and legal concepts are most accurately and rigorously described. It involves the examination of legal reasoning, legal interpretation, and the efficacy of laws and legal systems"[1]. Also known as clarificatory jurisprudence, this category is composed of two interrelated spheres, known as "substantial" and "methodological." Before the 1980s, this was mostly known as "substantive," as it was characterised by the creation of theories with the aim of analysing the nature of law, the relationship between legal provisions and the system governed by laws and the relationship between morality and the law. Subsequently, this jurisprudence took a methodological turn characterised by the idea that philosophy aims to understand the nature of law. In this way, analytical jurisprudence has come to be considered as a conceptual analysis of law.[2] According to Bix, conceptual analysis in law is mainly related to two activities: a) "to explain what is important or essential about a class of objects" and b) "to establish an evaluative test for the concept-word" (Bix 1995, Himma 2021).

Analytical jurisprudence is a legal approach found in jurisprudence since the beginning of the 20th century and which has been utilised by a good

---

[1] The definition is given by Oxford Reference.

[2] Definition of analytical jurisprudence on Encyclopedia.com, www.encyclopedia.com

number of labour lawyers. It responds to the need for stability, which is opposed to the need for change, a theme that is expressed by the more sociological branch of philosophy. The incrementing relevance of this legal approach has created increasing interest among labour lawyers whose object of jurisprudence is positive law. In other words, labour law itself is made up of different laws, which give life to the bodies of other labour laws. These are underpinned by the principles which are relevant for the interpretation of jurisprudence. Among the same principles, which are generally common to several systems, a differentiation can be made between the necessary and the unnecessary. Necessary are, for example, definitions such as "right", "duty", "freedom" or distinctions such as that between laws which are promulgated and those which are not. The unnecessary are those whose presence is not essential for the functioning of the system, such as the distinction between "laws of people" and "laws of things" (Pound 1927). In this context, jurisprudence should concentrate only on the fundamental concepts of law, analysing them in its ordinary use in the professional field.

A real change in analytical jurisprudence was brought about in the second half of the 20th century, when Hart proposed that emerging linguistic theories should be taken into account in jurisprudential debates. Normally, in the legal process of understanding, the definition *"per genus et differentiam"* is used, but sometimes the application of this method is not possible. In fact, the lexicon used in the legal field is anomalous and differs profoundly from the words of the ordinary lexicon. This situation translates into uncertainty and perplexity due to the absence of a corresponding term in the material world. Represented from Hart's point of view, this is a weak point in analytical jurisprudence, which results in an attachment to definitions and the need for further explanations to be fully understood.

According to this philosopher of law, it was important to focus attention on linguistics, with a sociological approach to law, highlighting the benefits that jurisprudence would derive from linguistics itself. His intention was to analyse in a descriptive and prescriptive way the problems that arise in the specific context of the law, and to then solve them (Bix 1991). In this, one could find similarity with the spirit of labour law, notably that labour law needs other disciplines besides itself to be better defined (Hart 1957). Somehow, from a legal philosophy viewpoint, the indeterminacy of the law is eliminated by the interpretation and application of the law, two aspects that should be considered jointly and indissolubly (Viola 1974).

In essence, analytical jurisprudence does not provide a particular interpretation of legal terms. It limits itself to the assertion of a certain interpretation of a specific term, in the search for a solution to a problem. These particular decisions are up to the judge and not to the philosopher of law, who only has the task of highlighting when a given interpretation is logical and reasonable. In sum, the increasing interest in analytical jurisprudence has promoted the philosophical dimension of labour law, especially in the common law tradition (Lacey 2006).

Normative Jurisprudence

Normative jurisprudence "involves the examination of normative, evaluative, and otherwise prescriptive issues about the law, such as restrictions on freedom, obligations to obey the law, and the grounds for punishment" (Himma 2021). To this, it should be added: "Normative jurisprudence aims to reinvigorate normative legal scholarship that both criticizes positive law and suggests reforms on the basis of stated moral values and legalistic ideals" (West 2011). Normative jurisprudence questions general issues that contemplate the interaction between values and law, and can translate into what exists between labour law, politics and ethics. Even more, it encompasses issues related to constitutional principles and democracy in the workplace.

Normative jurisprudence is based on the consideration that stating the law is no different from saying what the law should be. The philosophers of normative jurisprudence believe that the law is not adequately explained without recourse to moral evaluations. As some legal philosophers have stated: "the task of characterizing law 'as it is'" is closely linked to an individual's understanding of how law morally should be (Himma 2015).

In this regard, labour lawyers are interested in three common themes of jurisprudence, notably the extent and modalities in which the laws can intervene in citizens' freedoms by limiting them; the nature of the obligation to obey the law; and the justification of the sanction in cases of the law being violated. In terms of the first point, criminal and civil laws limit the freedoms of human beings, but considering that human freedom deserves moral respect, it is necessary to identify the times and manner of these limitations. In this regard, Mill argues, "[T]he sole end for which mankind are warranted, individually or collectively, in interfering with the liberty of action of any of their number is self-protection. The only purpose for which power can rightfully be exercised over any member of a civilized community against his will is to prevent harm to others. His own good, either physical or moral, is not a sufficient warrant. Over himself, over his own body and mind, the individual is sovereign" (Mill 1906, 12f.). Limitations on freedom can occur based on different approaches. As a first example, one can take into consideration legal moralism, which delineates the limitation of freedom by the law as being justified only when it is used as an instrument for eliminating behaviour that is in conflict with collective morality.

Another approach is that of legal paternalism, which could be defined as the interference of the state in the behaviour of citizens for the wellbeing of the same. In cases such as when protecting the health and wellbeing of the human person, coercive intervention by the state, such as during the Covid-19 pandemic, is justified (Himma 2021).

Regarding the second issue, namely the nature of the obligation to obey the law, some authors believe that there is a moral obligation to obey the law for societies that are founded on social cooperation. This argument has received some criticisms, as it does not provide the explanation in relation to an obligation regardless of the content of the law, and citizens are not offered the possibility to refuse the benefits they derive from the law itself and its compliance. Other arguments are problematic too, such as that of consent as, in the case of the acceptance of benefits that cannot be refused, real consent is not implied (Himma 2021).

Critical Theories of Law

When examining the critical theories of law, which have their roots in Hegelian Marxism (Christodoulidis 2019), one could find an innovative approach to the more traditional forms of the philosophy of law (Himma 2015). Their starting point is realism. Boyles wrote, "it is a commonplace that to understand critical legal thought one must first understand legal realism" (Boyle 1985). A common and distinctive trait of the theories falling into this category is the rejection of any cognitive claim and doubt about legal knowledge. During the 1970s and 1980s, important debates of critical theorists mainly revolved around which concept of law was the best one (Balkin 2009). The liberal claim was that the law could not be apolitical and impartial, because it is understood as being a political tool that hides the reality characterised by oppression and domination (Sinclair 2010). The Critical Theories of Law marked a significant debate around the philosophy of law. Among others, mention should be made of critical legal studies, minority jurisprudence and women jurisprudence.

Critical Legal Studies

Critical legal studies is an intellectual movement which believes that the law is not free from moral values and politics. Members of the movement use the term politics not to mean "class struggle" but as a reference to the role of economic and social actors within society (Kennedy 1992). This point of view is reflected in their conception of jurisprudence, no longer seen as a system of accumulated wisdom over time, but as an unfair instrument of power. This movement is openly left wing and advances a project of change in society that it sees as unjust and unequal (West et al. 2020).

The movement attempts to expand Marxist ideas into a critique of traditional liberal jurisprudence. Their thinking is opposed to that of the realists who, according to them, underestimate the indeterminacy of the law. Such indeterminacy of the law creates a sort of internal inconsistency, which allows judges to justify conflicting results. The indeterminacy contrasts with democratic principles because it leaves a great deal of space for the interpretative power of judges, who find themselves not only interpreting the law but also constructing it. In doing so, they run counter to democratic principles, which establish that legislators make the law and are accountable to the electorate (Himma 2015). The movement reached its peak in the 1970s, when it was a reflection of the profound dissatisfaction with the state of legal doctrine which, at the time, was considered excessively conservative and far from the role it should have been occupying. The term conservative can be interpreted in a broader sense that does not take into account morality and the effects of injustices, and does not seek to change the status quo. Perhaps the most lasting contribution of critical legal studies is the consideration that even the set of constitutionally guaranteed rights (e.g. the right to equality, the right to sexual freedom, the right to privacy, etc.) are instruments of subordination. In fact, they have the effect of alienating us from each other, legitimising the conviction of the need for subordination to the ruling classes. Some legal philosophers developed precisely this point by stating that the result of these rights proposed by the liberal legal system is to make humans distrustful of each other, leading them to live a life of anxiety in fear of being stabbed in the back by the other (West 2011).

In this argument, it is possible to identify a common point given by the desire to modify the social structure. In this regard, it is possible to say that labour law has two souls: one "moral" and one "jurisprudential". The path of the first one is to alleviate a moral suffering while the second one is to intervene in the indeterminacy of the law to make it an instrument for the elimination of subordination (West 2011).

The critical legal studies movement, starting from the critique to liberalism, has developed a cultural legacy. Through the cultural critique, it is possible not only to understand the function of labour law, but also to reach a real understanding of its meaning. Precisely through this full understanding of the law, it is possible to render it an instrument of social transformation (Torres 1988). At this point it is interesting to see the position of Audain, who believes it is possible to identify within this movement at least six distinct criticisms and two sub-categories of criticisms. The first of these is the "neutrality critique", according to which there are no discourses that are politically neutral. The second one, called "indeterminacy critique", focuses on the indeterminacy of the legislative dictate with the aim of demonstrating it. Then, the "entrenchment critique" allows the scholar to demonstrate how the law is an instrument that keeps power in the hands of those who already have it and continues to fulfil their interests. The "ideals critique" leads the scholar to affirm that the instrument of the law is not suitable for achieving the ideal objective that it had set itself. Finally, the "power critique" demonstrates how knowledge of the legal object contributes to conferring power on those who possess it. Audain, as previously mentioned, also identifies two subsidiary categories: the "mystification critique" and the "constraining critique". The first leadss the philosopher to show how the law leads to the deception of others, while the second how it fails to limit the exercise of power (Audain 1992).

The Increasing Relevance of Legal Rationality in Labour Law

In this regard, in every labour law system there is persuasion to comply with the law. This is seen as necessary in order to avoid unpleasant consequences, in the sense that compliance is considered just. Obedience to rules is requested because they are issued in accordance with just procedures and they are based on valid general standards applicable to all individuals. In this way, the law appears as a neutral and rational body of rules supplemented by objective principles, which require universal respect.

This kind of rationality in the legitimation of power of the dominant interest encompasses not only practices in the workplace but also much slower-paced rationality in the area of labour relations. Historically, the domination of capital was asserted through the instrumentality of the absolute rule of the employer in the enterprise, as reflected in work rules and the system of sanctions applicable in the workplace. In previous years, large employers were anxious to remove the stigma attached to their profit-making activities, which endangered the life of children and women, so they started to support the movement for protective labour legislation.

In this sense, labour law is not the outcome of a single philosophy of the dominant classes but the product of conflicting ideologies, and hence of different approaches to legal philosophy. Among the most common ideologies, mention should be made of the ideology of self-help, the ideology of state help, the ideology of patriarchy, the ideology of social Christianity, and the ideology of socialism.

In assessing the influence of all these ideologies supported by philosophical thinking, one could argue that the development of labour law does not end with the enactment of specific legislation. The instrumental aspect of the law requires enforcement and the adjudication of disputes as well. The philosophy of law in its various interpretations continues to be of relevance. This can be seen in the way labour law is applied in a proactive manner where, increasingly, prevention and a conciliatory mode is preferred to enforcement and sanctions. In addition, this is connected to the way the philosophy of law is understood within the framework of labour law. Certainly, the positivist theories of law emphasise the neutral role of legal rules in maintaining the interests of all groups within the pre-established "rules of the game". This makes labour law more interactive with the philosophy of law, in the sense that it aspires to provide "just rules and procedures" to be applied in the workplace. In this regard, an example is provided by the increasing relevance of women's jurisprudence.

Women's Jurisprudence

With the term women's jurisprudence or feminist jurisprudence, we mean the "examination of the relationship between law and society from the point of view of all women" (Audain 1992). This implies the use of ideas and principles of feminism in law. Consequently, feminist theories are the key to reading feminist jurisprudence. Feminist jurisprudence as a field of law studies and theories began to develop in the 1960s. With its intervention, feminist jurisprudence seeks to correct legal theory and practices of the tradition. It focuses on the ways in which the law has been structured to deny women's experiences and needs. Although feminist jurisprudence can be divided into different schools of thought, it is generally agreed that they all have a common aspect, namely that feminist jurisprudence is centred on analysing the position occupied by women in a patriarchal society and on methods to eliminate this patriarchy. Precisely because of their critique of the system, the thinking of feminist jurisprudence is closely linked to that of critical legal studies (Lacey 1990).

Feminist theorists distrust the law as it is and start from three fundamental points. First, fundamental legal doctrines are made by men and therefore are characterised by a fundamental male bias, even in cases where they appear neutral. Second, the diversity of women's lives compared to those of men means that the theories proposed by them are inapplicable to women. Third, feminist theory requires that women produce theories from their own perspective and from their own experiences (Baer 2011). As in many cases, the law is unable to see the dangers women face and the needs they have (Sinclair 2010).

A recurring topic in feminist jurisprudence is concern around respecting rights and equality. In particular, there is concern around equal treatment in the workplace. The recurring issue to be answered is how women are treated at work. This is of particular interest to pregnant women. The viewpoint of Herma Hill Kay is especially interesting in this respect, according to whom it is important to protect women from the loss of equal opportunities that could come from pregnancy (Kay 1985, Burchard 2021). Precisely on this issue of pregnancy, the same author theorizes different approaches and develops arguments of discrimination between men and women and the rights that must be recognised for all. In this regard, worthy of note is the thought of Littleton, who believes that the presumption of a difference between men and women must be accepted and that the choice should focus not on eliminating it, but rather on its effects. Therefore, equality should work in the sense of eliminating the costs of these differences. Empowerment models follow this path, rejecting differences as irrelevant, hence "equality [...] is understood as what balances power for groups and individuals, and dismantles the ability of some to dominate others" (Burchard 2021).

The critique of feminist jurisprudence extends to overwhelming even the law of contracts. In fact, it is characterised by a cold language that excludes the private and family spheres, with the effect of further penalising women by condemning them to subordination (Letwin 2005).

One of the most problematic knots for feminist jurisprudence to resolve is the determination of damage. In fact, since the system is characterised by a strong patriarchal vision, it is difficult to recognise harm to women in the first place. Women's jurisprudence has allowed the debate to be shifted towards three acts that are harmful to women — rape, sexual harassment and beatings — which, in some cases, were previously not even really considered by the legal system to be crimes. Cases relating to these three harmful acts are often united by the same profiles, which brings attention to some problematic issues, such as the fact that it is often the female victim who is blamed. Women's jurisprudence also extends its investigation to the evaluation of whether or not it is possible to have legal neutrality, that is, if it is possible to be judged by legal practitioners only for one's own actions. Thus, all efforts should be made to the inclusion of the prejudices of the person who is called on to be judged (Burchard 2021).

Legal doctrine is the result of human behaviour. Women were previously excluded from the legislative process, which is why the law was filtered from the point of view of men. Women's jurisprudence first emerged during the same period in which women entered the legal sector either as judges or lawyers. The laws were thus modified to include the point of view of women. Despite these interventions, male prejudice remains in the system, which still leads the legal doctrine to respond more to the needs of men than women. Both scholars and legal professionals know there is still a long way to go until equality and fairness is achieved in this respect (Baer 2011).

Conclusion

The philosophy of law and labour law have always interacted and have their roots in the past. They have been able to adapt to the needs of different historical periods, becoming a vehicle for the expression of the needs of different social classes and their on-going demands. Philosophers who have dealt with legal debates have questioned the law and its function as well as its *raison d'être* since the times of the ancient Greeks, giving rise to different movements of thought. Legal philosophy is intertwined with legal interpretation, where jurisprudence becomes the main tool for the interpretation of the law. It is precisely in this context that philosophy shows its incredible relevance, both when it comes to analytical jurisprudence and normative jurisprudence, but above all when it comes to critical legal theories and the feminist approach, which bring to the fore social problems of profound actuality. All of this nurtures labour law. Thus, we can observe how, over the years, the study of the nature of jurisprudence has evolved into including a political dimension that goes beyond questions of morality and which endeavours to seek tangible and pragmatic answers to reality.

Overall, we can conclude that while jurisprudence and the legal system have evolved through time to meet the needs of societies, there is an increasing sense that political, social, economic and technological advancements will increasingly question, and thus demand, a rapid change to its status quo. If the legal apparatus of countries fails to address this ongoing trend, and labour lawyers do not actively question the pre-conceived notions of legal philosophy, there is a risk that the jurisprudential system could see a complete overhaul of its powers conferred to it by society and the state.

Bibliography

Audain, L., "Critical Legal Studies, Feminism, Law and Economics, and the Veil of intellectual Tolerance: A Tentative Case for Cross-Jurisprudential Dialogue," *Hofstra Law Review*, Vol. 20, Issue 4, Article 5 (1992)

Baer, J. A., "Feminist Theory and The Law," In *The Oxford Handbook of Political Science*, edited by Goodin, Robert E. (2011)

Balkin, J. M., "Critical Legal Theory Today," In *On Philosophy in American Law*, edited by Mootz, Francis J. (Cambridge University Press, 2009)

Bix, B. H., "Conceptual Questions and Jurisprudence," *Legal Theory,* vol. 1, no. 4, December (1995)

Boyle, J., "The Politics of Reason: Critical Legal Theory and Local Social Thought," *University of Pennsylvania Law Review*, vol. 133, no. 4, April (1985)

Burchard, M., "Feminist Jurisprudence," In *Internet Encyclopedia of Philosophy*, ISSN 2161-0002, https://iep.utm.edu/, accessed on 7 August 2021

Christodoulidis, E., "Critical Theory and the Law: Reflection on origins, trajectories and conjunctures," In *Research Handbook in Critical Legal Theory*, edited by Christodoulidis, E, Dukes, R., and Goldoni, M. (2019)

Coyle, S., "Three approaches to jurisprudence," In *Dimensions of Politics and English Jurisprudence*, (Cambridge University Press, 2013)

Finnis, J., "What is the Philosophy of Law?" *The American Journal of Jurisprudence*, vol. 59, no. 2 (2014): pp. 133-142

Hart, H. L. A., *Essay in Jurisprudence and Philosophy* (Oxford: Oxford University Press, 1983)

Heidegger, M., *Discorsi* (Genova, 2005)

Himma, K. E., "Conceptual Jurisprudence. An Introduction to Conceptual Analysis and Methodology in Legal Theory," *Revus [Online]* 26 (2015)

Himma, K. E., "Philosophy of Law," In *Internet Encyclopedia of Philosophy*, ISSN 2161-0002, https://iep.utm.edu/, accessed on 7 August 2021

Kay, H. H., "Equality and Difference: The Case of Pregnancy," *Berkeley Women's Law Journal* (1985)

Kennedy, D., "Nota sobre la Historia de Cls en los Estados Unidos," 11 Doxa 283, (Alicante, 1992)

Lacey, N., "Analytical Jurisprudence Versus Descriptive Sociology Revisited, Leon Green '15 Lecture in Jurisprudence," *Texas Law Review* (2006)

Lacey, L. J., "Introducing Feminist Jurisprudence: An Analysis of Oklahoma's Seduction Statute," vol. 25, issue 4 Symposium on Feminist Jurisprudence, *Tulsa Law Review* (1990)

Letwin, S., "Political Jurisprudence I: From Realism to feminist jurisprudence," In *On the History of the Idea of Law* (Cambridge University Press, 2005)

Mill, J. S., *On Liberty* (New York: Alfred A. Knopf, 1906)

Pound, R., "The progress of the Law. Analytical Jurisprudence, 1914-1927," *Harvard Law Review*, vol. 41, no. 2 (1927)

Sinclair, A., "Introducing critical jurisprudence," In *International Relations Theory and International Law: A critical Approach*, (Cambridge University Press, 2010), pp. 61-86

Torres, G., "Local Knowledge, Local Color: Critical Legal Studies and The Law of Race Relations," *San Diego L. Rev.*25 (1988): p. 1043

Villa, V., "A Pragmatically Oriented Theory of Legal Interpretation," *Revus* 12 (2010)

Viola, F., *H. L. A. Hart e la Struttura Aperta del Diritto, in Interpretazione e applicazione del diritto tra scienza e politica* (Palermo: Edizioni Celup, 1974)

West, R., *Normative Jurisprudence: An Introduction* (Cambridge University Press, 2011)

CHAPTER 2

THE CRITICAL CONCEPT OF WORK AS A KEY TO JUSTICE

LEONOR SUÁREZ LLANOS

The Relevance of the Concept of Work

The history of societies is the history of their representative, cyclical, successful, urgent, convinced, violent, peaceful, silent, lasting transformations and of the reading of these transformations by the different economic, cultural, political, legal, artistic and religious bodies, and whether or not they promote the recognition of people.

In this history of stories, any conceptualisation that is not strictly descriptive of a given and scientifically demonstrable positive fact — and there are few of these for various reasons of concreteness, value assessment and proof — incorporates a structure of evaluative and normative justification that puts "innocent" concepts at the service of "ideologies."

One of these concepts is that of "work" which, when contemplated through its law, proves to be fertile, interesting and relevant because of its capacity to influence the set of transformations, changes and daily revolutions that go beyond work and alter and define our vital status in a broad sense. I am thinking here, for example, of the successive computerisation and robotization of production; of teleworking; of the young people who are rapidly being spun out of the labour market into precarious working conditions or into systemic-structural unemployment. I am also thinking of workers from the age of forty-five onwards who do not comply with the youth parameters of current markets and management strategies; and of the belligerent scenarios in which women encounter glass walls and ceilings and the gaps, stigmas, prejudices, uncertainties and fallacies that prevent them from accessing all professions and hierarchies.

The aim of this work is to investigate a critical concept and justification of what work is: its reifying (see Lamo de Espinosa 1981, Díaz 1999, 255), alienating (cf. Alonso Olea 1974, on "alienation" and its history in the field of labour law), redistributive and recognition scope, through a deconstruction and a reconstruction aware of the complexity of the concept and the need to reasonably manage its conditions, objectives and consequences, without "occurrences."[1]

The critical perspective that I work with, therefore, is projected onto the "object" to be known, assuming, on the one hand, that there is a concrete society segmented by multiple and contradictory claims to knowledge that will be appropriated and used by the will to power in the current capitalist, legal, social and market framework. Therefore, the interest of critical theory is to account for the evaluative conditions on which a concept is constructed which, in its apparent innocence and descriptive simplicity, normatively imposes the conditions of labour injustice or justice. And, for this reason, the critical concept I am pursuing demands both to follow different paths from those established by the simple understanding of work as a mere activity of paid production, and to abandon the metaphysics of definition and the objective and universalising presumptions about the identity and subjectivity of those who work.

On the other hand, this critique is confronted with a universal and objective approach, acting as a true critique of society and its theories. After all, each of these theories expresses a reflexive moment that arises from society itself and that accounts, as Lukács emphasised, for the knowledge that reality has of itself and of the objects of knowledge whose concept it refers to.

To this end, I will bear in mind the Marxian contribution in a more Western (Perry Anderson) and less orthodox critical sense, at the service of emancipation and self-possession. Further, I will follow paths that are taken with the impulse of different critical motors of legal conceptualisation which, from the critique of the Enlightenment by Adorno and Horkheimer, point to an alternative, externalised perspective of foundation, rooted in personhood and his or her recognition. These are critical motors that, in different ways, make use of the insights offered by post-structuralism and post-modern conceptions, and also point to post-positive legal approaches. However, labels are the least of it, and they can also present us with undesirable travelling companions who can lead us astray from our destination, tempting us into an unedifying nominalist drift.

[1] Work done in the context of the research project AUNAS: Alternatives for an effective Trade Union Action in the new company model. Ref: RTI2018-093458-B-I00.

The Complex and Value-Driven Nature of the Concept of Work

As I pointed out, no matter how neutral and aseptic it may seem, every concept of work is based on, and finalises, important value reasons and consequences that substantially affect the activity, conditions and perception of those who work, to the point of being a cause and consequence of the political-legal, economic, intellectual, etc. frameworks, as well as the conditions of identity, wellbeing, dignity and recognition.

Thus, from slavery[2] to algorithmic programming, to chain production, whatever and however work is conceived to be is constitutive of what at any given moment is and is understood to be and can be a person. Therefore, the history, present and future of work responds to its social and political history (see Pérez Leñero 1961, 22), which is already part of the concept of work, and *vice versa*. Consequently, reducing the concept to the idea that someone spends some time and effort on behalf of another in exchange for remuneration simplifies the prospect of regulation, but at a very high cost that perhaps we should no longer have to bear. And that is why I insist on the need to go deeper into the problematic, complex and dynamic nature of the concept of work as a precondition for the analysis of labour relations and also of the possibilities of representation that are based on them (see Noguera 2002, 163ff.).

In broad terms, I would say that work has been viewed philosophically, sociologically and historically in a negative[3] way. But many approaches

---

[2] I am thinking not only of ancient slavery, but also of the factual and speculative formulation that drives the modern colonising and racial state; slavery in which someone essentially surrenders all or part of themselves without freedom in order to end the situation. This institution was reviled by Victoria who, already in 1532, in contrast to many contemporaries and other thinkers who would succeed him, considered colonial slavery absolutely inadmissible. It was taken up by Kant who, beyond anachronisms, has given a good account of his lack of recognition of sectors historically constructed by the will to power as vulnerable, such as women or domestic servitude. For Kant (1943), with various flourishes by way of concretisation, and in addition to the slavery of the offender, domestic slavery (servitude) is justified under the absolute power of the father of the family (husband-father-master), people who are possessed by the simple will of the owner "as long as and wherever he exists" (*ibid,* 102-103, 67). In contrast to the common service tenancy, which is rented for a specific job, the domestic "is obliged to do everything that is permitted for the good of the household" (idem. 193). This is a Kantian approach which Hegel confronts in his *Philosophy of Law* (p. 67), mainly because freedom is inalienable. See in this respect, comp., Alonso Olea (1979).

[3] Plato derives the concept of work from the ideal of the Greek man who finds his

also view it positively, either as a form of collaboration with the community or as a means of personal significance.

In the latter sense, Renaissance approaches, beyond their dispersion, already underline the importance of the development of the human spirit, of a "humanist" that enables the person to become effectively active in the world and in events and activities. For example, Giordano Bruno extols the union of the intellect and the will of the person who not only wants, but also wants to want, affirming a will of mastery over things and revealing the virtuous possibilities of work. Later, some representatives of modern idealism strengthened this idea by establishing work as the fundamental factor of life insofar as it deepens and extends the very concept of the person. The developments of this classical idealism successively adopt very interesting forms which, on occasions, as with Bergson, promote the valorisation of productive work, linking the very dignity of the person to his dimension as a worker, in such a way that *homo faber* is identified with *homo sapiens* (see Pérez Leñero 1961, 21).

Marx, who drew so much from Hegel's idealism, his dialectics and his vision of history, defined labour in terms of the capitalist market, which values it for its capacity to generate surplus value that is invested in the productive capital itself, and not in the human element of the worker who drives and makes this production possible. This approach demonstrated its great capacity to fix the distinction of classes and rights according to the ownership of the means of production[4] that generates this surplus value, announcing important tensions that today we can take for granted, such as the concentration of capital, the growing division of classes or the consolidation of a growing consumerism that strengthens the network of productive "slavery" chains, multiplying the needs of accessible satisfaction, etc.

From then until now, at least in Western economies, it is as if labour is torn between the utopia of Edward Bellamy's *Looking Backward* (1887),

---

dignity in his activity and who tends to imitate and approach divinity thanks to the intellect. This is why wisdom and intellectual training mark the highest levels of perfection, bringing to light the worker-thinker antithesis — a line maintained by his conservative and traditionalist disciple, Aristotle, to highlight the highest virtue of the thinker as opposed to those who carry out the material tasks of the organic community of virtue, which are less virtuous and inferior to the reflection of philosophers and magistrates. This characterises the "labour" structure of *areté* and social classes.

[4] An approach taken up by Marx (in his *Poverty of Philosophy*) from Hegel but, to turn it on its head, that the division between classes stems from the division of labour and wealth.

which was published 20 years after *Das Kapital* (1867) and is about mechanising and specialising production for all people, but only until they are 45 years old, when they will be able to aspire to leisure, and the dystopia of *News from Nowhere* (1890), in which William Morris replies to Bellamy in an effort to move from capitalism to socialism by reorienting activity, the mode of production, consumption and the elimination of pollution, in favour of a conception of work and of those who work that allows for the development of expressive and narrative capacities and makes work activities pleasurable.

The Concept of Work as a Broad Concept and as a Productivist Critique

The current approach, according to which labour identifies its value with the market price of its product, with some nuances, is the end of capitalism. The problem is that the market price does not correspond to what is valuable in itself, but depends on multiple variables that are difficult to justify and control.

This objectification of value and price around uncritical considerations of the capitalist market trivialises the value of the worker by reducing the value of his production, as can be seen, for example, in the low price of the ideologically worthless but essential and highly profitable activity of cleaning, or in certain hotel and catering activities. This trivialisation consolidates undervaluing the rights of the person who provides the activity, to which we are not usually sensitive.

Indeed, the usual terms of "precarious," "blurred" and "indecent" are not adjectives for work, but real situations in the labour market that impose social identification models of "lack of recognition in a dense sense" of the person. These are real life situations that correspond to activities whose specific and quantifiable value participates in cultural, traditional and group values that harm, oppress and discriminate against entire sectors of the population, while favouring other power groups. In this way, the traditional ideological struggle, which is culturally bound to established models and structures, is reinforced by the vital and essential instrument of labour as a material violence. This is supported by the various deep-rooted concepts, social categories and criteria of success (see Honneth 2018, 112), which have a vital institutional effect. It is an ideological struggle to which specific imaginaries, which have already been fed by a favourable economic distribution, or naturalistic concepts of duty towards others, such as domestic work or migrant workers, are to a large extent linked. In turn, the limitation of freedom and the threat to equality is aggravated by a market capitalism which, promising just the opposite, shapes an implicit concept of work that both deepens the traditional axiological divisions between men and women, city/countryside, intellectual/manual work, reason/emotion, and introduces the new "rupturist" and alienating distinction between those who work and the means of production and those who work and the hierarchical structures that fragment and distort the very conception of the self (Foster 2017, 9).

In the face of this, the pretension of incorporating the critical dimension in the conceptualisation of work and investigating the theory of such conceptualisation allows us, on the one hand, to understand the disruptive contradictions of representation and the "intrinsic dynamics" of struggle and contradiction found in the social base on which work is developed and, on the other hand, to understand that work is not reduced to a peaceful reified activity of labour accepted in the abstract without contradiction and without dynamism. It becomes a universal, homogeneous and omnipotent fetish that neutralises the person both in their need and in their preconceived working reality.

The fact is that the world and the law that "seem" to be positive do not have to be what they are or what they should be or, therefore, what has to be represented. This requires us to "do away with the fetishism of the concept (and) place social antagonism at the center of the analysis of labor" (see Foster 2017, 291).

I would say, then, that the radical critique of the concept of labour starts from the fact that labour has become a central category of social organisation, classification and valuation, ahead of private property,[5] and this centrality and beatification of the capitalist economic category of productive labour according to market value, turns people into productive slaves whom capital can impose to work, either as employees or as unemployed, in a standardised labour subjected to the social, economic, aesthetic, vital, ethical, etc. conditions of a market founded on power relations.

The Archaeology of the Concept of Work: Diversity, Globalisation and Postmodernity

In the face of the standardisation and stabilisation of work, an archaeology of knowledge[6] is needed to understand that work is more than the mere

---

[5] In fact, "instead of describing capitalism in terms of private ownership of the means of production, we can say that it is a social system based on the taxation of labour." Cleaver 1985, 33.

[6] It is necessary to inquire into the conditions of knowledge and into its pretensions

employment relationship (see Castillo 2000, 58-59) and that the "entity" to which work is given is also more than a workplace, a company or an employer.[7]

This archaeology of knowledge about work, and thus about forms, purposes and subjects, on the one hand accounts for the conceptual framework of established meanings and how it conditions and limits people's perspectives on the conditions, nature, purpose, value, etc. of work. On the other hand, it makes us aware of the incompleteness, the "sociology of absences" and what is often left out: the "sociology of the absent,"[8] the blurred, indeterminate, non-dependent, undeclared work, necessity and the will itself, etc. because, as I have already pointed out, the concept of work refers to the objective dimension of activity and the subjective dimension of value classification in a system of power relations (see De la Garza 2000, 32), emotions, aesthetics, everyday reasoning and the real, complex and social needs of the person who would claim a full right to "a procedure capable of creating a mutual intelligibility between possible and available experiences without destroying his identity" (see Sousa de Santos 2005, 153). This is a recognition that allows him to elaborate and pursue his own conception of good and the good life.

A post-structural and post-modern approach risks the frequent criticisms against legal post-modernism, on this occasion, because the claimed "heterogeneity" in the understandings and definition of the working class would prevent the collective representation of the working class.[9]

In the face of this objection, I believe that what matters is to understand that accepting diversity does not "anarchise" the possibilities of analysis and classification, but only brings us closer to the existing reality of work in society, even if it is at the cost of demanding new visions and instruments that allow us not to remain petrified in a reactionary conservatism of established positive security. Moreover, it is striking to see how the company diversifies, makes flexible and adapts its structure and mobility to the new reality and needs, logically using its workers, while to a large extent

---

of use and appropriation. This is strategic in order to "know" knowledge itself and therefore to discover the object that this knowledge pretends to know. See Foucault 2002, 306-307.

[7] Comp. on the inadequate confusion of the three terms. Nieto 2015, 143.

[8] That explains to us that what does not exist is actively produced as non-existent, there is an "interested concealment" in the face of which it is necessary to rehabilitate the social fragments not socialised by indolent reason, transforming impossible objects into possible ones and absences into presences. Suárez Llanos 2018, 59.

[9] I discuss these critical approaches, their actual foundations and possible responses in Suárez Llanos 2018.

the static concept of the universal, permanent, industrial worker, formatted to the traditional market standards of value, time, occupation and remuneration, seems to be indispensable for the homogeneous representation of their interests. However, such formatting is neither indispensable nor ineffective at representing, classifying and regulating diversity. In fact, this is one of the causes of the crisis of labour representation. In addition, it is worth noting two issues.

The first is that labour and market globalisation are characterised by an inverse development of those who work and those who receive work, in such a way that the continuous economic and political strengthening of the company, in addition to the globalisation process, corresponds to a process of the gradual weakening of the representation of the interests of those who work, especially in emerging and less traditional sectors that do not offer previous structures of supranational organisation, which can serve transnational trade union federations, etc.[10] Both processes, in turn, are framed in the context of the progressive loss of power, domination and control of sovereign states.

The second issue is that what seems to be an insurmountable obstacle for those who offer themselves in the labour market, to integrate their diversity, is often valued inversely by the company, which shows a diversifying and changing agility in a complex process with important repercussions for the worker, and that two apparently antagonistic but complementary movements are developing: the business process of aggregation and the decentralising tendency. Both are movements that strengthen the power of the company while weakening the possibilities of representation for the worker.

It seems to me, as Patricia Collado also clearly sees, that the company has adapted very well to post-modernity, but not those who work. In some cases, the company absorbs a sector of workers into its identity and makes them part of its image and design, thus highlighting the element of adaptation of those who orientate towards those for whom they work. In other cases, when it comes to precarious and vulnerable workers, the company imposes total adaptation to their needs and changes in accordance with a vital clause of fixed subsistence in a labour and economic market in structural crisis (see Collado 2001, 70).

On this point, there is a need for a considered legal response that is capable of adapting to the needs of representation in a more appropriate way

---

[10] Because this globalisation implies a "loss of coherence between state, productive apparatus, currency and society [...] it reinforces that of large companies and multinationals, which can articulate organizational and distribution strategies [...] Much more effective than trade union organizations." Antenas Collderram 2008, 37.

than, for example, the Spanish legislator's provision for the analogical application to these situations of the representation of contractors and subcontractors by the representatives of the main company, even though the situations are undoubtedly changing and abundant[11] and make the regulatory possibilities more difficult.

The serenity and adaptability of legal responses to real needs, in any case, depends on at least two important factors: one formal and the other material. The formal factor stresses the need to incorporate dynamic jurisdictional and doctrinal regulations into legislation in an effort to make legislation into constant law, in order to respond to the "revolution of practical reason," which calls for guaranteeing adaptability to the needs of recognition in successive market scenarios, but also security in the recognition of the interests and rights of those who work.[12] The material warns that what is subject to regulation must be viewed from a critical, evaluative, normative and justifying perspective that makes it possible to overcome sclerotized conceptions of what, who, for what, how and with what reasons it is represented, precisely in favour of recognition as integrity. In this respect, the circular view of law is important, according to which validity is a concept that materially integrates meaning from and in relation to practice dynamically and in constant law.

In short, the concept of work to which I am referring, on the one hand, makes the interests of those who work more flexible and diversified and goes beyond prevention, trying to promote a dense recognition of those who work. For work, its lack, its mode, its model, its concept, its projection, etc. is a defining part of, and defined by, the understanding that everyone has or can have of themselves. It is thus a broad concept that incorporates instrumental and expressive elements.

On the other hand, it integrates redistribution as an essential conceptual element, beyond the centrality of[13] productivism, because it is a condition for recognition and dignity.

---

[11] I am thinking here, for example, of the precariousness often suffered by those who work in auxiliary companies, given the practical dependence that exists between the company that hires the person and the main company that contracts the service. In this sense, see Nieto 2015, 202 and also Merino Segovia, 2008, 25.

[12] I have already analysed this question in depth on different occasions. In general, see Suárez Llanos 2018, 338, 341ff; and in particular, see Suárez Llanos 2019, 69-96.

[13] "(O)nly in modern times has work come to occupy so much time and have so much importance in the lives of human beings, and it is not unreasonable to expect that this situation will not last forever." Noguera 2002, 147-148.

And, furthermore, representation is conceived as a fundamental instrument at the service of the two previous ones. Let us look at this in more detail.

Conceptual Justice: The Worker as a Universal Subject of Rights

The condition that justifies whether an action or organisational decision in the social sphere is rational, ethical, just or correct is the person. However, establishing the philosophical and political-legal concept of that person, of their needs, interests, reasons and evaluations is complicated, as the only objectivity is biological, and the scope of that objectivity and of all the subjectivities that go with it (gender, ethnicity, class, religion, property, etc.) has been and is contested from different narrative and power fronts.

After various historical vicissitudes, subject to numerous evaluative and normative interpretations, the Enlightenment conception led to the "recognition" of a universal "man" of rights. But this man, rather than being universal, was unique and closely linked to the white, property-owning man, and defined himself in a valuable way in terms of his own rights to the exclusion of all others, something clearly seen by Olympe de Gouges, who drew up a declaration of the rights of women and citizens equal to the declaration of the rights of man and citizens which had been published two years earlier. She was guillotined two years later and it is perhaps not surprising, therefore, that to this day there is still strong discrimination against different groups of people, not because of their status as persons, but because of their physical and metaphysical characteristics, their material conditions and the interpretation that was and is still held of them.

This idea that the conditions and characteristics of people act as a criterion that limits the rights of equality and freedom of people, favouring the interest of power and the injustice of partiality, served Rawls to design a constructive procedure of justice as impartiality oriented to justify the formal Kantism of rights but without ignoring our starting conditions. To do so, he made use of a veil of ignorance that does not prevent us from knowing who we are before writing the two principles, but who we are going to be and with what characteristics when those principles that we have previously elaborated then have to be applied to us. These principles took the form of the recognition of the widest possible range of rights for everyone and, as a subsidiary element, the provision of services for the most disadvantaged in terms of social and economic inequalities.

Habermas, a renewing heir to the critical theory of the Enlightenment, insisted on this same path of constructing procedures for justifying the criteria for the distribution of goods and rights, but this time seeking a subject of real autonomy that would have the power to be recognised both in its definition as a subject entitled to rights and freedoms and in its active capacity to construct and shape those rights, its freedoms and the conditions for their realisation. To achieve this, he wanted to avoid the imaginary Rawlsian construction and focus on the real person that each person is when they show and develop their universal rationality through their dialogical capacity. Therefore, what the political-legal structure must offer is a design that guarantees the possibilities of communication, dialogue and agreement, which again leads to the recognition of the rights (food, housing, health, education, work, expression, etc.) that allow the person to be a person with rights, that then enable the person to be a competent speaker in the "ideal speech community" in which agreements are developed and in whose constant dynamics the rationality and justice of each norm and decision is justified.

For the purposes that are of most interest here, Habermas' advance over static conceptions such as Rawls' is that he allows us to maintain the Kantian procedural formalism that does not condition *a priori* the content of rights but incorporates material perspectives thanks to the incorporation of the dynamics of interests, needs and criteria of distribution.

These legal-philosophical approaches to the justification of human rights have a lot to do with the struggle for labour rights, not only because all fundamental rights have a labour aspect/affection (Alonso Olea 1990, 28ff.), but also because labour law refers to the conditions that affect the vital development of each individual, both descriptively and prescriptively. Descriptively, because they describe a process in which initially a basic package of equal rights was demanded for workers to protect them against the company and capital through safety, health, working time limits and minimum wages, and then, successively, the demands addressed the improvement of personal working conditions and sectoral adequacy, thanks in large measure to trade union and unitary representation. These were closer and more sensitive to the particular conditions of those fighting for the application of the criteria of equality, freedom and redistribution (Rawls) and a recognition of the transcendence of the position of workers as subjects of rights and competent speakers (Habermas).

In terms of the prescriptive dimension of the struggle for labour rights, however favourable and necessary this evolution may be, it is also insufficient[14] in the current socio-labour frameworks and with regard to the

[14] There are various criticisms of Habermas, although they could be grouped into two levels (comp. Suárez Llanos 2001, 100ff., 127ff.). On the one hand, there are those who refer to his limited understanding of will, necessity and the vital narrative of each individual, which is trapped in the semiotic limits of language. On the other,

authentic recognition of the individual and his or her representation. The current scenario is post-modern, complex, diverse, global, transnational, precarious and in crisis. It shows a very unbalanced distribution of resources and rights and, moreover, is based on a stable, homogeneous and universal model of the worker, which is very useful to guarantee the continuity of the economic, political and social structure, but which has already been destroyed by the crisis. This model has been replaced by a society of people with very different needs, expectations, capacities and possibilities, and of workers who no longer fit into the static conception (see Maar 2005, 433-436) of a piece of production nor into a life modelled to fit into such a piece.

This being the case, I believe that the conception of rights justice in a post-modern scenario recommends articulating and conditioning the discourse around the three axes of "the three Rs": recognition-meaning, redistribution and representation.

R1: "Recognise Well" who Works. "Resignification" as a Logical *a priori*

The first element of the concept of work, which functions as a logical *a priori* for the understanding of the person, is "resignification," which starts from an awareness of the limits, conditions, obstructions and keys of understanding and valuation of the different social subsystems of meaning that act on the individual and, from there, discursively and structurally claims the identity and all its conditions through protest. Resignification accounts for the relevance of the successive and changing calligrams of our lives and the need for them to be read and recognised by our social context of realising rights, and by each one of us when we draw ourselves and fill that drawing with our life's narrative.[15] This is why resignification is the antidote to injustice and concealment, because it is born of the conflict itself but with the will and the capacity to resolve it by being internal to that same

---

there are the procedural limits, which are constrained by the traditional value keys and nuclei of meaning. These are two fronts of criticism that highlight the fact that nothing is foreseen in the procedure and in its conception of the subject to guarantee a true recognition of the moral keys and justice proper to each person. See Honneth 1991, 166-167.

[15] On this point, as on so many others, Butler is right when she directs the resignification to the living discourse capable of transcending and transforming the very context that determines it, which is why it has a subversive component that allows us to return, and be against, and to signify ourselves. This reverses the conservative condition of discourses towards the subversive and the the irreverent. Butler 1997, 98.

conflict, and not an external ideology without the capacity to have an impact.

The archaeology of knowledge with regard to this "resignification" is aimed at unravelling, deconstructing and reconstructing the constitutive foundations of the conception and belief that the person, in particular here, as a worker, has of him/herself. This is why it has a lot to do, because it is based on the concept of recognition which, in the field of work, is of great relevance.

The concept of "recognition" in a political philosophical context is linked to Hegel's approach, for whom the person is the result of successive family-society-state dialectics that are driven by, and materialise in, the reason of "*sencia*" (*aufheben*) history. This justification characterised the Hegelian identity-conservative approach which, in turn, gave impetus to communitarian developments of "recognition" which assume that the community sets the criteria of intelligibility, justice, practical reason and the common good of people, so that collective rights replace individual rights, thus benefiting the original and real sense of the person and not individual inventions and egoism.

The problem is that this Aristotelian-rooted metaphysical communitarian biology, which defines us as part of a whole, not the whole as the sum of its parts, is problematic for the individual considered through his or her differences and for a redistribution in the service of individual rights.

Obviously, this approach is a simplification of the dialectic of communitarianism (collective interest — Hegel) and liberalism (individual interest — Kant), but it already warns of the good performance in the field of labour law and of the struggle between the universal and homogeneous worker, predefined and affiliated to patterns of "collective interest and rights." This is a struggle between the universal, homogeneous, predefined worker who can be affiliated to "collective interests and rights" employers, who have more lobbying power and effectiveness than the various individual claims, but who also have increasingly serious problems with regard to the rights and interests of the real workers in the flexible, globalised and dynamic scenarios of our post-modern society.

One of the problems of collective rights is their limitation in "recognising" the person who is and on whom the whole construction and justification of the processes of representation and distribution are really based. The starting point is a universal individual affiliated with a unique history and narrative of his or her reality, goals, needs, ambitions, definition of identity, concept of dignity, etc... On this is built a provision for the compensation of basic needs.

A problem that affects the trade union approach is representing objectives, not individuals, in favour of uniformity and institutional strength in the face of corporate ambition. However, it has a high opportunity cost, which helps to explain the trade union crisis. Because the work scenario is not an accessory element of an industrial worker's subsistence, but rather a touchstone for the possibility of vital development, and because of its economic conditions, working hours, harmonisation, valuation and social structuring, as well as what we do being part of who we are, it gives us value and conditions what we do.

In other words, our "recognition" — the recognition that each of us has of ourselves — is and depends on social recognition, and this incorporates multiple factors that are beyond our control. But this recognition is often lacking, or is bad or unfair and assumes unjustified valuations of gender, ethnicity, class, age, maternity, etc. that support traditional narratives of the objectives of time and salary, and reify those who are not recognised or are poorly recognised and, thus, obstructs the justice of rights.

Therefore, recognition in a dense sense in the work context requires that narratives and discourses change substantially, to incorporate the affective, emotive, ideological, practical reality and self-concept elements that characterise the speaker and allow them to recognise and discover their vulnerabilities, humiliations and daily disrespect, or failed recognitions, and ways to overcome them. But it also requires a process of redistribution that removes barriers and biases that prevent the development and recognition of the diverse narratives that are so often silenced.

In short, truth, reason and the justification of law are strengthened, precisely in terms of a "post-truth critique" that brings to light the interest of each legal dogma and the need for a revision in the service of narratives that are concealed, vilified or socially, politically and legally sanctioned.[16]

It calls into question all the practical and speculative dogmas that favour the development of a labour market that multiplies geometrically its capacity to appropriate capital, but which appears to live in a permanent form of crisis that "justifies" the existence of new forms of labour slavery imposed by working conditions, wages or the social valuation of the activity.

Modern forms of labour slavery (day labourers, hotel cleaning staff, domestic service, hotel and catering, agriculture, sex workers, etc.) have a

---

[16] The aim is thus "a normative theory developed on the basis of experiences of disrespect, humiliation, contempt and moral offence which, on the basis of the negative, could reveal what constitutes the integrity of the person and which thus aims to overcome a normative deficit of a critical theory of society, suggesting elements for a real policy" (Campello 2012, 114).

marked traditional and value archaeology that fixes their margins, conditions and an absolute and vital dependence, strict necessity and are not renounceable to the master's will.[17] In this respect, it is enough to think of the evolution of servitude towards "domestic employment" (see Alonso Olea 1979, 129), even as a "live-in worker" and its conditions.

Injustices are normalised, linked to, and justified by "a structurally false form of praxis" (pre-theoretical praxis of loss of the original capacity for involvement) (Honneth) that accounts for the objectification, "reification" (Lukacs) and "self-reification" of the person,[18] fiercely projected onto the worker promoting the "forgetting [...] of the affective aspects of rationality" (see Campello 2012, 112).

R2: "Redistribution" as a Material *a priori.* Universal Income, Alienation and Labour Slavery

One of the important conditions in the fight against new forms of labour slavery and in favour of recognition is to start from an adequate redistributive scenario. In this adequacy, I include universal income (UK).

It is true that in the philosophical, political and legal context, redistribution can be linked to egalitarian approaches in material terms and is distrustful of capitalist rights, or the moderation of redistributive perspectives that inquire into the conditions of equal opportunity to access rights. It is in the

---

[17] On 24 July 2019 the SC (STS 396/2019) stated there is an attack on the dignity of many women who are being forced into prostitution in roadside clubs in what can be considered "the slavery of the 21st century." This extends "along the margins of our roads, where one can find one or more nightclubs where prostitution is practiced with forced, enslaved people, who are forced, enslaved, to whom they are forced to work. XXIst century slavery. [...These women,] without any shame, are bought and sold between the different establishments, while these human beings are forced to "pay" even the single ticket to their indignity" (FJ 10). Addressing this issue requires a multifaceted approach that includes extensive research and knowledge of the archaeology of prostitution, what we know and propose about it, and of the axiological keys, interest and power that have structured and articulated it. This is beyond the scope of this chapter.

[18] Lukács introduces the concept of reification in relation to the reifying pathologies of capitalism and which give, among other things, three areas of error in social development: the disintegration of self-identity; the disintegration of social identity; and the disintegration of nature. For his part, Honneth reinterprets this reification by adding important elements to capitalism in relation to the failure or "forgetting of recognition" (Honneth 2007, 83ff.) which occurs when, in the knowledge of and in the knowledge we have about other people, "we lose awareness of the extent to which both are due to prior involvement and recognition" (idem. 91).

latter sense that I use redistribution and the RU as an instrument. However, in accordance with an approach of removing the obstacles that prevent equal recognition of differences, a real removal warns us that isolated economic resources that are developed outside the labour context (which is a vital context) and the minimum welfare resources of certain social policies are insufficient, inappropriate and often counterproductive. Redistributive policies must be included in the context of labour recognition in an ambitious way, knowing, but not recognising, the alternative between misery and[19] traditional privileges.

In turn, the legal-philosophical and political-philosophical tension between redistribution (equality) and freedom is also reflected in social movements, to account for the fact that while economic redistribution seems to be affiliated with economic class claims, recognition claims would relate to criteria of identity, status, and ethnicity, etc. Thus it is not uncommon to find that those who base their claims on identity object to the individualistic aspirations and arguments of those who make economic class claims.[20]

---

[19] Rössler offers an interesting analysis of how a redistributive measure, which I handle with conviction here, can lead to the opposite effects to those that justify proposing it. He refers to the remuneration of domestic activities, since the various technical problems of the measure will be added, among others, to the complex issue of the incentive for women to continue to devote themselves to domestic activities, while men remain in public activities, in which they are particularly privileged and recognised. Rössler 2010, 140-149.

[20] In the context of her confrontation with Honneth, Nancy Fraser systematises the four axes on which the opposition between economic redistribution and recognition is usually based: 1). Their different paradigms of injustice. For one, economic injustice; for the other, cultural injustice rooted in social patterns of representation, interpretation and communication; 2). The different forms of solution which in the first case, could be the redistribution of income or wealth and, in the second, could be cultural or symbolic change; 3). Different conceptions of the subject or collectivity that suffers the injustice, in distributive injustice, classes or collectives similar to classes that are defined by an economic relationship with the means of production of exploitation or abandonment, and when the concept of economy is broadened to incorporate non-wage labour and gender converted into class, becoming an account of this injustice in general and in particular with respect to all levels. However, if the injustice is one of recognition, the group is characterised by its stigma, its difference and its less valuable character; 4). Referring to the valuation of the differences within the group, the injustice of distribution would be corrected by eliminating the differences, while the injustice of recognition would call for either re-evaluating the differences in order to value them or characterising them as malignant dysfunctions of a homogeneous form of identity and thus suppressing them. See Fraser 2018, 21-25.

However, looking at the approaches and criticisms from a certain perspective, the outcome can, and I believe must, be different. The different keys to vulnerability in terms of gender, ethnicity, age, ideology, etc... are already segmented by the economic claims of class and redistribution in a way that is not necessarily directly causal, although it is also complex and linked to an interpretative hermeneutic that warns us that discrimination is a "polycausal" whole with a strong hereditary component. Further, in respect of this, the distributive injustice is generally the cause and consequence of a global injustice based on interests, prejudices and fallacies and leads to a lack of recognition (Honneth 2018, 121). On some occasions, the economic distribution dimension will be more relevant and obvious, although the condition of recognition acts in parallel, and in other cases the other way around, even when the economic factor of injustice seems to act in isolation without being linked to any model of identity recognition. This is why policies are needed that are capable of combining the criteria of redressing economic injustices with those of overcoming the injustices of identity determination and recognition.[21] The axiological and cultural assumptions of inclusion and exclusion that segment macro and micro economic distributive decisions and inheritances are already at the causal basis of all economic and labour action. Therefore, in order to unravel and repair the injustices of distribution and recognition of the worker, it is necessary to identify and purify the axiological weaknesses of the concepts of work and its representation.

Indeed, the various actions in favour of redistribution or recognition will have effects on their respective travelling companion (see Fraser 2018, 65-67) and, just as a given line of economic decision-making goes beyond its own sphere by projecting its evaluative effects on people's dignity, so, conversely, the effect of recognition of diversity and identity has an effect on distribution.[22] An economistic conceptual approach to rights whereby

[21] I propose here a couple of examples close to those proposed by Fraser. A senior executive who is scared when she returns home on foot (women commonly return home scared) and, conversely, a structurally unemployed or a precarious but male, national and white worker. The apparent distributive justice of the first example and the recognition of the second are already burdened by their own imbalances and vulnerability factors. For her, because of what it requires for her to reach her position; for him, because of the vulnerability factor (age, orientation and training). This explains the distributive injustice. In the end, "maldistribution is not only a class injustice, in the traditional sense," but rather a matter of "subordinate genders, races, sexualities and nationalities [being..] subject to systematic economic prejudice." In Fraser 2018, 83.

[22]I take the example of sex work. A certain cultural reading can lead us to prohibit and sanction to try and suppress the activity. However, although well-intentioned,

social measures are not incorporated in the context of social rights linked to labour rights fosters a structure that is socially visible as welfare or charity, which is what comes after precariousness and which, apart from its rickety promotion of welfare and development of rights, fosters a cultural vision of the other "taking advantage" of benefits not obtained through personal effort and sacrifice when, in reality, social and labour rights are about reforming a deep and increasingly alienating class structure.

In this context and with these keys, the different economic, social and/or labour policies that can act in favour of the promotion of identity and dignity must be considered. That is why universal income in the labour context is as necessary as introducing the conceptual keys that act in favour of social and labour justice. This avoids an economic measure that is isolated from other labour and cultural measures and leads to deepening discrimination, inequality, the perpetuation of poorly paid, partial and undervalued jobs, and the confinement of women to the domestic sphere, etc. This is why a cultural reform in the labour sphere aimed at recognising diversity and difference and making work-life balance possible, and "making care work" and "making it profitable" will be effective in favour of the rights and equality of all citizens.

Justice requires a dynamic and complex perspective that makes it possible to identify and adjust objective (distributively) and subjective (ethically/valuationally) unjust situations. And the analysis of the justification and reasonableness of its actions depends on the identification of situations of vulnerability (simple and complex) as the unjustified impossibility of the person to elaborate and pursue his or her own conception of the good life, and to participate on an equal footing in all social agreements and practices[23] (legal, political, economic, religious, health, cultural, sporting and, of course, labour).

---

the measure can lead to the marginalisation of sex workers and the deepening of both their social alienation and their unacceptable economic and labour situation, as well as favouring a hidden and extraordinarily powerful economic enterprise from whose profits those who work do not benefit.

[23]In this context of recognition and redistribution, the concept of vulnerability, linked to that of dignity as a presupposition of the public order of realisation of rights, runs parallel to Fraser's concept of "parity of participation," according to which justice requires social arrangements for members of society to act on an equal footing, and also that at least two conditions are met: "the distribution of material resources must be made in a way that guarantees the independence and 'voice' of all participants [... and] requires that institutionalized patterns of cultural value express the same respect for all participants and guarantee equal opportunities to achieve social esteem" (Fraser 2018, 42).

It is to be understood that "recognition" is not oriented, as some of the first approaches of critical theory might suggest, towards the psychoanalytic "healing" of the self, but towards a cultural, social, political, ethical, legal and economic transformation that makes it possible to overcome the false values, justifications and interests that underlie the valuation of the position, definition and narrative of the other. This requires, on the one hand, "social recognition" in all areas. This includes the old social law and the current labour law that contemplated the extraordinary relevance of the "social question," but also a "self-recognition" which, in conjunction with the above, prevents those who work from having a negative understanding of themselves, from attacking the value of their self-identity or from self-sabotaging in their search for personal justice. On the other hand, the conditions of justice and distribution characterise the political-legal structure and bring to light the fact that identity erased by a lack of identification and valuation is the structural key to social injustice. The condition of adequate representation is of great importance here.

R3: Representation

Although I cannot now delve into the fundamental constitutive element of the critical concept of work, which is representation, I leave here the lines of analysis that I develop elsewhere.

At the time, and in relation to the representation and political and legal recognition of people and vulnerable groups, I highlighted the need to articulate the recognition of the person through a complex and polycentric citizenship, which aims at the political and legal accommodation of interests, value criteria and judgements representative of the real narratives of people in a system of "radical democracy."[24] And now, in the context of

[24] Radical democracy is articulated and reclaimed from affirmative and reconstructive postmodernism, from Conolly, Derrida, Kristeva, Rorty or Butler, Mouffe, Laclau, etc., as an instrument of visibility and real representation of the diverse interests of people. Not only because the undifferentiated human subject, the guarantor of universal reason, does not exist, but because it alone has already become the greatest obstacle to exploring the real democratic project. This is why the "revaluation of utopian values" of "identity," "recognition" and "difference" that question the undifferentiated *status* of citizenship in all spheres, including work, is needed. And so both essentialist positions that construct aprioristic universals of society, history or the subject, and foundationalist efforts to base theory on stable presuppositions on which theoretical systems can be built, are contested. To achieve this, a number of things are necessary. First of all, it is necessary to sectoralise democracy and fight against the hegemony that totalises society around the concept of class, concealing

work, I take up this approach in order to object to agglutinating and homogenising processes, and to seek instruments of representation in the face of the objectifying objectification of the person and an identification around standards of domination and subordination that can encourage vulnerabilities within the group and even turn the vulnerable group and/or some of its members into violators of the recognition of the other.

In this context, and for the purposes of representation, it is necessary, as I discussed in depth when addressing the keys to rationality in the theory of legislation,[25] that the social actors and agents affected by the rules, directly or indirectly (e.g. workers with dependent children, hotel cleaning staff, sex workers, etc.) participate representatively in the adoption of decisions, regardless of how this participation is formally institutionalised. And then the plausibility or otherwise of the proposals will have to be assessed in technical terms and in terms of their effectiveness for the recognition, redistribution and protection of the individual. Among other things, as I have been pointing out, this requires removing the accumulation of traditional axiological conceptions of value, price, status and merit.

Conclusions

First, work has become a central category of organisation, classification and social valuation of the development and protection of the individual, ahead of private property, which is why it is essential to approach the critical analysis of its concept.

Second, an archaeology of knowledge about work warns us that what falls normatively outside the concept becomes blurred, indeterminate, non-dependent work which is unrecognised and bad, and that labour is more than

---

social diversity and fragmentation. Secondly, it should be assumed that socio-political identities and the social arena are not closed and finalised structures, unstable, non-unified, contingent and open to a permanent process of negotiated articulation in a society that is discursively constituted as an unstable system of differences (Laclau and Mouffe). Thirdly, it should be understood that the structure of socio-economic relations is one of domination. Fourthly, it should be recognised that economic and social welfare are permanently negotiated and fought over in a network of multiple nuclei that the state no longer directs, but "coordinates from different levels of super-ordination" (Sousa Santos 2005, 366). Fifthly, a "redistributive democracy" should be promoted, centred on a redefinition of the relationship between democracy and capitalism in order to overcome the idea of participatory democracy in favour of its redistributive ingredient. See. comp. Mouffe 1988, Mouffe 1993, Laclau 1988.

[25] In particular, in Suárez Llanos 2013 and Suárez Llanos 2007.

and different to the mere employment relation, and incorporates a whole web of power and value meanings about selective disregard, overexploitation, growing consumption and unlimited production and devastation.

Third, the current scenario is post-modern, complex, diverse, global, transnational, precarious and in crisis. It shows a very unbalanced distribution of resources and rights and is based on a stable, homogeneous and universal model of "an" objective and universal worker that has already been replaced by a dynamic society of workers with very varied needs, expectations and capacities.

Fourth, it is therefore necessary to deconstruct the concept of work as instrumental and reifying of the person, but without abandoning the reconstructive expectation of a broad, non-central, non-productivist and instrumental/expressive concept of work that allows everyone to develop their own conception of a good life. And it is important to understand here that diversity does not "anarchise" the possibilities of analysis and classification, but only brings us closer to the existing reality of complexity, makes us more demanding and responsible and increases our capacity for advocacy and change, saving us from being petrified in a reactionary conservatism excused in established positive security.

Fifth, injustice in the recognition and rejection of diversity is the cause of distributive injustice and *vice versa*. This injustice is inflicted on vulnerable groups by preventing them from having equal access to their legal dignity in the political order of rights.

I stress that the conception of rights justice in a post-modern labour scenario recommends articulating and conditioning the discourse around the three axes of "the three Rs": recognition/resignification, redistribution and representation.

Sixth, the lack of or defective recognition of groups and individuals must be tackled as a matter of priority by means of a cultural labour reform that, among other things, assumes the objective of a redistribution, in which I include universal income, capable of eliminating the barriers and biases that prevent the development and recognition of one's own life narratives.

Seventh, the reorientation of the concept of work towards the person in a broad, ethical and redistributive sense of promotion and accommodation for recognition, thus avoiding reification. This does not devalue work, nor its representation, nor those who carry it out, nor the company. On the contrary, it humanises work activity whereby the person, deprived of the enslaving burden of need, works by putting his or her best abilities, aptitudes and interests at the service of cooperative development objectives, solidarity and personal development and re-signification.

Eighth, this humanisation rationalises the concept of work, puts it at the service of more ecological, solidarity-oriented and cooperative values, and confronts the ironic paradox that in the richest, most technologically advanced and developed world we have ever had, mass impoverishment, alienation and slavery multiply geometrically. There is no doubt in my mind that "(t)he universal crisis of our time necessitates an epoch of uncompromising revolutionary change [...] aimed at harnessing human energy for creative and socially productive work in an ecologically sustainable and substantively egalitarian world" (Foster 2017, 13).

Ninth, cultural reform in the field of work to recognise diversity and difference and to enable work-life balance. To "labourise" and "monetise" care will work effectively for the rights and equality of all citizens. As emancipation refers to overcoming structural obstacles and distortions to what we consider to be a good life or adequate enjoyment of our rights, labour law has great potential in this regard.

Tenth and final is that, beyond the technical and regulatory considerations to be determined, it is necessary to assume that the concept of work is a prior and indispensable category for social justice, and that the "social question" has segmented it since the 19th century. We must approach it in its complexity in order to avoid intuitionism and certain ideological drifts that could lead to the opposite point than that intended.

Bibliography

Alonso Olea, Manuel, *Alienación. Historia de una Palabra* (Madrid: Instituto de Estudios Políticos, 1974)

—. *De la Servidumbre al Contrato de Trabajo* (Madrid: Técnos, 1979)

—. *Las Fuentes del Derecho* (Madrid: Cívitas, 1990)

Antenas Collderram, Josep María, "Los sindicatos ante la globalización Hacia qué nuevas formas de solidaridad internacional," *Cuadernos de Relaciones Laborales*, vol. 26 (2008), no. 1

Campello, Filipe, "Axel Honneth y la renovación de la teoría crítica," In *Diálogos de Pensamiento Crítico*, eds. Javier Insausti, Jorge Vergara (Bilbao: Universidades País Vasco-Chile, 2012)

Castillo, Juan José, "La sociología del trabajo hoy: la genealogía de un paradigma," In *Tratado Latinoamericano de Sociología del Trabajo*, ed. Enrique de la Garza Toledo (Ciudad de México: FCE, 2000)

Cleaver, Harry, *Una Lectura Política del Capital* (Ciudad de México: FCE, 1985)

Collado, Patricia, "El trabajo y la posmodernidad," In *Utopía y Praxis Latina* (2001): no. 15

De la Garza, Enrique, "El papel del concepto de trabajo en la teoría social del siglo XX," In *Tratado Latinoamericano del Sociología del Trabajo*, ed. Enrique de la Garza Toledo (Ciudad de México: FCE, 2000)
Foster, John Bellamy, "The meaning of work in a sustainable society: A Marxian view," *Monthly Review*, vol. 69 (2017), https://www.cusp.ac.uk/themes/m/m1-3/
Foucault, Michel, *The Archaeology of Knowledge.* (Mexico: Siglo XXI, 2002), https://monoskop.org/images/b/b2/Foucault_Michel_La_arqueologia_del_saber.pdf
Fraser, Nancy, "La justicia social en la era de la política de la identidad: redistribución, reconocimiento y participación," In *¿Redistribución o Reconocimiento?*, trd. Pablo Manzano (Madrid: Morata, 2018)
Honneth, Axel, "La ética discursiva y su concepto implícito de justicia," In *Ética Comunicativa y Democracia* (Barcelona: Crítica, 1991)
—. *Reificación. Un Estudio en la Teoría del Reconocimiento* (Buenos Aires-Madrid: Katz, 2007)
—. "Redistribución como reconocimiento," In *¿Redistribución o Reconocimiento?* trad. Pablo Manzano (Madrid: Morata, 2018)
Kant, Immanuel, *Principios Metafísicos del Derecho* (Buenos Aires: Americalee, 1943)
Laclau, Ernest, "Politics and the limits of modernity," In *Universal Abandon*, ed. Andrew Ross (Minnesota: Minnesota University, 1988)
Merino Segovia, Amparo, "Nuevas formas de organización productiva y autonomía colectiva: sus reciprocas influencias," *Justicia Laboral*, Vol. 36 (2008)
Mouffe, Chantal, "Radical democracy: Modern or postmodern," In *Universal Abandon,* ed. Andrew Ross (Minnesota: Minnesota University, 1988)
—. *The Return of the political* (London: Verso, 1993)
Nieto, Patricia, *La Representación de los trabajadores en la empresa,* (2015) https://e-archivo.uc3m.es/bitstream/handle/10016/21492/patricia_nieto_tesis.pdf?sequence=1&isAllowed=y
Noguera, José Antonio, "El concepto de trabajo y la teoría social crítica," *Papers* (2002): no. 68
Pérez Leñero, José, "Concepto y valoración del trabajo en la Filosofía," *Revista de Política Social* (1961): no. 51
Rössler, Baete, "Work, recognition, emancipation," In *Recognition and Power*, ed. Bert van den Brink and David Owen (Cambridge: Cambridge University Press, 2010)

Sousa de Santos, Boaventura, *El Milenio Huérfano* (Madrid: Trotta, 2005)
Suárez Llanos, Leono, *La Teoría Comunitarista y la Filosofía Política* (Madrid: Dykinson, 2001)
—. *La Ley Desmedida. Estudios de Legislación, Seguridad y Jurisdicción* (Madrid: Dykinson, 2007)
—. "El juicio legal Tienen razón las leyes," *Anales de la Cátedra Francisco Suárez* (2013): no. 47
—. "El aguijón pospositivista del Tribunal de Justicia de la Unión Europea en el concepto de validez," In *Una Contribución a la Europeización de la Ciencia Jurídica,* coord. Paz Andrés Sáenz de Santamaría (Pamplona: Thomson Reuters, 2019)
—. *El Posmodernismo Jurídico y la Filosofía del Derecho* (Valencia: Tirant lo Blanch, 2018)

CHAPTER 3

RE-CONSTITUTING LABOUR LAW: HOW DIFFERENT IS IT TO THINK LABOUR RIGHTS AND IMPROVING THEM IN POST-MODERNITY?[1]

EDUARDO HENRIQUE RAYMUNDO VON ADAMOVICH

1. The Idea of Constitution and the Welfare State and its Progressive Evanescence in Post-Modern Times

It is undoubtedly known that the rise to constitutional level of social rights represented part of the basic structures for the economic and social phenomena of the welfare state or, in other countries, the socialist state or developmental state, at least in continental Europe and Latin America. It can also be explained as the rise to political power of the working class, as a consequence of revolutionary movements, such as in the case of the Soviet Constitution of 1918, or even the Mexican Constitution of 1917 and the German Constitution of 1919. In other cases, there was a movement for re-reading and reframing constitutional texts in order to assimilate collective liberties and union organisation as paths to allow the construction of social rights under liberal precepts.

It can also be said that this movement represented the consolidation of the "labour revolution", which began in the second half of the 19th century and reached its peak after WWI in the first half of the 20th century. Most remarkable in this sense is the Treaty of Versailles and its part in progressing social rights, with the creation of the International Labour Organization and,

---

[1] A special thank you is addressed here to Dr. Flavio Leardini, who has sent me a copy of his *La consistenza del diritto: limiti delle capacità regulative del linguaggio deontico*. Padua: CEDAM, 2011, which inspired some ideas that are presented in this paper.

most importantly, the clause prohibiting treating human labour as a commodity[2]. This is the rise of a new international order, intentionally built over material human dignity, far beyond the basis of strictly liberal equality, representing the overcoming of the liberal revolutions that buried the *Ancien Régime*. To make these legal purposes effective, it took decades and a bloody WWII. However, we should also note the insufficiency of these legal models to guarantee the persistence of the precepts constitutionally enshrined, whether in a formal written or a purely jurisprudential way. Paradoxically, its effectiveness also brought up perceptions of the insufficiency of these legal patterns, hitherto conceived to guarantee the persistence of material welfare.

The end of 20th century and the beginning of 21st have unquestionably demonstrated that the effectiveness of social rights depends more on economic efficiency than on incisive legal predictions. It can be confirmed, even by the fragmentation of the central figure of the employment relationship, which is being dismembered by new work relations, mostly because of new technological innovations, but surely under conditions that would be comparable to those of 19th century proletarians. In a short period of time, the social and economic basis of social rights have been undermined, even with consecrated constitutional features. In this sense, we may mention (even in an earlier period[3]) the works of Georg Brunner (1971), who compared the best results then obtained by western countries and its poorer legal texts to those of socialist states, which were more detailed in this matter and surely less successful in implementation; and that of Theodor Tomandl (1967), appointing the needlessness of a constitutional approach to reach a fundamental ranking of rights, which could be achieved by social recognition and concretisation in ordinary legal texts.

The realisation of a strict dependence of social rights from political and economic conditions, which has frequently demanded constitutional reforms (such as in Portugal and Brazil) in order for a liberalising approach of those rights, does not allow us to underestimate the correctness of some conclusions of jurists in the first half of the 20th century, no matter the fear we have of their authoritarian vocations. Specifically, we can mention the dependence of the effectiveness of constitutional rights on an underlying political and economic order, always noted by authors such as Schmitt

---

[2] This clause is nowadays integrated into International Labour Organization's Constitution, reaffirmed by the *Declaration of Philadelphia*. See >https://www.ilo.org/dyn/normlex/en/f?p=1000:62:8256090188154::NO:62:P62_LIST_ENTRIE_ID:2453907:NO#declaration<, access May, 20th, 2021.

[3] By the end of the 1960s, when it was almost a dogma to execute an imperative constitutional treatment of those rights.

(1995)[4] and Santi-Romano (1945).[5] We can also mention here the entirely different approach of Marxism (*cf.* Marx & Engels 1982, pp. 5-187)[6], which placed the legal order in a superstructure dependent on economic infrastructure. Following these guidelines, social rights should exist no longer than the means to satisfy them or even, in other words, it would be idle to search for any other legal or philosophical reasoning to sustain those rights as reality would not deny the possibility of regression in this field. Social rights and their constitutional recognition would be finite and there would be no limits to surpass them. Strictly said, fundamental social rights were not to be fundamental and should soon be buried along with their constitutional texts.

This weakening picture of social rights, which we see at the beginning of the 21st century, leaves no doubts that the chosen legal rules, mostly those of the constitutional rank, are no longer sufficient for this task. It would not be an exaggeration to say that so-called social constitutionalism is coming to an end. These first post-modern decades have been unable to ensure the same level of social security that was experienced, at least in the so-called developed countries, for most of the last century. Fundamental legal standards were constantly set aside by countless subterfuges and alleged innovations of legal reasoning, which invariably had the effect of weakening the bargaining power of workers and their hiring conditions[7]. Unemployment, technological and educational unpreparedness have created the rest, and even obtained union agreements to take backward steps and lose guarantees. Strikes and demonstrations took a diffuse character and the unions are no longer the only or preferred theatre of convergence of resistance forces in labour disputes. For those who believe that everything depends on economic and financial efficiency, there would be no legal limits for retrocession. Some of them even get to say that human dignity is a vain concept, which is usually invoked as a pretext to violate economic and financial rules of efficiency. From this point on, to deny authoritarianism and continue to affirm the validity of constitutional standards that guarantee social rights

[4] Carl Schmitt has pointed out (p. 78) the need for concrete and typical figures, issued from a concrete order, which are not recognisable, instead of through themselves.

[5] Santi Romano has developed the idea of institution underlying the state which, consequently, allows us to question the Kelsenian unity between state and law.

[6] To mention only one main idea, it is useful to point to the constitution as a formal reality, with a ceremony or a "lie" to be revealed in the content. The consideration of Marxist thinking really challenged those who believed in social-liberal constitutions and intended to seek socialist solutions in a legal way.

[7] To note how constitutional debate has become an instrument of setbacks of rights, see, for example, Concerning the USA (Getman 2016).

can become a mere rhetorical exercise.

To overcome this point, it is essential to find another anchor for the foundation of social rights than just a formal constitutional one. To scape a kind of theoretical idealism and a merely abstract notion of law, it is imperative to look at its underlying elements, even to find structuring instruments to master the bias and centrifugal forces that oppose the consecrated civilising values. It would be deeply disappointing to verify that, after almost 3,000 years of legal history, we have not yet been able to create instruments for the implementation of rights beyond abstractions or, on the opposite side, authoritarian casuistry. The foundations of labour law have been multiple and somehow paradoxical, from humanism to socialism, from positive to social law theories, not to talk about naturalistic ones and international labour standards, besides the casuistic construction of norms by collective bargaining. In some cases, the autonomy of single private law, or scientific investigation for new foundations can also be multiple and is not be restricted by ideological creeds. The width of the plain of theoretical possibilities is so vast that it comprises all the above-mentioned ways, but essentially it is equivalent to the vastness of human expressions of personality, of which work represents one.

It is otherwise certain that the best way forward for this investigation will never be an attempt to keep legal thought exactly as it was during the times of the welfare state, and the creed of that constitutional basis is sufficient to path legal grounds towards effective protection of social rights. As it was already clear to Plato and his dialogues in the *Republic* or the *Laws*, constitution is something that emerges from social practices before popular assemblies can impose them as statutes. Even those who believe in a sort of social contract or those who cultivate the “vines” of rationality, believing in deducing fundamental rules from strict reasoning, cannot deny the centrality of values and human social experience as the beginning and the end of law in space and time. Law, more than an ideal (an abstract one) is a continuous experience of values or, in other words, it aims to conduct and is simultaneously conducted by the social changes in life. Work is a branch of that. And when it is time to deduce new paths, it is to search for values that we shall not abdicate, otherwise we begin to believe that the ends justify the means and, then, there will be no more limits. To reach this purpose is to follow a method that is nearer to ancient law constructions, such as the Greeks or Romans, rather than modern ones. Instead of starting from ideal values subject to reasoning, it should be possible to observe social facts and several interconnected systems, which constitute the subjacent order, and then conceive means to conciliate this order and the values dictated by reason.

Just as it seemed clear to ancient legal thought, the task is not to analyse social structures and produce idealistic critics of it, calling this legal reasoning. From Aristotle to St. Thomas Aquinas, the meaning of natural law has not been restricted to a kind of naturalistic view of law, but rather to understand that it is by definition a conservative means of the *status quo*, in order to preserve a certain social equilibrium and with no necessary connection to political or, as we would say nowadays, public law or constitutional questions[8]. The abstraction of private law from the public or political dimensions of law and society can be understood as the secret or main goal of ancient law, which succeeded in creating means of solutions to private disputes by using the abstraction of legal concepts and enforcing them through the arts of *epieikeia* or *aequitas*, making them suitable to private and individual relationships in its most peculiar aspects with no need to appeal at any time to political or even philosophical discussions. In truth, *aequitas* was the connecting element between the abstractions of law and the subjacent social order, which allowed acquaintanceship between a dynamic and casuistic procedure of legal reasoning and autocratic political systems, such as during the Roman Empire. It is remarkable that the Roman Praetorian Law has found fair solutions to many problems brought by a strictly formal view of legal concepts, using the techniques of injunctions

[8] It is interesting to observe that, on the other side, Hobbes has concluded that law is a method of safeguarding inequality, in opposition to naturalistic equality between human beings. Thus, it is the paradox of those who suppose it is possible to conceive of egalitarian legal theories based on contractual theoretical foundations. To check: *De Cive*, Chap. III, XIII. The question of whether or not two men would be the more worthy, belongs not to the natural, but civil state: "for it hath been shewed before, Chap. I. Art. 3. that all men by nature are equall, and therefore the inequality which now is, suppose from riches, power, nobility of kindred, is come from the civill Law. I know that Aristotle in his first book of Politiques affirmes as a foundation of the whole politicall science, that some men by nature are made worthy to command, others only to serve; as if Lord and Master were distinguished not by consent of men, but by an aptnesse, that is, a certain kind of natural knowledge, or ignorance; which foundation is not onely against reason (as but now hath been shewed) but also against experience: for neither almost is any man so dull of understanding as not to judge it better to be ruled by himselfe, than to yeeld himselfe to the government of another; neither if the wiser and stronger doe contest, have these ever, or often the upper hand of those. Whether therefore men be equall by nature, the equality is to be acknowledged, or whether unequall, because they are like to contest for dominion, its necessary for the obtaining of Peace, that they be esteemed as equall; and therefore it is in the eight place a precept of the Law of nature, That every man be accounted by nature equall to another, the contrary to which law is PRIDE." (capital letters are from the original).

or exceptions, for instance, so that the equity jurisdiction could do well in the Common Law system, especially during English absolutism.

How absurd it would seem to an ancient jurist to speak of fundamental rights and their implementation in private legal relations. Law was then something that belonged to an elite without specific concerns about freedom, equality and so many other issues that are so important today. Workers and the poor were left out of most legal protection at this time, although it is true to say that those jurists did not depend on political systems or public law arguments to solve delicate legal problems or to build subtle solutions for them. Therefore, the aim of this article is not to try to reproduce or create a kind of post-modern Roman law to solve the problems of social rights brought about by the transitoriness of its constitutional foundations, like the German language doctrine building the Bourgeois-Roman civil law until the 19th century. The aim is just to bring about debate concerning the observation of those old techniques for solving legal problems, and try to build through this experience more appropriate solutions to the dynamics of postmodern society and the permanent need to assert civilised values in the face of a growing weakening of social protection, without having to "constitute" and "reconstitute," affirm or reaffirm the entire political system to each problem that needs to be solved.

It is time to realise that the constitutional anchor to social rights has proved to be insufficient in the face of economic, financial, environmental and technological crisises. Utilitarian or contractual views of legal reasoning have been shown to be incapable of imposing limits on the setbacks to social and civilising values, such as philosophical concepts like human dignity, if we do not link them by means of a permanent interconnection technique between the abstractions of legal norms and the dynamics of underlying social order. Establishing this connection seems to be the task that remains far beyond proclaiming or further refining legal reasoning, announcing new principles or new rights without connection to the underlying order, leaving them to fall into the void.

2. Labour Law: Talking about Dialects Instead of Grammar

As shown in the last topic, labour law is characterised by the plurality of theoretical and ideological bases. Structurally, it questions the ancient Roman *summa division* of law, between public and private law. Due to the emergence of a *tertium genus*, social law, coming from union entities and not from the state or individual legal relations, marks a real break with classical civil law science, conceiving that rules could come from those corporate entities. The historical outline of it is well known. In addition to the extensive existing bibliography on these subjects, it is never sufficiently emphasised that the structural techniques of producing legal norms rescued from ancient and medieval legal practices and highlighted during industrial modernity by labour law (and also by commercial law that has a comparable corporative base in its medieval beginnings) represents an advance in the theory of law, which cannot be ignored and deserves to be rethought in post-modernity. The main problem with these new times is the inadequacy of normative, *rectius*, abstract legal structures to a new social order that emerges. Rescuing equitable techniques seems to be more important than reaffirming old legal norms or announcing new ones.

The reforms known in most Western countries have started from a utilitarian primacy of the lowest cost with the greatest social benefit, guided by the imperative of economics or, at best, environmental possibility. The current Covid-19 pandemic has served to reinstate the human dimension as an imperative in the design of social measures, but without the possibility of the same commitment in terms of labour protection, given the economic debacle. The resumption of the human as central to the legal order can firstly be achieved in labour law exactly by subjecting the abstract regulatory framework to an equitable interpretation and application procedure, in which the highest level of human protection and shared access to wealth becomes structurally integral. It is also worth mentioning solidarity, as several papal documents emphasised this even before the pandemic.[9] Replacing the primacy of economic-financial efficiency or utilitarian pragmatism should be the first step. Far from representing a postulate of freedom that subordinates concessions to economic possibilities, this utilitarian pragmatism has been in force with the authoritarian imposition of certain rules of wealth division on immense contingents of people. There is nothing more authoritarian and politically distant from democracy and those

[9] John Paul II, Pope. *Encyclical letter **Centesimus annus***. Available in >https://www.vatican.va/content/john-paul-ii/en/encyclicals/documents/hf_jp-ii_enc_01051991_centesimus-annus.html<, accessed on May 27th, 2021. Especially relevant when it summarises the breadth of the concept: "In this way what we nowadays call the principle of solidarity, the validity of which both in the internal order of each nation and in the international order I have discussed in the Encyclical *Sollicitudo rei socialis*, 34 is clearly seen to be one of the fundamental principles of the Christian view of social and political organization. This principle is frequently stated by Pope Leo XIII, who uses the term 'friendship', a concept already found in Greek philosophy. Pope Pius XI refers to it with the equally meaningful term 'social charity'. Pope Paul VI, expanding the concept to cover the many modern aspects of the social question, speaks of a 'civilization of love.'"

"self-evident truths that all men are created equal…"[10]

It is true that economic, financial and environmental limitations must be taken into account, but the time and dimension to do so should be in union bargaining procedures and not by state imposition. If there is a rational imperative of norms, as Kant concludes, or even if their justice is in the materialisation of the meanings abstractly embedded in the norms, as Kelsen might say, it should not be forgotten that the legal legitimacy of the norm is given by its adaptation to the environment to which it is directed since, as Augustine or Aquinas would say, an unfair law is not a law. Going beyond the public statute that must protect workers in matters of health, safety and environment, the law must ensure minimum rules of sharing the fruits of labour, leaving the most to unions to bargain. At this point it should be noted that, if there is a crisis of union legitimacy, this is more about the method than the substance of worker participation in decision-making procedures. More recent means of communication, such as social networks and other platforms, almost allow the direct participation of workers in bargaining procedures. The question would be only to regulate these new forms of participation and to create methods that would allow a minimum consensus to be reached in the discussion of the terms of negotiation.

If it is true that strikes or demonstrations don't have the same effectiveness as they once did because of the legitimacy crisis of the union representation of workers and the fragmentation of industrial production, and a decrease in the need for a concentration of workers in the workplace, it is also noticeable that a certain reawakening of workers' interest for union membership is emerging, even where it would not be expected. This seems to be the case in some new large companies in the USA, which so far have had a reduced number of unionised workers but where this interest in collective membership is beginning to reappear. If the legal means to prevent unjust acts by employers against unionised workers and even their dismissal are still fragile in many countries, just the perception of workers' intentions to join unions could be enough to stimulate better wages and larger benefits. And when it comes to blue-collar employees, the benefits can be even better. In other words, it proves that union negotiation is not buried and still serves to promote a connection between the abstract and ideal worlds of norms and values that aim to protect workers and the

[10] The clause has become known for being used in the second paragraph of the United States of America's Declaration of Independence, to mean that government is established by consent between people. In any case, this consent is given to a certain division of goods in this society which results in inequality because it is the true social basis of a society, such as in America, whose society is historically based on slavery.

dimension of underlying social order.

It is foreseeable that many will say this formula of associating a minimum public statute protection to a collective negotiation of benefits to workers has already run out. In any case, nothing better has been proposed until now and the problem seems to be less with the method itself than with the means to adapt it to the current reality. Labour law has proved, well before its formal constitutional recognition, to be an efficient method of reconciling the interests of capital, the state and workers, showing itself capable of putting these three dimensions in reasonably peaceful communication. This has since been translated into the real meaning of benefits and economic strength. Well understood by social-liberal doctrines, labour law has made itself constitutional for Western democracies. Contrary to the belief that it may have been a mere concession from the capitalist state, or even that the ideal character of a constitution is the creator of a legal system, it was in fact labour law that sculpted the means of connection that gave real meaning and later legal validity to its ideals. If there were changes in capitalism and in the spatial and temporal dimensions of work, which made the norms and methods that had been efficient, lose their adequacy, the two extreme methods proposed in substitution have been shown to be even worse. Thus, the mere idealistic attachment to the constitutionally enshrined values, or even the attempt to ponder them through judicial courts, lacks economic and social assimilation. Further, the execution of this task without considering humanistic values, taking into account strictly economic imperatives, points to an unlimited setback.

It is not the duty of labour law to create job opportunities, nor has it been scientifically proven that the simple restriction, or even the abolition of social rights increases these opportunities. It is worth noting that this expansion is mainly due to economic and production reasons and legal rules can, at most, contribute to facilitate this eventual trend, but can also hinder it with excessive legal tightening. In other words, the role of law is secondary with regard to economic and financial results, but it is essential for the implementation of humanistic values and there is no sense in the economic dimension if it cannot serve those values. For this reason, rules that are strictly conceived economically fail and lead to misery and exclusion, leaving a large contingent of workers in conditions comparable to those of the 19th century. Similarly, at the opposite extreme, the isolated theoretical conception of an uncountable series of sophisticated rights remains a mere abstraction, far from reality. Both solutions fail because they do not conceive of law as a means of linking its ideal dimension to the real order. They start on an opposite path, believing that law must produce the world they desire and that there is no underlying order, or that it could be necessarily governed by law without other elements to be considered. The other side of the same coin is that law should be a mere reproduction of the underlying order. If we try to understand the problem using a linguistic or grammatical comparison, it may be easier.

If we think of a language, it can be said that "official" language is that recognised by the institutions in charge of determining its grammar and its best or correct uses. Grammar is to languages what statutes are to law. That is, an abstract rule or a system, enunciated by scholars or representatives based on the observation of social uses and the ideal forms they have studied. However, there is another "rule" or "grammar" of each language, which is its current use by its speakers or by those who eventually use it to express the ideas and needs of life. In many cases, there are still many "official" grammars for the "same" language, especially for those spoken in several countries which are geographically distant from each other (e.g. English, Spanish and Portuguese). It would be idle to remember the many dialects various languages have and how far or not each is from its official rules. In reality, how far away they are and the differences in their uses and "rules" and how these relate to official rules means that they can even, at times, come close to presenting as new languages. As with a statute, when it becomes inadequate to social practices, it is usually said that scripture dies, as with old grammatical systems and words which become dead languages. In order to understand this, it is essential to realise that the comings and goings between official and unofficial languages are dynamic and constant and that, in social life, one does not exist without the other, as both make up a single linguistic system. Many of them even coexist. It should also be noted that even different languages that share the same origins can preserve some degree of intelligibility between each other. For example, cultured Portuguese speakers generally understand written or spoken Spanish, or even formally separate languages that, in reality, are mere variations on each other, such as Portuguese and Galician. It is useful to remember that lawyers from civil law countries tend to understand each other's systems better than those from common law.

This comparison is useful to show how wrong it is to believe that law should only reproduce the literal meanings of statutes or other forms of positive norms. It would be like requiring people to speak only a grammatically correct language, which must rigorously reproduce the meanings of these positive rules in social life. The absurdity of the hypothesis is also that of strictly statutory legal theories. Like languages, legal systems must be permanently linked to the dynamics of social life. They are no longer alive if this interconnection is no longer possible. This seems to happen to some positive systems of constitutional social law, which have failed to guarantee the promised effectiveness of their protections to workers and other groups susceptible to special protection, such as in the Brazilian system. Even legislators and constitutional courts promote a real reinterpretation of the precepts of constitutional social law, under a strictly liberal inspiration, sometimes even an orthodox liberal view, which means the imposition of a whole new grammar, with the pretext that social changes demand the privilege of economic and business activities and its freedom. In doing so, those who move by strictly liberal ideological inspiration push defenders of social rights into the uncomfortable position of being defenders of the strictly positive meanings of the legal norms of social rights, producing the paradox of being a defender of social law supporting strict legality. Those who innocently or thoughtlessly assume this strict position in social law do not contribute in any way to its improvement. On the contrary, their sectarianism suggests the inadequacy of this branch of law for these new times. There is nothing worse for social law than to be considered overtaken by time. This is what opens the door to a regression in social rights presented as a requirement for progress.

Labour and social law must recover the dialectical capacity to communicate values to reality, not just through political struggle. Social legal thinking needs to recover its multiple theoretical foundations, connecting them to normative texts but also knowing how to represent the expression of these values in the social environment, through interpretations, decisions and theoretical constructions for an application to social reality, without depending on a formal or strictly legal standard. Human values imposed through equity rules or decisions are more important than legal texts. In reality, they precede formal texts. To show the difference, it is not a matter of seeking an interpretation that expresses values appropriate to the constitution or other legal texts. As values come first, there is no legal obligation to obey a text that contradicts values; and values are not legitimated by texts. On the contrary, it is the texts that justify their existence by consecrating values. Those who believe in improving social law by seeking new adequate interpretation to the constitutional texts deserve to be criticised, as they are trying to circumvent positivism, affirming, on the one hand, the validity of texts while, on the other, trying to reconstruct their meaning through creative interpretation. Thus, they try to use the mandatory character of a text, which has a determinate meaning, to impose another meaning, the product of their own creation, as if they were true legislators, without the duty to assume their ideological and philosophical contradiction to the text. That is why strict positivists call them corrupters of the law. It would be better to assume this contradiction and make it clear that if the official grammar no longer expresses the dialects spoken by people, then we already have new rules and, if we have them, it is best to study them and try to spell out a new grammar, or at least new rules for it, even if it requires overriding the preceding text.

The international, as much as the constitutional consecration of labour and social rights, as well as its improvement during the welfare period in Western Europe and even in the most developed countries of Latin America, may have given its defenders a kind of tranquillity and the belief that those rights would be eternal, mainly because they acquired this support in international declarations of rights. Many of the social rights were recognised as human rights, which is really extraordinary, if we think that less than a century ago its requests were considered to be breach of contracts or even criminal cases. Nobody would doubt or try to diminish the relevance of this consecration. No one should accept setbacks at this point. However, the economic crisis of capitalism proved that this problem would be more complex and that all this solid legal framework would not be enough to contain the setback. It seems to have been precisely this feeling of ease, which was due to the legal certainty of this framework which, at least with regard to legal thinking, has contributed to the loss of the original capacity of labour law to synthesise values extracted from social practice and communicate appropriate solutions to these concrete problems, to a formal legal plan. Instead of denying the meanings of legal texts, or recreating them, the theory of labour law was able to express the meanings extracted from social practices. No one would say that it was the intention of representatives of financial and economic power to create legal texts that would bring many fringe benefits to workers, or even some health or environmental procedures that would limit profits. They only gave in when they realised there was a reasonable justification for more real political advances, and the risk that those ideas could finally triumph.

Labour law has imposed itself as the best solution. Its theory and practice are failing in the same task, which is what this article has tried to show so far, while highlighting the need to rescue this capacity, go back to the roots and seek the elements that could assist in this purpose. This is what we will try to do in the next section or, at least point out some issues that should be considered in a new reworking of labour law theory.

3. Values Beyond States. Concrete Order Beyond Statutes

It can be said that the social state, based on social constitutionalism, was the last historical stage of consolidated nation states since absolutism. Since then, we have had globalisation, a virtual economy, transnational companies, and an information society. Nation states — the great empires born during the 19th and 20th centuries — have become competing and coexisting powers, in a more profound and exaggerated way than when they were separate power groups. Nation states are not yet dead, though. They coexist with transnational powers and some are even becoming transnational empires like the USA and China. One could say that this was also the case with the Roman Empire. We would add that this was precisely the beginning of the sunset for the latter, as it was for the British Empire, too, although it this case it does seem to have been a slower-setting sunset. In order not to abandon the British case as an element of comparison, we can point to a recent wave of nostalgic imperialism in the country, which has thrown it into the confusions of Brexit, and difficulties in re-establishing a border between Eire and Northern Ireland. If we were really in a time of national sovereignty of the state, it would be enough to re-establish control of passports and cargo. However, the complex relations of exchange, transit of people, services and information in postmodern societies show how difficult it is to return to the previous model, or even to move to a new one. So great is this paradox, it should be noted, that the Scots, or at least a considerable number of them, want to separate themselves from Great Britain and join the European Union. The admirable British civilisational work is in danger of being lost in the void, with the country having to re-establish, in a more costly way, the previously broken transnational ties.

All these considerations are justified in order to highlight that the dimension of national laws is somehow emptied by this transnationalisation, and so is constitutional law. As if anticipating it, labour law relies on the magnanimous performance of the International Labour Organization and its system of labour standards, especially conventions and binding international treaties, which establish basic principles and rights at work.[11] Mention should also be made of the numerous documents on this topic from the European Union.[12] The existence of those general rules originating from international or transnational organisations, binding national states, represents a kind of international minimum labour law which, in some cases, is repeated only by general constitutional precepts on the same matter. However, even in many of these cases, beyond international standards these precepts reflect consecrated human values, which would not even depend on positive rules to be bound unless governments or courts found no limits in those values, in a true transgression of civilization. These

---

[11] *Rules of the game: An introduction to the standards-related work of the International Labour Organization.* International Labour Office, Geneva, 2019, p. 18.

[12] An explanation of these standards can be found in >https://eur-lex.europa.eu/summary/chapter/1717.html<, accessed March 23th, 2021.

precepts are the ones that structure a system and could really be called "fundamental labour precepts," beyond constitutional texts. Therefore, they cannot be disregarded by national laws or court decisions and persist until a higher level of civilization is achieved. The lack of economic or financial conditions to improve these rights does not allow them to be denied or overridden under the pretext of a lack of material conditions. The task of governments, courts and unions, in an attempt to improve these rights, is equitable construction, and this should occur much more in ordinary cases or even in collective bargaining than in abstract legislative activity or judicial reviews of constitutionality. It is the domain of direct communication and not that of grammatical enunciation.

The privilege of positive law, or even of written statutes, that was chosen in some countries (mainly in Latin America) to protect social and labour rights, as we saw above, has fulfilled its task, and it is now time to look at its roots and the methods by which these rights emerged. However, it is also essential to realise that many of the ideas that once inspired labour law have influenced other legal branches, mainly civil and commercial law, and even if we leave aside labour law as an instrument of the protection of social rights, these ideas will continue to be observed in solutions to many cases in those other branches. Thus, if we decide to apply the rules of civil law to labour relations, the results would not be essentially different to those of labour law. The same principles, such as the protection of human beings, the prohibition of prejudice, good faith and fair bargaining, restricting interpretations of benefits, and prohibiting excessive advantage for one side in situations of excessive loss for the other, and so on, would continue and would contribute to avoiding the excesses of economic and financial power, and produce equitable results. In other words, the assimilation by other legal branches of many of the ideas that once inspired labour law opens up new ways to obtain legal protection for workers, and this does not depend on constitutional or higher court decisions in favour of these new constructions. They can be taken simply by applying positive rules and principles recognised by civil codes or other legal statutes outside labour law, or even the social branch of the law. By way of analogy, many other solutions could come, for instance, from environmental or consumer laws. There are many solutions that evoke these other branches, as the law today is much more complex than when it started to think about norms and principles to protect workers.

This finding cannot be interpreted as a waiver of the patrimony of labour law. On the contrary, it is to show that the principles and constructions arising from labour law are so solid and so widespread in other legal branches that very similar results could be achieved, if we tried to exclude legal labour protection. This is especially important for those new classes of workers and contracts that employers initially attempted to establish outside legal labour protection. Some employers insisted that they were simply civil contracts with no intention of characterising the typical subordination of the conduction of labour relations. In these cases, even in contract law, some constructions could be made to achieve results very similar to those that would come with labour law. The civilisational phase no longer allows denying the observance of the principles of protection of the human beings, good faith, and fair bargaining, under the pretext of excluding the protection of labour law to some classes of workers. Coalition rights, for instance, apply not only to workers in labour relations, but also to other classes of rights, such as civil rights defenders, consumers and other classes of people who may have common interests and reveal the intention to gather in favour of those common interests. A strike by workers on digital platforms, who are being denied labour protection in many countries, would be no different than a strike by regular employees and, perhaps, could bring much more disorder to some cities than one from, for instance, bank employees, whose work is being replaced by technological means. Countries that deny labour protection to workers on digital platforms, in this case, would have serious problems in trying to impose restrictions analogous to those that are usually imposed on the right to strike. If these digital workers are not employed and do not deserve the legal labour protection, how can we impose restrictions on them that are typical of these labour relationships?

This new figure of "autonomy" granted to many workers of this new digital or technological, virtual economy, is in fact a regression to the social conditions of the beginning of the 19th century, when there was no statute that guaranteed any type of minimum status to workers, and we are now faced with the paradoxical situation in which people who work in so-called "old fashioned" activities live in a dimension of comprehensive social protection guaranteed by law, at least formally. On the other hand, outside this vanishing dimension, the new-born system puts workers back in the past prior to the Treaty of Versailles, and places them under the conditions of "free" workers who offer their work as a commodity without prior legal protection, at least as the defenders of this new world seem to intend. Doctrine and jurisprudence of labour law was established in a certain way, imagining that statutes and social rights, such as legal grammar, would be eternal and would never have their meaning removed. This branch of law has lost much of its capacity for expansion and has been unable to extend its protection to these new types of labour contracts. The main flaw has been in not realising that individual rights, guaranteed by relatively strict statutes as constitutions, are not the best-suited attire to dress labour citizenship. Denying what is usually propagated, individual rights of freedom demand large sums of state investment to be guaranteed, from roads to public security, from health protection to military activities. To live and trade in a free country costs a considerable sum of money. When it comes to labour rights as the rule of state under liberal ideologies, the legal treatment of these rights as individual rights would also require major investment. There is also the paradox of formally guaranteed rights, for which state rulers usually refuse to provide increased investment and expenditure. It took the calamity of a pandemic to make them act differently, and there is no guarantee that it will continue in the same way once the health disaster is brought under control.

The mistake was to become embedded in legal structures with individualist roots and rely on the insulation of workers, who were transformed into consumers in the welfare society, supported by statutes of individualistic inspiration. This pushed workers out of the collective construction of rights and, consequently, caused the decline of the expansion capacity of labour rights. In order to continue using the linguistic comparison, labour law should be more dialectical than grammatical, since its mode of expansion should be equitable dialectical construction, taking rights as experiences in social trafficking. The environment of this expansion must be the workplace, such as streets and popular places, rather than the courts, even the highest ones. Courts must be the seats of the consolidation of advances or, at most, a means for opening popular expansion. When workers progressively lose their capacity to collectively bargain, which is the true ability to exercise their citizenship, they start to depend on political and judicial injunctions to expand labour protection beyond its traditional limits in post-industrial society. At the same time, they experience the ideological, political and economic limitations of this expansion, usually under the promise of a "new world" for work, which is promised to be freer, without the "chains" of statutes and with no limits for workers, as if they could be entrepreneurs of themselves. It is clear that such a framework could arise regardless of the existence of legal protection. The responsibility for that framework could not be attributed solely to that legal protection. However, the main mistake has been the delay in realising this protection is not enough to stop this situation. In the next section, to conclude this article, we will try to reveal some ideas to contribute to solving this problem.

4. Conclusion

The 20th century has been called the century of work. We are now at the end of one period or age and at the beginning of a new one. As Hannah Arendt described in her extraordinary *The Human Condition* (2019),[13] it is this centrality of work as a social phenomenon that introduces citizenship into the industrial society and creates the conditions for a range of rights derived from this condition of worker. More recently, other authors have noticed that the "invention" of individuality, which is an indispensable concept to link with fundamental and human rights, has been propitiated by liberal thinking (Siedentop 2015),[14] meaning the abstraction of work is something that could be hired in exchange for a certain sum of money. Proceeding from the Roman contract, *locatio conductio operarum*, this is an element that fits with the idea of the free individual who has the autonomy to offer his work as a commodity that can be acquired by anyone in a legal trade. It is public statutory protection, conquered by workers since social constitutionalism, that has guaranteed them a status and allowed them live in relative welfare during the last few decades of the 20th century. It has been said that if the contract binds the worker to the employer, that public statute frees him or her, in the same sense that the bourgeoisie freed itself from the nobility by means of liberal constitutions. If this mechanism worked very well for the bourgeoisie, since its underlying social and economic freedom was already concrete reality when they obtained the legal recognition of formal equality, it was not the same for workers. In this last case, legal protection was only a stage to reach minimum social and economic equality and it depended essentially on the persistence and the improvement of the mechanisms for the conquest of rights.

Let us note that the liberal state has great difficulty in dealing with collective rights and, since at least the 18th century and the emergence of capitalism in the Mediterranean, has used the technique of personification to do it, as if individual rights are juridical fiction, and it does not matter if a case deals with large patrimonial collectives and their owners or workers, or even consumers and civil rights fighters. The technique frames one or more persons representative of a collective group as a corporation, a union or an association, which ultimately means a way to conceive rights only through an individualistic sense. This concept is also present in the attribution

---

[13] Arendt has the merit of realising that work continues to occupy a central place in consumerist society.

[14] Siedentop traces extraordinary historical research, which allows for the conclusion that individuality is an abstraction which has contributed mainly to the liberal conception of state.

of property, or even in familiar statutes through the concept of monogamous marriage. It is a liberal concept that did not necessarily exist in ancient societies, from Egyptian to Roman, from Hebrew to African or American societies. This concept, in an abstract way, is closely related to the hierarchical structuring of law, initially with a sovereign and then with its abstraction in the form of a constitution — the abstract expression of the sovereign. This theoretical concept deals with the dimension of validity, a mandatory abstraction which depends on underlying social experience to acquire real semantic value. As everyday life, differently, occurs in a semantic dimension, which does not necessarily correspond to those abstract hierarchical structures, the conquest of statutory freedom may not dismiss the constant improvement of the means of gaining semantic value for this abstraction. The task, in other words, is more in the semantic dimension of rights than in its formal concept. It is useless to insist on the experiential dimension conforming to the abstract one. It is only partially possible, in an adapted way, and so a truly new semantic structure is born — a new dialect, perhaps, or even a new language.

How this is possible is the question that always arises and there is no precise or unique answer. Law is not an exact science and the concept of language as a collective and dynamic procedure refutes the idea of magic formulas. To give one unique answer: this is the procedure for constructing semantic values. These values are especially the result of social experience. If we ask why there are absurd propositions that could formally become statutory texts (although never seriously bind people), the answer is because there is also absurd signification for any reasoning human being in a determined time and place. It is the social assimilation of norms that dictates its significance and its obligatoriness and, of course, its correspondence to logical and scientific patterns (if applicable). Much of the reversal that social benefits have experienced in the last two decades has been due to the resignation of workers and their defendants. Their trust in the welfare state's legal structures allowed some accommodation, but this is totally incompatible with the constant clash of forces that underlies capitalist societies. To signify social benefits for workers, it is essential to make them more legal than formal texts. Above all, they must be the result of that clash of forces. If reason and common good dictate many of the legal norms, it is unquestionable that there are social and economic irrational forces that are opposed to reason, and legal enforceability starts to depend on the resistance of rational forces, which have to make reason not only the correct and abstract solution, but the socially accepted one, too. When irrational forces emerge, sustaining the denial of rational values and imposing a new rationality, which relegates human rights to a secondary position, there comes a new order and it is then time to seek new patterns of significance to support those humanistic values. It will often be useless to evoke the contrariness of legal patterns.

Just as the truth in social sciences sometimes seems to be the result of a choice between values and the enforceability of this truth first of all as a question of political preponderance, so too do labour rights and social benefits begin as political achievements justified by humanistic rationality. This starting point may never be neglected because the way of improving those rights, as said above, is the inverse of those of bourgeois freedom and equality. As these first become social and economic realities before they achieve legal recognition through liberal revolution, social and labour rights, the other side have to conquer this recognition as a way to improve them as social realities. When the bourgeoisie conquered legal equality to the noble classes during the American and French revolutions, its economic power was already a reality and many of the nobles, in fact, depended on financial aid coming from the state and, ultimately, the bourgeoisie. Social rights, in contrast, were imposed by reason and political clash before they could be felt as social realities. That is why they cannot expect to follow the same schemes of bourgeois liberties. They demand a continuous and dynamic procedure of construction. It is true that other liberties also demand this continuous "care" and can also be "caught" by irrational forces, but they are less subject to reframing movements because their sense is more elementary. They can more easily be called "self-evident truths" as they are not essentially bound to a certain form of state or economic order. Social and labour liberties are creations of social liberalism as a way, originally, to oppose socialism, so the task appears to reconstruct these social benefits in a new capitalistic order, as ancient irrational capitalistic forces resurface.

It cannot be ignored that, internationally, there remains an immense universe of normative construction to protect workers, especially in the form of the conventions and other documents of the International Labour Organization, and other norms from multilateral organisms such as the European Union. The "open" character of redaction of these norms rarely allows for their improvement directly to rule on concrete situations in labour conflicts. If these patterns cannot be properly called a grammar for regular use, they can always be remembered as patterns of ruling, or limits under which internal regulation or resolution of conflict must be guided. When internal legal limits erode, those international patterns can be called upon to restructure legal protections and to rationally support social bargaining for effective benefits. As expressions of humanistic values, those international legal norms must also be politically reinforced by governments and taken under consideration by labour unions and workers' political representatives, as an important chapter of their task. If they fall into the void and their limits are increasingly widened, sometimes even loosened, there can emerge a truly new rationality, progressively divorced from those original values, bringing to light (or to darkness, maybe) a new civilisation. We should never neglect that work makes up part of the central nucleus of the evolution of human societies and is its basis in many ways, over time and in many forms of civilisation. We can undoubtedly say that work means the verbal constitution of a society and, even when we think of one without work, it is also a great to prove its facticity. Perhaps the greatest failure of the defenders of labour rights in the last century, during the so-called "welfare period," was to believe that law and constitution could constitute the labour world and to forget that, in reality, it is the contrary. It is work that constitutes and gives significance to law and constitution in a society. When work changes, and underlying labour relations change, it is time to find new ways of continuing to express the same humanistic values. Essentially, human nature poses the same problems today as it ever has.

Bibliography[15]

Arendt, Hannah, *The human condition* (Chicago: Chicago University Press, 2019)

Getman, Julius, *The Supreme Court on unions:* why labor is failing American workers (Ithaca; London: ILR Press, an imprint of Cornell University Press, 2016)

International Labour Organization, *Rules of the game: An introduction to the standards-related work of the International Labour Organization* (Geneva: International Labour Office, 2019)

Leardini, Flavio, *La consistenza del diritto: limiti delle capacità regulative del linguaggio deontico* (Padua: CEDAM, 2011)

Marx, Karl, and Engels, Friedrich, *Gesamtaugsabe (MEGA)*, I/2 (Berlin: Dietz Verlag, 1982)

Santi Romano, *L'Ordinamento Giuridico* (Florence: Sansoni, 1945)

Schmitt, Carl, *Les trois types de pensée juridique*, transl. from German by Köller, Mira and Séglard, Dominique (Paris: Presses Universitaires de France, 1995)

Siedentop, Larry, *Inventing the individual:* The origins of Western Liberalism (London: Penguin Books, 2015)

[15] The bibliography contains only the books mentioned. Sites and other publications in the public domain are referred to in the footnotes.

CHAPTER 4

THE ADVENT OF LABOUR LAW: REREADING PHILOSOPHERS AND SOCIOLOGISTS

MARCEL ZERNIKOW

Introduction

From its advent, labour law has been defined as the subject governing legal relations that arise from the performance of work on behalf of others, whenever it is accompanied by subordination to an employer (Rouast & Durand 1951, no. 1). In this sense, our legal branch governs subordinate or dependent labour. Employing these terms – or their equivalent in French – the authors of the first textbooks on industrial legislation (*Législation industrielle*) answered the question of subordination that was crucial for the foundation of this new subject.[1] They also agreed upon re-baptising the latter into labour law, the term "industrial legislation" being not inclusive enough.

At that time, labour law was broadly conceived as the branch of law that governs the necessary occupation for earning one's livelihood. As such, it concerns, in general terms, the legal status of the subordinate worker (*salarié*) in society. Upon this terminology was based a binary reasoning, which consists of opposing the subordinate to the independent worker under French law. Whenever a person would not be concerned by any of these categories, social protection would provide for risk compensation related to the loss of one's job. Unemployment insurance is justified because the social security system, which was initially grounded on the idea of insuring

[1] One should note that there have been initial doubts about the characteristics of the dependency. Since the *Bardou* decision (*Cour de cassation, chambre civile*, 6 July 1931), it has been acknowledged that this dependency would describe a legal dependency rather than an economic dependency.

the workforce of the employer against events which would prevent its exercise, has become a general guarantee for the economic security of all residents in the country (Borgetto & Lafore 2019, no. 270 f.). Eventually, one must add that the French Constitution guarantees the right to work, which also reflects the importance of work as a source of income and of the participation of each person in the labour market (preamble of the French Constitution of 1946, paragraph 5, which has the force of a constitutional right).

In the following lines, we reflect on the protections which result from the application of labour law to a legal relationship more generally, before attempting to answer those questions arising in the current context of the "fourth industrial revolution," which combines all transformations resulting from the power of augmented intelligence (Schwab 2017, p. 23f.).[2] Given the global impact of this industrial revolution, our aim is to generalise this reflection, thereby attempting to take into account what is common to different labour law systems around the world. Setting aside the local, national or regional specificities, one should bear in mind that labour law exists in all countries. Generally speaking, it provides the necessary protection (health protection, working time limitation, etc.) to a certain category of the population exercising an activity in exchange for an equivalent remuneration. Notwithstanding the differences, it aims to respond to a similar purpose in all different legal systems.

This reading should be introduced by philosophical reflections and be based on sociological reflections. While sociologists are anxious to progress in the knowledge of social phenomena, sociologists of law respond by formulating divergent answers to questions which aim, for example, to discover the creation and evolution of law (*cf.* Weber 2012, who distinguishes *Rechtsquellen* and *Rechtsfindung*). We summarise that the sociology of law helps us to answer questions on law, from outside, such as on its failure to adapt to a certain social reality. Taking into account the function of law, one will suggest possible evolutions.

Affirming that labour law pursues a certain function is the rationale for our work, which will consist of reading labour law as a response to societal and economic changes that have taken place. One must remind oneself that labour law emerged as a response to the first industrial revolution that had led to the mechanisation of work. Thanks to electricity and chain production, the second industrial revolution arrived, and the third industrial revolution can be described as being enhanced by informatisation and numerisation (*cf.*

---

[2] According to Schwab, this revolution is characterised by the universal presence of the Internet in its mobile form, by more and more powerful sensors and by the emergence of artificial intelligence and machine learning.

Schwab 2017, p. 23 f.). A reading that is based upon the importance of work in society may be helpful for resolving current legal debates on the changes to the organisation of work. The current transformations of work, in the framework of the fourth industrial revolution (Industry 4.0) can be described as a fusion of technologies from the physical, digital and biological worlds (Schwab 2017, p. 15). They lead to the recomposition of all industrial sectors, with the emergence of new business models, the disruption of actors in place and the restructuring of production systems, consumption, transport and delivery (Schwab 2017, p. 15). Regarding work, one of the most important effects can be described as "uberisation," which leads to collaborative networks, thereby gradually replacing old-fashioned companies. These networks are based on new machines capable not only of coordinating each other's tasks, but of controlling and memorising their execution; they can even evaluate and reward those who do it well and disconnect those who do not (Supiot 2019, p. 15f.). By appearance, this occurs objectively, without human intervention (Supiot 2019, p. 15f.). Whereas economic, technological and societal changes have continued to evolve further in our different societies, subordinate labour persists as a restrictive legal category. One may ask, however, whether this category and its boundaries are still adequate.

Aimed at reconstructing the advent of labour law by rereading its theoretical foundations, our method should more precisely consist of presenting different reflections which deal with the industrialised society and the phenomenon of the subordinate worker, from the perspective of the social sciences. Doing so, we expect to observe an important interplay between political, societal and economic changes and the legal discipline. We consider that sociologists and philosophers hold the principal knowledge for our study. The focus should be on Central European – mainly German and French – authors who testified to the emergence of the concept of the subordinate worker.

Adopting a certain interdisciplinary approach, Raymond Aron, in his important *œuvre* reconstructing the emergence of sociology as a discipline, placed at the centre of his analyses the relationship between the phenomena of the economy and the political regime or the state, and regularly started from the interpretation that different authors gave of the societies they lived in (Aron 1976, p. 263). Likewise, our method should consist of exploiting reflections on the function of labour law made at its advent. The purpose of reading this and other authors is less to seek their answer to contemporary questions, but rather to interpret their thoughts for drawing conclusions on labour law as it continues to exist.

Interdisciplinarity has been identified as the strength of these authors. Going back to Marx's[3] sociological demonstration, for example, one will notice that the quality of his demonstrations lay in the excellent knowledge he had of the political economy of his time. After all, we consider this present essay as a contribution to the reconstruction of the foundations of the legal discipline in general and labour law in particular. Its aim is to present together a certain knowledge from philosophy and sociology on the one hand, and the legal discipline on the other hand, while recognising these are usually treated separately in the respective disciplines. Its joint presentation can be understood as an attempt, because interpretation difficulties may arise from the relations between philosophy and sociology (*cf.* Aron 1976, p. 195).

First of all, one has to justify the present method which consists of interpreting law by using philosophical and sociological references (1.). This part will be a necessary step before applying this method to labour law (2.).

1. Interpreting Law by Using Philosophical and Sociological References

Philosophy and the sociology of law can be conceived of as subjects that aim at gaining a view over law from outside of it. Whereas both subjects sometimes use similar terms, those terms have different significations within both. The sociology of law is understood as an evolution of early philosophical works that aim to explain a person-centred (individualistic) reading of law. Our presentation will naturally start with philosophical references. This brief outline of the different interactions between law and other disciplines also shows that law cannot be regarded as a discipline that does not interrelate with others. At the beginning, it was necessary to realise that the law was not a given, imposed from above (Ihering 2012). We will therefore start by effectuating a person-related interpretation of law which preceded the adoption of individual rights (1.1.).

Authors from the field of the sociology of law will then help us in our analysis. While one could also define law simply as techniques adapted to concrete social situations, using a sociological "outside" reading makes it possible to know its full social reality (Gurvitch 2012). According to Carbonnier, the purpose of legal sociology is to contribute to the

[3] As a controverted author, his sociological theories are too often ignored. On this occasion, we remember our classes on the sociology of law at the Humboldt University of Berlin.

establishment of a new conception of law which could serve the jurist (Carbonnier 2013).

The peculiarity of the different authors that we will study is that they necessarily consider the interactions between law, on the one hand, and society or economy, on the other. Starting with Karl Marx's sociological studies in a logical sequence, one will discover that economy determines directly or indirectly the legal and political domains. In other words, economy would determine society as a superstructure. Max Weber considers that the various spheres of social life (economy, law, power relations, etc.) maintain interdependent relationships, each also retaining its relative autonomy (Weber 2012). This knowledge will help us to conclude on the individual's role in society, and on how the conscience of it necessarily influenced emerging provisions on the collective (1.2.).

1.1. A Person-Centred Interpretation of Law: the Philosophy of Law

Scrutinising the classics of legal philosophy for their subtle references to an emerging labour law, one may first of all turn oneself to Hegel's *Grundlagen der Philosophie des Rechts.*[4]

One must note beforehand that Hegel considers that law defines the universal form of the relationship between men and nature as well as that of the relationships of men among themselves, insofar as those relationships are not consciously ordered to an ethical end (Hegel 2013, p. 59). In this context, Hegel gives special attention to the transformation of the particular into the universal right (Hegel 2013, p. 59). The passage from a particular to a universal right would be necessary for the constitution of law itself. This is also referred to as formalism in law. Furthermore, law is abstract, as opposed to concrete. Only the abstraction of law would make it possible to determine and effectuate those ideas contained in concrete and universal rights (Hegel 2013, § 30). More specifically, the objective of Hegel's demonstration is to underline the abstraction of private law as a guarantee of the universal validity of its principles. In other words, abstract law would need to be formalised.

In his classic, Hegel's particular concern is to forge the universal right of personality (Hegel 2013, § 10). To put it in different terms, he underlines the objectively universal tenor of the concept of personality. The free will resulting from it would be opposed to the acceptance of slavery or serfdom. This important conclusion can be interpreted as dictating a certain grammar

[4] When translated into English, the title is *Elements of the Philosophy of Right.*

to the positive law adopted at the time, under his influence, which was consequently based upon a person-thing relationship (Hegel 2013, p. 59, according to the "présentation" of the book by Kervégan). More precisely, one may find in the construction of this universal right the theoretical bases underlying the foundation of labour law.

As for the concept of personality of man, Hegel holds that it needs to be effective (Hegel 2013, § 57). It is not by his mere immediate existence in himself that man acquires his personality. Hegel points out that man is a natural being, external to his concept. It is only through the formation of his own body and mind and essentially by the fact that his self-consciousness is apprehended as free, that he takes possession of himself and becomes the property of himself to the gaze of others (Hegel 2013, § 57). This is the explanation founding Hegel's objection to slavery. The alleged legal institution of slavery as well as any historiographical vision of the law of slavery and domination rests on the point of view which consists in taking man as being-of-nature in general, according to an existence which is not appropriate to his concept (Hegel 2013, § 57). In other words, man needs to be aware by himself that he cannot be subordinated and be taken as a being-of-nature. These and other important developments on the concept of personality can be said to have influenced the foundation of private law at his epoch.

More precisely, they can be mobilised for explaining the existence of labour law. Hegel dedicated certain paragraphs of his classic to the division of labour (Hegel 2013, § 198). Starting with the enunciation of the universal right of personality, he holds that the work of the individual is facilitated thanks to the division of labour. Thus, the workers' talent and productions would increase permanently. As a counterpart, reciprocal dependence between men would become a necessity for reaching the satisfaction of their needs. The abstraction of the production processes would eventually make work become more mechanical and make it possible for men to replace themselves with machines (Hegel 2013, § 198).

Whereas Hegel is often identified as an idealist philosopher who conceives of historical becoming as the becoming of mind (Aron 1976, p. 197), Marx later takes a more active approach towards the construction of humankind. One might remind oneself of Marx's Feuerbach thesis, according to which, "philosophers have only interpreted the world in different ways, but now it is up to them to transform it" (Engels 1888, 11th thesis on Feuerbach by Karl Marx, translated into English). Marx studies the philosophical significance of the history of humanity. The history of humanity, as it unfolds through the succession of regimes and as it results in a non-antagonistic society, has a philosophical significance for Marx. It is through history that man creates himself; the culmination of history is simultaneously the end of philosophy. Some interpreters may read an influence from Hegel's philosophy in these developments.

The presentation of these developments on the concept of man of the 19th century was crucial for the construction of the sociology of law.

1.2. The Offspring of a Sociological Reading of Law

It is interesting to note that sociology was motivated at the same time. In France, Montesquieu can be considered as the forerunner of sociology for the considerations he made in *L'Esprit des Lois* (in this sense, Aron 1976, p. 22, if we define sociology as scientific knowledge of the social as such). Auguste Comte, then, is generally seen as the founder of sociology. A starting point for the theories evoked by sociologists was that of social unrest (*troubles sociaux*) (Aron 1976).

Trying to reach unity in human society, Auguste Comte starts by interpreting contemporary society. He observes that social unrest is being caused by the contradictions between a weakening theological and military social order and a simultaneously emerging scientific and industrial order (Comte 1854). To solve these tensions, he suggests the triumph of the scientific and industrial social order (Comte 1854). At the same time, he excludes any idea of a revolution. For the ongoing crisis to come to an end, it would be necessary to rapidly create a system of scientific ideas that would govern social order. In this ambit, Comte conceptualises sociology that has the function of solving the crisis of the modern world. According to him, sociology provides a system of scientific ideas that will preside over social reorganisation (Aron 1976, p. 91). His method is positivist, based upon that practiced in sciences. Thus, sociology is understood as a synthetic science that starts from the most general laws, from the fundamental laws of human evolution, and finds a global determinism that men could, in a certain way, use.

Comte, who concentrates on European societies, draws a temporal line between different societies. Interestingly, Comte advocates the model of industrial society as the model of society. He predicts that all of humanity would follow the road Western societies are following. Indeed, industrial society was a new fact at his time and was described as being characterised by a scientific organisation of work, an increase in wealth and a concentration of workers in factories. One might underline the creation of "masses of workers" (*salariés*). Comte notably wants a reform of spiritual power and would like this spiritual power to be exercised by interpreters of social organisation. Doing so, scientific organisation in industrial society would end up giving everyone a place in proportion to their abilities and would achieve social justice. The idea behind Comte's sociology is unitary: he claims that unity of society will be reached when all the guiding ideas that are adopted by the different members of the collective (*collectivité*) form a coherent whole. Thus, Comte provides us with reflections which can be helpful for constructing universal laws.

Parallel sociological reflections have been led in Germany by Marx who attempts to explain the necessity of sociology next to philosophy. Marx starts, in *Epicurie*, from the divorce between concept and empiricism (Marx 1970). This separation would have led philosophy to turn itself against the world which has become irrational. Philosophy would have to transform it (Marx 1970, p. 206f.). Starting from Hegel, Marx affirms that philosophy would turn to the concrete world and, in doing so, form intrigues with it. Once this separation was achieved, one would need to make a weapon of combat out of the concept for the struggle which makes the state adequate to its essence (Marx 1970, p. 207f.).

Whereas philosophers would have completed their task consisting of raising the experiences of humanity to explicit consciousness, it is up to man to realise the vocation of which he has been conscious (Aron 1976, p. 198). According to Marx, the real world would not conform to the meaning that philosophy gives to the existence of man (Aron 1976, p. 198). This reasoning created a necessity for sociology. One of the essential questions Marx tried to find an answer to is: Under what conditions can the course of history realise the vocation of man? Operating a historical analysis of society, Marx addressed his efforts to explain human nature. It would be advisable to study the individual from the angle of universality (*cf.* already Hegel 2013). Under the influence of universality, man has a double and contradictory situation. On the one hand, he is a citizen and participates as such in the state. His role is limited to formal democracy, that is, voting. On the other hand, man belongs to the "bürgerliche Gesellschaft" (civil society), that is to say, he exercises professional activities (comp. Hegel 2013, who also developed this concept). Concerning this latter situation, however, man would be locked into his peculiar situation and not communicate with the whole of the community. He would either be a worker under the orders of an entrepreneur or an entrepreneur separated from the collective. Thus, civil society would prevent individuals from realising their universal vocation. After all, he concludes that the individual accomplishes an essentially economic role. The challenge of achieving universality would be that of letting the individual participate in civil society. Until this universality was realised, one would continue with an opposition between universality and particularity. This study is of a philosophical character insofar as it analyses the universality of the individual before concluding that this universality would be limited to political order. In this respect, it would also constitute a transition towards a sociological analysis (Aron 1976, p. 199). One may remind oneself that Marx's analysis has been a philosophical one before becoming economic or sociological. Marx conceives men as complete beings, as opposed to those specialised by the division of labour (*division du travail*). In other words, Marx's theory reflects a certain protest towards the conditions made to the individual by industrial society.

Max Weber shared the characteristic with Marx that he did not exclusively dedicate himself to sociology, and was mainly an economist, but focused on the sociology of law. The object of his study was law as an *Erzwingungsstab* (enforcement mechanism). It would be characterised by orders that apply to the way one reacts; this would not necessarily imply a judicial instance (Weber 2012, position 767). Weber's analysis is important for identifying sources of law. He considers that not every applicable order necessarily has a general and abstract character and can be identified as law. However, he denounces an artificial separation between legal acts (*Rechtssätze*) and judicial decisions (*Rechtsentscheidung*), the latter having lately and wrongly been excluded from the designation as law. According to Weber, an "order" can also appear as an order of just a concrete state of affairs. What matters is the legitimate validity of the order which is attributed to it by actors in one of the following ways: a) by virtue of tradition; b) by virtue of affective (especially emotional) belief; c) by virtue of value-rational belief; d) by virtue of positive statutes in whose legality one believes. Concerning the last category of positive law, Weber considers that its legality can be considered legitimate either by virtue of the agreement of the interested parties or by virtue of enforcement (due to a rule of people over people that is considered legitimate) and obedience. One should principally note that this could have an impact on the sources of law which would be developed.

According to sociological analysis, law should be considered as enabling adaptations to societal evolutions. The observed crisis would provoke a certain harmony between law and society. Progressively, law professors started to consider law as a mechanism to respond to new societal needs whereas legislative acts were more and more considered as being inefficient. At the beginning of the 20th century, Sinzheimer considered that the healing power of law was still unshaken and reiterated that new social needs would have to be satisfied by new laws (Sinzheimer 1977, p. 182). He wrote: "One is dizzy when one looks back at the seemingly unmistakable mass of laws of the last decades and imagines where this legal mass production will lead to" (Sinzheimer 1977, p. 182, translated into English).

In other words, he doubted that the mass production of legal acts would be able to respond to the contemporary needs of society. A mass of state laws would rather hinder societal developments (Sinzheimer 1977, p. 182). Whereas one should consider to liberate the judge of excessively precise conditions, one should not let the judge be completely free, either. Sinzheimer, however, considers law as hindering societal progress as forms of life should be constantly evolving. In the end, one would need to come to the conclusion that judicial decisions, although based upon detailed legal norms, naturally include decisions of will and value judgments of a subjective nature (Sinzheimer 1977, p. 183). From this perspective, it is not evident to arbitrate different opinions on legal sources. After all, legal education would need to be adapted and include aspects of social sciences for guaranteeing the desired interpretation (Sinzheimer 1977, p. 183). In summary, judges should have a view of the legal whole (Sinzheimer 1977, p. 184).

While the first developments concerned sociologists, the latter is an example of how sociological theories were finally mobilised by lawyers and, more precisely, by labour lawyers.

2. Applying a Sociological Reading to Labour Law

These guidelines on the emergence of the philosophical and sociological analysis of law influenced (in substance) the progressively adopted norms. At that time, labour law emerged as a new branch of the discipline. André Rouast and Paul Durand still presented, in the mid-20th century, labour law as a branch of law that is "relatively recent: in its modern form, it only dates from the middle of the nineteenth century" (Rouast & Durand 1951, no. 1, translated into English). To know the characteristics of labour law it is necessary to look at its origins and, more specifically, the context in which it was born. For this purpose, it is particularly relevant to reread the authors of the sociology of law. They will serve as a starting point for a description of its birth. Here, it may be interesting to recall that sociologists of law observe the links between law and economics (e.g. Weber 2012), or rather between modern law and capitalism (Beaud 2021, p. 170).

Our essay, which tries to found the law on sociological observations (*cf.* Commaille 1982, p. 12f. who specifies that important sociological studies have been led in the field of labour law), starts by recalling that labour law was born to accompany the effects of the (first) industrial revolution, which caused the emergence of large collectives, the creation of repetitive and monotonous tasks and the establishment of hierarchical structures. How does the law manage to respond to the challenges imposed by the evolutions that have taken place in the world of work? The analysis provided herein will focus on economic and societal aspects that have favoured the advent of labour law (2.1.).

Moreover, the strength of sociologists of law is to link this description of the evolution of law to that of the science of law. Max Weber, for example, considers again that legal authors are actors in the development of law (Beaud 2021, p. 170). This brings us to our second point: discovering lessons from the sociological analysis on the future development of labour law (2.2.).

2.1. Describing the Advent of Labour Law: A Sociological Standpoint Enabling the Consideration of its Economic Context

There are different ways to describe the ascension of labour law.

According to one perspective, which we call the economic perspective, labour law emerged as an answer to the economic changes provoking a fundamental transformation of work. One of the first representatives of this school of thought that we identified was undoubtedly Marx, who set himself the task of constructing a philosophical vision of historical becoming (*cf.* Marx 1872). In other words, the aim of his work was to scientifically demonstrate the evolution of the capitalist regime. Thus, the study of work relations would necessarily need to envisage the interactions between law and its economic foundations.

The object of the following developments is to present the peculiarities of work relations that motivated the *naissance* of a specific law on this object. The emerging economic regime described by Marx was characterised by the exploitation of men by men, that is to say, the subordination of manual workers to a class which simultaneously held ownership of the means of production and political power. Marx explained the formation of the *prolétariat* in Germany as a consequence of emerging industrialisation. In fact, what led to the emergence of the *prolétariat* was not a naturally existing but an artificially produced poverty (Marx 2018). In other words, the *prolétariat* was not to be considered as the masses mechanically oppressed by the weight of society, but as the masses resulting from the acute decomposition of society and, after all, the acute decomposition of the middle class (Marx 2018).

What is striking about his theory, and what we attempt to explain as the economic reason of labour law, is the link he constructs between the economic system and the social evolution. Marx distinguishes different stages of human history according to prevailing economic regimes. The *bourgeois* economic regime would be characterised by wage labour. Given that this regime would also imply the exploitation of men by men, antagonistic social formations would necessarily be formed (Aron 1976, p. 181).

The description of these interactions between labour law and society or economy are echoed by the first comprehensive studies on labour law. Thus, labour law would need to be understood as exerting a hold on economic life (Rouast & Durand 1951 no. 6). But the organisation of the economy reciprocally exerts an influence on working conditions (Rouast & Durand 1951, no. 27). Depending on this equilibrium, one may possibly observe the advent of a labour law that pursues economic objectives (Rouast & Durand 1951, no. 27). In this context, one must add that, from the end of the 19th until the 20th century, one could observe the formalisation of society on the business model (Foucault 2004, p. 166). This led to the redefinition of legal institutions and the rules of law which are necessary for a regulated society starting from and depending on the competitive market.

This brings us to a second point: the sociological reasons for labour law. The strength of Marx's demonstration earned him the qualifier of sociologist-economist. One of the central concerns of his work is the conflict between the social productive forces and the relations of production. By relations of production we mean the relations of property as well as the distribution of incomes between individuals or groups of the collectivity. By further politicising his thought, Marx arrived at the description of class struggle between the *prolétariat* and the *bourgeoisie*. In this context, one must not forget that Marx's analysis of the evolution of the economic system was also a great contribution to the foundation of sociology.

One may summarise this theory, sharpening it a little, and say that it is man's awareness of his submission that counts. The challenge, however, to the transformation of the so-called capitalist regime, would be the antagonism between the relations of production and the exploitation of man by man, so that the required consciousness would not be facilitated. What characterises Marx's sociology is that he opposes social reality and consciousness: "It is not the consciousness of men that determines their social reality, on the contrary, it is social reality that determines their consciousness" (Aron 1976, p. 178, translated into English).

This helps us to summarise his thoughts as a sociologist: Marx tries to explain, based on the illustration of the functioning of capitalism, why men are "exploited" in the regime of private property, and why this regime is condemned, by its contradictions, to evolve towards a revolution that would destroy it (Aron 1976, p. 181). Marx considers that this general theory can possibly be used for describing other forms of society (Aron 1976, p. 195).

Other sociologists of that time analysed the divisions created in society by the emergence of new forms of labour. The division of labour was, in the 19th century, explained as favouring the emergence of a new type of society. It consists of the logic that everybody responds to a particular function in society which also leads to abandoning the "total" man. Thus, the division of labour exists as a condition of our societies (Comte 1854) and helps in understanding them. Theories on the division of labour need to be placed in their historical context. The creation of a collective work force composed of dependent workers in the 19th century seems to have contributed to the birth of labour law. Contemporary writers such as Émile Zola described the problems resulting from this new phenomenon (*cf.* Zola 2000).

As we noted above, the division of labour had been explained economically at the beginning, before it was analysed from a sociological point of view by Comte in France. Comte considered that large societies would only be able to maintain their equilibrium thanks to the specialisation of tasks. Thus, the division of labour would be one of the principal sources — if not the only one — of social solidarity. Social solidarity would be mainly constituted by the continuous distribution of the variety of human work; this would be the elementary cause of the extent and the increasing complication of the social organisms (Comte 1854). What is original about Comte is that he sought to apprehend the division of labour in its complete rational scope. He applied it to various operations instead of limiting it to simple material uses. Therefore, he considered the division of labour and, in particular, its social effects.

After Comte, it was Durkheim who sought to study the division of labour. He explained the causes of the progression of the division of labour. The economy would contribute to the creation of a new civilisation. According to the most widespread theory, the division of labour has no other origin than the desire of man to constantly increase his happiness (Durkheim 1893, *Livre* II). One acknowledges that the more the work is divided, the higher the output. Consequently, the resources it makes available are more abundant. As for the causes of the division of labour, Durkheim admits: "The division of labour varies in direct proportion to the size and density of societies, and if it progresses continuously in the course of social development, it is that societies are steadily becoming denser and very generally larger" (Durkheim 1893, *Livre* II, translated into English).

According to Durkheim, the division of labour is the rule that commands us to realise in ourselves all the attributes of the species. One duty can be contained and moderated by another duty, but not by purely economic necessities (Durkheim 1893, *Livre II*). The division of labour provokes the individual to renounce being a complete man. However, the attributes of the species cannot be limited by the contrary rule of the division of labour unless it is of the same nature, that is to say, it is moral. Durkheim considers that the division of labour needs be moral because the needs for order, harmony and social solidarity are considered to be moral.

The methodology he proposes is not that of subjective concepts but he says that "one should know a fact which could serve to measure the level of average morality and then observe how it varies as civilization progresses" (Durkheim 1893, translated into English). From there on, one can measure collective immorality and, consequently, make conclusions on a civilisation. In the context of an emerging industrial movement, Durkheim observed, in particular, crimes in industrial production where the division of labour was constituted only on an economic basis. As a result, one would have to conclude that a civilisation must not only be constituted on economic interests. Indeed, one would necessarily have to stop creating communities based solely on economic interests. To put it in Durkheim's words: "It is possible that the economic utility of the division of labour contributes to a certain result but, in any case, the division of labour goes infinitely beyond the sphere of purely economic interests because it consists in the establishment of a *sui generis* social order. Individuals are linked to each other who would otherwise be independent; instead of developing separately, they concert their efforts; they stand together" (Durkheim 1893, translated into English).

At the time, Durkheim considered that studying the division of labour would be of crucial importance, given that the question has made little progress since Adam Smith's studies on the division of labour from an exclusively economic perspective (Durkheim 1893). As industrialisation has led to the constitution of new collectives of labour, the latter would need to be the subject of analysis. This consideration can be interpreted as expressing an emerging need for the creation of rules of labour law that should not be based on purely individual interests.

The need to create a branch of law that takes into account the collective can be found in the following statement by Durkheim: "The most remarkable effect of the division of labour is not that it increases the output of the divided functions, but that it makes them interdependent. Its role in all these cases is not simply to embellish or improve existing societies, but to make possible societies which without it would not exist" (Durkheim 1893, translated into English). This statement also helps us to understand the opposition between the individual and the collective – or the common conscience – which underlies labour law. One can find several indirect references to these theories in the initial writings on labour law, such as in the *Précis* by André Rouast and Paul Durand (1951), who characterise the meaning of labour law for the constitution of a moral order, in the sense that law should always be moral.

Studies on the link between the collectivisation of labour and the economy have been redundant in sociology from the late 19th century onwards. In Germany, Weber chose *Gemeinschaften* (communities) as an object of his study. Interestingly, he addressed himself to the economic character of these collectives and, surprisingly, he considered that communities are economically justified. In other words, the economic interest in their continuous existence would always be primary, before that which concerns common ideals. Weber considers that it is therefore normal that people belong to a religious, student, political or other association, although they are absolutely indifferent to the interests cultivated there (Weber 2012).

Given this broad panorama, one may conclude that the economic origins of the societal mode of operation cannot be ignored while studying the emergence of labour law. They need to be read in conjunction with those theories on the sociology of law. In this context, it is not surprising that sociologists of the 19th century were also interested in the economic reasons for new societal models. Their developments are crucial for our essay, which attempts to reread the emergence of labour law from a sociological perspective. These writings have undoubtedly influenced the bases of labour law, which depend on a strong will to consider the collective interests, in a context where the individual is deliberately dissolved in collective structures and depends on economic structures.

2.2. Lessons to Be Learned from the Sociological Analysis of Labour Law

Following our preceding developments, one may understand labour law as an answer to economically provoked changes to the societal model. In other words, labour law cannot be completely separated from economic reasoning. A sociological reading helps us discover coherent answers within labour law to economic and societal evolutions. Such a reading might be a considerable contribution to the analysis of reforms in this field of law and anticipate its future evolutions.

Therefore, it is important to take into account the possible impact of progressive economic changes on labour law. With economic crisis provoking the reconsideration of expenses in the social system, it is susceptible to enhancing further economic productivity from a solely economic perspective. This reasoning could develop without considering necessary protections for the worker. However, one needs to take into account that economic measures aiming to create productivity possibly create new risks for workers which need to be considered before implementing them. The instauration of reduced working time, for example (Rouast & Durand 1951, no. 27),[5] is an economic measure which aims to save costs for the employer and therefore maintain a rather constant level of employment.

Before the crisis related to Covid-19, other contexts showed the evolution of mechanisms for reducing working time or suspending employment contracts for a limited time. To take a fluctuating debate in French labour law, one can observe that, in previous decades, the legislator tried to institute measures for reducing working time – and remuneration – by invoking economic reasons (French Ordinance No. 2017-1385 of 22 September 2017 on the strengthening of collective bargaining. Article 3 instituted *accord de performance collective*). While the employer cannot unilaterally impose them, the legislator created certain mechanisms to be instituted by collective agreements. These reforms were based on a rationale aimed at maintaining employment contracts (Auzero, Baugard & Dockès 2020, no. 329 ff.). What we have demonstrated here is that labour law's fluctuations over time are necessarily motivated by economic causes.

At the same time, using economic reasoning, labour law is sometimes considered to be a constraint for economic progress and standards are put at risk. Therefore, it would be necessary to institute rights that could apply regardless of economic challenges. Apart from the fundamental rights, which are guaranteed as ultimate limitations to the employer's power (Article L. 1121-1 of the French Labour Code), one has to note all those rights that cannot be derogated from, neither by collective agreements nor by contract (*ordre public*).

Analysing further the incidence of economic evolutions on labour law, one may evoke the temptation to create new forms of work, of which we consider the "platform economy" an example. Digital platforms aim to reserve certain types of activity from the benefits of constraining labour protection. In France, like in other countries, this evolution bypassed the adoption of a "secondary" labour law, by which only certain rights apply to these "service providers" (*cf.* Title VII of the Labour Code).

---

[5] The authors demonstrate that labour law is conceived of as an arm on behalf of economic strategies, as shown by the fact that working hours are reduced in contexts of crisis and that labour law as such pursues, among others, the aim of protecting against unemployment. The evolution of specific regimes of working hour reductions in combination with financial aid (*activité partielle*) in France and other countries (*Kurzarbeit* in Germany) was favoured by the pressure of the economic crisis, whereas in normal contexts such measures would have been difficult to pass through the legislative process.

Instituting a regime of independent labour for certain activities, the legislator favoured the creation of a new economic sector in which individuals asking for a service are connected with service providers via an algorithm. The employer being allegedly replaced by this algorithm, there has been debate in all countries hit by this new economic phenomenon, on the identification of the debtor of health protection, for example. In other words, economic change has provoked a new form of labour which is, initially, not submitted to national labour law and thus does not enter into habitual national legal reasoning. Eventually, this evolution might be considered as a new development of the manner in which work can be performed.

To clarify this statement, taking into account the economic evolution for understanding labour law does not mean, however, that modern society is based on the assumption that labour is a material good that must obey the laws of the market (Rouast & Durand 1951, no. 28). This has been recalled in the context of economic crisis, where important "guardrails" help guarantee the fundamental rights of the employee. Therefore, labour law reforms in times of crisis are necessarily accompanied by important debates on fundamental labour rights. One may repeat, in this context, that labour is not a commodity (Supiot 2021).

This helps us to illustrate that it is necessary to remember the fragility of labour law as a branch of law in the service of the economy. Reading works on the history of political economy, one has to admit, however, a decline in state regulation in essential fields such as health, hygiene, natality and race (*cf.* Foucault 2004). Foucault who studies bio-politics (i.e. the problems posed to governmental practice by phenomena specific to a group of living beings — members of a specific society) comes to the conclusion that the aforementioned phenomena were traditionally regulated by sovereign states before being abandoned to economic doctrine.

Labour lawyers have been aware of this problem. To put it in Rouast's and Durand's words, an economic policy has to be careful not to disregard the superior rights of the human person (Rouast & Durand 1951, no. 27). From its advent, labour law has been characterised as a specific branch of law based on the individual person. In this sense, labour law may precisely be considered as a reaction to a materialist philosophy.

From a sociological point of view, the aforementioned developments induce that societal changes have been orchestrated and are not happening by coincidence. This conscience brings into question the function of labour law in the face of these realities. Should labour law not precisely respond to insufficiencies of traditional legal reasoning? Sociological reflections should have particular importance for labour lawyers. Sinzheimer found that the protection of employees is a particular field where legislative evolution has caused protests (Sinzheimer 1977, p. 182). This evolution has contributed to the creation of specific types of norms (e.g. collective agreements, charters, etc.) which cannot be found in other fields of law. As we have noted before, the acceptance of a greater variety of norms has probably been favoured by the admission of a philosophical and sociological analysis of law.

Concerning the content of labour law, sociological analysis brings us to two conclusions on the characteristics of labour law.

Essentially, labour law is understood as the branch of law that aims at protecting the employee as being subordinate to his employer. This should be the main characteristic of labour law which deals with the protection of the "weaker" party. In France, this relationship continues to be described as subordination, whereas its definition needs to fit into more modern contexts. Would the traditional, strict criteria of subordination not impede worker protection benefits to those who actually need to be protected, such as workers of digital platforms?

Furthermore, labour law was instituted as a response to the deliberate or "artificial" creation of collectives of workers. Herein, workers resemble each other by their condition of being subordinate to an employer. Our branch of discipline emerged at a time when the mass phenomenon of factory work was new. As such, labour law institutes rights for the single employee to express his rights collectively. Thus, the subordinate nexus is compensated. Rouast and Durand commented on the adoption of the law on collective agreements of 1919 as favouring social peace: "It achieves this not only because it brings, like any legal rule, a certain order in labour relations, but above all because it expresses the feeling of justice of the social environment: A good organisation of labour relations is an element of peace in the State" (Rouast & Durand 1951, no. 5, translated into English).

To conclude, one may draw attention to the fact that work is a source of income for the majority of people and, thus, labour law concerns an important part of society. Starting from that, it might be interesting to imagine a future labour law that would also be based on the concept of labour as a means to accomplish oneself.

Bibliography

Aron, Raymond, *Les étapes de la pensée sociologique* (Paris: Gallimard, 1976)

Auzero, Gilles, Baugard, Dirk, and Dockès, Emmanuel, *Droit du travail* (Paris: Dalloz, 2020)

Beaud, Olivier, "Max Weber, les droits subjectifs et l'État," In *La pensée et les normes. Hommage à Jean-François Kervégan*, directed by Aubert, Isabelle, Djordjevic, Élodie, Marmasse, Gilles (Paris: Éditions de la Sorbonne, 2021), p. 167

Borgetto, Michel, and Lafore, Robert, *Droit de la sécurité sociale* (Paris: Dalloz, 2019)

Carbonnier, Jean, *Essais sur les lois* (Paris: LGDJ, 2013)

Commaille, Jacques, "Esquisse d'analyse des rapports entre droit et sociologie. Les sociologies juridiques," *Revue interdisciplinaire d'études juridiques,* vol. 8, no.1 (1982): p. 9

Comte, Auguste, *Système de politique positive ou Traité de sociologie, instituant la religion de l'humanité. Tome quatrième* (Paris: Librairie des Corps impériaux des ponts et chaussées et des mines, 1854)

Durkheim, Émile, *De la division du travail social* (Paris: Félix Alcan, 1893)

Engels, Friedrich, *Ludwig Feuerbach und der Ausgang der klassischen deutschen Philosophie (Mit Anhang Karl Marx über Feuerbach vom Jahre 1845)* (Stuttgart: Verlag J. H. W. Dietz, 1888)

Foucault, Michel, *Naissance de la biopolitique. Cours au Collège de France, 1978-1979* (Paris: Seuil, 2004)

Gurvitch, Georges, *Éléments de sociologie juridique* (Paris: Dalloz, 2012)

Hegel, Georg Wilhelm Friedrich, *Principes de la philosophie du droit,* edited by Kervégan, Jean-François (Paris: PUF, 2013)

Ihering, Rudolf von, *Der Kampf um's Recht* (Hamburg: Tredition Classics, 2012)

Marx, Karl, *Différence de la philosophie de la nature chez Démocrite et Epicure*, translated by Ponnier (Bordeaux: Ducros, 1970)

Marx, Karl, *Le Capital* (Paris: Maurice Lachâtre, 1872)

Marx, Karl, *Contribution à la critique de la philosophie du droit de Hegel* (Paris: Allia, 2018)

Rouast, André, and Durand, Paul, *Précis de législation industrielle* (Paris: Dalloz, 1951)

Schwab, Klaus, *The Fourth Industrial Revolution* (Switzerland: World Economic Forum, 2017)

Sinzheimer, Hugo, *Ein Arbeitstarifgesetz: Die Idee der sozialen Selbstbestimmung im Recht* (Berlin: Duncker & Humblot, 1977)

Supiot, Alain, "Introduction. Homo faber: continuité et ruptures," In *Le travail au XXIe siècle*, directed by Supiot, Alain (Ivry-sur-Seine: Les éditions de l'atelier/Les édition ouvrières, 2019)
Supiot, Alain, "Labour is not a commodity: The content and meaning of work in the twenty-first century," *International Labour Review*, vol. 160, no. 1 (2021): p. 1
Weber, Max, *Wirtschaft und Gesellschaft. Grundriß der verstehenden Soziologie* (Altenmünster: Jazzybee Verlag, 2012), e-book
Zola, Émile, *Germinal* (Paris: Le Livre de Poche, 2000)

CHAPTER 5

FUNDAMENTOS FILOSÓFICOS DO DIREITO DO TRABALHO: APLICABILIDADE DA TEORIA DA JUSTIÇA DE JOHN RAWLS

ANDRÉ JOBIM DE AZEVEDO & VITOR KAISER JAHN

Introdução

Diversos achados científicos apontam para a constatação de que o Direito do Trabalho está em crise. Pode-se dizer, inclusive com razoável grau de certeza, que esta é uma sensação comum entre os operadores e acadêmicos voltados à seara jurídico-laboral, a qual tem experimentado impactos significativos no seu objeto.

Isto porque, atualmente, há uma série de fatores extrajurídicos que entram em choque com institutos e soluções pensadas pela dogmática tradicional do Direito do Trabalho. Podemos citar, sem a pretensão de apresentar um rol exaustivo: *(i.)* a nova conjuntura política, social e econômica de uma sociedade pós-industrial (Dorneles 2019), na qual os sujeitos que compõem a relação de emprego típica divergem sensivelmente do modelo industrial que delineou a gênese do Direito do Trabalho (Ramalho 2015, 66-73); *(ii.)* as crises econômicas que vêm sendo enfrentadas globalmente de forma cíclica, demandando a redução de custos de produção (Ramalho 2015, 73-74); *(iii.)* a Quarta Revolução Industrial e suas tecnologias disruptivas, que modificaram sensivelmente os contornos em que se desenvolvem relações de trabalho, fazendo surgir o novo paradigma da "uberização laboral"; bem como *(iv.)* as perniciosas consequências da pandemia do novo coronavírus (COVID-19), que não só tem afetado de forma extremamente grave a saúde humana, ceifando milhares de vidas a cada dia que passa, mas, também, diversos setores da economia, à medida em que, além da redução do consumo inerente ao contexto pandêmico, as políticas de isolamento social para contenção da propagação do vírus envolvem o fechamento temporário de estabelecimentos comerciais classificados como não essenciais. Os fatores extrajurídicos citados, dentre inúmeros outros que também poderiam ter sido elencados, colocam em questão a própria sustentabilidade do sistema laboral e seu arranjo protetivo em tempos de crise.

Nesse contexto, classifica-se como de capital importância esta obra coletiva que propõe o resgate de pressupostos filosóficos do Direito do Trabalho com a nobre ambição de constituir um ferramental teórico que justifique a defesa dos valores juslaborais no cenário atual. À medida em que fornecem elementos de teorização abstrata, os fundamentos filosóficos permitem transplantar a compreensão dos institutos laborais para um cenário neutro, distanciando-se das distorções decorrentes do estado crítico presente.

Visando contribuir com o processo de revelação dessa fundamentação filosófica, o presente ensaio abordará a viabilidade de adequação dos institutos laborais à teoria da justiça defendida pelo jusfilósofo John Rawls, notadamente se as soluções fornecidas pelo Direito do Trabalho persistem hígidas após serem submetidas ao método procedimental da posição original e do véu da ignorância.

1. Fundamentos Filosóficos do Direito do Trabalho

Ainda que em apertada síntese pela natureza ensaística desta contribuição, faz-se necessário, preliminarmente, averiguar a viabilidade de o Direito do Trabalho socorrer-se de fundamentos filosóficos.

Ao contrário do esperado, uma revisão preliminar da literatura maximiza as dúvidas acerca da compatibilidade entre estas diferentes áreas do saber. Em nível nacional, constata-se aridez na aproximação teórica entre o Direito do Trabalho e a filosofia[1]. Expandindo a pesquisa para o âmbito internacional, confirma-se que, de fato, a literatura sobre os fundamentos filosóficos do direito laboral é escassa (Spector 2006, 1121).

Conforme Bogg, esse desligamento da filosofia não é tão surpreendente, ao passo que a pesquisa juslaboral possui um forte aparato em métodos sociológicos de investigação, com um caráter mais pragmático, havendo pouco espaço para uma teorização abstrata por si mesma. O autor enfatiza

---

[1] Um dos poucos livros publicados especificamente sobre o tema no Brasil: "O direito do trabalho na filosofia e na teoria social crítica", de Everaldo Gaspar Lopes de Andrade.

que, na experiência britânica, o Direito do Trabalho foi forjado pelas lutas sindicais travadas coletivamente pelos trabalhadores para alcançar a dignidade por meio dos seus próprios esforços, não se tratando, pois, de um fruto do exercício intelectual de codificação racional de princípios jurídicos, de tal modo que essa autoimagem relegou pouco espaço para a filosofia na doutrina trabalhista (Bogg 2017, 7-37)[2].Porém, especialmente na última década, tem havido um interesse crescente nas perspectivas filosóficas sobre o Direito do Trabalho, fazendo emergir como um novo campo de pesquisa hábil não só a justificar os fundamentos desse ramo jurídico, mas, também, a influenciar o seu próprio desenvolvimento no futuro. Como destacam Collins, Lester e Mantouvalou (2019), não é uma tarefa simples encontrar uma filosofia de base para uma área como a do Direito do Trabalho, que, por vezes, parece ser constituída por uma colcha de retalhos de leis concebidas para satisfazer políticas de curto prazo, prescindindo princípios jurídicos coerentes. Não obstante, segundo tais professores das Universidades de Oxford, Columbia e Londres, há motivação de grande envergadura que agora demanda a investigação dos fundamentos filosóficos do Direito do Trabalho, relacionada com a própria continuação da existência da área jurídica face aos ataques perpetrados pela concepção política libertária de que empregadores e empregados deveriam ser livres para conduzir seus negócios sem uma regulamentação detalhada. Segundo os autores, a filosofia é capaz de dar um forte apoio intelectual ao Direito do Trabalho para responder a tais ataques, precisando os conceitos de dignidade, liberdade e igualdade, bem como as estruturas mais amplas que tornam os trabalhadores vulneráveis à exploração.

Outrossim, a filosofia fornece um aparato científico bastante desenvolvido através de suas teorias da justiça, que foram desenvolvidas com notório êxito por insignes jusfilósofos. Essas teorias descrevem, justificam e promovem princípios morais que visam alcançar a justiça no que tange à distribuição de riqueza, poder, oportunidades, liberdades e outros materiais e capacidades necessários para o bem-estar (Collins, Lester e Mantouvalou 2019).

Originalmente, tais teorias da justiça possuem sua fundamentação voltada à organização do Estado e à eleição das políticas públicas a serem adotadas pelos governos para o alcance da justiça social no modo em que idealizada, havendo, por isso, uma visão convencional de que somente o direito público estaria no escopo dessa filosofia política (Kordana e

---

[2] Na doutrina brasileira também encontramos autores que denunciam o "mito da outorga", sustentando que o Direito do Trabalho nacional não fora concedido pelo Estado, mas somente alcançado pelas lutas travadas coletivamente pelos trabalhadores (Campana e Boschi 2009; Godoy 2017).

Tabachnick 2005).

No entanto, o presente ensaio propõe-se a desvendar se, para além da filosofia política, a teoria da justiça de Rawls apresenta repercussões relevantes também sobre o Direito do Trabalho, perquirindo se esta pode ser utilizada como ferramenta para a compreensão e justificação da racionalidade das bases de institutos juslaborais.

2. Teoria da Justiça de John Rawls

Em síntese, John Rawls apresenta sua teoria da justiça sob o fundamento de que, observado um determinado procedimento composto de quatro etapas, dois princípios básicos da justiça seriam intuitivamente eleitos pelos indivíduos racionais ao celebrarem o contrato social na posição original e cobertos pelo véu da ignorância, os quais sistematizariam a concepção de justiça.

De grande importância, pois, para a compreensão da teoria proposta por Rawls, a "posição original" corresponderia ao momento de celebração do contrato social, um *status quo* no qual pessoas racionais, numa situação inicial de igualdade, escolheriam os primeiros princípios da justiça responsáveis por reger a sociedade. Para o filósofo, tratar-se-ia de um elemento de relevância para que os consensos básicos estabelecidos fossem equitativos:

> A posição original é o *status quo* inicial apropriado para assegurar que os consensos básicos nele estabelecidos sejam equitativos. Esse fato delimita o conceito de "justiça como equidade" [...] O objetivo é excluir aqueles princípios cuja aceitação de um ponto de vista racional só se poderia propor, por menor que fosse sua probabilidade de êxito, se fossem conhecidos certos fatos que do ponto de vista da justiça são irrelevantes. Por exemplo, se um homem soubesse que era rico, ele poderia achar racional defender o princípio de que vários impostos em favor do bem-estar social fossem considerados injustos; se ele soubesse que era pobre, com grande probabilidade proporia o princípio contrário (Rawls 2002, 19-21).

Afigura-se importante frisar que a posição original "não corresponde a uma situação histórica real ou condição primitiva da cultura; pelo contrário, é entendida com situação puramente hipotética (Boquimpani 2002).

Soma-se à ficção da posição original a necessidade de que o indivíduo racional esteja coberto pelo "véu da ignorância", outro conceito fundamental da teoria rawlsiana. Significa dizer que, no momento da eleição dos princípios da justiça, as informações referentes às qualidades e características pessoais que os indivíduos terão na sociedade devem ser desconhecidas por estes, a fim de que reste excluído o conhecimento das contingências que criam disparidades entre os homens e que permitem que eles se orientem pelos seus preconceitos (Rawls 2002, 21). Para que o véu da ignorância reste caracterizado, todos devem estar privados de qualquer tipo de informação pessoal sobre os papeis que irão desempenhar na sociedade que está sendo formada na posição original.

Sob essa teorização, Rawls sustenta que a aceitação dos princípios básicos da justiça seria intuitiva[3]. Afirma o autor que em um cenário inicial de eleição dos princípios básicos que irão reger a sociedade (posição original) no qual os indivíduos tivessem excluído o conhecimento a respeito das características individuais que teriam na sociedade cujos fundamentos estão elegendo (véu da ignorância), necessariamente dois princípios seriam eleitos: o princípio da igual liberdade e o princípio da diferença.

No que tange à igual liberdade, Rawls conceitua o primeiro princípio que seria intuitivamente eleito como a compreensão de que "cada pessoa deve ter um direito igual ao mais abrangente sistema total de liberdades básicas iguais que seja compatível com um sistema semelhante de liberdades para todos" (Rawls 2002, 333). O filósofo afirma que as liberdades abrangidas pelo princípio podem ser delimitadas, estatuindo aquelas que julga como as mais importantes para a sua teoria da justiça:

> É necessário observar que é possível delimitar uma lista dessas liberdades. As mais importantes entre elas são a liberdade política (o direito de votar e de ocupar um cargo público) e a liberdade de expressão e reunião; as liberdades da pessoa, que incluem a proteção contra a opressão psicológica e a agressão física (integridade da pessoa); o direito à propriedade privada e a proteção contra a prisão e a detenção arbitrárias, de acordo com esse conceito de estado de direito. Segundo o primeiro princípio, essas liberdades devem ser iguais (Rawls 2002, 65).

Por sua vez, o princípio da diferença, segundo Rawls, diz respeito à necessidade de se ordenar as desigualdades sociais e econômicas de tal modo que, ao mesmo tempo, tragam maior benefício possível para os menos favorecidos e sejam vinculadas a cargos e posições abertos a todos em condições de igualdade equitativa de oportunidades (Rawls 2002, 333).

Quer dizer, segundo a concepção rawlsiana, se os indivíduos estivessem fictamente em uma posição original de escolha dos princípios regentes da sociedade em uma condição de ignorância sobre qual será a sua futura posição dentro desta, intuitivamente escolheriam que fosse a todos

[3] A posição original deve se amoldar à ideia de que as pessoas são iguais moralmente, possibilitando que os princípios sejam aceitáveis intuitivamente (Dresch 2018, 159).

assegurado o mais amplo rol de liberdades; o maior benefício possível aos menos favorecidos; bem como iguais condições de alcançar cargos e posições de destaque. Isto porque, se o indivíduo na posição original e coberto pelo véu da ignorância não sabe se será muito abastardo ou muito empobrecido, desejará, intuitivamente, ser livre para alcançar aquilo que lhe couber, contando com iguais condições às de seus concorrentes.

Diz-se que a teoria da justiça de John Rawls é procedimental, haja vista que, embora consubstancie uma ficção teórica, segundo o autor, "a qualquer momento podemos utilizar a posição original, por assim dizer, simplesmente obedecendo a um certo procedimento, isto é, argumentando em defesa de princípios da justiça de acordo com essas restrições" (Rawls 2002, 21).

Tal procedimento envolve uma sequência de quatro estágios para a aplicação dos princípios da justiça (Rawls 2002, 217). O primeiro deles é o da posição original, que, como visto, envolve a adoção dos princípios da justiça (princípio da igual liberdade e princípio da diferença) sob um completo véu da ignorância.

Após a adoção intuitiva dos dois princípios da justiça, o segundo estágio é chamado de convenção constituinte, no qual os indivíduos devem propor um sistema para os poderes constitucionais de governo e os direitos básicos dos cidadãos (Rawls 2002, 213-215). Rawls destaca que, nessa etapa, o primeiro princípio possui essencial relevância:

> O primeiro princípio da liberdade igual é o princípio primário para a convenção constituinte. Seus requisitos principais são os de que as liberdades individuais fundamentais e a liberdade de consciência e a de pensamento sejam protegidas e que o processo político como um todo seja um procedimento justo. Assim a constituição estabelece um status comum seguro de cidadania igual e implementa a justiça política (Rawls 2002, 215).

Eleitos os princípios básicos e realizada a convenção constituinte, parte-se para o terceiro estágio, o qual é voltado à produção de legislação ordinária por um legislador que não conhece seus dados particulares, mas busca conhecer melhor a sociedade. Nessa fase prepondera o princípio da diferença para maximizar as expectativas de igualdade de oportunidades e favorecimento dos mais fragilizados (Dresch 2018, 159).

Por fim, a teoria da justiça rawlsiana sustenta que, uma vez eleitos os princípios básicos da igual liberdade e da diferença, realizada a convenção constituinte (com preponderância do primeiro princípio) e elaborada a legislação ordinária (com a preponderância do segundo princípio), chega-se à quarta e última etapa, na qual se materializa a aplicação das regras aos casos particulares pelo Poder Executivo e pelo Poder Judiciário e a sua observância pelo cidadão. "Nesse estágio todos têm total acesso a todos os fatos. Não há mais limites ao conhecimento, uma vez que agora se adota um sistema pleno de regras que se aplica aos indivíduos em virtude de suas características e circunstâncias" (Rawls 2002, 216).

Ou seja, na teoria da justiça de Rawls, o véu da ignorância somente deve ser integralmente levantado no último estágio, quando realizada a subsunção do fato à norma, de modo a assegurar a completa imparcialidade e, ao fim e ao cabo, a igual liberdade. Nessa senda, além de viabilizar as intuições sobre a justiça, a posição original teorizada por Rawls tem o papel de auxiliar na precisão dessas intuições e proporcionar uma perspectiva de imparcialidade que permite avaliar situações opostas, uma vez que afasta os indivíduos de sua posição social concreta parcial (Dresch 2018, 160).

3. Aplicação da Teoria da Justiça Rawlsiana ao Direito do Trabalho

Quando apresenta sua teoria da justiça, Rawls afirma que os princípios da igual liberdade e da diferença, adotados na posição original, devem pautar a construção das instituições sociais, mas destaca que esses dois princípios são aplicáveis apenas na estrutura básica da sociedade. Assim, afigura-se de essencial relevância para o alcance do objetivo deste ensaio que se esclareça o que deve ser compreendido pela "estrutura básica da sociedade" na concepção rawlsiana.

Ocorre que, de acordo com Kordana e Tabachnick, pode-se vislumbrar um certo grau de ambiguidade por parte de Rawls quanto à definição daquilo que o jusfilósofo entende por "estrutura básica da sociedade". Os autores apontam que, em um primeiro momento, Rawls defende que a estrutura básica corresponderia a um rol bastante amplo, no qual estariam inseridos a distribuição de direitos fundamentais e obrigações, a definição dos benefícios da cooperação social, a constituição política, a definição das políticas econômicas e arranjos sociais, a proteção da liberdade de pensamento e consciência, os mercados competitivos, bem como a propriedade privada e a família, sugerindo que a estrutura básica seria composta por qualquer aspecto da vida social que afete as perspectivas de vida de alguém. Porém, Kordana e Tabachnick verificam que, em um segundo momento, Rawls define a estrutura básica da sociedade em uma concepção mais limitada, apresentando-a como as instituições que definiriam o fundo social, incluindo operações como tributação de renda e herança, que continuamente ajustariam e compensariam as inevitáveis tendências contrárias à equidade. Nessa segunda concepção, mais limitada, o direito privado não estaria compreendido dentro da estrutura básica e, portanto, não sofreria repercussões dos princípios da justiça, enquanto, na primeira, sim (Kordana e Tabachnick 2005, 609-614).

Soma-se, ainda, que a filosofia política parte de um grau mínimo de suposições, enquanto, por outro lado, a busca por uma teoria que explique os fundamentos filosóficos do Direito do Trabalho precisa partir daquilo que já existe, isto é, precisa haver uma relação de coerência com relação ao direito vigente. Claro que princípios e conceitos morais podem ser extraídos da filosofia política, mas é um equívoco simplesmente impor a sua aplicação às práticas juslaborais se eles não explicam o Direito do Trabalho (Collins, Lester e Mantouvalou 2019).

Fato é que, como já referido, a preocupação de Rawls fora estabelecer uma filosofia política, com percepções sobre a natureza de uma sociedade justa e sua forma apropriada de governo. Por via de consequência, não podem ser ignoradas as dificuldades inerentes ao transplante dos conceitos e princípios concebidos para a teoria política de Rawls ao âmbito do direito privado e, especificamente, do Direito do Trabalho (Collins, Lester e Mantouvalou 2019).

Kordana e Tabachnick defendem que, apesar das dificuldades na exegese de Rawls, o direito privado e, especialmente, o direito contratual (que foi objeto do estudo citado), possuem sim espaço dentro da teoria política de Rawls, destacando que se o primeiro princípio da justiça assegura a liberdade, ele garante o direito de contratar, enquanto que os detalhes daquilo que será contratado deverá atender o que o segundo princípio demanda, no sentido de maximizar a posição dos menos abastados mediante cláusulas de índole distributiva. Os autores ressaltam que, se o princípio da diferença exige que selecionemos, em comparação com esquemas alternativos, o esquema que maximize a posição dos menos favorecidos, devemos adotar a compreensão de que os princípios da justiça de Rawls repercutem também sobre o direito privado. Defendem que, se há um esquema no qual pelo menos algumas regras do contrato devem ser projetadas para alcançar efeitos distributivos desejáveis, os menos abastados estarão em um patamar mais elevado do que em um esquema em que a distribuição é realizada apenas através de impostos e transferências (Kordana e Tabachnick 2005, 616). Assim, concluem que o direito contratual deve ser governado (embora indiretamente) pelos dois princípios da justiça e que há uma porta aberta para uma compreensão mais profunda sobre o papel que o direito privado desempenha na filosofia política de Rawls (Kordana e Tabachnick 2005, 632).

Outra é a análise feita por Scheffler (2015), que vislumbra que da concepção de justiça de John Rawls podem ser retiradas duas diferentes injunções para o direito privado, sendo um distributivismo fraco e um distributivismo forte. O fraco levaria em consideração o princípio da diferença em combinação com os princípios das liberdades básicas e da equitativa igualdade de oportunidades, reconhecendo a prioridade destes dois últimos, de modo que o direito privado só deveria atender ao princípio da diferença caso, ao fazê-lo, não atentasse contra algum dos outros princípios. De outro lado, o distributivismo forte seria caracterizado por desconsiderar os limites à aplicação do princípio da diferença, demandando que o direito privado fosse conformado para beneficiar a situação dos menos abastados na maior medida possível. Scheffler defende que o princípio da diferença se preocupa com a distribuição geral de bens primários, enquanto o direito civil, na forma em que tradicionalmente concebido, trata das relações bilaterais que se formam entre particulares, com valores igualmente bilaterais, sendo, por esse motivo, incompatível com o princípio da diferença. Zanitelli critica essa conclusão, afirmando que um princípio não necessita responder a toda e qualquer dúvida atinente ao conteúdo de uma certa área do direito, podendo haver partes do direito privado cujo fundamento não será distributivo e poderá fazer jus aos valores bilaterais a que Scheffler se refere (Zanitelli 2019, 138-139).

Já os professores Collins, Lester e Mantouvalou, analisando especificamente a implementação da teoria da justiça de Rawls ao Direito do Trabalho, sugerem três mecanismos de transposição da teoria política, a saber: *(i.)* imitação metodológica; *(ii.)* replicação de conceitos-chave[4]; e *(iii.)* exegese de posições implícitas[5], embora reconheçam não ser possível ter certeza sobre o que Rawls efetivamente gostaria de dizer sobre o Direito do Trabalho. Daremos especial atenção à imitação metodológica, pela sua

---

[4] Os autores indicam como exemplos da utilização de conceitos-chave da teoria política para a compreensão do direito do trabalho e seus institutos: concepções de democracia aplicadas à negociação coletiva e à definição do sindicato representativo; e a proteção de direitos humanos específicos, como privacidade ou liberdade de expressão, aplicada às relações de emprego (Collins, Lester e Mantouvalou 2019).

[5] Os autores apontam que algumas regras ou princípios gerais sobre o direito do trabalho já estariam implícitos nas obras de teoria política, mesmo que não tenham sido elaboradas explicitamente pelos autores. Citam o princípio da igualdade de oportunidade, que poderia servir como sustentação de alguns direitos trabalhistas, principalmente das leis contra discriminação e proibição de exploração. Porém, destacam que a teoria política oferece pouco em termos de orientação explícita sobre o direito do trabalho, de modo que a tarefa corresponderia a uma leitura atenta dessas obras, a fim de argumentar que embora não haja suporte textual direto para um aspecto particular do direito do trabalho, uma regra ou princípio particular seria inerente às declarações explícitas dos filósofos, ou, então, uma inevitável consequência da adoção de uma determinada declaração explícita na teoria política (Collins, Lester e Mantouvalou 2019).

fertilidade teórica; as outras duas repercussões foram abordadas nas notas de rodapé respectivamente inseridas.

A imitação metodológica relaciona-se com o reconhecimento da natureza procedimental da teoria da justiça de Rawls que explicamos anteriormente, isto é, com a utilização das técnicas da posição original e do véu da ignorância (Collins, Lester e Mantouvalou 2019). Quer dizer, através da imitação metodológica, seria possível recorrer a um *status quo* hipotético no qual os indivíduos racionais, sem conhecer a posição que ocuparão no futuro (*v. g.* se serão empregados ou empregadores), deveriam firmar as bases do Direito do Trabalho (ou mesmo a inexistência deste).

Através desse método, não parece suscitar maiores dúvidas que os indivíduos racionais concordariam com a proteção de direitos humanos e fundamentais dos trabalhadores. Outrossim, para viabilizar o trabalho, acredita-se que concordariam com as características gerais da relação de emprego, incluindo a subordinação do empregado às demandas de desempenho do empregador. Collins *et al* acrescentam ser provável que, na posição original, os indivíduos desejariam garantias contra o abuso de poder por parte dos empregadores; bem como que, se suficientemente avessos ao risco, também concordariam com uma lei que exigisse "salários justos" ou, pelo menos um "salário mínimo" (Collins, Lester e Mantouvalou 2019, 15).

Outrossim, interessante estudo fora desenvolvido por Croucher, Kelly e Miles, no qual apresentam que é possível extrair uma base rawlsiana para os direitos fundamentais do trabalho. Tendo por base a Declaração da OIT sobre Princípios e Direitos Fundamentais no Trabalho, os autores sustentam que três princípios declarados já são explicitamente reconhecidos por Rawls em sua Teoria da Justiça como direitos fundamentais abrangidos por seu primeiro princípio de justiça, ou seja, como direitos que as pessoas na posição original identificariam como essenciais: *(i.)* a eliminação do trabalho forçado (cf. argumentação de Rawls de que a escravidão é injusta sob o primeiro princípio); *(ii.)* o combate à discriminação (cf. afirmação de Rawls de que a discriminação racial é obviamente injusta); e *(iii.)* a liberdade sindical (cf. afirmação de Rawls de que o governo não tem autoridade para tornar associações legítimas ou ilegítimas, implicando em liberdade para aderir os sindicatos). Quanto ao segundo princípio de Rawls (princípio da diferença), os autores destacam que os direitos trabalhistas em geral devem ser entendidos como necessários à justiça social (Croucher, Kelly e Miles 2012).

De outro lado, Spector defende que ainda que a atuação sindical e a legislação trabalhista possam contribuir para o fortalecimento do poder de barganha dos empregados perante os empregadores, tais institutos não cumpririam a justiça social. Isto porque, na teoria rawlsiana, as desigualdades econômicas só poderiam ser justificadas para a vantagem dos que estão em pior situação. A peculiaridade de Spector está em situar nos campos dos mais desfavorecidos os desempregados, e não os empregados em detrimento dos empregadores, bem como em vislumbrar uma via de consequência na qual o encarecimento da mão-de-obra pela legislação laboral e pela atuação sindical desencadearia a redução das vagas de trabalho oferecidas e, por isso, o desemprego (Spector 2006, 1134-1135).

A concepção de Spector, porém, é falha. Além de não estar amparada em dados concretos, ignora que incumbe ao Direito do Trabalho regulamentar direitos mínimos para retificar a relação assimétrica estabelecida entre os sujeitos da relação de emprego, no âmbito da qual, à toda evidência, os trabalhadores constituem o polo menos favorecido[6].

Embora os desempregados possam estar em uma situação inferior comparativamente aos empregados, o caminho contrário ao fortalecimento dos institutos de Direito do Trabalho, com a respectiva extinção das normas laborais de direito mínimo, prejudicaria as condições de trabalho asseguradas aos trabalhadores nessa relação pujantemente marcada pela dependência de uma parte à outra[7], além de não proporcionar a plena ocupação (e, portanto, não resolver o problema apontado por Spector). Portanto, não se afigura possível concluir que as normas laborais impeçam a justiça social preconizada por Rawls, mas sim que, muito pelo contrário, elas constituem umas das suas principais molas propulsoras!

Fato é que a teoria da justiça de John Rawls apresenta um comprometimento funcional com a maximização de igualdade de oportunidades e liberdades, de modo que, avaliado de acordo com a justiça distributiva que o caracteriza, é possível classificar o liberalismo igualitarista de Rawls como uma das

---

[6] Cesarino Jr. classifica como hipossuficientes aqueles economicamente débeis que "dependem, para viver e fazer viver sua família, do produto de seu trabalho", e, para tanto, subordinam-se às ordens de um empregador (Cesarino Júnior 1980, 44-45).

[7] Alain Supiot analisa de maneira bastante aprofundada a "tensão latente" que se estabelece entre a autonomia da vontade individual e o vínculo de subordinação que percorre o direito do trabalho. Para o autor, a sujeição contratual da vontade de um indivíduo à de outro é uma fonte inevitável de antinomias ao sistema jurídico do direito contratual, eis que este é dominado pelos princípios de liberdade individual e igualdade. Supiot observa a contradição estabelecida entre autonomia da vontade e subordinação sob a ótica de que "no contrato civil, a vontade compromete-se; no contrato de trabalho, submete-se. O compromisso manifesta a liberdade, a submissão nega-a", redundando em que o trabalhador não é apenas o sujeito, mas também o objeto do contrato de trabalho, de modo a impedir que os princípios jurídicos da autonomia da vontade sejam mantidos intactos, pois restam desfigurados pelo vínculo de subordinação e pela alteração da qualidade do sujeito de direito que ela envolve. (Supiot 2016, 147-163).

teorias fundantes da racionalidade do direito privado contemporâneo (Dresch 2018, 170), e, especialmente, fornece uma metodologia que justifica a estrutura protetiva fornecida pelo Direito do Trabalho ao hipossuficiente.

Considerações Finais

Em tempos de crise desencadeada pelo choque entre pressupostos extrajurídicos e algumas das soluções tradicionalmente fornecidas pelo Direito do Trabalho, voltam-se contra este diversas críticas, as quais, inclusive, colocam em questão a própria manutenção do ramo jurídico autônomo. Sendo alvo de tais ataques, o Direito do Trabalho pode socorrer-se dos fundamentos filosóficos, desenvolvidos em teorizações mais abstratas que retiram o intérprete do meio que condiciona suas especulações.

Por óbvio, não estamos a defender a completa absorção dos institutos juslaborais pela filosofia, tampouco que estes podem ser explicados, integralmente, pela teoria da justiça de Rawls. Com sua reconhecida autonomia dogmática, o Direito do Trabalho possui uma série de soluções que foram desenvolvidos no seu seio e que somente podem ser satisfatoriamente compreendidos através das construções próprias do âmbito juslaboral. Porém, se o que está em jogo é a discussão referente à sobrevivência do sistema laboral protetivo, a fundamentação apresentada autoriza concluir que o procedimento da posição original defendido na filosofia política de Rawls fornece elementos para avaliarmos o grau de justiça da intervenção Estatal nas relações de emprego, outorgando justificativa plausível para a sua reafirmação enquanto mecanismo de justiça social.

Afinal, não parece razoável que um indivíduo racional que estivesse na posição original e coberto pelo véu da ignorância arriscaria opinar pela inexistência do Direito do Trabalho, notadamente se o indivíduo pudesse, por motivos alheios à sua vontade, vir a ser um trabalhador subordinado, quiçá em condições análogas à escravidão (afinal, haveria algum limite em uma completa ausência do Direito do Trabalho?). O método de Rawls é interessante porque fornece elementos para o intérprete afastar-se de suas características e de seus interesses pessoais, viabilizando uma conclusão justa não só no âmbito da filosofia política, mas, também, em matéria de Direito do Trabalho.

Bibliografia

Andrade, Everaldo Gaspar Lopes de, *O direito do trabalho na filosofia e na teoria social crítica* (São Paulo: LTr, 2014)

Bogg, Alan. Labour, "Love and Futility: Philosophical Perspectives on Labour Law", *International Journal of Comparative Labour Law*, vol. 33 (2017): 7-37

Boquimpani, Eduardo Gonçalves, "Rawls e seus críticos: revisitando a teoria da justiça", *Revista de Direito Constitucional e Internacional*, vol. 40 (2002): 183-204

Campana, Priscila e Boschi, Olga Maria, "A falácia do discurso da doação das leis trabalhistas: recuperando outras memórias históricas", *Revista de Informação Legislativa do Senado Federal*, no. 181, janeiro-março (2009): 53-70.

Cesarino Júnior, Antônio F, *Direito Social* (São Paulo: LTr, 1980)

Collins, Hugh, Lester, Gillian e Mantouvalou, Virginia, "Does Labour Law Need Philosophical Foundations?" In *Philosophical Foundations of Labour Law*, edited by Collins, Hugh, Lester, Gillian e Mantouvalou, Virginia (Oxford: Oxford University Press, 2019): 1-32

Croucher, Richard, Kelly, Mark G. E e Miles, Lilian, "A Rawlsian basis for core labor rights," *Comparative Labor law and Policy Journal,* vol. 33, janeiro (2012): 297-320

Dorneles, Leandro do Amaral D. de, "Teoria geral clássica do direito do trabalho e sociedade pós-industrial: faces de uma crise e perspectivas para superação," In *Novas Tecnologias, Processo e Relações de Trabalho*, org. Fincato, Denise e Vidaletti, Leiliane Piovesani, vol. III (Porto Alegre: Lex Magister, 2019): 97-115

Dresch, Rafael de Freitas Valle, *Fundamentos de direito privado: uma teoria da justiça e da dignidade humana* (Rio de Janeiro: Processo, 2018)

Godoy, Arnaldo Sampaio de Moraes, "O tema da proteção jurídica do trabalho humano no contexto historiográfico da construção de mitos e heróis que fragilizam as lutas sociais: paradoxos e possibilidades", *Revista do Tribunal Superior do Trabalho,* vol. 83, abril-junho (2017): 82-111

Kordana, Kevin A. e Tabachnik, David H., "Ralws and contract law," *The George Washington Law Review*, vol. 73, no. 3, abril (2005): 598-632

Ramalho, Maria do Rosário Palma, *Tratado de direito do trabalho: dogmática geral* (Coimbra: Almedina, 2015)

Rawls, John, *Uma teoria da justiça* (São Paulo: Martins Fontes, 2002)

Scheffler, Samuel, "Distributive justice, the basic structure and the place of private law," *Oxford Journal of Legal Studies*, vol. 35, no. 2 (2015): 213-235

Spector, Horacio, "Philosophical Foundations of Labor Law," *Florida State University Law Review*, vol. 33, no. 4 (2006): 1119-1148

Supiot, Alain, *Crítica do direito do trabalho* (Lisboa: Fundação Calouste Gulbenkian, 2016)

Zanitelli, Leandro Martins, "Liberalismo igualitário, direito privado e valores bilaterais," *Revista Estudos Institucionais*, vol. 5, no. 1 (2019): 133-146

PART 2

THE ESSENCE OF LABOUR LAW: ON UNIVERSAL PRINCIPLES AND DIVERGING LEGAL RULES

A. Regional or Country-Specific Reports

CHAPTER 6

THE SOCIALISATION OF ECONOMIC RISK AND THE REDISTRIBUTION OF LIABILITIES[1]

NICOLE MAGGI-GERMAIN

Liability is a concept that provides structure to the law and has been described as an "institution" in the writings of eminent civil-law scholars (Jourdain 1998; Viney 2008). It is one of the fundamental concepts of legal life: to be liable is, firstly, in the etymological sense, to remedy the damage one has caused. This description of liability, according to Emmanuel Lévy (1939, p. 7), is the counterpart to the freedom recognised as a subject in law: "We become liable when we exercise our rights." It reveals the intricate relationship between the aptitude to exert one's rights and to be subject to obligations — criteria which characterise a legal personality.

Labour, or more precisely the transformation of the forms of organisation of labour linked to large-scale industry that was becoming widespread in the 19th century following the expansion of mechanisation[2], contributed to the redefinition of a part of civil liability law by opening the way to collective compensation mechanisms based on a liability that, from then on, would be without fault, based on the idea of "risk"[3] in the context of employment. The "general risks of industry" (Boissard 1910, p. 27) are thus fully integrated

[1] This article is an updated version of an article published in 2019 in a special multi-disciplinary issue of the journal *Sociologie du travail* on the theme of employment in search of liabilities. Special issue, vol. 61 - n°2, April-June 2019, coordinated by Michel Lallement and Bénédicte Zimmermann, accessible at https://journals.openedition.org/sdt/17619.

[2] "That is the use of sets of tools in which manual labour has been replaced by air, steam or electrical power." Romieu opinion in Cames judgment (Council of State 21 June 1895, in Sirey collection 1897.3.33).

[3] "Objective" liability, Council of State 21 June 1895 (Cames judgment) in Sirey collection 1897.3.33, Romieu opinion, Hauriou note and *Cour de cassation* 16 June 1896, (Teffaine judgment) Dalloz 1897, p. 432 ff., Saleilles note; Law of 9 April 1898 on liabilities in workplace accidents in which workers are victims.

into the liability framework and contribute to the transformation of its nature and objective.[4] The indemnification of damages (reparation) supplants the normative function, to ensure sanction of the faults that caused the damage (Viney 2008).

Classical analysis of the development of liability law allows us to examine the development of the functions attributed to it. The very significant debates that divided some legal scholars at the end of the 19th and the start of the 20th centuries nevertheless agree on the link between the economic context ("the pressure of the necessities of industrial life", Josserand 1897, p. 9) and the development of the law towards an "economic concept of risk" (Veniamin 1930, p. 415). The obligation of reparation, based on liability for the actions of others[5], is the counterpart of the benefits gained from the activity which generated them, summarised by the existence of a "law of connectivity between profit and risk" (Planiol 1909, p. 300).

While the slow transformation of civil-liability law caused by the development of large-scale industry opened the way to the "socialisation" of risk (caused by workplace accidents) and of the law, it also facilitated the increased autonomy of labour law, separate from the civil-law matrix based on the dogma of the equality of the parties to a contract. The fourth industrial revolution, and the place it occupies in the context of the globalisation of economic trade and digitalisation, has led to the emergence of new legal figures, of whom the most iconic today are workers on digital platforms. New forms of dependency are being created that are more insidious because they are clothed in the misrepresentation of the autonomy and freedom generated by information and communication technologies.

1. From the Socialisation of Risk Caused by the Development of Large-Scale Industry to the Fourth Industrial Revolution

The individualist spirit of the Civil Code of 1804 was followed by what legal scholars call the socialisation of law: "The law is not a large construct similar to the Classical theatre which only features general abstractions" (Demogue 1911, p. 169; see also Veniamin 1930, p. 401 ff.; Durand 1942).

---

[4] "Let us recognise that it is a legal obligation, an obligation based on the concept of risks and justified by this concept, that is so simple and equitable, that he who manages a business must bear the risks arising from it." Saleilles, op. cit., p. 439.

[5] Article 1384, paragraph 1 of the Civil Code which, in 2016, became Article 1242 following the ratification of Order n° 2016-131 of 10 February 2016 reforming contract law, the general regime and proof of liability.

Liability does not disappear, but changes in nature: "It becomes collective" (Savatier 1931). The way the law worked was significantly updated by the birth of "socialised" risks in the legal world, which responded to a particular legal regime. The recognition of objective liability that obeyed specific mechanisms of imputation and reparation allowed the law to evolve alongside the social and economic transformations of society and to mirror more general developments in the law and the state. We are witnessing a veritable paradigm shift with the invention of the theory of risk-based liability. Universal law, based on the "natural order" of the world and the concept of causality, that we find formalised in Aristotle's *Physis*[6], is being succeeded by laws of society based on the concept of finality (Ripert 1918). The individualist and liberal Napoleonic Code is being succeeded by so-called "social" legislation (Boulanger 1950, p. 73). The law can get involved in the most minor upsets in social life, replacing a relationship with nature with a "purely social relationship" (Ewald 1986, p. 541). The "workers' laws" that were first codified in the labour and providence codes in the early 20th century can be fully included in this legal order. It thus seems indispensable to replace the regulation of a workshop "worked by a single owner" with "special legislation on the conditions of validity of an employment contract" (Jay 1904). Employment relationships must be organised in the context of the development of large-scale industry.

The use of the concept of risk in the legal regime of civil liability shows the extent to which this legal category has become systemised within the contextual elements linked to economic developments. Subsequently, other risks associated with industrial activity, or simply with life in society, have emerged, leading to the creation of special regimes of liability that allow, for example, the guaranteed reparation of damages caused by traffic accidents and terrorist acts or the requesting of reparation for environmental damage (Trébulle 2016; Blin-Franchomme 2017; Boutonnet 2017)[7].

Related to the digitalisation of the economy, the expansion of globalisation — used as an argument which returns like a refrain in the texts explaining

---

[6] *Nomoi*, defined by humans, are derived from *Physis,* the natural law of things and humans. It is on this notion that theoreticians of natural law would rely, from St Thomas Aquinas to Montesquieu, right up to influencing one of the early drafts of the Civil Code which bore a preliminary title taken from a passage in Cicero's *Republic*, which states the principle that "a universal, immutable law exists that is the source of all positive laws; it is only natural reason in itself that governs all the peoples of the earth" (1st paragraph). "Individual and intelligent beings may have the laws they have made; but they also have those that they did not make […] Before there were made laws, there were relationships of justice" (Montesquieu, *The Spirit of Laws*, Book I, Chapter 1).

[7] Article 1248 and following articles of the Labour Code.

the reasons for new proposed laws — and its conception against the background of the progressive liberalisation of economic transactions has led states to integrate "economic risk" into their public policies, thus confirming the passing of "social functions" (Duguit 1912, p. 19 ff.) in favour of the economic finalities of labour law[8]. This socialisation of economic risk has been demonstrated by the adoption in the last decade of a series of reforms (among others) aimed at making the conditions for breaking employment contracts more flexible, while transferring legal control to judges, rather than protecting, under the aegis of the law, the weaker party in the employment contract (the employee), so as to re-establish a sort of equality in the employment relationship.[9] Should this be seen as an overall transfer of risks (Lokiec 2015, p. 114f.) within a system of labour law that has become an adjustable variable, and a manifestation of what Gérard and Antoine Lyon-Caen (1978, p. 620) called, from the end of the 1970s onwards, "triumphant economism"?

2. Economically Dependent Self-Employed Workers: The Example of Service Providers on Collaborative Platforms

Some recent developments that can be observed within and outside the framework of salaried employment deserve a mention as they create new forms of economic dependence at the same time as constituting a source of

---

[8] This also stresses the importance of the economic analysis of law. For an illustration of the reception of the theory by the legal establishment, see, for example, Bruno Deffains and Myriam Doriat-Duban (2010).

[9] Creation of the individual "rupture conventionnelle" (a mutual agreement for ending of a contract), outside the procedures applicable to redundancy and dismissal (Labour Code Article L. 1237-11 and following); law of 25 June 2008 modernising the labour market, then collective because it was determined by a collective agreement (Labour Code Article L1237-19 and following; order of 22 September 2017 concerning the predictability and securing of employment relationships); insertion into the Labour Code of standard redundancy letters (Articles L. 1232-6, paragraph 3, L. 1233-16, paragraph 3, and L. 1233-42, paragraph 3); possibility for the employer to give the reasons for redundancy in a letter after notifying the employee (Article L. 1235-2); establishment of a sliding scale to be imposed on judges when calculating compensation for redundancy without proper and serious cause (Article L. 1235-3); appraisal of the economic cause of redundancy decided in a business that belongs to a national group and no longer international groups, except in cases of fraud (Article L. 1233-3; Law of 8 August 2016 concerning employment, modernisation of social dialogue and securing career paths).

change to labour law. The inclusion in the Labour Code of regulations governing working conditions on collaborative platforms and the application of specific social rights to self-employed workers providing their services via these platforms, reverses a century of legislative, jurisprudential and doctrinal developments of labour law. For, indeed, it was the "invention" of employment contracts that allowed, by detaching them from the matrix of the Civil Code, the bringing together of "workers" in heterogenous working conditions under the same legal status, that of employees. In doing this, the law made possible the uniformisation of dependence figures[10] by referring to a flexible legal interpretation of the relationship of subordination ("lien de subordination juridique")[11] which allowed the recognition as employees who, however, have real autonomy in the organisation of their work[12].

Work done via collaborative platforms does not exhaust the multiple forms of "economically dependent work" (Antonmattei and Sciberras 2008), defined by the European Commission in its 2006 Green Book as work that "[…] covers situations that are not covered by the well-established concept of salaried work, nor that of self-employment. This category of workers does not have an employment contract. They cannot fall under the coverage of employment legislation because they occupy a 'grey area' between employment law and commercial law. Despite being formally "self-employed", they remain economically dependent on a single principal or client/employer for the source of their incomes" (Commission des communautés européennes 2006). Nevertheless, it recognised forms of work organisation that, while performed under the status of self-employed contractors, also borrowed from the criteria of salaried employment. Does this syncretism herald the creation of a new legal status, the extension of social rights to self-employed contractors, or does it presage a more general

[10] The relationship of dependence, be it economic, technical or legal, constitutes the main criterion used to categorise, in a legal sense, the employment contract (Cuche 1913).

[11] "Given that the legal status of a worker with regard to the person for whom he works cannot be determined by weakness or economic dependence of the worker but only from the contract between the parties; the status of the emplyee necessarily implies the existence of a legal link of subordination between the worker and the person that employs him." Civil Chamber of the Cour de Cassation, 6 July 1931, DPO 1931, 1, 121; Civil Chamber of the Cour de Cassation, 22 June 1932 (3 judgements) and 1 August 1932 (5 judgments), D.P. 193, 1, 45, note PIC.

[12] "What is still called subordination is now only, in a general sense in social law, a group of circumstances, which appear to be very diverse, that allow it to be confirmed that the worker is one of the human components that occupies a place in a business of which he is not the organiser: he is the person who belongs to a business" (Groutel, 1978, p. 57-58).

development in employment law?

The business objective of the operators of collaborative platforms – as they are described in Article L.111-7 of the Consumer Code – is to provide an electronic means of contact between clients and "self-employed" workers, who are tied to the platform by commercial contracts, for the sale of goods, the provision of services or the exchange or sharing of goods or services[13]. Uber defines itself in its standard contract for the provision of services as a "provider of technological services,"[14] while Deliveroo "ensures the contact between its clients, its portfolio of partner restaurants and self-employed delivery providers by offering the provision of a delivery service for meals to homes or workplaces."[15] The economic risk, in the sense of the loss of revenue linked to a decline in activity,[16] is borne in principle by the service provider who also receives the benefits derived from it and whose activity is characterised by autonomy. However, some platforms, such as Deliveroo, have set up mechanisms that generate competition between workers while at the same time organising a sort of control of their activity, from the moment that it is regulated by the platform which allocates delivery districts to a limited number of workers. Not all the workers can choose their working hours because they are determined by registration slots that are pre-set by the platform ("shifts" starting at 11am, 3pm and 5pm), which allows workers to build their weekly working plans on each Monday for the following week.[17] Yet the options for choosing the shift (i.e., to choose their working hours and districts) depends on statistics generated by the platform with regard to the individual worker's activity. Depending on his or her activity level,[18] the number of late cancellations,[19] or participation at peak hours,[20] the platform will automatically place the worker on one of the three shifts. If the statistics are good, the worker is offered the first shift starting at 11am, when few other workers will be

[13] Decree n° 2017-774 of 4 May 2017, concerning the social responsability of platforms that create electronic relationships. French Official Journal of 6 May 2017. Article L. 111-7, I, 2° of the Consumer Code.

[14] Version dated 1 February 2016.

[15] Standard contract for service providers, *Généralités, A.*

[16] The concept deserves deeper study, especially with regard to economic analyses, in particular to distinguish it from capitalist risk. For a first approach to this, see Marco (2012).

[17] 7.50am/9am; then every hour between 9am and 11.30am; 11.30am/1pm then every hour from 1pm to 2am.

[18] "Percentage of delivery shifts to which you are connected."

[19] "Percentage of delivery shifts cancelled at less than 24 hours' notice."

[20] "Number of connections during peak delivery shifts (8pm to 10pm Friday, Saturday & Sunday)."

working; whereas if the statistics are poor, the worker will be relegated to the 5pm shift and only given access to the hours and districts that have not already been booked by other workers. In addition, while the worker is connected to the Deliveroo app, he or she can be geolocated by both Deliveroo and the customer, who can track the delivery and the route taken. Any worker who turns off the app too often, according to Deliveroo, will not only see his or her statistics get worse but will receive a reprimand from Deliveroo which can threaten to end his or her contract. Originally, Deliveroo delivery riders were paid a fixed price per delivery (€5.75), but since the summer of 2018 they have been paid on a variable tariff (between €4.80 and €7.50 per delivery) which takes account of the distance travelled. At the same time, the delivery districts were enlarged. In theory, riders can refuse deliveries, and the number of refusals that day will appear on the app.

Setting aside the fact that such mechanisms bear a strong resemblance to disguised economic sanctions which create new forms of allegiance between workers (Supiot 2000, 2018), they also contribute to the creation of a work structure that is organised so as to give the service providers no decision-making power whatsoever – a criterion which prevents it from being described as (among others) self-employment, and thus could be seen to change the service-provider contract into an employment contract (Jeammaud 2017).[21]

In consequence, whether it be by promoting the employee's autonomy whose personal initiative has become a determining criterion for the law[22],

---

[21] Several internal complaints were made in different EU member states, including France. The *Cour de cassation* decided, in a judgement on 28 November 2018 (published as n° 17-20.079), that the existence of the power of direction and control in the execution of the delivery constituted a link of subordination and the existence of an employment contract. This was established from the moment that a company (Take Eat Easy) uses a web platform and an app that places its partner restaurants, the clients placing orders for meals via the platform, and bicycle delivery riders delivering those meals. Self-employed service providers were compelled to use an app containing a geolocation system which allowed the company to track the delivery rider in real time and the calculation of the total number of kilometres travelled by the delivery rider. In addition, the company had the power to sanction the delivery rider. Also, in the social chamber of the *Cour de cassation*, on 4 March 2020, n° 19-13316, published, discussed the "fictitious" status of self-employed service provider of an Uber driver.

[22] The example of the right to continuous professional training can be cited: the law of 4 May 2004 recognises this initiative as the directive principle that affects the applicable legal regime in the field of the obligations on the employer (Labour Code Article L. 6312-1). Also, see the judgement of the social chamber of the *Cour de cassation*, dated 16 January 2008, published in the official bulletin as n° 07-10095:

or by regulating in the Labour Code[23], forms of activity which would previously have been regulated by commercial law, employment law seems to have undergone a metamorphosis which raises the question of whether it has pushed "the bases of a new social model into the digital era"[24].

3. The New Figures of Dependence, "*Bases of a New Social Model in the Digital Era*"?

The conditions for exercising the activity generated by these platforms were set out in Article 60 of the law of 8th August 2016 cited above, in its second chapter, entitled, "Adapting employment law to the digital era." These provisions were added to the Labour Code as Articles L. 7341-1 to L. 7342-6, in the seventh part concerning "specific dispositions that apply to particular professions and activities."[25] Thus the law extends the field of the application of the Labour Code to workers technically designated as self-employed under Article L. 7341-1.

In the 21st century, as in the 19th, the law is accompanying the expansion of new ways of organising work — mechanisation on the one hand and digitalisation on the other — embedded in new economic models. But dependence has changed its appearance. The dematerialisation of collaborative

---

"And, given that it has been noted that the training activities linked to the 'Alliance' project has not been requested by the employees, they had concluded that, whatever their nature, these hours of training could not be debited from the training savings accounts, the Court of Appeal which has ruled that those debits made constituted a manifestly illicit offencee, was correct in law; and that the means was unfounded." See also on this subject Maggi-Germain 1999; Maggi-Germain 2014 and Gautié *et al.* 2015.

[23] Article L. 7341-1 and following the Labour Code. "This section is applicable to self-employed workers who have recourse, in the performance of their work, to one or more electronic contact platforms as defined in Article 242 bis of the General Taxation Code" (Article L. 7341-1 was introduced by the law of 8 August 2016 concerning employment, the modernisation of social dialogue and the securing of career paths).

[24] Title III: "Securing career paths and constructing the bases of a new social model in the digital era" of law n° 2016-1088 concerning employment, the modernisation of social dialogue and the securing of career paths.

[25] E.g. journalists, people who work in entertainment, advertising and fashion (Book 1); concierges and those employed in residential apartment buildings and domestic personal care workers (Book 2); sales representatives, branch managers, salaried entrepreneurs associated with cooperatives and workers who use electronic contact platforms (Book 3).

platforms (are we really dealing with enterprises here?[26]) makes new forms of control possible that may be less visible, but remain just as real. Furthermore, the disintegration of the workplace not only makes it more difficult to create a work cooperative (would it make any sense from a legal point of view?) but also encourages the deconstruction of collective protections that aim to be applied in the framework of the business. Here we could mention in particular the question of protecting the health of workers.

This dematerialisation also has an effect on the liability regime established by Article L. 7342-1 of the Labour Code, "when the platform determines the characteristics of the delivery of the service provided or the goods sold and fixes its price, it has, with regard to the workers concerned, a **social responsibility** that applies in the conditions described in this chapter." The established responsibility regime does not ensue from the relationship of salaried employment and the existence of a link with legal subordination, but rather the determination by the platform of the economic conditions under which the work is organised. This, so-called "social" responsibility is characterised by the replacement of the self-employed worker by the platform regarding the payment of some subscriptions (e.g. insurance premiums covering the risk of workplace accidents, Labour Code Article L. 7342-2) or social-security contributions (e.g. those to finance professional training, Article L. 7342-3) as soon as the worker reaches a fixed turnover threshold (Article L. 7342-4). Furthermore, some freedoms and social rights are recognised for these workers: "the right to professional training" (Article L. 7342-3, paragraph 1); the right to validation of prior experience (VAE – *Validation des acquis de l'expérience* Article L. 7342-3, paragraph 2), the support costs being assumed by the platform (Article D. 7342-3, paragraph 1 and Articles R. 6423-2 and 3) which pay an allowance to compensate for the loss or revenue caused (Article D. 7342-3, paragraph 2); the right to go on strike[27]which cannot, except when abused, "neither engage their contractual liability, nor constitute a reason for the ending of their relationships with the platforms, nor justify measures that penalise them in the exercise of their activity" (Article L. 7342-5); and the right to

---

[26] From a legal point of view, Article 242 *bis* of the General Taxation Code qualifies them as businesses, whereas the Labour Code only refers to the concept of a "platform."

[27] Which is not qualified as such, as Article L. 7342-5 refers to "movements of concerted refusal to provide their services organised by the workers" of the platforms "with the aim of defending their professional grievances." The classical definition of a strike is defined in jurisprudence as the "collective and concerted ending of work motivated by professional grievances" (e.g. Social Chamber of the Cour de cassation, 16 May 1973, published as n° 72-40541).

join or set up a trade union (Article L. 7342-6). The reference to the concept of "social" responsibility allows the delimitation of the field of legal liability of the platforms, rather than changing their nature, while at the same time placing the "business risk" (Maggi-Germain 2013b) on the platforms' workers.[28]

Concomitantly with the emergence of new figures of economic dependence, it is interesting to note that employment law mobilises, from now on, beyond the figure of the worker or salaried employee, the "person" (Maggi-Germain 2004, 2013a, 2017). Should this be seen as a form of emancipation or rather the resurgence of links of personal responsibility which permits the transfer of liability?

The slipping of the scope of social law from the salaried employee or even the worker towards the person is illustrated by recent creations of the personal training account (*compte personnel de formation)* and the personal activity account (*compte personnel d'activité*). Codified by the law of 8 August 2016 in the fifth part of the Labour Code dedicated to employment, the personal activity account aims, as a perpetuation of the personal training account, to bring together social rights which, although acquired under different legal statutes, can be exercised regardless of job status. It is about guaranteeing continuity in the exercise of social rights.[29] To permit this, the

---

[28] The existence of this risk, noted by the *Cour de cassation*, permits it to reserve itself the right to check the validity of the clauses in the employment contract that specify a variation in remuneration which could have the effect of making the employee bear the business risk. In the framework of its social responsibility towards its workers, law n° 2019-1428 of 24 December 2019, on the orientation of mobilities, provides that the platform can establish a "charter defining the conditions and processes for implementing its social liability, defining its rights and obligations and those of its workers with whom it has a relatonship." "These rules guarantee the non-exclusive nature of the relationship between the workers and the platform and the freedom of the workers to use the platform and to connect to it or disconnect from it, without having activity time slots imposed on them," and thus, among others, that "the processes aim to allow the workers to obtain a fair price for their provision of services." These charters, where they exist, must be submitted for approval by the administrative authority. They cannot be characterised by the existance of a link of legal subordination between the platform and the workers (Labour Code Article L. 7342-9).

[29] The concept of "social rights" in itself deserves to be researched from the point of view of the law. If the particularity of these rights is to express an ideal form of respect for human beings for the purposes of society (Michaélidès-Nouaros 1966. p. 235), then this means they can benefit from a specific legal regime characterised, for example, by the mutualisation and fungibility of their financing. Social rights were launched in the programme of the National Resistance Council of 15 March 1944 and emerged into the French legal order at the end of the Second World War in the

acquired rights are attached to the person, which also ensures continuity in their implementation. These social rights (e.g. the right to receive training) which at present are derived from the personal training account, the professional health and safety account and the civic engagement account,[30] can be different in nature and acquired under different statuses (Maggi-Germain 2016, 2017). If their use relies, in theory, on the person's initiative, the purposes laid down by the law concerns as much the conditions of their acquisition as their use, thus linking them more to the provision about flexi-security that to a mechanism of empowerment, which serves as a vehicle for the emancipation of individuals. If it is indeed the owner of the personal activity account that decides to make use of their rights, this must be under the conditions defined by the legislation concerning a system whose purpose is, above all, to overcome obstacles to social mobility by reinforcing the autonomy of this "owner."[31] If "the advent of the society of individuals is the recognition of the power human beings have over the organisation of their society" (Dumont 1956, p. 37), is not the society of individuals heralding the socialisation of economic risk, which translates into the setting up of competition between workers supported by "the desire of the legislators to go past the horizon of employment law" (Willmann 2016, p. 819)? The personal activity account and the personal training account seem, through the "new" social rights attached to the individual who guarantees their implementation, to be participating in an individualisation of the management of social risks and to be forcing workers to contribute to the management of economic risks. This specific question deserves to be asked in terms of the work done in management sciences around "agile" businesses that can adapt more easily, are more flexible, and which value free individuals (Barrand 2010, p. 19), or of the pronouncements about "talents," according to which "the individual who has chosen his/her own career path ("l'acteur-trajectoire") must pursue it through erratic situations,

---

preamble to the 1946 Constitution of the Fourth Republic, which proclaims as "particularly necessary in our time" the following political, economic and social principles: equality of men and women, the duty to work, the right to employment, the right to join a trade union, the right to strike, the right to access professional training and culture and the right to obtain from society the means required for an acceptable standard of living. These principles remain in legal force today. But here we are dealing with programmatic rights, that aim to give direction to political decisions without creating subjective rights that individuals could claim.

[30] Labour Code Article L. 5151-5.

[31] "The personal activity account's objectives are, through the use of the rights contained in it, to strengthen the autonomy and freedom of action of its holder and to secure his or her career path by reducing obstacles to mobility" (Labour Code Article L. 5151-1, paragraph 1).

trend reversals, critical incidents and cuts in resources" (Bourion *et al.* 2011, p. 2).

Conclusion

By making references to the "socialisation of the law", late-19th-century and early-20th-century legal scholars were attempting to take account of developments that had led to replacing an individual obligation with "a collective obligation that supports a social group" (Durand 1942, p. 83). Breaking with the individualist tradition of subjective rights, the socialisation of the law also presumes that the state abandons its role of guarantor[32] to become a welfare state. The developments described above only constitute part of general transformations that are more to do with the redistribution of liabilities, in our opinion, than with the taking of more responsibility (Bargain *et al.* 2014). The "socialisation of economic risk"[33] at first sight certainly seems to encourage salaried employees, workers and individuals by opening up to them, for example, "rights to training," whose declared objective is to secure their career paths by individualising them (Gautié *et al.* 2015), but it also contributes to rethinking the function of the company as embedded in public employment policies (Maggi-Germain 2014) by the extension of its obligations and liability towards its salaried employees.[34] These developments also transform the welfare state into a regulator state, subsumed into "public action," determined by its capacity to "create institutional systems that are adapted to the reality of public problems" (Duran 2009, p. 328). A reduction in the number of figures — transnational businesses, NGOs and international institutions — on the international stage (Delmas-Marty, 2015, p. 395) has also created a "post-national constellation" (Habermas 2000, p. 47) of democratic institutions and transnational public spaces in which the state becomes a player among

---

[32] "Freedom consists of being able to do anything that does not harm someone else: thus the exercise of natural rights by each individual is only subject to limits that ensure that other members of society can enjoy those same rights. These limits can only be determined by the law." Article 4 of the Declaration of the Rights of Man and the Citizen of 1789.

[33] The Council of State dedicated one of its annual reports to this, noting a "growing trend towards a "socialisation of risk" generated by the development of our society towards an increased desire for security and an increased demand for risks to be covered" (Conseil d'État 2005, p. 9).

[34] Businesses are required, for example, to maintain the professional capacity of their salaried employees (Maggi-Germain 2009).

others, charged with the "piloting of public action" (Duran 2009, p. 329).[35]

One of the main debates resulting from the developments described above is most certainly about the progressive development of employment law towards common employment law (Maggi-Germain 2010, 2019), which is a prescriptive corpus applicable to a group of workers (salaried employees, civil servants and self-employed workers), thus recreating a link with the ideal of universal law carried by the *jus commune* of the editors of the Civil Code. Based on what the eminent legal scholar Paul Durand (1952, p. 439) identified as the "different forms of human work," the principles common to all workers with distinct legal statuses can be stated — as was the case for salaried employees in the recodification movement beginning in 1989 (Maggi-Germain 2019)[36] — in new "activity codes" (e.g. the Energy Code and the Transport Code) the "perimeter"[37] of which will be defined by the economic activity itself. What logic or rationality will back up this common employment law? Can the extent of social rights be shaped by this economic activity? Will it always be a case of protecting the weakest party in compliance with an ideal of justice that "wants to ensure, above all, that the powerful do not oppress the weak" (Capitant 1922, p. 33)? Or will it rather be a matter of circumscribing, under the cover of an extension of the scope of the social rights that have so far been brought together in a "base" in exchange for a redistribution of liabilities? In other words, is it possible to extend the scope of common employment law to all workers or even to all "persons"[38] without questioning the historical functions of employment law or changing its very nature?

---

[35] State intervention can thus take multiple forms, such as the creation of independent administrative authorities, concomitant with the privatisation of industrial and commercial public services.

[36] Book 1 of the Energy Code contains a Title 6, which brings together the provisions concerning staff of electricity and gas utility companies (Articles L. L161-1 to 6) while a book of the Transport Code is dedicated to the social regulations that apply to transport (Articles L1311-1 to L1331-3).

[37] The term "perimeter" is gradually replacing "scope" in employment law in particular. This semantic shift is far from anodyne: it is one of the signs of the move from institutionalised law, characterised by its hierarchy of sources, to horizontal law determined by the subsidiarity of its sources.

[38] The scope of the Labour Code extends, in some of its provisions derived from recent laws, to "all persons": holders of personal activity accounts (Article L5151-2) and beneficiaries of career development advice (Article L. 6111-6) (cf. Maggi-Germain 2016 and 2017).

Bibliography

Antonmattei, Paul-Henri, Sciberras, Jean-Christophe, *Le travailleur économiquement dépendant: quelle protection?* Rapport au ministre du travail (November 2008)

Barrand, Jérôme (dir.), *L'entreprise agile. Agir pour une performance durable* (Paris: Dunod, 2010)

Bargain, Gwenola, Berthier, Paul-Emmanuel, Sachs, Tatiana, "Les logiques de responsabilisation au cœur des évolutions récentes du droit social français," *Le Droit ouvrier*, no. 797 (2014): pp. 784-810

Blin-Franchomme, Marie-Pierre, "Autour de la consécration de la responsabilité environnementale dans le Code civil," *Revue Lamy de droit des affaires*, no. 128 (2017): pp. 20-23

Boissard, Adéodat, *Contrat de travail et salariat: introduction philosophique, économique et juridique à l'étude des Conventions relatives au Travail dans le Régime du Salariat* (Paris: Bloud & Cie, 1910)

Boulanger, J., 1950, "Principes généraux du droit et droit positif," *in* Études offertes à Georges Ripert, *Le droit privé au milieu du XXe siècle*, tome I (Librairie générale de Droit et de jurisprudence, 1950) pp. 51-74

Bourion, Christian, Bournois, Frank, Igalens, Jacques, Thevenet, Maurice, "L'ère des talents," *Revue internationale de psychologie*, vol. XVII, no. 41 (2011): p. 2

Boutonnet, Mathilde, "Quelle action en responsabilité civile pour la réparation du préjudice écologique ?," *Énergie, Environnement, Infrastructures*, June, no. 6 (2017): pp. 39-43

Capitant, Henri, "Les transformations du droit civil français depuis cinquante ans," In *Les transformations du droit dans les principaux pays depuis cinquante ans (1869-1919). Livre du cinquantenaire de la société de législation comparée*, tome I (Paris: LGDJ, 1922), pp. 31-80

Charmont, Joseph, *Le droit et l'esprit démocratique* (Montpellier: Coulet & fils éditeurs, 1908)

Collectif Dalloz, *Proposition de code du travail* (Paris, Dalloz: 2017)

Commission des communautés européennes, "Moderniser le droit du travail pour relever les défis du XXIe siècle," document du 22 novembre 2006, COM (2006)-708-final

Cuche, P., "Le rapport de dépendance, élément constitutif du contrat de travail," *Revue critique de législation et de jurisprudence* (1913): pp. 412-427

Denoix de Saint Marc, Renaud, "Éditorial," In *Responsabilité et socialisation du risque (rapport public)*, by Conseil d'État, IInd part, 2005

Deffains, Bruno, and Doriat-Duban, Myriam, "Le procès : risque économique," *Revue générale du droit des assurances* 01/07, n° 2010-03 (2010): pp. 870-886

Delmas-Marty, Mireille, "Trois dynamiques pour responsabiliser les résultats et les entreprises transnationales," In *Prendre la responsabilité au sérieux*, directed by Supiot, Alain, Delmas-Marty, Mireille (Paris: Presses universitaires de France, 2015), pp. 393-408

Demogue, René, *Notions fondamentales du Droit privé. Essai critique* (Paris: Éditions La Mémoire du Droit, 2001 [1911])

Duguit, Léon, *Les transformations générales du droit privé depuis le Code Napoléon* (Paris: Librairie Félix Alcan, 1912), accessible online: http://gallica.bnf.fr/ark:/12148/bpt6k935172d/f9.image

Dumont, Louis, *Essais sur l'individualisme. Une perspective anthropologique sur l'idéologie moderne* (Paris: Point Essais, 1991 [1956])

Duran, Patrice, "Légitimité, droit et action publique," *L'Année sociologique*, vol. 59 (2009): pp. 303-344

Durand, Paul, "Rémunération du travail et socialisation du droit," *Droit social* (1942): pp. 83-85

Durand Paul, "Naissance d'un droit nouveau. Du droit du travail au droit de l'activité professionnelle," *Droit social,* July-August, no. 7 (1952): pp. 437-441

Ewald, François, *L'État providence* (Paris: Grasset, 1986)

Gautié, Jérôme, Maggi-Germain, Nicole, Perez, Coralie, "Fondements et enjeux des "Comptes de Formation": les regards croisés de l'économie et du droit," *Droit social*, no. 2 (2015): pp. 169-180

Groutel, Hubert, "Le critère du contrat de travail," In Collectif, *Tendances du droit du travail français contemporain : études offertes à G. H. Camerlynck* (Paris: Dalloz 1978 [1977]), pp. 49-61

Habermas, Jürgen, *Après l'État-nation. Une nouvelle constellation politique*, (Paris: Fayard, 2013 [2000])

Jay, Raoul, *Rapport de la commission de codification des lois ouvrières sur le livre premier [du Code du travail]: Les conventions relatives au travail* (Paris: Imprimerie nationale, 1904)

Jeammaud, Antoine, "Uber, Deliveroo: requalification des contrats ou dénonciation d'une fraude à la loi ?," *Semaine sociale Lamy* no. 1780 (2017): pp. 4-8

Josserand, Louis, *La responsabilité du fait des choses inanimées* (Paris: LGDJ and Arthur Rousseau, 1897)

Jourdain, Patrice, *Les principes de la responsabilité civile* (Paris: Dalloz, 1998)

Lévy, Emmanuel, *Les fondements du Droit* (Paris: Alcan, 1939)

Linhart, Danièle, "Imaginer un salariat sans subordination," *Le Monde diplomatique,* July, no. 760 (2017): pp. 20-21

Lokiec, Pascal, *Il faut sauver le droit du travail !* (Paris: Odile Jacob, 2015)

Lyon-Caen, Gérard, and Lyon-Caen, Antoine, "La doctrine de l'entreprise," In *Dix ans de droit de l'entreprise*, directed by Mousseron, Jean-Marc, Teyssié, Bernard (Paris: Librairies techniques, 1978), pp. 601-621

Maggi-Germain, Nicole, "À propos de l'individualisation de la formation professionnelle continue," *Droit social* no. 7 (1999): pp. 692-699

Maggi-Germain, Nicole, "La formation professionnelle continue entre individualisation et personnalisation des droits des salariés," *Droit Social*, no. 5 (2004): pp. 482-493

Maggi-Germain, Nicole, "La capacité du salarié à occuper un emploi," *Droit social,* no.12 (2009): pp. 1234-1245

Maggi-Germain, Nicole, "Mobilis in mobile: le Code du travail en mouvement," In *Nouveau Code du travail. Évaluation par les usagers et bilan des deux premières années d'application*, *Semaine sociale Lamy,* supplément, 20 December 2010, no. 1472 (2010): pp. 64-74

Maggi-Germain, Nicole, "Le compte personnel de formation," *Droit social* [numéro spécial "Loi relative à la sécurisation de l'emploi"], no. 9 (2013a): pp. 687-700

Maggi-Germain, Nicole, "La suspension de l'application de l'arrêté d'extension de la convention collective nationale de la branche de la production cinématographique par le juge des référés: prologue judiciaire ou clap de fin ?", *Droit social,* no. 12 (2013b): pp. 1016-1022

Maggi-Germain, Nicole, "L'entretien professionnel: de l'outil managérial au dispositif juridique instrument des politiques publiques de l'emploi," *Les Cahiers* sociaux, no. 267 (2014): pp. 597-602

Maggi-Germain, Nicole, "Le Compte personnel d'activité à la croisée des chemins," In *Compte personnel d'activité,* dossier coordonné par Maggi-Germain, Nicole, *Droit social* no. 10 (2016): pp. 792-799

Maggi-Germain, Nicole "Les droits attachés à personne, une nouvelle catégorie de droits sociaux? L'exemple du compte personnel d'activité," In *Los actuales cambios sociales y laborales: nuevos retos para el mundo del trabajo. Libro 1: Cambios tecnológicos y nuevos retos para el mundo del trabajo (Portugal, España, Colombia, Italia, Francia),* edited by Mella Méndez, Lourdes, Serrani, Lavinia (Bruxelles: Peter Lang, 2017): pp. 419-432, available at https://www.peterlang.com/view/product/80122?rskey=6mz9BG&result=5

Maggi-Germain, Nicole, "Existe-t-il un droit commun du travail?" In *La réforme de la fonction publique*, coord. by Maggi-Germain, Nicole,

Droit social no. 12 (2019): pp. 1034-1041

Marco, Luc, "Le risque chez Courcelle-Seneuil: une approche éclectique et libérale au milieu du XIXe siècle," *Vie & sciences de l'entreprise* no. 191-192 (2012): pp. 118-131

Michaelides-Nouaros, Georges, "L'évolution récente de la notion de droit subjectif," *RTD Civ.* LXIV (1966): pp. 216–235

Planiol, Marcel, "Responsabilité du fait d'autrui," *Revue critique de législation et de jurisprudence*, LVIII, tome XXXVIII (1909): pp. 282-301

Ripert, Georges, "Droit naturel et positivisme juridique," *Annales de la Faculté de Droit d'Aix*, no. 1 (1918): pp. 3- 47

Savatier, René, "Vers la socialisation de la responsabilité et des risques individuels," *Dalloz hebdomadaire*, chronique (1931): p. 9

Supiot, Alain, "La contractualisation de la société," In *Qu'est-ce que l'humain ?*, directed by Michaud, Yves (Paris: Odile Jacob, 2000), pp. 157-167

Supiot, Alain, "Et si l'on refondait le droit du travail?" *Le Monde diplomatique* no. 763, October (2017): pp. 1, 22 and 23

Supiot, Alain, "Introduction," In *Face à l'irresponsabilité: la dynamique de la solidarité*, directed by Supiot, Alain (Paris: Collège de France, 2018), pp. 7-17

Trébulle, François-Guy, "La consécration de l'accueil du préjudice écologique dans le code civil," *Énergie, Environnement, Infrastructures,* November (2016): p. 19

Veniamin, V.L., *Essai sur les données économiques dans l'obligation civile* (Paris: LGDJ, 1931)

Viney, Geneviève, *Traité de droit civil. Introduction à la responsabilité* (Paris: LGDJ, 2008)

Wilmann, Christophe, "Le compte personnel d'activité: être et avoir," In *Compte personnel d'activité,* coord. by Maggi-Germain, Nicole, *Droit social* no. 10 (2016): p. 812-822

Wolmark, Cyril, "Quelle place pour le travail dans le droit du travail?" *Droit social*, no. 5 (2016): pp. 439-445

CHAPTER 7

INDIVIDUAL RIGHTS AS A CRITIQUE OF LABOUR LAW COLLECTIVITY: LOOKING AT LABOUR LAW FROM THE PERSPECTIVE OF ITS OUTSIDERS[1]

EVA KOCHER

The individualising and subjectificating dynamics of law have repeatedly been exposed to fundamental critique. Labour law seems to be a particularly suitable subject for studying the dynamics of individual subjective rights, because collective labour law offers a very specific coupling of society, politics, economics and law. However, collective labour law has its specific objective in the vertical conflict between employees and employers. When it seeks to adequately integrate horizontal relationships of power and inequality, it often reaches its limits. At these limits, individual rights to equal treatment and reasonable accommodation emerge that often act in tension with collective action.

The following example may serve as illustration. Some time ago, the German Federal Labour Court (Bundesarbeitsgericht, BAG) had to deal with the case of an employee (let's call her W) who worked in the sales department of a DIY store (BAG 16.12.2008; this was also one of the cases that served as illustrative material for Kocher 2018). The DIY store employed a total of 24 workers and opened Monday to Saturday from 8:00am until 8:00pm. The employees in the sales department worked in a rolling shift system for five working days. W initially worked full-time, but

[1] This chapter is based on ideas I have developed in several articles in recent years (Kocher 2016; Kocher 2018). Basic ideas have already been developed in the course of the research project, "Soziales Recht der Arbeit", Kocher et al. 2013. Recently, I have been part of a research project that studies empirical issues of "law – gender – collectivity" (https://www.recht-geschlecht-kollektivitaet.de/en/projects/b-work-and-employment/ (accessed 13-03-2021).

then had a child and started working part-time during parental leave. At the time of the conflict, she lived alone with her son, who attended kindergarten daily from 8:00 am until 3:00 pm. That's why, at the end of her parental leave, W wanted to reduce her working hours from 37.5 to 30 hours per week, and divide these into timeframes Monday to Friday, from 8:30am to 2:30pm, with a maximum of two Saturdays per month. She invoked sections 8 (1) and (4) of the Act on Part-Time Work and Fixed-Term Employment (Teilzeit- und Befristungsgesetz, TzBfG), which require the employer to "agree to a reduction in working hours at the request of the employee and to determine their distribution in accordance with the employee's wishes, notwithstanding operational reasons to the contrary."

The employer refused, stating among other things that turnover was higher in the evenings and on Saturdays than at the times "A" wanted to work. She pointed out that the works council also did not support W's request, which was true. The works council chairwoman had written: "A rigid, fixed working time for an individual employee is not in line with the interests of other colleagues. Fixed working hours for a single employee would disturb industrial peace quite considerably." What the works council had in mind was the fact that the working hours during afternoons and evenings, as well as on Saturdays, were felt to be burdensome by all employees. Changing shifts had been introduced and laid down in a collective agreement on the level of the undertaking, to ensure that these shifts were distributed evenly among all.

The Federal Labour Court found, on the one hand, that the collective agreement conflicted with W's request to reallocate her working hours, but held, on the other hand, that the works council, when exercising its co-determination rights, must ensure the promotion of the compatibility of family care work and employment. In this "weighing of individual and collective interests" the parties to the collective agreement were awarded a margin of discretion which the Court found to have not been exceeded in the present case (BAG 2008, 43-45, 71-72). W therefore lost her case. If subsequently she felt forced to resign, she would not have been the first parent to be forced out of an employment relationship following parental leave (Bundesregierung 2017, 88-89).

The fact that and how collective and individual rights have been shown to be opposed to each other in this case, closely relates to the structures of labour collectivity. The problem with which W had to struggle is by no means of an individual nature; it is ultimately about the fundamental social question of the relationship between care work and gainful employment. In other words, it is a question of the compatibility of work in employment with work in the family — a question which is closely intertwined with gender relations that have a social and therefore collective character. The fact that this problem becomes perceived as an "individual" issue in labour law and enters into a contradiction with the equal treatment interests of other employees has to do with the construction of labour collectives. This is what I will deal with in this chapter.

1. Exclusive Collective Autonomy as a Gendered Relationship

Collective action is by definition representative action. Collective action always requires reference to an imagined collective (in detail: Kocher 2007, 55-66). This collective will be socially, communicatively, culturally, but also legally constituted. And its legal constitution is by no means something incidental, but is itself capable of shaping the social structures of the collective (e.g. Baer 2020, § 4, para. 155).

First of all, in labour law, there is a basic understanding that both the law and collective autonomy react to imbalances in the individual contract (in labour law, the latter is never something "individual" anyway, but a contract of adhesion that always forms part of a collective regulation for the order of the business) (Collins 1986). However, collective labour law is legitimised and organised quite differently from state legislation, despite similar objectives of employee protection (on the whole, see, e.g. Davidov 2016; Rebhahn 2010). In Germany, collective autonomy is constituted both as collective bargaining autonomy (Article 9 (3) of the basic law (Grundgesetz, GG) and within the framework of the Works Constitution Act (Sec. 77, Betriebsverfassungsgesetz, BetrVG. For a comparative view, see for example, Rebhahn 2010). Collective bargaining autonomy is mostly constructed on the principle of solidarity as countervailing power; it is not something that is granted, but something that has been fought for and is being fought for again and again (e.g. Zachert 2004 with reference to Weber and Sinzheimer). The result of these effects of power and counter-power is a legal protection of "collective" interests, which can by no means be equated with "public" interests (on this distinction see Kocher 2007, 72-80).

In German law, collective bargaining autonomy is clearly and directly linked to membership. In a narrow chain of legitimation, the legal effects of a collective agreement in this context are attributed solely on the basis of membership. According to Section 4 of the Collective Bargaining Act (Tarifvertragsgesetz, TVG), a collective agreement only applies to an employment relationship if the employee is a member of the contracting trade union and the employer is a member of the contracting employers' association (Franzen 2021, 5, 16). Anyone who is not a member of one of the parties to the collective agreement is literally referred to as an "outsider" (Franzen 2021, 29-31).

More strictly than other legal systems, German collective bargaining law is therefore based on the idea that, in labour law, solidarity in the form of collective action is only legitimate as action "with others," but not necessarily as action "for others." It assumes an understanding of solidarity based on commonality and an assumption of responsibility and cooperation (Supiot 2015; Gamillscheg 1973). Such a notion of solidarity in a group, which is reciprocal and oriented towards the particular, has a much more exclusive character than inclusive and group-transcending notions of solidarity (on different understandings of solidarity see Brunkhorst 2015; Lessenich, Reder and Süß 2020, 319-326; Altreiter et al. 2019; Bude 2019). That's why these collective processes of law-making are fundamentally different and more exclusive than the legislative process. In the context of German collective bargaining, the inclusive and exclusive effects of - solidarity and collective action are constructed through the social processes that produce and organise membership, meaning that minorities in a trade union organisation, as well as groups that are not unionised at all, are included in solidarity and participate only to the extent that, contrary to its legal construct, a solidarity concept of acting "for others" becomes effective in the organisation (see also below at 4.0 for this collision of logics).

Imbalances in representation exist in particular with regard to gender (Kocher 2018). Trade union membership structures and the imagined self-images of collective action clearly present themselves as hegemonically gendered (on the gendering of collective action in gainful employment see, for example, Funder, Dörhöfer and Rauch 2006; Stöger 2008; Schambach-Hardtke 2005; Greifenstein and Kißler 2014). These structures translate directly into gendered understandings and practices of solidarity, collective action and collective agreements (on the representation of gendered interests in works council action see, for example, Funder, Dörhöfer and Rauch 2006, fn. 18).

2. Compatibility of Care Work and Employment as a Problem of Labour Law

It is no coincidence that the exclusions that arise as a result of the specific organisation of collectivity are similar to those dealt with by the instruments of equal treatment and anti-discrimination rights (on the relevance of anti-discrimination law in the present case see, for example, Kocher et al. 2013, 79). However, the BAG had primarily relied on the right to family, as established in Article 6 of the Basic Law (Grundgesetz, GG).

Solidarity and collective action have limited scope in these contexts insofar as they are legitimised by the principle of countervailing power (i.e., by functions referring to the "vertical" imbalance between employees and employers). With this backdrop, the exclusions that equality discourses address present themselves as (horizontal) conflicts, which Guy Mundlak has rightly called the "third function of labour law" (Mundlak 2011; cf. Gamillscheg 1973), and the individualistic paradigms of anti-discrimination law are constructed in such a way as to protect interests that are not already represented in labour law collectives (cf. Zachert 2002).

Therefore, an important example of possible contradictions between collective autonomy and individual rights is the debate about whether collective agreements must also legally be measured against anti-discrimination law. In any case, the legal presumption that collective agreements contain an overall appropriate balance of interests can only be legitimated with regard to the conflict of interests between employer and employees. It can be to no avail with regard to different interests among employees (BAG 27.5.2004; ECJ 8.9.2011; ECJ 19.6.2014, para. 63 et seq.; explicitly: Art. 16 of Directive 2000/78/EC; Art. 23 of Directive 2006/54/EC; Kocher 2010; Dieterich 2001, 112 ff; Zachert 2002). It has been feared, with good reason, that no stone could be left unturned, should the principle of "equal pay for work of equal value" be taken to its end.

The case outlined at the beginning shows how gendered individual rights of parents can come into conflict with collective agreements and lead to these being put under stricter legal scrutiny. Collective agreements that unions conclude in their countervailing power function typically do not take care work by parents into account at all. For example, this can be seen in the regulations on working hours and place of work. Further, it is not uncommon for works councils to regard single mothers and fathers, whose interests have not been taken into account in the assumptions of the normality of everyday working life, as disruptions to everyday working life.

This is due to social and cultural structures. The organisation of private households and care work is closely intertwined with the social gender order. This can be traced historically, for example, in the emergence of a gendered division of spheres between private and public and is also structurally reflected in the gendered models of "male" autonomy and "female" caring (Beckmann 2013). The social invisibility and social devaluation of care work also means that this form of work is treated as a residual factor in the economy and labour society. In short, gainful employment is organised in such a way that those who take on care work have a compatibility problem (Bundesregierung 2017, 76 seq.).

3. The Transformation of Social Problems into Individual Rights

Due to the specific and exclusive structure of labour collectives, the third function of labour law can currently almost exclusively be mobilised through individual rights. In such situations, the law increasingly guarantees individual rights to those who are not adequately represented collectively. In Germany, individual rights exist, for example, for parental leave, caregiver leave, the transfer from daytime to nighttime work, and for a reduction in working hours. W had asserted the latter, thus subjecting the collective agreements at company level to some degree of legal scrutiny. Such scrutiny at the hands of a labour court does, however, create problems. Employee representatives do have an enormous and difficult task in developing counter-power through solidarity in a constant power struggle with the employer, which often leads them to neglect specific situations.

Against this non-consideration, W had only an individual right to assert. However, the legal form of individual rights itself has a specific subjectivating effect (i.e. it (re)produces an isolated legal subject endowed with subjective rights). The law itself presents the social problem of the compatibility of professional and family work as an individual problem. Through its structure, the law itself contributes to the fact that the relationship between care work and gainful employment in labour law is not addressed as a societal issue, but as an issue of individual outsiders who, in turn, come to be considered disruptors.

The decision of the Federal Labour Court amounted to legally obliging the parties to the collective agreement to take individual legal positions into account at any point. Such a right to consideration amounts to a right to reasonable accommodation, thus enabling objections to general rules that are not specific enough to consider vulnerable groups (Kocher et al. 2013) – these individual rights can therefore function as a very interesting form of an "immanent critique" of the collective (Wihl 2021).

4. Solidarity First?

a) The Critique of a Human Rights Approach to Labour Law

In labour law, there has always existed a fundamental critique of the legalisation of collective bargaining through individual rights. This evolved from a critique of the juridification of political processes (Erd 1987; Teubner 1984, 289). In the 2000s, it was directed against using individual human rights as an anchor for notions of justice in worklife. As Jay

Youngdahl (among others) argued, such a human rights approach could lead to the displacement of notions of solidarity, democracy in the workplace, and economic justice (Youngdahl 2009, 31, 46-47; by contrast: Compa 2009, 38; for a detailed discussion of this debate, see Kocher 2012). The critique focused in particular on forms of human rights activism: the human rights movement was accused of envisioning justice as an end rather than merely a means, thus overlooking the fact that collective representation, trade union and works council action is usually the most effective means of asserting employees' interests in the workplace, in particular if compared with NGOs that operate outside the workplace, without direct legitimisation from workers.

Even if modern trade unionism itself increasingly relies on civil society action and, for example, involves the general public in collective debates and actions (e.g. Schmalz and Dörre 2013; Brinkmann, Choi and Detje 2008), fundamental tensions with human rights approaches remain. Reference to human rights is often associated with a discourse of care for victims (solidarity *for others*) and not with an empowerment and promotion of collective action (solidarity *with others*, which relies on reciprocity and thus has a more exclusive character than human rights activism) (for a summary of the arguments, see Kolben 2009, 449).

Criticism of EU anti-discrimination law has sometimes taken a parallel line, describing it as an Anglo-American regulatory model, incompatible with the European Social Model and its orientation toward collective bargaining. Some authors have considered anti-discrimination law in welfare states as either superfluous or as promoting a reorientation of social policy from insider protection to a mere protection of access opportunities (i.e. as opening markets and dismantling social policy) (Somek 2011; on the other hand, Schiek 2012; and basically on this debate Schieck 2014).

All these critiques ultimately refuse to take seriously the contradictions described above that arise from the incomplete representation of the collective in labour law.

b) Contradictions in the Use of Legal Categories

A completely different critique of individual (and equality) rights has to do with a paradox of antidiscrimination law. If categories such as "gender" are used, they threaten to reproduce the social inequalities and power relations that anti-discrimination law is supposed to address. Anti-discrimination law is in fact partly based on "groupism" (Brubaker 2007; Baer 2012, 23-46; Young 1988/89), establishing and constructing social groups in order to determine whether discrimination has occurred. If, on the other hand, we dispense with categories, it may no longer be possible to address power and discrimination appropriately (see the discussions on a post-categorical antidiscrimination law by Liebscher et al. 2012 and Hartmann 2019, 24).

In a research project on the relevance of gender in legal collectivisation processes, we examined such dynamics in two case studies. One study dealt with a campaign by the German Metal Workers' Industrial Union (IG Metall) for flexible working hours (Hensel and Höllmann 2021). The campaign had started with a gender equality discourse, which gradually faded into the background as the campaign was communicated more widely within the organisation and to the public. In the end, the campaign refrained from any debate on discrimination and instead mostly articulated arguments referring to plural interests of employees, and the promotion of individual self-determination for all employees. Although the collective agreement that has emerged is still suitable for tackling gendered conflicts regarding reconciling employment and care work, it remains to be seen how the individualising discourse can be abandoned in implementation.

Another study dealt with a campaign by the German Education Sector Union (Gewerkschaft Erziehung und Wissenschaft, GEW) and focused on the question of how the union used anti-discrimination law to fight for the equal pay of primary school teachers and teachers at secondary schools. GEW used the invocation of gendered legal positions to summarise individual situations into collective narratives and to mobilise the collective memory of the law – an interesting case of "strategic essentialism" (Spivak 1988). Here, collectivisation was, after all, partly an effect of legal categorisation processes (Hensel 2020).

c) In Search of Actors

Having said all this, individual rights, especially in the German legal system, entail further specific problems. Their opportunities only unfold if the right is being invoked and used. In situations of social inequalities and power, this requires a considerable will of individuals to resistance, and action that often depends on the solidarity of others. In the end, solidarity and collectivity do not only function as a means of collective autonomy and collective bargaining; a supportive collective context is often also indispensable for an effective enforcement of individual rights (an interesting approach can be found in Griffiths 1999, 313-330).

This is one of the unsolved questions of labour law: how can we enable the putting-into-effect of the law in social situations where the law is most important, but where the individual resources necessary for its use are non-existent (e.g. in companies without a works council where no trade union officials show up)? Precariousness and the lack of structures for collective representation depend on each other. Even external administrative control can be rendered ineffective in situations without resistant actors in the workplace itself. Even administrative control will ultimately depend on someone being willing to disclose their name and put themselves into play as a witness or affected person (for an example of pay review in home work see Kocher and Pfarr 1998, 149; a fundamental example is Apelt, Dosdall and Trautwein 2020, 445). Class action and collective litigation evidently also rely on collectivity (unfortunately still current: Kocher 2002).

It is therefore no coincidence that the promotion of collective organisation and mobilisation processes is increasingly seen as a policy objective in its own right. In Germany and Europe, a number of policy proposals have recently been made regarding how membership in associations could be promoted on both sides. On the employer's side, the main aim would be to make it more difficult to escape collective bargaining; on the union side, positive incentives through differentiation clauses or trade union access to the workplace have been discussed (Deinert and Walser 2015, 386; Deinert 2017, 24-32; with a comparative approach see Fornasier 2017, 239-254; Krause 2016). The former German government planned to create a digital access right for trade unions (Federal Ministry of Labour and Social Affairs and Federal Ministry of Finance 2021), and the European Commission, in its proposal for a directive on adequate minimum wages in the European Union, wants to promote collective bargaining in wage setting by increasing collective bargaining coverage. Member States will be required to take action to promote the capacity of social partners to engage in collective bargaining in wage setting (European Commission 2020). Unfortunately, the exclusive effects of solidarity are hardly discussed in these contexts.

5. Individual Rights as Immanent Critique

Labour law protection is about offering employees options for action. This is true both for collective autonomy and for individual rights. In both cases, labour law ultimately establishes forms in which autonomy can be mobilised against powerful organisations, either with the help of countervailing power (collective autonomy) or through legal procedures (individual rights). The two processes can interfere with each other. However, this interference exposes social contradictions in the law.

Tim Wihl has called this function of individual rights "immanent critique" and, following Hegel, has described the normative potentials of individual rights to equal freedom (individuality) as "threefold abrogation"; they "blow up the order and the legal system from within." In this sense, the rights discussed in this text can be understood as "second-level" abrogation rights, which "raise an objection to rules that are not specific enough to address relevant particularities, especially of vulnerable individuals" (Wihl 2019; my translation). The radical effect of rights in consideration of the family in labour law, in particular, would become even more apparent if one tried to rethink labour law from the perspective of single parents (thus my suggestion in Kocher 2016), and to conceive of a generalised right to reasonable accommodation (Wenckebach and Kocher 2013), not only considering the perspective of the parties to the labour contract, but including the perspectives of friends, partners and the children of employees, i.e. the perspectives of persons whose claims to time and attention compete with the claims to time and attention that the modern world of work places on employees (thus the proposal of Möhring-Hesse 2007, 356-357).

Individual rights can thus create transformative situations. But they need resistant, autonomous, free individuals to mobilise them. Solidarity and collective autonomy provide a framework for this. But there is still a long way to go before they can really function in an inclusive way. The law can at best contribute to this development by creating spaces for conflict, while relying on the critical dynamics of individual rights.

Bibliography

Altreiter, Carina, Flecker, Jörg, Papouschek, Ulrike, Schindler, Saskja, and Schönauer, Annika, *Umkämpfte Solidaritäten: Spaltungslinien in der Gegenwartsgesellschaft* (Wien: Promedia, 2019)

Baer, Susanne, "Rechte und Regulierung. Das Problem des Gruppismus für die Grund- und Menschenrechte," In *Verschleierter Orient – entschleierter Okzident?* Edited by Dennerlein, Bettina, et al. (München: Wilhelm Fink, 2012) 23-46

Baer, Susanne, *Rechtssoziologie: Eine Einführung in die interdisziplinäre Rechtsforschung* (Baden-Baden: Nomos, 2020)

Beckmann, Sabine, "Women and Care: Subjectification in Times of the Rising Adult Worker Model - An Intersectional Perspective," In *AG About Gender - International Journal of Gender Studies* (2013): 2 (4). http://www.aboutgender.unige.it/ojs/index.php/generis/article/view/92

Brinkmann, Ulrich, Choi, Hae-Lin, and Detje, Richard, *Strategic unionism: Aus der Krise zur Erneuerung? Umrisse eines Forschungsprogramms* (Wiesbaden: VS Verlag, 2008)

Brubaker, Rogers, *Ethnizität ohne Gruppen* (Hamburg: Hamburg Edition, 2007)

Brunkhorst, Hauke, *Solidarität unter Fremden* (Fischer, 2015)
Bude, Heinz. *Solidarität: Die Zukunft einer großen Idee* (Müchen: Carl Hanser, 2019)
Bundesregierung, *Zweiter Gleichstellungsbericht* (2017) https://www.bmfsfj.de/resource/blob/117916/7a2f8ecf6cbe805cc80edf7c4309b2bc/zweiter-gleichstellungsbericht-data.pdf
Collins, Hugh, "Market Power, Bureaucratic Power, and the Contract of Employment," *Industrial Law Journal* 15 (1986): 1–14
Compa, Lance, "Solidarity and Human Rights. A Response to Youngdahl," In *New Labor Forum* 18(1) (2009): 38
Davidov, Guy, *A Purposive Approach to Labour Law* (Oxford: Oxford University Press, 2016)
Deinert, Olaf, "Gesetzliche Anreize für die Verbandsmitgliedschaft zur Stärkung der Tarifbindung," *Social Law* (2017): 24-32
Deinert, Olaf, and Walser, Manfred, "Tarifvertragliche Bindung der Arbeitgeber," *AuR* (2015): 386
Dieterich, Thomas, "Die Grundrechtsbindung von Tarifverträgen," In *Tarifautonomie für ein neues Jahrhundert: Festschrift für Günter Schaub zum 65. Geburtstag*, edited by Schlachter, Monika, Ascheid, Reiner, and Friedrich, Hans-Wolf (München: Beck, 1998), 117–134
Dieterich, Thomas, "Bindung der Tarifvertragsparteien an den Gleichheitssatz," *Recht der Arbeit (RdA)* (2001): 112
European Commission COM(2020)682 final (Art.4)
Erd, Rainer, *Verrechtlichung industrieller Konflikte* (Frankfurt am Main: Campus Verlag, 1987)
Federal Ministry of Labor and Social Affairs and Federal Ministry of Finance, *Cornerstones for the Further Development of the Minimum Wage and Strengthening of Collective Bargaining Agreements* (March 2021) https://www.bmas.de/SharedDocs/Downloads/DE/Arbeitsrecht/fairer-mindestlohn.pdf;jsessionid=908485EF574AE68DCDF28AB32D6A43DF.delivery1-replication?__blob=publicationFile&v=2#page=1&zoom=auto,-22,848 (accessed 12-03-2021)
Fornasier, Matteo, "Wege zur Stärkung der Tarifbindung. Ein rechtsvergleichender Streifzug zur Untersuchung funktionaler Äquivalenten der Allgemeinverbindlicherklärung von Tarifverträgen," *SR* (2017): 239-254
Franzen, Martin, "§4 TVG," In *Erfurter Kommentar, 21st edition,* (München: Beck, 2021)
Funder, Maria, Dörhöfer, Steffen and Rauch, Christian, *Geschlechteregalität – mehr Schein als Sein. Geschlecht, Arbeit und Interessenvertretung in der*

Arbeits- und Telekommunikationsindustrie (Edition Sigma, 2006)

Gamillscheg, Franz, "Die Solidarität als Rechtsbegriff," In *Festschrift für Erich Fechner*, edited by Wannagat, Georg, and Gitter, Wolfgang (Tübingen: Mohr Siebeck, 1973), 135–53

Greifenstein, Ralph, and Kißler, Leo, *Wen Betriebsräte repräsentieren. Sozialprofil von Interessenvertretungen und Belegschaftsstrukturenen: Spiegelbild oder Zerrbild?* (Edition Sigma, 2014)

Hartmann, Felix, "Diskriminierung durch Antidiskriminierungsrecht? Möglichkeiten und Grenzen eines postkategorialen Diskriminierungsschutzes in der Europäischen Union," *EuZA* (2019): 24

Hensel, Isabell, "Recht und Geschlecht als gewerkschaftliche Strategien. Mit Hilfe der Geschlechterkategorie in der mittelbaren Diskriminierung zu einer Höherbesoldung von Grundschullehrer*innen?" In *Arbeit | Grenze | Fluss - Work in Progress Interdisziplinärer Arbeitsforschung* Nr. 4 (Frankfurt (Oder): Viadrina, 2020)

Hensel, Isabell, and Höllmann, Judith, "Vergeschlechtlichtes Recht als Strategie in arbeitsrechtlichen Kollektivierungsprozessen," *Feministische Studien* (2021)

Kocher, Eva, "Funktionen der Rechtsprechung: Konfliktlösung im deutschen und englischen Verbraucherprozessrecht," *Beiträge zum ausländischen und internationalen Privatrecht* 86 (Tübingen: Mohr Siebeck, 2007)

Kocher, Eva, "Die Anpassung diskriminierender Tarifverträge an das Recht," *djbZ* (3) (2010): 128–31

Kocher, Eva, "Solidarität und Menschenrechte – Zwei verschiedene Welten?" In *Erzählungen vom Konstitutionalismus: Festschrift für Günter Frankenberg*, edited by Lindemann, Helena, Malaviya, Nina, Hanebeck, Alexander, Hanschmann, Felix, Nickel, Rainer, and Tohidipur, Timo (Baden-Baden: Nomos, 2012), 151–62

Kocher, Eva, "Das Andere des Arbeitsrechts," *AuR* (8-9) (2016): 334–38

Kocher, Eva, "Arbeit, Kollektivautonomie und Solidarität," In *Autonomie im Recht – Geschlechtertheoretisch Vermessen*, edited by Susanne Baer and Ute Sacksofsky (Baden-Baden: Nomos Verlag, 2018), 331–47

Kocher, Eva, Groskreutz, Henning, Nassibi, Ghazaleh, Paschke, Christian, Schulz, Susanne, Welti, Felix, Wenckebach, Johanna, and Zimmer, Barbara, *Das Recht auf eine selbstbestimmte Erwerbsbiographie: Arbeits- und sozialrechtliche Regulierung für Übergänge im Lebenslauf* (Baden-Baden: Nomos, 2013)

Kocher, Eva, and Pfarr, Heide, *Kollektivverfahren im Arbeitsrecht: Arbeitnehmerschutz und Gleichberechtigung durch Verfahren* (Baden-Baden: Nomos, 1998)

Kolben, Kevin, "Labor Rights as Human Rights?" *Virginia Journal of International Law* Vol. 50 (2009): 449

Krause, Rüdiger, "Digitalisierung der Arbeitswelt – Herausforderungen und Regelungsbedarf: Gutachten B," In *Verhandlungen des 71. Deutschen Juristentags Essen 2016*, edited by Deutscher Juristentag (München: C.H.Beck, 2016)

Lessenich, Stephan, Reder, Michael, and Süß, Dietmar, "Zwischen sozialem Zusammenhalt und politischer Praxis: Die vielen Gesichter der Solidarität," *WSI-Mitteilungen* 73/5 (2020): 319-326

Liebscher, Doris, Naguib, Tarek, Plümecke, Tino, and Remus, Juana, "Wege aus der Essentialismusfalle: Überlegungen zu einem postkategorialen Antidiskriminierungsrecht," *KJ* (2) (2012): 204–18

Möhring-Hesse, Matthias, "Wie Rechtsbrechern zu ihrem Recht verhelfen? Arbeitsrecht unter den Bedingungen subjektivierter Arbeit," *KJ* 40 (4) (2007): 347–57

Mundlak, Guy, "The Third Function of Labour Law: Distributing Labour Market Opportunities Among Workers," In *The Idea of Labour Law*, edited by Davidov, Guy, and Langille, Brian (Oxford: Oxford University Press, 2011) 315–28

Rebhahn, Robert, "Die Zukunft der Kollektivautonomie in Europa - Tarifautonomie im Rechtsvergleich," *EuZA* 3 (2010): 62–87

Schambach-Hardtke, Lydia, *Gender und Gewerkschaften, Der Kampf von Frauen um politische Partizipation im organisationalen Handeln* (Verlag Barbara Budrich, 2005)

Schiek, Dagmar, "Review: Somek, Engineering Equality, 2011," *CML Rev.* (2012): 842–44

Schiek, Dagmar, "Zwischenruf: Den Pudding an die Wand nageln? Überlegungen zu einer progressiven Agenda für das EU-Anti-Diskriminierungsrecht," KJ (2014): 396

Schmalz, Stefan, and Dörre, Klaus, *Comeback der Gewerkschaften? Machtressourcen, innovative Praktiken, internationale Perspektiven* (Frankfurt am Main: Campus, 2013)

Somek, Alexander, *Engineering Equality. An Essay on European Anti-Discrimination Law* (Oxford, 2011)

Spivak, Gayatri Chakravorty, "Can the Subaltern Speak?" In *Marxism and the Interpretation of Culture*, edited by Nelson, Cary, and Grossberg, Lawrence (Urbana: University of Illinois Press, 1988), 271–313

Stöger, Ursula, *Aus Frauensicht. Eine Analyse des Deutungsmusters "innerbetriebliche Interessenbeziehungen" von weiblichen Betriebsratsmitgliedern* (München, 2008)

Supiot, Alain, "Der Rechtsgrundsatz der Solidarität," *SR* (2015): 133 = FS Armin Höland, 167 ff.

Teubner, Gunther, "Verrechtlichung - Begriffe, Merkmale, Grenzen, Auswege," In *Verrechtlichung von Wirtschaft, Arbeit und sozialer Solidarität: vergleichende Analysen,* edited by Friedrich Kübler (1984), 289

Wenckebach, Johanna, and Eva Kocher, "§ 12 AGG als Grundlage für Ansprüche auf angemessene Vorkehrungen," SR (2013): 17–28

Wihl, Tim, *Aufhebungsrechte: Form, Zeitlichkeit und Gleichheit der Grund- und Menschenrechte* (Weilerswist: Velbrück Wissenschaft, 2019)

Wihl, Tim, "Immanente Kritik durch "Aufhebungsrechte"," *KJ* 2/2021 (2021)

Young, Iris Marion, "Polity and Group Difference: A Critique of the Ideal of Universal Citizenship," *Ethics* 99 (2) (1988/89): 250–74

Youngdabl, Jay, "Solidarity First. Labor Rights Are Not the Same as Human Rights," In *New Labor Forum* 18(1) (2009): 31, 46-47

Zachert, Ulrich, "Individuum und Kollektiv im Arbeitsrecht: Alte Fragen – Neue Probleme," *AuR* (2002): 41ff.

Zachert, Ulrich, "Legitimation arbeitsrechtlicher Regelungen aus historischer und aktueller Sicht," *RdA* (2004): 1

Cases

BAG (German Federal Labour Court). May 27, 2004. 6 AZR 129/03

BAG (German Federal Labour Court). Dec. 16, 2008. 9 AZR 893/07

BAG (German Federal Labour Court). Nov. 20, 2014. 2 AZR 755/13

BVerfG (German Federal Constitutional Court). July 29, 2020. 1 BvR 1902/19

ECJ (European Court of Justice). Sep. 8, 2011. C-297/10 and C-298/10 (Hennigs and Mai), ECLI:EU:C:2011:560

ECJ (European Court of Justice). June 19, 2014. C-501/12 to C-506/12, C-540/12 and C-541/12 (Specht et al.), ECLI:EU:C:2014:2005

CHAPTER 8

THE CARROT RATHER THAN THE STICK! AN ITALIAN INTRODUCTION TO PROMOTIONAL LABOUR LAW

VINCENZO PIETROGIOVANNI

Introduction

The present contribution aims to present, through reflections of a theoretical-philosophical nature, as well as a legal technical one, the subject of positive sanctions in Italian labour law. By resorting to positive sanctions, labour law seeks the promotion of behaviours considered desirable rather than discouraging unlawful and prohibited behaviours with negative sanctions. Throughout the Italian experience, with its refined reflections of legal scholars such as Norberto Bobbio, and its regulatory standards in legislation related to labour matters, this chapter aims to develop a debate, at comparative and international level, on the role of sanctioning techniques in labour law, even in the light of those that are generally underestimated, as the positive sanctions actually are.

The Sanction as a Juridical Act

In jurisprudence, the term 'sanction' indicates the reaction of the legal system to a relevant behaviour carried out by the addressee of a legal rule (Gavazzi 1997). More commonly, however, it is intended to refer to the reaction to a violation of an obligation or a prohibition, thus preferring the 'negative' sense of the term. 'Sanction' takes on different meanings in relation to the fields in which the term is used: from the general theory of law, to private law or to public law, and to criminal law, in particular.

Other social disciplines, such as social psychology, pedagogy, sociology and anthropology, have also made their contribution to a very broad diversification of the term. And this is one of the two difficulties encountered in trying to find a univocal definition of the concept of sanction. The second difficulty derives from the influence that the concept of the law to which one might adhere exercises on this notion, with particular regard to the function attributed to the law in society. After all, "dealing with the notion of legal sanctions means nothing more and nothing less than dealing with the concept of law" (Gavazzi 1978).

Yet, there are those who look at the sanction with very critical eyes: some do not consider it "a rigorous juridical notion, indeed not even a correct notion" (Allorio 1956). Others, in defining it bluntly as the "*inconnue du droit*" (Jestaz 1987), underline its evanescent and elusive character. These authors, in essence, even deny its right of citizenship in legal science and, accusing it of ambiguity, uselessness and harmfulness, affirm that it could disappear without any difficulty from the legal vocabulary (Morand, 1990). Norberto Bobbio believes that there are only two hypotheses of normative systems in which the sanction has no reason to exist: "a) a perfectly rational system for perfectly rational beings; b) a system, even if not rational, for completely automated beings" (Bobbio 1976). Through this minimal anthropology (D'Agostino 1989), Bobbio reveals the proper dimension of the sanction and, more generally, of the law, which belong exclusively to human beings, synthetic creatures between perfection and automation or, as Aristotle put it, between divinity and bestiality. This middle-land condition is the only one in which normativity is conceivable, a reflection of a non-absolute freedom, in which there are rights and duties with respect to which the sanction is a juridical consequence.

It is clear that the theme of the sanction refers to the theme of freedom, in the concrete form that it assumes in the being of humans, that of *responsibility*, which exists "whenever a man acts in the world, he intervenes, that is, following rules and principles, rather than abandoning himself to the impersonality of naturalistic occurrence" (D'Agostino 1993). Responsibility is the effect of human beings' exercise of their free will, through which it is possible to formulate an accusation that establishes a link between human behaviour and the sanctioned juridical rule.

The person who sanctions is the person who observes the world, understands it and makes it their own. The judgement underlying the sanction is nothing more than an intellectual process of anthropomorphisation, intended for the creation of an order that is built on values and principles that affirm, first of all, and then guarantee, the existence of a given social community. The human being places herself in the world with her "juridical gaze" — as Natalino Irti had the opportunity to affirm when speaking of the effectiveness of the law (Irti 2011) — and creates a reality different from the natural and factual one in which she is immersed, that is, the *legal reality*, which is not the description of the real *datum* but, rather, represents its *configuration*: hence, "the high-sounding dichotomy between ought to be (Sollen) and to be (Sein)" (Voza 2009).

The Italian verb *sancire* (to set forth) is built on the radical *sak-*, which means to render something in the same state indicated by the term linked to it. According to many authors, *sak-* translates as 'to exist'; sanctioning would therefore indicate "that particular activity through which something acquires the specific dimension of existence, which is within the possibilities of man to contribute to making it so" (D'Agostino 1989). The sanction is understood as an exclusively anthropic trait: the human being is the actor and yardstick of the world to which, through the law, she gives her own rationality, the rationality of a human being as such. The sanction is, therefore, "a fundamental existential act, in which the recognition of human coexistence, the capacity for judgment and discrimination, the awareness of the distance that exists between naturalistic causality and ascription of responsibility for actions are mixed" (D'Agostino 1989).

The sanction brings us, perhaps better and more directly than any other juridical concept, to the "constitution normative de l'être humain" (Supiot 2005), being synthetic between perfect rationality and automation.

The Sanction in the General Theory of Law

The general theory of law makes a macro-distinction between primary norms and secondary norms: the former prescribes a conduct, which can consist of an obligation or a prohibition; the second ones establish the reaction of the legal system to the violation of the primary norm (Hart 2002). The sanctions, therefore, are contained in the secondary rules which, for this reason, are also known as sanctioning rules.

"The only way to understand what 'sanction' means is to answer the question 'what is it for?' That is, to try to understand what its function is" (Bobbio 1976). In this way, Bobbio expresses the centrality of the functional approach, not strictly in contrast to (but, so to speak, in extension of) legal positivism and the structural or systematic conception of law, among whose greatest advocates there is, of course, Hans Kelsen.

After World War II, Bobbio says, "finally there was a democratic constitution and a growing legislation that responded to the ideals of the Resistance against Nazi-Fascism"; consequently, "respect for the State as the only source of law and respect for single norms as an expression of a democratic order were the understandable needs of those who rejected a law applied according to external principles: legal positivism, therefore, not natural law, whatever form it assumed" (Losano 2007). Bobbio is convinced that the general theory is a prisoner of a concept of law whose corollary is the simplistic idea of the state as "an organism that establishes the rules of the game and an arbiter" (Bobbio 2007). Reducing the concept of law in terms of negative sanctions and coercion presupposes as a systematic archetype a model of social organisation that was 'absorbed' in the aftermath of World War II: the 'Gendarme State' that pursued limited ends through equally limited legal techniques.

Public bodies, on the other hand, are no longer called upon to only carry out the tasks of police and to repress behaviours that violate commands and prohibitions, in order to guarantee social peace, as it was believed they had exclusively in the liberal 19th century conception of state (Hegel 2004). The new tasks the state is called upon to carry out require a more or less direct intervention in socio-economic dynamics, by virtue of general interests to be protected which can be identified in four legal macro-assets: health, education / instruction, the environment and employment (understood in its double meaning of protection of employment right as well as the right to work).

There are numerous interventions by the legislator who, on the thrust of constitutional norms, puts a new face to public authorities, who are no longer formal guarantors of the rights and duties of citizens, but propulsive actors (Morand 1991; moreover, Cassese 1991) of socio-economic dynamics. Labour law in general, and collective labour law (*diritto sindacale*) in particular, have known one of the greatest expressions of the so-called 'promotional legislation', particularly with the Workers' Statute of 1970 (Freni, Giugni,1971; Ghezzi, Mancini Montuschi Romagnoli 1972; Giugni 1979). Starting from the model of auxiliary legislation, implemented for the first time in the United States during the New Deal as the result of Keynesian policies in the trade union field (Kahn Freund 1974), promotional legislation (of which the statute represents the highest expression in the field of collective labour law) not only changed its language, expressing itself with prepositions constructed differently, but above all it changed its technical-legal apparatus. The prohibition, as well as negative obligations in general, turned out to be an institution no longer sufficient in itself to guarantee all fundamental rights and freedoms recognised by the democratic constitution.

In Bobbio's view, the introduction into the legal system of encouragement techniques denotes the most important innovation in the legal control system, no longer characterised by an increase in the number of commands and prohibitions, but by the increasingly widespread tendency to increase stimuli for the execution or super-execution of those very same commands and prohibitions (Bobbio 2007).

As well as the promotional techniques emerging in the 20th century, the central place was occupied by positive sanctions, common since the 19th century but which only in the changed socio-cultural context of the second post-war period began its slow path of emancipation in the more traditional legal institutions. This change in the conception of law differs from the conception common to all currents of legal positivism, ranging from Austin to Kelsen, without neglecting Jhering, according to which the proper purpose of law is essentially repressive and is perfected through the organisation of negative sanctions (Kelsen 1994). In particular, according to Thomasius, in order to be clearly distinguished from individual and social morality, law must be considered as a set of negative norms, whose main precept can be summarised in *neminem laedere* (Thomasius 2013). According to Kelsen, the distinction between the legal norm and the other social norms is found in coercion (Kelsen 2000).

This is what characterises the law so much as to lead to a substantial overturning of the jurist's point of view towards unlawful behaviour: the offence has usually been understood as a moment of rupture, of violation of the legal order to which the latter reacts to restore its effectiveness, and does so precisely through sanctions; for the pure doctrine of law, however, the offence is not constituted by the antisocial element of the fact not pleasing to the legislative authority but by the circumstance of the "position of the fact within the juridical proposition: that this is a condition for the specific reaction of the law, for the act of coercion" (Kelsen 2000).

The Kelsenian theory holds that the law is the institution of a coercive measure, of a sanction, for that conduct called 'illegal', that is, for an offence, "and this conduct has the character of 'illicit' because, and only because, it is a condition of the sanction" (Kelsen 2000).

The general premise of Kelsen's study is that the pure doctrine of law, limiting itself to the knowledge of positive law and excluding from this knowledge both the philosophy of justice and the sociology of law, considers the purpose of law irrelevant, as an element extraneous to the law, the legal system being understood in its normative autonomy. And it is precisely the structuralism conceived in this way that, according to Norberto Bobbio, does not accept the full recognition of positive sanctions as a regulatory technique worthy of citizenship among fundamental legal institutions, since the excessively formal approach neglects the function that legal propositions perform, even at a legal level, not only at sociological and philosophical levels.

Positive sanctions, in fact, are a 'foreign body' (Gavazzi 1978) within the theories that put coercion at the core of law, which in general tend to exclude such sanctions even to be considered as proper sanctions. This is true both for Austin and Kelsen, of course, as well as for other authors such as Alf Ross (Ross 1979), Herbert L.A. Hart (Hart 2002) and Karl Olivecrona (Olivecrona 1939), who seem to reach these conclusions from a mere necessity rather than from a methodological premise.

It can therefore be affirmed that only with the advent of that particular form assumed by the legal system with the birth of the welfare state (Beveridge 2010; Goodin and Marshal 1988; Jordan 1976; Lloyd 1970; Marsh 1980; Sabattini 2009), "one of the most extraordinary inventions of Western political intelligence" (Habermas 1998), can positive sanctions, although already used and present in positive legal systems, gain a prominent place within the general theory of law.

Growing industrial development, which began with the first industrial revolution in the 18th century, laid the foundations for overcoming the rule of law in the mid-19th century: the new ruling class, the capitalist bourgeoisie, had no more need to defend their interests through natural law, as was the case when feudal aristocracies were still in power. "After having produced its own equal law, it has also created its own political power, its own State" (Barcellona 1996) which, therefore, was no longer in opposition to the interests of the bourgeoisie but, on the contrary, promoted them.

The radical changes introduced by the new production processes brought with it enormous social impact, especially for the industrial proletariat which, in order to cope with the conflict of interest *vis-à-vis* the capitalists, organised itself collectively. Soon, however, workers' organisations also addressed their claims against the state, asking for adequate safeguards for their unhealthy working conditions. On these instances was born a series of legislative interventions known as social legislation, which "presents itself in an exceptional position with respect to the system of private law, as a response of the legal system to the social question that arose as a result of the industrialisation process [...] and magnified by its consequences" (Ghera 2011).

This process of economic and social change brought its legal results to completion in the middle of the last century, within the constitutional charters born after the Second World War, apart from a first prototype during the Weimar Republic (Arrigo and Vardaro 1982).

The welfare state distanced itself from the camouflage imposed by the rule of law, breaking the veil that covered the conflict between the principle of formal equality and actual substantive inequality, with the indirect effect of certifying the failure of the market as a place of just and orderly composition of the tension between the opposing interests within industrial societies.

According to Piero Barcelona, the objective of the welfare state, through the unification of "the horizon of social meanings around the principle of 'general accessibility' to 'economic goods'", is resolved in "realising the 'promise' of capitalist economy to satisfy the needs of everyone" (Barcellona 1996). The *face* of the state changes, as well as of its bureaucratic apparatus, because what changes is its appearance in the social imagination that it intends to produce or modify: "the image of the State that takes care of the wellbeing (*summum bonum*) of its citizens" (Barcellona 1996). In short, the state becomes teleological, in the sense that the aims that private individuals set themselves in the exercise of their economic activities also become a relevant aspect from a legal point of view.

The scope, therefore, within which the legal system can legitimately affect the sphere of private economic activity – or individual economic freedoms – is that defined through prescriptive/prohibiting techniques (essentially, the technique of mandatory rules) or through completely new interventions that take the form of programs or incentives aimed at social control (Rodotà 1977).

Giuseppe Guarino flawlessly analyses a normative phenomenology composed of laws endowed with particular characteristics, which the author himself defines as direction laws, to which contract laws and incentive laws belong. These are tools through which the state and public authorities in general direct and coordinate private economic initiatives towards social goals deemed worthy of intervention. In addition to the traditional prescriptive/prohibiting forms, the tendency of the state to use incentives as a social control tool is increasingly emerging, by virtue of the fact that they direct economic initiative without affecting private autonomy in any way — in fact, on the contrary, acting right through their autonomy (Guarino 1961).

Guarino specifies that "with them the State (*but we could say, any public power*) intends to provoke, in the collective interest (*today we would say general interest*) the fulfilment of a specific activity by private individuals; the addressee of these laws is therefore always a private subject; the activity desired by the legislator may be generically social, but it is almost always of an economic nature" (Guarino 1961). From this clear description, the promotional character of this normative device clearly emerges, giving impetus to individuals in order to take on a certain activity or to take it on in a certain way. We are thus within the horizon of the promotional norm.

Overcoming the limits of an excessively functionalistic approach, as in some ways hoped for by Bobbio, Guarino looks at the structure of these particular types of law and identifies a second characteristic element: in order to obtain a specific activity or its specific modality from the private individual, the law offers an advantageous position, which takes the form of a counter-performance by public authorities.

The synallagma between the activity desired by the public authority and carried out by the private subject, on the one hand, and the advantageous situation promised by the public authority to the private subject which complies with the law, on the other, is demonstrated, according to the author, from the fact that if the activity is not undertaken or is undertaken in a different way, the advantage is not recognised.

Continuing, "the third element of identification is that the activity requested by the State, if there were no law, would not be carried out or would be carried out in forms or in quantities other than those deemed most suitable for the collective interest" (Guarino 1961). This third element, on the other hand, which is more in line with functionalist theory, enhances the teleological moment of the norm and introduces a peculiar aspect of promotional norms, namely constituting a factor that alters the calculation of private interests.

Formally, incentive laws do not have any authoritarian character as they do not prescribe obligations (Viola 1979) nor do they prohibit anything. Incentive laws develop their effects only through a voluntary adherrance by the private individuals – if and when they decide to adhere.

The positions of advantage for individuals set up by incentive laws can vary between different forms: from a financial, fiscal or contributory advantage, such as exemptions or concessions, to a *strictu sensu* legal advantage, which may be the right to derogate, for example, to some particular mandatory rules.

Beyond the specific form of the envisaged mechanism, it is certain that the disbursement of the advantage to the private subject by the public administration is a legal consequence of the actual performance of the activity envisaged by incentive laws (Giannini 1964; Falzone 1960). The advantage, therefore, is conditioned by the private individual's desire to conform or not.

Positive Sanctions

In a stipulative way (Bernardini 1999; Scarpelli and Di Lucia 1994), by positive sanction we mean legal consequence consisting of an advantageous position, with respect to a relevant behaviour envisaged by a provision of the legal system.

Analysing it from a structural point of view, it seems plausible to argue that this definition fits perfectly into the scheme of the Kelsenian hypothetical judgement: "if A is, then B ought to be."

The differences emerge if only the diversified elements of apodosis and protasis are analysed. In fact, it must be specified that, in Kelsen's model, the condition of protasis, or A, corresponds to a delict, and the consequence of the regent apodosis, or B, corresponds to a negative sanction, or a punishment or disadvantage. In terms of positive sanctions, on the other hand, A coincides with a conduct considered desirable by the legal system and, for this reason, promoted, stimulated, encouraged through B, which consists of a reward or an advantage.

The sanction understood as the juridical consequence of a given behaviour identified by a rule of law allows a partial unification of the *genus* which, in turn, knows the two species of positive and negative sanctions. In this way, moreover, this construct undoubtedly has the merit of not making the subsistence of the sanction depend on a primary norm in the Hartian sense (Hart 2002; Jori 1977), i.e. on a norm that prescribes an obligation, something that is often easy to find in positive law. All this, therefore, technically makes positive sanctions into sanctioning norms, that is those provisions which, wishing to take up the systematics introduced by Hart, are qualified as secondary norms.

In positive sanctions there is no coercion: the conduct taken into consideration by the law, in fact, is neither mandatory nor prohibited. The typical instruments of the prescriptive-repressive law (prohibitions and commands) are extraneous, at least directly, to these normative devices. Conduct, on the other hand, is only incentivised, which means that private individuals conforming to it only concerns their free choice. In his opinion, Bobbio explains the core of the differences between the two types of sanctions from a functionalist point of view: "the initial moment of a discouragement measure is a threat; the initial moment of an encouragement is a promise" (Bobbio 2007).

The first reflections about the impact of positive sanctions on the structures of labour law start from the most immediate evidence: the analysis of current techniques for guaranteeing effectiveness requires an abandonment of the traditional concept of sanctions as a negative reaction to a breach. Sanctioning techniques have long been conceived in the exclusive context of mandatory rule, but labour law very often resorts to sanctions that escape the traditional prohibitive-repressive approach. Positive sanctions undermine the monolithic image of a labour law interpreted in a purely imperativist key (Bobbio 1959), that is, of a system of mere coercion that acts in a unilaterally and authoritarian fashion, prescribing prohibitions and obligations, and establishing negative sanctions in cases of non-compliance.

The interests worthy of protection have expanded considerably, which has consistently led the legal system to diversify regulatory techniques in order to operate in the most effective way at the level of socio-economic assets.

These techniques may appear as the reflection of a "mild law" (Zagrebelsky 2005), a concept for indicating in the image of meekness the essential character of the law of today's constitutional state of rights, in which the constitution operates as an instrument of integration for the multiform dynamics of a pluralistic society that finds its new paradigms in 'liquidity' (Bauman 2003).

While admitting the undisputed fascination that these interpretations of the problems inherent in the contemporary state generate, however, we prefer the analyses that allow us to grasp the incentive techniques in their juridicality. A sanction that rewards or facilitates certain behaviours, in fact, is an indication of a radical innovation in the relationship between the state bureaucratic systems and citizens, a relation that goes beyond the classic vertical dynamic to become horizontal, affirming itself in terms that we could define as 'contractual' (Gaudin 2007; Bifulco and Vitale 2005).

Far from giving an account here of the neo-contractualist theses (Rawls 2008), for our purposes it is sufficient to point out that, as noted, the common element to these reinterpretations is the passage (which curiously seems to recall the historical evolution of labour law) from citizenship understood as status, in the framework of which citizens, as such, are recipients of services established on the basis of universalistic or categorical entitlements, to citizenship understood as a contract, which tends to attribute to the recipients the status of active subjects and contractors, especially through individualised measures and interventions (Vitale 2005).

Social policies — in which, in many ways, labour law is grafted — are the privileged terrain for the affirmation of contractual relationships with the public administration. Let's think of active labour market policies, for example, in which between an unemployed person and the employment service, as seen, a contractual relationship arises, followed by specific obligations of the unemployed person who is, at the same time, a public service user and a contracting subject (Lagala and D'Onghia 2010; Spattini 2008; Liso 2006; Garofalo 2004).

The horizontal relations between private individuals and public authorities represent the context in which various positive sanctions are used. The incentive technique represents one of the indicators of how the compactness of contemporary law can vary in intensity according to the different possible legal policy options.

What does it take for a rule to be normative without being coercive? To find the answer to such a question, some reflections on the concept of normativity seem appropriate (Thibierge 2009).

Assume that for normativity – or normative force, as it is usually indicated – we refer to the ability of a sentence to become a rule, or norm, precisely. It is distinguished from effectiveness on the basis of the point of view from which it analyses the norms. The latter, in fact, observes their implementation at a social level, while the former evaluates from a strictly technical-juridical point of view the mechanism by which the norm aims to provoke certain behaviours. Therefore, it is possible to affirm that the highest possible degree of normativity is reached when the legal system, choosing to qualify a given behaviour as mandatory, intervenes in an authoritarian way through the provision of a mandatory rule and prepares, to guarantee its compliance, typically negative sanctions. If the legal system, on the other hand, deems such behaviour legitimate without imposing it, it acts through the provision of a permissive or authorising rule (Scarpelli 1963), also accompanied by negative sanctions. Finally, if the behaviour in question is only desired, the legal system resorts to positive sanctions. In this case the minimum possible degree of normativity is reached.

The conduct, even if not prescribed but encouraged, is in any case subject to a legal rule, since the recipient of the positive sanction, when she freely chooses to comply with the provisions therein – thus becoming sanctioned – satisfies the condition (or the conditions) for its application, creating for the sanctioning public power a legal constraint (obligation or burden) aimed at providing the promised advantageous position. By overturning the classic approach to the relationship between sanction and sanctioned, the normativity of positive sanctions can in fact also be understood in the binding nature of its payment.

This allows us to affirm that a labour law that resorts to positive sanctions does not yield fragments of the juridicality of its system to more or less latently extra-juridical mechanisms (considered, at one time, to be economic, financial, fiscal or social security instruments) but, on the contrary, it uses a precise sanctioning technique. Therefore, when we talk about positive sanctions and define them as facilitations, incentives or rewards, for example, undoubtedly, we are not mistaken, since such terms refer to their functional dimension (in order to facilitate, encourage or reward). However, these terms play a purely descriptive and, therefore, non-legal role. If they refer to norms that respect the Kelsenian conditional structure of "if A, then B ought to be," from the technical-juridical point of view they shall be defined as positive sanctions.

However, if they are structurally sanctioning rules, as they establish the consequence of a given conduct, then they must be systematically connected to the sanctioning apparatus of a given regulatory measure, as well as related sanctions (civil, administrative or criminal ones) of a negative type. It is believed, that is, that the interpreter, when she wants to analyse the sanctions of a certain legislative act, must necessarily also contemplate the possible positive sanctions provided for therein, because only in this way could she fully understand the overall meaning of the sanctions disposed in that particular act or law. The experiment, perhaps too daring, that this contribution intends, is also that of inducing the interpreter not to separate, in her exegetical exercise, the two sanctioning aspects, as unfortunately often happens.

It is a question of looking with a new perspective on an institution that has existed for a long time in our legal systems. The task is not at all simple since it proposes to structurally review a way of operating which is now largely established. Nevertheless, it is believed that this interpretative remodelling is suitable for ensuring a more correct legal analysis.

Alternativity or Coexistence between Positive and Negative Sanctions?

A guarantee of the effectiveness of law is the primary purpose of sanctioning rules, whether they are negative or positive. Negative sanctions, as we know, take the form of a threatened (and, in case, applied) position of disadvantage to the person who violates a rule of primary conduct (non-compliance with an obligation or a duty), or as a disavowal of the effects of the action that is non-compliant with the law, declaring its invalidity (in terms of nullity, annulment or ineffectiveness) (Ghera 1979).

Positive sanctions, alongside negative sanctions, constitute the complex and articulated sanctioning apparatus prepared by the legal system: tools or techniques of social control and surveillance that are completely static, and which conform and adapt socio-economic dynamics to the model prefigured by the rules and principles, including constitutional ones, which give body (and, one might say, soul) to labour law.

The reflection of the imperativity of certain rules that, marked by the protection of super-individual interests or the particular interests of the worker as a weak contractor, impose themselves on different private will. They operate for three distinct purposes: to guarantee essential assets and interests; to correct certain asymmetries of contractual power; or to ensure a certain level of regulatory uniformity.

The consequences that the legal system envisages in the event of a violation of the mandatory legislation do not immediately relate to its foundation and are linked to the sanctioning side profile: from ablative mechanisms (Art.1418 of the Italian Civil Code) to the substitutive ones of the content of the contract (Art. 1339 of the Italian Civil Code), to the various regulatory modalities of partial nullity (Article 1419, paragraphs 1 and 2, of the Italian Civil Code) and the supplementary sources of the effects (Article 1374 of the Italian Civil Code) (Cester 2008).

Always in line with the imperative-mandatory approach, the legislator resorts to further types of sanctions. We might think of the reinstating sanction following an unlawful dismissal (reintegration pursuant to Art. 18 of the Workers' Statute) (Mazzotta 2005; Sandulli, Vallebona and Pisani 1990) or the restitutive sanction related to the repression of anti-union conduct (Art. 28 of the Workers' Statute), or to administrative sanctions related to the inspection activities of the apparatuses in charge of the public administration (Inspectorate of the Ministry of Labour and, in many ways, of the INPS), which ultimately, are sanctioning instruments with a complementary or alternative function in respect to civil or criminal liability.

Then, we might think of the various criminal sanctions of so-called criminal labour law. They undoubtedly represent the pinnacle, at sanctioning level, of the imperative conception of labour law with the highest degree of normativity. This area of criminal protection consists of sanctions protecting health and safety at work, moral freedom and the dignity of workers, as well as social security and welfare benefits (Musacchio 2010).

Summarising the mechanisms underlying the current techniques of law enforcement (Polinsky and Shavell 2007; Becker and Stigler 1974) in labour law, we could affirm that with the imperative rule a given structure of interests between private individuals is prescribed, by imposing a given discipline of an institute or certain rules of conduct aimed at achieving inderogability (D'Antona 1994), which is the technique through which private individuals are prevented from regulating some businesses in a different way from the law (through the so-called agreements in derogation), and negative sanctions, which punish the violation and non-observance of primary rules. In the event that negative sanctions are not able to ensure a sufficient degree of effectiveness, or in the event that the ordinary legislator has not laid down any mandatory rules, positive sanctions are used.

In the light of what we have seen so far, the need arises to understand whether positive sanctions represent an alternative sanctioning technique to negative sanctions and whether this alternative is resolved in terms of incompatibility.

There are many areas of labour law where positive sanctions operate alongside prohibitive-repressive rules. Consider the case, for instance, of the fine imposed on the employer who does not carry out the assessment of all H&S risks and, consequently, does not fully complete the relevant documents required by law; or the arrest in the case where she does not designate a head of risk prevention and protection service, as emerged from the regulations referred to in Legislative Decree 81/2008.

Despite the use of these sanctions, which ensure the highest degree of deterrence, the level of ineffectiveness is H&S is such that the legislator has decided to make available, at the same time, to companies that improve their levels of protection through training and organisational processes, a series of incentives and concessions. Many of these incentives are, as we have seen, positive sanctions that produce the effect of making compliance with mandatory rules more convenient (or less burdensome).

In this case, compatibility between incentive rules and the prohibitive-repressive ones is evidently peaceful, also due to the fact that the former present themselves in a 'surrogacy' guise, compensating, that is, for the widespread ineffectiveness of the latter ones. Positive sanctions here do not exclude the validity of the mandatory rules but act on the mere level of their (poor) observance.

This is confirmed by the fact that there are other areas of labour law in which the incentive technique and the mandatory one coexist, such as in disciplines against undeclared or irregular work. Again, in such areas, prescriptive rules and related negative sanctions have by no means been replaced by positive sanctions.

In the promotion of disabled workers, the coexistence between the two techniques assumes a different structure, as the positive sanctions established within Act 68/99 are functional to exclusively incentivise the hiring of subjects with a very high percentage of disability, who are among the most vulnerable workers in the labour market. Here the positive sanctions affect only a part of the larger area covered by the obligation to hire, namely workers for whom, reasonably presumptively, the greater disability corresponds to greater difficulty in working. However, also in this case, coexistence between the sanctioning techniques, even if reduced to a particular sector of the field of application of the precept, is peacefully assured.

Moreover, there is legislation promoting equal opportunities between men and women, which is presented as a wise combination of the two techniques. On the one hand, in fact, conduct aimed at achieving the objectives of equal treatment and non-discrimination is encouraged through incentivised positive actions, whilst on the other hand, conduct detrimental to legal precepts is repressed through the prohibition of discrimination, direct and indirect, and the related sanctions (Voza 2002). The legislator thus intended to ensure coexistence between positive and negative sanctions by functionalising them to the maximum, based on their respective ontological structures: the former promotional, the latter repressive.

It is in the more general discipline of the promotion of employment – apart from the case just seen of targeted groups – that the legal system does not resort in any way to negative sanctions.

What is known as the "imposeable of a workforce" (which refers to an obligation for farmers to hire a certain number of workers established by law) has long since been expelled from the Italian legal system. Therefore, there are no provisions whatsoever that require employers to hire anyone without their consent. Precisely the epilogue of such a legal institution in agriculture, however, shows us that the choice of the legislator is not simply inspired by mere opportunity, as it could also be argued. More than anything else, it turns out to be an obligatory choice, dictated by the need to safeguard the constitutionality of the legal discipline of access to work.

The sentence of the Constitutional Court n. 78/1958 defined the margins of the question in a sufficiently clear manner, which we think it is appropriate to retrace. The Court examined the institution's constitutionality with reference to Art. 41 Cost. (freedom of conducting business), considering that this investigation provided absorbing and decisive arguments also with reference to Articles 38, 42 and 44 of the constitution, with which disputes had also been raised.

The Constitutional Court expressly stated that Art. 41 of the Italian Fundamental Charter does not tolerate provisions that interfere and seriously affect free private economic initiative. This is also with regard to the free evaluation and consequent self-determination of elements suitable for sizing the company and providing for its internal organisation. Therefore "the Court cannot recognise the legitimacy of rules which, rather than informed by a general vision in the proposed directions, are designed in such a way as to interfere in the economic activity of individual operators, disturbing and compressing that private initiative which is guaranteed by the paragraph of the same article. The obligation imposed on operators to hire workers even against their evaluation of the organisation of their own company remains extraneous to the provisions of the third paragraph and cannot be part of the general provisions provided for therein."

The fundamental principle that the Court affirms is that the freedom of economic initiative prevents the use of any mandatory rule that compresses it and, in particular, that compromises two of its aspects: the freedom to size the company; and the freedom to establish its actual needs.

It is also for these reasons, moreover, that the only type of mandatory provision regarding recruitment (i.e., those provided for by the discipline of targeted placement (previously defined even mandatory) (Law no. 482 of 2 April 1968)) has always passed the constitutionality test. In fact, the Constitutional Court, repeatedly referred to the question, has always held that this mechanism does not compress the two profiles just highlighted, since the recruitment of disabled people is only pro-quota and the self-determination of entrepreneurial needs is subject to the choice of the type of worker to be hired. In essence, the Constitutional Court has always held that targeted placement respects the balance between the freedom protected by Art. 41 Const. and the mandatory duties of solidarity – pursuant to Art. 2 Const. - and the task of the Republic to "remove the obstacles of an economic and social nature which, by limiting the freedom and equality of citizens, prevent the full development of the human person and the effective participation of all workers in the political, economic and social organisation of the country" (Art. 3, para. 2 Const.).

An irrefutable fact emerges: the constitutional arrangements thus outlined preclude the ordinary legislator from prescribing a general obligation to contract. However, it is not certain that the latter cannot legitimately intervene in any way on certain portions of the freedom to conduct a business, that is, by juridifying some aspects in order to orient them according to specific purposes. In fact, this is the ideal proscenium in which positive sanctions act in their highest degree of promotional capacity.

The use of the promised advantageous positions passes through the respect of conducts which, in the incentive technique, are not subject to obligations or prohibitions but represent the conditions of access.

Conditionalities can be explained on several levels. They range from a general level (e.g. possession of the DURC, a document on compliance within the rules for the protection of OSH and the application of collective agreements), which establishes conditions useful for all positive sanctions aimed at companies; to more specific levels, at which the varying conditions functionalise and specialise the sanctions themselves with respect to the purpose(s) that the legal system intends to pursue.

The employer who wants to use manpower that involves less burdensome economic and management costs than so-called "standard" manpower, can decide to hire a weak or disadvantaged worker. In this way, the economic or regulatory benefits that the legal system promises are the product (*rectius*: the consequence) of an autonomous conformation (or self-conformation or super-conforming behaviour) to the conditions set by the incentive provisions.

And here we come to the central aspect of the (meta) discourse: the incentive technique assumes the freedom of the sanctioned person as a structural presupposition, unlike the negative sanctions which, on the other hand, leave it aside to the point of compelling it to itself or repressing it if it occurs in a discordant sense.

Therefore, without prejudice to the prerogatives of freedom of the employers, positive sanctions represent the only regulatory technique capable of legitimately affecting some of their subjective positions, since, even in an attempt to conform their behaviour, they do not compress their constitutional protections.

We just have to deal with the last relevant aspect that significantly differentiates the two techniques. It has been said that imperativity is the regulatory technique that ensures the uniform application of the discipline of a given institution. The classic sanctioning techniques of a prohibitive-repressive type, therefore, are the remedial tools to which the effectiveness of the mandatory-uniformity combination is entrusted.

From this point of view, numerous positive sanctions show the intention to give effect to the principle of equality but through a different path. Think of general discipline in equal opportunities, or in the employment of certain categories of disadvantaged workers. In these cases, as has already been emphasised, the legal system considers the *de facto* inequalities relevant and, to remedy them, it provides different disciplines.

A positive sanction triggers a mechanism that acts as an exception (or special rule) to the general rule of equal treatment, which the legal system places precisely for the prescriptive or mandatory rule to protect.

It is easy to see, therefore, that this happens not because the two techniques move from two different conceptions of the principle of equality. The prohibitive-repressive rules that labour law adopts are functional to the affirmation of *de facto* equality as well as positive sanctions. The difference lies in the technique through which one tends to achieve the same goals.

Here too, coexistence is not only possible but even desirable, because, precisely under the egalitarian profile, the two techniques are perfectly complementary (and therefore, not sufficient if they lack mutual contribution).

In fact, the equality ensured by the mandatory rule would only remain formal if it were not also realised at the level of concrete socio-economic assets, with respect to which the relevance of the related sanctioning apparatus emerges. This does not mean that the difference between formal and substantial equality runs along the dividing line between the imperative norm and the incentive norm, but certainly the principle of equality, in a completely compulsory and not at all proactive system, will be necessarily less effective.

In light of all that has been said so far, despite the alternative (as defined above) between positive sanctions and traditional negative sanctions, we fully agree with the thesis according to which "both from a technical point of view and in terms of right, no impediment to a peaceful coexistence - within the same subject or institution - between the traditional intervention of a compulsive type, aimed at invalidating *contra legem* acts and behaviours, removing their effects through mechanisms to varying degrees and – possibly – replacing them with compliant ones, and the rewarding intervention, aimed at stimulating – without imposing – the adoption of practices oriented to the ends desired by the law" (Voza 2002).

On the other hand, it is unthinkable that positive sanctions can fully replace the mandatory rule and its typical sanctions, for two main reasons. The first is of a financial nature: the state and public authorities in general would never be able to incentivise all relevant conduct, since this would over-engage public budgets which are already challenged by notoriously huge deficits (Brancaccio 2008; O'Connor 1979). The second reason is, so to speak, common sense: encouraging everything would mean, in fact, not encouraging anything (Garofalo 1999).

Therefore, the coexistence of the mandatory technique and the rewarding technique is not only possible but is even considered desirable, as it is probably upon their well-planned mixture that the effectiveness of labour law depends.

These considerations are completely in line, moreover, with those that Edoardo Ghera already formulated in his 1979 essay on civil sanctions in the protection of subordinate work, where positive sanctions are analysed within the complex sanction system established by the Italian legislator. There the author recognises specific functions of legal mediation (Garofalo 1979) within the conflict of interest underlying the employment relationship between the freedom of private economic initiative and the interests of the person-worker, a terrain in which classic civil protections appear insufficient (Montuschi 2007).

Bibliography

Allorio, Enrico, "Osservazioni critiche sulla sanzione," *Rivista di Diritto Civile* (1956): 1-35

Arrigo, Gianni, and Vardaro, Gaetano, *Laboratorio Weimar. Conflitti e diritto del lavoro nella Germania prenazista* (Roma: Edizioni Lavoro, 1982)

Barcellona, Pietro, *Diritto privato e società moderna* (Napoli: Jovene, 1996)

Bauman, Zygmunt, *Modernità liquida* (Roma – Bari: Laterza, 2011)

Becker, Gary S., and Stigler, George J, "Law Enforcement, Malfeasance, and Compensation of Enforcers," *Journal of Legal Studies* (1974) 3: 1

Bernardini, Gianni, *Realtà e conoscenza giuridica* (Rimini: Guaraldi, 1999)

Beveridge, Williamo (a cura di), *Alle origini del welfare state. Il rapporto su assicurazioni sociali e servizi assistenziali* (Milano: Franco Angeli, 2010)

Bifulco, Lavinia, and Vitale, Tommaso, *La contrattualizzazione delle politiche sociali e il welfare locale*, In, *Le nuove politiche sociali: temi e prospettive emergenti*, edited by Bifulco Lavinia. (a cura di) (Roma: Carocci, 2005)

Bobbio, Norberto, "Sanzione," *Novissimo Digesto Italiano*, edited by Azara Antonio and Eula Ernesto (Torino: UTET, 1976)

Bobbio, Norberto, *Dalla Struttura alla funzione. Nuovi studi di teoria del diritto* (Bari: Laterza, 2007)

Bobbio, Norberto, *Teoria della norma giuridica* (Torino: Giappichelli, 1958)

Brancaccio, Emiliano, "Deficit commerciale, crisi di bilancio e politica deflazionistica," *Studi economici.* (2008): 96, 3

Cassese Sabino, "Les finances comme moyens d'action des pouvoirs publics," In *L'Etat propulsif. Contribution à l'étude des instruments d'action de l'Etat*, edited by C.A. Morand (Paris: Publisud, 1991), 155-164

Cester, Carlo, "La norma inderogabile: fondamento e problema del diritto del lavoro," *Giornale di Diritto del Lavoro e di Relazioni Industriali* (2008): 3

D'Agostino Francesco, *La sanzione nell'esperienza giuridica* (Torino: Giappichelli, 1993)

D'Agostino, Francesco, "Sanzione (teoria generale)," *Encilopedia del Diritto* (Milano: Giuffrè, 1989)

D'Antona Massimo, "L'autonomia individuale e le fonti del diritto del lavoro," In *Autonomia individuale e rapporto di lavoro*. Atti del X Congresso nazionale di diritto del lavoro 1991, AA.VV. (Milano: Giuffrè, 1994)

Falzone, Guido, *Le obbligazioni dello Stato* (Milano: Giuffrè, 1960)

Frenim, Antonio and Giugni, Gino, *Lo Statuto dei lavoratori: Commento alla legge del 20 maggio 1970* (Milano: Giuffrè, 1971)

Garofalo, Domenico, "Organizzazione e disciplina del mercato del lavoro. Dal collocamento al rapporto giuridico di lavoro," In *Lavoro e diritti*, edited by Curzio Pietro (Bari: Cacucci, 2004)

Garofalo, Mario Giovanni, "Tecnica degli incentivi e promozione dell'occupazione," *Rivista Giuridica del Lavoro* (1999) 3: 74

Gaudin, Jean-Pierre, *Gouverner par contrat* (Paris: Science Po, 2007)
Gavazzi Giacomo, "Sanzione," *Encilopedia del Diritto* (Milano: Giuffrè, 1997)
Gavazzi, Giacomo, "Le sanzioni nel diritto: problemi vecchi e nuovi," *Il Politico* (1978) 43, 3: 393-409
Ghera, Edoardo, "Le sanzioni civili nel diritto del lavoro," *Giornale di Diritto del Lavoro e di Relazioni Industriali* (1979): 305
Ghera, Edoardo, *Diritto del lavoro* (Bari: Cacucci, 2009)
Ghezzi, Giorgio, Mancini, Giuseppe F., Montuschi, Luigi and Romagnoli, Umberto. *Statuto dei diritti dei lavoratori* (Bologna: Zanichelli, 1972)
Giannini, Massimo Saverio, *Le obbligazioni pubbliche* (Roma: Jandi Sapi 1964)
Giugni, Giugni, *Lo Statuto dei lavoratori: Commentario* (Milano: Giuffrè, 1979)
Goodin, Robert E., and Marshall, Cohen, *Reasons for welfare: The political theory of the welfare state* (Princeton: Princeton University Press, 1988)
Guarino, Giuseppe, "Sul regime costituzionale delle leggi di incentivazione e di indirizzo (a proposito della questione della legittimità costituzionale della L. 27 dicembre 1953 n. 959 e della L. 30 dicembre 1959 n. 1254 sui sovracanoni elettrici)," *Atomo, Petrolio ed Elettricità - Rivista giuridica internazionale delle fonti di energia* (1961): 3-22, now also in Giuseppe Guarino, *Scritti di diritto pubblico dell'economia e di diritto dell'energia*, (Milano: Giuffrè, 1962): 174.
Habermas, Jürgen, *La nuova oscurità. Crisi dello Stato sociale ed esaurimento delle utopie* (Roma: Edizioni Lavoro, 1998)
Hart Herbert L. A., *Il concetto di diritto* (Torino: Einaudi, 2002)
Hegel, Fredrich, *Lineamenti di filosofia del diritto* (Bari: Laterza, 2004)
Irti, Natalino, *Diritto senza verità* (Bari: Laterza, 2011)
Jestaz, Philippe, "La sanction ou l'inconnue du droit," *Droit et pouvoir*, volume I, *La validité*, edited by Rigaux and Haarscher (Bruxelles: Edition Story-Scientia, 1987)
Jordan, Bill, *Freedom and the welfare state* (London: Routledge, 1976)
Jori, Mario, "Esiste una funzione promozionale del diritto?" *Sociologia del diritto* (1977): 2
Kahn-Freund, Otto, *Il lavoro e la legge* (Milano: Giuffrè, 1974)
Kelsen, Hans, *Lineamenti di dottrina pura del diritto* (Torino: Einaudi, 2000)
Kelsen, Hans, *Teoria generale del diritto e dello Stato* (Milano: Etas, 1994)
Lagala, Canio, and D'Onghia, Madia, eds., *Politiche di attivazione dei disoccupati in Europa. Le esperienze realilzzate in Belgio, Danimarca, Francia, Germania, Inghilterra, Spagna e Svezia* (Roma: Ediesse, 2010)

Liso, Franco, "I servizi per l'impiego," In *Percorsi di diritto del lavoro,* edited by Garofalo, Domenico and Ricci, Maurizio (Bari: Cacucci, 2006)

Lloyd, Trevor O, *Empire to welfare state: English history 1906-1967* (Oxford: Oxford University Press, 1970)

Losano, Mario G., *Prefazione* a Bobbio, Norberto, *Dalla Struttura alla funzione. Nuovi studi di teoria del diritto* (Bari: Laterza, 2007)

Marsh, David Charles, *The welfare state: concept and development* (London: Longman Higher Education, 1980)

Mazzotta, Oronzo, *Il recesso. La giustificazione del licenziamento. La tutela reale. Vol. 1* (Milano: Giuffrè, 2005)

Montuschi, Luigi, "*Attualità della sanzione civile nel diritto del lavoro,*" *Argomenti di Diritto del Lavoro*, (2007) 6: 1188

Morand, Charles A. ed. *L'Etat Propulsif* (Paris: Publisud, 1991)

Morand, Charles A, "La sanction," *Travaux CETEL*, n. 36, Mars 1990, Genève

Musacchio, Vincenzo, *Il sistema penale del lavoro* (Roma: Franco Angeli, 2010)

O'Connor, James, *Crisi fiscale dello Stato* (Torino: Einaudi, 1979)

Olivecrona, Karl, *Law as Fact* (London: Sweet & Maxwell, 1939)

Polinsky, A. Mitchel, and Shavell, Steven, "The Theory of Public Enforcement of Law," In *Handbook of Law and Economics*, edited by Polinsky, A. Mitchel, and Shavell, Steven (Amsterdam: Elsevier, 2007)

Rawls, John, Una *teoria della giustizia* (Milano: Feltrinelli, 2008)

Rodotà, Stefano, *Il controllo sociale delle attività private* (Bologna: il Mulino, 1977)

Ross Alf, *Direttive e norme* (Milano: Edizioni di Comunità, 1979)

Sabattini, Gianfranco, *Welfare state. Nascita, evoluzione e crisi. Le prospettive di riforma* (Milano: Franco Angeli, 2009)

Sandulli, Pasquale, Vallebona, Antonio, and Pisani, Carlo, *La nuova disciplina dei licenziamenti individuali* (Milano: CEDAM, 1990)

Scarpelli, Uberto, and Di Lucia, Paolo, ed., *Il Linguaggio del Diritto* (Milano: LED, 1994)

Scarpelli, Uberto, "Il permesso, il dovere e la completezza degli ordinamenti normative," *Rivista Trimestrale di Procedura Civile* (1963)

Spattini, Silvia, *Il governo del mercato del lavoro tra controllo pubblico e neocontrattualism*o (Milano: Giuffrè, 2008)

Supiot, Alain, *Homo juridicus. Essai sur la fonction anthropologique du Droit* (Paris: Seuil, 2005)

Thibierge, Catherine, ed., *La force normative. Naissance d'un concept* (Paris: LGDJ, 2009)

Thomasius, Christian, *Fundamenta iuris naturae et gentium* (Firenze: Nabu Press, 2013)
Viola, Francesco, *Behemoth o Leviathan? Diritto e obbligo nel pensiero di Hobbes* (Milano: Giuffrè, 1979)
Vitale, Tommaso, "Contrattualizzazione sociale," *Rivista di Previdenza Sociale* (2005): 1/05
Voza, Roberto, "Oltre i confini del lavoro dipendente: la valorizzazione della imprenditorialità femminile dalla L. 215/1992 al D.P.R. 314/2000," In *Lavoro delle donne e azioni positive. L'esperienza giuridica italiana*, edited by Garofalo Mario Giovanni (Bari: Cacucci, 2002)
Voza, Roberto, *A lezione di diritto* (Roma: Edizioni Conoscenza, 2009)
Zagrebelsky, Gustavo, *Il diritto mite, Legge diritti giustizia* (Torino: Einaudi, 2005)

CHAPTER 9

COLLECTIVE LABOUR LAW AND TRADE UNION PARADOXES IN THE SLOVAK REPUBLIC

MONIKA UHLEROVÁ & MAREK ŠVEC

Introduction

The main aim of this chapter is to point out, analyse and define selected phenomena in labour law and collective labour law in the conditions of the Slovak Republic. The authors call these phenomena "trade union paradoxes." It is assumed that these phenomena are influenced by social, political, societal and economic developments and have a direct impact on the operation and functioning of trade unions in Slovakia. They have also influenced internal decisions, systemic failures and mistakes made by trade unions over the last three decades of their existence under the conditions of the independent Slovak Republic (since 1993). In addition to outlining the current legal status of the issues in question, the chapter also sheds light on the basic socio-political concept of trade unions. The analytical part of the chapter focuses on the transformation of trade unions in Slovakia after the fall of communism and its consequences, important for their further functioning.

I. Paradoxes of Labour Law in the Slovak Republic

To evaluate the development of labour law in the Slovak Republic, a quote from Eduard Rabofský from 1959 comes to mind: "chaotic relations in labour law — promoting the leading role of capitalism in productive relations — leads employers to deceive employees and deny their legitimate social claims." This statement seems to be characteristic of the pandemic and post-pandemic period, which many employers exploit to shape and redefine employment relationships according to their own wishes. In doing so, they often choose the way of latent capitalism instead of progressive liberalism, where labour is reduced to goods. Such an approach is in direct conflict with the constitution of the International Labour Organization.

The position and importance of labour law in the Slovak Republic can be addressed from two points of view. At the primary level, labour law can be described as a set of legal norms, the aim of which is to regulate the relations arising in connection with the activity a natural person performs for another natural or legal person. Although the above view is typical of liberal and neoliberal movements in particular, the prevailing view has also another specific function — in the context of its historical development in the Slovak Republic, labour law is perceived as a means of the *ultima ratio* for safeguarding the social rights of working persons. Therefore, in addition to its regulatory function, its protective function is also important[1]. However, the protective function of individual labour law also depends on the orientation of national policies and political views. While the social democratic parties emphasise the social dimension of labour law and promote the strong legal position of employees and their representatives in labour relations along with the basic principles of socialist labour legislation, right-wing political parties prefer legislative interventions aimed at strengthening the flexibility of labour law provisions, which ultimately may weaken the protection of employees. Some legislative interventions aim to strengthen the "flexibility" of individual labour laws in order to enable better and faster adaptation of business processes to the changing conditions of the market economy. The gradual improvement of the legal position of one of the parties to the employment relationship (employer) means the gradual marginalisation of the protective elements of labour law — fundamental changes in the position of employee representatives, a reduced possibility of enforcing legal rights at the end of employment (severance pay, shorter notice period, etc.), and strengthening the employer's legal position when deciding on the way work is carried out by removing existing legal limits, etc. Therefore, if we perceive labour law primarily as a protective element ensuring the preservation of social rights and the human dignity of employees, and given the developments of the last period, we must naturally come to the conclusion we are heading towards a labour law crisis (Černy 2005).

Thus, the provisions of labour law are no longer governed by basic ideas of moral imperatives and the generally accepted concept of human rights and fundamental freedoms, but by boundless liberalism and the desire for greater dominance of capital. Low socio-political quality of labour

[1] In this context, it should be mentioned that the German legal system introduced yet another designation for labour law: the so-called *Schutzrecht*, which clearly indicates its fundamental function in society.

legislation is something we should pay attention to. The existing traditional employment relationships are often replaced by various contracts based on civil and commercial law (e.g. work contracts and nominal contracts) as employers try to break out of existing employment protection regulations (no protection against termination of employment, entitlement to leave, obstacles to work with the compensation of wage, etc.). The flexibility requirement is implemented in labour relations under the so-called “atypical” employment contracts. These are characterised by the frequent presence of dodgy statements requiring the employee to carry out “precarious work”. As a result of the above, a new social phenomenon is on the rise: so-called "working poverty."[2] However, the quality and culture of working conditions is not only reflected in the field of labour law and social security law, but also significantly affects the private and family life of employees. Work-life balance in today's labour market is far from what it is supposed to be.

Labour law describes the risks brought about by economic and social changes resulting from the transition to a post-industrial society — the so-called "new social risks". New social risks target younger employees, women and low-skilled people, as they directly affect the entry and integration of these groups into the labour market and childcare/household chores. While the "old risks" were mainly related to retirement or incapacity for work (effectively eliminated through income redistribution strategies), today's social policies must respond to current developments and effectively protect at-risk populations (Taylor-Gooby 2004). The quick increase in new social risks was boosted by the collapse of the world economy, due to the closure of national economies, accompanied by the adoption of "new" regulations on dependent work aimed at supporting the domestic economy by lowering labour standards to make the workforce cheaper and more flexible, thereby helping the employer "survive" the crisis. Repeated calls for respecting the dignity of employees are lost in the often violent efforts to promote labour law liberalisation and flexibility. The demand for the liberalisation of labour law is thus slowly becoming an axiom – the issue is not discussed, it is just taken as it is (Galvas 2011; Caruso 2002).

---

[2] Precarious work is typical for low labour protection and the disadvantaged position of the employee in the field of social affairs. Unambiguous features of precarious work are considered to be low job security, low remuneration for work performed, part-time or fixed-term work, a lack of representation in the workplace in social dialogue, and insufficient protection against dismissal, etc..

II. Paradoxes of Collective Labour Law in the Slovak Republic

In post-communist countries, the role of employee representatives, especially trade unions, is ambivalent, as they try to ensure effective protection of employees and minimise the "damage" caused by individual policies and legislation, as well as their impact on labour or collective labour law. Recently, the term "trade union paradox" has found its ways into Slovak labour law theory. The term refers to the situation where trade unions — historically the strongest and most widespread form of employee representation in the workplace — clash with the efforts of right-wing and liberal-oriented governments to change the nature of collective labour relations, thus leading to an overall weakening of the position of trade unions and their representative organisations in the public space. In general, three trade union paradoxes exist. These are based on the social changes and collective labour relations in the Slovak Republic. Even though collective labour relations experienced a renaissance in the form of additional recognition of certain competencies in the field of employment and wage conditions after social democratic governments came into power, the recent right-wing governments have pushed towards change in the overall paradigm of trade unions and their position in the workplace.

The first trade union paradox is a phenomenon characterised by a general decline in trade unionism, despite the strengthening position of trade unions in the legal order of the country concerned. The changes to legal regulations on the establishment and operation of employee representatives in general has significantly strengthened the position of employee representatives in the Slovak legal system, especially in relevant labour legislation and particularly over the last 12 years of social democratic governments. Historically, several amendments to the legal order were adopted, especially amendments to the Labour Code (the most significant change in recent years with effect from 1 January 2013) which, on the one hand preserved the competencies of trade unions as the most important form of employee representation in the workplace, including maintaining the exclusive right to collective bargaining, compared to other forms of employee representation in the workplace. On the other hand, though, amendments to legislation were implemented which strengthened the position of employee representatives in other labour law areas (e.g. the Social Fund Act, Section 7, par. 4 regulating the possibility of co-deciding on special employer funds aimed at building the employer's corporate social policy), as well as the importance and significance of trade unions in the legal order and in society itself (the law on tripartite consultations – the tripartite). Even the obvious and significant strengthening of competencies and the position of trade unions in Slovakia did not stop the decline in the membership in trade unions in the Slovak Republic. The more significant the strengthening of the competencies of trade unions, the more significant the decline in the number of trade union members in existing trade unions.

The second trade union paradox takes into account the indicated potential stability of the legislation on collective labour relations. It can be characterised as a phenomenon in which the legal regulation of collective labour relations is maintained in contrast to the need to amend it due to changes in the labour market, the redefined nature of dependent work and individual employment relationships. The aim of the second paradox is to assess the relevant labour law elements regulating the powers of employee representatives in the workplace, as well as the very purpose of its own existence. Thus, despite the structural changes in the Slovak economy and labour market; the emergence of new jobs and different types and kinds of employers; changes to the nature of employers, and large enterprises, medium-sized enterprises and micro-enterprises having fewer employees who do not tend to associate with each other and whose business activity is not based on manual work or work performed in one location, there were no significant changes made to the legal regulations on employee representatives which would reciprocate these changes. In light of the above, some regulations became obsolete. The changes include, in particular, changes to working-time scheduling and the drastic onset of working from home and teleworking, flexible changes in the employees' place of work, and the shift towards the contractual negotiation of remuneration.

The third paradox confirms the general approach of the legislator or trade union elites to the quality of existing and adopted legislation in the field of activities of employee representatives. This points to the fact that, even though employee representatives were granted certain competencies and rights, these are vague and of no real benefit in terms of more effective protection of employees' rights. Despite the fact that trade unions were granted several new competencies (e.g. the right to negotiate the introduction of a control monitoring mechanism with the employer) and rights (e.g. the right to leave to perform trade union activities) in recent times, the quality of employee protection did not increase significantly. The new labour rights of trade unions failed to bring any improvement in the performance of their activities due to insufficient and often vague wording of the relevant legal regulations. Thus, although the labour code constructed a new basic principle which became part of the normative text of the labour code 13 years ago (the text introduced the obligation of the employer to discuss with employee representatives the introduction of a monitoring mechanism with the employer to protect the right to private and family life), there is still no legal definition of the term "control mechanism." The lack of explanation causes fundamental disagreements between employers and employee representatives.

Taking into account all three trade union paradoxes, we may discuss whether the declared stability of the legal regulation of collective labour relations should be seen as an advantage or a reluctance to solve the problems (or a move to postpone them). If we take into account the general reluctance of trade union elites to accept any changes to the legal regulation of collective labour relations, then we should not be surprised by problems for those who wish to form and operate a trade union facing the employer. The emergence of anti-system destructive trade unions, in the absence of relevant legislation, block collective bargaining with employers as well as social dialogue. Along with fake quasi-legal theories without legal relevance, these are the most common problems resulting from the situation. These problems weaken the position of standard trade unions established by employees in order to improve their working and wage conditions.

III. The Confederation of Trade Unions of the Slovak Republic as a New Social and Political Actor in Shaping Labour Law

With regard to labour law in the Slovak Republic, trade unions (stakeholders able to influence the development of labour law) also find themselves in a difficult position. Following the Velvet Revolution of November 1989, trade unions in Slovakia found themselves in a difficult situation, as they became part of the social and economic transformation process. This process of transition required trade unions to transform into independent organisations operating under democratic principles. In the first years of its existence, the Confederation of Trade Unions of the Slovak Republic (hereinafter the Confederation: CTU SR), as the largest organisation covering trade unions in Slovakia after the establishment of the independent Slovak Republic in 1993, struggled to find its place in the new political system and establish itself on the international stage. It also had to create new structures and transfer its property from the Revolutionary Trade Union Movement, a body operating under the previous regime. Later, the Confederation focused on three basic areas of problems: defining and finding its position in the tripartite government and social partners; defining its position in political parties and movements; and activating the membership base which, given the turbulent years, began to decline. The Confederation's program reflected the efforts of trade unions to strengthen their position in society and move towards social partners, promoting their interests through alliances with the relevant left-wing political parties.

Studies by various authors examining trade unions in the post-communist countries of Central and Eastern Europe confirm that trade unions bear the heaviest burden of the previous regime's legacy (Ekiert and Kubik 1998; Crowley 2004; Čambáliková 2003; Uhlerová 2014). For this reason, the Confederacy took a neutral stance towards political parties and decided to enforce its views outside of the political arena. It was not until the 1998 election that the Confederation participated in an election campaign for the first time. It mobilised its members to vote in the elections, thus contributing to efforts to change the then way of governing Slovakia and restore democracy. The involvement of CTU SR in the election campaign was marked by deteriorated relations with the then government and the subsequent departure of trade unions from the tripartite. Following the 1998 elections, the Confederation focused on enforcing the legislative onto the tripartite institution, and succeeded. However, the relationship with the then government deteriorated, too, due to the program statement of the government which aimed to remove corporatist elements in the economic and social spheres (i.e. to eliminate the influence of social partners on the government and diminish their interests in the tripartite). The deterioration of relations with the government and the inability to enforce their demands at the tripartite meetings forced the unions in Slovakia to look for their political allies among the political parties and to find a union-friendly partner in the government. This process led to the signing of an agreement on cooperation between the CTU SR and the Social Democratic Party, SMER. After the 2006 elections, and again after thc early elections of 2012, as well as the general elections of 2016, when SMER became the governing party (the party governed alone between 2012 and 2016), it seemed that this "partnership" could bring certain benefits to the unions. During the period SMER was in power, the unions acquired significant competencies. That meant they no longer needed to redefine their own position as new powers, such as in the areas of limiting agency employment, scheduling working hours or wage negotiation, which meant at least a partial win for the unions and an increase in trade union membership. Over time, however, employers have come up with other ways of negotiation, thus circumventing "stricter" labour legislation fought for by the unions. The power of unions weakened once again.

IV. Internal Transformation of CTU SR: Obstacle or Future Challenge?

In terms of internal organisation, an effective response to external stimuli and internal decision-making systems, trade unions in Slovakia have not undergone significant changes since 1990. The reason is simple: the Confederation rather focused on defining its activities and priorities, its attitude towards other subjects of the political system and addressing various external factors that influenced its activities. The Confederacy gradually became a reactive socio-political actor rather than a major "agenda setter." Furthermore, a strong inertia factor and a strong staff continuity prevailed in the internal structure of the unions, resulting in a reluctance to start internal reforms and to name and solve internal problems. Even though the internal structure and decision-making process can be considered highly democratic and built from the bottom up, they slowed down the efficiency and dynamism of the Confederacy. It should be noted that decisions made within the CTU SR by associated trade unions are not enforceable and are not subject to sanctions. This hinders the practical implementation of decisions (even though the internal democratic conditions based on collective decision-making are upheld). The situation weakens the position of trade unions, as it has a negative impact on the internal mechanism of taking and implementing not only strategic decisions, but also the effectiveness of social dialogue and the very internal communication and functioning of trade unions. As a result, the Confederacy is increasingly dependent on political alliances and decisions of the government.

The membership base is one of the sources of uncertainty in the unions. In Slovakia, the union membership shows a continuously declining trend. This trend is caused by a number of external and internal factors. External factors are difficult to influence. The only thing the organisation can do is to adapt to them and try to eliminate their negative impact as much as possible. With the loss of members comes a weaker position in collective bargaining and the loss of benefits. Political and external issues influencing the activities of the Confederation seem to "distract" its attention from the need to solve internal problems, its own reorganisation, qualitative analysis and internal audit in order to name the causes of problems and find new suitable and modern forms by way of solution.

In recent years, trade unions have begun to argue over their future direction and views, thus giving rise to an imaginary rivalry. On the one hand, there are unions holding on to traditional modes of action (collective bargaining in sectors and social dialogue at tripartite level), and on the other hand there are trade unions declaring dissatisfaction with the outcome of negotiations who seek new tools and ways to satisfy their needs. The second group of "new" unions is more radical and uses more tools of coercion to influence society. In general, more radical actions seem to bring unions more success and attention than traditional social dialogue and collective bargaining could ever bring. While these types of instruments strengthen internal organisation, mobilisation and human resources of trade unions, they undermine the traditional pillars of industrial relations, social dialogue and collective bargaining. These new trade unions "parasitise" on the possibilities offered to them by the current legislative framework and use them not to defend the rights and interests of employees, but to gain certain benefits or weaken already established trade unions.

It will therefore be necessary for trade unions in Slovakia to adapt their internal structures in the near future so that they will be able to face the challenges and problems and transform labour law into a more socially acceptable legislation. Decision-making structures and processes will need to be more dynamic, streamlined and ready to face the challenges posed by the modern (digital) age, such as new types and forms of work, innovative forms of communication, the need to reach more young people, the requirement to strengthen professional capacities and cooperate with research institutions at the domestic as well as at the international level, and the need to eliminate the risks of politicisation and the penetration of party interests in the activities of trade unions.

At present, staff inertia (the so-called dinosaur's extinction principle) still prevails at all levels of trade union management. This phenomenon slows down and sometimes even prevents the necessary changes and transformations and there is much-needed generational change. All of the above should be part of the trade union revitalisation scenario. Trade unions in Slovakia[3] also have a lot of room to expand their membership base by representing and integrating new types of workers, provided they accept innovative approaches and strategies and remove existing internal structural and institutional obstacles.

---

[3] We can identify several groups of workers who are not represented by a trade union (especially in terms of supply and the interest of active representation of their interests): agency staff, platform workers, people working from home, migrant workers, immigrants, students, and the unemployed, etc.

V. Tripartism as a Gateway to Influencing the Creation of Labour Law Legislation and the Future of Labour Law

Institutionalised social partnership at the top (national) level — tripartite — creates an opportunity for trade unions represented by CTU SR to consult, express themselves and be informed about important social and economic measures taken by the government. The tripartite is also a formal "gateway" to exclusive access to the government. Slovakia's experience with institutionalised social dialogue after 1990 indicates that this approach may bring success (not only formally) only if the government respects and acknowledges the importance of social dialogue. The state (government) has a dominant position in the tripartite and is a determining factor in how social dialogue at the national level develops. The government's attitude to the principles, functions, philosophy, and actors of social dialogue and partnerships influences and determines their importance, effectiveness and significance. It follows from the above that, despite the fact the social dialogue has undergone some legal and social changes and established itself at an institutional level over the last 30 years, it is still subject to the political influences, affinities and preferences of the government. The state (government) should create the preconditions and space for conducting social dialogue and stop using it as a tool for presenting its ideological preferences, personal sympathies and political aversions. Unless the social partners manage to get rid of these tendencies, the institutionalised social dialogue will not be respected and socially accepted.

Despite the legally defined mandate, tripartite rule has been weakening in Slovakia for a long time. The current legislative framework does not motivate the social partners to agree on issues and, instead of dialogue, they seek political support and agreements directly with the government. In a 2019 study by the Central European Institute for Labour Research (CELSI), representatives of the social partners themselves pointed out the main factors of the inefficiency of social dialogue, as well as the fact that the tripartite is not a decision-making body but only an advisory body to the government without a mandate to influence the government's decisions. The social partners are inadequately prepared and lack time to study the documents in detail and prepare their own analyses. The result is often politically-motivated decisions. Informal interaction between trade unions and employers' unions in the preparatory phase of negotiations is insufficient, often resulting in divergent views. Employers feel fragmentation within their ranks and a lack of will to better coordinate their positions. Instead of focusing its role on creating the conditions for dialogue between trade unions and employers, the state exercises its power and dominates the negotiations. For this reason, too, trade unions and employers prefer to enshrine their proposals in legislation instead of collective bargaining. Rather, the social partners choose the path of seeking quick profits at the expense of building long-lasting relationships through social dialogue. Circumventing the tripartite by submitting legislative proposals and the existing legislative measures triggered in the event that the social partners do not agree also seriously interferes with the position and importance of the tripartite (Kahancová et al. 2019).

The end of the 1990s and the beginning of the new millennium brought about a new trend: trade unions in Slovakia tended to affiliate with the views of social democracy represented by the SMER-SD political party in an effort to strengthen their position with the government. Such an alliance can bring certain benefits as well as a "more comfortable" life for unions if teamed with the government. However, this political partnership also brings to the table a policy of concessions and restrictions on pressure the trade union may exert on the government. Efforts to strengthen labour law during times when the social democrats are in power means a favourable legislative framework for trade unions on the one hand but, on the other hand, "empties" the space and opportunities for collective bargaining, weakening trade unions at company level (Švec 2020).

Trade unions in Slovakia have long focused on influencing legislation through their direct access to government using the tripartite and their political supporters. Under the government led by SMER-SD, the unions enjoyed political support at a national level. However, the government increasingly came under the influence of business interests, which also shed negative light on the political resources of trade unions and the legitimacy of their activities in the future. These developments suggest that unions should create a more balanced mix of resources in order to reduce their political dependence. Actions likely to strengthen the legitimacy and position of trade unions include the enrolment of new members, as well as professions and sectors not previously affiliated with them, possibly from more flexible parts of the labour market; making strong international contacts with European and international trade union federations; more active involvement in domestic socio-economic issues; and taking an active role in discussions within and outside the sectoral social dialogue. At sectoral and company levels, trade unions consider collective bargaining and the conclusion of collective agreements to be of key importance. Despite this position, collective agreements cover only 25% of the workforce. This can be explained by the low social and organisational strength of trade unions.

Concluding Remarks

In Slovakia, in general, trade unions have long sought to find a compromise between their own requirements, the expectations of citizens and union members, the current political, economic and social situation, and the measures implemented by the government. The functioning of trade unions in post-communist countries is very specific. Their power is based mainly on economic and political principles, but also depends on real-life conditions, the expectations of a particular government, current political representation and political actors, the political context and ad hoc agreements (Uhlerová 2012). We assume this kind of unstable model of functioning will persist, even after the crisis triggered by Covid-19 and unfavourable economic and social conditions are over (Martišková and Uhlerová 2016). In particular, the political situation and political representation at a national level, and the attitudes and experience of politicians will seriously affect the level of social dialogue and the involvement of trade unions in the adoption of economic and social measures (Uhlerová 2020).

After 2020, Slovak trade unions also find themselves at a crossroads. They will have to decide whether to follow the conservative strategies of communication, recruitment, access to collective bargaining and the content of collective agreements, political expectations (and failures) and the overall conservative setting of collective labour relations, or whether they will follow the path of revitalisation, transformation and innovation in all areas of their activities. Should they choose conservative strategies and approach, they will get sidelined and gradually lose their prominent position as the basic guarantor of employees' social rights in the upcoming new digital era. It must be borne in mind that the strategies and tools used to promote the interests of those working in the economic and social conditions of the 1990s may no longer be relevant and effective in the new millennium and in the digital age. Ignoring the reality will only accelerate what has so far been a gradual fall from grace. The importance of trade unions at national level will gradually decline and the (illusory) neo-corporatist model of interest policy will weaken. However, in this scenario, the importance of "bread-and-butter" unionism and the position of trade unions at (in traditional terminology and scope) the enterprise level may be strengthened. Attention should be paid to the emergence of various "independent" trade unions which are not members of larger union bodies. The aim of these independent trade unions (usually operating in the virtual space) is to defend the interests of a certain group of workers without any further (e.g. political, wider social) involvement. One of the reasons these trade unions do not wish to be affiliated with higher union bodies (e.g. CTU SR) may be the inability of these bodies to respond adequately to new conditions, the emergence of new professions and forms of work and failure to adapt structures and decision-making dynamics to these conditions. The structure of CTU SR, as well as other trade unions not affiliated with it, is still based on the principle of grouping the traditional professions into individual trade unions, typical of the industrial or post-industrial era. In this scenario, the rivalry of trade unions (the operation of several trade unions with different or no affiliation to the employer) as well as the emergence of other forms of representation, such as civic associations and initiatives, could not be excluded.

If we are to believe that labour law will "survive" and continue being the element dominating the human rights agenda and ensuring the ability of natural persons to enforce their basic rights and social needs, the legislators must change their approach. To assume that this will be possible without taking the above into the account is wrong, especially in post-communist countries like the Slovak Republic. Continuing stagnation in the trade union movement will ultimately result in drastic changes to collective labour relations (as well as labour law itself), as the only option for improving the working and wage conditions of employees in crisis and post-crisis times.

Bibliography

Caruso, Bruno, "The Future of Labour Law: Traditional Models of Social Protection and a New Constitution of Social Rights," *WP Centro Studi di Diritto del Lavoro Europeo "Massimo D'Antona,"* no. 10 (2002): 3-15

Crowley, Stephen, "Explaining Labor Weakness in Post-Communist Europe: Historical Legacies and Comparative Perspective," *East European Politics and Societies 18*, no. 3 (2004): 394-429

Čambáliková, Monika, "Začlenenie a vylúčenie v období transformácie a integrácie (Inclusion and Exclusion in a Period of Transformation and Integration)," *Sociológia 35*, no. 4 (2003): 285-306

Černy, Josef, "Anmerkungen zur Krise des Arbeitsrechts," In *Krise des Arbeitsrecht. Symposium zur Erinnerung an Eduard Rabofsky*, edited by Oberkofler, Anja (Wien: Alfred Klahr Gesellschaft, 2005), 21-24

Ekiert, Grzegorz, and Kubik, Jan, "Contentious Politics in New Democracies: East Germany, Poland, Hungary, and Slovakia," *World Politics 50*, no. 4 (1998): 547-581

Galvas, Milan, "Úvahy o perspektivách liberalizace pracovního práva v ČR (Reflections on the Perspectives of Labor Law Liberalization in the Czech Republic)," In *Možnosti a hranice liberalizácie pracovných vzťahov (Possibilities and Limits of Liberalization of Labor Relations)*, edited by Barancová, Helena (Bratislava: Sprint dva, 2011): 57-65

Kahancová, Marta et al, *Enhancing the Effectiveness of Social Dialogue Articulation in Europe, Country Report Slovakia. CELSI Research Report no. 29/2019* (Bratislava: CELSI, 2019)

Martišková, Monika, and Uhlerová, Monika, *Union Organizing in the Automotive Industry in Slovakia in the Times of Crisis: Do They Help Workers or Protect Themselves? Working Papers Series* (Budapest: Central European University, Center for Policy Studies, 2016)

Švec, Marek, *Odborová organizácia. Postavenie a pracovnoprávne nároky (Trade Union. Status and Employment Rights)* (Bratislava: Wolters Kluwer, 2020)

Taylor-Gooby, Peter, *New Risks, New Welfare. The Transformation of the European Welfare State* (Oxford: Oxford University Press, 2004)

Uhlerová, Monika, "Inštitucionalizovaný sociálny dialóg a jeho dosahy na postavenie odborov v post-komunistických krajinách strednej Európy. Prípadová štúdia Slovenska (Institutionalized Social Dialogue and its Implications for the Position of Trade Unions in the Post-Communist Countries of Central Europe. Case Study of Slovakia)," *Political Science* 15, no. 1 (2012): 8-33

Uhlerová, Monika, "The Role of Trade Unions and Social Dialogue during the Crisis: The Case of Slovakia," *Central European Journal of Labour Law and Personnel Management* 3, no. 1 (2020): 61-76

Uhlerová, Monika, "Transformácia odborov na Slovensku po roku 1989: Možnosti a limity vplyvu na verejnú politiku (Transformation of Trade Unions in Slovakia after 1989: Possibilities and Limits of Influence on Public Policy)," In *Bariéry a paradoxy demokracie (Barriers and paradoxes of democracy)*, edited by Kulašik, Peter and Tichá, Karolina (České Budějovice: Vysoká škola evropských a regionálních studií, 2014), 383-393

B. Universal Principles

CHAPTER 10

COLLECTIVITY – AN ORIGINAL FEATURE OF LABOUR LAW

MIROSLAW WLODARCZYK

1. The birth of capitalism, assessed in the context of relations between employers and employees, was of an individualistic nature. This feature developed mainly from the domination of the liberal doctrine at that time (the turn of the 19th century), which emphasised the notion of freedom and the freedom of the individual to conduct economic activity (Dziadzio 2014, 55 ff.). At that time, any collective actions which could have threatened this liberty were subject to victimisation. In particular, the collective actions of those employed in factories and industry were considered such a threat. Workers soon learned that the effectiveness of influencing factory owners was significantly greater when they acted collectively. When one or more of these individuals protested, it provided the opportunity for others to identify with them and join the action. At the same time, it should be noted that while such actions being in concert was commonplace, the entrepreneurs treating all or most employees equally badly were also the norm (Dziadzio 2014, 60 ff).

One of the basic principles governing employment relations is the right to unite, the essence of which is the formation and association of trade unions. Fundamental to this right is the possibility of group action by persons performing work in defence of their own economic interests, and thus the realisation of their social interests. Freedom of association was legally guaranteed in European countries in the 19th century. Trade unions were legalised in the United Kingdom in 1825. In other European countries, this happened later. In France, trade unions were banned until 1884, and in Germany until 1869 (Szubert 1960, 8; Grzybowski & Swiatkowski 1984, 54-55). The right of trade unions to conclude collective-bargaining agreements was confirmed in the second half of the 19th century and the early part of the 20th century: in the United Kingdom in 1875, in France in 1919, and in the United States in 1932 (Grzybowski & Swiatkowski 1984,

55; Dziadzio 2014, 61-73). The international community recognised the right to unite as a universal labour right only in the mid-20th century (Convention No. 87 of the International Labour Organization of 1948 on the Freedom of Association and the Protection of the Right to Organise).

What reasons dictated the struggle of the employed for the right to unite? It was primarily the economic leverage of the employer over the employee. A worker acting alone was not a significant counterpart to an entrepreneur. A worker acting in isolation, who did not agree to the conditions dictated by the employer, could be replaced by another candidate seeking work. There were plenty of free labourers in the early capitalist working environment. The replacement of one contractor who disagreed with the conditions of employment with another person could be made almost without halting the company's operations, especially since at that time most jobs did not require long-term vocational training. The leverage of the entrepreneur was eliminated only by the group action of employees. When a group of protesters was large, serious disruptions to production would occur and the replacement of numerous protesting contractors required time — was necessary to find suitable candidates, and to train them in how to perform their work — therefore, significant problems for the entrepreneur arose only when the scale of such resistance was large enough, in which case it became necessary to resolve the conflict through negotiation and settlement.

The essence of protecting the interests of employees, in the above context, is realised primarily in the form of self-protection through their organisation, and solidarity in pursuit of the adopted objectives. The *sine qua non* of such action appears to be the right to unite and the principle of the freedom of association (Tomaszewska 2014, 253 ff.). The latter rule is intended to guarantee the existence of independent workers' organisations, which only then can articulate the content of their interests. The state in this process becomes the guarantor of the realisation of these rights. The development of labour law in the last 200 years in Western European and North American countries demonstrates such a state of affairs (Florek & Sewerynski 1988, 87 ff.).

The collective action of the employed has given labour law a specific notoriety. This reputation tends to be initially acquired by the manner of creating labour law, determined mainly by social partners, employers, and employees. The abovementioned is evidenced by the development of labour law, especially the institution of collective bargaining (Szubert 1960, 8-31; Wlodarczyk 2014, 411 ff.). Agreement law, which should be considered fundamental to labour law, was created by the representatives of employees and employers. Employees are always represented by their organisations (usually trade unions); employers act collectively when the agreement is of an over-institutional character. Thus, the subject of these regulations is always connected with the interests of a specific group: factory workers, employees in a given industry, or professional associations, on the one hand; or, on the other hand, employers operating in each industry, field of production, or category of services. Regardless of the subjective scope of a collective-bargaining agreement, it always considers the interests of specific social groups, either employees or employers. It is worth pointing out that, in such situations, the interests of each of the two groups are pursued initially, and thus the general interest is not pursued, as is the case with universally binding law. The general interest is considered indirectly, as a rule, through restrictions imposed by the state on social partners.

The above practice reflects the need to differentiate the situation in particular fields of activity for which employees are engaged. This diversity of detailed solutions results from the fact that it is not possible to regulate the situation of all employees in the same way. The wide-ranging variety of economic relations means that this aspect of social life avoids the possibility of regulation by universally binding law in the vast majority of cases. This universally binding law establishes only general principles or minimum standards of protection; law created collectively (collegially) adjusts regulations to the interests and needs of individual groups of employees and entrepreneurs (Wlodarczyk 2010, 389 ff.). This also has a direct impact on the competitiveness of companies and on their economic efficiency.

It should be further added that the formation of universal (statutory) labour law was usually a consequence of the level of regulation established in collective agreements (in particular, with respect to the minimum wage, working time, annual leave, etc.). For the future, it would also be desirable to formulate the thesis that the collective method of lawmaking should always be used in the process of creating collective-bargaining law; while in the process of creating general (state) labour law, it would be advisable to give it a dominant, or at least an initiating, role (Szubert 1960, 60; Wlodarczyk 2015).

The essence of this collectivity thus consists of the following tenets: (1) labour law is created by employee representations (i.e., by a group of employees in agreement with an employer or a group of employers); (2) labour law is always created for a group of employees (i.e. the interests of a given group of employees are taken into account); (3) at the same time, the interests of the opposing party are accommodated in negotiations on the content of the law; (4) in the creation of labour law, the methods of collective action by employee groups are used; (5) as a consequence, the group of employees who created this law is the guardian of the enforcement of the law so enacted.

The indicated prerequisites are necessary for the establishment of the real protection of employee rights instituted under this procedure. This protection assumes that only employees have the possibility of the ongoing supervision of the processes of employment and of the provision of work; therefore, they can directly, and on a continuous basis, observe the application of this right and take immediate action in the event of its violation. Other ways and forms of protecting employee rights (e.g. labour inspection and common courts) are less effective in this respect.

From a subjective point of view, it is important that the association which is a participant in the creation of law on behalf of the employee or the employer is of a voluntary character — we cannot recognise as such all types of associations created by law, membership of which is compulsory (e.g. institutions of professional or economic self-government) (Szubert 1960, 141). Forcing a dialogue in the form of various "workers' councils" imposed by universally binding law is not of a collective character, as it does not create a social bond or responsibility for group matters (group interests), creates a power which is used by a formally appointed representation which does not have social trust or support (Wratny & Bednarski 2010).

The collectivism of labour law undoubtedly reaches its culmination in the sphere of activities related to the conclusion of collective-bargaining agreements (Szubert 1960, 75 ff; Wlodarczyk 2014, 418 ff). Such agreements come into effect through a bilateral legal act (i.e. it requires the consensual declaration of will by two parties). To be effective, labour law requires the acceptance of social partners, so at its basis there is agreement or consent. In this agreement there is also a bond of obligations of its participants, which at least implies the duty to cooperate in the implementation of the provisions of this law. These obligations are an additional guarantee of compliance with its provisions, because social partners making a genuine contribution to the creation of labour law will also act as its guarantor. Participants in the agreement are contracting parties in these relations, and this requires ensuring legal equality and the freedom of action, allowing them to decide independently on the content of the act, and on its binding force. Labour law will be authentic when the social partners independently present their expectations in this sphere and agree to be bound by this law. Agreements should only be concluded by participants who occupy a certain social position and represent certain interests. In capitalist relations, they have an antagonistic stance, are autonomous of each other, and are also independent of the state. At the same time, the conclusion of such agreements is always conditional on the balance of the economic power of both parties. On the employees' side, there should only be autonomous organisations (usually trade unions); on the employers' side, there might also be self-determined employers in addition to organisations. The contents of collective-bargaining law are conditions of individual employment contracts. This law uniformly regulates the content of employment relationships and protects the rights of employees by imposing set standards on individual employers and employees, while excluding the possibility of formulating individual contracts which are contrary to its content.

2. Examples of collectivism in labour law can be found in every national legal system. The Polish law of 23 May 1991 (on trade unions) designates the rights and interests of employees as a collective and as individuals, in Article 7 (Florek 1990; Gozdziewicz, Myszka & Piatkowski 1991, 15 ff; Florek & Pisarczyk 2019, 298-301). With regard to the first type of issue, trade unions represent all employees, irrespective of their trade-union membership (i.e. including those who do not belong to a trade union); whereas with regard to individual cases involving the employment relationship, they represent only their members. In both aspects, an employee who is part of a collective structure is in a more-advantageous position, guaranteeing more effective protection of his or her personal rights and interests. To show more clearly the value of the above-described feature of labour law, it seems appropriate to show what an employee loses when he or she acts outside a trade union within the contemporary Polish legal order (Wlodarczyk 1997).

Regarding collective matters, it must be assumed there is no company trade-union organisation at a given employer. Employees working for that employer would not then benefit from such measures as the laws created by trade unions and the employer (collective agreements). In the Polish legal system, such acts include collective-bargaining agreements, or remuneration rules and working regulations created through such agreements. Similar arrangements may be established for the plans around taking annual leave. In the absence of trade unions, matters which are set out in these documents are determined by the employer itself. In such a situation, the consideration of employees' needs might be limited. Even if, in some cases, the employer consulted employee representatives, it does not seem that the position of such delegates could be compared to that of a trade union.

On the other hand, in individual employment matters, persons who do not belong to a trade union would not enjoy the protection of this organisation, in two types of situations. The first is provided for by the measures establishing the legal obligation for the employer to cooperate with the trade-union organisation representing the employee in individual matters concerning the given employee. Under Polish law, such matters include, in particular, the trade union's right to give an opinion on the employer's intention to terminate an employment contract for an indefinite period of time, and on the termination of the working conditions; to give an opinion on the employer's termination of an employment contract without notice; to give an opinion on the employer's decision to award an employee with a citation or a distinction; to express a position on the imposition of a disciplinary penalty by the employer on an employee; to express consent to termination without notice due to the fault of an employee subject to an employment contract during pregnancy and maternity leave; and to agree with the employer on the termination of an employment contract with a woman during pregnancy and maternity leave, in the event of the announcement of the employer's bankruptcy or liquidation (Polish Labour Code).

The second group, in turn, includes several labour-law institutions whose application does not require formal cooperation with trade unions, but where the trade union is always a guarantor of their proper functioning. In all such situations, it is the ongoing supervision resulting from the permanent presence of trade-union activists in the workplace, and their immediate interventions, which facilitate the real application of the legal regulations favourable for the employee. The role of the company's trade-union organisation in such cases must also be seen in the context of at least two circumstances. First, that an employee usually avoids conflicts with his or her supervisor during the employment period in order not to be exposed to the supervisor's animosity. Second, that the state labour inspectorate can only occasionally supervise compliance with labour laws, given the extremely limited staffing for such needs. For example, such cases could include situations in which the activities of a trade union might contribute to the elimination of the practice of concluding civil-law contracts with employees, instead of an employment contract; to scale down the practice of renewing fixed-term employment contracts; for the use by the employer of the written form when concluding an employment contract; for the employee to exercise the right to terminate an employment contract without notice, due to a serious breach of obligations by the employer; for the formulation of an anti-competition clause in such a way that it does not serve as a tool for disciplining employees; to ensure that an employee has the right to substitute remuneration with an overtime bonus of a day off — the lack of monitoring by a trade union means that it is usually the employer who decides when the employee will receive his or her remuneration; to eliminate cases in which an employer forces an employee to take unpaid leave; or to use the right of an employee to refuse to perform dangerous work (Polish Labour Code).

3. Considering the above-mentioned remarks, the thesis stated at the beginning of this chapter does not raise any doubts. It is unnecessary to repeat that an employee can be defended effectively only by a strong trade union (i.e. an organisation which is able to challenge the employer). The latter circumstance, in turn, depends not only on the organisational shape of the given union and the composition of its activists, but above all on the attitude of its rank-and-file members, which is expressed in the effective support of trade-union officials acting in their defence.

In the picture of a trade union presented above, the confrontational character of this type of organisation has been emphasised. However, it should also be borne in mind that trade unions in the workplace, being a guarantor of the implementation of most standards of labour law, have also become a serious factor stabilising this sphere of social relations. This aspect of their existence emerges when the established rules of conduct are respected. Resulting from the right to be present in the workplace, the possibility to directly supervise the application of labour law obliges trade unions to immediately respond to any irregularities. The prompt disclosure and resolution of disputes at an early stage — in cooperation with the employer, of course — is the very guarantee of a stable and undisturbed functioning of the employer's enterprise, but also of the peaceful course of the employee's career.

In the above context a question arises about the future of the Polish labour-law model. In its current form, it appears to be a law which primarily performs a protective function (i.e. a regulation guaranteeing decent working conditions to employees and other persons performing paid work for entrepreneurs). In the classical view, dominant in the 20th century, it was assumed that the way to ensure such a result was the activity of trade unions through the conclusion of collective agreements. Such a model did not function in the Polish reality during the period after World War II (i.e., under the doctrine of real socialism). It was the state and the political forces governing it which decided on employment standards. After the political transformation of 1989, the situation changed to the extent that the trade union movement gained significant influence on the content of labour law created by parliament. Trade unions became an important entity shaping this law. However, this role of trade unions resulted from the fact that they used the political power they had gained during the period of struggle against communism in the 1980s (Wratny 2010). Thus, the standards of labour law in Poland are still being created by the Polish Parliament. The forms of agreement are of negligible importance. Under these circumstances, it is worth asking whether a return to the contractual form of labour law is feasible. The practice of the last 30 years is in favour of a negative answer. This means that it is the state which plays the primary role in the creation of labour law, sets employment standards, and determines the standard of working conditions, but it also dictates the rules of the operation of social partners (e.g. trade unions and employers' organisations). The latter are granted a certain degree of influence on the shaping of these principles. However, the extent of this influence is not determined by their activities in the field of determining the conditions of employment through the conclusion of collective agreements, but rather by their political position, which depends on their ability to influence the results of elections to government bodies (central and local), and to influence public opinion.

In depth research on the developmental direction of the model of Polish labour law is still to be conducted by Polish labour-law scholars. This is not to say that these issues have gone unnoticed until now (Florek 2010; Sanetra 2015; Liszcz 2015; Sobczyk 2015; Wlodarczyk 2017). Although to a large extent the direction of this development is, in the author's opinion, fixed (Dukes 2014), it nonetheless requires the indication and specification of detailed elements in this model.

Bibliography

Dukes, Ruth, *The Labour Constitution. The Enduring Idea of Labour Law* (Oxford: University Press, 2014)

Dziadzio, Andrzej, "Zarys historii rozwoju zbiorowego prawa pracy," In *System prawa pracy. Tom V. Zbiorowe prawo pracy,* edited by Baran, Krzysztof W. (Warszawa: LEX a Wolters Kluwer business, 2014), 59-96

Florek, Ludwik, *Ochrona praw i interesów pracownika* (Warszawa: PWN, 1990)

Florek, Ludwik, *Ustawa i umowa w prawie pracy* (Warszawa: Oficyna a Wolters Kluwer business, 2010)

Florek, Ludwik, and Pisarczyk, Lukasz, *Prawo pracy* (Warszawa: C.H. BECK, 2019)

Florek, Ludwik, and Sewerynski, Michal, *Międzynarodowe prawo pracy* (Warszawa: IWZZ, 1988)

Goździewicz, Grzegorz, and Myszka, Zbigniew and Piatkowski, Jan, *Uprawnienia związków zawodowych w stosunkach pracy* (Gdańsk-Toruń: KK NSZZ Solidarnosc, 1991)

Grzybowski, Marian, and Swiatkowski, Andrzej, "Wolność związków zawodowych. Aspekt prawny i ustrojowy," In *Kompetencje związków zawodowych,* edited by Swiatkowski, Andrzej (Warszawa-Kraków: PWN, 1984), 51-98

Liszcz, Teresa, "Niech prawo pracy pozostanie prawem pracy," In *Przyszłość prawa pracy. Liber Amicorum. W pięćdziesięciolecie pracy naukowej Profesora Michała Seweryńskiego*, edited by Hajn, Zbigniew, and Skupien, Dagmara (Lodz: Wydawnictwo Uniwersytetu Lodzkiego, 2015), 277-90

Sanetra, Walerian, "Przyszłość prawa pracy z perspektywy istniejących dla niego zagrożeń," In *Przyszłość prawa pracy. Liber Amicorum. W pięćdziesięciolecie pracy naukowej Profesora Michała Seweryńskiego*, edited by Hajn, Zbigniew, and Skupien, Dagmara (Lodz: Wydawnictwo Uniwersytetu Lodzkiego, 2015), 69-80

Sobczyk, Arkadiusz, *Wolność pracy i władza* (Warszawa: Wolters Kluwer, 2015)

Szubert, Waclaw, *Układy zbiorowe pracy* (Warszawa: PWN, 1960)

Tomaszewska, Monika, "Wolność zrzeszania się w organizacjach związkowych i organizacjach pracodawców," In *System prawa pracy. Tom V. Zbiorowe prawo pracy*, edited by Baran, Krzysztof W. (Warszawa: LEX a Wolters Kluwer business, 2014), 253-98

Włodarczyk, Miroslaw, "Wpływ przynależności do związku zawodowego na sytuację pracownika," In *Polskie prawo pracy w obliczu nowelizacji Kodeksu pracy*, edited by Stadniczenko, Stanisław L. (Opole: Wydawnictwo Uniwersytetu Opolskiego, 1997), 71-75

Włodarczyk, Miroslaw, "Swoiste źródła prawa pracy," In *Zarys systemu prawa pracy. Tom I. Część ogólna prawa pracy*, edited by Baran, Krzysztof W. (Warszawa: LEX a Wolters Kluwer business, 2010), 389-466

Włodarczyk, Miroslaw, "Pojęcie kompetencji związków zawodowych," In *System prawa pracy. Tom V. Zbiorowe prawo pracy*, edited by Baran, Krzysztof W. (Warszawa: LEX a Wolters Kluwer business, 2014), 403-47

Włodarczyk, Miroslaw, "Udział partnerów społecznych w tworzeniu ustawowego prawa pracy," In *Przyszłość prawa pracy. Liber Amicorum. W pięćdziesięciolecie pracy naukowej Profesora Michała Seweryńskiego*, edited by Hajn, Zbigniew, and Skupien, Dagmara (Lodz: Wydawnictwo Uniwersytetu Lodzkiego, 2015), 481-92

Włodarczyk, Miroslaw, "Indywidualne prawo pracy a polityka społeczna," In *System prawa pracy. Tom II. Indywidualne prawo pracy. Część ogólna*, edited by Grzegorz Goździewicz (Warszawa: Wolters Kluwer, 2017), 96-112

Wratny, Jerzy, "Związki zawodowe. Znaczenie w życiu politycznym i społeczno-gospodarczym," In *Związki zawodowe a nie związkowe przedstawicielstwa pracownicze w gospodarce posttransformacyjnej*, edited by Wratny, Jerzy, and Bednarski, Marek (Warszawa: IPSS, 2010), 27-45

Wratny, Jerzy, and Bednarski, Marek, ed., *Związki zawodowe a niezwiązkowe przedstawicielstwa pracownicze w gospodarce posttransformacyjnej* (Warszawa: IPSS, 2010)

CHAPTER 11

THE IMPORTANCE OF TRADE UNIONS AND THEIR ROLE IN SOCIAL PROTECTION AT TIMES OF CRISIS

NELSON MANNRICH
& ALESSANDRA BARICHELLO BOSKOVIC

Introduction

The historical role played by trade unions is undeniable, particularly in the context of collective bargaining and the resolution of collective labour disputes. In fact, not only the union movements, but also (and especially) collective bargaining, have led to the acquisition of numerous rights and a more appropriate adjustment of government rules to the technical, cultural, and social specificities of each economic activity or locality.

In times of crisis, such as the one we are currently living through because of the coronavirus pandemic, unions are even more relevant. If well conducted, union actions can mitigate the adverse effects of the crisis on working conditions and on the maintenance of jobs.

This evidences the need to strengthen social movements that, as will be further analysed herein, have experienced their own crisis of representativeness in recent decades. Therefore, the Brazilian trade union system must necessarily be reformed, especially to finally implement the genuine freedom of association, as advocated by the ILO and other international players. This is what we discuss in this text.

1. The Historical Role of Trade Unions in Gaining and Consolidating Social Rights

Trade unions have always played a significant historical role in the acquisition of social rights, especially labour rights. From 1917 to 1920,

Brazilian unions promoted several strikes for better working conditions. Such trade union movements resulted in the acquisition of several labour rights (e.g., the prohibition on children under the age of 12 being able to work) during the 1920s and 1930s.

At the beginning of the 20th century, Brazil underwent an intense urbanisation process, resulting in the industrialisation movement. As Caio Prado Júnior points out, industrialisation occurred mainly due to investments made by coffee farmers (Prado Junior 2008, p. 264). Capitalist accumulation was still an essentially restricted individual practice in Brazil. Only individuals who had managed to raise enough funds to establish themselves on their own and independently invested capital in the industry made huge profits with their crops, particularly coffee. For example, after 1907, when coffee allowed a large margin of income thanks to the valuation policy, but its planting was limited, in addition to the fear of recurrence of the crisis, many of those profits were applied to manufacturing. Actually, from 1910 on, industrialisation developed very rapidly.

At the end of the 19th century, the city of São Paulo rapidly grew into a manufacturing centre, especially because it was located near the main coffee-growing areas. However, the rapid industrialisation process was not accompanied by a corresponding increase in workers' rights. Working conditions were precarious, and the presence of children in industrial complexes was amazingly common.

Therefore, social movements were intense during this period. Souto Maior points out that, from 1917 to 1920, just in São Paulo, 108 labour strikes occurred (Souto Maior 2017, p. 130). Undoubtedly, the 1917 General Strike, which lasted for several days, stands out. Boris Fausto lists the main demands of the 1917 strike: wage increases; prohibition of employing minors under 14 years of age; the abolition of night work for women and workers under the age of 18; a limit of an eight-hour workday, with a 50% mandatory pay increase for overtime; an end to work on Saturday afternoons; job tenure; respect for the right of association (Fausto 2003, p. 300).

Labour movements of the time were organised around the unions, largely as a consequence of the high immigration flow, mainly of Italian workers, who had brought such ideals with them. Souto Maior highlights how essential trade unions were to the workers' movements, pointing out that revolutionary unionism was an effort to build a working identity, as well as a tool for defending the unity of the working class and the fight for better living and working conditions (Souto Maior 2017, p. 134).

Due to popular and trade union appeals, labour legislation underwent profound changes in the subsequent period. The Federal Constitution of

1934, promulgated by President Getúlio Vargas, raised social rights, especially labour rights, to constitutional level.

During this period (1920-1934), some executive orders establishing workers' rights stand out. Executive Order No. 3,724, of January 15, 1919, regulated occupational accidents (art. 1), imposing on employers a duty to indemnify the injured worker or his family, except in cases of *force majeure* or exclusive fault of the employee (art. 2). Executive Order No. 4,982 of December 24, 1925, established the right to a remunerated annual rest period of fifteen (15) uninterrupted days (art. 1). In 1927, Executive Order No. 17,943-A of October 12 prohibited minors under 12 years of age from working (art. 101). Executive Order No. 21,364, of March 4, 1932, set limits on working hours in the industry – eight hours per day and 48 hours per week (art. 1). For employees at banks and banking institutions, Executive Order No. 23,322 of November 3, 1933, established six hours as maximum daily working hours, with a weekly total of 36 hours (art. 1).

As it turns out, the outstanding labour rights had a legal framework. In 1934, however, the number of rights increased and they became constitutionally secured. The following stand out: a) prohibition of different pay for the same job, based on age, gender, nationality or marital status (art. 121, Paragraph 1, "a", of the CF/34); b) minimum wage (art. 121, Paragraph 1, "b", CF/34); c) prohibition of employing minors under 14 years of age (art. 121, Paragraph 1, "d", CF/34); d) weekly rest, preferably on Sundays (art. 121, Paragraph1, "e" of CF/34); e) daily working hours limited to eight (art. 121, Paragraph1°, "c", CF/34); f) indemnity to the employee dismissed without cause (art. 121, Paragraph1, "g", CF/34).

Unlike what is often thought, social rights were not freely and spontaneously granted by the government. These rights were achieved by the workers' struggles and demands. Indeed, social rights are different from government charitable activities. Norberto Bobbio points out that one of the main characteristics of human rights, in which social rights are included, is their historicity (Bobbio 2004, p. 31). Human rights are historical rights: they gradually emerge from struggles and consequent changes in living conditions. Moreover, the conquest of rights related to work in Brazil could not be dissociated from historicity.

Thanks to the trade union movements, orchestrated by the unions and guided by revolutionary unionism, the government began to intervene in labour relations to guarantee minimum rights.

Amauri Mascaro Nascimento reports that unionism emerged as a workers' reaction, based on solidarity and the defence of their interests on the one hand, and, on the other, as a revolt against the capitalist mode of production (Nascimento 2005, p. 41).

For a long time, coalitions were considered crimes in several countries. Until the first half of the 19th century, laws in France, England and the United States provided for imprisonment. Due to the rise of liberal thinking, governments around the world began to repeal laws that criminalised coalitions (Nascimento 2005, p. 46).

From then on, all over the world, trade unionism began to be structured following two main concepts: the liberal type, in which "law took care of organising the system, regulating the means, not the ends," ensuring freedom of union and collective bargaining and sealing anti-union practices; and the Soviet-Leninist type, which rejected free-trade unionism and maintained trade unions controlled by the government (Nascimento 2005, p. 51-53).

The corporate trade union system led to the organisation of social classes through government regulatory actions and, according to Nascimento (2005, p. 54), invalidated the spontaneity of unionism. Its main techniques were: limitations on union plurality (union unity); official union framework imposed by the state; union recognition letter granted by the state in a discretionary way; and compulsory union dues, among others.

In both the liberal and the corporatist union systems, the strength of the union movements stems from their leaders' bargaining power, which is manifested in scenarios of claims and strikes, as well as in collective bargaining.

Trade unions contribute to the achievement and consolidation of social rights not only because they force public authorities to secure rights, but also because they secure specific guarantees and protections to their leaders through collective labour agreements. This second path has gained even greater relevance in times of economic or social crisis, like the current scenario of the new coronavirus pandemic.

Erik Olin Wright acknowledges the existence of two major sources of bargaining power that can be used by workers to enforce their interests regarding their employers: associational power and structural power (Wright 2000, p. 962).

Associational power derives from the collective organisation of workers through unions. Although not as effective as structural power, Wright believes that this is the main form of power given to workers in general because it is up to them, and only them, to build a strong organisation, so that any worker, in theory, can enjoy associational power.

On the other hand, workers may enjoy structural power only because of their position in the economic system, and this is subdivided into "power within the labour market" and "power within the workplace."

Power within the labour market results directly from restricted labour markets, whether due to scarce skills and high demand from employers, low levels of general unemployment, or workers' ability to exit the market and survive from sources of income other than their salaries.

Power within the workplace comes from the strategic location of a certain group of workers in a key industrial segment. This power is conferred on workers involved in well-integrated production processes, in which a stoppage at an essential point is capable of causing disruption at a much larger scale than at just that point. This is the case when entire production lines are hampered by unrest in only one of its segments, or when corporations that rely on just-in-time supply are completely paralysed by a strike by workers in the rail industry.

When workers began to use their bargaining power in defence of their interests in a systematised way, capital began to respond with three main measures, which follow a recurring pattern: spatial, technological or product/financial nature (Silver 2005, pp. 53-81).

The spatial solution is to shift the production to new locations where the workforce is relatively cheaper and more easily controllable. The technological solution consists of process innovation by introducing significant changes in production organisation, especially through automation, reducing dependence on human labour. Finally, the product solution is characterised by the displacement of capital to new segments and product lines less subject to competitiveness in more radical situations. Industry capital might migrate to financial speculation (financial solution).

The above-mentioned dynamics may have been responsible for weakening union movements around the world in recent decades. This crisis in trade union representation seems to have even more pronounced contours in developing countries, such as Brazil. This is what will be discussed below.

2. Crisis in Trade Union Representation

Even before the labour law reform of 2017 (Law No. 13,467/17) – which made it optional to pay union dues and, therefore, abruptly reduced the main source of funding of trade unions – it is possible to see evidence of a crisis of unionism.

A study conducted by the Brazilian Institute of Geography and Statistics (IBGE 2002, p. 29) shows that the rate of unionisation of the economically active population remained constant from 1992 to 2001, at 23%. However, the number of workers' unions has grown much more rapidly than that of unionised workers. As a result, the average size of labour unions, measured by the relationship between the number of members and trade unions, decreased between 1992 and 2001. By way of example, unions representing urban employees and liberal professionals shrank, respectively, by 23% and 19% (IBGE 2002, p. 30).

The downward trend of union activities, even before the 2017 reform, raises questions about the causes thereof. Among the culprits are employers, governments and the unions themselves. Fiorito, Jarley and Delaney explain:

> Among the "suspects" are union themselves. Various observers have cited undemocratic practices, insufficient rationalization, unwillingness to innovate, overly narrow goals, insufficient or poorly focused organizing effort, and reliance on a 'service model' of unions that fails to activate rank-and-file workers. [...] Although many of the criticisms are complementary, some are potentially in conflict: too little versus too much centralization, for example, or a need for greater rationalizations – operating in a more 'business-like' manner – versus a need for more democracy (Fiorito, Jarley & Delaney 1995, p. 614).

Peter Fairbrother and Charlotte Yates clarify that the trend of contraction of union participation is global and stems from structural factors, especially significant changes in the labour market, such as greater flexibilisation of labour standards and the migration of industrial activities to the services segment (Fairbrother & Yates 2003, p. 1).

But the most used argument to explain the alleged crisis of union movements is that, at the end of the 20th century, the hyper-mobility of productive capital established a peculiar labour market, in which workers around the world are compelled to compete with each other.

By moving – or simply threatening to move – production to other regions or countries, large corporations have created strong competitive pressure among the growing mass of disorganised workers, which has weakened workers' bargaining power, starting what Beverly Silver (2005, p. 21) calls the "race to the bottom" in terms of wages and working conditions on a global scale. The hyper-mobility of capital has indeed weakened the sovereignty of states. And when governments become unable to effectively control capital flows, their ability to protect the wellbeing of their citizens and some other workers' rights, including welfare state and substantive democracy, will also diminish (Silver 2005, pp. 21-22).

Bargaining power has weakened because governments that choose to maintain expensive social pacts are subject to mass abandonment of capital, as corporations worldwide prospect the highest possible return on their investments. From this point of view, the greatest consequence of the race to the bottom would be the pressure suffered by governments to reduce social welfare costs and provide the highest possible profitability in their territories, in order to attract (or maintain) investments (Martin & Schumann 1998, pp. 17-22).

Another argument supporting the existence of a crisis in union movements is based on the characteristics of the current productive market. During the 20th century, industrial activity was the highlight of the international market, but at the end of the 20th century and the beginning of the 21st century, the service segment became an important share of this market – which has become even more prominent with several new technologies.

According to the World Trade Organization (WTO 2012), in 2011 international trade in goods and services handled US$18.2 trillion and US$4.1 trillion, respectively. Of all business transactions in that year, 18.6% referred to services.

There is reasonable doubt around whether workers in this segment will have enough bargaining power to lead the trade union movements in the 21st century, as workers in the automotive industry did in the last century. This is because the services modality is generally intended for individual customers, and therefore workers are geographically dispersed. Thus, the workers in this segment have very little structural bargaining power in the workplace, which was precisely one of the main reasons for the great automobile union force in the 20th century.

When the structural bargaining power of workers is small, their victories will depend on strong associative power. It is possible for workers to be organised in strong trade unions, as is the case in some of these segments. Thus, despite little bargaining power in the workplace, associative bargaining power can strengthen structural market bargaining power, thus reinforcing the importance of the association of the view that the right to strike is an important tool in the search for balance between capital and labour relations.

In addition to the hyper-mobility of capital and the specific characteristics of the contemporary productive market, another relevant factor for the alleged crisis of the union movements is the growing individuality present in a "post-moralist society".

According to Gilles Lipovetsky, current individualism does not stem from greater selfishness of contemporary individuals, but rather from a greater social acceptance of the individualistic character of their preferences: "the novelty is precisely this: thinking only about themselves is no longer regarded as something immoral" (Lipovetsky 2005, p. 107).

While in the eyes of the moral ideal individuals do not enjoy rights, because they are only in charge of performing duties, the post-moralist culture overvalues the legitimacy of subjective rights and undermines the spirit of sacrifice, the ideal of giving precedence to others. The new individualist era atrophied in consciences the high regard that the altruistic ideal used to enjoy, redeemed self-centrism and legitimised the right to live only for oneself (Lipovetsky 2005, p. 107).

Often, the charitable-supportive spirit (minimalist and intermittent) becomes present only when there is some kind of identification between the individual, who gives himself, and the person or group receiving charity. Richard Rorty argues that the solidarity feeling finds its maximum intensity when those with whom we sympathise are recognised as "one of us" (Rorty 2007, pp. 314-315).

The expression "one of us" is adopted by Rorty to represent something more specific than merely belonging to the human race. According to him, people sympathise with each other not simply because they are all human beings, but in the presence of another element that subjectively gives them the feeling of closeness and belonging: nationality, age group, life history, family conditions or any other characteristics whereby a person identifies with another. And that is exactly why the union environment is conducive to restoring the spirit of solidarity, since several points of affinity are established among the unionised.

Michael Yates points out that the major union achievements in the 1930s in the United States were largely due to the basic principle that "an injury to one is an injury to all" (Yates 2009, p. 52). With the growing individualism present in society, this principle has lost strength and meaning.

Thus, trade unions must resume their spirit of a true "union movement", based on group identity. The expression "trade union movement" is used by Julius Getman (2010) in his work "Restoring the power of unions: it takes a movement" to designate something more than simple union activity.

Trade union movements presuppose activity empowered by the activism of unionised workers, producing a force that transcends money, affiliates and economic power:

> "Organized labor needs to rekindle the spirit of the activist member-powered movement that has guided its past successes. Organized labor today is a progressive interest group, but it is not a workers' movement. A "movement" entails something more than money, members, and economic power – all those factors are significant thought. A movement requires activating and using the energies of workers. It means fostering solidarity across unions and occupations. It requires leaders who are willing to trust and who are committed to sharing power with the union's rank and file. The spirit of movement also requires a concern for issues beyond the economic wellbeing of the members, such as environmental justice, racial equality, and the rights of immigrants" (Getman 2003, p. 1).

Thus, even if we recognise the existence of a series of factors that signal a crisis in union movements in these first decades of the 21st century, none of these elements is absolute or irreversible. It is in this sense that, in the 1990s, Fiorito, Jarley and Delaney stated: "Even if union decline is primarily due to external forces, there is little questioning that unions' responses have been largely ineffective" (Fiorito, Jarley & Delaney 1995, p. 614).

A study conducted by Peter Fairbrother and Charlotte Yates (2003, p. 2) showed that in the early 2000s, many national trade unions and labour movements in several countries were already undergoing a process of reevaluating their strategies in response to the crisis of trade unionism.

This strategic reassessment ushered in a period of rapid change for many unions in order to rebuild union movements and restore their strength to employers and governments. The main actions adopted were mergers between trade unions, attempts to organise non-union workers and, in some cases, tests of new forms of partnership between unions and companies (Fiorito Jarley & Delaney 1995, p. 614).

Rescuing union movements is imperative, especially in economic and/or social crisis scenarios, such as the one we are facing due to the coronavirus pandemic.

3. Freedom of Association and other Challenges: An Urgent Review of the Current Union Model in Brazil

3.1 Freedom of Association: The Basis of Trade Unions

In order to enable the rescue of union movements, as mentioned above, it is imperative to urgently review the Brazilian trade union model. The most elementary aspect of reform is implementing freedom of association, which can be considered the cornerstone of trade union organisation in the world.

Freedom of association is one of the pillars of trade union law. Through this fundamental guarantee, workers organise themselves for greater efficiency at collective bargaining (second pillar), the main assignment of unions in Brazil. They use strikes (third pillar) when necessary and as a last resort to "force the employer" to get to the bargaining table. But, as can be seen, it all revolves around a fundamental principle: freedom of association.

In other words, if the main function of unions is collective bargaining and the latter is their main *raison d'être*, freedom of association appears as the basis of collective self-protection and, therefore, their first generation fundamental law.

Freedom of association implies autonomy enjoyed by groups to organise themselves freely, according to their own interests, respecting the laws governing the country.

The debate involving freedom of association and collective bargaining itself is not only linked to the fundamental rights aspect and the guarantees thereof *vis-à-vis* the state, as will be seen later, but especially because of the importance that unions have in collective labour relations, in a scenario of permanent advancement and transformations of the labour laws to ensure the improvement of workers' conditions.

This has been demonstrated since the first unions emerged during the Industrial Revolution and has continued to this day. In this long trajectory, unions have proven their ability to overcome enormous obstacles and vicissitudes in such combative and conflicting relationship between capital and labour and in the permanent need for adaptation, especially nowadays, when there is an actual reconstruction of labour laws in progress.

Hence the importance of this topic in the field of international law, particularly from the tireless effort of the ILO (International Labour Organization) to provide a safe ground to serve as a basis for the actions of national governments, especially in view of the governability of collective labour disputes. In this sense, there is an important set of international rules as far as the ILO is concerned: Conventions 87 and 98, always referred to and celebrated, because they refer to certain sensitive aspects such as freedom of association and collective bargaining.

If international law, especially in the context of international labour conventions, is fertile in terms of flexibility and possible adaptability, favouring the adoption of its treaties by the most different countries, it is not in regard to certain doctrines, such as freedom of work, non-discrimination and, particularly, freedom of association. This principle is adamant, not subject to arrangements to accommodate anyone's interests. Its implementation is fundamental, not only in the scope of collective labour relations, but because of what it represents for strengthening and consolidating democracy in general and substantiating all fundamental rights in particular.

Oscar Ermida Uriarte points out three assumptions for implementing an appropriate union system: interdependence between trade union rights and other human rights; promotion of trade unionism and recognition of total freedom of association (Uriarte 2000, p. 116).

(i) interdependence between trade union rights and other human rights.

For the aforementioned author, the first presupposition for implementing freedom of association has to do with the effectiveness of human rights. This is because the development of freedom of association or its actual implementation depends on the pre-existence of other human rights and vice versa: freedom of association depends on the full exercise of human rights.

In other words, freedom of association is not self-sufficient – its existence depends on other civil and political freedoms – the latter constituting the basis of the former and at the same time thereby being conditioned. In this sense, the very effectiveness of individual rights depends on a system of effective freedom of association. Such freedom is so relevant that it is presented as an "indispensable element to real democracy" (Uriarte 2000, p. 117).

Ermida Uriarte also notes that democratic consolidation is not limited to political pluralism, as the effective implementation of the rule of law is linked to free actions by both trade unions and employers' associations. This is because trade union law is not only enforced by the recognition of freedom of association, it is also linked to "the freedoms of man as a whole" (Uriarte 2000, p. 118).

(ii) promotion of trade unionism.

According to Article 11 of Convention 87, member states that ratify it are obliged to take the necessary measures to ensure that workers and employers can freely exercise the right of unionisation. In other words, it is up to the member state to promote the organisation of the union[1], as well as to sanction laws supporting union activity.

(iii) recognition of total freedom of association.

There must be unrestricted freedom for the creation of trade unions, their organisation and membership. It also implies adequate protection for exercising freedom of association.

3.2 Freedom of Association in the Context of Public Freedoms

For Montesquieu, freedom is the good that allows individuals to enjoy the other individuals, which also applies to freedom of association.

Freedom of association was recognised in France only in 1884. Before that, there was no sense in discussing the topic because trade unions as we know them today simply did not exist (in this respect, cf. Israel 2005, p. 583).

According to Jean-Jacques Israel, the expression "public freedoms" has

---

[1] The Constitution of Uruguay has followed this line since 1934, as Oscar Ermida Uriarte points out.

been traditionally preferred to "human rights" in France since the 19th century, although the notion of human rights is older, as can be seen in the Declaration of Human and Citizen Rights of 1789 (Israel 2005, p. 6).

In Marcel Waline's teaching, public freedom corresponds to any and all faculties recognised and guaranteed to citizens by the constitution, or at least by law (Waline 1963, p. 651). Therefore, public freedoms indicate the set of civil and political rights to which citizens are entitled, and in the space of which the state can only practice abstention, as occurs with the right to property and the right to freedom of movement, among others.

According to Georg Jellinek, it is up to the state to recognise human rights to emphasise the positivist character thereof, to the detriment of a naturalistic view. Consequently, in addition to recognising the positivist character of these rights, they will take form in an unequal relationship between the individual and the state (Jellinek *apud* Ramos 2018, p. 55).

Within this perspective, one of the situations in which the individual comes before the state, in addition to the status of submission or subordination, is in the subjective status, which Jelinek calls *negative status libertatis*. According to André Ramos de Carvalho, here we are faced with a set of limits that are imposed on the government, forcing it to respect individuals' own rights in their private lives (Ramos 2018, p. 56).

According to this standing, the government is supposed to perform negative action, i.e., to abstain from acting. It is in this scenario that throughout history the limitations that individuals have imposed on monarchs and power holders since the Magna Carta of 1215 have been observed[2].

The theory of generations or dimensions of human rights was built in this perspective, but this study is only interested in those of the first generation, which imply negative actions by governments, with regard to the rights of freedom, integrated by so-called civil and political rights. They are related to the liberal revolutions, as André Ramos de Carvalho explains (Ramos 2018, p. 58).

Therefore, freedom of association, because it integrates the set of public freedoms, in addition to representing an important achievement for citizens in the face of the oppression of the state, is an expression of collective self-protection.

In this scenario of public freedoms, freedom of association gains greater contours when examining classical texts, such as in the writings by John Stuart Mill. The author was one of the most celebrated representatives of

---

[2] Signed by King John, better known as John Landless, before ecclesiastical authorities and barons. On this topic, for all, check COMPARATO, 2013.

the English liberal movement of his time, which he expressed in the book *On Liberty* (Mill 1859).

Celso Lafer, in the presentation of Mill's book, translated into Portuguese, addresses the distinction between modern freedom and ancient freedom. The latter, characterised by the participation of citizens in collective decisions, was based on the Athenian democratic model; the former is characterised by the power that individuals have to act within the framework provided by law, within the "sphere of non-impediment" scope that is aimed at imposing limits on power, and restricting the interference of people or even the government in the private sphere of individuals. According to Celso Lafer, Stuart Mill "deals basically with modern freedom, i.e. (...) the nature and limits of power that society can lawfully exercise over the individual" (Mill 1991 (orig. 1859), pp. 18-19).

According to Stuart Mill, even democratic processes with balance of powers are not free from oppression brought about by the "social tyranny of the majority", so it is essential to ensure spaces that will facilitate the expression of several forms of freedom, including freedom of association.

Stuart Mill does not address what is referred to as freedom from want, but only civil or social freedom, when examining what he calls the "nature and limits of power that society legitimately exercises over the individual". For the author, at the time, freedom was understood as "protection against the tyranny of political rulers", so that the community would draw the limits of power that would be tolerated by the ruler. But when the interest and will of the rulers were identified with those of the people, it would make no sense for the nation to protect itself against its own will (ibid, pp. 45-47).

However, the notion that "people need not limit their power over themselves" was possible when a popular government was nothing but a dream. In view of that, it is possible that some people might want to oppress part of their own, and there is need for caution against any type of abuse of power (ibid, p. 48).

Elizabeth Balbachevsky explains that in the lifetime of Stuart Mill (1806 to 1873) "the hearty question that challenged the imagination of English political elites was the 'peaceful' incorporation of the mass of workers depleted by industrialization, who knocked on the doors of the political system". In such a context, one must take into account the thoughts of Stuart Mill, whose work intends to be "a compromise between liberal thought and the democratic ideals of the 19th century": political participation is not a privilege of minorities. According to Elizabeth Balbachevsky, Stuart Mill is a pioneer with regard to two very dear concepts in political science: "defense of pluralism and social diversity against interference of the State and of public opinion (the latter, the tyranny of 'prevailing opinion', is the worst, because it is more systematic and recurrent); and the perspective of open, multipolar systems, in which the administration of dissent predominates over the imposition of broad consensuses" (Balbachevsky 1985, pp. 193-198).

As it turns out, although many view classical authors such as John Stuart Mill with skepticism, their reading remains obligatory, as it is still valid and inspiring.

3.3 The Distant Freedom of Association: A Revision of the Brazilian Model

Even in the 21st century, Brazil has not yet implemented freedom of association, resulting in serious damage to genuine collective bargaining, which ends up compromising the consolidation of democracy. But what can explain this omission?

In a seminal text, Amauri Mascaro Nascimento examines this issue in depth. He begins his argument by recognising undeniable efforts to implement modern trade union legislation, which ended up not happening. But in the face of new attacks, the matter deserves to be revisited (Nascimento 2007, p. 647).

Is it possible to identify and evaluate the causes of the failure to implement freedom of association? Nascimento asks: what are the problems that have made union reform impossible? Is the nature of such problems legal, political or both? But, after all, are the unions interested in such reform?

For Amauri Mascaro Nascimento, the first reason is cultural: the weight of this set of ideas about the union system is very heavy; it corresponds to inherited beliefs that our will does not seem to want to abandon. The preservation of this heritage by the unions is linked to something they do not want to give up.

For the author, there is also another level: the regulatory framework. There are records of laws from 1903 and 1907, which today have only historical value. Despite the repercussions of anarcho-syndicalism, the movement was muffled without leaving supporters. Our true history goes back to the "Estado Novo"[3], which laid the roots on which our unionism flourished. There is our "union genetic heritage", which has lasted to this

[3] *Estado Novo*, or the Third Brazilian Republic, was the Brazilian political regime established by Getúlio Vargas on November 10, 1937, which was in force until January 31, 1946, and which was characterised by the centralisation of power, nationalism, anti-communism and authoritarianism.

day, and the cradle of Brazilian unionism, on which unions have been shaped and become accustomed to surviving in the shadow of the government and without any kind of competitiveness.

The rupture with this corporate model, which should have already occurred in the 1946 Constitution, as occurred in European countries from which we partially copied such a model, was put on the agenda by the ABC[4] movement, in a strong confrontation with the military government in force in Brazil at the time.

The most significant union leaders of that time, among which Luiz Inácio Lula da Silva stands out, demanded prompt reform, dissatisfied with the continuity of the outdated union model. This movement gained strength when the National Labour Forum was installed (already under the administration of President Lula), with emphasis on important leaders, such as José Francisco Siqueira Neto. Osvaldo Martines Bargas was its coordinator and the Minister of Labour and Employment at the time, Ricardo Berzoini, its president. According to the movement, the proposed amendment to the constitution would "enable a broad union reform, within the principles of freedom and union autonomy."

The government at the time acknowledged the structural outdatedness of union laws and was committed to making changes. It intended to create free and autonomous unions in the face of the state, and thus promote collective bargaining with a view to resolving disputes and strengthening democracy. In order to implement broad freedom of association and union autonomy, it was necessary to overcome certain constitutional obstacles, especially Article 8 of the 1988 Brazilian Federal Constitution.

Therefore, in addition to the draft constitutional amendment, the National Labour Forum – a tripartite and equally-balanced body – was in charge of drafting the bill that would finally implement union reform. This bill was based on the so-called Final Report on Trade Union Reform, forwarded to the President of the Republic, in 2004.

Although ambitious, the bill was not even sent to the National Congress,

---

[4] The "ABC Paulista" is an industrial region located in Greater São Paulo, Brazil. The expression refers to three smaller cities south of São Paulo city: Santo André, São Bernardo do Campo, and São Caetano do Sul. The ABC region is widely known in Brazil and abroad because of the great number of international companies, particularly car manufacturers, in its area. National media and organisations consider ABC a powerful industrial pole and birthplace of the labour union movement that fought against dictatorship in the 1970s and 1980s. In this region the Workers' Party ("Partido dos Trabalhadores" - PT) was created the activities and popularity of which made the unionist Luiz Inácio Lula da Silva, or just Lula, known nationally. He became president of Brazil in 2002.

for several reasons, despite expectations that fuelled the hope that finally everything would be changed, as the political scenario was extremely favourable: the president of the Republic was the same union leader who had dared to rise up against the old regime in the ABC Paulista.

The failure of the National Labour Forum was not just the result of the complexity of the topics being proposed, which generated resistance and mistrust. It was more than that: it was Brazilians' old habit of resisting any kind of change that came into play. Moreover, the bill was nothing but an adjustment of old ties (which were criticised so much, but which Brazilian society was not prepared to address, and so continued with merely apparent changes). As Octavio Bueno Magano said, it was necessary to demolish this old building to facilitate the reconstruction of a new building, on flattened and clean land.

In short, as soon as it was published, the report of the National Forum "was condemned by the union bases,"[5] not only for the excess of powers conferred on the central unions, but by the unbalanced strengthening of union summits. Amauri Mascaro Nascimento concludes that the obstacle for the trade union movement to approve that bill was to import the "irradiation system of representativeness" (Nascimento 2007, p. 651).

Despite innovations, two points included in the Draft Union Relations Law that generated consternation can be highlighted: the matter of representativeness (art. 10); and the scope of action of the unions (which would be allowed up to the limit of the municipality – art. 14). It is clearly perceived that maintaining government intervention was considered important, according to the old expression: "everything within the State, nothing outside the State, nothing against the State".

Concerning the proposal for representativeness, as suggested by the aforementioned draft law, in order to better understand the intended setback, it is interesting to mention the case of Italy, where representativeness has become measured in the scenario of companies, not union summits, as in the proposal by the National Forum. In Italy, according to Article 19 of Law 300 of May 20, 1970, trade union representation can take place in any production unit, and 15 employees suffice (art. 35). In view thereof, Mattia Persianni concludes that the law sealed the aspiration of unions to be present in the factories (Persianni 2011, p. 51). For Amauri Mascaro Nascimento, this model of representation in Italy "results from the ability of the bases to impose themselves on the employer" (Nascimento 2007, p. 649).

As for the scope of union representation in Brazil, there is widespread

---

[5] It is curious to observe this reaction signalled by Prof. Nascimento: how did the unions react to a project in which they all participated?

fear, even today, of losing control of the unions if doors are opened for the organisation of business unions, which is a contradiction, if the desire to achieve freedom of association is sincere. But it is well known that this was the formula found to make the leadership of traditional unions unviable while at the same time strengthening the central unions. In short, everyone wants to change, as long as everything remains as it has always been.

Final Comments

This analysis highlighted the important historical role played by unions in achieving better working conditions. Social movements, especially strikes and collective labour negotiations, have made it possible for several rights to be obtained and government standards to be adapted from the general to the particularities of each economic activity or locality.

This important role is even more relevant during times of crisis. Truly effective and representative trade union movements have the power to mitigate the damaging effects that social and economic crises cause, contributing not only to the improvement of working conditions, but also to the maintenance of jobs.

The coronavirus pandemic is an excellent example of how collective rules regulating telework and work carried out from home have become usual in Brazil, securing the necessary legal basis.

The relevance of trade unions in times of crisis shows how important it is to strengthen social movements that, as discussed above, have been facing their own crisis of representativeness for years. To this end, it is imperative to reform the Brazilian trade union system in order to break with constitutional limitations and democratise the organisation of trade unions.

Undoubtedly, the main premise of this reform is implementing freedom of association, as recommended by the ILO, among other international players. However, the main challenge is not legal, but cultural.

Bibliography

Balbachevsky, Elizabeth, "Stuart Mill: liberdade e representação", In *Os clássicos da política*, organised by Wefort, Francisco C. (São Paulo: Ática, 1985)

Bobbio, Norberto, *A era dos Direitos* (Rio de Janeiro: Editora Elsevier, 2004)

Comparato, Fábio Konder, *A afirmação histórica dos direitos humanos* (São Paulo: Saraiva, 2013)

Ermida Uriarte, Oscar, *La Flexibilidad* (Montevideo: Fundación de Cultura Universitaria, 2000)

Fairbrother, Peter & Yates, Charlotte A. B. Unions in crisis, unions in renewal? In *Trade unions in renewal – a comparative study*, coordinated by Fairbrother, Peter & Yates, Charlotte A. B.) (New York: Continuum, 2003)

Fausto, Boris, *História do Brasil* (São Paulo: Editora da Universidade de São Paulo, 2003)

Fiorito, Jack, Jarley, Paul & Delaney, John Thomas, "National union effectiveness in organizing: measures and influences," In *Industrial and Labor Relations Review,* Vol. 48, No. 4, July (1995)

Getman, Julius, *Restoring the power of unions: it takes a movement* (New Haven: Yale University Press, 2010)

IBGE, *Sindicatos: indicadores sociais 2001* (Rio de Janeiro: IBGE, 2002)

Israel, Jean-Jacquies, *Direito das Liberdades Fundamentais* (São Paulo: Manole, 2005)

Lafer, Celso, "Apresentação à obra", In Mill, John Stuart, *Sobre a Liberdade*, (Ed. Petrópolis, Ed. Vozes, 1991)

Lipovetsky, Gilles, *A sociedade pós-moralista: o crepúsculo do dever e a ética indolor dos novos tempos democráticos* (São Paulo: Manole, 2005)

Maior, Jorge Luiz Souto, *História do Direito do Trabalho no Brasil: Curso de Direito do Trabalho, Volume I: Parte II* (São Paulo: LTr, 2017)

Martin, Hans-Peter & Schumann, Harald, *A armadilha da globalização: o assalto à democracia e ao bem-estar social* (São Paulo: Globo, 1998)

Mill, John Stuart, *Sobre a Liberdade* (Ed. Petrópolis, Ed. Vozes, 1991)

Nascimento, Amauri Mascaro, *Compêndio de Direito Sindical* (São Paulo: LTr, 2005)

Nascimento, Amauri Mascaro, "Problemas que dificultam a reforma sindical", In *Revista LTr*, vol 71, no. 6, junho (2007)

Persianni, Mattia, *Diritto Sindacale* (Pádua: CEDAM, 2011)

Prado Junior, Caio, *História Econômica do Brasil* (São Paulo: Editora Brasiliense, 2008)

Ramos, André de Carvalho, *Curso de Direitos Humanos* (São Paulo: Saraiva, 2018)

Rorty, Richard, *Contingência, ironia e solidariedade* (São Paulo: Martins Fontes, 2007)

Silver, Beverly, *Forças do trabalho: movimentos de trabalhadores e globalização desde 1870* (São Paulo: Boitempo, 2005)

Waline, Marcel, *Droit Administratif* (Paris: Sirey, 1963)

World Trade Organization, *World Trade Report 2012,* online http://www.wto.org/english/res_e/booksp_e/anrep_e/world_trade_report12_e.pdf

Wright, Erik Olin, "Working-class power, capitalist-class interests, and class compromise", In *American Journal of Sociology*, v. 105, n. 4, January (2000)

Yates, Michael D, *Why unions matter* (New York: monthly review press, 2009)

Chapter 12

O Direito Fundamental à Adaptação Razoável em Casos de Discriminação de Minorias nas Relações de Trabalho*[1]

Alexandre Agra Belmonte

Introdução

O que têm em comum as pretensões de usar barba por motivo religioso em restaurante que não admite o uso por questões de higiene; da mulher, de usar véu islâmico no trabalho ou ali o muçulmano de ter pausas durante a jornada para rezar; o judeu, o adventista do sétimo dia e o muçulmano, de folgarem no dia correspondente às suas crenças; do deficiente físico, de também lhe ser possibilitado lavar a marmita na copa, como os demais trabalhadores, e não somente no banheiro, único lugar onde a altura da pia permite a prática?

Assim como ocorre na sociedade, o ambiente de trabalho é plural e envolve várias circunstâncias, porque reúne pessoas com crenças, hábitos, tradições e ideologias as mais diversas.

No entanto, não atender aos reclamos das chamadas minorias, quando possível, é comportamento que encontra justificativa de recusa meramente num padrão que deve ser seguido ou, ao contrário, pode significar tratamento diferenciado em relação a esses trabalhadores, por serem componentes de minorias com crenças ou necessidades peculiares?

O dilema a ser enfrentado é, portanto, o fato de que atender a diferenças de minorias pode significar uma interferência na forma de estruturar o empreendimento. O que coloca em xeque o poder diretivo do empregador, a quem cabe organizar por conta própria a atividade, estabelecer a disciplina de conduta ambiental e o serviço a ser feito, o *modus faciendi*, fiscalizar o cumprimento e penalizar o descumprimento. Mas, por outro lado, não

---

* First published in *Revista de Direito do Trabalho e Seguridade Social*, vol. 218, ano 47, julho/agosto (São Paulo: Editora Revista dos Tribunais, 2021): 19-55.

atendê-las coloca em xeque o exercício de direitos fundamentais garantidos pela Constituição Federal.

Estará a sociedade preparada para encontrar regras de convivência que superem, de lado a lado, as diferenças ou, em outras palavras, o preconceito e o estigma que podem levar à intolerância e à discriminação em relação aos trabalhadores que não se encaixam num padrão médio ou socialmente aceito?

Em casos como esses, a ponderação de princípios em antinomia, normalmente utilizada em comparação de interesses fundamentais, para estabelecimento de uma proporcionalidade, importaria em que esse sopesamento poderia acabar inibindo um deles para permitir a concretização do outro, se utilizada a ponderação de princípios em antinomia.

No entanto, a Teoria do Impacto Desproporcional, pela especificidade de aplicação a situações de discriminação de minorias, está fundada nos efeitos discriminatórios indiretos de uma norma ou situação de fato, sendo potencialmente apta a dar tratamento capaz de propiciar a conciliação ou acomodação de interesses contrapostos, por meio de uma solução intermediária, que realize simultaneamente os interesses antinômicos.

Tentaremos neste artigo demonstrar a viabilidade da utilização da Teoria da Adaptação Razoável como apta a acomodar múltiplos interesses, permitindo ao empregador, sem abrir mão do seu poder diretivo contido no direito fundamental ao exercício da livre iniciativa, por meio da assunção de um ônus razoável, possibilitar que o trabalhador possa exercer um direito que sem essa adaptação, na organização da empresa, lhe seria impossível usufruir.

Ao final, investigaremos um acórdão em que, como relator, pioneiramente utilizamos a teoria para solucionar a pretensão de uma mãe, de se ausentar do trabalho para acompanhar na terapia um filho portador de síndrome de Down, procedimento indispensável para o seu desenvolvimento sadio e potencial melhoria de integração social.

Evidentemente, para se chegar à possibilidade de utilização prática da teoria da adaptação razoável, é preciso reavivar alguns conceitos, o que faremos a seguir.

Direitos fundamentais

Inspirada na Revolução Americana de 1776 e nas ideias iluministas, em meio à Revolução Francesa foi editada em 26 de agosto de 1789 a Declaração dos Direitos do Homem e do Cidadão. Ela proclamou as liberdades e os direitos fundamentais do homem, estabelecendo, no art.1º, que eles são livres e iguais em direitos (França, *Déclaration des Droits de l'Homme et du Citoyen*, Assembleia Nacional Constituinte, 1789: https://br.ambafrance.org/A-Declaracao-dos-Direitos-do-Homem-e-do-Cidadao, acesso em 20 de julho de 2021).

Portanto, os direitos fundamentais podem, numa primeira abordagem, ser agrupados em três dimensões distintas. Essas dimensões seguem os postulados da Revolução Francesa de 1789: liberdade, igualdade e fraternidade (ou solidariedade).

Os direitos de primeira dimensão, nascidos no Estado Liberal, decorrem da reação aos excessos do absolutismo, com inspiração no liberalismo político e no individualismo jurídico. Trata-se de dimensão de direitos baseada na defesa ou proteção contra as intervenções coativas estatais na esfera jurídica privada, e na igualdade. São os direitos civis ou pessoais (direitos e garantias individuais) e os direitos políticos (liberdades públicas), caracterizando, no conjunto, os direitos humanos.

São, portanto, direitos humanos os direitos básicos, inatos e universais de proteção ou defesa da liberdade e igualdade, inerentes à pessoa humana. Destinam-se a resguardar a integridade física, moral e psicológica da pessoa perante seus semelhantes e o Estado, garantindo-lhe a dignidade e o bem estar social, sem discriminação de qualquer espécie. Tais direitos, fundamentais por natureza, são, basicamente, aqueles previstos no artigo 5º, da Constituição Federal de 1988 e os incorporados ao ordenamento por força de tratados internacionais aprovados pelo Brasil.

Direitos humanos e direitos fundamentais, contudo, não se confundem. Os direitos humanos são, por natureza, fundamentais, mas a abrangência destes é maior.

Direitos fundamentais são os direitos essenciais positivados na esfera da ordem constitucional de determinado Estado, assegurados por um conjunto de princípios e regras de enunciação e de garantias, que lhes confere um regime jurídico diferenciado de imediata observância e concretização.

Direitos humanos, por sua vez, são os direitos inatos e assim naturalmente indispensáveis e inalienáveis em relação a qualquer ser humano, integrando a moral jurídica universal. *"A vigência dos direitos humanos independe de sua declaração em constituições, leis e tratados internacionais, exatamente porque se está diante de exigências de respeito à dignidade humana exercidas contra todos os poderes estabelecidos, oficiais ou não"* (Comparato 2008, p. 227).

Direitos humanos e direitos fundamentais também podem ser diferenciados com base no critério da titularidade: direitos humanos têm sempre como titular a pessoa natural, mas os direitos fundamentais podem ser atribuídos também a pessoas jurídicas e sujeitos de direitos que não integram a espécie humana. As pessoas jurídicas têm direito fundamental à livre iniciativa, ao nome, ao devido processo legal e à imagem, por exemplo.

Compreendemos assim como direitos fundamentais os positivados na ordem constitucional, conforme o momento histórico, político, cultural e social, para garantir integral defesa e realização material e espiritual do homem, individual e coletivamente. A garantia do FGTS é direito fundamental na Constituição Federal brasileira de 1988 e não o é em outras constituições de épocas anteriores. Também não é direito de reconhecimento internacional, como ocorre com os direitos humanos, embora fundamental na referida Carta Magna.

Enfim, os direitos humanos são fundamentais, mas nem todo direito fundamental é direito humano em sentido estrito. O trabalhador tem, além dos direitos humanos previstos no art. 5º da Constituição Federal de 1988 (liberdade de trabalho, vedação à escravidão), os direitos fundamentais inseridos nos artigos 7º a 11. E as pessoas jurídicas podem ser detentoras de direitos fundamentais, a exemplo do nome, da imagem, da livre iniciativa, da recuperação econômica e do segredo empresarial.

Entendemos como direitos fundamentais, na dimensão juslaborativa, as prerrogativas de que os trabalhadores necessitam, no relacionamento com o Estado e nas relações privadas de trabalho, para lhes assegurar uma existência livre, igualitária, fraterna e socialmente justa e lhes oportunizar o alcance da realização material e espiritual.

Os direitos de segunda dimensão dão prosseguimento ao processo de afirmação dos direitos do homem. Situados em momento histórico a partir de 1917 (Revolução russa e Carta Mexicana, Carta de Weimar - 1919, Grande Depressão 1929), caracterizam-se pela busca da igualdade material ou real que visou minorar os desajustes sociais decorrentes do liberalismo. São, pois, os direitos sociais. Eles foram implementados pelo interventor Estado Social, visando a pacificação dos conflitos derivados da Questão Social.

Esses direitos compreendem aqueles em que o homem é partícipe de coletividades, assim os direitos sociais, econômicos e culturais. Entre os sociais, destacam-se educação, saúde, moradia, segurança, lazer, trabalho, segurança, previdência social, proteção à maternidade, aos desempregados e à infância.

Como tais direitos requerem disponibilidade orçamentária, investimentos e programas governamentais visando melhor distribuição de renda, diminuição dos abismos sociais, assistência social e incentivos à busca do pleno emprego para o alcance de uma vida digna, isso exige a cobrança por uma atuação do Estado em prol da respectiva concretização e progressão. Daí porque esses direitos têm conteúdo prestacional, de natureza positiva, de postura promocional ativa do Estado.

Os direitos de terceira dimensão coincidem com o surgimento de um novo modelo de Estado, não um estado interventor, mas sim promotor, que requer a participação da sociedade, que é o Estado Democrático de Direito, decorrente de uma série de fatores iniciados nos anos 70: a crise do petróleo, o esvaziamento do Estado, a globalização, o colapso do comunismo e a extinção do modelo bipolar. Correspondem aos direitos metaindividuais de fraternidade ou solidariedade. Decorrem do avanço da tecnologia e do surgimento das sociedades de massa. São os direitos coletivos e difusos, como os direitos à paz, ao desenvolvimento, ao meio ambiente, de comunicação, de defesa do consumidor e de propriedade sobre o patrimônio comum da humanidade e ao direito de comunicação.

O fato dos direitos fundamentais constituírem garantias do cidadão contra o Estado, não significa que também não devam ser proporcionalmente observados em suas relações particulares.

A respeito, Daniel Sarmento observa: *"reconhece a doutrina contemporânea a existência de uma dupla dimensão dos direitos fundamentais, porque este constituem, simultaneamente, fonte de direitos subjetivos que podem ser reclamados em juízo e as bases fundamentais da ordem jurídica, que se expandem para a proteção e promoção dos ideais humanitários que alicerçam os direitos fundamentais, os quais serão enriquecidos com o reconhecimento da sua dimensão objetiva"* (Sarmento 2006, p. 107).

Daí decorre que já não mais satisfaz ao homem e às coletividades em que agrupados, a postura estatal passiva, de se abster de violar os direitos fundamentais. É preciso que os Poderes Públicos os protejam contra as agressões e ameaças provindas de terceiros, assim transcendendo o domínio das relações entre cidadãos, para expandir a aplicação dos direitos fundamentais ao âmbito das relações privadas.

Enfim, se os direitos fundamentais norteiam as ações e limitam a ingerência do Estado nas relações com os cidadãos, devem igualmente repercutir nas relações entre particulares, de forma a limitar os abusos que possam afrontar a eficácia das garantias estabelecidas na Constituição. Assim é que se os cidadãos têm direito à saúde, à integridade física e à vida, o empregador, na relação de trabalho estabelecida com o empregado, precisa prevenir o ambiente de trabalho contra os riscos da insalubridade e insegurança, respondendo inclusive pelas doenças profissionais e acidentes típicos do trabalho causados em decorrência da prestação de serviços.

Há doutrinadores defendem a existência dos direitos de quarta dimensão. Em sua visão vanguardista seriam os direitos decorrentes da globalização política, relacionados à democracia, à informação e ao pluralismo (Bonavides 2006, p. 563).

E há doutrinadores que vão além, ao defenderem a existência de uma quinta dimensão: direito à paz, decorrente do terrorismo; e da intolerância de crença e costumes (Honesko 2008, p. 195 e seg.).

Antinomia ou colisão de princípios e direitos fundamentais

Na aplicação ao caso concreto, pode ocorrer antinomia ou aparente colisão de princípios e direitos constitucionais, diante do confronto de interesses contrapostos, ambos justificados pelo exercício de direitos fundamentais. Nesta hipótese, incide o caráter interpretativo dos princípios, a exemplo dos princípios da proporcionalidade e da razoabilidade, que devem ser utilizados na busca da harmonização ou da identificação do direito fundamental capaz de realizar, nas circunstâncias, os objetivos da Constituição.

Com efeito, a Constituição Federal de 1988 enuncia direitos fundamentais e princípios que no caso concreto podem entrar em aparente choque, mormente diante de normas polissêmicas. Essa antinomia de normas constitucionais pode ocorrer entre princípios constitucionais, entre direitos fundamentais e entre direitos fundamentais e outros valores e interesses constitucionais.

Quer diante de normas polissêmicas, que geram várias significações, para se interpretá-las visando a que garanta maior eficácia e ao mesmo tempo se evite o sacrifício total de um bem jurídico em relação a outros; quer diante do aparente choque entre princípios, direitos fundamentais e entre direitos fundamentais e outros valores e interesses constitucionais, é preciso, por um lado, fazer-se ponderação, segundo critérios de peso e importância, para o alcance da melhor proporção entre os meios utilizados e os fins perseguidos e, por outro, mediante utilização de critérios de equidade, encontrar-se solução razoável, numa justa medida de adequação.

A finalidade dos direitos fundamentais é assegurar que a pessoa seja tratado de forma digna perante o Estado e em repercussão horizontal, nas relações privadas.

O princípio da dignidade da pessoa humana

Quando se diz que a Constituição de 88 colocou a pessoa humana no centro das relações jurídicas, é porque, nos termos do inciso III do art.1º, A república Federativa do Brasil, consubstanciada em Estado Democrático de Direito, tem como um de seus fundamentos a *dignidade da pessoa humana*. Toda a normatividade contida na Constituição está voltada a assegurar esse valor social, porque só assim o indivíduo pode vir a ostentar a condição de ser integral, capaz de se realizar material e espiritualmente.

Não bastasse, enuncia o art.170, da Constituição Federal, que a ordem econômica tem limites e um deles é de natureza moral. Daí a garantia constitucional de que a livre iniciativa deve atuar de forma a assegurar a todos *existência digna*, conforme os ditames da justiça social.

A dignidade da pessoa humana consiste no respeito às qualidades essenciais que caracterizam a sua integral existência. Uma existência digna é a que permite à pessoa humana, sem discriminação e com preservação dos atributos que compõem a sua integridade física, moral e intelectual, uma atuação individual dotada de vontade livre, de modo a permitir o desenvolvimento da sua autonomia espiritual, bem como um tratamento igualitário, justo e solidário, que lhe permita uma real participação social capaz de influir no próprio destino e no da sociedade em que vive.

A dignidade deve, portanto, considerar o sujeito: a) em seu aspecto moral, ou seja, em igualdade de condições perante os demais, sem discriminação de qualquer espécie e pleno acesso aos bens e oportunidades; b) em sua integridade psicofísica, de maneira que preserve os direitos da personalidade; c) no respeito à sua liberdade, de forma a permitir a autodeterminação de escolhas individuais; e, d) em sua consideração como parte do grupo social que integra, a exigir o respeito a um tratamento justo e solidário, que lhe garanta a igualdade substancial.

O respeito à legislação trabalhista e à pessoa do trabalhador é condição para o desenvolvimento sustentável da sociedade e para o cumprimento dos objetivos fundamentais do Estado Democrático Constitucional brasileiro, constantes do art. 3º da Lei Maior – bem como para a observância dos princípios fundamentais da República, em especial o respeito aos valores sociais do trabalho e à dignidade da pessoa humana (Constituição Federal da República Federativa do Brasil de 1988, artigo 1º, III e IV).

A dignidade da pessoa humana é o "*princípio mais relevante de nossa ordem jurídica, que lhe confere unidade de sentido e de valor, devendo por isso condicionar e inspirar a exegese e aplicação de todo o direito vigente, público ou privado. Além disso, o princípio em questão legitima a ordem jurídica, centrando-se na pessoa humana, que passa a ser concebida como 'valor-fonte fundamental de Direito'. Desta forma, alicerça-se o direito positivo sobre profundas bases éticas, tornando-o merecedor do título de 'direito justo*" (Sarmento 2006, p. 86).

Para Arion Sayão Romita a dignidade da pessoa humana é "*a pedra filosofal dos direitos fundamentais. Não constitui um direito fundamental: é o valor que possui a maravilhosa propriedade de dar nascimento aos direitos fundamentais e de lhes atribuir sentido*" (Romita 2007, p. 156).

A dignidade da pessoa humana é, assim, o fundamento último dos direitos humanos, podendo ser compreendidos os direitos fundamentais como manifestações da dignidade da pessoa humana. Quando houver violação de direito fundamental, seja a qual for a família ou dimensão a que esse direito pertença, haverá, por conseguinte ofensa à dignidade da pessoa humana.

Discriminação

Neste ponto do estudo nos dirigimos de forma mais concreta ao seu objetivo de encontrar aplicações para a teoria da adaptação razoável na resolução de certos conflitos entre direitos fundamentais e para os quais os princípios da proporcionalidade e da razoabilidade não teriam aplicação adequada.

O contrato de trabalho é, por natureza, inibitório de direitos fundamentais, a partir do momento em que, diante da subordinação jurídica e da pessoalidade que o caracteriza, boa parcela de autonomia se esvai, tornando-o hipossuficiente. Some-se a esse aspecto o fato do trabalhador ser estrangeiro, islâmico, do sexo feminino, negra, homossexual e deficiente física. Ou contar com pelo menos alguma ou algumas dessas características.

Seria um contrassenso o trabalhador ser, como cidadão, um ser integral igual aos demais e dotado de liberdade, mas não sê-lo no ambiente de trabalho, onde lhe seriam negados direitos como as liberdades de crença e expressão, de orientação sexual, de igualdade de gênero e, dependendo de sua capacidade física, de mobilidade e adaptação para o acesso ao trabalho. Daí a garantia dos direitos fundamentais assegurados por atitudes prestacionais do Estado, destinados, por exemplo, a possibilitar aos deficientes físicos aceder ao mercado de trabalho ou a dar igualdade de tratamento em relação aos demais aspectos. Mas, ainda assim, um sem número de situações, inclusive em relação aos deficientes físicos, não encontra abrigo expresso, exigindo interpretação e concretização sob a ótica da superação à discriminação indireta ou silenciosa.

A Organização Internacional do Trabalho - OIT foi criada pelo Tratado de Paz assinado em Versalhes, em Junho de 1919. A OIT é a agência mais antiga do Sistema das Nações Unidas. Foi constituída com o objetivo de definir e promover políticas sociais em nível internacional, numa fase marcada pela revolução industrial.

Em 02 de maio de 1944, a Conferência Internacional do Trabalho, por meio da Assembleia-Geral da Organização, reunida em Filadélfia, nos Estados-Unidos, aprovou declaração relativa aos fins e objetivos da OIT, conhecida pela Declaração de Filadélfia. Ela reafirma os princípios orientadores da OIT, inspiradora da política a ser adotado pelos países membros e que são os seguintes:

- o trabalho não é uma mercadoria;
- a liberdade de expressão e de associação é uma condição indispensável para um progresso constante;
- a pobreza, onde quer que exista, constitui um perigo para a prosperidade de todos;
- todos os seres humanos, qualquer que seja a sua raça, a sua crença ou o seu sexo, têm direito de efetuar o seu progresso material e o seu desenvolvimento espiritual em liberdade e com dignidade, com segurança econômica e com oportunidades iguais.

Por meio do Decreto Legislativo nº 24, de 1956, o Congresso Nacional aprovou a Convenção no. 100, OIT, vindo a ser promulgada pelo Presidente da República por meio do Decreto nº 41.721 em 25 de junho de 1957. Adotada pela Conferência em sua Trigésima Quarta Sessão, em Genebra, a 29 de junho 1951, ela prevê a igualdade de remuneração para a mão de obra masculina e feminina por um trabalho de igual valor.

A Convenção nº 111, OIT, adotada pelos países membros em Genebra, em 25 de Junho de 1958, foi aprovada pelo Congresso Nacional através do Decreto Legislativo nº 104, de 1964 e promulgada pelo Presidente da República por meio do Decreto nº 62.150, de 19 de janeiro de 1968.

A referida Convenção repudia qualquer distinção, exclusão ou preferência que tenha por fim alterar a igualdade de oportunidades ou tratamento em matéria de emprego ou profissão.

A Constituição da República Federativa do Brasil, de 1988, em seu preâmbulo, demonstra destinar-se a assegurar, entre outros valores, *"a igualdade e a justiça como valores supremos de uma sociedade fraterna, pluralista e sem preconceitos"* (Brasil, Constituição da República Federativa, 1988).

O direito fundamental à igualdade, previsto no art.5º, *caput*, da referida Carta Magna determina que *"todos são iguais perante a lei, sem distinção de qualquer natureza, garantindo-se aos brasileiros e aos estrangeiros residentes no País a inviolabilidade do direito à vida, à liberdade, à igualdade, à segurança e à propriedade, nos termos seguintes: I – homens e mulheres são iguais em direitos e obrigações, nos termos desta Constituição."* (Brasil, Constituição da República Federativa, 1988).

A conjugação do art.5º, caput e inciso I com o art.3º, IV da referida fonte constitucional, leva ao princípio da isonomia, quer na vertente da igualdade, quer na da não discriminação.

O princípio da não discriminação atua tanto na preservação do direito à diferença, como na eliminação de tratamento injustificadamente diferenciado.

Em termos de igualdade, a Constituição Federal de 1988 não está se referindo à igualdade formal proposta pelo Estado Liberal, limitada à utilização de critério uniforme de tratamento, mas à igualdade do modelo de Estado Social, recepcionada e desenvolvida pelo Estado Democrático de Direito, em que a intervenção estatal, por meio de medidas positivas coercitivas ou incentivatórias, prevê meios destinados ao tratamento das desigualdades com igual valor, na busca da igualdade material e que, no modelo de Estado Democrático de Direito, atua de forma a garantir a dignidade da pessoa humana.

A respeito, *"a igualdade que orienta o Direito laboral não é a igualdade formal e abstrata do liberalismo, segundo a qual "todos são iguais perante a lei" – uma lei cega que não distingue entre pobres e ricos, entre poderosos e débeis, entre possuidores e despossuídos – senão a igualdade real ou material, que intenta corrigir aquelas diferenças"* (Uriarte 2011, prefácio, XII).

Mas a Constituição Federal vai além e veda a discriminação, ao determinar, no art.3°, inciso IV, que constituem objetivos fundamentais da República Federativa do Brasil, entre outros, promover o bem de todos, sem preconceitos de origem, raça, cor, sexo, idade e outras formas de discriminação (como nacionalidade, naturalidade, orientação sexual, opção política, religiosa, ideologia etc).

Discriminação, portanto, pode ser definida como a conduta atentatória e injustificada da igualdade de oportunidades ou de tratamento, destinada a distinguir pessoas ou grupos com base em preconceito, estigma ou outro meio de desqualificação.

> *"O princípio da igualdade é o maior, que inclui o de não discriminação. Este é um derivado daquele, uma concreção, efeito ou reflexo da igualdade ... um instrumento da igualdade ... a igualdade opera verticalmente (reduzindo a diferença entre capital e trabalho), enquanto que a não discriminação opera horizontalmente, procurando que não se prejudique (ainda mais) aos trabalhadores mais débeis ou expostos"* (Uriarte 2011, prefácio, XV).

De forma prática, como corolário do princípio da isonomia, não se admite a distinção entre trabalho manual, técnico e intelectual (art.7°, XXXII, Constituição Federal); a mesma Constituição Federal atribui igualdade de direitos entre o trabalhador com vínculo empregatício permanente e o trabalhador avulso (art.7°, XXXIV); a todo trabalho de igual valor corresponderá o mesmo salário (art.461, da CLT[1]); o art.3°, parágrafo único,

[1] Brasil, Decreto Lei n° 5.452, de 1° de maio de 1943 (Consolidação das Leis do

CLT, veda distinções à espécie de emprego, condição do trabalhador e ao trabalho intelectual, técnico e manual; os arts. 460 e 461, CLT, dispõem, respectivamente, sobre salário equitativo e equiparação salarial sem distinção de qualquer natureza, ressalvadas as hipóteses justificadas por lei e quadro de carreira; e, o art.12, a, da Lei nº 6.019/74,[2] determina a isonomia remuneratória do trabalhador temporário aos trabalhadores efetivos do tomador.

Já o tratamento diferenciado por motivo de gênero, raça, etnia, cor, religião, idade, naturalidade, nacionalidade, orientação sexual ou política, origem social, deficiência física ou qualquer outro parâmetro desqualificante da pessoa, decorre de ofensa ao princípio da não discriminação. A título de exemplo, o artigo 7º, XXX (proibição de diferença de salários, de exercício de funções e de critério de admissão por motivo de sexo, idade, cor ou estado civil), XXXI, da Constituição Federal de 1988 (proibição de qualquer discriminação no tocante a salário e critérios de admissão do trabalhador portador de deficiência) e a Lei nº 9.029/95,[3] que proíbe a exigência de atestados de gravidez e esterilização, e outras práticas discriminatórias, para efeitos admissionais ou de permanência da relação jurídica de trabalho, e dá outras providências, vedam especificamente essa espécie de discriminação como impeditivo ao tratamento igualitário. Os concursos públicos são democráticos porque permitem o acesso sem qualquer tipo de discriminação e de forma positiva ainda facilitam, contornando os obstáculos, que a eles concorram deficientes físicos.

Tipos de discriminação

Ao mesmo tempo em que a Constituição Federal de 1988 estabelece a punição por qualquer discriminação atentatória dos direitos e liberdades fundamentais (art.5º, XLI) ou estabelece a proibição de qualquer discriminação no tocante a salário e critérios de admissão do trabalhador portador de deficiência (art.7º, XXXI), dá competência concorrente à União, aos Estados e ao Distrito Federal para legislar sobre a proteção e integração social das pessoas portadoras de deficiência (art.24, XIV) e estabelece reserva, por lei, de percentual dos cargos e empregos públicos para as pessoas portadoras de deficiência (art.37, VIII). Ou seja, a não

Trabalho), disponível em http://www.planalto.gov.br/ccivil_03/decreto-lei/del5452.htm, acesso em 20/07/2021.

[2] Brasil, Lei nº 6.019, de 3 de janeiro de 1974), disponível em http://www.planalto.gov.br/ccivil_03/leis/l6019.htm, acesso em 20/07/2021.

[3] Brasil, Lei nº 9.029, de 13 de abril de 1995), disponível em http://www.planalto.gov.br/ccivil_03/leis/l9029.htm, acesso em 20/07/2021.

discriminação pode se apresentar de forma negativa, com base na proibição de tratamento injustificadamente diferenciado, ou de forma positiva, em que o Estado, de forma prestacional, age para possibilitar o tratamento sem discriminação.

Para Sidney Madruga "o caráter negativo traduz-se na vedação da discriminação, que em determinadas circunstâncias poderia gerar desigualações indesejáveis. É o caso da igualdade de direitos entre homens e mulheres; (...) a proibição de qualquer discriminação no tocante a salário e critérios de admissão ao trabalhador 'portador de deficiência', dentre outros" (Madruga 2016, p. 99 e seg.).

Já o caráter positivo decorre do princípio da igualdade material estabelecido na Constituição. "O texto constitucional discrimina positivamente, para promover a igualdade de oportunidades e afastar os fatores de desigualdades entre os menos protegidos: (...) na reserva percentual de cargos e empregos públicos às pessoas portadoras de deficiência (Madruga 2016, p. 100).

As políticas afirmativas decorrem do caráter positivo da discriminação, para concretizar a igualdade de oportunidades ou que todos possam exercer os seus direitos fundamentais. Em relação às chamadas minorias, é o meio adequado a compensar discriminações culturalmente arraigadas, como forma de desmistificar os preconceitos sociais e investir numa consciência coletiva plural e heterogênea. Também chamadas de políticas de reconhecimento fundadas na constatação de que a igualdade de tratamento muitas vezes não se mostra capaz de materializar a isonomia *in concreto*, objetivam assim corrigir desigualações sociais em relação a grupos historicamente estigmatizados pela sociedade e pelo Estado.

Chega-se à conclusão de que o princípio da isonomia tem por fim estabelecer igualações e desigualações para que todos possam exercer os seus direitos fundamentais e assim garantir a dignidade ou bem estar de todos. É deveras angustiante se sentir humilhado, injustiçado, estigmatizado ou escanteado por não ser tratado de forma igual ou não poder ter acesso às mesmas oportunidades dos demais em razão de uma característica física, territorial, intelectual ou espiritual.

Mas há outro aspecto que deve ser considerado em se tratando de discriminação. Ela pode se revelar de forma direta e indireta. Direta, quando o comportamento alheio contém em si o *animus* de tratar a pessoa de forma desqualificante, em função de uma característica individual ou de grupo. Nesse caso, o comportamento ilícito é intencional, cabendo à vítima, exceto nas hipóteses em que, pelas circunstâncias, leva-se à presunção do tratamento diferenciado, o ônus de comprovar o ato discriminatório praticado. É o caso de preterir uma promoção à pessoa mais qualificada para o cargo, pela condição de gênero, religião ou orientação sexual.

Cabem, no entanto, observar que há casos em que o não aproveitamento é justificado, a exemplo da não contratação de uma mulher para integrar a equipe masculina de futebol.

Já na forma indireta, a diferença de tratamento, intencional ou não, surge de maneira dissimulada, com efeitos advindos de práticas aparentemente neutras, mas que resultam em discriminação.

O direito estadunidense, que primeiro identificou essa vertente da discriminação, a denominou de Teoria do Impacto Desproporcional, consubstanciada em desigualdade não oriunda de atos concretos ou manifestação expressa e direta, mas de práticas administrativas, empresariais ou políticas públicas, aparentemente neutras e prospectivas, mas que revelam, nos resultados, grande potencial discriminatório. Revela-se muito comum em planos de cargos e salários que terminam por privilegiar certos grupos em detrimento de outros.

Origem do princípio da adaptação razoável

Como consequência natural de um país de imigrantes, que reúne grupos e pessoas com diferentes crenças, ideologias, convicções, costumes e tradições diversas, desde 1962 os estadounidenses já utilizavam a teoria da adaptação razoável em julgados, ao menos de forma a buscar a adequação de interesses de grupos religiosos minoritários marginalizados frente à predominância da proteção à religião das maiorias nos procedimentos estatais, sociais e empresariais.

Assim, não é de se estranhar a edição, em 1972, por meio do *Equal Employment Opportunity Act,*[4] tenha ocorrido o primeiro registro legislativo da teoria denominada *The Duty of Reasonable Accommodation* (ou dever da acomodação ou adaptação razoável).[5] Teve como finalidade inibir as constantes discriminações religiosas no ambiente laboral e atribuir ao empregador o dever de respeito à religião do empregado, com a acomodação que se faz necessária para o ajuste entre a atividade laboral do empregado e o exercício do seu credo, nas circunstâncias em que tal não acarrete sério inconveniente para o empregador.

Vê-se que o prejuízo excessivo foi inicialmente compreendido como um sério inconveniente, mas em seguida tornou-se necessária a substituição da

---

[4] EUA, Equal Employment Opportunity (EEO) laws, disponível em https://www.dol.gov/general/topic/discrimination, acesso em 22/02/2021.

[5] EUA, The United States Department of Justice, disponível em https://www.justice.gov/jmd/reasonable-accommodation, acesso em 20/07/2021.

expressão pelo termo *hardship* ou encargo excessivo, que tem mais concretude do que a subjetividade de um sério inconveniente.

Também na língua pátria ocorreria o mesmo problema de compreensão terminológica. Há profunda diferença entre sério inconveniente, pela subjetividade; sério prejuízo, pela concepção puramente financeira; e encargo excessivo, de conceito ao mesmo tempo concreto e mais aberto, a revelar incontornável ônus sob o aspecto administrativo ou financeiro na dinâmica empresarial.

Ao longo do tempo, vários julgados envolveram a acomodação ou adaptação razoável na proteção ao direito das minorias religiosas. Como exemplo, o Wisconsin V. Yoder, de 1972,[6] em que o direito das famílias da comunidade religiosa Amish de não permitir que seus filhos estudassem em escolas, sendo educados por suas famílias, na manutenção da tradição, foi reconhecido pela Suprema Corte. Cita-se ainda o caso Sherbert V. Verner, de 1963.[7] A Corte decidiu pela acomodação razoável de um empregado, que reivindicava não trabalhar aos sábados em razão da sua religião.

Como as possibilidades físicas e intelectuais das pessoas com deficiência são diferentes, mas podem ser produtivas diante de oportunidades inclusivas de acesso ou se adotadas certas adaptações em ambientes públicos e empresariais, em 1990 os Estados Unidos ampliaram a aplicação da teoria da adaptação razoável por meio da promulgação da lei *Americans with Disabilities Act* (ADA),[8] de natureza trabalhista, para estendê-la aos portadores de deficiência contra a discriminação injustificada nas empresas, e de forma explícita utilizando as expressões acomodação razoável e encargo excessivo.

O *Americans with Disabilities Act* remete ao Pacto de Direitos Civis de 1964,[9] que tornou a discriminação baseada na raça, religião, sexo, origem nacional e outras características estigmatizantes ou preconceituosas e ainda exige dos empregadores instalações condizentes para trabalhadores com deficiências e observância de requisitos de acessibilidade em acomodações públicas.

A teoria da adaptação razoável adquiriu visibilidade universal a partir de sua adoção pela Convenção sobre Direitos das Pessoas com Deficiência

---

[6] EUA, US Supreme Court, Wisconsin v. Yoder, 406 U.S. 205 (1972), disponível em https://supreme.justia.com/cases/federal/us/406/205/, acesso em 20/07/2021.

[7] EUA, US Supreme Court, Sherbert v. Verner, 374 U.S. 398 (1963), disponível em https://supreme.justia.com/cases/federal/us/374/398/, acesso em 20/07/2021.

[8] EUA, Americans with Disabilities Act, disponível em https://www.ada.gov/, acesso em 20/07/2021.

[9] EUA, Civil Rigth Act, 1964, disponível em https://www.ourdocuments.gov/doc.php?flash=false&doc=97, acesso em 20/07/2021.

(CDPD) em 2006, na ONU, passando assim a ficar vinculada aos direitos humanos, na proteção dos direitos das minorias.

O Brasil adotou a Convenção sobre os Direitos das Pessoas com Deficiência da ONU em 30 de março de 2007, em Nova Iorque. Pelo Decreto Legislativo nº 186/2008, aprovado pelo quorum qualificado previsto no art.5º, §3º, da CF pelas duas Casas do Congresso Nacional e sancionado pelo Decreto nº 6.949/2009,[10] passou a constar do ordenamento jurídico brasileiro a adaptação ou acomodação razoável, integrando a Constituição brasileira, como equivalente às emendas constitucionais, segundo dispõe o art.5º, §3º, CRFB/88.

Convenção sobre os direitos das pessoas com deficiência e a Lei brasileira de inclusão

Conforme art.1º, o propósito da Convenção ratificada pelo Brasil *"é promover, proteger e assegurar o exercício pleno e equitativo de todos os direitos humanos e liberdades fundamentais por todas as pessoas com deficiência e promover o respeito pela sua dignidade inerente."*

Em complementação, o dispositivo define que *"Pessoas com deficiência são aquelas que têm impedimentos de longo prazo de natureza física, mental, intelectual ou sensorial, os quais, em interação com diversas barreiras, podem obstruir sua participação plena e efetiva na sociedade em igualdades de condições com as demais pessoas."*

Conforme art.3º da Convenção, a não discriminação; a concretização da inclusão e participação ativa na sociedade; o respeito pela diferença em relação aos não deficientes e sua aceitação; a promoção da igualdade efetiva de oportunidades; e a acessibilidade compensatória das deficiências físicas são, entre outros, os princípios que orientam a promoção de ações e políticas públicas, destinadas a garantir a concretização dos objetivos da Convenção.

No artigo 5º, ao tratar da igualdade e não discriminação, estabelece no item 3 que para a promoção da igualdade e eliminação da discriminação, os Estados Partes adotarão todas as medidas apropriadas para garantir que a adaptação razoável seja oferecida. E no artigo 2º define que *"Adaptação razoável significa as modificações e os ajustes necessários e adequados que não acarretem ônus desproporcional ou indevido, quando requeridos em cada caso, a fim de assegurar que as pessoas com deficiência possam gozar ou exercer, em igualdade de oportunidades com as demais pessoas, todos*

---

[10] Brasil, Decreto nº 6.949, de 25 de agosto de 2009, disponível em http://www.planalto.gov.br/ccivil_03/_ato2007-2010/2009/decreto/d6949.htm, acesso em 20/07/2021.

os direitos humanos e liberdades fundamentais".

A Lei nº 13.146, de 2016 (Lei Brasileira de Inclusão – LBI),[11] em texto similar dispõe, *verbis*:

> *"Art. 3º. Para fins de aplicação desta lei, consideram-se:*
>
> ....
>
> *VI – adaptações razoáveis: adaptações, modificações e ajustes necessários e adequados que não acarretem ônus desproporcional e indevido, quando requeridos em cada caso, a fim de assegurar que a pessoa com deficiência possa gozar ou exercer, em igualdade de condições e oportunidades com as demais pessoas, todos os direitos e liberdades fundamentais."*

Nas relações de trabalho podemos definir como adaptação ou acomodação razoável em relação aos deficientes físicos, o dever de utilização dos meios, instrumentos, práticas e regras indispensáveis ao ajuste do ambiente de trabalho para assegurar igualdade de condições e de oportunidades para que as pessoas com deficiência possam exercer os direitos e liberdades fundamentais.

Esse ajuste ou adaptação do ambiente deve considerar as necessidades de cada pessoa com deficiência, de maneira que torne possível excepcionar ou flexibilizar regras e práticas gerais que evitem estigma, humilhação, constrangimento e segregação.

A incorporação dos tratados internacionais no ordenamento jurídico brasileiro e o controle de convencionalidade

Nos termos do §1º do art.5º, da Constituição Federal da República Federativa do Brasil, as normas definidoras dos direitos e garantias fundamentais têm aplicação imediata.

O §2º do art.5º dispõe que os direitos e garantias expressos na referida Constituição não excluem outros decorrentes do regime e dos princípios por ela adotados, ou dos tratados internacionais em que a República Federativa do Brasil seja parte.

Contudo, o artigo 5º da *Lex Fundamentalis* não definiu o *status* ou grau normativo dos tratados e convenções internacionais sobre direitos

---

[11] Brasil, Lei nº 13.146, de 6 de julho de 2015, disponível em http://www.planalto.gov.br/ccivil_03/_ato2015-2018/2015/lei/l13146.htm, acesso em 20/07/2021.

fundamentais, humanos ou não, aprovados pelo Brasil no plano externo e finalmente ratificados para adoção no plano interno. Daí que o entendimento era o de que os tratados sobre direitos humanos eram equiparados a leis ordinárias.

Em 2004, por meio da Emenda Constitucional nº 45, foi acrescentado à Constituição Federal o §3º que agora consta do art.5º. Ele define que os tratados que versem especificamente sobre direitos humanos são equivalentes a emendas constitucionais, se aprovados em cada Casa do Congresso Nacional em dois turnos, por 3/5 dos votos dos respectivos membros.

Diante da natureza de emenda constitucional conferida aos tratados sobre direitos humanos frente às normas infraconstitucionais hierarquicamente inferiores (isto se observado o *quorum* estabelecido pelo §3º do art.5º, da CF), surgiu a indagação a respeito da força normativa dos tratados que versam sobre direitos humanos adotados pelo Brasil anteriormente à Emenda Constitucional nº 45/2004,[12] ocasião em que esse *quorum* não era exigido e essa condição de emenda constitucional não era atribuída a essas normas internacionais. E, de igual sorte, Bem como em relação aos tratados sobre direitos humanos aprovados posteriormente à EC nº 45/2004 com *quorum* inferior ao previsto no referido §3º.

Respondendo à indagação, para Valerio Mazzuoli todos os tratados internacionais sobre direitos humanos ratificados pelo Estado brasileiro têm nível de norma constitucional, não importando o *quorum* de aprovação do tratado. Esse *status* constitucional, para o jurista, deriva do disposto no art. 5º, § 2º, da CF/88 (Mazzuoli 2011, p. 58).

Concordamos, em parte, com Mazzuoli, porque até o inserção da restrição prevista no §3º do art.5º, da Constituição Federal, os tratados internacionais ratificados pelo Brasil sobre direitos humanos se agregavam à Constituição enquanto vigentes, não importando o *quorum* qualificado ora previsto no citado §3º, que era exigido para o alcance desse status.

Todavia, a restrição que passou a vigorar a partir da inclusão do §3º, deixa claro que os tratados versando sobre direitos humanos aprovados dali para a frente sem esse quórum de 3/5 com dupla votação em cada Casa do Congresso Nacional não adquire o status de emenda constitucional.

Prosseguindo em sua investigação, Valerio Mazzuoli entende que os tratados internacionais sobre direitos humanos em vigor no Brasil funcionam como paradigma de controle da produção normativa infraconstitucional. É o que denomina de controle de convencionalidade das

---

[12] Brasil, Emenda Constitucional nº 45, de 30 de dezembro de 2004, disponível em http://www.planalto.gov.br/ccivil_03/constituicao/emendas/emc/emc45.htm, acesso em 20/07/2021.

leis, a ser observado tanto na via de ação (controle concentrado), quanto na de exceção (controle difuso) (Mazzuoli 2011, p. 90).

Quanto aos demais tratados internacionais, para ele possuem *status* de supralegalidade, de igual sorte contando com um controle jurisdicional da convencionalidade das leis na produção normativa doméstica e ainda com um controle de supralegalidade das normas infraconstitucionais, deixando a Constituição de ser o único paradigma de controle das normas de direito interno. Ou seja, são paradigma de controle dessa produção normativa os tratados internacionais de direitos humanos (por meio dos controles difuso e concentrado de convencionalidade) e os instrumentos internacionais comuns (por meio do controle de supralegalidade).

O jurista aponta então, principalmente a partir da EC 45/2004, quatro modalidades de controle de normas infraconstitucionais: de legalidade, de supralegalidade, de convencionalidade e de constitucionalidade.

E conclui que caso os tratados internacionais sobre direitos humanos não tenham sido aprovados com essa maioria qualificada, seu *status* será de norma materialmente constitucional, como paradigma de controle somente difuso de convencionalidade; caso tenham sido aprovados (e entrado em vigor no plano interno, após sua ratificação) pela sistemática do art. 5º, § 3º, tais tratados serão material e formalmente constitucionais, servindo de paradigma dos controles difuso e também concentrado de convencionalidade, como meio de retirar a validade de norma interna que viole um tratado internacional de direitos humanos em vigor no país, ainda que compatível com a Constituição (Mazzuoli 2011, p. 68-69 e 132).

Em relação aos tratados internacionais comuns, servem de paradigma do controle de supralegalidade das normas infraconstitucionais. A incompatibilidade com estas invalidaria a disposição legislativa contrária ao tratado, que prevalece.

Decidindo no RE 466.343-SP questão sobre a prisão do depositário infiel, o STF decidiu que os tratados não incorporados na forma do art. 5º, § 3º, da Constituição Federal não adquirem a natureza de normas constitucionais e sim a de normas supralegais (Supremo Tribunal Federal, RE nº 466.343-SP, Relator Ministro Cesar Peluso, Tribunal Pleno, decisão unânime, DJe 05/06/2009).

Com base no instituto da proscrição, decidiu-se que os tratados sobre direitos humanos, incorporados antes ou introduzidos posteriormente ao art.5º, §3º, da CF, paralisam a eficácia de todo o ordenamento infraconstitucional em sentido contrário. Pelo que concluiu o Supremo Tribunal Federal do Brasil, por meio do voto condutor do Ministro Gilmar Mendes, que o art. 5º, inciso LXVII, que dispõe sobre a prisão do depositário infiel não foi revogado pela ratificação do Pacto Internacional dos Direitos Civis e Políticos, promulgado pelo Decreto nº 592, de 6 de julho de 1992, art. 11[13] e da Convenção Americana sobre Direitos Humanos, art. 7º, 7,[14] mas deixou de ter aplicação diante do efeito paralisante que a ratificação desses tratados impuseram à legislação infraconstitucional que disciplina a matéria.

Da decisão decorre que independentemente de sua hierarquia constitucional, os tratados operam como parâmetro para o controle de outros atos normativos que lhes são — ou não — hierarquicamente inferiores.

Essa decisão é aplicável, por arrastamento, às demais hipóteses, pelo que os tratados e convenções internacionais sobre direitos humanos, a exemplo, da Declaração Universal dos Direitos Humanos, da Convenção de Viena sobre tratados e da Convenção Americana sobre Direitos Humanos, por não terem sido recepcionados na forma prescrita no § 3º do artigo 5º da Lei Fundamental, permanecem na condição de normas supralegais. E com esse *status* paralisam todo o ordenamento infraconstitucional que com elas não se conforme.

Reconheceu-se assim, além do controle de constitucionalidade, o controle de convencionalidade destinado a afastar a aplicação de norma interna de matriz infraconstitucional, contrária ao tratado. Mas, diferentemente da doutrina de Valério Mazzuoli, o STF estabeleceu apenas três controles: o controle difuso de convencionalidade (ou de supralegalidade), que não se confunde com o controle de legalidade (por exemplo, entre um decreto e uma lei) e nem com o controle de constitucionalidade (antinomia entre uma lei e a CF/88). E determinou que as normas supralegais, não contando com valor constitucional, servem de paradigma apenas para o controle difuso de convencionalidade ou de supralegalidade.

Quanto aos tratados aprovados pela maioria qualificada do § 3º do art. 5º da CF/88, porque contam com *status* constitucional, servirão de paradigma ao controle de convencionalidade concentrado (perante o STF) ou difuso (perante qualquer juiz, incluindo-se os do STF). Neste caso, o controle de convencionalidade concentrado (perante o STF) tem o mesmo significado do controle de constitucionalidade concentrado, porque os tratados com aprovação qualificada equivalem a uma Emenda constitucional.

Em relação ao controle de convencionalidade concentrado (só cabível, repita-se, quando observado o § 3º do art. 5º da CF/88) cabe admitir o uso

---

[13] Brasil, Decreto nº 592, de 6 de julho de 1992, disponível em http://www.planalto.gov.br/ccivil_03/decreto/1990-1994/d0592.htm, acesso em 20/07/2021.

[14] OAS, Convenção Americana de Direitos Humanos, disponível em https://www.cidh.oas.org/basicos/portugues/c.convencao_americana.htm, acesso em 20/07/2021.

de todos os instrumentos desse controle perante o STF, ou seja, é plenamente possível defender a possibilidade de ADIn (para eivar a norma infraconstitucional de inconstitucionalidade e inconvencionalidade), de ADECON (para garantir à norma infraconstitucional a compatibilidade vertical com a norma internacional com valor constitucional), ou até mesmo de ADPF - Arguição de Descumprimento de Preceito Fundamental para exigir o cumprimento de um "preceito fundamental" encontrado em tratado de direitos humanos formalmente constitucional. Embora de difícil concepção, também não se pode desconsiderar a ADO (Ação Direta de Constitucionalidade por Omissão);

Enfim, a adequação das leis com a Constituição é denominada de controle de constitucionalidade. Mas além de compatíveis com a Constituição, as normas internas devem estar em conformidade com os tratados internacionais ratificados pelo Brasil e em vigor no país. À verificação dessa conformidade se dá o nome de controle de convencionalidade, ou seja, de conformidade dessas *convenções* com a lei interna do país ou vice-versa. Tal controle, assim como ocorre no caso do controle de constitucionalidade, se dá, portanto, conforme o STF, em virtude da hierarquia das normas, ou seja, com prevalência sobre as de inferior hierarquia.

A expressão controle de convencionalidade significa a verificação do respeito ao que foi convencionado pelo Brasil no plano internacional e internamente adotado. Além de compatíveis com a Constituição, as normas internas devem estar em conformidade com os tratados internacionais ratificados pelo governo brasileiro e em vigor no país. A esse procedimento é denominado controle de convencionalidade.

Com base no entendimento adotado pelo STF, a diferença entre tratados com *status* equivalente aos de emenda constitucional e demais tratados que revelem hierarquia supralegal, está em que os primeiros passam, para efeito interno, a integrar o bloco de constitucionalidade, como parâmetro tanto de um controle de constitucionalidade, como de um controle de convencionalidade, já que o tratado não se incorpora ao texto constitucional propriamente dito. Os tratados de direitos humanos não internalizados pela dita maioria qualificada, passam a ser paradigma apenas do controle difuso de convencionalidade ou conformidade com a Constituição.

Como a Convenção sobre os direitos das pessoas com deficiência foi aprovada de acordo com o *quorum* qualificado previsto no §3° do art.5° da Constituição Federal, adquiriu status de emenda constitucional, e as normas infraconstitucionais editadas sobre a matéria estão sujeitas a controle de constitucionalidade.

A extensão do princípio a todas as situações que envolvam discriminação indireta de minorias

Considerando que o real fundamento da adaptação razoável é coibir a discriminação indireta, por meio do ajustamento ou acomodação às necessidades particulares das minorias no ambiente empresarial, de forma que possam desfrutar dos mesmos direitos da maioria, tem-se que não pode ficar adstrita à deficiência física.

Logo, em que pese a ratificação da CDPD e o conceito ligado à deficiência física, é evidente que o seu campo de atuação é infinitamente maior.

Com efeito, o terreno aqui vislumbrado é o das políticas afirmativas, na busca do alcance de um patamar de igualdade material, por meio de instrumentos que permitam o harmônico convívio multiculturalista nas empresas.

Assim, com fundamento no disposto no art.7º, *caput*, da Constituição da República Federativa do Brasil *("São direitos dos trabalhadores urbanos e rurais, além de outros que visem à melhoria de sua condição social: .... ")* e no que dispõe o art.8º, *caput*, da CLT *("As autoridades administrativas e a Justiça do Trabalho, na falta de disposições legais ou contratuais, decidirão, conforme o caso, pela jurisprudência, por analogia, por equidade e outros princípios e normas gerais de direito, principalmente do direito do trabalho, e, ainda, de acordo com os usos e costumes, o direito comparado, mas sempre de maneira que nenhum interesse de classe ou particular prevaleça sobre o interesse público.")*, é impositiva a aplicação analógica iuris da CDPD aos demais casos de discriminação indireta de minorias nas relações de trabalho, não podendo o magistrado trabalhista recusar a sua aplicação sob o fundamento de "falta de amparo legal específico". E ao assim proceder, também não estará se substituindo ao legislador, posto que a sua atuação discricionária e interpretativa é, no caso, autorizada expressamente por lei.

Conceito e natureza jurídica

Nas relações de trabalho podemos definir como adaptação ou acomodação razoável o dever de utilização dos meios, instrumentos, práticas e regras indispensáveis ao ajuste do ambiente de trabalho para assegurar igualdade condições e de oportunidades para que as minorias possam exercer, concretamente, os direitos e liberdades fundamentais com a mesma amplitude das maiorias.

O direito à adaptação razoável é de natureza fundamental, destinado a corrigir discriminação indireta.

Esse ajuste ou adaptação do ambiente deve considerar as necessidades de cada pessoa componente de minorias, de maneira que torne possível excepcionar ou flexibilizar regras e práticas gerais que evitem preconceito, estigma, humilhação, constrangimento, preterição, segregação ou, afim, tratamento injustamente diferenciado.

A acomodação razoável: a) é democrática, porque permite a inclusão; b) visa preservar o emprego mediante adaptação; c) concretiza a dignidade e os valores sociais do trabalho.

O limite para a realização da adaptação razoável: ônus indevido

O conceito de onerosidade excessiva, de longa monta aplicável a relações civis e administrativas no terreno do negócio jurídico, notadamente o contratual, está atrelado a malícia (arts. 156 e 157 do Código Civil brasileiro)[15] ou a fatos imprevistos (arts.373 e 478/480, do referido diploma).

No direito estadounidense a evolução do conceito levou à percepção de que a impossibilidade de exercício de um direito fundamental por preconceito gera a necessidade da empresa fazer adaptações em suas instalações ou em seu regramento interno, desde que isso não imponha a ela um encargo excessivo ou desproporcional, assim entendido como o ônus incontornável sob o aspecto administrativo ou financeiro na dinâmica empresarial.

Vê-se, portanto, que a gênese em relação à onerosidade excessiva é a mesma, variando, no entanto, o âmbito de aplicação, a justificar uma denominação própria para o limite da adaptação que, na prática, importa numa revisão de procedimento.

No caso da onerosidade excessiva civilista ou administrativa, o desequilíbrio entre as prestações das partes leva à revisão ou resolução do negócio. A natureza da onerosidade é econômica. Mas em se tratando de adaptação, ela é razoável quando, por meio de ajustes na organização empresarial, torna-se possível ao credor em situação de discriminação indireta, o exercício de um direito fundamental, portanto, de conteúdo extrapatrimonial, ficando à consideração do trabalhador dar por rompido o

---

[15] Lei nº 10.406, de 10 de janeiro de 2002, disponível em http://www.planalto.gov.br/ccivil_03/leis/2002/l10406compilada.htm, acesso em 20/07/2021.

contrato ou exigir o ajuste.

Em síntese, o limite para a adaptação razoável (esforço factível de inclusão em obrigação de fazer) é o ônus indevido ou desproporcional que a pretensão possa acarretar em termos de ajuste (dificuldades insuperáveis no âmbito organizacional, custo material excessivo em relação ao benefício a ser obtido, prejuízo insuportável para os demais trabalhadores em comparação ao benefício de um só ou alguns).

O ônus na adaptação razoável não se confunde com o modo ou encargo civilista, que consiste num ônus em troca de uma liberalidade. A adaptação é um dever se razoavelmente não importar em ônus material ou imaterial desproporcional em relação ao benefício.

Para o ajuste é preciso verificar a finalidade da medida destinada a excepcionar por meio da adaptação, para então comparar custos materiais e imateriais e benefícios diretos e indiretos.

O ônus é indevido quando a adaptação mostra-se demasiadamente custosa (em sentido material e imaterial) em proporção aos benefícios individuais, necessidades empresariais e afetação de direitos coletivos.

Numa empresa em que trabalham adventistas do sétimo dia, muçulmanos, católicos e judeus, é possível conceder folga no dia correspondente à crença de cada um desses fieis, se esse procedimento for factível conforme a natureza do empreendimento. Seria possível numa padaria ou numa fábrica que funcione de segunda feira a domingo, mas em princípio inviável num escritório que tenha funcionamento de segunda a sexta-feira.

Direito comparado

Sobre a adaptação razoável nos Estados Unidos da América já se fez referência ao *Equal Employment Opportunity Act* e ao The *Duty of Reasonable Accommodation*, tanto em relação ao aspecto religioso, como no tocante à deficiência física, nos dois casos admitindo a acomodação se o encargo não for excessivo para o empregador (*hardship*).

No Canadá, a Comissão de Direitos Humanos de Ontario (The Canaddian Human Rights Commission) estabeleceu que empregadores não podem discriminar a contratação, promoção, condições laborais ou o término do contrato com base apenas no fato de que uma pessoa precisa cuidar de um membro da família ("the coast of caring").[16]

Por outro lado, a referida Comissão esclarece:

---

[16] Canadá, Ontario Human Rights Commission, *Direitos Humanos e Condição Familiar*, disponível em http://www.ohrc.on.ca/pt/direitos-humanos-e-condi%C3%A7%C3%A3o-familiar, acesso em 19/02/2021.

"What is the Duty to Accommodate?

Employers and service providers have an obligation to adjust rules, policies or practices to enable you to participate fully. It applies to needs that are related to the grounds of discrimination. This is called the duty to accommodate.

The duty to accommodate means that sometimes it is necessary to treat someone differently in order to prevent or reduce discrimination. For examples, asking all job applicants to pass a written test may not be fair to a person with a visual disability. In such cases, the duty to accommodate may require that alternative arrangements be made to ensure that a person or group can fully participate."[17]

Traduzindo,

"Os empregadores e prestadores de serviços têm a obrigação de ajustar as regras, políticas ou práticas para permitir que você participe plenamente. Aplica-se a necessidades relacionadas com os motivos de discriminação. Isso é chamado de dever de acomodar.

O dever de acomodar significa que às vezes é necessário tratar alguém de forma diferente para prevenir ou reduzir a discriminação. Por exemplo, pedir a todos os candidatos a emprego que passem em um teste escrito pode não ser justo para uma pessoa com deficiência visual. Em tais casos, o dever de acomodar pode exigir que arranjos alternativos sejam feitos para garantir que uma pessoa ou grupo possa participar plenamente."

E apresenta como exemplos:

- *Fornecer tela especial e software para pessoas com deficiência visual;*
- *permitir que um trabalhador tire uma folga para comparecer a uma consulta médica;*
- *gerenciar a agenda de um funcionário de uma forma que equilibre seu trabalho e obrigações de cuidar;*
- *disponibilizar o acesso de cadeiras de rodas para pessoas com deficiência."*

Na Espanha, a acomodação razoável foi tratada especificamente pela Lei nº 51/2003, que adota conceito semelhante ao disposto no art. 2º, da Convenção da ONU.[18]

---

[17] Canadá, Ontario Human Rights Commission. *What is the Duty to Accommodate?,* disponível em https://www.chrc-ccdp.gc.ca/eng/content/what-duty-accommodate, accesso em 22/02/2021.

[18] Espanha, Ley 51/2003, da Igualdad de Oportunidades, No Discriminación y Accesibilidad Universal de las Personas con discapacidad, disponível em https://www.bienestaryproteccioninfantil.es/fuentes1.asp?sec=17&subs=213&cod

Na França, em caso de ser vítima de discriminação, o deficiente pode recorrer ao Défenseur des Droits, "responsável pela proteção dos direitos humanos e defesa da liberdade, inclusive em matéria de trabalho, como assédio moral contra pessoas com deficiência, discriminação contra pessoas com deficiência, falta de adaptação razoável ou contra autoridades que não promoveram o encaminhamento das pessoas com deficiência ao local de trabalho" (Resende 2016).

Em Portugal, embora sem referência expressa, a adoção da adaptação razoável permeia os direitos da personalidade do trabalhador.

Realmente, ao adotar *o normal funcionamento da empresa*, acolhe a ideia de ônus indevido como limite ao exercício dos direitos da personalidade.

Vejamos, *verbis*:

> *"Artigo 14.º*
> *Liberdade de expressão e de opinião*
> *É reconhecida, no âmbito da empresa, a liberdade de expressão e de divulgação do pensamento e opinião, com respeito dos direitos de personalidade do trabalhador e do empregador, incluindo as pessoas singulares que o representam, e do normal funcionamento da empresa.*"[19]

Adaptação razoável e técnica de ponderação de princípios: distinção

Com alto grau de abstração, impregnados do ideal de justiça e servindo de base norteadora da construção das regras jurídicas, os princípios serviam para a interpretação lógica e sistemática das regras ou subsidiariamente, para a construção de regras no silêncio do legislador.

A partir da Teoria dos Princípios de Dworkin, passaram a ser vistos por meio do seu real caráter, ou seja, de norma jurídica.

Para Dworkin os princípios indicam um fim ou meta, mas não as consequências, e aplicados mediante ponderação em caso de colisão entre princípios, deve verificar-se a dimensão de grau de cada um envolvidos no caso em questão, para a escolha da solução que se revelar a mais moral ou principiológica, posto que os princípios teriam limites imanentes (Dworkin 2010, p. 127-203).

A partir dessa discussão, Robert Alexy difere na concepção dos princípios e, consequentemente, em sua aplicação em caso de conflito,

=1949&page, acesso em 06/08/2021.

[19] Portugal, Lei 7/2009 (Código do Trabalho), disponível em https://dre.pt/legislacao-consolidada/-/lc/34546475/view, acesso em 22/02/2021.

adotando-os como mandados de otimização. Partindo da ideia de que os direitos fundamentais possuem uma eficácia irradiante, funcionando como vetor interpretativo e axiológico do ordenamento, e de que a regra, com razões subjacentes, é fruto das ponderações, os princípios, como mandados de otimização, precisam alcançar um fim indicado, em ponderação com a realidade e com as outras normas do ordenamento jurídico (Teoria Externa dos Direitos Fundamentais), e não com os limites sugeridos por Dworkin. Daí que, pelo pluralismo social os princípios necessariamente colidem e sua acomodação deve ser feita por meio do Princípio da Proporcionalidade, que trabalha com três vetores: adequação, necessidade e proporcionalidade (Alexy 2008, p. 85-120).

A adequação exige que se olhe se aquela ação atingirá o fim a que se destina; a vedação do excesso importa em que, de todas as medidas analisadas, deve-se escolher a que melhor atinja os fins com a menor negatividade possível; e a proporcionalidade específica deve comparar a análise do custo frente ao benefício, considerando o peso concreto dos princípios analisados.

Como a proporcionalidade gera regra, deve-se tomar extremo cuidado para que o uso dos princípios não desrespeite as regras jurídicas democraticamente produzidas pelo Legislativo e sancionadas pelo Executivo, ou que mitiga a segurança jurídica e a separação de poderes.

A Teoria do Impacto Desproporcional difere da técnica da ponderação de princípios. O uso do sopesamento não torna iguais a ponderação de princípios e a adaptação razoável. A distinção reside na finalidade, eis que na ponderação a sobreposição de princípios é necessária e resolvida por si mesma, ou seja, pelo critério comparativo, com exclusão ou sobreposição de um direito em detrimento de outro. Já na adaptação razoável há condicionamento para a sua realização: a sobreposição só ocorrera se possível for a acomodação dos interesses sob a ótica da razoabilidade do encargo.

A Teoria do Impacto Desproporcional é específica e está fundada nos efeitos discriminatórios indiretos de uma norma ou situação de fato. Daí surge o Direito à Adaptação Razoável destinado a permitir que o discriminado busque modificações e ajustes necessários e adequados a corrigir a distorção, para que, sem que isso acarrete ônus desproporcional ou indevido, possa exercer, em igualdade de oportunidades com as demais pessoas, um direito fundamental colocado em risco.

De forma prática, permitir que o fiel, cozinheiro em um restaurante, possa, com uso proteção para que de sua barba não caiam pelos por questão de higiene; que o muçulmano possa ter pausas para rezar durante a jornada, fazendo a compensação dos intervalos; que o judeu, o adventista do sétimo dia e o muçulmano possam folgar no dia correspondente às suas crenças numa instituição que funciona de segunda a domingo; ou que o deficiente físico possa, com adaptação da pia da copa para atingir a altura da cadeira de rodas, lavar a marmita na copa, como os demais trabalhadores, e não somente no banheiro, único lugar onde a altura da pia assim permite, são situações que ensejam a incidência da Teoria da Adaptação Razoável.

Já para a situação de uma apresentadora de programa infantil diário de televisão, que resolve paralelamente atuar em filmes pornográficos, a Teoria da Adaptação Razoável não serve, quer porque no caso da empresa resolver despedi-la não haverá discriminação e sim conduta necessária diante da incompatibilidade do contrato com os atos da vida privada, quer porque essa incompatibilidade é resultado de outra teoria, exatamente a da ponderação de princípios.

A adaptação razoável na Justiça do Trabalho: *leading case* do Tribunal Superior do Trabalho

Tivemos a oportunidade de, como Relator, identificar no processo TST-RR-11.204-62.2017.5.15.0144 a hipótese de aplicação da teoria da adaptação razoável diante do dilema de uma professora de ensino público não poder se ausentar do trabalho em dias e horários determinados para acompanhar o filho acometido de síndrome de Down às atividades terapêuticas indispensáveis ao desenvolvimento sadio e à integração social da criança. Sem elas, torna-se impossível o atingimento do maior estágio de evolução do deficiente para o regular convívio social.

A hipótese se resume ao fato de que trabalhadores com encargos parentais necessitam, para a conjugação com o direito fundamental ao trabalho, que o empregador promova as adaptações razoáveis que evitem a discriminação por associação familiar.

A hipótese é prevista no art.4º da Convenção 156, da Organização Internacional do Trabalho - OIT, *verbis*:

Com vista ao estabelecimento de uma efetiva igualdade de oportunidades e de tratamento para homens e mulheres trabalhadores, serão tomadas todas as medidas compatíveis com as condições e as responsabilidades nacionais para:

a) dar condições a trabalhadores com encargos de família de exercer seu direito à livre escolha de emprego e

b) levar em consideração suas necessidades nos termos e condições de emprego e de seguridade social.[20]

---

[20] Convenção 156, da OIT, disponível em

A adaptação imposta pela decisão judicial adotou a compreensão de que seria ônus razoável a ser suportado pelo empregador a adequação da jornada da trabalhadora, por meio da substituição das atividades pedagógicas presenciais por Horas de Trabalho Pedagógico Livre (HTPL), sem diminuição de sua remuneração, diante do benefício social que o procedimento traria para a criança deficiente.

Eis a ementa e o dispositivo do acórdão da Terceira Turma do TST, unâmime, julgado em 02/12/2020 e publicado no DEJT de 04/12/2020:[21]

> **ACÓRDÃO NO RECURSO ORDINÁRIO PUBLICADO APÓS A VIGÊNCIA DA LEI Nº 13.467/2017.**
>
> **I – AGRAVO DE INSTRUMENTO EM RECURSO DE REVISTA DA AUTORA.**
>
> **TUTELA INIBITÓRIA – OBRIGAÇÃO DE FAZER – PRETENSÃO DE REDUÇÃO DA JORNADA DE TRABALHO, SEM DIMINUIÇÃO PROPORCIONAL DA REMUNERAÇÃO E SEM A COMPENSAÇÃO DE HORÁRIOS, A FIM DE QUE A TRABALHADORA ACOMPANHE SEU FILHO DE SEIS ANOS DE IDADE, PORTADOR DA SÍNDROME DE DOWN, EM ATIVIDADES TERAPÊUTICAS INDISPENSÁVEIS AO DESENVOLVIMENTO SADIO E À INTEGRAÇÃO SOCIAL DA CRIANÇA. EFICÁCIA HORIZONTAL DOS DIREITOS FUNDAMENTAIS DA IGUALDADE SUBSTANCIAL E DA ADAPTAÇÃO RAZOÁVEL. PRESENÇA DE TRANSCENDÊNCIA SOCIAL.** Discute-se desde 2017 o direito de uma mãe e professora de ver reduzida em algumas horas a jornada de trabalho perante o Município de Bariri, sem a obrigatoriedade de compensação de horários e sem prejuízo da remuneração que provê o sustento da família, a fim de que ela acompanhe o filho, que completou seis anos de idade no dia 20/10/2020, nas atividades terapêuticas indispensáveis ao seu pleno desenvolvimento enquanto portador da Síndrome de Down. Considerando que a proteção à infância e a assistência à pessoa portadora de necessidades especiais, bem como o direito ao trabalho são direitos sociais assegurados pela Constituição, reconhece-se a transcendência da matéria trazida no recurso de revista, nos termos do art. 896-A, §1º, III, da CLT. A razoabilidade da tese de violação do art. 5º, *caput*, da CF justifica o provimento do agravo de instrumento. **Agravo de instrumento conhecido e provido.**

---

https://www.ilo.org/brasilia/convencoes/WCMS_242709/lang--pt/index.htm, acesso em 19/02/2021.

[21] Brasil, Tribunal Superior do Trabalho, Terceira Turma, acórdão unâmime, julgamento em 02/12/2020 e publicação no DEJT de 04/12/2020. Disponível em https://tst.jusbrasil.com.br/jurisprudencia/1237547033/recurso-de-revista-rr-104098720185150090/inteiro-teor-1237547169, acesso em 20/07/2021.

II – RECURSO DE REVISTA DA AUTORA.

TUTELA INIBITÓRIA – OBRIGAÇÃO DE FAZER – PRETENSÃO DE REDUÇÃO DA JORNADA DE TRABALHO, SEM DIMINUIÇÃO PROPORCIONAL DA REMUNERAÇÃO E SEM A COMPENSAÇÃO DE HORÁRIOS, A FIM DE QUE A TRABALHADORA ACOMPANHE SEU FILHO DE SEIS ANOS DE IDADE, PORTADOR DA SÍNDROME DE DOWN, EM ATIVIDADES TERAPÊUTICAS INDISPENSÁVEIS AO DESENVOLVIMENTO SADIO E À INTEGRAÇÃO SOCIAL DA CRIANÇA – EFICÁCIA HORIZONTAL DOS DIREITOS FUNDAMENTAIS DA IGUALDADE SUBSTANCIAL E DA ADAPTAÇÃO RAZOÁVEL - CONCESSÃO DE HORÁRIO ESPECIAL POR MEIO DO AUMENTO DAS HORAS DE TRABALHO PEDAGÓGICO LIVRE (HTPL) E DIMINUIÇÃO EQUIVALENTE DA JORNADA PRESENCIAL – APLICAÇÃO DOS ARTS. 98, §3º, DA LEI Nº 8.112/1990 E 11 DA LEI MUNICIPAL Nº 4.111/2011 – PONDERAÇÃO DOS INTERESSES EM CONFLITO, SEGUNDO O ART. 2 DA CONVENÇÃO INTERNACIONAL SOBRE OS DIREITOS DAS PESSOAS COM DEFICIÊNCIA – PROVIMENTO PARCIAL DO PEDIDO. Discute-se desde 2017 o direito de uma mãe e professora de ver reduzida em algumas poucas horas a jornada de trabalho perante o Município de Bariri, sem a obrigatoriedade de compensação de horários e sem prejuízo da remuneração que provê o sustento da família, a fim de que ela acompanhe o filho, que completou seis anos de idade no dia 20/10/2020, nas atividades terapêuticas indispensáveis ao seu pleno desenvolvimento enquanto portador da Síndrome de Down. O juízo de primeiro grau, em caráter liminar *inaudita altera pars* autorizado pelo art. 300, *caput* e § 2º, do CPC, deferiu a antecipação dos efeitos da tutela. Já em sede de cognição exauriente, cassou a medida de urgência e julgou improcedente a pretensão. O Tribunal Regional negou provimento ao recurso ordinário da autora. Utilizando como fundamento nuclear a ausência de previsão legal que respaldasse o pedido, o Colegiado acrescentou que os princípios constitucionais não autorizam o Poder Judiciário a impor obrigações não previstas em lei, notadamente as que representam impacto financeiro. Destacou que a efetivação do que pretende a trabalhadora em juízo deve ocorrer por meio de políticas públicas abrangentes. No entanto, a Constituição Federal de 1988 consagrou a dignidade da pessoa humana e os valores sociais do trabalho como fundamentos nucleares da República Federativa do Brasil (art. 1º, III e IV). O poder constituinte originário erigiu a construção de uma sociedade justa e solidária e a promoção do bem de todos, sem preconceito ou discriminação, ao *status* de objetivos fundamentais do Estado brasileiro (art. 3º, I e IV). Os direitos humanos foram alçados ao patamar de princípio norteador das relações externas, com repercussão ou absorção formal no plano interno (arts. 4º, II, e 5º, §§ 2º e 3º). Já o catálogo de garantias e direitos fundamentais deixou de assumir a conformação vertical do constitucionalismo clássico para constituir o principal fundamento sobre o qual repousa todo o ordenamento jurídico nacional. A denominada *Carta Política*, de feição marcadamente liberal e que se propunha, essencialmente, à imposição de limites ao poder do Estado na vida privada, deu lugar a uma *Carta Fundamental*, de caráter dirigente, programático e de alcance muito mais abrangente e concretizador. O processo histórico de ***horizontalização*** **dos direitos fundamentais** adquiriu assento constitucional expresso (art. 5º, §1º), de modo que, diferentemente do que sugere o acórdão recorrido, **os valores mais caros à sociedade possuem aptidão para alcançar todos os indivíduos de forma direta e eficácia plena, sem a necessidade de que sejam veiculados por meio de** ***pontes infraconstitucionais***. Nesse sentido, a matriz axiológica da Constituição não somente pode, mas, sobretudo, deve servir de fonte imediata para a resolução de demandas levadas à tutela do Poder Judiciário, notadamente aquelas de alta complexidade. De todo modo, a ausência de norma infraconstitucional específica não seria capaz de isentar o magistrado de, com base nos princípios gerais de direito, na analogia e nos tratados internacionais ratificados pelo Brasil, dentre eles o Pacto de San Jose da Costa Rica, reconhecer a incidência direta dos direitos sociais em determinados casos concretos, mesmo porque aqueles nomeados exemplificativamente no texto constitucional, inclusive no que diz respeito aos trabalhadores, encerram cláusulas gerais ou de conteúdo indeterminado, mas de aplicação imediata (arts. 6º e 7º, *caput, in fine*). O Tribunal Regional não deixa de ter razão quando afirma que o dever da sociedade, de assegurar o exercício de direitos aos grupos em situação de vulnerabilidade, deve ser aperfeiçoado por meio de políticas públicas de alcance abrangente. Essa responsabilidade, no caso específico dos deficientes e dos portadores de necessidades especiais, é de competência concorrente dos entes federativos, nos termos dos arts. 23, II, e 24, XIV, da CF e se encontra prevista em diversos pontos da própria Constituição, notadamente nos seus arts. 203, IV, 208, III, e 227, §1º, II, bem como na legislação específica, a exemplo do art. 8º da Lei nº 13.146/2015 – Lei Brasileira de Inclusão da Pessoa com Deficiência (Estatuto da Pessoa com Deficiência). Neste sentir, é mesmo dever do Estado promocional, por meio de seus Poderes, dar conteúdo prestacional aos direitos sociais, agindo de forma ativa a concretizá-los. Ocorre que a ainda claudicante atuação do Poder Público na adoção de medidas efetivas ao bem-estar da população vulnerável e, sobretudo, o alcance mais restrito da pretensão declinada na exordial, permitem que este Colegiado examine a controvérsia sob ótica diversa. Felizmente, está ficando para trás o tempo em que a pessoa portadora de deficiência física, mental, intelectual ou sensorial, inata ou adquirida, era considerada apenas um peso a ser suportado por terceiros, fosse no âmbito familiar ou social ou ainda sob as expensas do Estado. Impulsionada pela medicina, pela psicologia, pela sociologia e por outras áreas do saber, a sociedade tem evoluído, passando a enxergar os integrantes dessa parcela da população como indivíduos sujeitos de prerrogativas e obrigações, no exercício, às vezes pleno, às vezes mitigado, de sua capacidade e de sua cidadania. O direito brasileiro não ficou alheio a essa evolução, de modo de que

documentos construídos no plano internacional com o intuito de proteger e salvaguardar o exercício dos direitos dos deficientes e portadores de necessidades especiais vêm sendo absorvidos pela ordem jurídica pátria com força de emenda constitucional, a exemplo da Convenção Internacional sobre os Direitos das Pessoas com Deficiência e do Tratado de Marraqueche; da revogação dos incisos I a III do art.3° do Código Civil brasileiro quanto à caracterização dos incapazes; e, o art.1783-A, do Código Civil, sobre a tomada de decisão apoiada. A nossa ordem jurídica, mesmo que de forma incipiente, tem procurado promover e garantir os direitos e liberdades fundamentais desses indivíduos, visando à sua inclusão social, em igualdade de condições e oportunidades com as demais pessoas. Expressões de conotação depreciativa, como a outrora paradigmática "loucos de todo gênero", deixaram de ser utilizadas nos textos legais, ao passo que a não-discriminação negativa passou a ser a palavra de ordem em documentos oficiais. No âmbito da Administração Pública, a Lei n° 13.370/2016 alterou o art. 98, §3°, da Lei n° 8.112/1990 para estender o direito ao horário especial ao servidor público federal que possui cônjuge, filho ou dependente com deficiência e para revogar a exigência de compensação. Especificamente no que toca ao Direito do Trabalho, tramita no Congresso Nacional o Projeto de Lei n° 110/2016, da relatoria do senador Flavio Arns, que pretende reduzir em 10% a jornada dos trabalhadores que tenham sob sua guarda filhos com deficiência, sem prejuízo da remuneração. A par de tudo o que já foi considerado, há de se ter em mente que **os anseios por uma sociedade justa não podem passar ao largo da percepção de que os seus integrantes são plurais e de que a <u>igualdade substancial</u> é valor que coloca em alto relevo as diferenças de ordem pessoal**. Tratar pessoas diferentes com isonomia não significa tratá-las segundo a mesma régua ou de acordo com os mesmos parâmetros. A aplicação do primado da igualdade sem qualquer temperamento costuma apenas aprofundar as desigualdades ainda tão presentes em nossa realidade social. É certo que os funcionários da municipalidade recorrida não têm seus horários de trabalho adequados a fim de que possam acompanhar seus filhos em atividades educacionais ou recreativas, mormente sem a redução de salários. Ocorre que **o filho da autora possui características particulares que não apenas o diferenciam da maioria das outras crianças, mas, também, representam um desafio superior tanto ao seu desenvolvimento como pessoa quanto à sua afirmação enquanto agente socialmente relevante**. Destaque-se, por oportuno, que a ciência não estabelece gradação à Síndrome de Down, não havendo que se cogitar de sua incidência severa ou moderada. Daí a importância do seguinte questionamento: **ao negar um horário diferenciado à sua mãe, o reclamado não estaria adotando um tratamento uniforme para crianças em situações flagrantemente desiguais? Pensamos que a resposta seja positiva**. A **Convenção Internacional sobre os Direitos das Pessoas com Deficiência**, aprovada pela Assembleia Geral das Nações Unidas em 13 de dezembro de 2006 e chancelada pelo Congresso Nacional por meio do Decreto Legislativo n°

186/2008, conforme o procedimento do art. 5º, §3º, da CF, reconhece que **a deficiência "é um conceito em evolução" e que "resulta da interação entre pessoas com deficiência e as barreiras devidas às atitudes e ao ambiente que impedem a plena e efetiva participação dessas pessoas na sociedade em igualdade de oportunidades com as demais pessoas"**. Estabelece, no art. 3º, os seus "princípios gerais", dentre os quais se destacam o **"respeito pela diferença"** e a **"igualdade de oportunidades"**. Prevê, no art. 5.1, que **"todas as pessoas são iguais perante e sob a lei a que fazem jus, sem qualquer discriminação, a igual proteção e benefício da lei"**. Especificamente quanto à criança, determina, no art. 7.1 que **"os Estados Partes tomarão todas as medidas necessárias para assegurar às crianças com deficiência o pleno exercício de todos os direitos humanos e liberdades fundamentais, em igualdade de oportunidades com as demais crianças". Referidos dispositivos não apenas ratificaram o já consagrado princípio da igualdade material insculpido no art. 5º, *caput*, da CF, mas, também, lhe conferiram refinamento temático expresso. Assim, o direito das crianças com deficiência, de serem tratadas pelo Estado e pela sociedade em igualdade de condições e segundo as características peculiares que as diferenciam dos demais indivíduos, passou a ser literal na Constituição brasileira** a partir de 25 de agosto de 2009, data da publicação do Decreto presidencial nº 6.949. Existem julgados do Tribunal Superior do Trabalho, inclusive da 3ª Turma, nos quais o cuidado diferenciado que deve ser dirigido às crianças portadoras de necessidades especiais justificou a alteração de turno de trabalho de seus pais. É evidente que **a transposição de um ideal de justiça de uma decisão judicial para a realidade concreta nem sempre é tranquila, ou mesmo factível. O alto grau de abstração de um princípio constitucional deve sempre ser levado em consideração pelo juiz no exame da exequibilidade e das repercussões econômicas e sociais de sua decisão.** Assim, é de toda pertinência a preocupação do Tribunal Regional com impacto financeiro e/ou administrativo de uma sentença desfavorável ao réu. Nesse sentido, o art. 5.3 da Convenção diz que, **"a fim de promover a igualdade e eliminar a discriminação, os Estados Partes adotarão todas as medidas apropriadas para garantir que a adaptação razoável seja oferecida"**. Já o art. 2 conceitua a **"<u>adaptação razoável</u>"** como as **"modificações e os ajustes necessários e adequados que não acarretem ônus desproporcional ou indevido, quando requeridos em cada caso, a fim de assegurar que as pessoas com deficiência possam gozar ou exercer, em igualdade de oportunidades com as demais pessoas, todos os direitos humanos e liberdades fundamentais". Prover "adaptação" significa adotar os esforços necessários para que os portadores de deficiência possam usufruir dos direitos humanos e fundamentais, em igualdade de condições com os demais indivíduos. A razoabilidade dessa acomodação encontra limite apenas na eventual desproporcionalidade entre os benefícios que podem ser alcançados com a sua adoção e os possíveis custos dela decorrentes.** Diante dessa perspectiva e tornando ao caso concreto, **cabe à Justiça do Trabalho conciliar os interesses divergentes entre as partes para que a criança possa ser acompanhada por sua mãe nas atividades multidisciplinares, sem que isso proporcione um ônus para o qual o réu não esteja preparado ou não consiga suportar**. Conforme o quadro fático expresso no acórdão recorrido, ***"a reclamante acumula dois contratos na função de Professor de Educação Básica II, ambos com a municipalidade reclamada, cada um com carga horária semanal de 31 horas"***. O pedido formulado na inicial consiste na obrigação de que a municipalidade autorize a sua ausência do serviço às terças-feiras, de 13h00 às 17h00 (quatro horas) e de 18h20 às 21h10 (duas horas e cinquenta minutos), e às quintas-feiras, de 12h30 às 17h00 (quatro horas e trinta minutos). Ou seja, **a autora pede para que lhe sejam reduzidas, sem prejuízo de sua remuneração, 11 horas e 20 minutos dentre as 62 horas semanais por ela despendidas no ofício de professora de Geografia da municipalidade ré**. Já **o município requer a total improcedência da reclamação trabalhista** ou ***"que seja encontrada outra solução para o próximo ano letivo, para a professora poder acompanhar o seu filho no tratamento e também não haja prejuízos tanto para os alunos da rede municipal, tanto quanto para o erário municipal"*** (sic). De um lado, sabe-se que **o acompanhamento da criança por sua mãe tende a desempenhar papel muito importante na sedimentação das competências adquiridas e/ou estimuladas nas atividades terapêuticas, mesmo porque o contato direto e reiterado da genitora com os membros da equipe multidisciplinar deve repercutir positivamente na estimulação adicional promovida no âmbito familiar**. Ademais, a ciência diz que a estimulação precoce é de extrema relevância para a maior eficácia das técnicas adotadas pelos profissionais. Diante desse contexto, uma eventual improcedência da pretensão poderia ensejar até mesmo um pedido de desligamento da trabalhadora, o que prejudicaria sobremaneira os rendimentos da família e colocaria em risco a própria subsistência do filho deficiente. De outro lado, entende-se que **a procedência integral do pedido demandaria uma série de expedientes do réu, a fim de que seus alunos não ficassem prejudicados e de que o impacto orçamentário fosse minimizado. Afinal, a readequação da grade horária dos docentes de Geografia, com o consequente pagamento de horas extras, ou mesmo a contratação de outro profissional, seja em cargo efetivo ou pela via do contrato emergencial, certamente resultaria em ônus administrativos para a municipalidade e financeiros para o erário, embora suportáveis em confronto com a manutenção do contrato de trabalho e o direito de acompanhamento do deficiente, em prol de uma melhor integração na sociedade.** Conforme ressaltado alhures, **a Lei nº 8.112/1990 assegura a concessão de horário especial ao servidor ou à servidora que possui cônjuge, filho ou dependente com deficiência, sem prejuízo do salário e sem a necessidade de compensação de horário**. Ora, **se o dependente do funcionário federal possui tal prerrogativa, entendemos que o filho de uma professora municipal deve desfrutar de direito semelhante. Pessoas**

em situações análogas não podem ser tratadas de forma absolutamente desigual, sob pena de violação do multicitado princípio da igualdade substancial, previsto tanto na Constituição Federal quanto na Convenção Internacional sobre os Direitos das Pessoas com Deficiência. No caso específico dos professores do município de Bariri, **a Lei Municipal nº 4.111/2011 determina que parte da jornada de trabalho seja realizada por meio de atividades pedagógicas extraclasse, coletivas ou individuais, as chamadas Horas de Trabalho Pedagógico Coletivo (HTPC), Horas de Trabalho Pedagógico Individual (HTPI) e Horas de Trabalho Pedagógico Livre (HTPL), sendo as últimas cumpridas em local e horário de livre escolha do docente, nos termos do art. 11, §6º**. Cabe destacar que o §3º do mesmo artigo diz que o professor de Educação Básica II poderá ampliar ou reduzir a jornada de trabalho definida no início do ano letivo, a critério da Administração, ao passo que o §4º estabelece que o número de horas de trabalho pedagógico sofrerá alteração conforme o número de horas/aulas que o docente assumir. A petição inicial alerta para o fato de que as 62 horas semanais de trabalho seriam compostas por 42 horas presenciais com os educandos, 4 horas de HTPC, 8 horas de HTPI e 8 horas de HTPL. **Imaginando-se, em adaptação ou acomodação razoável, um cenário em que as HTPL pudessem ser aumentadas e as horas presenciais diminuídas na mesma proporção, a autora certamente teria a possibilidade de administrar os seus horários para que pudesse ter a liberdade de acompanhar o seu filho nas sessões multidisciplinares. Adotando-se esse horário especial, ainda que haja, em adoção do princípio da solidariedade, a necessidade de remanejamento da jornada dos demais professores de Geografia, ou mesmo o pagamento de horas extras para a substituição da autora nos períodos de impossibilidade de sua docência presencial, o custo adicional para a municipalidade, seja financeiro ou administrativo, certamente não seria substancial a ponto de superar os benefícios individuais e as repercussões sociais decorrentes da procedência do pedido. A "adaptação", neste caso, atenderia plenamente o requisito da razoabilidade previsto no art. 2 da Convenção Internacional sobre os Direitos das Pessoas com Deficiência**, ainda mais quando se considera que esse ônus deve ser mitigado por um aumento de produtividade da professora, que, livre da preocupação de não poder acompanhar o seu filho nas atividades de que ele necessita, tende a preparar as aulas com maior qualidade e a ministrá-las com maior empenho e profundidade, em evidente benefício de seus alunos. Por fim, colaciona-se julgado do Superior Tribunal de Justiça em que uma demanda de portador de deficiência foi examinada sob a ótica do Princípio da Adaptação Razoável. **Recurso de revista conhecido, por violação do art. 5º, *caput*, da CF e parcialmente provido.**

....

ACORDAM os Ministros da Terceira Turma do Tribunal Superior do Trabalho, por unanimidade, **I** – conhecer e dar provimento ao agravo de instrumento para determinar o processamento do recurso de revista e **II** –

conhecer do recurso de revista, por violação do art. 5º, *caput*, da CF, e, no mérito, dar-lhe parcial provimento para condenar o reclamado na obrigação de fazer, consistente, em adoção do princípio da adaptação ou acomodação razoável vigente na legislação brasileira por ratificação de tratado internacional, **a adequação da jornada da jornada de trabalho** da reclamante por meio da **substituição das atividades pedagógicas presenciais por Horas de Trabalho Pedagógico Livre (HTPL), sem diminuição da remuneração**, a fim de que ela se ausente do trabalho às terças-feiras, de 13h00 às 17h00 e de 18h20 às 21h10, bem como às quintas-feiras, de 12h30 às 17h00, enquanto houver a necessidade de acompanhar o seu filho nas atividades terapêuticas de que ele necessita, que deve ser comprovada anualmente mediante laudo médico especializado. Ressalva-se o direito da criança a eventuais alterações dos dias e horários das sessões multidisciplinares, mas sempre respeitado o limite de 11 horas e 20 minutos semanais fixado na petição inicial. O decreto condenatório deve ser cumprido independentemente do trânsito em julgado, nos termos do art. 300 do CPC, até o primeiro dia do calendário letivo da educação pública do Município de Bariri no ano de 2021, sob pena de multa diária no valor de R$ 1.000,00 (mil reais). Custas de R$ 800,00 (oitocentos reais), das quais o reclamado se encontra isento, nos termos do art. 790-A da CLT e do Decreto-Lei nº 779/1969, calculadas sobre o montante de R$ 40.000,00 (quarenta mil reais), ora arbitrado à condenação.

Brasília, 2 de dezembro de 2020.**ALEXANDRE AGRA BELMONTE - Ministro Relator** (BRASIL, TERCEIRA TURMA DO TRIBUNAL SUPERIOR DO TRABALHO, 2020)

Conclusão

O direito à adaptação razoável é de natureza fundamental, destinado a corrigir discriminações indiretas, que inibem a concretização de direitos que podem ser exercitados mediante procedimentos destinados à acomodação de interesses.

O limite para a adaptação razoável (esforço factível de inclusão em obrigação de fazer) é o ônus indevido ou desproporcional que a pretensão possa acarretar em termos de ajuste (como dificuldades extremas, custo material excessivo etc).

Para o ajuste é preciso verificar a finalidade da medida destinada a excepcionar por meio da adaptação, para então comparar custos materiais e imateriais e benefícios diretos e indiretos.

O ônus é indevido, quando a adaptação mostra-se demasiadamente custosa (em sentido material e imaterial) em proporção aos benefícios individuais, necessidades empresariais e afetação de direitos coletivos.

Numa empresa em que trabalham adventistas do sétimo dia, muçulmanos, católicos e judeus, é possível conceder folga no dia correspondente à crença de cada um desses fieis, se esse procedimento for factível conforme a natureza e funcionamento normal do empreendimento. Seria possível numa atividade de restaurante ou numa fábrica que funcionam de segunda-feira a domingo, mas, em princípio, inviável num escritório que desenvolva o seu negócio somente de segunda a sexta-feira.

A Teoria do Impacto Desproporcional é específica e está fundada nos efeitos discriminatórios indiretos de uma norma ou situação de fato. Daí surge o Direito à Adaptação Razoável, destinado a permitir que a pessoa discriminada busque modificações e ajustes necessários e adequados a corrigir a distorção, para que, sem que isso acarrete ônus desproporcional ou indevido ao empresário, possa exercer, em igualdade de oportunidades em relação aos demais trabalhadores, um direito fundamental colocado em risco.

A técnica da ponderação de princípios não tem por fundamento necessário a discriminação e está fundada no conflito entre direitos fundamentais, para escolha daquele que puder, nas circunstâncias, atuar de forma otimizada, segundo graus de importância.

O Brasil adotou a Convenção sobre os Direitos das Pessoas com Deficiência da ONU em 30 de março de 2007, em Nova Iorque. Pelo Decreto Legislativo nº 186/2008, sancionado pelo Decreto nº 6.949/2009, passou a constar do ordenamento jurídico brasileiro a adaptação ou acomodação razoável, integrando a Constituição brasileira, como equivalente às emendas constitucionais, segundo dispõe o art.5º, §3º, CRFB/88.

Considerando que o real fundamento da adaptação razoável é coibir a discriminação indireta, por meio do ajustamento ou acomodação às necessidades particulares das minorias no ambiente empresarial, de forma que possam desfrutar dos mesmos direitos da maioria, tem-se que não pode ficar adstrita à deficiência física.

Logo, em que pese a ratificação da CDPD e o conceito ligado à deficiência física, é evidente que o seu campo de atuação é infinitamente maior.

Consequentemente, nas relações de trabalho podemos definir como adaptação ou acomodação razoável o dever de utilização dos meios, instrumentos, práticas e regras indispensáveis ao ajuste do ambiente de trabalho para assegurar igualdade condições e de oportunidades para que as minorias possam exerce, concretamente, os direitos e liberdades fundamentais com a mesma amplitude das maiorias.

Com efeito, o terreno aqui vislumbrado é o das políticas afirmativas, na busca do alcance de um patamar de igualdade material, por meio de instrumentos que permitam o harmônico convívio multiculturalista nas empresas.

O processo TST-RR-11.204-62.2017.5.15.0144, da Terceira Turma do Tribunal Superior do Trabalho, em julgamento unânime datado de 02/12/2020 e publicado no DEJT de 04/12/2020, em que foi Relator o Ministro Alexandre Agra Belmonte, pode ser considerado como *leading case* sobre a matéria na Justiça do Trabalho.

Decidiu-se caso em que foi aplicada a teoria da adaptação razoável diante do dilema de uma professora de ensino público não poder se ausentar do trabalho em dias e horários determinados para acompanhar o filho acometido de síndrome de Down às atividades terapêuticas indispensáveis ao desenvolvimento sadio e à integração social da criança. Sem elas, torna-se impossível o atingimento do maior estágio de evolução do deficiente em sociedade.

A adaptação foi possível porque importou em ônus razoável a ser suportado pelo empregador diante do benefício social que o procedimento trará para a criança deficiente, considerada a possibilidade de adequação da jornada de trabalho da trabalhadora por meio da substituição das atividades pedagógicas presenciais por Horas de Trabalho Pedagógico Livre (HTPL), sem diminuição da remuneração.

Bibliografia

Alexy, Robert, *Teoria dos Direitos Fundamentais*, trad. Virgilio Afonso da Silva (São Paulo: Malheiros, 2008)

Bonavides, Paulo, *Curso de Direito Constitucional* (São Paulo: Editora Malheiros, 2006)

Comparato, Fábio Konder, *A afirmação histórica dos direitos humanos* (São Paulo: Saraiva, 2008)

Dworkin, Ronald, *Levando os Direitos a Sério* (São Paulo: Saraiva, 2010)

Honesko, Raquel Schlommer, "Discussão Histórico-Jurídica sobre as Gerações de Direitos Fundamentais: a Paz como Direito Fundamental de Quinta Geração," In *Direitos Fundamentais e Cidadania,* coord. por Fachin, Zulmar (São Paulo: Método, 2008), p. 195

Madruga, Sidney, *Pessoas com Deficiência e Direitos Humanos* (São Paulo: Saraiva, 2016)

Mazzuoli, Valério de Oliveira, *O controle jurisdicional de convencionalidade das lei* (São Paulo: Editora Revista dos Tribunais, 2011)

Resende, Emerson Albuquerque, *O Direito Fundamental ao Trabalho da Pessoa com Deficiência no Brasil: caminhos para a eficácia social*, Dissertação de Mestrado (Universidade Federal de Sergipe, 2016), disponível em https://ri.ufs.br/bitstream/riufs/4385/1/EMERSON_ALBUQUERQUE_RESENDE.pdf, acesso em 19/02/2021

Romita, Arion Sayão, *Direitos fundamentais nas relações de trabalho* (São Paulo: LTr, 2007), p. 156

Sarmento, Daniel, *Direitos Fundamentais e Relações Privadas* (Rio de Janeiro: Lumen Juris, 2006)

Uriarte, Oscar Ermida, *Teoria da Discriminação nas Relações de Trabalho* (Rio de Janeiro: Campus Jurídico, 2011)

CHAPTER 13

LOS PRESUPUESTOS TEÓRICOS Y DOGMÁTICOS QUE EXIGE EL DEBER JURÍDICO DE LA DEBIDA DILIGENCIA. UN DESAFÍO DE RECONVERSIÓN DEL PENSAMIENTO

DIEGO LEDESMA ITURBIDE

1. Introducción y propósito

Existe una frase de alcance, diría, universal, que en esencia postula que no vemos las cosas como son sino como somos. Se trata de una proposición que pareciera sugerir que aquello que aprendemos resulta, en mayor o menor medida, producto y resultado de su vinculación con algo que ya sabemos y según cómo lo sabemos. En otros términos, en otra perspectiva, que todo proceso de aprendizaje no resulta en una mera y pura incorporación de saberes que se vuelcan en una hoja en blanco, sino que existe un rol activo del sujeto cognoscente que incide sobre el objeto de conocimiento, dándole sentido. Una intervención transformadora que ciertamente se encuentra, entonces, teñida, condicionada y determinada por los saberes previos.

En este entendimiento, los caracteres de la relación que se da entre objeto de conocimiento y sujeto cognoscente, y que es común a todo proceso o acto de aprendizaje, debiera determinar al individuo a un irrenunciable e inclaudicable ejercicio de indagar en torno a la consistencia y volumen de sus saberes adquiridos. Una vocación que exige siempre tematizarlos, explicitarlos, exponerlos, revisarlos y revisitarlos incansable para, llegado el caso, reconvertir tales saberes y reconvertirse con los nuevos. Todo ello se entiende necesario si lo que se pretende es aspirar a un razonamiento auténtico, a un conocimiento cientificista y de resultados mejores en términos de solidez y coherencia.

Ciertamente que la evocación de estas proposiciones luce particularmente pertinente en su consideración de cara a la comprensión de aquello que constituye el telón de fondo de lo que pretenderé desarrollar en estas líneas, lo que ha sido el móvil o inquietud general expresada en la convocatoria a participar en esta obra colectiva, la problemática sobre una supuesta falta de eficacia y crisis en general del derecho del trabajo en la actualidad. Y ello así en tanto la señalada resulta ser una cuestión de la mayor amplitud, extensa y extendida, histórica y compleja. Un desarrollo que al abordarse desde la perspectiva de Jurista, supone y compromete, necesariamente, muchos y muy diversos y variados saberes previos y, además, de naturaleza interdisciplinaria. Saberes previos con la virtualidad de comprometer y condicionar absolutamente no sólo la adecuada comprensión de la problemática referida, en cualquiera de sus múltiples aspectos, sino también el modo mismo de identificarla.

Con tal marco conceptual, el propósito de este trabajo será tematizar algunos de tales saberes previos o fundamentales involucrados, poner allí la lupa, cuestionar lo que se suele expresar y brindar respuestas que se suponen alternativas y mejores. Todo ello, por supuesto, en la convicción de que los resultados que se alcancen mediante tal práctica reflexiva tendrían, por sí mismos, la virtualidad de alcanzar a reconfigurar, modificar y transformar para mejor, el entendimiento de cuestiones más específicas, puntuales y de coyuntura.

Como se anticipó, estas líneas se apoyan sobre la problemática general de la supuesta falta de eficacia y crisis en general del derecho del trabajo. Ciertamente que no pretendo siquiera evocar aquí las enormes dificultades y graves cuestionamientos que enfrenta y desafían a la disciplina laboral en la actualidad, con impugnaciones que en algunos casos distan mucho de ser novedosas. Ni tampoco me resulta siquiera posible enumerar las circunstancias que causan o contribuyen a causar disfuncionalidad en la disciplina y que propician una crítica consecuente con aquello. En lugar de eso, me propongo utilizar como basamento o punto de partida para realizar el propósito anunciado, una mera alusión o evocación de un escenario complejo creado a partir de la aparición y difusión de las denominadas cadenas mundiales de suministro y del impacto que ello ha significado en el mundo jurídico en general y según sus caracteres actuales.

El acontecimiento elegido y que resulta ser el surgimiento y propagación global del fenómeno indicando, ciertamente que constituye un auténtico desafío al Jurista de cara a su tarea de interpretarlo, de conceptualizarlo y darle sentido en el contexto de un sistema de prescripciones con el cual aquél dialoga e interactúa. Un sistema normativo que luce hoy signado y modelado por los principios del estado constitucional de derecho y del derecho transnacional de los derechos humanos, por la entronización jurídica de la prescripción fundamental de la debida diligencia y del consecuente deber de las organizaciones de implementar sistemas adecuados de autorregulación.

Según mi humilde parecer, todo ello, toda esta puesta en escena, la práctica organizacional y su interacción, interrelacionamiento y diálogo con un contexto normativo que le brinda sentido y significado jurídico, conforman en conjunto un estado de situación dinámico, en desarrollo y evolución constante, que representa, insisto, un desafío al Jurista en su tarea de comprenderlo y dimensionarlo adecuadamente. Y ello así, ya sea porque la realidad pareciera contradecir reglas y saberes tradicionales, que son sus instrumentos de comprensión, lo que causa natural perplejidad en el intérprete; o porque las circunstancias existentes colaboran en impedir logre el Jurista intuir las soluciones posibles a las distintas problemáticas que el fenómeno plantea y suscita; o incluso, le obstaculizan siquiera advertir que existen ya vías de solución en curso y evolución; o porque el escenario pareciera invitar a un escepticismo en torno a la propia riqueza de la función de Jurista, que le limita a tan solo describir los hechos como un espectador de una realidad que no alcanza a comprender del todo.

El cúmulo de dificultades que el sentido y tratamiento jurídico del fenómeno de las cadenas mundiales de suministro entiendo suponen y traen aparejado aparece, entonces, como una oportunidad por demás propicia para darse a la tarea de revisar la consistencia de saberes previos. Por cierto que negarse a hacerlo supondrá arriesgarse a emplear nociones equivocadas y con ello, y en relación a la problemática en especial, a comprometer definitivamente las posibilidades del Jurista de colaborar elaborando una doctrina que fundamente y amalgame una reacción normativa que el fenómeno de por sí ha causado o contribuido a desarrollar, y con la cual dialoga y se interrelaciona. Una reacción normativa que ciertamente ocurre, se despliega y evoluciona, no obstante, en el terreno de los hechos. Por todo ello es que el fenómeno indicado resulta especialmente interesante y útil a los fines de este trabajo orientado, precisamente, a revisar conceptos de fundamento.

2. El escenario de las cadenas mundiales de suministro y el derecho transnacional de los derechos humanos. La prescripción de la debida diligencia y los sistemas de regulación empresarial

Las cadenas mundiales de suministro son una realidad global y ocurren y producen efectos sin mediar sistemas normativos efectivos que les gobiernen, tal es la magnitud del problema. El carácter transfronterizo del fenómeno, las razones económicas e ideológicas que le propician, promueven e incentivan, así como su propia complejidad, resultan en una cuestión que directamente inhibe y rechaza una adecuada sujeción de aquél a los mandatos jurídicos vigentes, tanto locales como internacionales o transnacionales. Esto apuntado no oculta, por cierto, el efecto positivo que tales emprendimientos indudablemente aparejan en términos económicos, de productividad y de generación de empleo. Sin embargo, tal ausencia indicada de vigilancia y control suficiente, adecuado y razonable, conduce a favorecer la producción de resultados disvaliosos y en múltiples sentidos (medioambiental, social, económico, etc.). En materia de derecho social, específicamente, no existen garantías ni mecanismos institucionales que aseguren allí, a lo largo de todo su entramado, la vigencia efectiva de condiciones de trabajo decente.

El problema que significan las cadenas mundiales de suministro es global y por dos razones. En primer lugar, a partir de las propias características transfronterizas del fenómeno y, en segundo lugar, porque los principios de un actualmente vigente Estado constitucional de derecho, obligan a ejercitar una visión integrada de las prescripciones de derecho social (de fuente local e internacional) con los mandatos provenientes del derecho transnacional de los derecho humanos, con sus normas, instituciones y prácticas.

Precisamente, en relación a esto último, desde el derecho transnacional de los derechos humanos se prescribe que la empresa, sea pública o privada, y cualquiera sea su tamaño e importancia, es siempre responsable por eventuales violaciones a los derechos humanos, y de todos ellos (civiles, políticos, económicos, sociales, culturales y medioambientales). También resulta incontrovertido allí que el alcance de la responsabilidad que se le atribuye a la empresa resulta comprehensiva no solo de la propia actuación sino también de la que llevan a cabo las terceras empresas con las cuales aquélla entabla relaciones. Este cúmulo obligacional y de atribución de responsabilidad se completa con el deber de observar una debida diligencia organizacional orientada, no sólo a evitar o prevenir daños o violaciones a derechos fundamentales sino, antes bien, a favorecer el máximo nivel de goce posible de tales derechos, según sus posibilidades.[1]

Otro aspecto insoslayable desde la perspectiva del derecho, y que resulta

---

[1] Todas estas resultan prescripciones que encuentran tratamiento exhaustivo en el ámbito internacional y se abordan bajo el título “Empresas y Derechos Humanos”, de donde destaca el instrumento de los “Principios Rectores sobre las empresas y los derechos humanos” (UNGPs), adoptado en el ámbito del Consejo de Derechos Humanos de Naciones Unidas por Resolución 17/4 del 16 de junio de 2011.

ser el correlato natural del deber de debida diligencia señalado, son los sistemas de autorregulación empresarial. Instrumentos de diseño e implementación voluntarios y que han merecido atención destacadísima y desarrollo encomiable en los más prestigiosos y encumbrados ámbitos institucionalizados de diálogo internacional y multilateral (ONU, OIT, OCDE, etc.). Herramientas que si bien entiendo estaban originariamente orientadas a asegurar la vigencia global de los principios del libre mercado, ética pública y lucha contra la corrupción, bien pueden también cumplir un papel ciertamente destacable e irremplazable para las corporaciones multinacionales en su indelegable tarea de dar adecuado cumplimiento al conjunto de mandatos que con toda Justicia le endilga el derecho trasnacional de los derechos humanos.

3. La noción de derecho como saber previo fundamental. El concepto de sistema normativo y su centralidad

Este escenario complejo descripto, que comprende a la práctica organizacional, la disfuncionalidad jurídica y el contexto normativo vigente, entiendo que resulta ser una ocasión por demás propicia para ensayar una revisión de la noción misma de derecho que utilizamos. Una noción que involucra muchos y muy variados saberes y que es absolutamente central. En este sentido, deberá considerarse que la determinación misma del sentido o relevancia jurídica de cualquier práctica o fenómeno, tanto como la comprensión o valoración de cualquier institución o herramienta jurídica supone, siempre y en todos los casos, un concepto o idea sobre lo que es el derecho. Un concepto o idea que aun cuando no surja patente en el discurso su tratamiento, tiene la virtualidad de afectar y teñir definitivamente aquella determinación, comprensión o valoración. Es más, la idea en torno al derecho constituye el medio y es la medida de la inteligencia y el procesamiento racional de cualquier fenómeno en perspectiva jurídica y bajo cualquiera de sus aspectos sensibles o perceptibles. Es por ello que reflexionar en torno a la noción de derecho que se posee y se utiliza, merece siempre del Jurista una atención prioritaria e impostergable.

Lo primero que debiera advertirse sobre este tema es que la discusión en torno a qué debiera entenderse por derecho no está concluida ni mucho menos, y que existen opiniones contradictorias al respecto[2]. Por mi parte,

[2] El derecho ha sido reconocido o identificado por diferentes escuelas *iusfilosóficas* como conjunto de normas; como práctica social estilizada; como conducta en interferencia intersubjetiva; como declinación de la Ley eterna; como racional organización de la convivencia social; y como sistema de expectativas

he adoptado como base de referencia y comprensión, ciertos postulados esenciales formulados por la denominada Teoría Egológica del Derecho, de Carlos Cossio. Se trata de una teoría que aspira a ser expresión de verdad científica y que define ontológicamente el objeto del derecho como conducta en interferencia intersubjetiva, es decir, un hacer compartido con otros. Esta auténtica escuela iusfilosófica adopta el método fenomenológico de Edmund Husserl, toma para sí los avances de la lógica jurídica formal de su época, e intenta dar una explicación sistemática de la experiencia jurídica, concebida como una praxis que integra tres elementos: a) la estructura lógica de la norma jurídica, que expone el modo de razonar propia y específicamente jurídico; b) los contenidos dogmáticos por ella mentados; y c) la valoración jurídica existente. La nominación de "egológica" se desprende del dato de que el objeto a conocer, que no es otro que el sentido jurídico de la conducta en interferencia subjetiva, es un objeto que a su vez ha de conocerse como tal, un conocimiento que parte de la propia conducta y que vuelve reflexivamente sobre ella.[3]

La Teoría Egológica del Derecho se distingue claramente de concepciones que son expresión de lo que juzgo un irreflexivo "positivismo legalista", el cual persiste, no obstante, en el discurso actual. Una línea de pensamiento, ésta última, que identifica derecho con el conjunto de normas generales, válidas y vigentes sancionadas por el legislador; y donde el legislador es el funcionario facultado por el Estado para crear, procedimiento legal mediante, el "derecho" que el juez deberá aplicar a los casos concretos sometidos a su conocimiento; donde las normas son consideradas objetos independientes y autónomos; donde conocer textos de normas es conocer derecho y; donde la aplicación de las normas a los casos concretos requiere de recurrir a uno o más métodos objetivos de interpretación. Todo esto postulado por el "positivismo legalista" es falso y se sostiene tan solo en motivaciones de tipo ideológico (Cossio 1961; Cárcova 2009).

Los postulados del "positivismo legalista" y no obstante su falsedad evidente, parecieran gozar de buena salud y se exhiben, entonces,

---

congruentemente generalizadas, y ello sólo según las vertientes más divulgadas (Cárcova 2009).

[3] Desde ya que la evocación que realizo de ciertos postulados esenciales formulados por la Teoría Egológica del Derecho, de Carlos Cossio, es elemental, precaria y no alcanza a presentar a esta teoría de un modo integral ni completo. En efecto, esto que presento es un recorte de ideas o, mejor dicho, mi interpretación de estas ideas. Se trata de nociones que si bien considero principales, debieran complementarse con la lectura de bibliografía específica y, preferentemente, de la elaborada por su propio autor, para lograr así un conocimiento acabado y mejor valoración y dimensionamiento de la teoría en sí.

incuestionados en calidad de saber previo y constituyendo algo así como una especie de sentido jurídico común[4]. La aplicación de los principios que caracterizan al "positivismo legalista" comporta una práctica deficitaria y con la potencialidad de afectar de manera irremediable y definitiva la calidad de la comprensión jurídica y, lógicamente, de la producción doctrinaria que resulta ser su medio de materialización. Nótese que el cambio en la concepción del derecho, y por caso, la adhesión e internalización de los postulados fundamentales de la Teoría Egológica del Derecho, de Carlos Cossio, conduce a tener una perspectiva bien diferente de todo el fenómeno jurídico en general y de manera integral. Así, por ejemplo, y lo destaco aquí, a erigir como idea central al concepto de sistema u ordenamiento jurídico o normativo y reconocer la funcionalidad que allí ostenta.

En efecto, el empleo de los postulados de la Teoría Egológica del Derecho, entiendo, conducen al descubrimiento del concepto de sistema u ordenamiento jurídico o normativo. Por cierto que este elemento resulta ser, como se anticipó, una parte central, definitoria y determinante del fenómeno jurídico y de su comprensión misma. A continuación procuraré caracterizarlo mediante el relevamiento de algunos de sus aspectos esenciales o definitorios, para luego procurar ensayar el impacto e influencia que tendría en la práctica de Jurista y de cara a la intelección del escenario complejo elegido.

a) Un sistema normativo está conformado por prescripciones cuya finalidad o propósito esencial es procurar una determinada realización de Justicia y que se expresa en forma de normas jurídicas generales. Ahora bien, cada una de tales normas jurídicas generales, y a diferencia de lo que sostiene el "positivismo legalista", no resulta ser un objeto autónomo e independiente, sino que es solo una estructura lógica, el modo de pensar estrictamente jurídico. Por otro lado, tal conjunto de prescripciones conforma el contenido dogmático o material del sistema normativo, siendo el resultado de la práctica de la función legislativa. Se aclara que la referida "función legislativa" es aquí una práctica o ejercicio cuya expresión más tradicional, aunque no la única, resulta ser la aprobación de disposiciones normativas o leyes, en sentido material, y que consiste, básicamente, en la selección e individualización de circunstancias de hecho a las se les imputa cierto determinado tratamiento, efecto o consecuente normativo, como

---

[4] Tal cosa se hace evidente tras un rápido análisis de los argumentos jurídicos usualmente utilizados en los textos de los especialistas. Así, por ejemplo, cuando se limita el análisis crítico o propositivo a lo que pueda figurar o no como texto en disposiciones normativas, como si tal cosa bastara para modificar la realidad e ignorando, por caso, la importancia de la función judicial.

debiendo ser[5]. En la norma jurídica individual, en cambio, que deriva necesariamente de la norma jurídica general, tal contenido dogmático o material será resultado de la práctica de la "función judicial", lo que ocurre perceptible empíricamente y que constituye la experiencia jurídica.[6]

b) Un sistema normativo posee una naturaleza ideal o conceptual y existe sólo como tal. Un concepto o idea del mundo del "deber ser" que alude al conjunto de prescripciones válidas y vigentes en un lugar y tiempo determinado, y cuyo cumplimiento está asegurado por la coerción. Existen múltiples sistemas jurídicos, tantos como sean reconocibles, y el modo de reconocer y de conceptualizar o delimitar conceptualmente a un sistema jurídico como tal y en su individualidad, es mediante el ejercicio de la función judicial. En efecto, y así como conocemos del contenido y de la singularidad de cualquier concepto por los elementos que se juzgan denotados por la expresión, sabremos del contenido y singularidad de un sistema jurídico en particular a partir del ejercicio generalizado de la función judicial. En este sentido, el ejercicio generalizado o extendido de la función judicial, más allá de su propósito próximo de atribuirle sentido jurídico a un comportamiento dado, visto en perspectiva intersubjetiva, tiene también un inocultable efecto constitutivo y delimitador de un sistema jurídico determinado. En otras palabras, un sistema jurídico es tal solo en la medida de su reconocimiento mediante la práctica extendida de la función judicial.[7]

---

[5] La función legislativa es una práctica que no debe resultar asociada a ningún órgano en particular. No obstante, en el ámbito del derecho, en tanto dicha función resulta en prescripciones de carácter obligatorio, su ejercicio válido deberá vincularse necesariamente con alguna entidad dotada de autoridad suficiente como para crearlas (vgr. la razón, la naturaleza, una divinidad).

[6] Surge así y con claridad, una nítida distinción entre la función legislativa y la función judicial. La primera, ya descripta, y donde el resultado se manifiesta en forma de prescripciones que se integran y fusionan luego en el sistema jurídico, completándolo y modificándolo. La función judicial, en cambio, es una práctica que consiste en decidir acerca del sentido jurídico que debe atribuírsele a un comportamiento intersubjetivo dado a la percepción, ya sea éste real o hipotético. Tal sentido va a ser indefectiblemente provisto por el contenido dogmático del sistema jurídico. La realización de la función judicial implica y conlleva la subsunción de una determinada actuación dentro del ámbito de aplicación de disposiciones normativas generales determinadas. Dicho con más precisión, la conclusión de que aquella verifica el presupuesto de hecho normativo previsto en una determinada norma jurídica general y debiéndose aplicar, entonces y como derivación, el tratamiento o efecto jurídico allí dispuesto como debiendo ser.

[7] Esta noción puede válidamente asimilarse a la idea de la "regla de reconocimiento" de Hart, H. L.A., plasmada en su célebre obra *El concepto de Derecho,* solo que en el pensamiento del prestigioso jurista inglés, la misma aludía al reconocimiento de

c) Un sistema normativo dado contiene y expresa un propósito político determinado y pretende realizar ciertos valores y postulados más o menos fundamentales mediante prescripciones o proposiciones del "deber ser". Dicho contenido con ideario no es, por cierto, materia cristalizada ni cosa que permanezca estática en el tiempo, sino que evoluciona al ritmo de la sanción de cada nueva disposición normativa particular válida, por insignificante que sea. Evoluciona y se transforma también con la sanción de un nuevo proceso para la adopción de prescripciones normativas de carácter general, o con un nuevo modo de comprenderlo o de atribuirle sentido de Justicia a sus prescripciones, entre otras maneras posibles. La evolución en los sistemas normativos también alcanza a conformar estadios o períodos con características bien marcadas y contrastantes a nivel global. Así ocurrió, por ejemplo, con la sucesiva conformación de lo que se denominara Estado Liberal de Derecho, Estado Social de Derecho y del actual Estado Constitucional de Derecho, cada uno con sus caracteres definitorios y bien diferenciales.

d) Un sistema normativo posee carácter de organización plena y totalitaria o totalizadora. La totalidad lleva la pluralidad a la unidad, siendo la síntesis de los conceptos de unidad y pluralidad. Esto implica, concretamente, que todo sistema normativo jurídico y cualquiera sea el número de prescripciones que se considera que contiene, no tiene carencias normativas o "lagunas". Lo que significa, a su vez, que quien ejerce la función judicial siempre encuentra y cuenta con una norma jurídica general en la que basar su decisión.[8]

4. Reflexiones en torno al impacto de la aplicación práctica de la idea de sistema normativo expuesta en la práctica de la función de Jurista y de cara a la comprensión jurídica del escenario complejo indicado

Si bien para el estudioso del derecho resulta algo de por sí positivo mejorar los conceptos que se utilizan, lo cierto es que el empleo de conocimientos

---

normas legales válidas y vigentes y aquí se emplea en relación al reconocimiento en torno a la individualidad o singularidad de un sistema normativo determinado.

[8] Cossio enfatiza en que el derecho no tiene lagunas porque hay jueces. Que ser Juez significa administrar justicia, donde la necesidad de juzgar en que están los jueces resulta una verdad de razón, con lo que su enunciación en un código está de más, y que un Juez no cumple su función sólo cuando se abstiene de sentenciar, lo que es usualmente denominado denegación de justicia. La verdad de estas conclusiones yace en el hecho de que, como se afirmó, la función judicial es inmanente al derecho, o en otros términos, de que no hay derecho sin función judicial (Cossio 1939).

más depurados tiene un innegable impacto práctico en la labor del Jurista y, lógicamente también, en la comprensión del escenario complejo descripto. Y ciertamente que cuanto más general y profundo sea el concepto, mayor será tal impacto. En este sentido y sin pretender agotar el tema ni mucho menos, procuraré esbozar algunas reflexiones que a título de simples pinceladas, tenderán a poner de manifiesto la trascendencia del empleo allí de algunas de las ideas indicadas y asociadas al concepto mismo de derecho y de sistema normativo, de cara a ciertas cuestiones que en forma de interrogantes o inquietudes ha suscitado el escenario escogido.

Uno primero, frente al déficit de eficacia normativa en las cadenas de suministro trasnacional ¿Es necesaria la sanción de normas jurídicas adecuadas, especiales, o la adopción de instrumentos normativos vinculantes del derecho internacional para asegurar allí y con coerción el imperio de la ley en toda su extensión? ¿Existe aquí un escenario de carencia de norma?

La posición que propicio relativa a la noción misma de derecho y de sistema normativo, conducen a responder negativamente al interrogante planteado, por lo menos en carácter de necesidad. Destaco, en fundamento, la idea ya evocada y relativa a que las normas no son objetos independientes, que no existe derecho sin ejercicio de la función judicial, y que las prescripciones normativas son expresiones de un sistema normativo que no posee "lagunas". En este punto y con la mirada puesta ahora en el contenido dogmático de los sistemas normativos, de su carácter y del sentido de Justicia que expresan, relevar que el tiempo actual no pareciera exigir en absoluto la sanción de norma adicional alguna para reconocer la obligación jurídica y positiva que pesa sobre los Estados y las empresas de garantizar y respetar de manera progresiva, integral, interrelacionada e irrenunciable, la totalidad de las prescripciones provenientes del derecho trasnacional de los derechos humanos, que existe una conciencia jurídica global consolidada en torno a ello y que entonces y en definitiva, no podría reconocerse allí déficit alguno.[9]

En todo caso, el problema cuya solución se procura versaría en asegurar la coerción de las prescripciones exigibles. Ello así en tanto se percibe que la empresa multinacional no responde eficazmente, que no recibe sanción jurídica alguna por las consecuencias disvaliosas que cause, o que contribuya a causar, en función de eventuales incumplimientos suyos de mandatos provenientes del derecho transnacional de los derechos humanos y no obstante estar positivamente obligada a respetarlos. Será, así y

---

[9] Esto señalado, no va en desmedro de la sanción de disposiciones normativas que especifiquen obligaciones y/o que resulten tendientes a asegurar los mandatos del derecho internacional mediante la imposición de conductas o procedimientos específicos.

entonces, un problema de ineficacia normativa y no de ausencia de norma. Una situación por demás relevante en tanto el carácter imperativo u obligatorio del derecho, la coerción, resulta ser elemento propio e indisociable de su misma conceptualización, en tanto no hay derecho donde no existe coerción. Pero insisto, se trata de un problema cuya solución definitiva no podría nunca depender o derivar de un texto dado a un instrumento normativo cualquiera, en tanto éste será siempre un concepto que se integrará al sistema normativo y que requerirá luego del ejercicio de la función judicial para alcanzar naturaleza sensible o perceptible y ser susceptible, entonces, de conocimiento empírico mediante el desarrollo de la experiencia jurídica, que es experiencia positiva y no ideal o conceptual. Así las cosas, el problema esencial que plantean las cadenas mundiales de suministro no puede ser nunca un problema de ausencia de norma o de "laguna". Ello en función, por un lado, de que los sistemas normativos no poseen "lagunas" y, por el otro, que existe consolidado a nivel del derecho trasnacional de los derechos humanos el deber positivo en cabeza de los Estados y las empresas, de garantizar y respetar los derechos humanos, respectivamente. En cualquier caso, pareciera haber un déficit de jurisdicción, de inexistencia o insuficiencia de órganos o instituciones con atribuciones suficientes para "decir" el derecho con el alcance transfronterizo que el fenómeno reclama, o de que se reconozca válida, de que se respete y de que se cumpla lo que allí se decida y con coerción y eficacia.

Un segundo planteo o reflexión que practico está relacionado al deber de realizar una debida diligencia y en torno a la implementación de sistemas de autorregulación organizacional o *Compliance* ¿Resultan instrumentos o expresiones de *Softlaw*?, ¿Constituyen una flexibilización o atenuación de la exigibilidad de obligaciones jurídicas? ¿Materializan una autorización para que cada quien elija qué obligaciones cumplir y en qué medida?

Como se señaló, el contexto normativo vigente reclama, impulsa y brega por una universalización de los principios del estado constitucional de derecho, y entonces, de sistemas normativos nacionales que resulten permeables a las prescripciones fundamentales adoptadas en la instancia trasnacional. Así, en la Organización Internacional del Trabajo, en su calidad de organismo especializado de Naciones Unidas, como desde el seno mismo de los sistemas universal y regional de protección de los derechos humanos. Por su parte, que desde el mismo ámbito trasnacional surge exigible el deber de practicar una debida diligencia en materia de derechos humanos. Un deber consagrado a texto explícito como deber propio de las organizaciones, de todas ellas, públicas o privadas y cualquiera sea su tamaño, carácter, actividad en la que se desenvuelva, producto que elabore, servicio que brinde, etc., por el documento cardinal de los Principios Rectores sobre las Empresas y los Derechos Humanos de las Naciones Unidas (UNGPs). Una auténtica declaración de principios de Naciones Unidas en la materia, cuya importancia y trascendencia resulta hoy día insoslayable.[10]

El deber de debida diligencia resulta ser una prescripción clara, práctica y directamente operativa, que ha sido definida como "la medida de prudencia, actividad o asiduidad que cabe razonablemente esperar, y con la que normalmente actúa, una (persona) prudente y razonable en unas circunstancias determinadas" (Oficina del Alto Comisionado de las Naciones Unidas para los Derechos Humanos 2012). Un deber de debida diligencia que pesa sobre los Estados[11], en tanto garantes de la efectiva vigencia de los derechos, como también, y directamente, sobre las empresas, quienes deben respetarlos fundamentalmente mediante la implementación sistemas adecuados de autorregulación empresarial. Surge así y con claridad meridiana, que las empresas resultan directamente responsables del deber de prevenir y reparar cualquier daño que pueda ocurrir por abuso o afectación nociva de los derechos humanos reconocidos en la Carta Universal de derechos humanos. Un deber que, por otra parte, les resulta directamente atribuible y exigible, y sobre el que deben dar cuenta independientemente de la capacidad o voluntad de los Estados. Por cierto que también surge expresado allí, en el ámbito trasnacional, y con elocuencia y determinación, que el deber jurídico de debida diligencia no resultará tan solo una herramienta apta o idónea para que la empresa cumpla con eficacia y suficiencia la responsabilidad que sobre ella pesa en materia de respeto de los derechos humanos, sino, más bien, que su implementación resulta ser auténtica condición para que pueda siquiera aspirar a lograrlo. Especialmente necesaria resulta la práctica en la empresa multinacional, en

---

[10] El documento de los Principios Rectores, cabe destacarlo, constituyen un auténtico punto de referencia global en la materia y registra recepción expresa en importantes instrumentos del sistema universal de protección de los derechos humanos. Por su parte, tanto la Declaración Tripartita de Principios sobre las Empresas Multinacionales y la Política Social de la OIT, como el documento Líneas Directrices de la OCDE para Empresas Multinacionales, se han actualizado para comprender la novedad que resultó ser su adopción.

[11] Así surge de las Directrices de Maastricht, del año 1997, que en referencia a la actuación de las entidades privadas o particulares (incluidas las empresas transnacionales) prescribe que "...Los Estados son responsables de las violaciones a los derechos económicos, sociales y culturales que resultan cuando no controlan con la debida diligencia la conducta de dichos actores sociales" (Directrices de Maastricht sobre Violaciones a los Derechos Económicos, Sociales y Culturales, Maastricht 1997)

función de su propia complejidad, de su carácter transfronterizo y de las problemáticas que suscita. La debida diligencia es, entonces, una herramienta fundamental y necesaria en la lucha por el respeto por los derechos humanos en las cadenas de valor transnacionales. Es una práctica organizacional virtuosa y necesaria, dirigida a prevenir, mitigar y reparar con eficacia eventuales violaciones de derechos humanos, entre ellos, los laborales.

Por otro lado y en carácter de auténtico correlato al deber de debida diligencia, se encuentran los sistemas de autorregulación o de cumplimiento (Compliance), que son, como ya se señaló, el modo mejor (¿único?) de cumplir adecuadamente con el deber de debida diligencia. Se trata, en definitiva, de instrumentos cuyo alcance, eficacia y eficiencia está determinada por el propio interés de quien lo diseña y pone en funciones, y que usualmente es también quien lo controla y lo supervisa en exclusividad y sin interferencias de terceros. Este carácter eminentemente voluntarista y privado de la herramienta, esta ausencia cuanto menos inicial o decisiva de heteronomía, es lo que conduce a su natural descalificación como dispositivo apto o idóneo para garantizar siquiera el cabal cumplimiento de las obligaciones jurídicas que la propia organización asume mediante aquél. Es más, suele atribuirse la opción por su instauración a una intención empresarial de satisfacer mediante él y únicamente, sus propios intereses. Ahora bien, y no obstante la sospecha razonable y justificable que pesa sobre el instrumento y según sus características señaladas, lo cierto y constatable es que los mismos han visto aumentada su importancia y centralidad en el concierto internacional. En efecto, sea por la razón que fuere, lo que no por otra parte no corresponde sea analizado aquí, lo cierto y constatable es que la herramienta ha despertado y estimulado un decidido interés internacional en desarrollarlo, y que se han precisado las exigencias o estándares que aquél debiera cumplir para ser considerado seriamente y según su funcionalidad y potencialidad, y no una mera formalidad[12]. En este sentido y en general, podría sostenerse que un buen sistema de autorregulación debiera: a) ser adecuado a la empresa, en el sentido de exhibir correspondencia con su dimensión, con su capacidad económica y

[12] En este sentido y provenientes del ámbito internacional, destacan los estándares fijados en la Evaluación de programas corporativos de Compliance del Departamento de Justicia de los EE.UU; la Guía de Buenas Prácticas sobre Control Interno, Ética y Cumplimiento de Normas y el Manual de Ética y Cumplimiento contra la Corrupción para las Empresas de la OCDE; y el Programa anticorrupción de ética y cumplimiento para las empresas de la UNODC, entre otros. Por su parte, también alcanzaron notoriedad las normas internacionales ISO 19600 de Sistemas de Gestión de Compliance o ISO 37001 de Sistemas de Gestión Anti-Soborno.

con los riesgos específicos y particulares a los cuales se halle expuesta; b) facilitar el descubrimiento de las inconductas por parte de la propia organización y, en tal sentido, tender a romper los pactos de silencio y facilitar un sistema de denuncias internas, con garantías suficientes a la seguridad del denunciante y con el debido resguardo de la privacidad de los datos que colecte; c) contar con apoyo al más alto nivel en la organización y con personas designadas directamente responsables de su cumplimiento a nivel interno; d) ser conocido y con previsión del desarrollo de programas específicos de capacitación; e) abarcar procedimientos y prácticas de debida diligencia también hacia terceros con los cuales se entablen relaciones; f) contemplar instrumentos para el monitoreo de su funcionalidad y correcta operatoria; g) actualizarse de manera periódica; h) resultar susceptible de ser explicado en su razonabilidad frente a su eventual requerimiento por parte de las autoridades.[13]

La idea de sistema normativo como totalidad deriva en comprender al deber de debida diligencia y los sistemas de autorregulación empresarial no como prescripciones de fuente privada, ni tampoco como obligaciones autónomas o independientes. Tampoco podrían considerarse prescripciones que están por fuera de los ordenamientos normativos, ni que vienen a sustituirlos, o a dialogar con ellos, o siquiera que les complementen como elementos distintos. En cambio, y según mi parecer, el deber de debida diligencia y los sistemas de autorregulación resultan prescripciones que nutren y se integran al sistema normativo, conformándolo en su unidad, en su totalidad. Así las cosas, tanto el deber de debida diligencia como el de implementar un buen sistema de autorregulación y su resultado, el instrumento en sí, serán, ambas, prescripciones que son expresiones de un sistema normativo determinado.

La situación de integración señalada causa que el contenido dogmático del sistema normativo se vea modificado, enriquecido y alterado por los nuevos deberes, al tiempo que como totalidad que es, éste tiña, module, matice y especifique, el alcance mismo de tales prescripciones y según su propio ideario. El deber de debida diligencia encuentra sentido, entonces, en su consideración y articulación junto con el resto de las prescripciones que expresa un sistema normativo determinado. En este sentido y desde la instancia transnacional se aclara que la debida diligencia es un presupuesto necesario y útil, pero cuya implementación no exime de responsabilidad a

---

[13] En la Argentina, la cuestión figura entre las preocupaciones y actividades de los organismos públicos. Así, su Oficina Anticorrupción publicó en el año 2018 sus "Lineamientos de integridad para empresas y otras personas jurídicas", que desde el año 2019 cuenta con una "Guía Complementaria" para pequeñas y medianas empresas.

las empresas. Resulta, entonces, insuficiente por sí sola y, en todo caso, les permite mostrar a las empresas que tomaron todas las medidas razonables para evitar cualquier participación en una supuesta vulneración de los derechos humanos.[14]

Un tercer planteo, el carácter transfronterizo del fenómeno y su reacción normativa de cara a la caracterización de los sistemas normativos contemporáneos.

Como se señaló, uno de los aspectos más problemáticos que suscitan las cadenas de valor es el de la ineficacia normativa. Un problema que involucra, atañe o afecta directa o indirectamente a los Estados "sede" tanto a los Estados de "destino" de las empresas y conglomerados internacionales, quienes por acción u omisión, por impotencia o interés, favorecen, aumentan y hacen propicio o perpetúan tal déficit señalado aumentando el riesgo de vulneración de los derechos humanos. Ahora bien, frente a tal circunstancia, lo cierto y constatable es que ha existido una reacción internacional evidente, encabezada por el derecho transnacional de los derechos humanos, con sus normas e instituciones. Una reacción que interactúa y dialoga con el fenómeno, puesto que la respuesta jurídica surge y se desarrolla a medida de exigencias políticas, fundamentalmente. En términos de análisis jurídico, se trata de una reacción que ha tenido la virtualidad de transformar la configuración, los contornos y las características de los sistemas normativos existentes. Así, desde una concepción estrictamente nacional de los sistemas normativos a una permeada, atravesada y teñida por los valores e instituciones del derecho transnacional de los derechos humanos. Un fenómeno cuya importancia y trascendencia ha justificado considerar el fin de la vigencia de los principios característicos y definitorios del denominado Estado Social de Derecho, sustentado y basado en un respeto categórico al principio de la soberanía estatal y el advenimiento en su lugar de la principiología del Estado constitucional de derecho, con sus rasgos distintivos de internacionalidad creciente. Resulta hoy evidente que los sistemas normativos contemporáneos expresan puntos de contacto, e incluso de obediencia y sumisión, en relación a lo que sucede en los ámbitos del derecho internacional y transnacional de los derechos humanos, al tiempo que dialogan y se relacionan activamente con otros sistemas normativos nacionales construyendo instancias y canales de coordinación y cooperación de acciones.

Esta interacción relevada no oculta por cierto el hecho de que los

[14] Comentario al Principio Rector Nro. 17.

sistemas normativos continúan siendo entidades o instituciones ligadas a la idea de Estatal Soberano. Un dato que resulta absolutamente razonable a partir de considerar que los Estados son los únicos entes que detentan el monopolio de la fuerza y que pueden así asegurar la coerción que el derecho necesita, por definición. Pero también resulta cierto e incuestionable que los Estados son también sujetos de un sistema normativo transnacional que les impone obligaciones; que los Estados, todos y cada uno de ellos, actuando de manera individual o en coordinación con los demás, son los garantes de que todas las personas y todas las organizaciones actúen con respeto de los deberes que impone el derecho transnacional de los derechos humanos; y que tal rol principal e indelegable de los Estados supone el deber de desplegar una actuación orientada, no solo a hacer efectivo el respeto de tales derechos, sino también a protegerlos, garantizarlos y promoverlos[15]. Es más, a partir de tal plafón conceptual y obligacional, resulta claro que el primer deber de los Estados es ejercitar ellos mismos una debida diligencia en la materia y con el empleo de hasta el máximo de los recursos disponibles[16]. Una expresión esta última que, desde luego, no debiera interpretarse aludiendo a recursos económicos únicamente sino y especialmente al recurso Estatal de implementar políticas públicas idóneas y de poder dictar disposiciones normas generales y obligatorias (poder legal), como también al poder de "decir" el derecho (poder jurisdiccional). Poderes con la virtualidad de generar obligaciones y responsabilidad jurídicas por la actuación desplegada por las personas incluso fuera de los límites geográficos de los Estados, en el ámbito extraterritorial.

Así las cosas, y en términos de legislación, una primera conducta esperable y diligente del Estado en procura de cumplir con sus propias e indelegables obligaciones en la materia y con adecuado empleo de sus recursos legislativos puede válidamente ser la dictar normas dirigidas a imponerle a la empresa transnacional nacional la obligación de adoptar

---

[15] En este sentido y a fin de distinguir adecuadamente las obligaciones indicadas, enseña G. J. H. VAN HOOF que "…Las obligaciones de *respetar* el derecho en cuestión se definen por el deber del Estado de no injerir, obstaculizar o impedir el acceso al goce de los bienes que constituyen el objeto del derecho. Las obligaciones de *proteger* consisten en impedir que terceros injieran, obstaculicen o impidan el acceso a esos bienes, las obligaciones de *garantizar* suponen asegurar que el titular del derecho acceda al bien cuando no puede hacerlo por sí mismo. Las obligaciones de *promover* se caracterizan por el deber de desarrollar condiciones para que los titulares del derecho accedan al bien" (Courtis 2002). El destacado en cursiva me pertenece.

[16] Cfr. Pacto Internacional de Derechos Económicos Sociales y Culturales (PIDESC), art. 2.

medidas de control de sus cadenas mundiales de producción para el respeto de derechos humanos fundamentales, incluyendo los medioambientales[17], o la de exigir una declaración de ejercicio de debida diligencia[18]. Otro medio posible de actuación Estatal directa orientado a la promoción del diseño y puesta en práctica por las empresas de medidas eficaces de control en las cadenas mundiales de producción es condicionar la contratación o la provisión de colaboración o soporte político, legal y/o financiero, a que la empresa y sus socios comerciales cumplan con sus deberes de respeto de los derechos humanos, mediante sistemas de autorregulación empresarial u organizacional de debida diligencia[19]. O de trabajar, por ejemplo, en la elaboración de instrumentos internacionales que establezcan estándares cuyo cumplimiento por parte de los sistemas de autorregulación organizacional resulten tendientes a garantizar con eficacia que los procesos de debida diligencia organizacional cumplan y alcancen con autenticidad los fines y propósitos a los que están orientados. O de fomentar y estimular el ejercicio de tal debida diligencia organizacional mediante la posibilidad de que mediante tales iniciativas las empresas puedan ver atenuada o hasta resultar incluso eximidas de responsabilidad civil y/o penal por violaciones a los derechos humanos. En cualquier caso, deberá siempre priorizarse el derecho de las víctimas a obtener remedio.

5. Reflexión final

El deber de debida diligencia importa una auténtica novedad del instrumental jurídico contemporáneo. Una novedad que exige un hacer activo de las organizaciones, de todas ellas, sean públicas o privadas. No se

[17] Tal como lo hizo la ley francesa sobre el deber de vigilancia de las transnacionales, LEY N ° 2017-399 de 27 de marzo de 2017.

[18] Tal como prescribe una ley de los Países Bajos que entró en vigor en el mes de enero del 2020, aunque limitada a la lucha contra el trabajo infantil. Lo propio efectiviza la Ley de Esclavitud Moderna del Reino Unido, la Ley de transparencia sobre cadenas de suministro en el estado de California en Estados Unidos, o la Ley de Esclavitud Moderna en Australia

[19] En este punto destaco que en el ámbito regional americano rige el principio de responsabilidad extraterritorial de los Estados por violaciones de derechos humanos que tengan lugar en zonas que se encuentran bajo su autoridad o control efectivo ("doctrina del control efectivo"). Un criterio de atribución de responsabilidad que bien puede ser de útil y de aplicación también en circunstancias que existe un déficit de conducta diligente de los propios Estados, al tiempo que les legitima y obliga a implementar medidas de promoción del tipo de las indicadas al principio de este párrafo y que están también específicamente mencionadas en el Comentario al Principio Rector Nro. 4 y en ejercicio, entonces, de su poder de influencia.

trata, entonces, solo de cumplir con disposiciones normativas determinadas para evitar la sanción prevista como consecuente, sino de asumir la iniciativa de procurar satisfacer las exigencias y obligaciones jurídicas del mejor modo posible. Se trata de un deber cuya cabal realización demanda el máximo compromiso y esfuerzo de las organizaciones, medido de acuerdo a sus posibilidades reales y considerando, también, la situación de necesidad de los eventuales damnificados en sus derechos.

El deber de debida diligencia conduce a relativizar así la importancia de la norma legislada y propicia, en cambio, el diseño y puesta en práctica de acciones positivas, políticas públicas integrales a cargo del Estado y con participación de los actores sociales, y de la implementación de buenos sistemas de autorregulación por las organizaciones privadas. El deber de debida diligencia promueve abandonar expresiones como la clásica y difundida tesis individualista que sostiene que el derecho de unos termina donde comienza el de los demás, y procura, en cambio, acentuar su carácter comunitario y relevar el necesario compromiso de cada uno para asegurar y hacer posible el goce efectivo de los derechos humanos por parte de los demás.

En términos de dogmática jurídica se trata que el Jurista relacione el deber de debida diligencia y lo integre al concepto de sistema normativo y a su contenido dogmático, específicamente. Que en ejercicio de su función conceptualice y describa los caracteres actuales de tales sistemas normativos y el modo como los mismos dialogan, interactúan y se relaciona con otros sistemas nacionales, transnacionales o internacionales. Que colabore en construir y establecer una cultura jurídica global que comprenda a la debida diligencia organizacional como una práctica necesaria e inseparable del deber de respeto de los derechos humanos que pesa sobre las organizaciones empresarias y de manera directa.

Se trata también de crear conciencia crítica en relación a los postulados del "positivismo legalista", de entender que tal punto de partida, tal saber previo o de fundamento es irremediablemente falso y que su utilización conduce, y de manera invariable, a la descalificación apriorística de cualquier análisis, y ya sea que aquél surja explícito o permanezca implícito en el argumento. Si el saber previo es defectuoso no existe modo de que lo se construye a partir de él resulte válido, y con mayor razón lo será si tal saber tiene que ver con el concepto mismo de derecho. Tal como ha sido dicho, un saber inauténtico encuentra en sí mismo las razones de su propia decadencia.

Por otro lado, este trabajo propone que la perspectiva de análisis que debe ejercitarse es la que pone el acento y foco en los sistemas normativos y en el ejercicio de la función judicial. Una determinación que viene apoyada y sustentada en términos dogmáticos por el propio concepto de derecho que utilizo y que considero verdadero. Ciertamente que es tarea del Jurista describir los sistemas normativos contemporáneos, identificar y reconocer su contenido dogmático, sus instituciones, determinarlos en su extensión y alcance, y reconocerlos en su individualidad.

En conclusión, entiendo que el deber jurídico de la debida diligencia reclama y exige una reformulación de los presupuestos teóricos y dogmáticos tradicionales, de la reformulación de los saberes previos y del cuestionamiento de un sentido jurídico común existente basado en la aplicación de los postulados del "positivismo legalista", todo lo cual comporta un auténtico desafío de reconversión del pensamiento.

En cualquier caso, y más allá de la posición que se adopte, entiendo que el Jurista debe tener clara su función de análisis, comprensión y descripción del sistema normativo y del fenómeno jurídico en general, de todos sus componentes y condicionantes. Que la práctica de Jurista requiere no prescindir nunca de la tarea de ajustar, integrar, purificar y actualizar siempre sus saberes y así, pensar y reflexionar; viajar al pasado, volver al presente y asomarse al futuro; construir y deconstruir, elaborar y reelaborar; vivenciar, atribuir significado y luego resignificar lo vivenciado y, con ello, su propio parecer.

Bibliografía

Cárcova, Carlos M., *Las Teorías Jurídicas Pos Positivistas* (Buenos Aires: Ed. Abeledo Perrot, 2009), pp. 3 y 4

Cárcova, Carlos María, *¿Hay una traducción correcta de las normas?,* en *Revista Electrónica del Instituto de Investigaciones Ambrosio L. Gioja,* Año III, Número 4 (2009)

Cossio, Carlos, *La gnoseología del error*, La Ley (Buenos Aires: Ed. La Ley, 1961) T° 101, pp. 1079 y sstes.

Cossio, Carlos, *La Plenitud del Ordenamiento Jurídico* (Buenos Aires: Ed. Los Andes, 1939), especialmente, pp. 179, 181,188 y 202

Courtis, Cristian, *Los derechos sociales como derechos*, en *Los derechos sociales como derechos exigibles. Derecho al trabajo, salud, vivienda, educación y seguridad social* (Madrid: Trotta Editorial, 2002), p. 13

Cracogna, Dante, *El legado de Carlos Cossio*, en *Isonomía*: *Revista de Teoría y Filosofía del Derecho*, núm. 12, abril (2000), pp. 197-209, accesible en http://www.scielo.org.mx/scielo.php?script=sci_arttext&pid=S1405-02182000000100197

Directrices de Maastricht sobre violaciones a los Derechos Económicos, Sociales Y Culturales, Maastricht, numeral 18, 22-26 de enero de 1997

Oficina del alto Comisionado de las Naciones Unidas para los Derechos Humanos, *La Responsabilidad de las Empresas de Respetar los Derechos Humanos: Guía para la interpretación* (2012), p. 7

Sanguineti, Raymond, Wilfredo, *Las cadenas mundiales de producción y la construcción de un derecho del trabajo sin fronteras,* ponencia inaugural (Salamanca: XXIX Congreso AEDTSS, 2019)

CHAPTER 14

THE RIGHT TO LAZINESS: THE MISSING LINK IN TERMS OF THE DEVELOPMENT OF THE BASIC INCOME

ALEXANDER DE BECKER & FLORE CLAUS

1. Introduction

For many years, the right to a basic income which is available to everyone has been the subject of an interesting debate. The idea of a basic income dates back to the Middle Ages and was explicitly mentioned in the work of Juan Luis Vives *De Subventione Pauperum* (Vives 1526), where he launched the idea of a subsistence minimum for the poorest inhabitants of a municipality.

The idea was frequently echoed in the 18th and 19th centuries and reappeared in the 20th century in the United States and the United Kingdom. In the last few decades, Northern and Western European thinkers have been defending the idea of introducing a basic income (Van Parijs and Vanderborght 2017) and the idea gained political support in the Netherlands during the 1970s and 1980s, with the Dutch *Politieke Partij Radicalen* launching the idea in their program. It even led to a debate in the framework of the Scientific Council for Government Policy, which published a scientific report on a partial basic income (Van Parijs & Vanderborght 2017). However, the legal transition has not yet been made.

A further initiative to introduce a basic income was organised in Finland (Perkiö 2020, 103-124). The idea continues to reappear frequently in economically or philosophically inspired academic contributions.

However, the legal foundation for any basic income still has to be identified. Legal conventions and legal charters are based on the idea that work is linked to the generation of an income. An income is the result of the execution of work. This contribution tends to research how a basic income can fit into the existing international legal framework. The contribution shall therefore focus on the question of which fundamental social or human rights need to play a role in order to establish a legal framework for a (universal or at least European) basic income. The research uses a pure positivist approach. This choice is made on purpose as it aims to identify the current legal issues with regard to the right to a basic income.

The first focus will be on the role of the right to work in the current legal framework. What lies at the core of the right to work and what are its links and its boundaries? The second focus will be on the search for an existing right which might be useful for the basic income to be founded upon. Which right can be considered to be suitable and under which circumstances?

Both elements should lead us to recommendations on how a basic income can be introduced in a legal framework which fits with its aim.

2. The Right to Work in the Current Legal Framework

2.1. The Development of the Concept of the Right to Work at the Drafting Stage of the Universal Declaration of Human Rights

2.1.1. Right to Work

World War II formed a catalyst for the international community to develop a universal set of human rights (Universal Declaration of Human Rights (adopted 10 December 1948 UNGA Res 217 A(III) (UDHR) UN Doc A/810; Morsink 1999, 36-92). During the drafting process of the Universal Declaration of Human Rights, international relations came under high tension. The schism between a capitalist approach and the communist approach really appeared in the debate on the interpretation of the right to work (Risse, 1999, 5-8).

On the one hand, the Latin-American countries and the USSR felt strongly about the development of a second generation of human rights: (individual) economic, cultural and social rights. On the other hand, most of the capitalist Western countries did not want an extended version of social rights since they considered it a symbol of social ideology and unnecessary restrictions on the internal market (Geldon 2000, 252-253). Eleanor Roosevelt, the Chairman of the Drafting Committee (Geldon 2000, 251), expressed the opposing views as follows: "*The right to work in the Soviet Union means the assignment of workers to do whatever task is given them by the government without an opportunity for the people to participate in the decision that the government should do this* [but...] *we would not consider in the United States that we had gained any freedom if we were compelled to follow a dictatorial assignment to work where and when we were told. The right of choice would seem to us an important, fundamental freedom.*" (Roosevelt and others 1949, 6-7).

During the drafting process, a balance was sought between the two opposing ideologies. John Humphrey, a Canadian human-rights advocate and professor, was asked by Eleanor Roosevelt in 1947 to prepare a first draft of what this "international bill of rights" should contain (Morsink 1999, 2-4 and 157-158). It is incorrect to think that those social rights were a concession to the Soviet Union from the United States drawing the UDHR (Mundlak 2009, 190-194). Although the country was in favour of the creation of fundamental social rights, John Humphrey studied various constitutions and treaties leading up to this first draft. Drafting the first articles of the UDHR, he read the Inter-American Convention, Frederick the Great's Prussian General Code, and several constitutions, including those of Brazil, Norway and France, where he found inspiration for a wide range of fundamental social rights (Geldon 2000, 257-258). The states agreed that the right to work was a fundamental right. The question was how this right was to be interpreted. John Humphrey described the "right to work" broadly and proposed at least five different articles, such as "everyone has the right and the duty to perform socially useful work" and "everyone has the right to such equitable share of the national income as the need for his work and increment it makes to the common welfare may justify" (United Nations Commission on Human Rights, Drafting Committee (1947) UN Doc E/CN.4/AC.1/3, 14; Morsink, 1999, 2-4 and 159). It is the first time that the right to work was coupled with a right to (a share of) an income.

Following John Humphrey's first draft, René Cassin was appointed to revisit the organic interpretation of the "International Bill of Rights" and to make a more logical arrangement (Geldon 2000, 254). Cassin, a French lawyer, professor and former French representative for the League of Nations, was added to the Drafting Committee because of the discontent of the European continent regarding a lack of representatives (Geldon 2000, 254). René Cassin added an important element: "Everyone has the right and duty to perform socially useful work to the full development of his personality." In this, he bore in mind the French Constitution of 1946 (United Nations Secretariat, Plan of the draft outline of an International Bill of Rights (1947) UN Doc E/CN.4/AC.1/3/Add.2). Despite his efforts, the U.S. vetoed his proposal because of the phrase "duty of work" as it could "in some countries be interpreted as forced labour" (UNCHR, Summary record of the 9th meeting (1947) UN Doc E./CN.4/AC.1/SR.9; 11; Geldon 2000, 257). A possible explanation could be the economic crisis after WWII where the U.S. and several other states were confronted with high unemployment rates (cf. also Morsink 1999, 162). Also, the French-inspired "development of his personality" never made it to the final version of the “right to work” because some parties (the U.K. and Chile, for example) felt that one could already read this into article 29 of the UDHR. Therefore, in an effort to distinguish the main principles from further interpretation or details, this part of the article was deleted (UNCHR, Summary record of the 14th meeting UN Doc E/CN.4/AC.1/SR.14, 6).

Next to the right to access a job, the right to useful work to the full development of one’s personality, as well as the right to free choice of employment were considered. After the first draft by the Drafting Committee, Lebanon, Cuba and the U.S. proposed the inclusion of another phrase regarding the right to work: “the right to work under proper conditions and to follow his vocation freely, in so far as existing conditions of employment permit” (UNCHR, Drafting Committee second session (1948) UN Doc E/CN.4/AC.1/SR.42, 7; Morsink 1999, 160).

This paragraph expresses the right of every person to decide about his “mode of life” (Eleanor Roosevelt and others 1949, 3).

Again, the right to choose a vocation did not make it into the final article for the same reasons surrounding the right to self-development. For many countries, the motto was "the shorter, the better." The interpretation behind the article was therefore largely left out but it should not be forgotten that the final article must also be interpreted in this way (e.g. the United States, the Union of South Africa, the United Kingdom and the Netherlands were in the third and final drafting session, which was critical regarding the implementation of social rights (cf. UNCHR, Third Session (1948) E/CN.4/85; Eleanor Roosevelt and others 1949, 6-7).

To conclude, the right to work must be interpreted in the light of drafting the UDHR as a right “to access a job.” But, in the preparatory works it is made clear that it has a broader perspective and must be interpreted in accordance with the other articles of the UDHR, in particular article 29, allowing for a right to develop oneself at work and the right to free choice of employment (Morsink 1999, 161-162).

An explanation for the urge to shorten the article was that, during the drafting of the declaration, there was a fine line between an unenforceable declaration that would not be able to impose obligations on states and, at the same time, a universal framework containing human rights that cannot be trampled on.

2.1.2. The Link between the Right to Work (Art. 23 UDHR) & the Right to Leisure (rt. 24 UDHR)

At the beginning of the drafting process, there was no direct link between the right to leisure and the right work. The main reason was that the concept of "leisure" was interpreted differently depending on the ideology of every state. While Humphrey based his formulations on the constitutions of, for example, Brazil and Costa Rica, and wrote that "everyone has the right to a fair share of rest and leisure," Cassin added that "everyone has the right to a fair share of rest and leisure and to a knowledge of the outside world" (Morsink 1999, 161-162).

In this way, the right to leisure was part of the right to education and not only workers, but every human being had a right to leisure. China did not agree and pointed out that "knowledge of the outside world" was already contained in the right to education and could not be separated from the right to work (UNCHR, Drafting Committee International Bill of Rights first session (1947) UN Doc E/CN.4/AC.1/SR.15, 2).

Originally, the "right to leisure" had a socialistic origin since it was only found by Humphrey in the constitutions of Latin-American countries (Costa Rica, Brazil, Ecuador, Guatemala, etc…) and the Soviet Union (Geldon 2000, 254). The Soviet Union emphasised that the right to leisure was part of the right to work and the right to fair working conditions. Nevertheless, some Member States had a more holistic view about what this "right to leisure" could mean. France, for example, interpreted this as a right to a social, cultural life and self-development (UNCHR, Third Session. Communication received from the French Government (1948) E/CN.4/82/ Add.8, 6. See also the Joint Amendment of the Philippines and Argentina. UNCHR, Joint Amendment to Article 24 of the Draft Declaration (1948) UN Doc. A/C.3/3583).

In the final phase, the right to rest and leisure was placed after Article 23 UDHR. The view that it was directly related to the right to work weighed in, although this right was interpreted differently amongst the Member States. It was finally Brazil that noticed this article should be placed directly after Article 23 UDHR (cf. UNCHR, Third Session (1948) E/CN.4/85, 45).

The debate, which was held during the drafting process of the Universal Declaration of Human Rights, did not lead to the development of a right to leisure or laziness. The right to laziness has never been the scope of the debate. The right to leisure was situated as another right beside the right to work. However, both fundamental rights were fully recognised (The Vienna Declaration of 1993 emphasises that all human rights are universal, indivisible, interdependent and interrelated. The Vienna Declaration and

Program of Action (adopted 12 July 1993 and entered into force 20 December 1993) UNGA Res 48/121 UN Doc A/CONF.157/53, art. 5).

2.2. The Right to Work Interpreted as a Negative Obligation

Unlike Article 23 UDHR, there is no separate article delineating the right to work in the European Convention of Human Rights (ECHR). An explanation may be that the draft ECHR had a different point of view than the UDHR, simply because its binding nature differs (Mantouvalou 2014, 317-320).

Article 4, §2 of the European Declaration approaches the right to work from the perspective of prohibiting forced labour and slavery: "No one shall be required to perform forced or compulsory labour" (European Convention for the Protection of Human Rights and Fundamental Freedoms (ECHR) as amended by Protocol nos. 11, 1994 ETS 155 and 14, 2010 ETS 194, originally opened for signature 4 November 1950).

The European Court of Human Rights (ECtHR) created a difference between the concepts of "forced" and "compulsory" labour in their case law (Dermine 2014, 758). Where "forced" implies a physical or mental coercion, "compulsory" includes a (legal) compulsion or obligation (Dermine, 2014, 758; *Vander Mussele v. Belgium* (1983) Series A No. 70 [34]).

Applying this article in its jurisprudence, the European Court of Human Rights (ECtHR) also interprets the article with regard to existing international instruments, in particular ILO No. 29, the Forced Labour Convention. Evaluating a possible violation of Article 4 EDHR, the Court considers if the two criteria in the ILO Convention No. 29 are met: (1) the work or service is exacted under the menace of a penalty; (2) the task is undertaken involuntarily (ILO Forced Labour Convention 1930 (adopted 28 June 1930, entered into force 1 May 1932); *C.N. and V v. France* App. No 67724/09 (ECtHR, 11 October 2012)). The ECtHR refers to the Convention in *Vander Mussele v. Belgium* which concerns a pupil advocate who did not want to perform *pro bono* work for indigent clients. Since he did not receive any remuneration and his refusal could evoke a sanction by the Judicial Code of Belgium if he did not want to represent this indigent client, *Vander Mussele* argued for the ECtHR that this obligation was a violation of Article 4, §2 ECHR which prohibits forced labour. The Court noticed that Article 4, §2 ECHR did not define the concept of "forced or compulsory labour" but since it was mainly based upon Article 2, §2 ILO Convention No. 29, this interpretation formed a starting point regarding this case: "All work or service which is exacted form any person under the menace of any penalty and for which the said person has not offered himself voluntarily." (*Vander Mussele v. Belgium* (1983) Series A No 70 [32]-[34]; *Graziani-Weiss v.*

Austria App no. 31950/66 (ECtHR, 18 October 2011).

Nevertheless, the European Court of Human Rights considers Article 4 as a living instrument that has to be interpreted in "present day" conditions (European Court of Human Rights, *Guide on Article 4 of the Convention – Prohibition of slavery and forced labour* (2021) 6 <www.echr.coe.int/documents/guide_art_4_eng.pdf.> accessed 20 June 2021).

In *Stummer v. Austria,* the applicant worked in prison and argued that the fact that he is not entitled to the pension system is a violation of Article 4, §2 since this is no longer "work required to be done in the ordinary course of detention" (*Stummer v. Austria* ECHR 2011-V 3 [131]-[134]). While the Court recognised the evolution in the field of penal policy, there was no "sufficient consensus on the issue of the affiliation of working prisoners to the old-age pensions system" (*Stummer v. Austria* ECHR 2011-V 3 [132]). In this case, there was no violation of Article 4 of the Convention but the motivation of the Court underlines the attention towards changed circumstances in welfare states.

Article 4, §3 ECHR excludes four categories from the term "forced or compulsory labour": detention, military character, any service in the case of an emergency or calamity, and any work or service which forms part of the national civic obligations (ECHR art. 4, para 3). In the three Dutch cases of *X.* (1976), *Talmon* (1997) and *Schuitemaker v. the Netherlands* (2010), in (slightly) different circumstances, all the applicants argued that the loss of their social unemployment benefits because of their refusal to work was a violation of Article 4, §3 ECHR. Despite the fact that the cases were ruled admissible but ill-founded, the boundaries of the possibility of work conditions in unemployment benefits were explored. While in the first two cases the European Commission of Human Rights ruled that it could not form a prohibition of forced labour, the European Court of Human Rights ruled in the latter case that they could not decide *in abstracto*, without concrete circumstances, if there was a violation of Article 4 or not (Dermine 2014, 775). Even if the motivation of the Court emphasises a case-by-case approach, there has not been any case law yet in which the Court ruled that work conditions tied to unemployment benefits formed a violation of Article 4, §3 ECtHR (Paz-Fuchs 2020, 16).

It seems that the right to work is limited by the prohibition to be forced to execute labour when it comes to the case law of the ECHR. However, no basis is granted to the possibility of not exercising one's right to work. Is it possible and plausible for every human being to enjoy the fundamental right to life, as part of a right to a decent life, without using the right to work? Further evolution will sharpen this debate.

2.3. The Right to Work Interpreted as a Positive Right

2.3.1. An International Perspective: Article 6 ICESCR

Article 6 of the International Covenant on Economic, Social and Cultural Rights (ICESCR) takes a holistic approach, referring to the right to work as "essential for human dignity" (Committee on Economic, Social and Cultural Rights (CESSCR), 'General Comment No. 18: The Right to Work (Art. 6 of the Covenant)' (2005) UN Doc E/C.12/GC/18, 1.). It includes the right to be provided with work, not to be prevented from work, and the prohibition of forced labour. The preparatory work points to a broad approach and refers to the different ways in which the right to work should be interpreted in this article. States should guarantee the right to work or should take measures "to implement concretely the enjoyment of the right" (Committee on Economic, Social and Cultural Rights (CESSCR), 'General Comment No. 18: The Right to Work (Art. 6 of the Covenant)' (2005) UN Doc E/C.12/GC/18, 1). A strikingly cited point is that, in the preparatory works, it was formulated as "proposed to guarantee the right to work with the aim of creating conditions that would exclude the threat of death by hanging or starvation" but that this statement was immediately nuanced to "it would represent too low a standard in respect of the right to work" (United Nations General Assembly (UNGA) 'Draft International Covenants on Human Rights. Chapter VII. The economic, social and cultural rights' (1955) UN Doc A/2929, 300).

Remarkably, the general approach of the right to work in the ICESCR differs from Article 4 of the ECHR, as mentioned above. Article 6 defines the right to work as "the right of everyone to the opportunity to gain his living by work which he freely chooses or accepts, and will take appropriate steps to safeguard this right" (International Covenant on Economic, Social and Cultural Rights (Adopted 16 December 1966, entered into force 3 January 1976) 993 UNTS 3.) It has a more profound interpretation than the ECHR. Not only does it contain a prohibition of forced labour, but it also anchors a positive right: the right to be employed (Harvey 2002, 380).

In the General Comment No. 18, the right to work is further explained (Committee on Economic, Social and Cultural Rights (CESSCR), 'General Comment No. 18: The Right to Work (Art. 6 of the Covenant)' (2005) UN Doc E/C.12/GC/18, 1; Mundlak 2007, 204-205). The essence of this right as contained in Article 6 of the ICESCR echoes what was already stipulated in Article 23 of the UDHR. What differs between the two international instruments is their binding nature. As a consequence, Article 6 of the ICESCR contains obligations for the parties in stimulating their national employment rates. During the drafting process of the UDHR, the states were reluctant to attach certain obligations to states regarding the right to work. However, South Africa, Brazil and the United States did not agree (UNCHR, Third Session (1948) E/CN.4/85; Harvey 2002, 377).

The right to work defined in Article 6 includes the right "to gain his living" but the preparatory works were even more sharply defined, as mentioned above (United Nations General Assembly (UNGA) 'Draft International Covenants on Human Rights. Chapter VII. The economic, social and cultural rights' (1955) UN Doc A/2929, 300). This definition of the right to work is immediately linked in both Article 6 of the ICESCR and Article 23 of the UDHR to the right to human dignity. In the drafting process of the UDHR, Eleanor Roosevelt formulated it as follows: "an offer of income support in lieu of a job will not secure the right nor will assurances of non-discriminatory access to available jobs" (Roosevelt and others 1949; Morsink 1999, 183). This view is also expressed in ILO Convention No. 168: "Emphasizing the importance of work and productive labor in every society, not only because of the resources they create for the community, but also because of the income they provide for workers..." (ILO Convention No. 168 on Employment Promotion and Protection against Unemployment (adopted 21 June 1988, entered into force 17 October 1997).

Looking at the motivations of the Human Rights Committee, suspending unemployment benefits can be tolerated if the unemployed person does not want to accept a job offer or training. In the case of *Fauré v. Australia*, an unemployed woman had her unemployment benefits suspended for two months because she did not participate in the *Work for the Dole* project of the Australian Government. The Human Rights Committee ruled that since the activity was not considered degrading or dehumanising, it did not meet the criteria of forced labour (in this case it was a possible breach of Article 8, §3, a) of the International Covenant on Civil and Political Rights (ICCPR); UNHRC, Communication *Fauré v. Australia* (2005) Comm. 1036/2001 UN Doc A/61/40 2005; Dermine 2014, 767). In that regard, the current international regulations seem to link the right to a decent life to the execution of the right to work (Mantouvalou 2014, 318).

The right to work is not considered to be a freedom. A freedom (such as the freedom of association) includes both positive and a negative angles. One may become a member of an association but one may also choose not to become a member. With regard to the right to work, the elaboration of this right does not leave the possibility (in order to live a decent life) of not using this right.

2.3.2. A European Perspective

Article 1 European Charter of Social Rights.

The European Social Charter (ESC) does not delineate a concrete "right to work" but it does attach obligations to this right for Member States to promote employment. Unlike the ICESCR, the Charter is considered more as an "aspirational document" rather than a (ratified) covenant (European Social Charter (revised) (1996) CETS No. 163 (ECS) art. 1 (1); Gundt 2014, 351).

Article 1 ESC stipulates the right of the worker to earn his living in an occupation freely entered upon (ESC (revised) Art. 1 (2)). Ensuring this right to work, several obligations for the parties are listed in Article 1 of the ESC. From these enumerated obligations, it can be inferred that, once again, the view is taken that the right to work includes the right to access the workplace (Council of Europe Committee of Social Rights, '*Digest of the Case Law of the European Committee of Social Rights*' (2018), 56 <https://rm.coe.int/digest-2018-parts-i-ii-iii-iv-en/1680939f80> accessed 20 June 2021). If the parties neglect the obligations, the consequence could be sanctions. The European Committee of Social Rights sets the bar and formulates a bottom line which a party may not reach: "an economic system providing for a permanent pool of unemployed" (Council of Europe Committee of Social Rights, Conclusions 1, 14; Gundt 2014, 352).

To maintain or achieve a high and stable level of employment, the parties may impose conditions on unemployment benefits such as taking a job or attending training. According to the Committee of Social Rights, this is in line with the right to work unless the work is not appropriate (e.g. it is below the level of the person's knowledge, pays less than the minimum monthly wage, or is too far from home). However, there are some exceptions (Council of Europe Committee of Social Rights, '*Digest of the Case Law of the European Committee of Social Rights*' (2018), 61 <https://rm.coe.int/digest-2018-parts-i-ii-iii-iv-en/1680939f80> accessed 20 June 2021).

Looking at the rationale and guidelines of the Committee of Social Rights, the question is to what extent this "right to work" will not *de facto* result in a "duty to work". Legally, one cannot be required to work, but it is tolerated that, if one does not want to work, one can and may lose unemployment benefits. In line with the previous legal instruments, the right to work, Article 1 (2) of the ESC emphasises this: "… to protect effectively the right of the worker to earn his living in an occupation freely entered upon." (Council of Europe Committee of Social Rights, '*Digest of the Case Law of the European Committee of Social Rights*' (2018), 57 <https://rm.coe.int/digest-2018-

parts-i-ii-iii-iv-en/1680939f80> accessed 20 June 2021).

Article 15, the European Charter of Fundamental Rights.

Article 15 of the European Charter of Fundamental Rights (CFR) delineates the right to work as "the freedom to choose an occupation and right to engage in work." Unlike Article 1(1) of the ESC, this article does not formulate any obligations regarding employment level but it does refer to Article 1(2) of the ESC: "to protect effectively the right of the worker to earn his living in an occupation freely entered upon." The European Union places the internal market first as a priority in which access to the labour market is crucial, which explains why no obligation is included for states to promote employment (Mundlak 2007, 205; NGundt 2014, 353).

As indicated in the case law of the Court of Justice of the EU (*Nold, Hauer* and *Keller*), Article 15 is based on the constitutional treaties of all member states ("Explanations relating to the Charter of Fundamental Rights" (2007) OJ C302/02). Given that it is contained in every constitution, it is considered a general principle of law or, as the Court puts it in the case of Keller, "the freedom to pursue one's trade or profession is part of the general principles of law, the observance of which it ensures" (Case 234/85, *Staatsanwaltschaft Freiburg v. Franz Keller* (1986) ECR 2827 [8]). This article has a social function to protect the right to work: "In respect of the freedom to pursue trade or professional activities, the right thereby guaranteed, far from constituting an unfettered prerogative, must likewise be viewed in the light of the social function of the activities protected thereunder" (Case 44/79, *Liselotte Hauer v. Land Rheinland-Pfalz* (1979) 3727). At the same time, it is not an absolute prerogative and may be restricted if justified on the grounds of public interest (Case 4/73 *Nold v. Commission* (1974) ECR 497, [12]-[14]; Case 44/79, *Liselotte Hauer v. Land Rheinland-Pfalz* (1979), 3727; Case 234/85, *Staatsanwaltschaft Freiburg v. Franz Keller* (1986) ECR 2827 [8]).

2.4. The Right to Work vs. the Right to a Basic Income

In taking an overview of the role of the "right to work" in the current legal framework, the right to work is interpreted in the most international/European legal instruments as a right to have access to a job. However, the ECHR interpret the "right to work" as a negative right: "a right *not* to work in compulsory or forced labour". The current legal framework establishes boundaries between the right to work and the right to human dignity (Mantouvalou 2014, 321-322). According to the preparatory documents of the ICESCR, initially, the right to work could even be described as "the right to work with the aim of creating conditions that would exclude the threat of death by hanging or starvation" (United Nations General Assembly (UNGA) 'Draft International Covenants on Human Rights. Chapter VII. The economic, social and cultural rights' (1955) UN Doc A/2929, 300). This right to work would guarantee, in other words, a right to human existence and would, as a result, exclude anyone who chooses not to pursue their right to work.

Except for Article 15 of the European Charter of Fundamental Rights (see also ILO Convention No 168 on Employment Promotion and Protection against Unemployment (adopted 21 June 1988, entered into force 17 October 1997) art. 2; Gundt 2014, 353), states are obliged to create employment levels which are as high as possible (Committee of Social Rights, Conclusions 1, 14; Gundt 2014, 352). With regard to this obligation, states may take steps to discourage unemployment, such as linking the acceptance of a job offer or training to conditions of unemployment benefits. In international and European case law, these measures are tolerated (*Vander Mussele v. Belgium* (1983) Series A No. 70 and UNHRC, Communication *Fauré v. Australia* (2005) Comm. 1036/2001 UN Doc A/61/40 2005). The ECtHR choses a case-by-case approach but has never ruled that the activating measures were a violation of Article 4 of the EDHR until now (*Schuitemaker v. The Netherlands* App. No. 15906/08 (ECtHR, 4 May 2010) and *Talmon v. The Netherlands* App. No. 30300/96 (ECHR, 26 December 1997) and *X v. The Netherlands* App. No. 7602/96 (ECHR, 13 December 1976); Mantouvalou 2014, 327).

The Committee of Social Rights of the Council of Europe reaffirms that these measures are in line with the right to work unless the offer is inappropriate in terms of distance to work, wage, capacities, etc… Tolerating the link between the activation of the unemployed and the fundamental right to work could form a *de facto* duty to work for a lot of people in order to obtain a decent life (Mundlak 2007, 196-197).

Who would not want to work and would lose their unemployment benefits and thereby sacrifice their own human dignity? In other words, there is no choice without the loss of the right to earn a living and the threat of poverty.

The right to a basic income is based on another approach: the right to work no longer constitutes the basis for a decent life (Mundlak 2007, 199-202). A decent life is provided by the authority where the right to work should evolve towards a freedom to work.

3. The Right to Leisure: Not Enough as a Legal Basis

3.1. What?

The Second Industrial Revolution led to increased productivity and introduced workers to a relatively new concept: leisure. The worker was given time to engage in other pursuits or, as F. Kelly described it at the time: "The breadwinning task of today too often stupefies and deforms the mind; and leisure is required to undo the damage wrought in the working-hours, if the worker is to remain fit for citizenship in the Republic" (Kelley 1910, 109).

In the preparatory works of the Drafting Committee of the United Nations, it was not clear if the right to leisure would be included in the draft for the Universal Declaration of Human Rights. Some countries saw the right to leisure rather as a duty for the states than a right that should be included in the UDHR (at the final vote, the Netherlands, Belgium, China and the United Kingdom voted negative. Morsink 1999, 189-190; Risse 2009, 7). However, in the final and third Drafting Session, Article 24 of the UDHR was put on the table. The scope of the article in the draft was interpreted more broadly than the final Article 24 of the UDHR. It described the right to leisure as: "1. Everyone has the right to rest and leisure. 2. Rest and leisure should be ensured to everyone by laws or contracts providing in particular for reasonable limitations on working hours and for periodic vacations with pay" (UNCHR, Third Session (1948) E/CN.4/85, 45), whereas the final Article 24 of the UDHR defines the right to leisure as: "Everyone has the right to rest and leisure, including reasonable limitation of working hours and periodic holidays with pay."

It is notable that in the second part of the article, the phrase *"rest and leisure should be ensured to everyone by laws or contracts providing..."* was deleted. Due to the dissatisfaction of several states (e.g. the United States, the United Kingdom and the Republic of South-Africa), this article could imply state obligations. In the words of the South African government: "Many of the provisions inserted here do not comprise fundamental human rights at all but rather the duties of states" (UNCHR, Third Session (1948) E/CN.4/85, 11-12). In addition, other states (e.g. the Netherlands) felt that the provision was too vague and ill-framed from which to derive an enforceable right (UNCHR, Third Session (1948) E/CN.4/85, 2). Unlike other countries from the North Atlantic block, France was supportive of this provision and wanted to see the right to leisure provided for as broadly as possible. The interpretation of the right to leisure in their eyes was not limited to working hours or paid leave, but was also about the right of each person to develop himself (UNCHR, Third Session.

Communication received from the French government (1948) E/CN.4/82/Add.8, 6. See also the Joint Amendment of the Philippines and Argentina. UNCHR, Joint Amendment to Article 24 of the Draft Declaration (1948) UN Doc. A/C.3/3583). However, this interpretation was not supported amongst all Member States and the final Article 24 of the UDHR remained restricted to the following: “Everyone has the right to rest and leisure, including reasonable limitation of working hours and periodic holidays with pay.”

In line with the right to work, as mentioned above (UN Division of Human Rights, Drafting Committee (1947) E/CN.4/AC.1/3, 14. See 2.1. ‘The development of the concept of the right to work in the drafting stage of the Universal Declaration of Human Rights’), the right to leisure was interpreted differently during the drafting process depending on the ideology of each state. It was Humphrey who formulated the right to leisure, which he found in the constitutions of most Latin American countries (e.g. Brazil, Mexico and Costa Rica), whereas the French, Philippine, Argentinian, Egyptian and Panamanian interpretation of the right to leisure was more about the need to include the right to self-development or described as “rest and leisure for his spiritual, cultural and physical wellbeing” (cf. the Joint Amendment of the Philippines and Argentina. UNCHR, Joint Amendment to Article 24 of the Draft Declaration (1948) UN Doc. A/C.3/3583 and the Amendment of France UCHR, Amendment to Article 24 of the Draft Declaration (1948) UN Doc. A/C.3/357; Geldon 2000, 254). Due to the strong incentive to create a Universal Declaration of Human Rights that “everyone should know by heart” (UNCHR, Third Session (1948) E/CN.4/85, 4-5 and Eleanor Roosevelt et al. Human Rights and Genocide: Selected Statements, United Nations Resolutions, Declaration and Conventions, Washington, D.C., Dept. of State, Division of Publications (Office of Public Affairs 1949) 11), several countries, such as the United States, the Netherlands and the United Kingdom applied pressure by formulating alternative shortened proposals of the Universal Declaration. As a result, important nuances were sometimes lost, as also evidenced by the incomplete integration of the right to leisure into the (inter)national legal order (cf. title 3.2. ‘How did the right to leisure disappeared in the current legal framework?’ The different opinions are made clear in the third (and final) Draft. See UNCHR, Third Session (1948) E/CN.4/85 and Morsink 1999, 187).

3.2. How Did the Right to Leisure Disappear in the Current Legal Framework?

Initially, the two criteria that were exemplary of the right to leisure ("reasonable limitation of working hours" and "periodic holidays with pay") were not included in the article. The representatives of the USSR and Yugoslavia wanted the article to contain the right to rest and leisure and for this to be implemented. This right mentions periodic vacations with pay explicitly because "there is no rest without pay" (UNCHR, Second Session (1947) E/CN.4/SR/40, 14).

After the proclamation of the UDHR, the right to leisure receded more. Some reasons can be given for this. First, it can be noted that the right was insufficiently demarcated in the draft process. Concrete examples were given of what this right to leisure would look like, but not what the scope of the right would be. Therefore, the Netherlands, Belgium, China and the United Kingdom also voted against it because they did not consider this right as a human right, with local authorities being free to further define it (Morsink 1999, 189-190; Mundlak 2007, 190-194). The core of the right to leisure was initially found in a WHO guideline, which René Cassin took as a starting point during the drafting of the article "human labor is not treated as a merchandise." The final article is far from the initial goal of including this as a universal human right, as it is limited to implying what the right might look like. The drafting process of Article 24 of the UDHR underlines the difficulty of finding a balance between establishing a "core" of fundamental rights, the absence of legal values, and the possibility of implementing concrete obligations (Morsink 1999, 190).

Another reason for its disappearance is the misinterpretation of this article, which lies in its phrasing. In the final version of the article, the word "including" refers to the two given examples. These examples are not exhaustive (UNCHR third session (1948) Un Doc A/C.3/ 359). Other countries (the U.K. and South Africa) proposed a different article, without "including," which would limit its scope. It eventually became "in particular" which underlines the broader scope of the article and goes beyond these two examples. The preparatory phase showed that the vision of the right to leisure was divergent. One side opted for the socialist interpretation of the right to leisure, especially with the focus on the right to work, while the other side chose a more holistic approach and considered the right to leisure as a right to self-development. Even though the right to leisure was immediately placed behind the right to work, this does not mean that the vision of the right to leisure as a right to self-development was definitively dropped (UNCHR, Third Session (1948) E/CN.4/85, 45. See the Joint Amendment of the Philippines and Argentina. UNCHR, Joint Amendment to Article 24 of the Draft Declaration (1948) UN Doc. A/C.3/3583 and the Amendment of France UCHR, Amendment to Article 24 of the Draft Declaration (1948) UN Doc. A/C.3/357).

Finally, it should be pointed out that when the UDHR was drafted, at no point did states provide an interpretation of the concept of "leisure." Given the spirit of the time, this was difficult since the different ideologies were at odds in this regard. Michael Walzer formulates it as the following: "freed from these distortions, free time will be experienced and enjoyed by the members of a free society in all the different ways they can collectively or individually invent" (Walzer 1983, 196; Morsink 1999, 190).

3.3. The Right to Leisure vs. the Right to a Basic Income: Not Sufficient (A Right to Laziness is Necessary)

In looking for an existing right upon which to found a basic income, the right to leisure should be considered. Human rights are an evolving phenomenon. As already stipulated above, time has stopped on the interpretation of the "right to leisure." The article mentions limitations on working hours and annual paid leave but, in many countries, this has been normal practice for several decades. The right to leisure only includes the possibility for a human being to develop. However, there has never been an aim to ground the possibility of not working.

In the preparatory documents of the drafting process of the UDHR, the right to laziness was briefly invoked as part of the interpretation of the right to leisure. States feared that the right to self-development would guarantee the creation of a right to laziness. That is another possible reason why the article was placed immediately after the right to work (Morsink 1999, 190. The view of the Cuban delegate, Pérez Cisneros, was included with the current explanation of Article 24 on the website of the United Nations Human Rights Committee <https://www.ohchr.org/EN/NewsEvents/Pages/DisplayNews.aspx?NewsID=23966&LangID=E> accessed 20 June 2021). However, the social climate has since changed and continues to do so; the right to self-development is now largely accepted as a human right (Declaration on the Right to Development, UNGA Res. 41/128 (4 December 1986), art. 1).

In a modern state governed by the rule of law, taking into account the growth of prosperity, there is no doubt that the right to leisure must be reviewed and interpreted differently. During the drafting phase of the UDHR, the right to leisure was seen by some countries as the right to self-development (see the Joint Amendment of the Philippines and Argentina.

UNCHR, Joint Amendment to Article 24 of the Draft Declaration (1948) UN Doc. A/C.3/3583 and the Amendment of France UCHR, Amendment to Article 24 of the Draft Declaration (1948) UN Doc. A/C.3/357). Why, in the 21st century, is this view not taken? Why has a teleological interpretation of Article 24 of the UDHR not been chosen instead of a textual one?

3.4. The Right to Laziness, the Right to Self-Development and the Right to Work

The right to laziness has been invoked by Lafargue (Lafargue 1996, 43; Bueno 2017, 472). However, his thoughts did not include a real and full right to laziness. His plea was to limit working time to three hours a day through legislation (Lafargue 1996, 81). Bertrand Russell based his work on the ideas Lafargue had put forward and wrote that a working day should stop after four hours (Russell 1935, 25).

Once again, the right to laziness, even as a pure philosophical concept, was linked to the right to work. The right to self-determination was also linked (after the Second World War) to the right to work (see points 2.1 and 3.2).

However, the approach in legal and philosophical scholarship is not necessarily linked to the positivist approach this article has taken as a starting point. The authors of this article are aware of the limitations of this approach. It does not lead to a wider foundation and acceptance of the right to a basic income.

It is nevertheless necessary to indicate that the right to work blocks the development of another approach to provide a decent life. As Bueno correctly indicates, the right to work does not fully include a freedom to work in the current legal framework (Bueno 2017, 476). The plea for a human economy which should lead to more freedom to work is an important step, even if it currently remains a theoretical shift towards another economic model (Bueno 2017, 473-480).

This new economic model, which may be needed, also includes a necessary fundamental modification of the treaties with regard to human rights and socio-economic rights (Risse 2009, 33-37). The right to work has to shift towards a freedom to work. The link between the right to work and the right to a decent life needs to be cut.

In our opinion, the most fundamental shift in thinking is the development of a full and individual right to laziness. The right to laziness includes the choice not to work (the negative freedom to work) but it goes even further because the right to a decent life as fundamental right needs to be combined with the right to laziness. It therefore implies a fundamental shift in the existing recognition of human rights (including socio-economic rights).

4. Conclusion

The right to a basic income has been at the heart of economical and philosophical debate in the last few decades. As mentioned before, legal scholarship has not contributed a lot to this debate. The aim of this article was to clarify to what extent the current legal framework, as it has been developed in international legal treaties, underpins the development of a right to a basic income.

It seems that the right to a basic income is blocked in the current legal framework. In Utopia, the right to a basic income would bloom from a freedom to work and from a dissolution of the right to work and the right to a decent life. The crown jewel would be the development of a human right to laziness. It would underpin the major idea of the right to a basic income. Everyone would receive money no matter what they did and even pure laziness would be financed. It may remain utopian but each dream carries hope.

Bibliography

Books

Lafargue, Paul, *Le droit à la paresse. Réfutation du droit du travail de 1848* (Paris: Le temps des cerises, 1996)

Morsink, Johannes, *The Universal Declaration of Human Rights: Origins, Drafting, and Intent* (Philadelphia: Pennsylvania Press, 1999)

Roosevelt, Eleanor and others, *Human Rights and Genocide: Selected Statements, United Nations Resolutions, Declaration and Conventions* (Washington, D.C.: Dept. of State, Division of Publications, Office of Public Affairs, 1949)

Russell, Bertrand, *In Praise of Idleness* (London: George Allen & Unwin Ltd., 1935)

Van Parijs, Philippe, and Vanderborght, Yannick, *Basic Income. A radical proposal for a free society and a sane economy* (Cambridge: Harvard University Press, 2017)

Vives, Juan Luis *De subventione pauperum* (Bruges: De Crook, 1526)

Walzer, Michal, *Spheres of Justice* (New York: Basic Books, 1983)

Contributions in Books

Paz-Fuchs, Amir, "Workfare's Persistent Philosophical and Legal Issues: Forced Labour, Reciprocity and a Basic Income Guarantee," In *Welfare to Work in Contemporary European Welfare States: Legal, Sociological and Philosophical Perspectives on Justice and Domination,* edited by Eleveld, Anja, Kampen, Thomas and Arts, Josien (Bristol: Bristol University Press, 2020), 27-48

Articles

Bueno, Nicolas, "From the right to work to the freedom from work." *Journal of Comparative Labour Law and Industrial Relations* 33, no. 4 (2017): 463-88

Dermine, Elise, "Activation Policies for the Unemployed and the International Human Rights Case Law on the Prohibition of Forced Labour," *European Journal of Human Rights* (2014): 746-76

Geldon, Mary Ann, "John P. Humphrey and the Drafting of the Universal Declaration of Human Rights," *J Hist Int'L* no. 2 (2000): 250-60

Harvey, Philip. "Human Rights and Economic Policy Discourse: Taking Economic and Social Rights Seriously," *Colum Hum Rts L Rev* no. 33 (2002): 363-471

Mantouvalou, Virginia, "The Protection of the Right to Work Through the European Convention on Human Rights," *Cambridge Yearbook of European Legal Studies* no. 16 (2014): 313-32

Mundlak, Guy, "The Right to Work Linking Human Rights and Employment Policy," *Int'l Lab Rev* no. 146 (2009): 189-215

Perkiö, Johanna, "From Rights to Activation: The Evolution of the Idea of Basic Income in the Finnish Political Debate, 1980–2016," *Journal of Social Policy* 49 , no. 1, January (2020): 103-124

Risse, Matthias, "Labor Rights as Human Rights," *L & Ethics Hum Rts*, no. 3 (1999): 5-8

PART 3

NEW PARAMETERS FOR THE EVOLUTION OF LABOUR LAW

CHAPTER 15

CHANGES IN LABOUR RELATIONS DUE TO DIGITAL PLATFORMS

JORDI GARCÍA VIÑA

1. Statement of the question

Technology and the entrepreneurial spirit have made possible the development of an ecosystem of new enterprises, created as start-ups and which are now technological giants. In 2008, *Airbnb* was born; in 2009, *Uber*; in 2011, *Cabify* evolved in the new Spanish catering sector, along with companies such as *Deliveroo*, founded in 2013, and *Glovo*, founded two years later.

With this new way of offering and buying services, technology creates a new way of working more flexibly and on demand. This new system has been spreading, affecting other economic sectors, and impacting young people, not only in terms of their status as workers, but also consumers (ILO 2021, 34).

It is common for great technological advances to always be ahead of regulation, which is why, at present, the activities carried out through platforms are operating in a legislative context that, at the time of their creation, did not even contemplate their existence.

In this scenario, there is no doubt that the legal relationships of the people who provide services through these digital platforms must be regulated in a clear and secure way, because only in this way is it possible to ensure the rights and obligations of the workers, companies and the market itself.

These fit artificially in a new work organisation model that is the reality within a framework devised before the invention of the internet or the digitisation process in general. Therefore, it might be necessary that the legislators of the different countries, before making definite decisions, take into account all the aspects that this new reality entails.

Flexible work is a model that will increase in the coming years, fostered both by technology, which makes it possible to work anytime and anywhere, as well as by society, which increasingly values flexibility, especially when it comes to digital consumption.

The European Union has played an active role in establishing guidelines and regulations in the context of the digital economy and computer commerce. Some of the most relevant documents are the European Agenda for the collaborative economy, of June 2, 2016, of the European Commission; European Parliament Resolution 2016/2003 (INI) of June 15, 2017, on a European Agenda for the collaborative economy; as well as European Parliament Resolution 2016/2276 (INI) of June 15, 2017, on online platforms and the digital single market.

In the labour market and the digital economy, Directive 2019/1152/EU of June 20, 2019, of the European Parliament and the Council, on transparent and predictable working conditions in the European Union, provides for its application to digital platform workers if they meet certain conditions. Furthermore, a proposal for a Directive of the European Parliament and of the Council on improving working conditions in platform work has been published in December 2021.

In addition, the Court of Justice of the European Union has resolved, to date, two relevant issues.

First, in the judgement of December 20, 2017, case C-434/15, Professional Elite Taxi Association and Uber Systems Spain, SL, it holds that the service provided by *Uber* is not limited to an intermediation service between supply and demand but organises and plans the transportation service.

Second, the request for a preliminary ruling from the Watford Employment Tribunal (United Kingdom) on 19 September 2019, B / Yodel Delivery Network Ltd, Case C-692/19, examines the legal link between this company and delivery men. Although it concludes that there does not appear to be a subordination relationship, it does not resolve the merits of the matter. It does, however, determine the criteria to be considered for a worker to be considered as autonomous or independent:

- Use subcontractors or substitutes to perform the service that you have agreed to provide;
- Accept or not the various tasks offered by your employer or unilaterally set the maximum number of those tasks;
- Provide their services to third parties, including the employer's direct competitors;

- Set your own "working" hours within certain parameters and tailor your time to your personal convenience and not solely to the interests of the alleged employer.

Faced with this regulatory solution, at the European level, social partners, especially sectoral ones, have tried to find solutions, for example, through the so-called "Frankfurt Document on the Platforms" of December 2016, or the recommendations of trade unions and European employers' associations of temporary work agencies of May 2018.

While analysing certain countries of the European Union that have regulated this issue or whose courts have assessed whether this provision of services is salaried, one can observe how the same evidence is used both for the argumentation of the judgements in favour and against, with minimal distinction (*European Commission,* 2018). The confusion is such that courts in the same country, in charge of cases on workers from the same digital platform and with the same conditions, have decided differently. For example, the Supreme Court in the United Kingdom has understood that Uber drivers are not autonomous (see the decision of February 19, 2021).

In France, various rules related to this type of relation between riders and platforms have been adopted. Law 2016-1088, of August 8, 2016, on work, the modernisation of social dialogue and ensuring professional careers. Title IV is dedicated to workers who use an electronic connection platform, which contemplates the social responsibility of the platforms towards these workers, under certain conditions if it determines the price and characteristics of the service provided or goods sold. Protection against accidents at work and the right of access to continuous professional training, to be supported by the platform, receive support and compensation costs and the right to organise, unite and promote their collective interests are regulated. These worker protection and training rights are subject to the worker's turnover on the platform, since not all of them are applicable when such volumes are below a threshold defined by the standard.

Law 2019-1428, of December 24, 2019, on mobility orientation, which aims to create the legal conditions for a new mobility, introduced a regulation of new forms of mobility and strengthened the social responsibility of the link platforms. Nevertheless, initially, this law intended to exclude the existence of a subordinate link provided that the platform fulfilled a series of commitments with its own-account workers, which was declared unconstitutional by a decision of the Constitutional Council of December 20, 2019 *(Décision d'inconstitutionnalité numéro 2019-794 DC*, 2019).

This law also determines the platform operator's obligation to verify compliance with the legal conditions relating to the exercise of the transport activity and regulates certain rules regarding working conditions of the workers of the digital platforms dedicated to transporting people or delivering goods in all kinds of vehicles; not penalising for rejecting a job proposal or disconnecting during the chosen hours; and transparency in information or the payment of social security contributions.

In addition, it determines that the platform can establish "documentary evidence" that determines the conditions and procedures for the exercise of its social responsibility, defining its rights and obligations, as well as those of the workers with whom it is in contact, mainly regarding payments for the provision of service, access to information and working conditions, modalities of control by the platform to carry out the activity, and, if necessary, the complementary social protection guarantees negotiated by the platform from which workers can benefit. Finally, the right of workers to access all data related to their own activities within the platform is established, as well as to receive this data and the right to transmit it.

Finally, Decree 2021-1461 of 8 November 2021 related to the organisation and operation of the Labour Relations Authority for employment platforms has been published in November 2021.

Nevertheless, in the courts of justice there is no consensus between decisions since they have issued rulings with contrary content.

Thus, the decision of November 9, 2017, of the Paris Court of Appeals, declared that the worker was not bound by an employment contract with the Deliveroo France company, on the basis that the service provider carries out its activity with total independence without being subordinate in any way to the platform; the company is duly registered in the commercial and corporate registry and makes its payments of social contributions, fees and taxes; there is no exclusivity clause; and it uses its own worker team and the latter does not receive instructions or orders by the platform.

In contrast, decision number 1737, of the Paris Court of Cassation, November 28, 2018, declared an employment relationship based on the principle of the primacy of reality. It confirms the existence of a power of direction and control of the execution of the service and affirms that there is a clear relationship of subordination. In the same way, decision number 374, of the Paris Court of Cassation, March 4, 2020, dismissed the decision of the Court of Appeals and revalidated the qualification of the legal relationship as an employment contract of *Uber* with one of its workers.

However, recently, decision number 19/08046, of the Lyon Court of Appeals, dated January 15, 2021, denies that *Uber* drivers are employees.

In Italy, through Legislative Decree 81/2015, protection was extended beyond the traditional scope of the labour relationship -*lavoro subordinato*- considering the protection of the *lavoro etero-organizzato* worker. However, the application of this norm presented problems of interpretation in its application. As a consequence, it was modified by Decree Law number 101, of September 3, 2019, as well as by means of law number 128, of November 2, 2019.

At present, in this country, the collaborative relationships that are carried out in a predominantly continuous and personal way are included within the concept of labour relationships. Thus, labour law rules apply if the way in which the service is carried out is organised through digital platforms (Malzani 2020).

In addition, a space-time requirement, and the requirement of exclusivity of the personal performance of the employee has been eliminated and replaced by the concept of prevalence. It has also been added that the organisation of the service modes can be carried out through digital platforms. Furthermore, the regulation established in terms of collective agreements guaranteeing protection measures and standards, instead of the legal protection granted by law, was preserved.

Regarding the courts, it is worth noting the first instance decision number 778/2018, of the Turin Court, which determined that there was no subordination, given the freedom of drivers to choose schedules and shifts, since they were self-employed and were performing the tasks under their own planning and organisation. This decision was appealed, and resolved by the Court of Appeal, in decision number 26/2019, of January 11, 2019, which confirmed there was no subordination.

The case was taken to the Supreme Court, which by decision number 1663/20, of January 24, 2020, indicated that there is a legislative policy option designed to guarantee the worker the same protection that subordinate work enjoys. Therefore, it is not considered necessary to frame in a *tertium* genre, an intermediate between autonomy and subordination.

In addition, it considered that the legislator, when issuing this norm, aware of the complexity and variety of the new forms of work and of the difficulty of returning to the unit of typology, and of the variable results of litigation, by virtue of establishing a labour relationship, had limited itself to assessing certain factual indices considered significant (personality, continuity, hetero-organisation) and sufficient to justify the application of the discipline dictated for the subordinate labour relationship, exempting the judge from any additional investigation. Subsequently, in the most recent decisions this idea of employment has been maintained.

Thus, in decision number 3570/2020, of November 24, 2020, by the Court of Palermo, it was declared that a true employment relationship existed between the applicant and the *Glovo* platform, and considered it useless to investigate the existence of the assumptions based on facts referred to in the rule, since the worker did not intervene in any way in the organisation of his work, which was the exclusive prerogative of the platform, coupled with the disciplinary power to which he is subject by the platform. For its part, ruling number 2949/2019, of the Ordinary Labour Court of Bologna, on December 31, 2020, in a case against the Deliveroo platform, established that it is not possible to doubt the need to extend to these workers, regardless of the *nomen iuris* attributed by the parties to the employment contract, a total subordination and in this regard, the discipline to protect the worker from any discrimination in access to employment.

In Spain, the steps taken in relation to regulating this type of service provision have been diverse and, among them, stand out from different actions taken by the Labour and Social Security Inspection and specifically, the definition of a specific campaign in "Platforms within the Master Plan for a Decent Work 2018-2019-2020," or the fact that one of the recommendations of the *Toledo Pact* is to avoid informality or underpricing in activities carried out through digital platforms and to fight with the resource to the figure of the false self-employed.

In the same way, in the field of collective bargaining, in the modification and extension agreements of the V National Labour Agreement for the Hotel Industry, dated March 19, 2019, the functional scope includes "the service of distribution of prepared or prepared meals and beverages, on foot or in any type of vehicle that does not require administrative authorization established by transport regulations, as a provision of the establishment's own service or commissioned by another company, including digital platforms or through the same."

In addition, there are various decisions of the social courts and the social chambers of various Superior Courts of Justice that have ruled on this issue and which, analysing the same facts, interpret them in a different sense.

Eventually, *FILT CGIL, FIT-CISL UIL Trasporti* and *Just Eat* signed a collective agreement in March 2021.

Between 2018 and 2020, some decisions were pronounced against Glovo or Deliveroo, of which several initially denied the labour nature of the relationship between the platform and the worker (SJS 39 Madrid, 284/2018, of September 3; SJS 24 Barcelona, of June 29, 2019; SJS 17 Madrid, 12/2019, of January 11; SJS 1 Salamanca, 215/2019 of June 14; STSJ of Madrid 715/2019, of September 19), and other judgments declared the labor nature of the relationship (SJS 24 Barcelona, of May 21, 2019; SJS 6 Valencia, 244/2018, of June 1; SJS 5 Valencia, 197/2019, of June 10; SJS 31 Barcelona 193/2019, of June 11; SJS 1 Madrid, 128/2019 of April 3; SJS 1 Madrid, 134/2019, of April 4; SJS 1 Madrid, 130/2019, of April 4; SJS 3 Oviedo, 329 / 2019, of 5 July; SJS 1 Gijón, 61/2019 of February 20; SJS 21 Madrid, 119/2020, of June 11; SJS 19 Madrid, 188/2019, of July 22; SJS 2 Zaragoza 123/2020, of April 27; STSJ of Madrid 40/2020, of January 17; STSJ of Catalonia, 1034/2020 of February 21; STSJ of Catalonia, 1432/2020, of 7 May; STSJ of Castilla y León, Valladolid, 291/2020 of February 17; STSJ of Madrid 68/2020 of February 3; STSJ of Madrid 1223/2019, of December 18; STSJ of Madrid 1155/2019 of November 27; and STS 805/2020, of September 25).

In a final way, at least to date, the decision of the Supreme Court (plenary of the social chamber) of September 25, 2020, on the Glovo company, declares that there is not a mere intermediary in the contracting of services between businesses and distributors. It is based on the following elements (Barcelo Fernandez, 2020):

- ✓ The platform does not limit itself to providing an electronic intermediation service, but rather it performs a work of coordination and organisation of the productive service.
- ✓ The company sets the price and payment conditions for the service, as well as the essential conditions for the provision of the said service.
- ✓ It is the owner of the essential assets who carries out the activity.
- ✓ It establishes instructions that allow it to control the production process and has sanctioning power.
- ✓ Through the digital platform, it carries out the control in real time of the provision of the service, without the delivery person being able to carry out his task unrelated to the said platform.

The Spanish Ministry of Labour and Social Economy has decided in favour of establishing a specific regulation that determines, without a doubt, that the situations of the distributors who provide services on the platforms are included within the category of employment relationship.

To this end, some documents have been prepared for the proposal of a regulatory change that have been negotiated in successive social dialogue meetings during 2020, including, even in the first of the texts, dated at the end of October, the "Draft Law against the flight from Labour Law through new technologies."

On November 11, 2020, the Ministry issued a document that regulates the presumption of employment. In response to this document, the social partners sent their observations on November 19, 2020.

Subsequently, the Ministry presented a document at the social dialogue table of November 26, 2020, very simplified, since it only regulated the inclusion of this benefit within the scope of the workers' statute and the creation of a tripartite observatory on platforms.

Later, the social partners received a version of the proposals dated January 19, 2021 where, in addition to reiterating the inclusion of this benefit into the scope of the workers' statute and the creation of a tripartite observatory on platforms, the conditions of the "platform" companies are regulated. A previous idea was recovered, although modified, to increase the possibility of issuing a prior report by the legal representation of the workers to the implementation and review of work organisation and control systems, studies of times, establishment of bonus and incentive systems and job evaluation, adding the expression "included when derived from mathematical calculations or algorithms."

Finally, on March 11, 2021, the Ministry of Labour and Social Economy, trade union organisations and business organisations, reached an agreement on the regulation of the labour relations of distributors, by which they introduced into the workers' statute a presumption of employment of the activity of the people who provide remunerated services consisting of the distribution or distribution of any consumer product or merchandise, by companies that exercise the business powers of organisation, direction and control directly, indirectly or implicitly, through the algorithmic management of the service or working conditions, through a digital platform.

This agreement has become the Law 12/2021, of September 28, 2021, for the guarantee of the labour rights of people dedicated to distribution via digital platforms.

2. Thinking about Employment

Digitization is a phenomenon that is transforming all areas of our lives, since it changes the form of commercial exchange and the way people act in their role as consumers, It facilitates access to goods and services from anywhere in the world in only hours or immediately and, of course, it also radically alters the job market. This reality allows workers from all over the world to provide their labour in different sectors for companies that are in other countries or even without a defined location (Digital Future Society 2019, 36).

These new forms of work in digital service platforms present clear degrees of flexibility for service providers. They also raise other elements for assessment: the contribution of work instruments by the worker; the freedom to accept or reject orders or tasks within digital platforms; freedom in the way tasks are performed; control (or not) over the performance of work; being subject (or not) to the organisation and the direction of digital platforms; and whether the legal relationship that exists between the digital service platforms and the providers of these services must be situated in the field of the employment relationship or if it must be considered an example of a commercial relationship between two subjects that are considered as real companies (ETUI 2020).

To solve these questions, following the classic scheme present in most of the countries of the world, it is necessary to analyse whether there are employment grades of dependency or subordination and alienation. Although the so-called grey areas between the borders of the labour and commercial relationship have existed since the beginning of time (Martín Valverde 2020, 21), the truth is that working for digital platforms allows this dilemma to be retaken with force, with multiple arguments and positions, leading these workers to be at the centre of this discussion, between dependent or independent work.

Although the concept of employment relationship is not unique, it does present certain common characteristics that have been adjusted over time, mainly through jurisprudential interpretations. However, if a recurrent revision of this idea is necessary, it is even more so because of the generalisation of these work situations on platforms, since the phenomenon of digitization introduces new aspects, from all points of view: the concept of the company, the worker and the provision of service itself.

The future of work is clearly influenced by digitization, robotics, big data, autonomous vehicles, artificial intelligence, the automation of things, the ability to collect, store and process a large amount of data, and the economics of digital platforms, etc. These new challenges are changing not only people's lifestyles, but also the way in which services are provided and tasks are performed and, therefore, the work itself (World Economic Forum 2020).

Therefore, it is necessary to take advantage of the benefits of technology and the opportunities it offers, not only for economic growth from all spheres and to enhance the skills and capacities of the population, but also to promote new workspaces, which do not end up transformed into assumptions of underground or informal economy, within a pertinent normative context of protection.

This transformation must involve the adaptation of current regulatory frameworks, incorporating the novelties that these new phenomena introduce (International Lawyers Assisting Network, 2021).

The original purpose of labour law is the protection of the worker who develops services within the provision of services called an employment relationship, whatever its form, to eliminate any type of imbalance that exists between the employer and the worker and avoid arbitrariness or abuse that may be committed within this relationship.

For years, there has been debate about whether atypical work modalities present the characteristic notes of alienation and dependence, so it is not a new phenomenon. This discussion returns now, but with more force, due to the disruptive elements that digitization introduces into the job market.

The characteristics of dependency and alienation, which are part of this classic concept of the configuration of the employment relationship, and which allow us to justify the very existence of labour law, when they have been analysed by the courts, have always presented fuzzy defining lines (Lane 2020).

It is evident that, within the digital economy, this debate has been accentuated, since, although these people are usually hired as self-employed workers, the aspects that make up the provision of work on digital service platforms generate in many cases strong indications of employment and, in general, the will of these people is usually to prefer a position as a salaried worker (Eurofound, 2018).

One option is to adjust the current concept of labour law to the new work modalities by adopting specific legislation for this group of platform workers. However, it is also possible to consider these workers as independent or self-employed. In either of these two positions, important questions arise not only in the field of the employment relationship itself, but also in other close areas, such as, for example, how social security coverage is provided to these workers or how to guarantee their rights to freedom of association and collective bargaining (ETUI, 2020).

In this hypothetical modernisation of the concepts of alienation and dependence, there are several aspects that must be analysed and/or transformed.

Regarding alienation, the double concept of alienation in the risks and in the products must be considered.

In relation to alienation in the risks, this must be considered if the worker does not charge for the service or it does not materialise, so he assumes its good end assuming the risk and fortune of this, or he assumes the risk derived from the use of the tools used, the costs of which are his responsibility, receiving the company's remuneration based on the services provided. Likewise, if the worker has or does not intervene in the agreements established between the company and third parties or if it is the company that agrees on the prices that customers pay and unilaterally sets the rates that it receives for the activities it carries out, including additional amounts (Kilhoffer, Lenaerts & Beblavý 2017, 36).

With respect to alienation in products, it must be ascertained whether or not there is a difference between the economic importance of the company and the material resources of the worker, since the essential means of production in this activity are not those normally provided by the worker, but rather by the digital platform, aside from which the provision of the service is not feasible.

Regarding dependency, in addition to other indications that can be considered relevant, such as who has the freedom to choose working times, the activities to be carried out or the way of providing the service, the possibility of rejecting part of this activity, the existence of an exclusivity pact, linked to the possibility of executing the service in an undifferentiated manner, or the non-need to justify absences, there are two main issues that must be taken into account.

First, it is necessary to determine who has the productive infrastructure, as well as the materials necessary for the exercise of the activity when, in this activity they are economically relevant, especially when they are accessory or complementary means, since the essential infrastructure for the exercise of the activity, for example, in the case of platforms, is the computer program developed by the company.

Second, it is essential to conclude who determines the organisation of the activity, whether the company carries out a work of coordination and organisation of the productive service or is a mere intermediary in the contracting of services between clients and workers. In this sense, it must be clarified whether the worker can organise the productive activity on his own, negotiate prices or conditions with the owners of the establishments he serves or receive his remuneration from the end customers.

In this matter, it is crucial to know if the worker has true capacity to organize his work provision, having autonomy to do so and assessing whether this activity is subject to the organisational guidelines set by the company. If so, an exercise of business power is revealed in relation to the mode of provision of the service and a control of its execution in real time that shows the concurrence of the dependency requirement of the employment relationship.

Finally, the most innovative element and that presents the greatest opportunity for the redefinition of these two classic concepts are digital applications, which usually assign services based on the assessment that each worker receives. This decisively conditions the theoretical freedom of choice of schedules and activities. Clarification is required on whether, through the platform, the company carries out a real-time control of the provision of the service, without the workers being able to carry out their tasks detached from the said platform, meaning they have a very limited autonomy that only reaches out to secondary issues.

To sum up, there are many challenges that labour law experts have in the coming years, and we have to face them by thinking about how we would like work to be in the future (ILO 2019).

Bibliography

Barceló Fernández, J., "Siege of the false self-employed on digital platforms. Notes on the thread of the judgment of the Supreme Court 805/2020, of September 25," *General Journal of Labor and Social Security Law*, 57 (2020)

Digital Future Society, *The future of work in the digital era: The rise of labour platforms* (December 2019)

Eurofound, *Digital Age, Employment and working conditions of selected types of platform work* (2018)

European Committee of the Regions, *A European framework for regulatory responses to the collaborative economy (2020/C 79/08), DOUE, March 10, 2020*

European Economic and Social Committee, *Decent work in the platform economy*, SOC/465, July 17, 2020

ETUI, *Will trade unions survive in the platform economy? Emerging patterns of platform workers' collective voice and representation in Europe*, https://www.etui.org/publications/working-papers/will-trade-unions-survive-in-the-platform-economy-emerging-patterns-of-platform-workers-collective-voice-and-representation-in-europe

ETUI, *Working on Digital Labour Platforms. A trade union guide for trainers on crowd-, app- and platform-based work* (ETUI: Brussels, 2020)

ILO, *Centenary declaration for the future of work adopted by the conference at its one hundred and eighth session* (ILO: Geneva, 21 June 2019)

ILO, *World Employment and Social Outlook. The role of digital labour platforms in transforming the world of work* (ILO: Geneva, 2021)

International Lawyers Assisting Network, *Taken for a ride: litigating the digital platform model*, March 2021

JRC, *European Commission, Platform workers in Europe*, 2018
Kilhoffer, Z., Lenaerts, K. and Beblavý, M., *The Platform Economy and Industrial Relations Applying the old framework to the new reality* (CEPS, 12/2017)
Lane, M., *Regulating platform work in the digital age*, Going Digital Toolkit Policy Note, 1, 2020, https://goingdigital.oecd.org/toolkitnotes/regulating-platform-work-in-the-digital-age.pdf
Malzani, F., "Work in the gig economy between legal qualification and health protection. The case of riders in Italy," *Work and Law*, 61 (2020)
Martín Valverde, A., "Fronteras y zonas grises del Derecho del Trabajo en la jurisprudencia actual (1980-2001)," *Revista del Ministerio de Trabajo y Asuntos Sociales*, 38 (2002)
Martínez Girón, J., "La laboralización de los trabajadores al servicio de plataformas digitales por la jurisprudencia, en Alemania. Un estudio comparado con el derecho español », *Revista Crítica de Relaciones de Trabajo, Laborum.* 1 (2021)
World Economic Forum, *The Future of Jobs report 2020*, https://www.weforum.org/reports/the-future-of-jobs-report-2020

CHAPTER 16

THE FUNDAMENTAL RIGHT TO STRIKE: REPLACING HUMANS WITH MACHINES AS A RESULT OF TECHNOLOGICAL DEVELOPMENT AND THE VIRTUAL STRIKE

CLÁUDIO TEIXEIRA DAMILANO
& GILBERTO STÜRMER

Introduction

Strike is an important tool for workers to protect themselves, by making complaints or seeking to uphold their rights with their employer. This tool was first used at the end of the 18th century and over the years it has gone through several different phases of development. Depending on the type of government (fascist, totalitarian or democratic), strikes have either been banned or authorised under the legal system. At this point in history, society is going through a fourth industrial revolution, in which the rate and degree of technological change is having an impact on labour relations.

Labour relations have also been affected by the economic crisis, which has been aggravated by the Covid-19 pandemic that started in March 2020, and nobody can be certain, at the moment, when normality will return. The fact is that labour law has constantly been changing and adapting to suit society's needs.

Therefore, if there is a risk of workers being replaced by machines (Industry 4.0) or losing their livelihood due to the economic crisis, it is of fundamental importance to examine how strikes can be used as a mechanism to ensure equality and help workers negotiate their rights. Therefore, it is important to analyse the position of the strike under Brazilian law and how other countries deal with this subject. In particular, we will analyse whether the Brazilian legal system allows humans to be replaced by machines during the suspension of activities, as well as the phenomenon of virtual strikes. The methods used in this research will be historical and comparative, while the interpretation method will be sociological, using bibliographical and documentary sources.

Therefore, the intention of this research is to analyse the historical development of legislation that has either prohibited or authorised strikes in Brazil, and the concept of them. Finally, we will examine the potential for replacing humans with machines while work activities are suspended, and in regard to this there is a decision from Spain that will be discussed. In addition, the idea of a virtual strike will be examined, as well as how it can be carried out, and we will consider some examples from Italy, in this regard.

The Strike under the Brazilian Legal System

There is no reference to striking in the constitutions of 1824 and 1891, since at that time labour service tended to be provided by slaves (Prado 2015). The Penal Code (Decree No. 847, dated Oct 11, 1890), however, prohibited (art. 205 and art. 206) the "cessation or suspension of work, in order to force the workers or employers to accept an increase or decrease in their amount of service or wages," even peacefully.

This prohibition only lasted two months, as Decree No. 1162, dated Dec 12, 1890 (art. 205 and art. 206), only restricted the ability to strike if threats or violence were used. This is therefore the first recognition of the right to strike in our country (Nascimento 2012, p. 536). This change to the legislation was in accordance with the trend in European countries to treat striking as a democratic action, which featured the right not to work in order to seek rights and better working conditions and to prevent abuse or excess, such as bodily harm, assault, unlawful imprisonment, etc. (Nascimento 2012, p. 536).

It is therefore important to mention that on Jun 14, 1920, the Federal Supreme Court ruled on Habeas-Corpus No. 5910, in which the reporting Justice was Pedro Mibielli and the Patient, Manoel L. Carvalho. On that occasion, the Federal Supreme Court concluded that peaceful strike is a right that can be freely exercised (Revista do Supremo Tribunal Federal 1920).

From the 1930 revolution onwards, there was a period when the right to strike was more restricted, although it was not mentioned in the 1934 constitution. This is because, on Apr 04, 1935, Law No. 38 (National Security) was published, which criminalised (art. 7, art. 8, art. 18 and art. 19) the incitement to peacefully strike in respect of public services and striking in solidarity, i.e. striking for reasons other than their own work.

The 1937 constitution, in art. 139, stated that "strikes and lockouts are antisocial actions, which are harmful to labour and capital and are incompatible with the more important interests of national production." Decree-Law No. 431, dated May 18, 1938, made it a crime to incite workers to strike; Decree No. 1237, dated May 02, 1939, which later became art. 723 of the CLT, provided, through art. 81, for punishment with penalties of suspension or dismissal for workers who, collectively and without previous authorisation from the labour court, abandoned their work or disobeyed the decision of the court; and the Penal Code (Decree-Law No. 2848, dated Jul 12, 1940), provided punishment for taking part in collective action to suspend or abandon work, "take part in violence against anyone or anything" (art. 200); "take action that leads to the interruption of public works or services in the public interest" (art. 201); or break into or occupy an industrial, commercial or agricultural establishment, prevent or hinder the normal course of work, or for the same purpose, damage the establishment or the things within it or dispose of them (art. 202) (Nascimento 2012, p. 537).

The *Chapultepec* Conference held in Mexico between Feb 21 and Mar 08, 1945 was attended by several nations, including Brazil. The final agreement contained a recommendation at *item g, number 1, item 11 – "Reconhecimento del Derecho de Associación de los Trabajadores, del Contrato Coletivo y del Drececho del Huelga"* (Rangel, Rodrigues, Naud & Martins 1964, p. 08f.). As a result of the Conference in *Chapultepec* and because Brazil was one of the signatories, Decree-Law No. 9070, dated Mar 15, 1946, was published, which provided for the collective suspension or abandonment of work, and allowed strikes to take place as a supplementary action should legal remedies fail to resolve the issue. It should be noted that Decree-Law No. 9070, of Mar 15, 1946, despite being published under the 1937 constitution, which expressly prohibited strikes, was declared constitutional by the Federal Supreme Court (RE No. 48207-SP, Reporting Justice Gallotti) which considered that the two legal positions were compatible, which also became the guidance from the Upper Labour Court (Nascimento 2012, p. 538).

The 1946 constitution put an end to the discussion by recognising the right to strike in art. 158, the exercise of which was regulated by further legislation. In addition, art. 28 of the ADCT granted an amnesty to all "workers who have suffered disciplinary penalties as a result of strikes or labour disputes."

On Dec 15, 1961, Legislative Decree No. 18 granted amnesty to workers who took part in any strike, as well as students who, as a result of striking or failing to attend during such a period, were at risk of failing the year, along with any who had received disciplinary penalties.

However, on June 1, 1964, as a result of the political changes that took place (Nascimento 2012, p. 539), law no. 4330 was published, which regulated the right to strike. This legislation, which was referred to as the Anti-Strike Law (Nascimento 2012, p. 541), brought in art. 2, which included the concept of and certain requirements for striking. In art. 4 there was a ban on strikes by public servants. In articles 6 to 9, the conditions for exercising the right to strike were established. The fundamental activities were established by articles 12 to 16. The guarantees for strikers were listed in art. 19, such as: no coercion, ability to collect donations, the use of non-offensive advertising posters, banning the sacking of strikers who take part peacefully in the strike and banning strikebreaking. A strike would be declared illegal (art. 22) if the deadlines and conditions established under the law were not met, if the claim had been rejected by the labour court within the last year, if it was declared for political, party, religious or social reasons, in support or in solidarity, without any direct or legitimate interest in the particular work area, or if its purpose was to change a standing condition of the legal system or rulings of the labour court, unless the supporting basis had been fundamentally altered.

The 1967 constitution recognised the right to strike in the private sector, art. 158, item XXI, but prohibited striking in public services and essential activities, art. 157, para 7. On Dec 17, 1978, Law No. 6620 (National Security) was published, which introduced several punishments for strikers who paralysed public services and essential activities (art. 9, para. 1, art. 27, art. 35, art. 36 and article 37, sole paragraph). Furthermore, Decree-Law No. 1632, dated Aug 04, 1978, prohibited strikes in public services and essential activities in the interests of national security. Art. 6 even established a penalty of "serious misconduct, punishable by dismissal or suspension, for a public official who takes part in or supports a strike."

Law no. 6833, dated Aug 28, 1979, granted (art. 7) an amnesty to employees of private companies who had been dismissed from their work, or removed from administrative positions or union representation, due to taking part in strikes or in any disputes or complaints covered by social legislation.

The Federal Constitution – enacted on Oct 05, 1988 – was not the first to enshrine the right to strike. It was, however, an important milestone for this institution because, as well as guaranteeing the right to strike for workers in the private sector (art. 9), it acknowledged the aforementioned right for public servants too (art. 37, VII), which was an advance on the position held by the 1967 constitution and constitutional amendment no. 1 (1969). Striking was elevated to a fundamental social right (Stürmer 2014, p. 106). The concept of the strike was also expanded and the rules were changed on ownership, which gave assurance to the worker, "defining expressly and exclusively that from the point they exercise their right, they will be protected under the constitution" (Boucinhas Filho 2019, p. 531). As a result, strikes were now allowed in all areas, including those deemed essential, but there were still restrictions. Members of the Armed Forces (art. 142, para. 3, IV), for example, and the military police (art. 42, para. 1, of the CF) were not allowed to strike.

In 1989, Provisional Measure no. 50, 1989 was published, which tried to limit the right to strike. However, it was not approved into law by the National Congress. As a result, the executive branch amended Provisional Measure No. 59 to include the same content as Provisional Measure No. 50, 1989, which enabled the National Congress to have more time to analyse the content and reach a consensus. Provisional Measure No. 59, 1989, in the end, became Law No. 7783, dated Jun 28, 1989, which provided the legislation regarding strikes and was considered to be more flexible, while in line with the federal constitution of 1988 (Nascimento 2012, p. 544).

The Concept of Striking

The scholar Alain Supiot states in his book "A Critique of Labour Law" which analyses the strike in France:

"The strike was also conceived in France as an individual freedom to act collectively. As a freedom, the strike is a choice that is available to individuals. It is a choice that implies the freedom not to strike, in other words, the freedom to work. This individual and 'negative' aspect has been included since the first 'acknowledgement' of the right to strike in the law from 25-27 May 1864, which replaced the offense of coalition (i.e. the offense of striking) with one regarding the attack on the freedom to work, which made it possible to criminalize the violation of the freedom not to go on strike" (2002, p. 189).

In Brazil, the CF/88 did not introduce the concept of striking, but established it in a more extensive form, by stating (art. 9) that it is up to "the workers to decide on how to exercise it and on the interests that they intend to defend by using it." The effect of this is that the wording of the constitution gave workers the ability to declare a strike at their convenience and to whatever purpose they decide (Nascimento 2012, p. 544-545). Note that a strike declaration is made by the union, but who decides individually whether or not to join the action is the workers themselves.

Striking, according to CF/88, "is a fundamental individual right to make a collective demonstration" (Boucinhas Filho 2019. p. 533). The worker must be free to join the movement or choose to continue to work. In other words, the worker cannot suffer reprisals from his employer for joining a strike, such as being discriminated against or dismissed (art. 6, para. 2 and art. 7, sole paragraph of Law No. 7783/89), nor can he/she be coerced by his/her colleagues or the union into joining the action (art. 6, item I of Law No. 7783/89).

Any stoppage has to be peaceful (art. 2 of Law 7783/89), not only with regard to people, but also with regard to things, anything else would be an abuse of rights.

The legal concept of the strike is "the combined stoppage of work in order to make a complaint to the employer; the jurists state that a stoppage by a single worker is not a strike, therefore its nature assumes that it is made by a group with a common interest" (Nascimento 2012, p. 507). In a similar way, the intention of the strike is not to terminate the employment contract, but to suspend its activities temporarily as a way to pressure the employer to either improve the contract or keep it unchanged. Therefore, there is no need to refer to a strike as abandoning a job, as the stoppage is not definitive and there is nothing about it to indicate that the intention is to terminate the employment contract. As mentioned, the purpose of the strike is not to terminate the employment contract, but to suspend the legal relationship until the rights that are being claimed have been obtained or upheld (Nascimento, 2012, p. 511). To strike is the right not to work.

Accordingly, Antônio Monteiro Fernandes, who discusses the Strike in the "Brazilian Dictionary of Labour Law," states that:

"In fact, a strike is the non-compliance with contractual obligations, without intending to terminate the contract; and it represents a phenomenon that the law is designed to prevent: direct action to defend and support particular interests. The principle of collective self-protection – which the right to strike is a typical expression of – carries with it the recognition that the legal system is insufficient to resolve collective labor conflicts and to effectively represent workers' interests. Furthermore, the right to strike is also linked to the principle of freedom to work, in the sense that it is a right to refuse to work when it is imposed. Both of these fundamentals are, when it comes to the right to strike, considered priorities, relative to contractual commitments and the social needs that the products of normal work are intended to meet" (2013, p. 225).

"Striking is a collective, not an individual action, which is why this right does not apply when carried out by a single person. In other words, when an employee refuses to do something because he considers it illegal, unworthy or arbitrary, his act is one of resistance and is not an act of insubordination. In any case, a strike does not need to include the entire group of employees, and its extent may be total or partial, whether it is only some employees, several, a particular category, part of a category, several categories or all workers in an area or from a section (Nascimento 2012, p. 511) […] department or branch, or only those on hourly pay, those on hourly and monthly pay, workshop personnel, or administration personnel, etc." (Nascimento 2012, p. 546, translated into English).

Another discussion related to the concept of strike is whether the stoppage of activities should be total or not. In other words, "whether work should be suspended for the entire shift or for part of it only; whether work should be suspended for overtime only and not affect normal working hours; whether it is possible to suspend work for only one shift or to split the stoppage across several periods" (Nascimento 2012, p. 526, translated into English).

However, it is important that when there is a stoppage of work by employees, there are economic consequences to the employer's activities or production, so that they are pressured into accepting the complaint. The aim of the strike is to affect or paralyse production for the sole purpose of claiming a specific change to the working regulations or to stop a commercial proposal, that is restrictive or contrary to the interests of the workers, from being effective (Pineda 2018). Similarly, there is "what is known as work to rule, during which the employees remain on duty. However, they ensure while working that work takes place more slowly, which also acts as a form of boycott," which can't be ruled out (Nascimento 2012, p. 545, translated into English).

Replacing Human Workers with Technology and a Virtual Strike

The development of technology has had two consequences for the workers' right to strike: the replacement of human labour by technology and the virtual strike (Martins 2015).

Law 7783/89 in art. 7, sole paragraph, prohibits the "rescission of employment contracts during a strike, as well as the hiring of replacement workers, except in the following cases: (i) where the stoppage may result in "irreparable damage due to the irreversible deterioration of goods, machinery and equipment, or the maintenance of whatever is essential to be able to resume the company's activities when the industrial action is over" (art. 9); and (ii) where a stoppage continues after an agreement or decision by the labour court (art. 14).

It should be noted that Law No. 13429/2017, which includes para. 1 of art. 2 of Law No. 6019/74 also prohibits "the hiring of temporary workers to replace workers who are on strike, except where legally allowed to do so". Up until then, according to Sérgio Pinto Martins, there was no legal impediment to "hiring a specialized company to provide strike-breaking services."

Now, the purpose of art. 7, sole paragraph of law no. 7783/89, is to ensure the effectiveness of the fundamental right of workers, because if employers were allowed to replace striking workers, it would render the action ineffective and prevent it from being successful, as it would lose its force and make it an empty gesture. Therefore, if there was no impediment to hiring a specialised company or to outsource the service, then this would violate the fundamental right to strike. In any case, law no. 13429/2017, which included para. 1 of art. 2 of law no. 6019/74 (temporary work) reinforces the prohibition on any hiring that is intended to weaken or reduce the effectiveness of industrial action.

Although legislation has been extended to ensure workers' fundamental right to strike is effective, there is an important issue that needs to be debated and, perhaps, subjected to regulation: the development of technology (Industry 4.0) that has been slowly diminishing this right to strike as humans have been replaced by machines. Is it possible to replace striking workers with robots?

Replacing humans with robots for some tasks is inevitably going to happen. Some research has suggested that this will lead to much unemployment (Bôas 2019), while other research has suggested that the advancement of technology will improve living standards, wages and create markets that did not previously exist, and that it will offset the eventual replacement of humans by robots (Matsuura 2015).

In the Brazilian legal system there is no specific rule preventing an employer from replacing striking workers with robots. Article 7, item XXVII of the CF/88 provides for "protection in the face of automation" but there has been no regulatory law despite this being a "social right inscribed for current and future generations of workers" (Feliciano & Moraes 2019). Bill No. 1091/2019 is currently progressing through the National Congress, which is intended to regulate for the provisions of item XXVII, of art. 7, of CF/88, but it does not refer to the potential for robots to replace striking workers.

If we make use of the comparative law provision, in accordance with art. 8 of the consolidation of labour laws, then it is important to note that Spain has already considered the issue of replacing striking workers with technology (technological esquirolaje) that is already available to the company. The latest ruling regarding *esquirolaje tecnológico* on Feb 02, 2017 made by the Constitutional Court (SENTENCIA 17/2017) involved *Sindicato Confederación General del Trabajo* and *Ente público Radio*

Televisión Madrid y sus Sociedade (Court, 2017).

On this occasion, the Constitutional Court believed that (i) there was no rule prohibiting a business person from using technology that is already part of their routine work to continue their activities and (ii) the use of technology that is already part of their routine work is compatible with the right to strike, and the existing prohibition in art. 6.5 del Real Decreto Ley 17/1977 which establishes the following:

"En tanto dure la huelga, el empresario no podrá sustituir a los huelguistas por trabajadores que no estuviesen vinculados a la empresa al tiempo de ser comunicada la misma salvo caso de incumplimiento de las obligaciones contenidas en el apartado número siete de este artículo"[1]

This being the case, the Constitutional Court concluded that the right to strike is not violated when a business person makes normal use of resources they already have available in the company, as part of their management of the organisation. The program could be broadcast because the company already had the technical means to do so and a number of workers did not join the strike. In other words, the technology to replace the striking workers already existed in the company – it was not specifically acquired to break the strike – and the workers who did not join the strike movement did not carry out any activities that were different to those they would normally engage in. Therefore, according to the Constitutional Court of Spain, the right to strike was respected.

In any case, both the Spanish and Brazilian legal systems, as they are interpreted based on the constitution, prohibit replacing striking workers with "new" machines, as this would weaken and undermine the industrial action they take and which has been given to them as a fundamental social right.

On the matter of the virtual strike, this has two meanings: (i) a strike that is not real and (ii) a strike carried out on the Internet.

When we refer to a "virtual strike" that "is not real", this is a form of action in which workers continue to work and the company continues to produce normally, but neither side receives anything from the other. In other words, the employee does not receive a salary for the service provided and the employer does not receive anything for the sales or services carried out. The money for salaries may go to the government, a charity, or even be passed on to customers (Ayres & Nalebuff 2002). The purpose of a virtual strike is that it enables the parties to negotiate without affecting customers

[1] As long as the strike lasts, the employer may not replace the strikers with workers who were not linked to the company at the time it was communicated, except in the case of non-compliance with the obligations contained in section number seven of this article.

by suspending activities.

According to the Yale Professors Ian Ayres and Barry Nalebuff, this is not something new and untested, as the virtual strike has already been used on several occasions: (i) the US Navy used it to resolve a labour dispute at the Jenkins Brothers valve plant in Bridgeport, Connecticut during World War II; (ii) it was used for bus transportation in 1960 in the city of Miami; (iii) it was used in the airline industry in Italy when pilots and flight attendants for Meridiana Airline held the first virtual action in 1999 and when the Transport Union of Italy lost USD 50,000 during a virtual strike by 300 of its pilots in 2000.

A professor at LUMSA University, Antonio Nicita, also includes this example of a virtual strike: "nel 1989 dai piloti aerei dell'Anpac; nel 1995 dai poliziotti della Sap; nel 1999 dai medici dell'Anmi; nel 2000 dagli autoferrotramvieri ATM; nel 2002 dagli elicotteristi" (Nicita 2009). The various virtual strikes in Italy led to the drafting of Bill 1170/2008 (Della Republica, 2008) to regulate this situation. However, it has not yet been approved by the Italian senate.

In a virtual strike – unlike a normal strike – workers try to reduce the social cost to consumers by explaining their demands so that, in one way or another, there is "external" support. In this situation, it encourages consumers to support the industrial action by posting messages on social media or choosing not to purchase products and services from the employer (Nicita 2009).

This format was used in a strike by workers for IBM Italy in 2007, where they used the virtual world, *Second Life,* to hold protests. At the time, Second Life had 10 million registered users, and IBM itself had invested millions of Euros to open departments, business centres and support services in the virtual world. Workers took advantage of this business by creating 2,000 avatars and protesting online for 12 hours in over 30 countries, claiming real rights with posters, slogans and banners. The "virtual strikers" occupied 07 of the 30 islands IBM had created in the virtual world, paralysing the business centre for several hours and disrupting an online meeting of managers (Carra 2008). This type of virtual strike action had a big impact in the media and after a month of protesting on *Second Life*, IBM gave in to the pressure and gave them the 2007-2010 award, their national health insurance contributions, and committed to continue negotiations on industrial strategies and improving internal conditions (Nicita 2009).

Several Google employees went on strike on Nov 01, 2018 in London, Dublin, Zurich, Berlin, Tokyo and Haifa, to complain about the sexual harassment and discriminatory treatment of women and other minorities.

The way that the workers managed to embarrass and force Google to change its position was to send photos of the staff on Twitter standing on the streets and at work with the following phrase: "I'm not at my desk because I'm walking out in solidarity with other Googlers and contractors to protest sexual harassment, misconduct, lack of transparency, and a workplace culture that's not working for everyone." Google, in response to the action, sent a notice to staff about the measures taken to eliminate sexual harassment, including dismissing 48 employees, including the director of Google X (O Globo 2018).

In Brazil, workers at PROCERGS — The Information Technology and Communication Centre of the State of Rio Grande Do Sul S.A — held a virtual strike on Jan 18, 2021, because they were working from home as a result of the Covid-19 pandemic. Their agenda included claims for increases that had been "frozen from 2019 (2.25%) and from 2020 (5.3%) - and retention of ATS (Length of Service Bonus), which the state government were proposing to do away with" (Lobo 2021).

As we can see, a "not real" virtual strike can be combined with one carried out on the Internet or in isolation and *vice versa*. In fact, the old model where employees paralysed city traffic or disrupted people's lives in order to draw attention to their demands, is being replaced by action on the Internet and social media. These changes to the way strikers and union workers can act, as seen in the cases of IBM and Google, has proved to be more efficient and effective in winning or maintaining rights.

Conclusion

As technology has evolved, it has brought about great changes in how we relate socially and, this is no different in the field of industrial relations. There are increasingly more opportunities to replace humans with machines, which makes it harder for workers to choose to strike. On the one hand, a systematic interpretation of the law means it is possible to conclude that the Brazilian legal system prohibits the replacement of employees through technological means. However, on the other hand, the lack of any formal regulation of art. 7, item XXVII of the CF/88 does not prevent, once normal work is resumed, striking workers from being replaced by machines.

Given this, the study has shown how workers and unions can take action on two fronts that are not mutually exclusive, but can be complementary. The first of these is the virtual strike to pressure the company into giving in to demands, not by suspending working' activities, but by appealing to consumers and damaging its image online.

The second front that unions must address is the upskilling and training of the workers they represent. There is provision within the CLT (art. 513, Sole paragraph and art. 514, Sole paragraph, letter "b") for unions to create a placement agency, and to establish and maintain schools for literacy and vocational skills. In other words, because workers will need to learn how to adapt to changes in technology in the future, the union needs to take on the function of training and upskilling the workers. Although technology may replace humans in certain activities, it will also create other jobs that did not exist previously and people need to have the skills necessary to remain part of the labour market.

Bibliography

Ayres, Ian and Nalebuff, Barry, "The Virtues of a Virtual Strike", published in 2002, accessed Mar 29, 2019, https://www.forbes.com/forbes/2002/1125/128.html?sh=c3ef90542713

Bôas, Bruno Villas, "Máquinas podem ficar com metade dos empregos no Brasil", published in 2019, accessed Oct 04, 2019, https://valor.globo.com/carreira/noticia/2019/10/03/maquinas-podem-ficar-com-metade-dos-empregos-no-brasil.ghtml

Boucinhas Filho, Jorge Cavalcanti, "Art. 9º É assegurado o direito de greve, competindo aos trabalhadores decidir sobre a oportunidade de exercê-lo e sobre os interesses que devam por meio dele defender", In: Martinez, Luciano; Teixeira Filho, João de Lima (org.). *Comentários à Constituição de 1988 em matéria de direitos sociais trabalhistas (arts. 6 a 11)* (São Paulo: LTr, 2019), pp. 531-537

Carra, Ilaria, "Sciopero virtuale, effetti reali i lavoratori Ibm cantano vittoria", published in 2008, accessed Mar 29, 2019, https://www.repubblica.it/2007/04/sezioni/scienza_e_tecnologia/second-life-news/scoperi-sl/scoperi-sl.html

Court, Spanish Constitutional, "SENTENCIA 17/2017, de 2 de febrero", published in 2017, accessed Feb 24, 2021, http://hj.tribunalconstitucional.es/en/Resolucion/Show/25242

Della Repubblica, Senato, "Disposizioni in materia di sciopero virtuale", published in 2008, accessed Mar 29, 2019, https://www.senato.it/service/PDF/PDFServer/DF/208505.pdf

Feliciano, Guilherme Guimarães; Moraes, Paulo Douglas de Almeida, "Automação e trabalho: sobre monturos, futuros e apuros: breves comentários ao pl n. 1.091/2019, da câmara dos deputados. Breves comentários ao PL n. 1.091/2019, da Câmara dos Deputados", published in 2019, accessed Oct 13, 2019, https://www.jota.info/paywall?redirect_to=//www.jota.info/opiniao-e-analise/colunas/juizo-de-valor/automacao-e-trabalho-sobre-monturos-futuros-e-apuros-11102019

Fernandes, Antônio Monteiro, "Greve," In *Dicionário Brasileiro de Direito do Trabalho*, organized by Pinto, José Augusto Rodrigues, Martinez, Luciano and Mannrich, Nelson (São Paulo: LTr, 2013), pp. 224-225

Hodges-Aeberhard, Jane; Dios, Alberto Odero de, *Princípios do Comitê de Liberdade Sindical Referentes a Greves* (Brasília: Organização Internacional do Trabalho, 1993), 20 p. Translated by Edilson Alkmim Cunha

ILO, International Labour Organization, "R092 - Recomendación sobre la conciliación y el arbitraje voluntarios, (núm. 92)", published in 1951, accessed Feb 18, 2021, https://www.ilo.org/dyn/normlex/es/f?p=NORMLEXPUB:12100:0::NO:12100:P12100_INSTRUMENT_ID:312430:NO

Lobo, Ana Paula, "Trabalhadores da Procergs entram em greve por aprovação de acordo coletivo 2020", published in 2021, accessed Jan 27, 2021, https://www.convergenciadigital.com.br/cgi/cgilua.exe/sys/start.htm?UserActiveTemplate=site&UserActiveTemplate=mobile&infoid=55904&sid=46#.YDcU-2hKjIU

Martins, Sergio Pinto, "Greve e Substituição de trabalhadores grevistas", published in 2015, accessed Feb 04, 2021, http://www.cartaforense.com.br/conteudo/colunas/greve-e-substituicao-de-trabalhadores-grevistas/14863

Matsuura, Sérgio, "Tecnologia cria mais empregos do que destrói, aponta estudo", published in 2015, accessed May 14, 2019, https://oglobo.globo.com/economia/tecnologia-cria-mais-empregos-do-que-destroi-aponta-estudo-17228160

Nascimento, Amauri Mascaro, *Compêndio de Direito Sindical* (São Paulo: LTr, 2012)

Nicita, Antonio, "Sciopero Virtuale e Incentivi Reali", published in 2009, accessed Mar 29, 2019, http://www.nelmerito.com/index.php?option=com_content&task=view&id=528&Itemid=159

O Globo (Rio de Janeiro) (ed.), "Após escândalos de assédio sexual, funcionários da Google fazem greve". published in 2018, accessed Apr 02, 2019, https://oglobo.globo.com/sociedade/apos-escandalos-de-assedio-sexual-funcionarios-da-google-fazem-greve-23204155

Pineda, Carmen Grau, "El impacto de las nuevas tecnologías en el derecho de huelga: a propósito de la sustitución de huelguistas por medios tecnológicos", *Nueva Revista Española de Derecho del Trabajo*, n. 206, (2018) Oct. 16, Monthly [digital]

Prado, Ney, "A Greve na Constituição de 1988", published in 2015, accessed May 26, 2015, http://www.editoramagister.com/doutrina_26826623_A_GREVE_NA_CONSTITUICAO_DE_1988.aspx

Rangel, Leyla Castello Branco; Rodrigues, Rogério Costa; Naud, Lêda Maria Cardoso; Martins, Norma Izabel Ribeiro, *Direito de Greve* (Brasília: Serviço de Informação Legislativa, 1964), p. 309

Revista do Supremo Tribunal Federal. 1920. "Habeas-Corpus No. 5910", Rio de Janeiro: STF, v. 25, n. 1, 1920. Oct/Dec Page 149-150. published in 1920, accessed Feb 19, 2021, https://sistemas.stf.jus.br/dspace/xmlui/handle/123456789/1455

Siqueira, Gustavo S., "O STF no Egito: greve e história do direito no recurso extraordinário n.º 693.456/RJ", *Revista Direito e Práxis* v. 10, n. 2 (2019): 1016-1045

Stürmer, Gilberto, *Direito constitucional do trabalho no Brasil* (São Paulo: Atlas, 2014). p. 146

Supiot, Alain, *Crítica do Direito do Trabalho* (Lisboa: Fundação Calouste Gulbenkian, 2002), p. 368. Translated by António Monteiro Fernandes

Thome, Candy Florencio, "Greve". *In Dicionário de direito do trabalho, de direito processual do trabalho e de direito previdenciário aplicado ao direito do trabalho*, org. Schwarz, Rodrigo Garcia (São Paulo: LTr, 2012), pp. 499-502

CHAPTER 17

A LABOUR REALITY IN CONSTANT TRANSFORMATION: THE NEED FOR NEW CONCEPTS

ALFREDO SÁNCHEZ-CASTAÑEDA

Labour law has been, for many years, reclining on a couch, with an identity crisis. Globalisation and a supposed uniformity have brought about abrupt changes throughout its history. Coupled with a dominant discourse that talks about the disappearance of labour law, there is a conceptual criterion that continues to be anchored in its origins, and which demands a different reading. This new reading should not neglect the past but understand that labour law requires new philosophical foundations.

I. Labour Relations between Globalisation and a Fictitious Uniformity that Masks Inequalities

The globalisation of all kinds of human relations is the main feature of the 21st century, whether it is at the level of sociability, recreation, consumption, production, health or work. Its guiding axis is always globalisation. People communicate through diverse electronic portals (*Twitter, Facebook, Spasnack*, etc.); entertainment shows which are shown in one country are repeated in another one (*Fear Factor, Exathlon*, etc.); people buy through companies with presence all over the world (*Amazon, Alibbaba*, etc); the production of goods and services is done through global chains which are supported on delocalisation and outsourcing; people's health and mobility are affected by the Covid-19 pandemic and; finally, labour relations participate in this concert called globalisation.

These features make it possible to think that we live in a uniform world, without any differences, where human relations are characteristically homogeneous. They are so alike that even poverty has been democratised. Before, poverty only appeared in developing countries, but it has now also emerged in developed countries. Now, the new poor, as the World Bank points out, will probably live in urban spaces to more of an extent than people who are chronically poor; their jobs will be informal and in manufacturing less than in agriculture and they will live in overpopulated urban spaces and work in sectors which are more likely to be affected by lockdown measures and other restrictions imposed on mobility (Bah 2009).

It is true that regionally there are structural differences, and this remains true between developed and developing countries (Ocampo 2020). While in Asia the standards of living have risen despite their unequal growth, African countries are the countries which suffer most from poverty.

The United Nations Program for Development (UNDP), in their 2019 report, pointed out that the poorest countries were: Niger, Central African Republic, Chad, South Sudan, Mali, Eritrea, Burkina Faso, Sierra Leona, Mozambique and the Democratic Republic of Congo.

Latin America and the Caribbean will have their largest contraction in the last 100 years. The GDP per capita levels from 2020 will regress to levels detected in 2010 and there will be an important deterioration in employment, poverty and inequality.

On the other hand, globalised labour relations have generated a new international division of labour: growing unemployment in developed countries; a parallel transfer of part of the industrial production process to developing countries; the decomposition of complex production processes; an intensive use of technology, the reduction of production costs and the intense use of labour in developing countries (Fröbel, Heinrich & Kreye 1978); the emergence of an unidentifiable or underground economy (mainly in developed countries) (OECD 2002); and informal workers (mainly in developing countries) (ILO 2009).

As we can see, the world of work seems homogeneous. Nevertheless, we must not stop pointing out the still existent heterogeneity among countries, particularly when it comes to the recognition of labour rights, or rights with high or low labour standards in terms of occupational health and safety (ILO 2011), labour matters in general (OECD, 2001), and even in recoil (Clauwaert and Schömann, 2012). We cannot stop mentioning countries that, even with high protections in labour standards, suffer great problems in terms of compliance (effectiveness) (ILO 2010).

The 21st century seems to be the century of migration. However, historically migration has been a means of mobilisation and the constant provision of cheap and specialised labour, whether it be in a slave system, undocumented migration, or national or binational programs for temporal or permanent migrant workers. Through these schemes, migrations have been one of capitalism's development factors (ECLAC 2006).

Unfortunately, migration is usually linked to topics related to interior politics and national security rather than regional cooperation, not criminalising irregular migration and establishing a principle of non-discrimination and equality among every nation and migrants. Meanwhile, migrants often suffer theft, discrimination, extortion, kidnapping, human trafficking, murder, disappearance, sexual violence, abuses of authority, the excessive use of force, a lack of access to justice and impunity, etc. (Inter-American Commission on Human Rights 2013).

Modern Western societies must also be given another adjective: patriarchal. Their supposed modernity has been built under the footprint of inequality and discrimination between men and women, and also in matters related to sex and gender. Discrimination in education and the job market in terms of employment and wages have put women in a situation of historical disadvantage in relation to men (ILO 2006). Such disadvantages are increased in developing countries, or when a woman possesses more than one feature commonly discriminated against, such as being a migrant woman who is poor and illiterate. Under these circumstances, in labour as in other fields, gender perspectives are essential to outcomes (ILO 2009).

II. A Changing Labour Law

A worker understood in a modern sense appears when societies transit from pre-capitalist modes of production to capitalist ones, namely, industrial production, the purchase of workforce to obtain surplus value and the accumulation of capital (Marx & Hobsbawm 2009). Stemming from such development and not only from these modes of production, but from the ideology that derives from them, is how labour law appears, in a modern sense. This happens when people find themselves in a situation of legal equality (far from the situation of slaves in ancient Rome and Greece and a servant's situation in feudalism) and are obliged to sell their workforce to whomever holds the means of production, in order to survive.

It is exactly the idea of legal equality which led to what is considered the sale of the worker's workforce as a relation ruled by civil law, where a person "freely" sells his or her work to another person. Such freedom in reality puts the workers in a situation of labour exploitation which was clearly explained by Engels in his famous book, *The Condition of the Working Class in England.*

Without a doubt, constant social manifestations at the end of the 19th century led to the signature of the Treaty of Versailles at the beginning of the 20th century, which ended World War I, and which would enact the following:

- Universal and lasting peace can be established only if it is based upon social justice;
- Where conditions of labour exist involving such injustice, hardship and privation to large numbers of people as to produce unrest so great that the peace and harmony of the world are imperilled, an improvement of those conditions is urgently required;
- Where the failure of any nation to adopt humane conditions of labour is an obstacle in the way of other nations which desire to improve the conditions in their own countries, this should be remedied.

This background serves to point out that labour law, in little more than a century and a half, has transited vertiginously through diverse stages:

- Prohibition. The repression and punishment of and towards the labour movement. This stage is usually exemplified in the French Criminal Code of 1810 and the Chapelier Law.
- Tolerance. The absence of the recognition of rights but with a presence of a certain permissive attitude from the state. In this regard, England's parliament recognised freedom of association in 1824. France ruled that punishment for the creation of professional associations and strikes would be eliminated (1864).
- Reglamentation. The recognition of worker's rights in some European countries and its constitutional inclusion, which can be seen in the Mexican Constitution of 1917 (Fix-Zamudio 1985; Alfie 2012 and Sánchez Vázquez 2016), Weimar's Constitution in 1919 (P.E.M. 1921), and at the international level in the Treaty of Versailles from 1919.
- Labour flexibility. Inverting the paradigm of the previous stage of reglamentation and transitioning from the adaptation of the company to the worker, towards the adaptation of the worker to the company's needs.
- Flexicurity has remained much more of a pipe dream, facing the continuous diminishment of workers' rights (Blyton 1995), or even the disappearance of labour rights (Reynoso 2000).

As discussed, it is hard to understand a legal discipline when it constantly changes; in this case the nature of labour law is challenged every few years. Not only is it hard in the present, but it has always been difficult to understand the scope and ends of this legal discipline.

III. The Discourse of the Disappearance or Decrease of Labour Law

Without a doubt, another explanation of the "crisis" which labour law is undergoing has to do with the reconsideration of outsourcing and the appearance of atypical forms of labour: temporary employment, part time work, agency temporary employment, and other multi-party labour relations, as well as undercover labour relations and economically dependent independent work (ILO 2016).

It is precisely the continuing decline in workers' rights or even the disappearance of labour rights that characterises the last quarter of the 20th century and the beginning of the 21st century. After labour law was an instrument to deliver welfare to labour, we now find ourselves facing a situation in which a person who works is not necessarily classified as a worker, or in the best scenario is situated in an intermediate classification, between independent and subordinate work.

It seems that the new conditions in which a subordinate and paid activity is performed imply expelling working people from labour law, because their activity is not necessarily classified as subordinate and, in that sense, in the case of not being subordinate, is situated far away from the benefits which labour law recognises for performing a personal subordinate job (Romagnoli 1992).

We point out that it seems we may possibly find ourselves facing a mirage, created by the emergence of new types of employment which run away from or aim to repel labour law, because they allow for labour law's evasion. This diminishes the costs of labour which, in other scenarios, would have to be covered under a scheme of labour subordination, or in another scenario the labour relation would be hidden as false autonomous work (Supiot 1999).

IV. A Labour Law with 19th Century Thought

As mentioned before, continuous and accelerated changes are a feature of labour law. Because of this we can state that those who study this subject have difficulty understanding the changes and finding new categories which explain those changes. The labour relation or labour contract, marked by the subordination of a person to another person, could have very well explained, for more than a century, the need for the emergence of labour law.

Over the last quarter of a century, there have been numerous changes: the onset of triangular labour relations (outsourcing); the real or simulated increase in independent work which has brought a significant amount of workers back to private law who question the notion of labour subordination (Supiot 2009; Megnoni 1986; Giappichielli 1998; Supiot 1998); an increase in work which is situated outside of the labour market; children's upbringing and care (labour) which are vital for society, but which are ignored by economic indicators (Bettoni & Cruz 2001; Moreno, 2021; Carrasco 2019; Carrasquer 2013; and Tiraboschi 2019); a fourth industrial revolution which is changing what remains of labour law's profile of identity (Mendizábal, Sánchez Castañeda & Kurczyn 2019); no rights for small business people who are single providers (a small employer, in contrast to an employee, is the owner of his/her work instruments and works under his/her own account and responsibility, which means he/she only faces risks of the activity on his/her own, absorbing all the benefits and risks simultaneously); and finally the emergence of an increasingly important category of poor workers, or in other words, having a subordinate job is not a guarantee of escaping poverty (Lyon-Caen 1995). In this sense, labour law has found itself exceeded, without identity (Lyon-Caen 1995) for many years now, which requires the assignment of a new conceptual framework.

Constant changes in labour relations, a discourse which claims the disappearance of labour law and the continuation of 20th century categories explains why today, labour law moderately responds to past and present necessities. Here arises the need to find explanations and answers.

V. New and Old Philosophical Foundations of Labour Law

Law as we know it is a modern law. The categories we know and use stem from the consolidation of modern states. So, labour law as we know it takes its first conceptions from the liberal legal reasoning of the 19th century. State abstentionism was translated into a social state of law, which was even constitutionalised by some states, as in the cases of Germany and Mexico. In this period, labour law was thought to be consolidated.

Nonetheless, since the last quarter of the 20th century, work and the way it is performed and regulated has undergone continuous legal changes, that even come to question its *raison d'etre.* In part, this was due to the change of paradigms that edged states, starting with the United Kingdom, towards a return to liberal politics that kept echoing labour relations.

The speed, quantity and diversity of changes that labour law has undergone in the last two centuries are incomparable in relation to other legal disciplines. There lies, in part, the difficulty writers have faced in trying to understand what has happened, and what is still happening. However, since reality does not await comprehension, we can observe a set of new and old situations: precarious labour, informal labour, poor workers, and vulnerable workers.

The lack of labour law's response, in the middle of a globalisation marked by false uniformity, can be explained by several elements: its permanent mutation; the imposition of a discourse which speaks about the disappearance of labour relations; that despite proposals thought about over the last few years, in general terms, an answer is still being searched for; this answer is searched for within philosophical concepts created in the middle of the 19th century, and which lasted for the whole of the 20th century — a labour relation marked by subordination.

From our point of view, we should depart from at least five categories which coexist in order to allow an explanation of labour performed in the 21st century.

First, we should not put subordinate labour aside, because in a minor or major measure it will continue to exist.

Secondly, it is necessary to uncover false autonomous work and the discourse of an alleged disappearance or decrease in labour law. The increase of entrepreneurship, autonomous work and the apparition of semi-subordinate work is not ignored. Nevertheless, these demonstrations must not serve as an excuse to present subordinate workers as false autonomous workers.

Thirdly, labour law requires us to walk in parallel to what some authors have named employment law and the law of activity. A discipline which starts from a set of rights and obligations that a hired person, and another person who hires the first person must have, independent of the existence or not of subordinate labour relations. Every person that performs a job, for one or more people (employers or not), must accumulate enough to allow him or her to have a decent job in terms of the ILO (non-discrimination, equality of opportunities in labour and occupation, association and collective negotiation rights, and the prohibition of the worst forms of child labour, and social security or social protection schemes).

An employment law or a law of activity without any categories or labels is needed; a law which recognises rights for every person who performs an occupation, independent of the subordinate labour relation he or she may or may not perform; rights which allow him or her to live with dignity. This requires understanding labour within a market, labour without a market, or even without market value (Tiraboschi 2019).

On this subject, the dimension which French law has taken with the *Loi pour la liberté de choisir son avenir professionnel,* which is oriented towards the person's wellbeing and the certification of competences in contexts of non-formal and informal learning, also implies a *compte personnel d'activité.*

Fourthly, we should understand labour not just as a means of subordination, but also as human emancipation. Arendt considers that the *Homo Faber* is the man who performs labour; the *Homo Laborans* is the worker; and the man endowed with action is the man capable of starting a search for his emancipation (Jaccottet Freitas 2013).

On this subject, we must consider Hannah Arendt's distinction among work, labour and action (Arendt 1995):

> "… Active life, in other words, is not only what most men are engaged in but even what no man can escape altogether. For it is in the nature of the human condition that contemplation remains dependent upon all sorts of activities — it depends upon labor to produce whatever is necessary to keep the human organism alive, it depends upon work to create whatever is needed to house the human body, and it needs action in order to organize the living together of many human beings in such a way that peace, the condition for the quiet of contemplation is assured.
> [...]
> "… And the first thing of which you might have become aware by now is my distinction between labor and work which probably sounded somewhat unusual to you. I draw it from a rather casual remark in Locke who speaks of "the labor of our body and the work of our hands." (Laborers, in Aristotelic language, are those who "with their bodies administer to the needs of life.") The phenomenal evidence in favor of this distinction is too striking to be ignored, and yet it is a fact that, apart from a few scattered remarks and important testimony of social and institutional history, there is hardly anything to support it.
> "Against this scarcity of evidence stands the simple obstinate fact that every European language, ancient or modem, contains two etymologically unrelated words for what we have come to think of as the same activity: Thus, the Greek distinguished between ponein and ergazesthai, the Latin between /aborare and/acere or/abricari, the French between travailler and ouvrer, the German between arbeiten und werken. In all these cases, the equivalents for lahor have an unequivocal connotation of bodily experiences, of toil and trouble, and in most cases they are significantly also used for the pangs of birth. The last to use this original connection was Marx, who defined labor as the "reproduction of individual life" and begetting, the production of "foreign life," as the production of the species.
> "If we leave aside all theories, especially the modern labor theories after Marx, and follow solely the etymological and historical evidence, it is obvious that labor is an activity which corresponds to the biological processes of the body, that it is, as the young Marx said, the metabolism between man and nature or the human mode of this metabolism which we share with all living organisms. By laboring, men produce the vital necessities that must be fed into the life process of the human body. And

since this life process, though it leads us from birth to death in a rectilinear progress of decay, is in itself circular, the laboring activity itself must follow the cycle of life, the circular movement of our bodily functions, which means that the laboring activity never comes to an end as long as life lasts; it is endlessly repetitive. Unlike working, whose end has come when the object is finished, ready to be added to the common world of things and objects, laboring always moves in the same circle prescribed by the living organism, and the end of its toil and trouble comes only with the end, i.e., the death of the individual organism." (Arendt 1987)

The Industrial Revolution made the dimensions of work and labour match. Meanwhile, labour today is an extensive concept which applies not only to the manufacture or participation in its productive process, but also to services, especially if they are produced at an industrial level. On this subject, economy has elevated labour to a single object of work, mistaking it and overlaying it, an error which Arendt attributes to Marx, and which could be extended to Smith and Ricardo: work as a necessity.

Currently, the transformation of labour suggests that the object of study and of labour law's protection can and must be: "…not just the workplace but work's place in personal, social, and economic life, in social reproduction, and in offering possibilities for and imposing constraints upon human self-realization" (Klare 2002).

Fifthly, we should explore the ethical dimensions of labour. In modern societies, voluntarily or involuntarily, we think about productivity, about new modes of production, work or employment, and on this path we have forgotten about the ethical dimension that legal norms ought to have.

Even Locke's, as the father of liberalism, held in his *Treatise on Civil Government* that "no one must harm another in what concerns his life, health, freedom or possessions." In the same way, for Kant, men have in front of them a fundamental categorical imperative which prescribes an action independently from personal desires, that is, treating people as ends instead of a means to an end. Throughout his work, Kant exposes diverse formulations of the categorical imperative: the Formula of Universal Law (act only in accordance with that maxim through which you can at the same time will that it becomes a universal law); the Formula of the Law of Nature ("act as though the maxim of your action were to become, by your will, a universal law of nature"); the Humanity Formula ("so act as to treat humanity, both in your own person, and in the person of every other, always at the same time as an end, never simply as a means"); the Formula of Autonomy (act that your will can regard itself at the same time as making universal law through its maxims); the Formula of the End in Itself ("act in accordance with the maxims of a member giving universal laws for a merely possible kingdom of ends" (Kant 2002).

Labour law definitely has to have an ethical discourse as its foundation, approached by authors with different perspectives who agree on the same purpose, such as Habermas, Dworkin or Amartya Sen, allowing them to ethically reach social agreements which are plausible for all.

For some authors, labour law must part ways from a liberal lecture that tries to uselessly conciliate means and ends, because they are an essential part of the law (Conaghan 1987). According to Trubek, "gaps between legal ideals and legal behaviour and between legal norms and social structure, are inherent and fundamental features of the life and consciousness of liberal society" (Trubek 1977). We must set aside the liberal discourse coming from modern societies, which distanced itself from normative deontology and has approached utilitarianism, egotism and ethical consensualism.

As long as labour law is kept under schemes coming from liberalism, it will change very little. Because of this, if we want to exit the contradiction that liberalism imposes on labour law, we must think about all labour norms in ethical terms, even if this implies separating from liberalism. Maybe labour legislation's failure and contradiction is that it developed under liberal schemes. In this regard we must remember that the only times that ethical discourse has prevailed in normativity has been when societies have placed the person and society over market interests.

Bibliography

Alfie, Ana Clara, "Conflicto y Derecho de Huelga: Reflexiones a partir del caso Argentino", *Revista Latinoamericana de Derecho Social*, Núm. 15 (july-december de 2012): 16

Arendt, Hannah, "Introducción de Manuel Cruz", in *De la historia a la acción*, (Barcelona-Buenos Aires, México, Ediciones Paidós. I.C.E. de la Universidad Autónoma de Barcelona, 1995): 92-97 and 93-94

Arendt Hannah, "Labor, Work, Action", in *Bernauer S.J.J.W.* Edited by Amor Mundi and Boston College Studies in Philosophy, vol 26 (Germany, Springer, Dordrecht, 1987)

Bah, El-hadj, "Structural Transformation in Developed and Developing Countries", *Proceedings of the German Development Economics Conference*, No. 42 (Frankfurt, Verein für Socialpolitik, Ausschuss für Entwicklungsländer, 2009)

Ballestrero, M.L. "L'ambigua nozione di lavoro parasubordinato", in *Lavoro e diritto* (Italy, 1987), p. 41

Bettoni, Analía y Cruz, Anabel, "Voluntariado en Uruguay: perfiles, impacto y desafíos, III Encuentro de la red latinoamericana y del caribe de la sociedad internacional de investigación del tercer sector (ISTR) "Perspectivas latinoamericanas sobre el tercer sector" in *Ciudadanía, voluntariado y participación* (Spain, Dykinson, 2011)

Bhorat, Haroon; Kanbur, Ravi; Stanwix, Benjamin; Compliance with labor laws in developing countries, *IZA World of Labor* (2010)

Blyton, Paul; Royaume-Uni: le cas de l'industrie métallurgique, p. 97; in; *La flexibilité du temps de travail. Négociations collectives et intervention de l'État,* edited by OECD/OCDE (Paris, 1995): p. 231

Carrasco, Cristina, *El trabajo de cuidados: Historia, teoría y políticas,* Los Libros de la Catarata, 2019: p. 440

Carrasquer Oto, Pilar, "El redescubrimiento del trabajo de cuidados: algunas reflexiones desde la sociología", *Cuadernos de Relaciones Laborales*, Vol. 31, Núm. 1 (2013) 91-113. p. 368

CEPAL, *Migración internacional, derechos humanos y desarrollo,* (CEPAL, August, 2006), p. 368

Clauwaert, Stefan and Schömann Isabelle, "The crisis and national labour law reforms. A mapping exercise", *European Labour Law Journal*, vol. 3(1) (2012), pp. 54-69

Conaghan, Joanne. "Critical Labour Law: The American Contribution" *Journal of Law and Society*, vol. 14, no. 3 (1987), pp. 334–352

García Ramírez, Sergio, "Tres textos precursores en el constitucionalismo social", *Boletín Mexicano de Derecho Comparado*, Núms. 2-3, México, (1969), p. 472

Fröbel, Folker, Heinrich, Jurgüen y Kreye, Otto, "La nueva división internacional del trabajo. Sus orígenes, sus manifestaciones, sus consecuencias", *Comercio exterior*, Mexico, 28(7), july (1978). pp. 831-836

Fix-Zamudio, Héctor, "El Estado social de derecho y la Constitución mexicana", in *La Constitución mexicana: rectoría del Estado y economía mixta*, México (UNAM-Instituto de Investigaciones Jurídicas, Mexico, 1985), p. 119

Heintz, J., Globalization, economic policy and employment poverty and gender implications, Employment Strategy Paper, *Employment Policy Unit* (Geneva, ILO, 2006)

ILO, *Guidelines on gender in employment policies* (Geneva, ILO, 2009)

ILO, *Non-standard employment around the world: Understanding challenges, shaping prospects,* International Labour Office (Geneva, ILO. 2016), p. 20

ILO, *Resolution and Conclusions concerning Gender Equality at the Heart of Decent Work, International Labour Conference*, 98th Session (Geneva, ILO, 2009)

ILO-Pontificia Universidad Católica de Chile *Comparación internacional de sistemas de salud y seguridad laboral* (Santiago, Oficina Internacional del Trabajo, 2011): p. 139

ILO-World Trade Organization, *Globalization and informal jobs in developing countries* (Geneva, ILO-WTO, 2009)

Instituto Internacional de Estudios Laborales, *La eficacia de la legislación laboral: Un análisis multidimensional para el caso de Chile* (Geneva, ILO, 2010)

Inter-American Commission on Human Rights. Rapporteurship on the Rights of Migrant; *Derechos humanos de los migrantes y otras personas en el contexto de la movilidad humana en México / [Preparado por la Relatoría sobre los Derechos de los Migrantes de la Comisión Interamericana de Derechos Humanos]* (USA, ICHR, 2013): pp. 37-104

Jaccottet Freitas, Gustavo, "La labor, el trabajo, la acción y la emancipación del ser humano para el goce de la condición humana en Hannah Arendt y Karl Marx", *Prisma Jurídico*, vol. 12, núm. 2, julio-diciembre, 2013: pp. 579-602

Kant, I. *Fundamentación de la metafísica de las costumbres* (Alianza Editorial. España, 2002)

Klare, Karl, 'The Horizons of Transformative Labour and Employment Law' in *Labour Law in an Era of Globalization,* edited by J. Conaghan, R. M. Fischl, and K. Klare (Oxford: Oxford University Press, 2002): p. 20

P.E.M. "La Constitución Alemana de 11 de agosto de 1919", *Revista Nacional de Córdoba*, Y.8, N.º 8-9-10, (1921), October, November, December

Lagala, C., "La nouova tutela previdenziale per le attività di lavoro autonomo, libero-professionale e di collaborazione coordinata e continuativa", in *La roforma del sistema pensionistico*, edited by Cester, C. (Turin, Giappichelli, 1998): p. 170

Lyon-Caen, Gérard, *Le droit du travail. Une technique réversible* (Dalloz, Paris, 1995): p. 30

Maraniello, Patricio and Parisi, Néstor Sebastián, "El constitucionalismo social en la Constitución mexicana y su vasta influencia en el derecho argentino", *Revista IUS*, vol.10, no.38 (2016), July-December

Marx, Karl and Hobsbawm, Eric, *Formaciones precapitalistas* (México, Siglo XXI, 2009)

Mendizábal Bermúdez, Gabriela, Sánchez-Castañeda, Alfredo y Kurczyn Villalobos, Patricia (eds.), *Industria 4.0 Trabajo y Seguridad Social*, (Mexico, UNAM, 2019): p. 440

Mengoni, L., "La question de la subordinazione in due trattazioni recenti", *Rivista italiana di dirritto del lavoro* (1986), no.1. p. 5

Moreno i Gené, Josep, "El personal investigador en formación ¿becarios o trabajadores?", *Revista andaluza de trabajo y bienestar social*, Nº 78, 2005: pp. 95-138

Ocampo, Rolando, "El impacto económico del COVID y el panorama social hacia el 2030 en la región". *Covid 19, las Metas de Salud de los ODS y las Equidad* (Chile, CEPAL, 2020)

OECD, *International Trade and Core Labour Standards* (Paris, OCDE, 2001): p. 122

OECD/IMF/ILO/CIS STAT. *Measuring the Non-Observed Economy: A Handbook* (París, OECD/IMF/ILO/CIS STAT, 2002)

Palomeque López, Manuel Carlos, "Las relaciones jurídicas de formación a través de beca o estipendio", *Revista del Ministerio de Trabajo e Inmigración* (2009), N. 83

Pera, Giuseppe, "Sulle prospettive di estensione delle tutele al lavoro parasubordinato", Rivista italiana di diritto del lavoro, Anno XVIII, 1998, pp. 371-385

Reynoso Castillo, Carlos, "Deslaboralización", *Alegatos*, México, núm.45, mayo-agosto, 2000

Romagnoli, Umberto, "Las transformaciones del derecho del trabajo", *Debate Laboral*, Revista Americana e Italiana de Derecho del Trabajo, San José Costa Rica, año V, núm. 12(3), (1992), p. 7

Ronconi, Lucas, "Enforcement and Compliance with Labor Regulations", *Industrial & Labor Relations Review*, July, 63 (4) (2010)

Sánchez Vázquez, Rafael," La trascendencia del constitucionalismo social en América Latina (Caso México)"; *Cuestiones Constitucionales*, No. 27, Mexico, (2012), Jul./Dec.

Supiot, Alain, Au-delà de l'emploi. Transformations du travail et devenir du droit du travail en Europe (Rapport pour la commission européene), (Fammarion, Paris, 1999): pp. 32-33

Supiot, Alain, "The transformation of work and the future of labour law in Europe: A multidisciplinary perspective", *International Labour Review*, volume 118, (1999) Issue 1

Supiot, Alain, "Et si l'on refondait le droit du travail…" in *Le monde diplomatique*, October, 2017

Tiraboschi, Michele, *Persona e lavoro tra tutele e mercato. Per una nuova ontologia del lavoro nel discorso giuslavoristico* (ADAPT University Press, Italy, 2019): p. 262

Trubek, David M., "Complexity and Contradiction in the Legal Order: Balbus and the Challenge of Critical Social Thought about Law." *Law & Society Review*, vol. 11, no. 3 (1977), pp. 529-569

CHAPTER 18

THE KEY TASK OF LABOUR LAW IN THE POST-COVID PERIOD: HOW DO WE PROVIDE FOR EMPLOYEES´ HEALTH AND HELP THE AFFECTED?

MARTIN ŠTEFKO[1]

1. Introduction

The purpose of this article is to identify two key legal issues that need to be addressed in relation to Czech labour law in the post-Covid period as quickly as possible.[2] At the time of writing, Czech society is in the pandemic epicenter. The Czech Republic is, virtually on a worldwide scale, the "best at Covid," which is why the healthcare system is on the verge of collapsing. Czech political representatives have not yet been able to agree on basic conceptual measures to protect society, the country or the economy. The indebtedness of the country and individuals is rising and so is mortality, as are the rates of domestic violence. Czech society is split, both ideologically and as far as the discourse between generations is concerned. On the one hand, there are those who want to protect themselves while, on the other, there are those who want to live, even at the expense of those facing a threat.

However considerable the problems may be, it has also become apparent that following the one year-long Covid-19 experience, the time to change

---

[1] This article has been written and published thanks to the financial support of the grant project *"Cooperatio"*, identity code SOC.

[2] Further legal issues that are in no way less urgent and should not be ignored are, in particular, home-working and addressing the plurality of trade unions with one employer. Home-working has become an essential element to protect society; it has been recommended by the government and is expected by employers; but our legislation has not changed, as is the case with many other problems.

has arrived. Consequently, it can be argued that prior to the Czech parliamentary elections in the autumn, the conditions are well set to solve problems whose solutions would otherwise not be pragmatically conceivable. There are politically interesting, understandable, and therefore solvable topics.

Although we can presume that the country's recovery plan will strive to get us back to levels that existed prior to the epidemic, this generation will remember the lesson it learned. The fundamental lesson is that there is no such thing as a free lunch. There are not just rights, but also obligations, and luck is usually on the side of those who are prepared. Seen from the labour law perspective, if the state intends to survive, it has to provide for a functioning labour market even in these times.

As we are going to demonstrate in sections two and three, the most important requirement is the prevention of infectious diseases. The second problem deals with critical infrastructure, namely volunteer firefighters. Again, this is not intended to indicate that it is the most important element, but rather this topic is addressed in order to exemplify an ineffective approach and highlight a specific issue which can be improved. As the civil defence units are hardly visible and the active reserves are very small, volunteer firefighters have taken on a key role following professional firefighters, and have had to help the undersized army and overburdened police for a long time. However, they are performing this task while being insufficiently protected against the consequences of an occupational accident.

2. Labour Law and Critical Infrastructure

If it is obligatory to undergo Covid-19 testing or have a Covid-19 vaccination, then the starting point for this is the employer´s duty to prevent detriment to health or damage to the property of employees and third parties. In this sense, the Czech Republic is primarily bound by the key International Labor Organization Convention No. 155 on the Safety and Health of Workers and on a Safe Working Environment of 1981,[3] ILO Convention

---

[3] See no. 20/1989 Coll. ILO Convention No. 155, which lays down in articles 4 and 5 the basic principles and preventive principles in the field of occupational safety and health, and in Article 8 regulates the cooperation with employees' representatives (trade unions) to address occupational safety and health issues. In Article 9 it provides for the presumption of independent state supervision over the area of occupational safety and health; and in Article 11, for the reporting and investigation of occupational accidents and occupational diseases.

No. 161 on Occupational Health Services, 1985[4] and Convention No. 187. As far as specific protection against certain risks is concerned, we should mention conventions No. 115 of 1960, No. 139 of 1974, No. 148 of 1977, No. 162 of 1986 and No. 170 of 1990. The legal basis for the EU legislature's activities is laid down in Article 151 *et seq*. TFEU, in accordance with the European Social Charter and the 1989 Community Charter of the Fundamental Social Rights of Workers. Pursuant to Article 153 par. 1 Letter a) of the TFEU, it is the EU´s task to promote its member states to cooperate in improving working environments so that the employees' health is protected, and to do so in relation to achieving the general objectives set out in Article 151 TFEU (see Article 156 TFEU). Article 31 of the EU Charter of Fundamental Rights regulates the right to decent and fair working conditions. According to paragraph 1 of this article, every worker has the right to working conditions that mind his/her health, safety and dignity. The most important piece of legislation in this area is Directive 89/391/EEC, on the introduction of measures to encourage improvements in the safety and health of workers at work, as amended. The national regulation is laid down in Act No. 262/2006 Coll. the Labour Code, as amended, Act No. 309/2006 Coll. as amended, and the implementing labour law regulations on the issue of safety and health at work.

According to Act No. 262/2006 Coll. the Labour Code, as amended, each and every employer is obliged to set aside sufficient material and personnel resources to implement risk prevention measures at his facilities. These risk prevention measures thus form an integral and equal part of all an employer´s activities at all management levels. In other words, managers at all management levels are responsible for them within the scope of their tasks. Every employer is obliged to keep records of the search for and the evaluation of risks.

Act No. 258/2000 Coll., on the protection of public health and on the amendment of some related acts, as amended, regulates the procedure for detecting an infectious disease incidence, including obligations affecting natural and legal persons as well as natural persons running a business. The regulation concludes with a sanction mechanism and a definition of the elements of the offences, including violations of the provisions governing

---

[4] See 145/1988 Sb. ILO Convention No. 161 which regulates the obligation to introduce company-internal health services at the national legal system level, which the Czech Republic subsequently did in the shape of so-called occupational medical services. According to Act No. 373/2011 Coll., the occupational health service provider's task is, in accordance with ILO convention no. 161, to provide for the prevention of health damage, including the protection of health against occupational diseases and other occupational injuries and the prevention of accidents at work.

vaccinations or non-compliance with special measures pursuant to Act No. 258/2000 Coll. The key provisions are contained in Art. § 46 of Act No. 258/2000 Coll.

The Czech labour code lays down the basic regulation of working and wage conditions for employees and is implemented by a number of special legal regulations. Of course, the labour code did not anticipate a pandemic and neither was it prepared for its arrival. Act No. 240/2000 Coll., on crisis management and on the amendments to certain acts, as amended (hereinafter only referred to as the *"Crisis Act"*) serves these purposes, along with the regulation of critical infrastructure, which was implemented into the Crisis Act in connection with Council Directive 2008/114/EC of 8 December 2008, on the identification and designation of European critical infrastructure and the assessment of the need to improve their protection.

Basic terminology is defined in § 2 of the Crisis Act.[5] Other critical infrastructure regulation is contained in government regulation no. 432/2010 Coll., on the criteria for determining the critical infrastructure element, as amended. The Czech Republic government´s resolution no. 140/2020 Coll. defines critical infrastructure employees as "employees of critical infrastructure entities" according to § 2 letter k) of the Crisis Act, and these employees anticipate, within the scope of their work tasks, providing for the functioning of a critical infrastructure element in the sense of government decree no. 432/2010 Coll., on the criteria for determining a critical infrastructure element, as amended by government decree no. 315/2014 Coll.[6]

In particular, the specific rules, set of duties and restrictions in relation to critical employees are defined by government resolution no. 377, with

---

[5] In general, a critical infrastructure element "means in particular a building, facility or public infrastructure, determined according to interdisciplinary and sectoral criteria; if the critical infrastructure element is part of a European Critical Infrastructure, it shall be considered as a European Critical Infrastructure element." In order to understand the context, it would be appropriate to add that the Crisis Act defines critical infrastructure protection measures as "measures to reduce the risk of a critical infrastructure element being disrupted" and that a critical infrastructure entity is "critical infrastructure element operator; if it is the operator of a European Critical Infrastructure element, it shall be considered as a European Critical Infrastructure Entity."

[6] Resolution No. 140/2020 Coll. was not formally repealed, but was supplemented by further government resolution no. 1185 in conjunction with government resolution no. 957, which defined critical infrastructure employees as employees whose presence at the workplace is required to provide for the functioning of relevant critical infrastructure and who are designated by the critical infrastructure entity in the sense of § 2 letter k) Crisis Act.

effect from 2 April 2020, as it "provides that critical infrastructure entities which are classified as employers in the sense of point III. Government resolution no. 332 of 30 March 2020, on the adoption of a crisis measure, promulgated under no. 140/2020 Coll., may identify critical staff whose presence in the workplace is necessary to provide for the function of the relevant critical infrastructure element, to which the prohibitions and obligations set out in points I., II. and IV. of government resolution no. 332 of 30 March 2020 will be applied." With effect from October 5th 2020, a similar authorisation is contained in government decree UV 957: "Critical infrastructure entities may designate critical staff whose presence at the workplace is required to provide for the functioning of the relevant critical infrastructure element to which prohibitions and obligations will apply."

In the case of the spread of the contagious Covid-19 disease, the public interest that the population be healthy is exhibited by the existence of the crime of spreading a contagious human disease, according to Art. § 152 of the Criminal Code and by the existence of the crime of spreading a contagious human disease due to negligence, according to par. § 153 of the Criminal Code. Annex No. 1 to government order no. 453/2009 Coll. Which contains an exhaustive enumeration of contagious human diseases. Covid-19 has also been added to this list. If an employee breaches his/her duties, thus spreading Covid-19, he/she may, depending on the circumstances of the case, fulfill the elements of the offence of spreading a contagious disease through negligence. If such an act is committed in the course of another event seriously threatening the life or health of people, public order or property, the offender may be imprisoned for up to three years.

3. (Non) Obligatory Testing

An employer is obliged to provide for a safe working environment. However, there is no labour law authorising the employer to check on the employee's health. This interpretation is backed by the wording of Art. § 106 of the labour code. Thus, there is no applicable private law provision that would permit an employer to impose an obligation towards an employee to be regularly or one-off Covid-19 tested. This is one of the fundamental principles stemming from the autonomy of contractual will.

The obligation to present a negative test result to be admitted into the workplace, or rather to be permitted to work, cannot be enforced by the employer in the shape that he would define this obligation as a work performance related requirement. The reasons for this are restrictions imposed by legislation on the employer, mainly statutory prohibitions concerning reviewing the employee's health condition, discrimination due to health status and protection of the employee's personality. The employer may not decide himself/herself whether it is required or appropriate to subject employees to Covid-19-testing and, at the same time, he/she can neither assess their health condition in any other way, as he/she is simply not competent to do so. To be able to do so, employers need special legislation, or rather a binding decision made by the competent public authority or courts.

Referencing the obligation to provide for the safety and health of employees, the Ministry of Labour and Social Affairs of the Czech Republic published the interpretation that the employer is entitled to call upon his/her employees to undergo an examination at an occupational health service provider or at his/her general practitioner when returning from a Covid-19 affected area in particular, if it is justified in relation to the work performed or if the employer suspects that the employee is not qualified to perform the work.[7] In this context of interpretation, we would like to point out that the Czech Ministry of Labour and Social Affairs has in no way been legally authorised to issue a binding opinion in the sense of Article 2, paragraph 3 of Act No. 1/1993 Coll. the Constitution of the Czech Republic, as amended, as well as Article 2 (2) of the Charter of Fundamental Rights and Freedoms,[8] or rather § 2 paragraph 1 of Act No. 500/2004 Coll., administrative procedure code, as amended. This fact is important from the point of view of the legality principle, which also applies to so-called binding opinions, which makes further procedures conditional in the relevant proceedings. These findings are also backed by correspondence practice in individual matters. When answering such individual questions, the Ministry of Labour and Social Affairs has repeatedly denied that it would be entitled to issue a binding interpretation of the given provisions from the labour code or a relevant implementing regulation.[9]

---

[7] The given press release furthermore reads as follows: "In this case, an extraordinary occupational medical examination at the occupational medical services provider is possible, i.e. in the sense of § 12 of Decree No. 79/2013 Coll., on occupational medical services and on certain assessment care types." The press release is available at https://koronavirus.mzcr.cz/informace-pro-zamestnance-a-zamestnavatele (Cited on: 15.1.2021).

[8] The document was published as an appendix to Constitutional Act No. 23/1991 Coll. introducing the Charter of Fundamental Rights and Freedoms as a constitutional law of the Federal Assembly of the Czech and Slovak Federal Republic and published under No. 2/1993 Coll. The Charter has been declared a constitutional law in articles 3 and 112 of the constitution.

[9] The following notice is contained in these words: "Employees and employers are provided with basic information and counselling on labor relations by the regional labour inspectorates (Act No. 251/2005 Coll., On labor inspection)." The competence,

According to applicable regulations, the employer is not entitled to order employees to undergo Covid-19 testing. The employer cannot straightforwardly request and enforce Covid-19 testing, nor can he derive legal consequences for the performance of work from such a fact.

Explicit legislation is missing, and the protectionist jurisprudence does not yet give us solid hope that an employee's absence from work due to refusing to undergo a Covid-19 test could automatically be considered as an unexcused absence or unpaid employee-related hindrance. This will always depend upon the circumstances of the particular case as well as the reasons why the employee refuses to undergo an employer-paid Covid-19 test. However, without adequate provisions, such a procedure cannot be explicitly recommended.

The Ministry of Labour and Social Affairs had been at least partially trying to remedy the lack of enforceability by proposing that the employer send such an employee to an extraordinary preventive medical examination. However, at present, such a recommendation is completely unrealistic in a number of districts, as even the patients themselves cannot access their general practitioners without prior appointment, and the doctors' work frequently resembles telemedicine.

3.1. Temperature Measurement and Test Obligation

Apart from ordinary employees, different rules were set up for the so-called critical infrastructure concerning indispensable employees. After the initial surprise phase, the state decided to protect its personnel (the so-called indispensable critical employees) and critical infrastructure. On the basis of § 5 and § 6 of the Crisis Act and under the resolution of the government of the Czech Republic, a critical infrastructure entity was authorised[10] to

---

which is not included in the cited law, cannot be inferred even by judicial interpretation. As stated by the High Court in Prague in its decision with file no. 6 A 59/93: "When interpreting and applying the law, the court has to proceed on the basis of what has been formulated by the legislator in the Act, not on what he may have wanted to state but did not do so; when applying unclear, contradictory and interstitial provisions, the court is for sure obliged to use generally accepted rules of interpretation. However, it is not possible to interpret something that is not in the law, or to come to such a conclusion by interpretation."

[10] See resolution no. 145/2020 Coll. of 1 April 2020 No. 377, on the adoption of a crisis measure (critical infrastructure entities) with effect from 2 April 2020. The resolution of the government of the Czech Republic no. 391/2020 Coll. of 30 September 2020, on the declaration of a state of emergency contains a similar authorisation.

identify so-called indispensable critical staff whose presence in the workplace is required to provide for the relevant element of critical infrastructure functioning, and who are subject to increased reporting obligations with regard to their health and the obligation to be re-tested for Covid-19 under certain circumstances. Making this resolution, the government amended the rights and obligations of critical infrastructure employees with effect from 30 March 2020.[11] The government has further ordered the critical infrastructure entities operating a critical infrastructure element to fulfil several obligations in this regard, yet mandatorily testing all critical employees for Covid-19 is not yet included in these obligations. This is also backed by the list of published recommendations by the Critical Infrastructure Association.[12] The Czech Republic's Chief Hygienist issued methodical instructions on the single procedure for regional hygienic stations to decide whether or not to order quarantine measures to persons who were in close contact with a person who had been diagnosed with Covid-19 via a laboratory examination, and whose employer declared them to be indispensable in operating the state's critical infrastructure, or to ensure activities that are similarly indispensable. These instrcuctions provide for

---

[11] The government prohibited that critical employees, i.e. employees in critical infrastructure who, while performing their tasks, contribute to providing the critical infrastructure element work, take leave during a state of emergency, with the exception of quarantine-ordered persons. Furthermore, critical employees were also obliged to immediately inform the employer upon finding out that they were in so-called "risky contact" without adequate personal protective equipment, i.e. in direct contact with a person whose Covid-19 disease was confirmed. The government ordered that critical employees showing no clinical symptoms who had risky contact and whose work is indispensable, according to the employer's decision, in order to provide that the relevant element of critical infrastructure work is operated by the relevant employer, are to comply among others with these rules:

- Temperature measurements ahead of each shift immediately before starting work and informing their superior about the temperature measurement result and current state of health or any health problems;
- Undergo a nasopharyngeal swab, including a RT-PCR examination for Covid-19 for five days after any risky contact and, at the same time, have a capillary blood rapid test to check for the presence of IgM and IgG antibodies;
- If both above-mentioned examinations are negative, continue working and undergo a second nasopharyngeal swab including a RT-PCR examination for Covid-19 14 days after any risky contact and, at the same time, have a capillary blood rapid test to check for the presence of IgM and IgG antibodies.

[12] A list of recommendations is available here https://www.mpo.cz/assets/cz/rozcestnik/pro-media/tiskove-zpravy/2020/4/AKI_MPO-Opatreni-Covid-19.pdf (Cited on 15.1.2021).

general preventive testing, MZDR 38651/2020-4/OES.[13]

Furthermore, the government has also ordered that public health authorities and health care providers do not order quarantine for critical employees not showing clinical symptoms who have had risky contact and whose work is necessary, according to the employer´s decision to make the relevant critical infrastructure element work, if such an element is operated by the given employee. The quarantine is proclaimed if the employee and the employer concerned observe the above-mentioned procedures and none of the tests performed is positive.

Based upon another resolution, the government has stipulated that critical infrastructure entities may designate critical staff whose presence in the workplace is required to provide for the functioning of the relevant critical infrastructure, to which prohibitions and obligations apply. Another provision was adopted via government resolution no. 1185.[14] However, this provision is less stringent, particularly as it only instructs designated critical staff to measure body temperature at the beginning of each shift immediately prior to commencing work.[15]

---

[13] The instruction is available here: https://koronavirus.mzcr.cz/wp-content/uploads/2020/10/Metodick%C3%BD-pokyn-hlavn%C3%AD-hygieni%C4%8Dky-%C4%8CR-k-jednotn%C3%A9mu-postupu-krajsk%C3%BDch-hyg.-stanic-p%C5%99i-rozhodov%C3%A1n%C3%AD-o-na%C5%99%C3%ADzen%C3%AD-karant%C3%A9ny-osob%C3%A1m-kter%C3%A9-byly-v-%C3%BAzk%C3%A9m-kontaktu-s-pozitivn%C3%AD-osobou.pdf (Cited on 15.1.2021).

[14] Published under no. 462/2020 Coll. Although government resolution no. 332 has not been formally repealed, there are reasonable doubts concerning its effectiveness. According to one of the interpretations, government resolution no. 332 (as well as government resolution no. 377) was to cease to have effect upon the state of emergency ending under which it had been declared, i.e. to end on 17 May 2020. However, the biggest problem is whether the Crisis Act allows that employees be ordered to be Covid-19-tested. Some of the doctrinal views support this by referring to the opinion that the Crisis Act provides for entirely replacing another (any) legal regulation, as it is a special regulation for crisis situations such as a state of war or emergency. Yet unfortunately, it is also true that the Crisis Act itself does not explicitly refer to the existence of a pandemic. Given the absence of any other legal regulation, we tend to interpret government resolution no. 1185 not only in connection with government resolution no. 957, but also with government resolution no. 332 and 377.

[15] Government resolution no. 1185 instructs, *inter alia*, all critical employees, if they find that they have come into direct contact with a Covid-19 diagnosed person while not wearing adequate personal protective equipment (which is understood as risky contact), to immediately inform their employer thereof. The employer is then obliged to decide whether the critical employee performing his/her work is necessary to provide for the function of the relevant critical infrastructure element operated by

A critical employee violating the obligation to undergo a Covid-19 test represents an administrative violation in accordance with the Crisis Act. The crisis management body may impose a fine of up to CZK 20,000 on a critical employee when he/she commits such an act. Depending upon the circumstances of the relevant case, a critical employee may also have committed a criminal offence, i.e. spreading a contagious human disease and currently also spreading a contagious human disease due to negligence.

Yet neither the Crisis Act nor the implementing regulations provide that a critical employee may be penalised by the employer for breaching the obligations imposed on a critical employee. This is due to the somewhat controversial legal basis for imposing the testing obligations for Covid-19. It is thus relatively risky to punish employees for these acts according to labour law regulations. If the given case refers to a critical employee violating his/her obligations under the Crisis Act and a crisis measure, then the employer is obliged to report the critical employee violating his/her obligations to the crisis management body, and to then wait for instructions from the crisis management body. If the critical infrastructure entity has a reason to believe that the employee is infected with Covid-19 and is spreading this contagious disease intentionally or negligently, it is entitled

---

the employer in question. If the critical employee is not indispensable to the relevant critical infrastructure element operated by the employer, then the employer has to inform the locally competent public health authority, which then orders the critical employee to quarantine. If the critical employee is able to work despite a potential Covid-19 infection, and if the critical employee´s work performance is necessary to provide for the relevant critical infrastructure element functioning, then the relevant employer shall inform the locally competent public health authority and this indispensable critical employee shall, among other things:

- Measure his temperature ahead of each shift immediately before starting work, and inform his superior about the temperature measurement result and current state of health or any health problems;
- Undergo a nasopharyngeal swab including a RT-PCR examination for Covid-19 five days after the risky contact and, at the same time, have a capillary blood rapid test to check for the presence of IgM and IgG antibodies;
- If both above-mentioned examinations are negative, continue working and undergo a second nasopharyngeal swab including a RT-PCR examination for SARS-CoV-2 14 days after the risky contact and, at the same time, have a capillary blood rapid test to check for the presence of IgM and IgG antibodies.

Only if the results of both tests are negative will the critical employee continue performing work in the usual work mode. If the critical worker is diagnosed with any known clinical Covid-19 symptoms, or if any of the test results are positive within 14 days from the risky contact, then the employer concerned shall inform the local public health authority, which will then order quarantine or isolation for that critical worker.

to call upon the police of the Czech Republic to help further prevent the spread of contagious human disease.

After almost one year, the Czech Parliament decided that the situation is severe and there is no hope of restoring efficient health care without Covid-19 testing. The respective statute was passed (Act No. 94/2021 Collection on Emergency Measures Against Covid-19 (in Czech: o mimořádných opatřeních při epidemii onemocnění Covid-19 a o změně některých souvisejících zákonů) and the government issued a few measures ordering Covid-19 testing for all employees and for the majority of freelancers.

4. (Non) Obligatory Vaccination

Labour law refers to an employee´s obligation to undergo vaccination. Paragraph §103 par. 1 let. d) sets forth in combination with § 106 par. 4 let. b) of the labour code that an employer is entitled to expect employees to undergo vaccinations related to work performance. However, compulsory vaccination needs to be provided for by special legislation or by a decision made by the competent public health authority. The employer itself does not stipulate mandatory vaccinations for employees that have entered labour law relations. He is not authorised to do so.

A special vaccination regulation is contained in the government decree of 12 December 2007, no. 361/2007 Coll., laying down the conditions for occupational health protection, as amended. According to § 38 of the cited regulation in connection with Annex No. 7, when performing activities which are potentially dangerous for one´s health due to a biological agent, the countermeasures may include vaccination, if appropriate, especially in the case of employees who are not immune to biological agents to which he/she might be exposed at work.

Given the by-law nature of the government regulation and the diction of it including its textual conditionality, one cannot derive the obligation to accept vaccination against Covid-19. For this reason, employees are not ordered to undergo Covid-19 vaccination until special legislation is adopted. The reason is that experts have articulated their concerns as well, which were formalised into a recommendation made by the Czech Society of Allergology and Clinical Immunology of the Czech Medical Association of Jan Evangelista Purkyně (České společnosti alergologie a klinické imunologie ČLS JEP) about vaccinating against SARS-COV-2, 22 December 2020, which explicitly does not recommend vaccinating certain categories of persons.

The compulsory vaccination issue is regulated by Title III. Act No. 258/2000 Coll., on public health protection and on the amendment of some related acts, as amended. Mandatory vaccinations are stipulated by decree no. 537/2006 Coll., on vaccination against infectious diseases, as amended (hereinafter the "Vaccination Decree"), including mandatory revaccination dates (Sivák 2020, p. 8). The Vaccination Decree stipulates in § 10 "special vaccinations against the hepatitis A virus and hepatitis B virus." More precisely, "the vaccination shall be carried out for the employees and members of the basic integrated rescue system units stipulated by the Integrated Rescue System Act for staff newly employed or hired to serve." There are no other specific regulations for members of the security forces or entities pertaining to the IRS. The Vaccination Decree does not contain them. Given that the last amendment to the cited decree has been effective since 1. 1. 2018, the logic of the matter itself and the temporal context reveals that the Vaccination Decree cannot contain vaccination against Covid-19.

The cases stipulated by Act No. 258/2000 Coll. state the option to order so-called "emergency vaccination." According to § 69 par. 1 let. g) Act No. 258/2000 Coll., emergency vaccination is included among the counter-epidemic measures in the event of an epidemic or threat of an epidemic. According to § 80 par. 1 let. g) of Act No. 258/2000 Coll., the Ministry of Health orders to take extraordinary measures when an epidemic occurs or if there is such a threat, and in accordance with letter (i), emergency vaccination is authorised. It should be added that a similar procedure was applied in the past, in the army of the Czech Republic, for example, when emergency vaccination was ordered against influenza as a general measure. In this case, it was *an emergency measure* according to par. § 80 of the Public Health Protection Act.

Consequently, police officers and firefighters can therefore be ordered to undergo extraordinary vaccination (this may be for measles, but also influenza or even Covid-19) by the Ministry of the Interior in accordance with Art. § 83 paragraph 2 of Act No. 258/2000 Coll.[16] If the Ministry of the Interior orders extraordinary vaccination based upon a legal procedure, compulsory vaccination with Covid-19 becomes acceptable and mandatory for members of the security forces. However, the Ministry of the Interior is not authorised to act alike in relation to social service provider employees. Within this context, we can also draw attention to the public proclamation made by the Head of the Communication Department of the Human Resources Management Section at the Ministry of the Interior — General

---

[16] https://stavbeznouze.cz/blog/jak-se-to-ma-s-povinnym-testovanim-a-ockovanim-hasicu-a-policistu/, cf. https://www.irozhlas.cz/zpravy-domov/ockovani-spalnicky-hasici-nedostatek-vakciny-zachranari_1905171117_cha, , https://www.army.cz/scripts/detail.php?id=1672

Directorate of the Fire and Rescue Service of the Czech Republic, Col. Mgr. Rudolf Kramář on 11 January 2021, for Studio ČT24, who concluded that Covid-19 vaccination is not obligatory, even for members of the security forces, as there is no clear legal regulation imposing the vaccination.[17]

Yet publicly available sources show that vaccinating critical employees is envisaged.[18] If it was ordered by a special law or based upon the Crisis Act via the respective measure, then we can expect that it will become obligatory and that the observance of this measure will have to be insisted upon in accordance with the legal opinion expressed by the constitutional court judgement, plenum of 27. 1.2015, file no. Pl. ÚS 16/14 – 1.

5. Volunteer Firefighters

There are a total of 6,698 firefighting units (in CZ: *"JPO,"* an abbreviation of *"Jednotka požární ochrany"*) registered within the Czech Republic, 237 of which pertain to category JPO II, 1,356 to JPO III and 5,105 to JPO V. All in all, there are more than 67,149 volunteer firefighters (as of 2019). There are also a further 3,013 firefighters in an employment relationship serving in company-internal firefighting units in the Czech Republic.

Given the nature of their activities, firefighters are in a dangerous environment, facing an increased risk of injury or death. When being deployed, firefighters are constantly exposed to adverse environmental impacts including various life-threatening dangers. The most serious cases include exposure to hazardous substances, extremely high or low temperatures, combustion products, road-work hazards, risks resulting from working at high altitudes and above free depths, electric shock hazards, infectious diseases, and many other hazards when rescuing people. When intervening in an emergency case, standard procedures commonly applied under usual conditions are frequently not abided by. This quite often refers to the use of technical means not listed in the instruction manuals, exceeding recommended

---

[17] See https://www.ceskatelevize.cz/porady/10101491767-studio-ct24/221411058260111/. The sequence in question starts at 4:40 min.

[18] See: https://www.mzcr.cz/mimoradne-opatreni-plan-ockovani-osob-urcenych-k-ockovani-s-ucinnosti-od-14-1-2021-do-dovolani/; https://www.mzcr.cz/mimoradne-opatreni-povinnosti-poskytovatelu-k-hlaseni-do-narodniho-dispecinku-ockovani-s-ucinnosti-od-14-1-2021/; https://covid.gov.cz/situace/ockovani; https://covid.gov.cz/situace/ockovani/kdo-bude-ockovan-jako-prvni; https://koronavirus.mzcr.cz/wp-content/uploads/2021/01/Metodický-pokyn-pro-očkování-plán-provedení-a-centrální-rezervační-systém_TK_05012021_Blatny.pdf (feeling.: 15.1.2021).

limits, with limited options for safety protection, etc.[19]

While professional firefighters are members of the security forces and are employed as well as properly insured for an accident at work or an occupational disease, if a volunteer firefighter gets injured or dies, a problem arises. Volunteer firefighters are in various difficult legal relations with their manager (mostly corresponding to the municipality where they are located). They frequently carry out this activity free of charge or for a symbolic fee in an employment relationship established by an agreement to complete a job. If such a firefighter gets injured or dies, the victim or his/her family receives little or no support.[20]

The compensation provided for a volunteer firefighter who is an employee and suffers damage is regulated by Act No. 133/1985 Coll., on fire protection, as amended (hereinafter only referred to as the "Fire Protection Act"), as well as by the labour code.

According to the opinion stated by the Ministry of Labour and Social Affairs of the Czech Republic, file no. 2009/60163-51 of 21.8. 2009, a volunteer firefighter who suffers a health impairment is entitled to seek reimbursement according to § 393 of the labour code and also according to § 29 par. 1 let. b) of the Fire Protection Act. If a volunteer firefighter is injured during his/her training or when being deployed, then his/her insurance for the damage is primarily governed by labour law, if he/she is in an employment relationship.

5.1. Employer Liability for Damage Caused to Employees

The insurance of an employee in case he/she suffers from an occupational disease or an occupational accident is still not addressed by accident insurance in the Czech Republic, but rather by employment law regulations and the employer's liability for damages (Act No. 266/2006 Coll., on accident insurance, has not yet become effective as far as most of its provisions are concerned (cf. § 99 cit. of the Act) and according to the decision made by the government, this will not happen in the future). This is due to the employer´s strict liability concerning the result and for the health impairment (damage) that an employee suffers while performing

[19] In 2020, firefighters were deployed more than 42,700 times, with municipal volunteer firefighters participating in 31.5% of those instances; company-internal firefighters 5.4% of the times; and company-internal volunteer firefighters 0.5%.

[20] Number of injured firefighters in recent years: 123 (in 2016), 209 (2017), 173 (2018) and 170 (2019). Statistical Yearbook 2019 (orig. in CZ: Statistická ročenka 2019). 2019. MV-General Directorate of the Fire and Rescue Service of the Czech Republic issued this as a supplement to its magazine 112, 3/2020.

work tasks or in direct connection with them. The employer is liable even if the damage is caused by another person and also if he doesn´t cause the damage. To the extent that an employer actually is liable for the damage, the employer is obliged to compensate the employee who has suffered an occupational accident or who has been diagnosed with an occupational disease, for loss of earnings, the pain suffered, increased difficulty in socialising, and for all medical treatment costs incurred and possibly also material damage. If an employee dies as a result of an occupational accident or an occupational disease, the employer is obliged to provide the following, within the scope of its responsibility: compensate the treatment costs incurred; appropriate funeral expenses; expenses for supporting surviving dependent family members; a one-off compensation for surviving dependent family; and possibly material damage compensation.[21]

According to § 386 par. 1 sentence one of the labour code, the following applies: "An employee who suffers [...] in a fixed-term employment relationship or when performing work under a fixed-term agreement to perform work shall be entitled to receive compensation for a loss of earnings only until the time when such an employment relationship is to end. When this period elapses, he/she is entitled to compensation due to loss of earnings if it can be assumed, depending on the circumstances, that the affected person would have been employed further on." Although the regulation in question governs only one of the claims of the injured employee, it is usually the financially most demanding one. The purpose of this regulation is to limit this entitlement to employees who are performing the gainful activity only occasionally or for whom the gainful activity does not represent their main source of income, which is why they have entered into a fixed-term employment relationship only on an occasional basis and would no longer work in that employment relationship, even if the occupational accident had not occurred. For this reason, it is also necessary to include employees performing work on the basis of an agreement to complete a job, although

[21] Based upon the Soviet model, the legal regulation in question was introduced virtually at the beginning of the 1960s and has not changed, even when the new labour code was adopted. Yet at present, it no longer corresponds to the fundamental changes in society and neither to those changes in the national economy that have taken place since then.[21] With effect from 1. 1. 1993, a new statutory insurance for damage caused to employees due to an occupational accident or an occupational disease was introduced, but this (then declared) temporary measure only mitigated the problem, without actually solving it. Unfortunately, the shortcomings in the current regulation are even more significant when it comes to volunteer firefighters. In this case, a volunteer firefighter´s activities are regulated only via an agreement to complete a job.

this type of employment relationship is not explicitly mentioned in the labour code. Otherwise, an absurd situation would arise where employees working quantitatively for the potentially shortest number of working hours would enjoy greater security than employees working on a fixed-term basis or an employment-law relationship established by an agreement to perform work.

An employment relationship or a type of employment relationship agreed for a definite period of time, which is usually the case with voluntary firefighters, terminates irrespective of the situation in which the employee finds himself. In such a case, the right of a third-country national to receive compensation for loss of earnings is conditional on the proof that, if the occupational accident or the occupational disease had not happened, he/she would have continued to have been employed. However, this is a complicated issue due to the secondary nature of such an employment, i.e. the dependence of the agreement to complete a job on the budgetary possibilities of the municipality and the amount of this income. Current Supreme Court jurisprudence also offers some space for interpretation in this regard. The entitlement to compensation for loss of earnings also arises when a volunteer firefighter's further employment can be assumed, depending upon the circumstances (see the Czech Supreme Court judgement of 6. 6. 2006 file no. 21 Cdo 2023/2005). We can reasonably presume such a situation only when taking into account the circumstances that existed at the time of the accident, indicating whether the employee had entered into a fixed-term employment relationship only occasionally (and would anyway not have worked after the agreed period), or whether the gainful activity was the main (basic) source of his income and the employee had been working regularly until then (and it can therefore be assumed, depending upon the circumstances, that he would have been re-employed after the termination of the employment relationship). "If a worker succeeds in proving this fact, compensation for the loss of earnings may be granted up to the amount of the average earnings which he achieved permanently at the organisation in which he suffered an occupational accident" (Assessment of the NS ČSR (Supreme Court of Czechoslovakia) from 27. 1. 1975, file no. Cpj 37/74 (R 11/1976, p. 51–52).

The significant problem consists in the difficulty of proving the amount of the loss of earnings. In accordance with applicable jurisprudence, when determining average earnings prior to suffering the damage, we cannot base this upon the income of the injured party received from the former employer, if it is about the right to compensation and damages for a period following the time when the employment relationship of the affected employee ended with that employer, and if the employment relationship ended due to reasons other than the impact of an occupational accident. The Supreme Court ruled that, in such a case, there is a causal connection between the occupational accident and the loss of earnings, and that loss of earnings would then be based on the average earnings that the injured employee would have demonstrably achieved from another employer for the work he would have done for him if the accident had not occurred (see the judgement of the Czech Supreme Court of 10. 12. 2002, file no. 21 Cdo 1185/2002 (R 64/2003)). In such a case, the injured employee is essentially forced to prove how much he would have been paid for work done for another employer if he had not suffered the occupational accident or occupational disease. The situation becomes much simpler if the injured employee becomes a job seeker. In such a case, the law defines that the earnings received after an occupational accident shall be regarded as equal to the minimum wage. However, if an employee had already been receiving compensation for the loss of earnings after the end of an incapacity to work prior to becoming a jobseeker, he shall be entitled to compensation equaling the amount to which he became entitled during the employment relationship.

6. Conclusion

When adequate regulation is missing, employers are unable to provide a safe working environment. Given the current legislation, an employer simply cannot require employees to measure their temperature, undergo Covid-19 testing or work from home. The inspiration for amending the labour law is the crisis law, according to which, based on a government resolution, critical employees were required to measure their temperature and communicate the temperature measurement result to their employer.[22] Critical staff who reported, based upon an epidemiological survey, that they had experienced close contact with a person who had been diagnosed with Covid-19, are classified into groups of "indispensable" and "dispensable" from the point of view of their work. This decision is made by the respective critical infrastructure entity. Indispensable critical staff who have to continue their work have to comply with increased testing and reporting obligations.

Given the absence of the right to order the appropriate crisis measures according to the Crisis Act, it is not possible to order compulsory

[22] This is due to a resolution of the government of the Czech Republic no. 140/2020 Coll. of 30 March 2020, no. 332, on the adoption of a crisis measure, or rather with effect from 17 November 2020 from 00:00, by government resolution no. 1185, published in the Collection of Laws under No. 462/2020 Coll.

vaccination for critical employees, which obviously poses a problem; so the question is whether employers should be offered a solution to what to do with employees who do not want to be vaccinated, if otherwise their safety in the workplace cannot be protected.

Last year particularly demonstrated that compensation for voluntary firefighters who suffer an injury is entirely inadequate and requires changes in order to be able to provide for occupational safety and the health of firefighters who diligently, voluntarily and constantly expose their health to hazards in order to rescue people at risk. Given the analysis of legislation and decision-making practice we have carried out, the most appropriate way seems to be to define within the relevant legislation that volunteer firefighters are those who do not undergo training and are not deployed as municipal employees, but consistently act as volunteer firefighters performing this activity free of charge. In this case, the state is obliged to provide compensation for the damage they suffer as if they had suffered it in their main employment where they earn their living.

Bibliography

Other sources such as websites are mentioned in the footnotes.

Sivák, J., "Očkování - povinnost či možnost z právní perspektivy. Soukromé právo (Vaccination - an obligation or an option from the legal perspective. - Private Law)," *In* Soukromé právo. - Roč. 8 (Wolters Kluwer, 2020), 1, p. 8

PART 4

THE FUTURE OF LABOUR LAW: REFLECTIONS ON THE ROLE OF LABOUR LAW IN FUTURE SCENARIOS

CHAPTER 19

CHALLENGES FOR LABOUR LAW

MANFRED WEISS

1. Introduction

To an increasing extent the function of labour law has become controversial. The debate is focusing mainly on whether, in view of the fundamental changes in the world of work, the traditional goals of labour law can be maintained or if a new paradigm is now essential. In order to take a position in this discourse it is necessary, first of all, to sketch these changes in the world of work and then link them to the traditional goals.

Labour law is a product of industrialisation. It has been developed in view of a social and economic reality which is no longer the reality of today. The point of reference for the development of labour law was the Fordist model (for an explanation, cf. Watson 2019). The workplace was embedded in a factory in the manufacturing industry, a more or less large unit, where employees – mainly blue-collar and only to a small extent white-collar – did not work in splendid isolation but as a collective entity. The employment contract was no longer conceived as a merely individual relationship between employee and employer but as an element of the collective relationship between the employer and the workforce. The workforce was relatively homogeneous as were the employees' interests. The prototype of this workforce was the male employee in an undetermined full-time employment relationship. This male employee was regularly functioning as the "breadwinner", responsible for the family's budget. Continuity and stability were features of employment. The enterprise was characterised by a clear structure of hierarchies. It was easy to define subordination and the employer's power to command and control as criteria for the employment relationship and, at the same time, as a reference point for labour law. Homogeneous interests of the workforce as well as the experience of being part of the collective were ideal preconditions for unionisation. Thereby protection by collective bargaining could be organised without serious problems. Labour law was focusing on the domestic labour market. Globalisation was not a real issue.

In today's post-industrial era practically everything in this scenario has disappeared. The factory as a location where employees cooperate with each other is eroding to an increasing extent. Outsourcing, networking, sub-contracting and similar dislocating strategies are on the agenda. The enterprise is often turned into a merely virtual entity. Vertical structures are replaced by flat hierarchies. Manufacturing is becoming an ever decreasing part of the economy and the service sector is increasing. Work organisation has changed dramatically as a consequence of technological changes. The workforce is no longer homogeneous; it is fragmented and segmented into core groups and marginal groups, with less traditional employment and more and more new forms of work. The number of part-time jobs and fixed-term contracts, as well as of temporary agency workers is significantly increasing. There are growing numbers of economically dependent self-employed. The labour market is no longer male-dominated; feminisation of the labour market has become an important feature. The male "breadwinner" model belongs to the past. The balance of work and family obligations, thereby, has become a serious problem. Globalisation puts pressure on national economies. The relocation of production to other countries is on the agenda. New communication technologies allow for dividing the process of production and providing services between different countries all over the globe.

These very sketchy and admittedly superficial and simplistic observations may be sufficient to illustrate that the reality of work indeed has changed dramatically. On this empirical basis this article will discuss whether the traditional goals of labour law are still appropriate to cope with this new reality of work, whether smaller or bigger adaptations may be sufficient, or if a total change of paradigm is needed.

2. The Goals of Labour Law

2.1. The Basic Concept

The key to understanding the goals of labour law is embedded in the core message of the ILO, namely the formula that "labour is not a commodity", enshrined in the Philadelphia Declaration of 1944. The implications of this formula are very complex. The de-commodification of labour is a relatively new insight in a long development (for a comprehensive overview of this development, cf. Evju 2012). The founders of economic theory in the 18th century had a totally different perception. Adam Smith (Smith 1999, p. 167ff.), along with other economists, considered labour to be a commodity, just like any other commodity. According to this approach, the same market rules had to apply as in any other market where products and services are the objects of trade. This conception remained predominant into the 19th century. It first came under attack by Karl Marx, who pointed to the fact that the object of the labour market is not labour but the worker, a person with flesh and blood, who sells the labour power. But the labour power is not an independent entity, since it cannot be separated from the worker as a human being. Therefore, the labour market cannot be the same as any other market and needs specific rules (Marx 1968, p. 559). How difficult it was to promote this critical approach against the mainstream economic theory can be best demonstrated by the fact that not even Friedrich Engels shared the view of Karl Marx. According to him, labour is a commodity, like any other, and its price is therefore determined by exactly the same laws that apply to other commodities (Engels 1961, p. 81ff.). In other words, in his view, demand and supply are the decisive factors in the labour market.

In view of this dominance of classic economic theory, it is no surprise that it took quite a long time until the formula, "labour is not a commodity" had been accepted on international level. Even the text of the preamble of the Constitution of the ILO in the Treaty of Versailles in 1919 remains rather cautious when it states "that labour should not be regarded **merely** as a commodity or article of commerce." In other words: labour is a commodity but not an ordinary one, a formula which left much room for interpretation. It was only in 1944 in Philadelphia, where the focus was set on human rights, that "labour is not a commodity" as an internationally agreed unconditional formula became part of the ILO Declaration. It has been reconfirmed many times since. However, in spite of the fact that this formula is stressed and reconfirmed, it may well be doubted whether it is understood and accepted everywhere. Therefore, it seems necessary to clarify its implications as concretely as possible.

2.2. Implied Goals

An important implication of the formula "labour is not a commodity" is the recognition of the asymmetric power relationship between employer and employee, leading to the need to overcome the power inequality by promoting the collectivisation of employees (Kahn-Freund 1979, p. 7). This link was confirmed very early by legislation, namely by the Clayton Antitrust Act of the United States of 1914[1] which not only confirmed that

---

[1] It was enacted on 15 October 1914 by the US Congress in order to clarify and strengthen the Sherman Antitrust Act of 1890.

"the labour of a human being is not a commodity or article of commerce" but concluded from this insight that labour unions and collective actions are to be exempted from competition law [...] Nothing contained in the antitrust laws shall be construed to forbid the existence and operation of labour organisations [...] or to forbid or restrain individual members of such organisations from lawfully carrying out the legitimate objects thereof; nor shall such organisations, or the members thereof, to be held or construed to be illegal combinations or conspiracies in restraint of trade, under the antitrust law" (section 6).

The possibility to act collectively, to get organised in labour unions and to conclude collective agreements with the employers' side, is of the utmost importance. As long as workers merely act as individuals competing with each other in the labour market, exposed to the mechanism of supply and demand, the danger of a race to the bottom is always present. In case the supply is lower than the demand for labour, impoverishment might be the result of individual competition between workers. Therefore, the restriction of competition between individual workers should not be forbidden but allowed and encouraged. Only if workers are able to join forces can they prevent the race to the bottom by negotiating and, if necessary, fighting via collective action for minimum standards fixed in collective agreements. This is the reason why freedom of association, including the right to collective bargaining and collective action is one of the basic pillars of labour law (ILO Declaration on Core Labour Standards of 1998). In other words, it is uncontested that one of the main implications of the formula "labour is not a commodity" is the compensation of unequal bargaining power between employer and employee. Of course, this compensation not only takes place with collectivisation but also by protective state intervention. The interplay between collectively developed rules and state legislation has always been a characteristic feature of labour law.

However, the compensation of unequal bargaining power is only one implication of the insight that labour is not a commodity. The underpinning idea of this formula, as O'Higgins in his seminal article of 1997 (Higgins 1997) has convincingly demonstrated, is the need to protect the human dignity of the worker.

The guarantee and respect for human dignity as the overarching goal of labour law is explicitly mentioned in quite a few international legal documents. For example, the key concept of the ILO's decent work agenda is human dignity. And it is particularly prominent in the texts of the EU. It is not only the predominant right of the Charter of Fundamental Rights of the EU as a whole, but is particularly mentioned in its chapter on solidarity which contains the fundamental social rights. According to Article 31, paragraph 1, "every worker has the right to working conditions which respect his or her [...] dignity." This reference to human dignity is, by the way, decisive for the interpretation of all fundamental social rights contained in this chapter of the Charter.

Of course the notion of human dignity is as vague as the principle that labour is not a commodity. The literature is full of attempts to develop a definition and to specify the different aspects of this broad concept (cf. for example Kresal 2019). Without engaging in this debate, it should be clear that the reference to human dignity is not an empirical description of labour law, meaning that labour law already corresponds to this ambitious goal. Human dignity is a normative concept which indicates how labour law is to be developed. It goes without saying that, of course, it requires respect for human rights in its broadest sense.

Instead of trying to elaborate a comprehensive definition of human dignity in the labour context, I would rather just like to mention some evident implications for the sake of illustration.

First of all, respect for human dignity means to put the protection of the worker as human being in the centre of all reflections on labour law. This, by the way, is also the message of the recently published report of the Global Commission on the Future of Work (Global Commission on the Future of Work, Work for a brighter future, ILO 2019). This report was written in order to shape the politics of the ILO at the occasion of its centenary. The report stresses that "people and the work they do are to be placed at the centre of economic and social policy and business practice" (Ibid., p. 3). This insight leads into a very controversial ideological debate.

In the last few decades, the dominating neo-liberal approach of economic theory has been insisting on the self-regulation by market forces. In this view, labour law focuses on workers' protection and has been denounced as an intolerable disturbance of the markets. The primary focus of this school is not workers' human dignity but economic efficiency. Thereby, labour law is becoming merely a residual category totally dominated by the tyranny of economic considerations. This leads, by necessity, to de-regulation, de-institutionalisation and de-collectivisation. A reduction in labour costs is the dominating goal of such a theoretical concept. It is evident that this view considers labour more or less as a cost factor and nothing else (for a critical discussion of the neo-liberal approach and a brilliant assessment of the proper role of labour law, cf. Deakin 2016). It evidently is not at all in line with the formula "labour is not a commodity".

The consequences of this approach could best be seen by the austerity measures imposed on some southern European countries in the course of the management of the crisis of the EU monetary union. These measures, based on neo-liberal thinking, led to the reduction of wages and pensions, a weakening of the protections against unfair dismissals and the deconstruction of the collective bargaining system. This crisis management may be categorised as an exceptional situation. However, it has been the normal strategy in the EU for the last few decades. The 'Lisbon Strategy' of 2000, or the follow-up strategy, 'Europe 2020,' have both subordinated labour regulation to the many instruments developed by the EU for macro-economic governance, culminating in the 'European semester.' The social dimension in this view has remained a residual category (for this development, cf. Weiss 2017). Therefore, it is of utmost interest whether the recently proclaimed European Pillar of Social Rights means a new start, emancipating labour law from economic dominance and finally putting labour regulation in line with the concept of human dignity (on this development, cf. Weiss 2019, p. 72ff.).

Another important implication of respect for human dignity is the fact that workers are not seen to be mere objects of management's decisions but must have an opportunity to influence this decision-making. Already the founding fathers of labour law were pleading for a democratic workplace as a precondition for labour law in line with human dignity (Sinzheimer 1976, p. 108). This insight of the founding fathers of labour law is as valid today as it was in the formative era of labour law.

A further evident example of an implication of respect for human dignity concerns respect for worker's privacy. This is not only an issue which has become dramatic in the era of digitalization. There has always been a danger that the employer tries to get as much information as possible on the worker's life, including his or her private behaviour, ideological and political preferences, religious affiliation, and economic situation, etc. The possibility of collecting all this data to process and save for possible future use has increased dramatically because of the availability of digital tools. Human dignity, however, requires that this possibility is limited and that the employer is only entitled to get an applicant's or worker's personal data to the extent which is absolutely necessary to perform the employment relationship.

These few examples of the implications of respect for human dignity, of course, could be extended with many other examples, such as those concerned with health and safety, the prohibition of discrimination, job stability, a decent remuneration, etc. However, they may be sufficient to indicate the enormous complexity of this notion.

The goals of labour law as described above are as valid today and in the future as they were in the past. Of course, they have to be balanced with other goals, be they economic or ecologic. This, however, is nothing new and goes without saying. The important message is that there is no need for a new paradigm of labour law. The problem is a different and much more difficult one. The question now arises how these goals can be achieved in view of the changes in the world of work. There is no doubt that the instruments have to be adapted to new conditions in order to achieve the above-mentioned goals. In what way does this have to happen? This is the big challenge for labour law today and in the future.

3. Adaptation to New Conditions

The institutional arrangements and the whole set of instruments of labour law have to be re-examined, in terms of whether and to what extent they are still appropriate, in view of changed conditions in the world of work. This is undoubtedly a giant task. In this sketchy chapter, it only can be briefly illustrated by presenting a few arbitrarily chosen examples.

3.1. Scope of Application

The question is whether the scope of the application of labour law has to be extended beyond the traditional employment relationship, particularly in view of all the technological changes up to digitalization. For quite a long time it has become evident that the demarcation line between employment and self-employment is very difficult to draw (Davidov & Langille 2006). To an increasing extent, there are persons labelled as being self-employed but in reality they are employees. The problem of drawing a demarcation line between employment and self-employed has become even more dramatic in the era of digitalization. The degree of autonomy in performing work makes it more and more difficult to categorise the persons involved in such work as employees, even if a closer look reveals that the autonomy is ambiguous because new mechanisms of more efficient control are in place. There is no doubt that, for example, many of those who participate in crowd-working are certainly not employees but rather self-employed.

The question is what to do with those who undoubtedly are self-employed and work alone without employees but are economically in a similar position as employees. They are not reached by labour law protection. They are not included in minimum wage schemes, in health and safety arrangements or in guarantees of decent working time, to just give a few examples. Theoretically, there are different possibilities to provide for them the necessary protection: the broadening of the notion of employee, the creation of a specific intermediate category or the extension of the scope of labour law to the economically dependent self-employed (so-called solo-self-employed).

The broadening of the notion of employee is the pattern presently to be observed in the many lawsuits all over the world determining the question of whether the persons who work on demand for platforms (Uber drivers etc.) are employees or self-employed. In many countries, the notion of employee has been extended significantly. However, this strategy has limits. If the notion is extended too far, it becomes meaningless and it will never be possible to include all economically dependent employees.

The introduction of an intermediary category between employment and self-employment might be a solution (for details on the German pattern, cf. Waas 2017, p 160 ff.). However, as the examples in quite a few countries show, such a third category has only provoked uncertainties and led to many controversies. It increases the complexity, thereby leading to more problems rather than fewer.

A more appropriate possibility would be the inclusion of solo-self-employed up to a certain wage level under the protective roof of labour law and social security law. As far as inclusion into the social security system is concerned, some countries – such as, for example, Austria – have followed this path already and it seems to work quite well. Whether, however, such a strategy might work for labour law as well may be doubted. It cannot be denied that many protective patterns are linked to the relationship between employer and employee in the employment relationship. The rules on protection against unfair dismissal might be a good example to illustrate what is meant. Therefore, a mere extension of labour law to the self-employed might not be a recommendable strategy.

A more radical approach perhaps might be more helpful. Instead of putting workers in different categories, the focus should be on the floor of rights all working people need, no matter what their status. This is in line with the universal labour guarantee, as suggested by the ILO Commission on the Future of Work (unfortunately no longer contained in the ILO Centenary Declaration of June 2019). It focuses on the protection of workers regardless of their contractual arrangement and their employment status. The focus should be on the shape of the protective umbrella, not on the boxes where workers are located. This, however, implies another problem: Who is responsible for providing the protection? The solution might be relatively easy in cases of platform work but it is certainly difficult for many other self-employed workers.

It is particularly necessary to guarantee freedom of association as a precondition of collective action for all workers, whether they are employees in a traditional sense or self-employed. This basic insight unfortunately is not yet generally recognised. For example, the Court of

Justice of the EU (CJEU) still considers the solo-self-employed as objects of the anti-trust rules which, therefore, cannot be included in collective agreements (ECJ, 4th December 2014, C-413/13, Kunsten Informatie en Media vs. Staat de Nederlanden). This narrow-minded view evidently misunderstands the function of anti-trust law which is meant to prevent the abuse of power in the market by forbidding cartels of companies. Collective agreements for the solo-self-employed evidently will not lead to such an abuse of market power and, therefore, should also be exempted from anti-trust-rules.

3.2. Workers' Participation in Management's Decision-Making

The more the world of work is changing, the more important becomes the workers' involvement in management's decision-making. Such involvement increases the legitimacy and thereby the acceptability of management's decisions. It is a necessary element of workplace democracy which – as shown above – is a traditional goal of labour law.

The transformation of working patterns is so speedy that the legislator evidently is not able to keep up with all these technological changes. Legislation can only provide a relatively flexible framework. Solutions balancing the needs of the companies and the workers are to be developed at a decentralised level, in the workplace and within companies.

However, there are preconditions for efficient functioning of workers' participation in management's decision-making: an identifiable workplace where employees are working together in the premises of the employer; a hierarchical structure between management and employees with more or less homogeneous interests; and a relatively clear method and easily recognisable criteria for identifying who is an employee and an identifiable employer, namely a company to which the employees belong. These preconditions have become more and more problematic. And this leads to the question whether and how workers' participation can survive in the future and how it has to be structured.

The fragmentation, segmentation and dislocation of the workforce has become an increasing trend. Not only due to the diversity of interests of the different groups of employees make it difficult to articulate a collective voice in participating, but isolation and individualisation prevent collective consciousness. The need to be present in the premises of the employer is fading away. Digitalization to a greater and greater extent allows that work can be performed from everywhere.

Vertical structures are increasingly being replaced by so-called flat hierarchies. Instead, subordination autonomy is becoming the new catchword.

But control prevails. Thereby the still existing conflict of interests between management and employees, of course, is not disappearing, it just becomes less visible.

There is not only an increase of fragmentation and segmentation of the workforce leading to very heterogeneous interests but – as already indicated – also the erosion of the company structures which makes it difficult to define who is the employer. It is quite a while since companies have achieved a 'new mobility' in terms of company patterns and cooperative structures. It makes sense to talk of a 'volatility' of legal structures, as virtual corporate networks emerge, areas are outsourced, companies are run without formal group structures and transnational cooperation is becoming more and more a common feature. Dislocating strategies are on the agenda. It often has become difficult to identify the employer. The "fissured workplace" has become a sort of catchword of this extremely complex development. Digitalization and globalisation are further and mutually pushing this trend (on this development, cf. Klebe & Weiss 2019, p. 270).

To sum up these observations: the more urgent the need for workers' participation, the more difficult it might be to maintain or establish such systems in the new world of work. There are quite a few obstacles which have to be overcome to maintain or establish functioning workers' representation in modern company structures, in particular in the platform economy.

First, it will be necessary to overcome the individualisation and isolation of workers. This applies in particular to tele-workers and to all types of workers in the platform-economy. It is necessary to create a collective consciousness. There are already many attempts, mainly organised by trade unions, to contact the respective workers using digital tools and bring them together in workshops where useful information is provided. These initiatives particularly try to enable digital workers such as crowd-workers to communicate with each other, thereby overcoming isolation. These initiatives are quite promising, even if they are still at an experimental stage.

Secondly, and also in this context, it becomes evident that it does not make sense to continue with the separation of employees and the self-employed. Integration is particularly needed here and it has to be clarified who is the counterpart on the management side. This is getting more and more difficult as more company structures are scattered. It is particularly difficult in the context of the platform-economy. To take just one example, in the case of crowd work, who is treated as an employer — the platform operator, the crowd-sourcer or both? The categorisation cannot be left to the platforms themselves. Objective criteria and a functional approach are necessary to identify the employer (Prassl & Risak 2016). The problem is particularly complex in a crowd-work structure, where it is not the platform operator but the crowd-sourcer as the client of the platform who is getting credit for the crowd-workers' achievements. In this tripartite structure, the employer's role might be split between platform and crowd-sourcer or fulfilled by one of the two actors.

Of course, the problem of tripartite structures is not new. It is well known in the context of temporary agency work. However, it has become much more dramatic in view of the platform economy. Therefore, efforts are to be taken to develop appropriate solutions to identify who is in such a constellation the employer and in what way.

The final challenge is the fact that the workforce, again particularly in the context of crowd-working, is trans-national. This leads to the question of whether schemes of workers' participation can be established covering all workers, no matter to which country they belong. All those workers might be included to vote for the workers' representatives, and the workers' representatives might possibly speak for all of them. This would need world-wide trans-national regulation, which is not easy to develop.

In short, and to make the point, whether and in what way functioning and effective workers' participation in management's decision-making can be established, is to a great extent an open question.

3.3. The Trans-Nationalisation of Labour Standards

In the course of globalisation, the trans-national sphere has become more and more important. Labour law can no longer be perceived from a merely national perspective. International rules are to be elaborated and applied in order to stop the race to the bottom and in order to guarantee respect for human dignity. There are attempts but they are not sufficient. Of course, the ILO, for more than a century has done a great job in setting universal labour standards (for an assessment, cf. Tapiola 2020). However, the problem is not so much the setting of standards but the low rate of ratification, the lack of adequate implementation, the deficiencies of the supervisory system and the lack of an efficient enforcement mechanism (for an assessment, cf. Waas 2020). The discrepancy between the efforts to develop international labour standards and the reality in many countries becomes particularly evident in the context of global supply chains.

More and more multi-national enterprises (MNE) make use of low standards in developing countries to obtain supplies for their products.[2]

[2] According to the *WTO Global Value Chain Report 2019 – Technological Innovation, Supply Chain Trade and workers in a Globalised World*, Geneva 2019, more than two thirds of global trade is performed by global supply chains.

Most prominent in this respect is the textile sector. Some states, (e.g. France (LOI n° 2017-399 du 27 mars 2017 relative au devoir de vigilance des sociétés mères et des entreprises donneuses d'ordre), the U.K. (Modern Slavery Act of 2015), the Netherlands (Wet Zorgplicht Kinderarbeid of 2020), Australia (Modern Slavery Act of 2019) and Germany (Lieferkettensorgfaltspflichtengesetz of 2021) have recently passed legislation to increase the responsibility of their MNE. The problem is not only that these laws are not satisfactory, but if only individual countries pass such legislation, this might lead to competitive disadvantages for mother companies situated in those countries. Therefore, comprehensive international regulation is indispensable.

The first international push for improving the situation came not from the ILO but from the United Nation's Human Rights Council. In 2011, this body endorsed the "Guiding Principles on Business and Human Rights" which were annexed in the famous Ruggie report. They define concrete, actionable steps for governments and companies to meet their respective duties and responsibilities to prevent human rights abuses in company operations and provide remedies if such abuses take place. The different member states were supposed to transform these principles into national action plans. This has been executed by now, of course, ending up not in binding rules but merely in recommendations.

When, in 2013, the Rana Plaza building in Bangladesh came crashing down, killing more than 1000 people and leaving thousands more injured, this served as a sort of wake-up call. It brought worldwide attention to death-trap workplaces within the garment industry. Not even a month after the event, the Accord on Fire and Building Safety in Bangladesh was concluded, a legally binding agreement between global brands, trade unions and the ILO designed to build a safe and healthy Bangladeshi ready-made garment industry. The agreement consists of an independent inspection program, public disclosure of all factories, inspection reports and corrective action plans, a commitment by the signatory brands for sufficient funds, democratically elected health and safety committees in all factories to identify and act on health and safety risks, workers' empowerment through an extensive training program and, last not least, complaint mechanisms. More than 200 companies have signed this accord, which first expired in 2018 and was extended for three more years. In the meantime, the Bangladeshi government expelled the foreign inspectors.

The accord could serve as a model of how regulation of global supply chains might look. But it should not be ignored that it only focuses on health and safety and targets just one sector in one country. Therefore, it was of utmost importance when, in 2014, Ecuador and South Africa initiated (in the UN Human Rights Council) a resolution for a comprehensive binding instrument to be elaborated on by the Open-Ended Intergovernmental Working Group (OEIGWG), aiming at an international and uniform solution that no longer relies merely on national action plans, and – above all – has a legally binding effect. The resolution was passed, but against the votes of all industrialised countries who are members of the Human Rights Council and whose MNE are profiting from the status quo. In July 2019, the OEIGWG presented a draft of a "Legally Binding Instrument to Regulate, in International Human Rights Law, the Activities of Transnational Corporations and other Business Enterprises."

The draft covers not only transnational companies but also those who only operate domestically. This is necessary to make sure that intolerable working conditions are not merely shifted to local companies without a transnational link. And the draft covers all human rights in the working context, not only the core labour rights, as contained in the ILO Declaration of 1998, but also those embedded in the UN international covenants which include the right to fair remuneration, guaranteeing an appropriate income for the workers and their families, as well as the right to appropriate limitation of working time and paid vacations, to give just two important examples.

The draft imposes on the member states the duty to prevent violations of human rights by specific mechanisms and procedures. In cases of transnationally operating companies, these responsibilities rest with the mother companies. In particular, the draft regulates the victims` access to courts or alternative independent and impartial bodies of conflict resolution, and establishes requirements for fair procedure, including a change to the burden of proof in favour of the victims. There are special chapters on liability. The draft also contains rules on applicable law and, in particular, on cooperation and mutual help between the involved states. Finally, the draft provides for a committee of experts who, among many other functions, are supposed to make "general comments and normative recommendations on the understanding and implementation of the legally binding instrument," based on reports by the states and other stakeholders. Thereby it would be guaranteed that the binding instrument would be understood in the same way in all the ratifying member states, and that it will not remain static but adapted to needs in practice.

Whether and when the draft of the intergovernmental working group will be turned into an international treaty, and whether the opposition of the industrialised countries can be overcome, remains an open question. So far, it is the most promising sign of hope. This is also true in comparison to the efforts made by the ILO.

In 2016, the ILO presented a report called "Decent Work in Global Supply Chains," to be discussed at the International Labour Conference. However, the result was disappointing. The trade union camp's request for a convention was pushed back and the debate ended in joint conclusions at the lowest possible denominator, according to which the ILO is supposed to develop an action plan on how to promote decent work in global supply chains, advise and support stakeholders, exchange information on best practices, and encourage companies to conduct "human rights due diligence". In short, and to make the point, everything remains voluntary for the companies. This has still not changed.

4. Conclusion

Globalisation and technological innovations have led to dramatic changes in the world of work and the reality for which labour law was originally shaped has largely disappeared. The reality of work today is, of course, not the end of this development, and it will continue to evolve. In spite of all the changes, the goals of labour law remain the same as ever. There is no need for a new paradigm. The challenge for labour law is how to adapt its scope as well as its instruments to the ever-changing reality. The few examples outlined in this article illustrate how necessary, complex and difficult this task is.

Bibliography

Davidov, Guy and Langille, Brian (eds.), *Boundaries and Frontiers of Labour Law* (Oxford/Portland: Hart Publishing, 2006)

Deakin, Simon, "The Contribution of Labour Law to Economic Development and Growth," In *Labour Law and Social Progress,* edited by Blanpain, Roger and Hendrickx, Franck (Alphen aan den Rijn: Kluwer Law International BV, 2016), 19 - 37

Engels, Friedrich, "The Principles of Communism", In *Selected Writings*, Vol. I, (Moscow: Progress Publishers, 1969), 81-97 (first published 1847)

Evju, Stein, "Labour is not a Commodity. A Reappraisal," *Working Papers in Labour Law (University of Oslo, Institute of Private Law),* no. 6 (2012): 1-9

O'Higgins, Paul, "Labour is not a Commodity – an Irish Contribution to International Labour Law," *Industrial Law Journal* (1997): 225-234

Kahn-Freund, Otto, *Arbeit und Recht*, (Cologne: Bund Publisher House, 1979)

Klebe, Thomas and Weiss, Manfred, "Workers' Participation 4.0 – Digital and Global?" *Comparative Labor Law & and Policy Journal* (2019): 263-284

Kresal, Barbara, "Human Dignity," In *The Charter of Fundamental Rights of the European Union and the Employment Relation*, edited by Dorssemont, Filip et alii. (Oxford/Portland: Hart Publishing, 2019), 191-208

Marx, Karl, "*Das Kapital*," In *Werke*, Bd. 23, by Marx, Karl and Engels, Friedrich (Dietz: Stuttgart, 1968), 557-564 (first published 1877)

Prassl, Jeremias and Risak, Martin, "Uber, Taskrabbit, and Co.: Platforms as Employers? Rethinking the Legal Analysis of Crowdwork," *Comparative Labor & Policy Journal* (2016): 619-651

Sinzheimer, Hugo, "Das Wesen des Arbeitsrechts," In *Arbeitsrecht und Rechtssoziologie,* Vol. 1, by Hugo Sinzheimer (Cologne: Bund Publisher House, 1976), 108-114 (first published in 1927)

Smith, Adam, *The Wealth of Nations*, Books I – III, Chapter VIII, Of the Wages of Labour (Munich: Penguin 1999), 134 (first published 1776)

Tapiola, Kari, "What happened to International Labour standards and Human Rights at Work?" In *International Labour Organization and Global Social Governance*, edited by Halonen, Tarja and Liukkunen, Ulla (Cham: Springer, 2020), 51-78

Waas, Bernd, "Crowdwork in Germany," In *Crowdwork - A Comparative Perspective*, edited by Waas, Bernd et alii. (Cologne: Bund-Verlag, 2017), 142-186

Waas, Bernd, "How to improve Montioring and Enforcement of International Labour Standards?" In *International Labour Organization and Global Social Governance*, edited by Halonen, Tarja and Liukkunen, Ulla (Cham: Springer, 2020), 79-96

Watson, Daniel, "Fordism: A Review," *Labor History* (2019): 144-159

Weiss, Manfred, "The future of labour law in Europe: Rise or fall of the European social model?" *European Labour Law Journal* (2017): 344-356

Weiss, Manfred, "The Social Dimension of the EU," In *Sixty Years of European Integration and Global Power Shifts*, edited by Chaisse, Julien (Oxford/Portland: Hart Publishing, 2019), 67-78

CHAPTER 20

THE WORKER WITHIN THE NEW PARADIGM OF LABOUR LAW: BETWEEN SOLIDARITY AND LONELINESS

RALUCA DIMITRIU

1. The Starting Point

Labour law broke away from civil law as soon as the ontological imbalance of forces manifested in individual bargaining began to be offset by the solidarity of workers bargaining collectively. Indeed, compared to civil law, the branch of labour law brought a significant peculiarity: the ability of one of the contracting parties to negotiate and act not only individually but also collectively, thus compensating with the power of the group the lack of power balance in individual negotiation. The issue of the imbalance of bargaining power continues to concern contemporary doctrine and, as has been shown, labour law has not departed from the founding ideas of Kahn-Freund (Davidov 2014, 10-12). The solidarity of workers and their collective organisation are what determined this "emancipation" of labour law from civil law, making the concept of collective interest a founding concept of labour law. Therefore, the history of labour law, in many legal systems, is that of its progressive "collectivisation," or "de-individualisation" (Adam 2005, 11). As a result, the employee appears bound not only by the employer, by virtue of the employment contract concluded, but also by the community to which he or she belongs. This belonging is the premise for the acknowledgement of some of the rights and freedoms.

As Barnard showed (2004, 213-14):

> Underpinning the idea of solidarity is the notion that the ties which exist between the individuals of a relevant group justify decision-makers taking steps, both negative and positive, to ensure that all individuals are integrated into the community, thereby enabling them to have the chance to participate

and contribute fully.

The collective component of labour law constituted the foundation of a balance of forces in the labour market, giving workers the opportunity to express themselves, through solidarity, with a unique voice.

But things seem to be changing.

The changes we are witnessing today, which concern not only the way in which the parties relate to the legal relationship under which the work is performed, but even the work itself, are not marginal. They are not natural correlates of technology and robotics. Rather, it is a paradigm shift with an effect on labour law as a whole, and I think the loneliness of the worker is one of the most significant trends.

Like Benjamin Button, over time, labour law seems to return to its own childhood.

Today, work performed within the family, in one's own household, acquires a relevance that no one suspected would be regained in the context of modern society. More people are working from their homes than at any time since the Industrial Revolution. The physical distance from colleagues (a pre-existing phenomenon but undoubtedly amplified by the Covid-19 crisis), contemporary management methods directed towards autonomy, and the increasingly direct relationship with the client, turned the worker into a lone wolf who obtains his resources in a universally competitive context and is expected to have a rather entrepreneurial attitude. Almost nothing that was defining for the work performed in large industrial companies — which occasioned the genesis of labour law on the basis of solidarity between employees working shoulder to shoulder — is indispensable today. If we look, for example, at the ILO Employment Relationship Recommendation, 2006 (No. 198), as well as at the criteria considered to be decisive for identifying an employment relationship, we can see how much dependent work has changed over the last 15 years.

Virtual labour relations can be distinguished from proximity-based labour relations both by aspects related to working conditions and the way work is performed, and by the way in which workers relate socially, in what used to be a community. But the loneliness of the contemporary worker, as I will argue, does not concern just the one who works remotely, but tends to extend to the most varied professional categories. Traditionally, the employee is in a potentially adverse relationship with the employer – the other contracting party with different, sometimes even opposite, interests. But today, the worker perceives many other categories of people as "enemies," becoming part of a general competitive realm.

However, the impact of these changes on collective labour relations cannot be left unnoticed. My perspective could be all the more pessimistic as I come from a part of the world characterised by a systemic crisis of collective labour relations (e.g. Poland: Pisarczyk 2019, Czech Republic: Myant 2010; Hungary: Kovacs 2019; Romania: Dimitriu 2016, etc.)

But even beyond that, one fact cannot be overlooked: often, the worker is alone.

2. How did the Worker End Up Alone?

Work has evolved in countless aspects — too many to list — but one of the most spectacular developments is that it has become, to a large extent, a solitary experience. Needless to say, we cannot make general assessments about all the categories of people who perform work because factories, warehouses or construction sites continue to exist, and many employees perform their work activity together with their colleagues, just as they have always done. But for an increasing number of workers (and of course, digital workers are the most obvious example) the physical proximity of their colleagues is no longer needed to carry out their work. Just as Netflix replaced cinemas, so did individual work in front of one's own computer replace the experience of collective work. Teams of workers have been replaced by virtual teams, often made up of colleagues who have never even met. This is not to say it is something good or bad, it is just an observation that there is a direct consequence of the worker's loneliness, in the physical sense, on her legal security. The worker is alone, also meaning "by herself," lacking the support that her colleagues could offer, including through the collective bargaining mentioned above. Indeed, as Arthurs noted (2013, 21):

> proximity traditionally fostered solidarity; it enabled workers to develop personal ties, identify potential leaders, reflect on their common fate, and respond collectively to a shared sense of grievance.

a) Digitalization

The employment relationship. Most of the traditional features of the employment relationship are no longer immediately visible to digital workers. They are often required to fulfil an obligation *of result* rather than an obligation *of means* and the provision of tools, materials and machinery by the party requesting the work is no longer necessarily requested by legislation. In many countries, such as Bulgaria, Greece, Romania, and Poland, for example, especially in the context of the Covid-19 crisis, rules were adopted around the possibility for the parties to agree on the use of the employee's own work equipment.

Integration into the organisation is weaker and the proximity of colleagues – the usual precondition of the manifestation of solidarity – is almost always absent. All of these factors diminished the collectivist dimension of work.

In addition, the duration of digital workers' contracts is often limited, as they are employed "on the project" or even to perform a micro-task, so that creating such solidarity is difficult, not only in terms of *where*, but also in terms of *when*.

The personality of the digital worker. The particularity of the digital worker lies in the fact that she expresses specific interests which are not identical to those of her colleagues. Digital employees rarely have the opportunity to express themselves in a single voice, they are not always animated by common goals, but they take advantage of a wide variety of possibilities and aspirations. As an expression of the concrete way of delivering the work, in the broader context of the tendency of "individualisation" of labour law, the possibility – and even the interest – of the exercise of collective rights is visibly diminishing, remaining the prerogative of standard workers. It is even argued that these difficulties can go as far as the denial (*de facto* or *de jure*) of the collective rights of digital workers (De Stefano 2015, 3). Indeed, digitalization is accelerating individualism, making workers perform their activities virtually alone, in an individual relationship with the beneficiary of their work.

Public expression. Digitalization has also brought with it the possibility of exercising individual freedom of expression. Until recently, the voice of the individual worker was rarely heard, so that the community provided a forum for expressing options that were validated by the number of those who shared them. Traditionally, for an opinion to reach outside of the workplace, to the general public, it had to be conveyed through channels that would allow it to amplify, such as trade unions. However, digitalization has changed this, and in terms of employment, the worker no longer needs a form of collective organisation to be heard. The Internet has created a global forum that provides individual voices access to the widest audience they have never dreamed of reaching. From this forum, the coalition of similar options and interests can be shaped easily, and the worker no longer needs to find, among colleagues, those who will listen to her or even share her opinions, being able to find followers at a great distance. Furthermore, access to policy-makers, which was impossible in the absence of the union vehicle, is today possible through the direct contact of the individual worker with the media.

The action. Traditional modes of action were directly associated with collective organisation. This is no longer the case today, when digitalization has allowed means of action that short-circuits the trade union association. From public denunciation of employer abuse ("name and shame") to raising awareness of customers and consumers, the means of action have not only developed in non-union areas, but do not necessarily claim any form of collective organisation.

b) Contemporary Methods of Human Resources Management

The way work is organised has shifted from pyramidal, hierarchical organisation to functional, decentralised modules. The worker gained autonomy but autonomy is just a euphemism for loneliness, because regardless of how much dependent work and its identification criteria have changed, the employer's right to control (directly, or through clients) has remained a defining feature. Control no longer regards the way the work is carried out, but often it is exercised on the results, amplifying the question of whether it is still true that the employee has an obligation of diligence, and not one of result.

The changes in production organisation and management theory, which have led to small, flexible and decentralised units, rather than large, bureaucratic entities, have some consequences for employment arrangements, disrupting the standard contract paradigm. The individualisation of human resources management is correlated with a new type of management of an integrative, participatory nature. The employee is addressed individually and personally; we are witnessing a "managerial revaluation of the individual" (Adam 2003, 203).

The repositioning of the standard labour relationship naturally accompanies the decline of the Fordist model of the large industry and the Taylorian organisation of labour. Production relations themselves are transformed from the vertical, hierarchical, national, standardised, Fordist organisation to the trans-national, post-Fordist and flexible organisation. This inevitably affects employment relationships.

c) Internal Competition

Solidarity between standard workers has lost its robustness because, among other things, in the organisational culture of the enterprise there is – in the period we are going through – a tendency towards internal competition. This development has led some authors to consider that labour law tends to turn, in reality, into "social competition law," having as tools, among others, "austerity policies (with impact on wages), flexibility of labour relations, intensive use of atypical contracts" (Schubert 2014, 29). The worker is put in a competitive position in relation to other workers, just like a company is in a position to compete against other companies. This obviously affects solidarity and the possibility of collective bargaining; competitive relationships are not conductive to solidarity, which is seen as weakened, not only at the international or national levels, but even at the level of a single establishment.

For instance, in sales companies, there are selective procedures to promote commercial agents who exceed their sales targets. They turn to fierce competition among themselves. Competition is a reality because, during the Covid-19 crisis, the number of jobs may decrease so that the employer is forced to make a selection from their employees.

Even when workers manage to unite their voices and bargain collectively, the results of such a negotiation often bear the mark of the competitive relations among them, because what employees obtain by collective bargaining is not always a "victory" over the employer but over other employees. In many cases, collective bargaining is not a regulator of relations between labour and capital, but is often a means of redistributing resources among workers. Thus, during collective bargaining, instead of the classic question: “Who will win — the workers or the employer?” we have to deal with another question: “Who will win and who will lose among workers?" Indeed, workers are no longer found in divergent relationships with just the employer, but also (and sometimes even primarily) with other workers from the same establishment (Dimitriu 2017, 394-95).

d) External competition

In relation to atypical and “very atypical” workers. Competition is not confined to the category of other standard employees, but – perhaps even more sustained – it targets the categories of atypical, casual or self-employed workers. Indeed, that which “stole” labour law from civil law is now re-appropriated by the latter by transforming a significant part of employees into self-employed and bogus self-employed workers. They return to the labour market in a new position, which not only exposes them to vulnerability and precariousness, but is also perceived by other workers as a danger — a form of unfair competition. The shift to atypical, unconventional and “very” atypical work relations has diminished the unity of the workers and the possibility for them to organize collectively. As Ursula Huws (2019, 53) showed:

> the actions taken by skilled tailors in mid-nineteenth century London to prevent the recruitment of less skilled stitchers are fundamentally little different from those of (…) licensed taxi drivers in the twenty-first century

organizing against Uber drivers operating in their cities.

There is thus a separation of the interests between standard workers and those who hold stable jobs with opportunities to be promoted (a working elite) from the large mass of precarious workers. There is a "hard core" of stable employees, surrounded by a mass of precarious, marginal workers who do not benefit from the right to collective bargaining and action. Some legal systems have lessened these issues by extending the right to collective bargaining to workers who, without having an employment contract, nevertheless share the relationship of economic dependence with employees. In Germany, for example, the law expressly allows unions to represent self-employed professionals under employee-like contracts (Klebe and Heuschmid 2019, 199). However, such rules are exceptions. In addition, they cannot be extended to self-employed persons, who are legally deprived of the chance to act collectively. In this respect, Rubiano pointed out (2013, 141):

> The limitation of the scope of labour laws to “employees” affects the right to collective bargaining as well (…) Even in cases where both “employees” and “self-employed” workers within the same (or similar) sector of activity have managed to join the same trade union, this does not imply that they can bargain collectively together, or that the trade union can negotiate on their behalf.

Self-employed independent contractors are subject to competition law. Self-employed workers can only bargain collectively if they are employees who are falsely labelled as self-employed, as the Court of Justice of the European Union has ruled in FNV Kunsten Informatie en Media C-413/13, an often criticised decision (e.g., Aloisi and Elena Gramano 2019). In this universally-competitive field, it is not surprising that it is competition law which imposes limits on collective labour law.

In relation to foreign workers. If employees working for the same employer often perceive themselves as competitors, such positioning is even more pronounced when it comes to employees of other employers, operating under different legal systems, possibly subject to another jurisdiction. At the EU level, the free movement of persons and the freedom of the provision of services determines workers not only being able to perform work in the territory of a member state, but in the territory of any other member state, and when the number of jobs is limited and unemployment is increasing, each worker is in fierce competition with any other European worker (Dimitriu 2017, 396). This significantly affects the chances of pan-European solidarity.

The lack of solidarity is also manifested in relation to migrant workers.

Analysing the so-called "isolated worker in the isolated state," Freedland (2018) presents two pillars of social inclusion: the employment relationship (personal relation) and migration law as having the same foundation. He points out that the two pillars are not adverse, as they seem, but present the same structural problems, leading to a double isolation of workers – by making their work and the state more precarious – which seeks to preserve this precarious job offer.

This leads to demonstrations by local workers against immigrants, against the various marginal categories of workers who, through the difficult economic situation in which they find themselves, accept lower working conditions and wages, thus putting pressure on the standard worker. We thus move from the antagonism of interests between labour and capital to a new antagonism, between the core of local employees, on the one hand, and peripheral workers and immigrants, on the other. Nationalist movements are inevitably isolationist: they tend to separate the local worker, who is denied a type of cross-border solidarity.

e) Cultural Differences

Even when working in the space organised by the employer, together with her colleagues, the worker may not share the same cultural values and customs with her co-workers, in the context of the current heterogeneity of the workforce. As we have shown above, she can even develop hostile, xenophobic attitudes towards those she perceives as different, to the detriment of the feelings of solidarity. Conversely, for certain categories of workers, especially belonging to ethnic or sexual minorities, phenomena such as harassment and discrimination in the workplace are common causes of loneliness and isolation. In addition, the possibility of relocation of employers has generated counter-reactions from the employees left "at home", hostages of a more protective legislative system which, paradoxically, they may perceive as representing a disadvantage in a global labour market.

Digital workers experience these types of feelings perhaps to a larger extent than proximity-based workers. Cultural and linguistic differences between digital workers (Aloisi 2019) are often characteristic of large transnational structures and can create barriers that are difficult to overcome.

However, we can hope that such cultural differences will be relevant in terms of professional organisation only in the "infancy" of diversity. Once citizens mature through education and public policies, they accept the heterogeneity of the workplace without this being a problem in terms of collective organisation.

f) Detailed Legislation

The option for more or less discreet state intervention in social dialogue differs from system to system and from period to period. From the collective *laissez faire* of the 1950s (as described by Otto Kahn-Freund) to actively encouraging collective bargaining, or sometimes even discouraging it (especially during and after the economic crisis), the models embraced by different European law systems are hugely diverse.

Essentially, when it intervenes in the space of social dialogue, legislation may in some cases allow the social partners to build their own legal constructions and, in other cases, may stimulate the creativity of social partners, encouraging self-regulation.

But even when it is in no way designed to discourage collective action, the legislation itself can be a brake on solidarity among employees. Often, in the context of very detailed legislation – common, for example, in Eastern European countries – employees may no longer perceive the need for collective, trade union intervention, since most rights are enshrined in law. The stronger the government intervention, the more the need for collective representation fades. In addition, there may be access routes for government decision-makers that can be perceived as simpler and as more effective than trade union ones.

g) Evolutions of the Worker's Psychology

Collective labour law was built on the foundation of the uniformity of the interests of those who work. However, with the diversification of contractual arrangements under which work is performed, this uniformity tends to diminish.

Psychologically, the worker has become more individualistic, eager to exercise her ability to express herself, and to formulate and pursue personal career and life goals. As we mentioned, the digital worker often feels she enjoys more freedom than the standard worker: more freedom in relation to the employer, to whom the subordination is apparently diminished, since the work itself is no longer closely supervised; more freedom in relation to society at large, which no longer has the same constraints, as in the case of traditional workers. It is precisely this sense of freedom that can reduce her desire for union association, an action that would presuppose *de plano* a certain limitation of individual freedom. On the contrary, freedom is associated with uniqueness and loneliness, such a worker having difficulties accommodating to the collectivism and concessions that it implies.

This reluctance of individuals to act collectively affects unions to the same extent as other organisations – churches or political parties. Concepts such as "professional success" or "career" have a strong individualistic element; they validate the person, not the collectivity and are constructed, if not by denying the professional associative structures, at least independently of them. In some countries (the US, for example, Margalioth 1998) the reduction of collectivist impulses may be based on a higher general degree of comfort, due to which solidarity is no longer seen as a chance for economic survival. As revealed (Triandis et al 1988), modern cultures are neo-individualistic, characterised by fixed-term social relationships, with low emotional impact.

Such cultural distinctions are extremely relevant to the psychology of the contemporary worker. An individualistic culture can come into conflict with the ontological-collectivist component of labour law. Moreover, Collins noted (1998, 117) that collective bargaining is constantly focused on pay and redundancies, rarely having regard to other interests, such as the human need for self-affirmation, respect and dignity at work.

In addition to their own cultural determinations, some historical ones (e.g. forced collectivism, typical of the communist period) may have generated individualistic counter-reactions for the Eastern European worker. Indeed, on the altar of the "trade union struggle," workers have traditionally been taught to sacrifice their individual interests in favour of those of the majority, thus subjecting themselves to a collective goal which usually does not preserve the identity of sub-groups and does not protect minorities (Dimitriu 2017, 399).

h) Covid-19 Crisis

During the pandemic, the limitation of certain activities, which could no longer be performed, given the rules of social distancing, had an effect on work-life balance and reshaped the role of work in the economy of the worker's time. Working from home, remotely, the worker:

- allocated a longer time for the activity carried out for the benefit of the employer (although often less productive, in conditions with more frequent breaks than the ones taken when working in the space of the company);
- re-internalised a series of activities that had been outsourced (the “pandemic-haircut” is a notorious example, but also other activities that had previously been carried out by third parties, in exchange for remuneration);

- opted for different budget allocations than before (lower purchases of durable goods, lower spending on services and goods in the entertainment industry, transport, etc., higher expenditure on vocational training, courier services or dedicated to purchasing display-screen equipment, licenses for operating systems and software applications). Also, part of the household expenses no longer exclusively benefitted the family, but also the employer, by allocating a space to carry out activities for their benefit, as well as using electricity and heat for the purpose of providing telework;
- left, in many cases, together with her family, the metropolises and large conurbations, in favour of less populated rural communities, etc.

But probably the most significant mutation in terms of collective labour relations is the isolation, resulting among other things, from the unprecedented expansion of remote work. For instance, according to Eurostat, in the European Union, an average of 12% of employees work from home, but in some member states, such as Finland, the percentage is 25%. Any worker who performs work that is even partially teleworkable has been sent to telework and this change has sometimes been implemented by contract, but often unilaterally by the employer: so-called forced telework (Fana et al 2020). As has been shown (Stickley and Koyanagi 2016), long periods of isolation in custodial care or quarantine for illness has detrimental effects on mental wellbeing. Loneliness is proposed to disrupt social integration, leading to increases in isolation; there is a vicious circle which makes the lonely worker "more segregated into his own 'constricted' space" (Banerjee and Rai 2020).

Working remotely presents its own challenges in terms of collective relations, but it should be noted that non-teleworkable employees also face their own problems. Thus, in the context in which the rules of social distancing were implemented, precisely in order to limit the effects of the Covid-19 pandemic, the employees working in the company were more exposed than those who stayed at home. They took on a number of additional risks, which they could not limit by avoiding contact with colleagues and the work environment. In this context, some authors consider that we are witnessing a new division of workers into white collars and blue collars: workers performing a teleworkable activity and workers performing a non-teleworkable activity.

As for collective labour law, it is still on standby today, alongside the production capacities themselves (against a background that includes blocking collective bargaining; in countries like Romania, for example, all collective bargaining agreements were automatically extended, and collective bargaining did not take place during the pandemic). I mention this because the protection measures specific to labour legislation in each country during the Covid-19 crisis are not strictly labour law rules. Far from regulating the relationship between employer and employee, most are social assistance rules, designed not to minimise the consequences of abusive or exploitative behaviour on the part of the other contracting party, but to distribute the effects of this case of *force majeure* that is the pandemic.

i) Fatigue of the Trade Union Movement

Traditionally, the expression of workers' solidarity is the trade union association: the fruit and at the same time the source of the development of labour law. Today, however, unionisation can be not only difficult, but also uninteresting for new generations of workers, who notice a certain loss of credibility of unions. In Eastern Europe for instance (Dimitriu 2017, 393), a causal link has been observed between, on the one hand, the participation of trade unions in the political arena, the numerous compromises without a mandate from the workers or a certain general perception regarding their rather anti-reformist position, and the decline in the popularity of trade unions, on the other hand.

Many unions show a certain lack of interest in principles such as non-discrimination or equal opportunities and treatment between women and men. Others have become unappealing through xenophobic or anti-immigration demonstrations.

The contemporary worker's need for flexibility also contributes to the phenomenon of avoiding collective forms of organisation, because "unions are often perceived as promoting rigidity, uniformity, job protections, and narrow job definitions" (Hendrickx, 2010, 65).

But if workers, especially digital ones, no longer have such a keen interest in trade union associations, unions do not seem to be very interested in mobilising them either. The unions are tailored to the traditional, typical employee profile. They are difficult to adapt to the profile of new categories of workers, who have atypical contractual arrangements and who use digital technology in their work. In some legal systems, there is little concern for the assimilation of tele-employees, because the "recruitment" of new union members is made easier in the company, in the production units where the employees are grouped, accessible and easy to mobilise. And the new generation of digital workers appears to the unions as a "market" less enticing than the traditional strongholds of stable workers, employed with permanent contracts, from the large industrial concentrations. Somehow, the rejection is mutual because "many such workers believe that unions are not necessary for them to achieve their career objectives" (Gumbrell-McCormick and Hyman 2013, 58), and unions do not immediately identify an interest in approaching digital employees.

3. Conclusions

In the above, I have tried to identify some of the causes of the phenomenon of the loneliness of the employee. In addition to psychological effects, this also generates immediate legal effects related to the diminishing of the collective component of labour law, which many legal systems are now experiencing.

Naturally, the human being is unique: she identifies herself with unique attributes and many of her goals are personal, not shared with others. But this does not mean that identity is not given by a certain sense of belonging to a community. The loneliness of the worker in the contemporary world has psychological as well as legal consequences. We find here one of the causes of the deterioration of the collective bargaining system, in many countries, as well as of the decline of the unionisation rate, reported in even more countries.

As far as workers are concerned, their active participation in associative structures at work, such as trade unions, attracts a wider participation in other types of organisations, non-governmental or political. In other words, solidarity in the workplace urges solidarity outside of it as well. And *vice versa*: the worker who does not interact socially tends to isolate herself in terms of civic activities which are distinct from the workplace. O'Neill and White (2018, 257) show, for example, that declining trade unionism coincides in many regions with declining political voter turnout.

Psychologically, the community fulfils some needs for attachment, approval, and social integration and provides a sense of belonging (Wright 2005). In the context of Amartya Sen's capabilities approach, as stated: "gaining the freedom to do the things that we have reason to value is rarely something we can accomplish as individuals" (Evans 2002, 69).

But collective labour law, the end of which has often been predicted, has a remarkable appetite for reinvention. In a way, the Covid-19 crisis has also had a positive effect: it highlighted the acute need for collective manifestation, and for forms of solidarity that do not stop at virtual relationships but involve the physical presence of each party. And the workers, both distant from the enterprise and from each other, experienced – and continue to do so – an unprecedented type of loneliness, which is likely to generate counter-reactions, post-Covid, from those who then rediscover the usefulness and significance of collective organisation.

Bibliography

Adam, Patrice, *L'individualisation du droit du travail* (Paris: Librairie Générale de Droit et de Jurisprudence, 2005)

Aloisi, Antoni, "Negotiating the Digital Transformation of Work: Non-Standard Workers' Voice, Collective Rights and Mobilisation Practices in the Platform Economy," *SSRN Electronic Journal* 3 (June, 2019): 1-41. http://dx.doi.org/10.2139/ssrn.3404990

Aloisi, Antonio, and Gramano, Elena, "Workers Without Workplaces and Unions Without Unity: Non-Standard Forms of Employment, Platform Work and Collective Bargaining," In *Employment Relations for the 21st Century. Challenges for Theory and Research in a Changing World of Work*, edited by Pulignano, Valeria and Hendrickx, Frank (Alphen aan den Rijn: Wolters Kluwer, 2019), 37-59

Arthurs, Harry, "Labour Law after Labour," In *The Idea of Labour Law,* edited by Davidov Guy, and Langille, Brian (Oxford: Oxford University Press, 2013), 13-30

Banerjee, Debanjar, and Rai, Mayank, "Social isolation in Covid-19: The impact of loneliness." *International Journal of Social Psychiatry* 66, no. 6 (2020): 525-27. https://doi.org/10.1177/0020764020922269

Barnard, Catherine, "The Future of Equality Law: Equality and Beyond," In *The Future of Labour Law: Liber Amicorum Bob Hepple,* edited by Barnard, Catherine, Deakin, Simon, and Morris, Gillian S. (Oxford: Hart, 2004), 213–28

Collins, Hugh, "Flexibility and Empowerment." In *Advancing Theory in Labour Law and Industrial Relations in a Global Context*, edited by Wilthagen, Ton (Amsterdam: Royal Netherland Academy of Arts and Science, 1998), 117-31

Davidov, Guy, "The goals of regulating work: between universalism and selectivity,*" University of Toronto Law Journal* 64, no. 1 (Winter 2014): 1-35. https://doi.org/10.3138/utlj.0115

De Stefano, Valerio, *Non-standard workers and freedom of association: a critical analysis of restrictions to collective rights from a human rights perspective* (Centre for the Study of European Labour Law "Massimo D'Antona", University of Catania, 2015), http://aei.pitt.edu/100462/1/20151111040547_destefano_n123-2015intpdf.pdf

Dimitriu, Raluca, "Provocări ale sindicalismului actual". In *Soluții normative sau jurisprudențiale criticabile prin prisma specificului raporturilor juridice de muncă,* edited by Ţichindelean, Mioara, and Gheorghe, Monica (Bucharest: Universul juridic, 2016), 32-42

Dimitriu, Raluca, "Unsettling trends in collective bargaining today." *Journal of Accounting and Management Information Systems* 16, no. 3 (2017): 389 – 405, http://dx.doi.org/10.24818/jamis.2017.03008

Fana, Marta, Tolan, Songul, Perez, Sergio Torrejon, Brancati, Maria Cesira Urzi and Macias, Enrique Fernandez, *The COVID confinement measures and EU labour markets* (Luxembourg: Publications Office of the European Union, 2020), https://publications.jrc.ec.europa.eu/repository/handle/JRC120578

Freedland, Mark, "Reinforcing the philosophical foundations of social inclusions: The isolated worker in the isolated state," In *Philosophical Foundations of Labour Law*, edited by Collins, Hugh, Lester, Gillian, and Mantouvalou, Virginia (Oxford: Oxford University Press, 2018), 322-36

Gumbrell-McCormick, Rebecca, and Hyman, Richard, *Trade Unions in Western Europe. Hard Times, Hard Choices* (Oxford: Oxford University Press, 2013)

Hendrickx, Frank, "The future of collective labour law in Europe," *European Labour Law Journal*, no. 1 (January 2010): 59-79, https://doi.org/10.1177/201395251000100106

Huws, Ursula, *Labour in contemporary capitalism. What Next?* (London: Palgrave Macmillan, 2019)

Klebe, Thomas, and Heuschmid, Johannes, "Colective regulation of contingent work: from traditional forms to crowdwork – a German perspective," In *Core and Contingent work in the European Union: A Comparative Analysis*, edited by Ales, Edoardo, Deinert, Olaf, and Kenner, Jeff, (Oxford: Hart Publishing, 2019), 185-205

Kovacs, Erika, "Do we really wish you were here? Hungary and distance work," In *Core and Contingent work in the European Union: A Comparative Analysis*, edited by Ales, Edoardo, Deinert, Olaf, and Kenner, Jeff (Oxford: Hart Publishing, 2019), 83-111

Margalioth, Sharon Rabin, "The Significance of Worker Attitudes: Individualisms a Cause for Labor's Decline," *Hofstra Labor and Employment Law Journal* 16, no 1 (1998): 133-65

Myant, Martin, "Trade Union Influence in the Czech Republic since 1989," *Czech Sociological Review* 46, no 6 (2010): 889-912

O'Neill, Martin, and White, Stuart, "Trade Unions and Political Equality," In *Philosophical Foundations of Labour Law*, edited by Collins, Hugh, Lester, Gillian, and Mantouvalou, Virginia (Oxford: Oxford University Press, 2018), 252-68

Pisarczyk Lukasz, “The Crisis of the Collective Bargaining System in Poland,” *International Journal of Comparative Labour Law and Industrial Relations* 35, no. 1 (2019): 57-77

Rubiano, Camilo, “Precarious work and access to collective bargaining. What are the legal obstacles?” *International Journal of Labour Research* 5, no. 1 (2013): 133-151, https://labordoc.ilo.org/permalink/41ILO_INST/1s2ok2m/alma994803663402676

Schubert, Jens M., “Instruments of Labour Law.” In *From Labour Law to Social Competition Law?* edited by Rigaux, Marc, Buelens, Jan, and Latinne, Amanda (Cambridge – Antwerp – Chicago: Intersentia, 2014), 21-33

Stickley, Andrew, and Koyanagi, Ai, “Loneliness, common mental disorders and suicidal behavior: Findings from a general population survey,” *Journal of Affective Disorders* 197, (June 2016): 81–7

Triandis, Harry, Bontempo, Robert, Villareal, Marcelo, Asai, Masaaki, and Lucca, Nydia, “Individualism and collectivism: Cross-cultural perspectives on self-ingroup relationships,” *Journal of Personality and Social Psychology* 54, no. 2 (1988): 323-28. https://doi.org/10.1037/0022-3514.54.2.323

Wright, Sarah Louise, *“Loneliness in the Workplace,”* PhD diss., University of Canterbury, 2005. https://core.ac.uk/download/pdf/35458935.pdf

CHAPTER 21

"BEYOND THE FENCE" – RE-THINKING, RE-SHAPING, RE-COMMODIFYING LABOUR

CALOGERO MASSIMO CAMMALLERI

Setting the Scene

Let us envisage an employment contract/relationship as a fence that functions as a rights and protections regulator and acts as a balancing device against attempts by both the supply-side and the demand-side of the labour market to respectively increase or restrict – and therefore unbalance – the warranties offered by the employment contract/relationship.

In a pre-globalised world, with its relatively simple production chain, that regulator worked very well but now, in the globalised era, it finds itself challenged on both sides of the fence.[1] On the workers' side, they try to push the fence forward, so that any personal work-relationship ("security-full") can be included within, that is, in an area where labour and social rights receive protection. But the regulator is also questioned on the employers' side, for they seek to pull that fence as close as possible to themselves, in order to keep flexible and precarious work relationships away from that protection area.

In dealing with this struggle around the fence, labour law scholars have built an epistemic cage in which they have eventually locked themselves. Looking at the protection against exploitation offered by the employment contract/relationship, rather than at the form of legal subjugation it brings about, on the one hand, those scholars seem to have forgotten the historical

[1] These aspects have not been examined in a dynamic perspective, like that considering outsiders vs. insiders. On the account that they both represent the same side of the market (i.e. supply), how such contraposition can be sorted out is not relevant for the line followed in this work.

process leading to that relationship. On the other hand, by rejecting any association between the employment contract/relationship and economics – which they too hastily and too often identify with mainstream, extreme neo-freemarket doctrine – they nevertheless end up bending the scope of the employment contract to what their ideology devises. Such a mindset legitimises the neoliberal tenet that the employment contract is not to be disposed of, but, in fact, has to be kept in place as it is, with all its Fordist requirements, on the assumption that in a globalised, supposedly post-Fordist world, everything has changed (as indeed it almost has). Counter-intuitively, the abovementioned epistemic cage has ended up providing the market with the best theoretical tool to rebuke any attempt to enlarge the area of labour and social rights protection.

In this light, the phrase "beyond the fence" in the title, does not express the intention of getting rid of the fence, but rather of re-shaping it in order to design a more effective regulator. Therefore, in order to climb over the fence, in this chapter I shall bring forward some proposals based on ideas that I have been developing since 2008 in a number of publications addressing specific aspects of labour, all connected toone another, as flexicurity (and its false promises), the historical origins of labour protections, manipulation of labour terminology, precariousness, AI/robots, and work through digital platforms (Cammalleri 2008, 2012, 2017, 2018, 2019).

I believe we are engaged in a trench warfare involving two opposing forces: the protectionists and the liberalisers. Paradoxically, both wish to tear down the same fence. Protectionists aim at making the definition of people involved in an employment relationship more inclusive, so that protective measures can also be applied to borderline workers – or, at least, to a fair share of them. On the opposite side, the liberalisers' goal is to dismantle the employment contract warranties and restrict their application, excluding borderline workers. The result is an apparent deadlock, but only in its appearance. In the globalised world of labour, vigorous defence of the employment contract as a paradigm of labour and social rights has been the best way for eluding their application. In fact, in one way or another, every employer has found an organisational structure allowing for a substantive control of jobs without the workers' formal control. The same can be said of any type of intermediate regulation.[2]

---

[2] This statement is confirmed by the many cases in which courts have applied criteria to establish whether an individual was actually employed (e.g. test of control and the like), to find out that employment features could in fact be isolated in many (phony) self-employed contracts. Today, the most popular cases are those regarding Uber drivers' and riders' work relationships classification. About the latter, see the

Thus, being the scope of labour law to protect the weakest individuals involved in "personal" work, for the workers to remain steadfast in the trenches means to lose not just a battle, but the whole war, for such a choice eventually effects a heterogenesis of ends. In fact, the employment contract is not a protective device but an oppressive one, since it was created as a substitute for slavery and servitude; a tool in the hands of the few (the employers) against the many (the working people) — a legal device of the price-makers. Similarly, a contract signed with a self-employed person is not a freedom device but an oppressive one, since it is a tool in the hands of the few (this time, the professionals) against the many (the people in general and the employers in particular): again, a legal device of the price-makers.

Going back to the warfare metaphor and the fence, labour law has sought to resist attacks coming from outside: namely, the demands of the free market that, thirsty for the water of economic freedom, has laid siege with their armies and tried to push back the fence. This said, the fence, as well as the employment contract, does not work anymore, and ostensibly so; it has ceased to function as a regulator for those in need of either protection or freedom of enterprise.

The fence failure will be the object of the first part of this chapter, mainly dedicated to labour, where I shall conduct an historical analysis of both law and literature. In the second part, dedicated to value and containing a flipped analysis of law and economics, I shall propose a reshaping of the criteria for the redistribution of labour and social rights among people who live off their work. An interlude on value-labour-price bridges the two parts and channels

---

Italian Foodora case (Trib. Turin – Sez. Lav. ruling of 7 May 2018, no. 778; Court of Appeal of Turin – Sez. Lav. ruling of 11 Jan.- 4 Feb. 2019 no. 26; Supreme Court of Cassation – Sez. lav. ruling of 24 Jan. 2020, no. 1663, forthcoming in English in temilavoro.it VI. 14 2022 – special issue "Old works new exploitation?" for the case see Cammalleri 2019 *Before,* p. 1 ff.). Lawmakers have made uncountable attempts at regulating trespassing across legal schemata. If we keep the focus on the Italian legal system, more than a dozen acts over the last 70 years, including l. no. 741/1959, art. 2 (so-called Legge Vigorelli); l. no. 533/1973, art. 1; l. no. 335/1995 art. 2 commas 25-26la; l. no. 38/2000 art. 5; l. no. 342/2000 art. 34 comma 2; l. no. 142/2001, art. 1 comma 3; d. lgs. no. 151/2001, art. 64; d. lgs. no. 276/2003 (so-called Legge Biagi) art. 43 comma 1; d. lgs. no. 276/2003 art. 61-69 bis; l. no. 183/2010 art. 32 comma 3 lett. b); arts. 39, 50, l. no. 92/2012 (so-called Legge Fornero); l. no. 76/2013; d. lgs. no. 81/2015 (so-called Jobs Act); l. 22 Maggio no. 81; d. lgs. 9 Agosto 208 n. 96. Thanks to the radical change in perspective it has brought about, the Jobs Act has proven to be the best legislative provision of them all, since it does not introduce any intermediate regulation or improvement in non-employee rights, but has put in place a radical remedy for every case in which the self-employed person's autonomy is unclear or not fully proved by the employer.

the discussion into the conclusions. Finally, the chapter ends with a demonstrative anecdote discussing an ILO's paper (Countouris 2019, pp. 2ff.).

Part I – Labour

In the beginning

In the beginning, there was just a word: labour. Its opposite was not non-idleness, but non-labour. Notions such as worker, employee, or self-employed person were unknown. There were, as a matter of fact, "free-lances"[3] and contractors (of what type is irrelevant here), but these words had different meanings than they do today. Labour was the activity of those who "worked." (Free) people did not work, "things" worked (slaves were indeed considered things). Work, "to work", that is, was just a verb – an action whose meaning was close to "to do" or "to make" or "to build." Consequently, the word labour was tied to suffering, poorness of slavery and servitude — an unpleasant term associated with an afflictive condition from which to break away: "in the sweat of thy face shalt thou eat bread, till thou return unto the ground" (Genesis 3:19 KJV. For a different view on this translation and its subsequent literal interpretation, see Cammalleri 2019, pp. 58 ff.).

At the end of the second industrial revolution, labour became a law and order issue (cf. Dickens 1854, *passim*) and a political one (Engels 1845). A number of social measures were taken to tackle labour as a law and order issue[4] whereas, for instance, the *Rerum Novarum* encyclical was delivered to address labour as a political matter (Mazzocchio & Notarstefano 2019, pp. 143 ff. For a different opinion, according to which *RN* was not a social but a political response against socialism, cf. Cammalleri 2019, p. 46). These actions played a key role in the drafting of the 1919 Versailles ILO's Constitution (Versailles's Treaty, Chapter VI, Part XIII), where labour, even if it was not yet an "article of commerce", came to be a special item.[5]

[3] Etymologically "free-lance" stands for "mercenary": "free" as a describer of the lance, lance as a synecdoche of the "lancer". Freelancers were soldiers ready to fight for those who offered them the highest pay, and were not enlisted in an (official) army, but, rather, constitued an army themselves. More precisely, they were free to perform the assigned task with no rule (cf. Massini 2016, p. 118).

[4] Consider, for example, Bismarck's Sickness Insurance Law of 1883, the Accident Insurance Law of 1884, or the Old Age and Disability Insurance Law of 1889.

[5] Annexe, Article 427 "labour should not be regarded merely as an article of commerce," *verbatim.*

However, in order to acquire a dignified meaning, the word labour had to wait for the 1945 Declaration of Philadelphia.[6] From that moment onward, labour could be conceived as something different tfrom a commodity;[7] it could also eventually take on the noble meaning that the word has today. Paradoxically, due to de-commodification of labour tied with the Fordist factory, the discourse on labour has produced the abovementioned epistemic cage.[8] Consequently, it was believed that, on the one hand, only the labour performed within the Fordist schema needed employment guarantees while, on the other, human work not performed within that schema, being neither labour nor a specific commodity, did not deserve any other regulation but the freedom granted by the contractual fiction.[9]

I believe that everything lies in the word. If we start by considering labour as a word, then we can construct a new paradigm of labour (and the law).

A non-legal, non-economic, non-sociological analysis of labour

One of the most in-depth inquiries into the word labour in the present-day labour crisis has been conducted by a dramatist. Stefano Massini's pamphlet, entitled *Lavoro* (which translates the English words "labour", "work", "employment", "service", "job", "task", and several others) is a significant starting point for our discussion. In the foreword, Massini affirms that he is neither a labour law scholar nor a sociologist, but a "worker of words", and adds that in his pamphlet he is not going "to talk of labour as a phenomenon, but as a word" (Massini 2016, p. 8). Further in the text, probably without

---

[6] ILO, Declaration concerning the aims and purposes of the International Labour Organisation (Declaration of Philadelphia), I, "The Conference reaffirms the fundamental principles on which the Organization is based and, in particular, that: (a) labour is not a commodity."

[7] I believe that Marx 1891, *passim*, esp. pp. 55-82, has been overrated with the aim of underestimating the historical perspective of the socio-economic analysis he conducted on workers' salaries. We can say that, wanted or not, a side effect of an anti-Marxist crusade, led through a de-commodification of labour, has been to detach labour from its value rather than from its (market) price.

[8] By mean of a Marxian (not Marxist) analysis, it can be said that, since the (labour as) commodity comes to existence thanks to the worker, the commodification of labour is a tool for the labour's exploiter subjugation. Anti-Marxist opponents adverse the core of Marxian discourse on salary with the idea of the de-commodification of labour. Where commodification was Marxism, de-commodification was simply 'de-marxisation.'

[9] For instance, within the EU, professionals – whatever their income – are subject to market competition rules (collective bargaining restrictions included).

realising the full implications of his reasoning, he states that "playwrights cannot but be sensible in the highest degree to the potential of each word, to the power they have to unleash effects, to create at once relation networks" (Massini 2016, p. 9). That is a crucial point. Labour as a phenomenon comes from the word. It is not the word labour that derives from labour as a phenomenon and describes it. Although this is no longer true today, it was in the beginning. The word creates and defines relational networks; the legal network is just one of its articulations.

As I have shown in *Was not the labour problem the same everywhere?* (Cammalleri 2019, pp. 74ff.) the archetypical structure of labour law and social security in pre-industrial, industrial and post-industrial eras even existed in biblical times. Labour is indeed a universal, immutable, and unique phenomenon, even in its digital dimension. Labour is double-bounded: tied to the notion of effort on one side, and to the necessity of asymmetrical regulations on the other. Because of these double-ended ties, all arguments aimed at abolishing the work relationship along with its labour and social rights have been disproven, since they would be based on the irrelevant assumption that the Fordist era with its relations of production is over. Incidentally, it has to be noted that the idea of avenging (or defending) the employment relationship well beyond the Fordist era fell sick with the same illness. Think, for instance, of the employment contract as a protection device. Its supporters argue that effective and real protections exclusively occur within the employment relationship, or that they cannot be included in or extended to any other legal schema. In consequence, there would be no other way to provide protection to needy workers unless by means of a second employment contract or by expanding it. I argue that this way of looking at the employment contract entails a parallax error,[10] which leads to a misunderstanding.

A misunderstanding of the employment contract function

An employment contract is a universal instrument of subjugation, irrespective of whether it also offers some form of protection. The reason why an employer hires an employee is the latter's subordination. Labour rights, often associated with employment status, are neither a natural effect

---

[10] Parallax (from Ancient Greek παράλλαξις ("parallaxis", "alternation'" is a displacement or difference in the apparent position of an object viewed along two different lines of sight. A measurement is made by viewing some marker's position relative to something to be measured subject to the parallax error if the marker is a distance away from the object of measurement and not viewed from the correct position. Source: https://en.wikipedia.org/wiki/Parallax

nor a purpose of the contract. In fact, since the workers are the price-takers, they do not have the power to claim labour rights, which are not (devices) for the workers' protection, but unwanted consequences of an escapable economic and organisational option.

Ostensibly, first protections did not come along with the standard employment relationship. It was after the employment relationship was established as a surrogate of slavery and servitude that, thanks to their struggles, the workers were able to secure labour protections. Frankly, these protections are patches on market failures and, as we shall see later, a way to rebalance labour value. Lawmakers have introduced protections and used the employment relationship to implement them for the sole reason the employment relationship was already in place and was the only tool available to employers to subjugate the workers.

Such a take on the matter is often neglected. Tests are run in order to establish if a certain worker is an employee or self-employed. This is, at least, what is typically described in academic papers or takes place in the courtroom. When a test fails to verify the existence of stringent criteria for subordination, the worker is left unprotected.[11] Regardless of his/her actual conditions in the real world, he/she is not, by definition, in a state of disadvantage in the legal realm (and *vice versa*). The rationale underlying those tests worked very well as long as the real world and the legal realm were two different ways of looking at and describing the same thing. It worked because the law appropriated the structures of the real world and, in the real world an employer could not help but hire people as employees. On the one hand, cases like these explain how employers have been forced to pay, and therefore fund, the labour and social rights that legally derive from an employment contract. On the other hand, a test of subordination, that is, a reverse engineering device,[12] yields positive results. Consequently, as reverse engineering devices do not work when the source code changes, tests of subordination do not work when the worker's involvement in the production chain changes. In turn, this failure leads to a no man's land where labour and social rights are unknown. Until recently, the phrase "standard employment relationship" (henceforth: "SER")[13] did not exist. Before that

[11] Less radical consequences can be observed in jurisdictions where there are not only employees and self-employed people but also *capitis deminuti* employees, namely workers. Cf. Kenner 2019.

[12] Reverse engineering is a process or method through the application of which one attempts to understand, with deductive reasoning, how a device, process, system, or piece of software accomplishes a task with very little (if any) insight into exactly how it does so. Source: https://en.wikipedia.org/wiki/Reverse_engineering.

[13] A full-time, open-ended ER. It has become the prototype of a standard and fully

time, to use SER to refer to an employment relationship would have been nonsense, as the latter must have certainly fallen into the category of the non-standard employment relationship (henceforth: "non-SER").[14] An employment relationship (henceforth: "ER")[15] was the sole legal device available to both employers and employees who wanted to enter into a relationship regulated by the law. If we consider SER as it is today, that is as a legal device offering full protection to the worker, one may forget that full protection involves costs for the employers — costs that they prefer to avoid. Now, since with a non-SER an employer can avoid those costs, it's worth asking, why didn't a non-SER exist before? From where has it popped up?

It would be easy to respond to the first question by saying that the ER has not always offered full protection (and therefore has never entailed full costs) but has, in fact, done so in the long run. In addition, the answer to the second question lies in that employers have begun avoiding entering an ER when the costs connected to the employment contract start to be unbearable for them in a globalised market. Indeed, in developing nations, where the work-employment relationship maintains its ancestral function and therefore subjugation without rights is deemed legitimate, neo-colonialist multinationals have no reason to invent new non-SER schemata for exploiting people. The ER bare structure adequately serves the purpose: the one dictates, the other obeys.

---

protected work relationship. SER has the advantage of being a useful term for comparison, because it is not tied to a specific jurisdiction. Practically speaking, there is an employment schema at the top of every worker's inverted pyramid of rights. By contrast, every kind of work relationship other than SER is defined as non-SER, which is not suitable for classification purposes. Due to its heterogeneity, non-SER comprises several contractual forms, even including fixed-term contracts, part-time contracts and TWAs – all forms that, for example, within the EU, must receive equal treatment as a comparable (S)ER. However, every jurisdiction features a working relationship, even employment, that is less favourable for the worker than SER. In other words, the non-SER is cheaper than SER practically everywhere.

[14] That is all ERs other than SER. See the previous footnote.

[15] Some legal systems (e.g. the UK and the USA) define the "worker" as "an intermediate category in UK law in between an 'employee' (the UK Employment Rights Act (ERA) 1996, s230(1)(3)(b)) who is obliged to work for an employer when required under her/his contract and has the greatest level of employment protection," and an independent contractor as someone "who works autonomously" (Kenner, *Uber drivers,* passim). Other jurisdictions/legal systems, including Italy, describe the worker differently. For example, in the Italian R. D. L. 13 November 1924, n. 1825, those who were not employees, according to this Act, were considered workers under the Civil Code. Today, this provision no longer applies.

The answers reported above are true but unsatisfactory. In fact, they both refer to the effects produced on the labour market by different worker hiring schemata. They merely take a snapshot of a state of affairs rather than identifying the causes of those effects. Before inquiring into its origins, as mainstream scholarship suggests, one has to investigate the phenomenon itself in a dynamic perspective (as human relational perspectives are). More than a static picture, a film would yield a better picture, a film whose title is...

"Was the labour problem the same everywhere?"[16]

Those who have read George Orwell's *Animal farm*, may remember, at the end of the book, the specious, rhetorical introduction to the final toast among humans and animals — "it was impossible to say which was which." In asking, "was not the labour problem the same everywhere?" we can answer that the labour problem has been the same since the remotest past because labour was, is, and will always be the same everywhere, as Rabbi Phineas'midrash has taught. He said that"

> If a man fell and died they paid no heed to him, but if a brick fell they sat down and wept, and said; 'Woe is us! When will another one come in its stead?'

Now, let's try to make the *midrash* contemporary and turn it into an Industry 4.0 newspaper interview, where "man" is replaced with "rider"; the "brick" is a strike for labour and social rights; and "they" are either employers or enlightened economists. Then, Rabbi Phineas' words would read as follows:

> If a rider fell and died employers paid no heed to him, but if a strike for labour and social rights stopped (the production), enlightened economists sat down and wept, and said: 'Woe is us! What will happen to an innovative sector, needy of flexibility, to accept (some) employers' responsibility? If so, a disaster is approaching!' (my emphasis).

The basic structure of human labour is made up of two positions and one relationship. The positions are "worker" and "employer." The relationship is the law. By means of the law, an owner exploits a slave. By means of the law, a lord exploits a servant. By means of the law, an employer exploits an employee. By means of the law, an entrepreneur exploits a self-employed

[16] Cammalleri 2019.

person. What the positions of the slave, the servant, the employee, and the self-employed person have in common is that they are weaker than their counterparts. What the positions of the owner, the lord, the employer, and the entrepreneur have in common is that they are price-makers (with "price" meaning "conditions"). Although each of the four relationships I have described is regulated by a different law, it is a law nonetheless and, as such, it legitimises the exploitation that derives from the asymmetrical power positions in the market. Without the law, there would be no mutual obedience. Even in the case of slavery and servitude, not everybody can be a slave or a servant: it is the law that states who has to be. The sequence of emancipating shifts – from slavery to servitude, from servitude to the employment contract, from slavery to the employment contract – is not the product of a free choice but an effect of changes in the law. Every shift has replaced an asymmetrical power relationship between two individuals. One may even venture to say that the law gives people the power they do not inherently possess.

Therefore, the employment contract has legitimised the freeman's slavery and the employer's exploitative power. All those protections, such as labour and social rights that today derive from an ER, are not its main goal, but merely secondary historical consequences. Of course, these considerations are by no means tantamount to neglecting the differences, even when hugely relevant, between the different types of laws and relationships described above, but are conducive to defining a specific field of investigation. Those differences, however, more than fragmenting the field of investigation, make it more cohesive: human work is a relational activity, and this relational dimension is connotative of the matter explored here; Keynesian policies, social charters and state constitutions[17] are grounded on this assumption.

Relational traits are indentifiable either between the weak and the strong, or among the weak. As a protection device, the employment contract is a

---

[17] See the first four articles of the Italian Constitution. According to Mortati 1954, pp. 149 ff.: "In order to understand the exact meaning of the constitutional provisions concerning labour and grasp the connections that bind them in a coherent and harmonious system, it is necessary to identify the fundamental principle that inspires them. This principle is enshrined in Art. 2 [of the Italian Constitution], in the part where it recognises the value of any man as an end in himself, therefore bestowing upon him, considered as an essence endowed with natural dignity, rights that are declared 'inviolable' in order to state their invulnerability even before the organs competent on constitutional revision." In a nutshell, labour is not just a right and a duty, but the very essence of mankind. It follows that its import and performative power in funding a society cannot be denied.

revolutionary upheaval in the relationship between the weak (the price-taker) and the strong (the price-maker), an effect of class consciousness and the establishment of a cooperative relationship among the weak. A sum of individual weaknesses becomes a collective non-weakness, which draws its strength from the very action of opposing. In pre-modern history, these (now) stronger groups were named "estates": the third and fourth estates are what interest us here. In the modern age, they took the name of the working-class. In the current post-modern Newspeak era, they coincide with the middle class.[18] In the modern, as well as in the post-modern age, class-consciousness is founded on the conviction of the essential role it plays in labour dynamics, and projects itself towards a future that is brand-new and possible .[19] Also, the deepest and more radical subversion has roots precisely in the state it aims to subvert. The transition does not need leaps; rather, it steps across a bridge walked on by the working-class struggle, that has been increasingly invigorated by the employers' accumulating need for subordination and integration. It has benefitted from the protections granted by (a transformed) employment contract (Cammalleri 2019, p. 75).[20]

So, at the struggle's endgame, labour is always "an issue" to be faced: be it the purpose of a contract or an effect of status. Because labour means to point to a human activity, labour framed in a legal relationship is to point at human exploitation. QED, the law is the tools allowing for this human

[18] In the Newspeak of the post-modern era (or "liquid era", as in Bauman's thought), working-class has been upgraded to middle-class, that is, in a higher position than the "low" class (law animal) of working-class itself. Being middle-class is not low-class, and neo-liberal storytelling convinced them that, if they were middle class, they were no longer "a problem to contend with." This also means, of course, that they can well be left without the old SER's protection. The only thing they needed was more competition and competitiveness. Cf. Bauman, 1998.

[19] According to Cover 1983, pp. 4-68, whose position I endorse, "law may be viewed as a system of tension or a bridge linking a concept of a reality to an imagined alternative – that is, as a connective between two states of affairs, both of which can be represented in their normative significance, only through the devices of narrative. Thus, one constitutive element of a nomos is the phenomenon that George Steiner has labelled 'alternity': the 'other than the case', the counter-factual propositions, images, shapes of will and evasion with which we charge our mental being and, using which, we build the changing, largely fictive milieu for our somatic and our social existence".

[20] One should consider social justice as an ontic character of the human being: like an unexpressed tension of solidarity towards one's neighbour, rather than merely a remedy against an allegedly ineluctable condition of inequality. That tension — which is by no means unavoidable — needs to be liberated from the box of contractual schemata, being the human condition of inequality observed everywhere.

exploitation; all the rest is just idle chit-chat.

Interlude: 'labour price – labour value'

But what about labour taking place outside a legal relationship? Was this a problem as well? Definitely. Stefano Massini reminds us that before any technical discourse (be it the law, economics or even sociology), "our primeval labour was to get food." And since getting food was a matter of survival, labour was, of course, a problem. Sticking to this elementary archetype, we have to agree that "getting food has been replaced by getting the money to buy access to nourishment […] to satisfy primal needs such as shelter […] and [...] clothing […]. Here, more than any other consideration, it is worth recalling Erasmus of Rotterdam's remarks (1511) about Plato's myth of the cave on how the development of social norms could foolishly turn the concrete, pressing need for a cave and a fur coat into fads and fashion" (Massini 2016, pp. 44-45, *passim*).

This could be the reason why rational mankind switched labour for money, and caves for mansions, and fur coats for fashion garments. Also, mankind has consigned to oblivion its animal nature! Food, shelter and clothing should not be dismissedly looked at with contemporary eyes and regarded as minimal needs, with a merely satisfactory remuneration of decent work standards. Food, shelter and clothing were a matter of survival. They were everything, and they were life. *Ça va sans dire,* decent life. They were so essential and satisfying that people put their lives at risk to get them. Exchanging labour in order to get them meant swapping labour for life. So labour was invested with the highest value imaginable – the value of life — that life.

Paradoxically, the switch from procuring food to getting money also had the side-effect of devaluing labour. Neglecting labour's quiddity, on the one hand, has meant to boldly assert its dignity, even that of exploited work, on the account that work is not just a mere means for survival. On the other hand, it has meant to forget that labour, which always has value, does not necessarily also have a price.[21] In other words, we can say that neglecting labour's quiddity has meant to forget that its price must be equal to its value[22] and, as we said above, that the value of labour is life. Moreover,

[21] Whatever the economics theory one follows, in all cases the price has to be referred to the value. There is a wide and heterogeneous array of theories dealing with measuring labour value, but even the marginalists do not deny that labour has value. In the end, even if the application of theories of value yield very different results, the price of labour is never detached from the value of labour.

[22] Here, a caveat is required. Surplus value is being evoked, which has not referred

since the ancestral swap of labour for food took place within the same primordial man, such a swap automatically found its balance point. The ensuing unbalancing was the effect of the exploitation of an individual's work by another individual. It is worth reminding ourselves that there is no unbalancing structural difference between slavery and servitude and (original) employment. The switch to money determines the surplus-value because the price of labour far from the value is an effect of market failures. However, it has been said that labour's value is in itself (Mortati 1958, pp. 173 ff., fn. 10). Universally, the workers' labour is their life. This way, labour is not a commodity. The worker's claims for better working conditions parallel the individual's claims for better living conditions.

In this light, the working-class struggle can be seen as a fight engaged to fill the gap between price and value, that is, between price and life. Two corollaries follow these adamant, although obvious, considerations. First, filling the gap has a dynamic dimension, as dynamic as life (i.e. labour). Consequently, food, caves and fur were labour's primordial fair counter-value, the same as SER-granted labour and social rights are today. Filling the gap has an oppositional and relational dimension, as every legal device for exploiting labour has. Therefore, in the labour exchange dynamic, moving away from labour price towards labour value does not make exploiters happy. In fact, they will oppose as much as they can. In their eyes, the improved conditions resulting in an SER represent unwanted limitations ("rigidities" in Newspeak). Nevertheless, in the Fordist chain, those improved conditions are unavoidable, for they derive from the legal subjugation device. Consequently, employers eventually accept those limitations to their power (including the fact of being no longer the sole price-maker), because they cannot resort to either servitude or slavery – the employment contract has replaced both. No other legal device allows the labour dynamic between the involved parties to be settled. Also, no other device could grant employers the subjugation power they needed. In other words, they were somewhat stuck with the (now limited) employment contract. This also partly explains why labour unions, in control of the labour offer, have been able to negotiate better employment conditions. For employers, not entering an SER would mean the loss of subjugation power, something irreplaceable in a localised Fordist organisational model. As a matter of fact, delocalisation is the best way to avoid entering into an employment contract.

Secondly, the price of labour, be it equal to the value or not or, at least, be it fair or not, is always a financial burden carried by an exploiter –

to Marx's labour surplus value as the sole foundation of the undertaking's profit. Instead, it is the imbalance between value and price, simplifying whatever the adopted value theory one is highlighting.

namely, over time, the owner, the lord, the employer. These burdens, directly and formally carried by employers, have arisen straightforwardly and promptly because they could not erode the living wage. Apparently, the connection between labour cost and salary has not affected the latter. Being the minimum pay, the living wage cannot easily absorb any financial burden. However, the imposition of such burdens – nominally on employers – slows down the growth of the nominal wage. On the other hand, the value of the real wage, and therefore the labour cost grows, because it incorporates the imposed burden and the nominal wage. Hence, the final sum of nominal salary and imposed burdens brings the value of labour close to its price.

The conclusion is that every single improvement of working conditions (whatever it is) has to be considered both an erosion of the surplus-value, from the worker's point of view, and an increase in cost from the exploiters (of whatever kind). An increase in cost corresponds to an increase in price. A price increase corresponds to a sum that, as we said above, is closer to labour value. From the end of the 19th century until the early 1990s, the employment contract was affected by this continuous, periodically resurfacing phenomenon, and has eventually surfaced in the SER schema and, as such, has worked best as a social justice device and a redistributive tool.

As I said earlier, employers have accepted the SER along with its (high) costs, just because it became unavoidable — no philanthropy here. In the best of cases, as soon as organisational requirements offer them the opportunity to avoid the SER, they opt to relinquish this schema. In the worst cases, as soon as inefficient legal provisions allow employers to get around the law, they do it promptly, adopting one of the many non-SER schemata available to them, or resorting to informal and undeclared work. The consequence is that it has been possible to observe a segmentation in the labour market — a separation between decent and non-decent work — even in the face of labour carried out by men and women in an identical way. All possible attempts that have been made to change the employment contract paradigm have failed, irrespective of whether they were aimed at extending labour and social rights beyond the SER scope, or at broadening it, or at enacting an intermediate regulation between dependent and independent contract schemata.

As I shall try to demonstrate in the following pages, all those who have looked at the SER as a protective tool have failed to solve the issue I have described so far, owing to two connected reasons. First, they focus only on the micro-level of the contractual relationship, discussing how to strengthen a single ring of the chain, but lose sight of the whole chain, which could be avoided if they just considered the macro-level of global interconnections.

Indeed, they all propose either to look at a unique (or, in the best cases, no more than two) compulsory legal device, typically a variation on the SER model which in fact can be easily eluded; or, alternatively, to resort to sub-contractors, informal work, and delocalisation in places where no rules and regulations apply.

Second, the SER supporters, so to speak, have remained entangled in the SER paradigm.[23] Indeed, they see the labour and social rights that come along with it as symbolic of the "triumph" of labour value over labour price, as the decent work flag to fly in the face of work exploitation. Unfortunately, the solution they propose is the product of an old-fashioned mindset, for it is linked to a progressive increase of labour price within the SER schema. Price increases for direct taxation are imposed, where the wage constitutes the taxable base. This system, that opts to impose a direct burden where labour is produced, that is on an SER rather than to tax labour indirectly, where it "disappears" (that is, in the global market), has numerous flaws and several traps into which it is very easy to fall.

As previously announced, the story of one of the last and the smartest academic proposals delivered for "defining and regulating for universal work relation"[24] is emblematic of the rationale underlying all those failed attempts.

As we can read in C. Fenweck's foreword to N. Countouris' paper mentioned above, it "was initially commissioned as a research paper input for the ILO's Global Commission on the Future of Work," that is, it was part and parcel of the scholarship on which ILO takes action to ferry labour into the next century. However, for the same undisclosed reasons – which, as the reader easily understands, have nothing to do with the quality of the legal arguments put forward, or the thoroughness of the analysis or, even less so, the nature of its conclusions – that essay was "downgraded" to a generic study on "governance" (although the object of such governance is not clear). Apparently, it was just another academic paper addressing "the important question of legal rules for an evolving and encompassing employment relationship," but certainly not a study on which the ILO would have based its strategy concerning the "Future of Work." Although undisclosed, the actual reason for the paper's devaluation (as can easily be

[23] So, in contrast to what Nicola Countouris, in *Defining,* meant with this expression. He highlights the actuality of the idea of protection included in a schema that is employment-shaped. For this reason, he pushes for a single schema related to all non-professional workers. Immobility in the text refers to the ER's ability to patch the market's distortions.

[24] One means the story about, not the paper of Nicola Countouris, *Defining*, for which see also below.

read between the lines) lies in the word "universal" — a frightening descriptor that could potentially solidify the liquid society (Bauman 1998) in which the ILO's three parties can keep waging their trench warfare. It's a study as brave as a global peace proposal presented to the board of a world association of weapon owners! Or a 'universal hirings' device that would have meant: *no way out* (!).

A gloss. This misleading trajectory is the result of looking at SER as a protection device and not as a tool for subjugation. Now, the tenet that a universal subjugation can be reached without an (expensive) SER and that any subjugation has to have the same treatment of an SER could be terrifying for employers, finally freed from the pressure of labour unions (maliciously, one could probably also add that this would be true for unions, too, for they would fear the loss of their perpetual battleground call, sometimes merely a mantra). End of *arrière-pensée*.

Part II – Value (and traps)

The SER trap

The SER trap looms large in both AI robotisation issues and in work performed in digital platforms. The most common response to these phenomena has been to anthropomorphise machines, considering either robot as employees or digital platforms as employers. A way to tackle the issues arising from these phenomena has been to trace them back to the SER schema – and thereby falling into the trap. Three examples will help elucidate this point. The first two are taken respectively from the EU's "Recommendation on Civil Law of Robotics ((205/2013) INL)),"[25] and from a well-known discussion paper on the so-called "independent worker" (Harris & Krueger 2015). The third one, in chronological order, comes from the abovementioned ILO paper (Countouris 2019). I have examined the first two in *Social Contributions on Robots and New Regulation for Labour Through Digital Platforms? Not Exactly the Right Way, but the Right Question!* (Cammalleri 2021), so it will suffice here to recap the conclusions. As for the ILO paper, its publishing vicissitudes reported above are quite self-explanatory, and I shall refer to it in this section when conducive to the discussion.

> The EU recommendation accurately and agreeably frames the issue: the development of robotics and AI may result in large part of the work now

[25] The proposal presented by MEP Mady Delvaux at the EU Parliament in 2003.

> done by humans being taken over by robots, so raising concerns about the future of employment and the viability of social security systems if the current basis of taxation is maintained, creating the potential for increased inequality in the distribution of wealth and influence.[26]

Unfortunately, a focus on the effects rather than the causes seeks to cancel out the former without removing the latter and, in so doing, falls into a vicious circle. Just think that, when a production plant is robotised, its workforce is squandered in the exact same way as when a firm delocalises a production plant to a state where employment contacts are cheaper and, therefore, offer less protection. To lose one's job due to delocalisation or robotisation makes no difference for the redundant employees.

To refer to the so-called formalisation of employment is irrelevant here. Let us consider the case of a delivery business that changes its traditional organisation, namely one where it is the employees who perform the services, into a freelance rider service working through an app. For the former drivers, who now become redundant due to the digitisation of services, it makes no difference whether they've lost their employment and social security protections to outsourcing or to their transformation into independent contractors, even when they are subsequently re-hired as self-employed individuals. In both cases, the SER protection has been greatly undermined. Of course, at the level of the firm's organisation, a company transforms ERs into either robots or digital work because these are cheaper than employees and, at the same time, grant employers a steady control on workers.

Historically, situations of this kind have followed a predictable pattern: a firm hires workers through the (primeval) employment contract (i.e. the subjugation device, merely), which is the only legal hiring device available. Then, since employers cannot escape the contract conditions, a process is activated whereby labour price gets closer to labour value. From the employees' point of view, as well as the perspectives of unions and labour scholars, the situation I have just described constitutes an improvement in terms of labour and social rights. Conversely, employers see it as an increase in costs. The increase in labour and social rights corresponds to an increase in employment contract and labour cost, hence a decrease in surplus-value. Thus, as the gap between labour price and labour value narrows because of SER – the best protective tool in everybody's mind – the employers shun away from it, or move to countries with weaker SER regulations, which results in an increase in the cost of the SER schemata adopted locally. Both

[26] The quotation is from the mentioned proposal. What follows re-elaborates the points I made in Cammalleri 2021.

attempts on the employers' part, especially if combined, are actions put in place to regain surplus-value, to again widen the gap between labour price and labour value. As a consequence, the introduction of direct burdens, financial or of another nature, that either extend labour rights and social security to other types of labour contracts, or expand the field of action of SER, would most likely only induce companies to delocalise in countries where there are no, or fewer, burdens, or where non-SER hiring is made easier and cheaper.

In recent times, a fulgid example of the trend of solving issues with ad hoc regulations has been proposed in what is arguably the most cited discussion paper on the matter: *A Proposal for Modernising Labour Laws for Twenty-First-Century Work: The "Independent Worker"* (Harris & Krueger 2015). According to its authors, the introduction of the contractual schema of the "independent worker," that is, of a third intermediate schema between that of the employee and the independent contractor (a device they are urged to adopt), should allow the re-shaping of protections for those who are not workers or employees. The discussion paper refers to US labour law, employment law, social security, and to the binary classification of non-professional personal performance, either in terms of workers or employees. This depends, among other factors, on the mutuality of obligations or lack thereof. Since the data used in the paper are specific to the US, one may think that to make here a closer commentary may not be fruitful. On the contrary, I argue that the study of the very structure of the article — on the account that it represents an excellent example of the typical mistake caused by the introduction of an intermediate regulation — helps define, by way of contrast, the terms of the issue.

When a production model works well, even with a degree of legal subjugation lower than that required by an SER, employers hire independent contractors with contracts containing clauses that include specific but, at the same time, loose duties, and that resemble or even mask employment contracts whose requirements would not pass the subordination test. As a consequence, troubles with classification lie exactly at the border between the description of employees' traditional duties and the clauses included in the contracts of the (new) independent contractors. The issue lies at the border. The introduction of a third contract – more protective and therefore more expensive than that of independent contractors' – would produce a duplication of relationships. One would be between the employee and the intermediate/third-contract; and the other between the intermediate/third-contract and independent contractor. As for the employers, since they prefer a lower level of subordination than that offered by either an employment contract or an intermediate one, they would be urged to invent new organisational models that do not include any intermediate contractual schema. It is not by chance that the intermediate area is also called the "grey zone." However, even if grey solves the black and white dilemma, it does not solve the issue. Moreover, since the colour grey has hundreds of shades, intermediate regulation would complicate the dilemma: which grey?

Classifications of both old and new regulations – that is, *ex-post* and *ex-ante* solutions, respectively – operate at the micro- and contractual levels. Both types of regulations have, explicitly or not, the employment contract as their touchstone. On the one hand, they both display criteria under which labour could be subsumed. On the other, they must both refer to a salary to calculate taxes and social contributions to fund rights and protections. However, these two classes of parameters are often missing. The inclusive criteria related to the employment contract as well as to the intermediate one and aimed at expanding protections, quickly become exclusive tools, because they are static and depend on production levels and local regulations. In a phony work relationship, the salary is often concealed, as is the real nature of the contract. Nevertheless, concealed or not, a salary is generally far too low to help the employee afford social security and private insurance outside of a genuine SER.

The pair of opposite relationships, namely the self-employed relationship and the ER, sustain one another, and depend on the historical context in which they were conceptually developed. As rights regulators, they were regarded very differently than they are today. In fact, the self-employment contract was designed to protect individuals who were free and powerful, certainly more powerful than firm/employers. The employment contract was envisaged to exploit individuals otherwise doomed to starvation, like slaves and servants. Have things changed nowadays? No, they have not. But a clarification is needed here. The comparison between then and now should not be made on the grounds of the measure of freedom: rather, it is about who is the price-maker or, on the opposite side, the price-taker. In theory, neither the price-maker nor the price-taker should exist. Their very presence signals a market distortion (and failure), and observing them at work is to look at the worst kind of exploitation. They describe a binary world where everything had a rule, a place and a goal.

Self-employed individuals had no legal protection, for they did not need it — they were self-protected. All the protections involved in an ER instead depended on employees' needs. In the above-mentioned binary world, the ER schema was not only cheap, but cheaper than other schemata, such as the self-employed one. Only on such preconditions could there develop an employment contract. As long as the self-employed individuals were strong enough to be able to charge fees higher than an employee's salary, they could keep their power and self-protection. That binary divide, on the one hand, depended on a binary setting of skills: labour and professional. On the other, it was connected to a specific demographic dimension: many unskilled workers, *vis-à-vis* few professionals (workers). Finally, skilled and unskilled individuals were non-fungible and hence, not replaceable.

What we have to focus on now is the fundamental structure of a system where the value of the work's outcome was incorporated into the global market, regardless of the place and the modalities in which that work (directly or indirectly human) was incorporated into the goods and services exchanged in the market. Furthermore, since the labour market, broadly conceived, and goods and services market (mutually communicating) were sections of the same (local) market, by consequence, the price of a product or service included the social costs for protecting working people. As a matter of fact, in both cases, the labour price was close to labour value.

This fundamental structure acted as the overarching frame, but two changes have occurred within. First, delocalisation has solved the issue of the high cost of unskilled employment. Secondly, the problem of the expense of skilled workers has been tackled with an organisational control's device, namely, by hiring self-employed contractors. These solutions have brought about a "dissociation" in the market: the solution applied to labour issues has produced labour cost; while that concerning goods and services has produced labour value. This dissociation is another trap that comes from an adverse selection. With Fordism, the SER was able to bring the labour value closer to its price. In post-Fordism, it does not. Consequently, taking SER as a paradigm of protection, rights selection, or anti-distortive tool effects an adverse selection.

The adverse selection trap

The question of how the SER has become a selector of labour rights is connected to the question of how it has been assigned the demanding job of protecting the weakest. In the binary world sketched above, an employment contract was the sole legal device in place to avoid the unfair exploitation of the weakest, whose destitute condition, in turn, depended on their low skills and inability to work as self-employed. To be sure, in theory, in a world like that there would not be needy people, except, of course, the unemployed. What does happen, then, with the shuffling of jobs and contractual schemata? When skilled, low-skilled and unskilled jobs are fungible, regardless of the contractual schema, unskilled jobs are left out of the SER and needy people become exploitable by means of non-SER schemata, even with the law's complacent consent.

The employment contract and well-functioning working models in general, instead of being rewarded as fair social practices, have been de facto indirectly penalised by lawmakers. As a matter of fact, the employment contract is affected by an adverse selection. To illustrate this perverse effect, it can be useful to refer to an Italian case concerning universal protection and the labour market.

A few remarks before we enter into the heart of the matter: Italy's national health service (SSN) is universal, meaning that it offers full coverage free of charge to all individuals, because a right to healthcare is a fundamental right pursuant to Art. 32 of the Italian Constitution. As such, the SSN has to be funded by general taxation. However, before this universal provision was implemented, the SSN was social, insurance-based and linked to social contribution and a working relationship (which is what currently happens in most parts of the world). So, the constitutional framing of the right to health as a universal protection came at the end of a process of transformation for its funding system: from a system based on social contribution to a tax-based one. At the end of this process, IRAP was introduced. IRAP is the tax, the revenue from which funds half of SSN expenditure; the other half is covered by general taxation.

The way in which IRAP works is emblematic of that perverse adverse selection. All firms with employees must pay this tax which, to put it very briefly, is based on the labour cost borne by the firm. IRAP works as if it were a tax on the ERs. When an employer swaps an SER for a non-SER, (or opts for informal or even undeclared workers), he or she does not have to pay IRAP. Still, independent contractors, informal, and undeclared workers have, as individuals, the same right to health as do employees. In the aftermath of that swap, however, IRAP is not paid on the former employees' wage in the way it would have been if salaries had been paid instead. Moreover, for the most part, IRAP revenue is levied on labour-intensive sectors (Oropallo & Proto 2005, 2006),[27] as happens in a social-contribution system. The same effects derive from every tax and social contributions linked to an ER and calculated on salaries. An in-depth analysis of labour price will show in a more precise way the adverse selection brought about by the imposition of a direct burden like IRAP.

The labour price has three main descriptors: the labour cost, the net wage, and the so-called "fiscal wedge" (the variance – mathematical Δ – between the labour cost and the net wage). The labour cost is how much an employer pays for labour for a single product unity; it includes gross salary,

[27] I would like to thank the authors for providing me with these difficult-to-find papers.

social contributions, taxes on labour, and indirect wages and benefits. This amount, like any corporate tax, is wholly reversed in the price of goods or services, so that, in the end, it is paid by the end consumer. The net wage is how much an employee has in his or her pocket after producing a single product unit; it also represents their purchasing power and the level of a decent life in the architectural frame of labour swapped for money, as described above. The so-called "fiscal-wedge" is the difference between labour costs and the employee's net wage. Theoretically speaking, the "fiscal-wedge" is made up of two components: tax and social contributions levied on the employer, and tax and contributions borne by the employee. In practice, however, the economic effect of both tax and social contributions constitute a portion of labour value. Indeed, the taxes and contributions that the employers pay in relation to the wages paid reduces the net wage, slows down its tendency to increase, and matches with the increase in labour productivity.

As it is intuitive, the higher the employment level, the lower the total divide between labour cost and labour value. The narrower the divide, the higher the labour cost is. The higher the labour cost, the lower the need for protection. Conversely, the lower the labour cost, the higher the general tax revenue needed for social protection. As a consequence, the employers with the lowest divide are those who contribute the most to social protection, while those who enjoy the best labour price produce the highest levels of exploitation. In conclusion, every issue can be traced back to the divide.

This divide has already been classified as "social pollution" (Cammalleri 2008 & 2012) which, in turn, has been likened to environmental pollution. When referred to a public good, pollution is a negative externality. The polluter, in our case, is an employer whose activity cannot be stopped, hence its polluting effects cannot be wholly avoided (as with a fossil fuel electricity plant); out of metaphor, the employer is exploiting a good that he or she does not own, since it belongs to society. This said, the law does not forbid a polluting employer, but seeks to internalise the externality by placing a burden on the polluter. If we apply this reasoning to labour and social protections, we can look at the SER as an internalising tool. By contrast, a non-SER becomes a pollution device, a negative externalising tool.

The t-shirt buyer example will help elucidate this point.

Some people are simultaneously workers (for example, in a T-shirt factory) and consumers (of those same t-shirts). They have rights both as consumers and as workers. Rights are not free; in fact, they are costly. Their cost is incorporated into the price of, for instance, a t-shirt, so it becomes the price of rights. While it is clear that it is the t-shirt buyer who pays the price of rights, it is not immediately evident to whom that quota of price — that is, the price of rights — is paid. This piece of information is somewhat hidden because the price is paid to three separate entities: first, to the employer, who uses a portion of the price to compensate the costs borne by the company for its employees' welfare: second, to the social insurance institutions, to which employers transfer a portion of the employees' salary (social contributions); and third, to the government, to which tax-payers transfer a portion of the employees' salary (taxes on the wage and the work).

This system of relation articulates as follows. A consumer pays the price of a good (e.g. a t-shirt) to a company. The company then splits the price into two parts: the first pays off the costs borne, the second is the profit. In turn, costs are distributed among departments to cover all sorts of costs: R&D investments, raw materials, labour cost, taxes, etc. Labour costs and taxes are respectively distributed among three different elements: finance, labour and social rights, and salaries and general tax revenues. All these three elements are SER-related. An employer in a SER has to finance labour and social rights. In contrast, an employer who has entered a contract schema which is different from the SER, produces little or no revenue for funding labour and social rights.

Still, individuals in a non-SER schema (who, in a Fordist plant, would have been in an SER) have their needs, which are going to grow as they age, independently of their being (or not) employees. Instead of being addressed through employment contract regulations, those needs are faced in two different ways: by means of the workers' solidarity (with an increase of the level of social contributions which is then diverted to under-protected workers), or by an increase in general revenue to tackle the increase in the level of social assistance (an increase that would have not taken place if the needy people in a non-SER schema had been in an SER).

Two corollaries follow. First, to keep a certain level of general protection steady, the labour cost differential between SER and non-SER is paid by the people who have entered an SER and by the tax-payers. Second, as non-SERs are still rather competitive, employers will try to swap SERs for non-SERs in order to fund their competitiveness to the detriment of those actors who use SER and the tax-payers. As a consequence, with a decreasing level of employees, to maintain the same level of labour and social rights for the employees, the cost of SER increases. So the higher the level of non-SER employees, the higher the cost of SER; an increment in competivity granted by non-SERs schemata will be matched by the adoption of a lower number SER schemata.

Some concluding (albeit intermediate) remarks. Any action affecting the SER schema triggers a vicious circle that simultaneously discourages employers from entering an SER and negatively effects competitiveness. This trigger comes irrespective of an enlarging area of its application; as an explanation of its typical protections toward other labour schemata, an "intermediate regulation", eventually becomes a 'universalisation' of the ER's concepts.

Therefore, everything is in the labour value divides. It follows that a reduction in labour value division cannot be pursued through an SER schema, namely catching non-SER schemata regulations without falling into a new trap — that of the labour-value divide.

The labour-value divide trap

From what we have just discussed, three considerations follow. First, the labour-cost labour-value divide is precisely the measure of the social protection divide. Second, those with a lower need for protection pay more for social rights, and *vice versa*. Third, *ceteris paribus*, the labour-value divide, stimulates unfair competition between "good" employers with a high-rate of SERs and "bad" employers with a high-rate of non-SERs operating in the same market.[28] Such an unfair competition produces a negative externality exploited by "bad" employers, as the latter do not pay any internalisation costs.

The three traps we have illustrated so far clearly show two things: first, that the struggling attempts at introducing work regulation aimed at tracking down and locating labour value in order to reduce the labour-value divide are ineffective, if not detrimental; second, that in a globalised market the employment contract is not a protection schema. So, it cannot be a valid "selector."

Free contracts with burdens on the added value of labour

A provisional conclusion is that schemata of legal contracts are not the solution – at least when the protective schema is more expensive than the others. Also, to improve the contractual conditions for the few who are already in a protected employment relationship will not work either,

[28] "Good" and "bad" employers are working definitions moulded on "good work" (and by contrast "bad work"), a phrase found in Crouch (2019), p. 92 who, in turn, quotes Taylor 2017. My lexical option is based on the binary track that he proposes in his work (see, for instance, pp. 40, 120, 121, 123, 127) which precisely matches the same conceptual framework I initially traced in the paper "Beyond Flexicurity," and later defined in the article "Flexicurity as" and used in other following publications (such as "Precarious Work").

because transformations of such a kind would eventually lead the employers to relinquish the improved contract in favour of stipulating less protective ones – precisely as happens with the SER. Moreover, enhancing labour rights and protections would entail a raise in costs: it would indeed trigger avoiding strategies that would eventually neutralise those measures.

Consequently, an effective solution to narrow the labour-value divide is to obtain an increase in value without affecting the regulation and, in so doing, leave employers free to hire through "good contracts" or "bad contracts." Every burden affecting regulation directly leads to its avoidance. This is why alternative solutions should be put in place — solutions that would levy non-regulated schemata.

Whatever labour value theory one likes to embrace, it cannot be denied that labour has value because it is only that which has value that can be exchanged and remunerate itself, as is the case with labour. Hence, if "labour is not a commodity" reminds us that labour is life, then labour value must be considered life value. Nonetheless, that "labour is a commodity" – owned by workers and solely by them – reminds us that labour is de facto tradeable, although solely by workers. It follows that, in the complex (and liquid) society, it has to have not a free price, but a decent life exchange value.[29]

Conclusively, as the Italian Constitution, whose Art. 4 defines labour as a duty/right, labour in the post-modern, globalised, and liquid era should be defined as a "commodity/non-commodity." To retrieve the dynamic character of labour as commodity means to give back effectiveness to its ontological nature of a tradeable non-commodity. After all, for economic efficiency it mean giving in to equity and social justice, by means of the very same economic devices used to disrupt the working people's class consciousness, and talk them into embracing the new servitude. This is a language manipulation causing the new poor to be happy "to be" middle-class.[30]

---

[29] See, for instance, Art. 36 of the Italian Constitution, which reads: "Workers have the right to a remuneration commensurate to the quantity and quality of their work and in all cases to an adequate remuneration ensuring them and their families a free and dignified existence."

[30] Huxley wrote the following to G. Orwell in 1949: "the lust for power can be just as completely satisfied by suggesting people into loving their servitude as by flogging and kicking them into obedience […], the nightmare of Nineteen Eighty-Four is destined to modulate into the nightmare of a world having more resemblance to that which I imagined in Brave New World (London: Chatto & Windus, 1932). [...] The change will be brought about as a result of a felt need for increased efficiency." Forty years later, Battiato (1971 & 1972) recalls Huxley's Brave New World: "Son felice di essere un beta / Il mio giorno non è duro / Dentro il mare mi posso vestire / Dai gamma e dai delta / Farmi ubbidire / Quando gioco non rompo mai niente / La violenza non ho nella mente."

Conclusions – Regulating Universal Protections

The regulation of work relations frames labour and social rights within specific regulations under a microeconomics balance. They remain considerations or remunerations of a way to work, so they remain a labour price. Again, changing its way will change its price. Universal work protections are human rights that identify labour value instead. Therefore, let the price change; it will not change the value.

It has been demonstrated that, owing to a misunderstanding about the contract's purpose, contractual schemata (as well as their re-shaping) are ineffective measures. Being exploitative in its very essence, a contract cannot have as its primary purpose to provide for the workers' lack of protection. In fact, such an effect is more to be likened to waste: as in chemistry, waste is an undesirable polluting by product (hence, a cost), so labour and social rights are an organisation's undesirable costs/effects. So, not unlike chemists that find a new process that avoids waste, and therefore switch to a better molecule, so an employer avoids labour and social rights costs by changing hiring contracts. Consequently, to find a new "wasteful" molecule, namely a new contract guaranteeing a high level of labour and social rights, is perfectly useless. A better solution is to have polluters clean up their mess or pay for their polluting. Therefore, it is possible to finance labour and social rights for weaker workers outside of any contractual schema by introducing an anti-pollution tax.

This way, there would be no need to find a universal work relation to extend the realm of protected workers, forcing employers to adopt a unique contractual schema moulded on the employment contract. Indeed, it would be the same as abolishing any other labour schema because, whether employers use it or not, a contract is, and by definition remains, at their disposal. Employers can dump any labour rights by discharging the power on the ground, namely, not using that contractual schema. Conversely, universal work protections that do not find their rationale in a contractual schema are not free for employers to use and, when financed with taxes, are (as everybody knows) "as certain as death."

Conclusively, this way, the labour-value is always encapsulated in the value chain, irrespective of the labour regulation schemata, so that the original scope of the asymmetrical regulation is granted, and so that, finally, giving value back to any labour, irrespective of contracts,[31] is the value of a decent life!

---

[31] *Addendum* – In this last footnote, I draw a possible implementation of funding labour and social rights through an SSFT (non-wage social security fake tax), Cammalleri 2018. As it is not theoretical, I believe that this *addemdum* fits well in here rather than in the text. Using this approach does not turn the philosophical

perspective of rewriting the rules of protection into an odd policy suggestion. Simultaneously, by leaving its content here, I try to prevent the easy allegation of presenting a purely imaginative utopia. The example of what an SSFT could implement about labour and social rights comes from the rider's issue. This issue (which can be extended to Uber drivers too) is well known. It is the mirror of today's work organisation. Moreover, it is a high-tech version of the so-called informal work dilemma. Let us change "informal" for "marginal" and "young people," and "under-developed countries" with "emerging and expanding sector." The dilemma will not change. Such a dilemma is an exemplary structure that shows the tension between the labour-value labour-price gap and tools for reducing that tension. As has been seen, regulations are ineffective devices. Furthermore, the employment contract is not always an answer. Since an employee has many more duties than a self-employed person, any riders dislike employment status, preferring the significant degree of freedom that comes with being self-employed. Nonetheless, on the one hand, these riders would like to enjoy some of the labour and social rights to which employees are entitled without losing their degree of freedom. On the other hand, delivery companies would comply with those rights as long as they had no impact on contract classification, for they need to maintain a certain degree of control. Besides, there are other cases where both delivery companies and riders agree to stay in an employment arrangement even within the same company. At this point, one should highlight three things that are in common in both arrangements. Firstly, the substantive rider's job is the same. It means that the job, as such, does not define the arrangement. Secondly, once the rider has accepted carrying out one single delivery, the company needs to control the performance. Given the company's potential liability towards both customers and restaurants, and that the contracts have the same scope, namely to carry food from point A to point B, such a control is closer to quality and compliance control of the object of the performance rather than a process control in itself. Consequently, this form of control is unsuitable for defining employment control, and suitable for service scope under a self-employed schema. It means that such a control cannot define the schema or be a labour and social-rights selector. Eventually, whatever is the contractual arrangement under which a rider performs her job, she has no control of the time and accepted delivery requirements. Waiting time is the main issue. Pathways and traffic conditions are the secondary ones. Taking a closer view, this is the real difference between the two schemata. The risk of wasting time (and to a certain degree the moral hazard) lies on the employer's side, in the employment relationship. It means that the value of the waiting time is encapsulated into salary, namely the labour price. Such a portion of the value and price is counterbalanced by control. In this case, quality and process controls are blurred. In a parallel way, the wasting time risk (but not the moral hazard one) lies on the rider's side, in the independent contractor relationship. Since the rider does not manage time, but the app does, the value of waiting and wasting time are not encapsulated into pay-per-delivery, namely labour price. Such a portion of the value, however, is not counterbalanced by a rider's freedom to maintain the control over her job. The regulation schema cannot neutralise the gap between labour-value and labour-price. There, the SSFT and umbrella companies take the field. Non-profit

Bibliography

Battiato, Franco, “Fetus,” In *Fetus,* edited by Franco Battiato (Roma: Bla Bla, 1971)

Battiato, Franco, “Beta,” In *Pollution,* edited by Franco Battiato (Roma: Bla Bla, 1972)

Bauman, Zygmut, *Globalization: The Human Consequences* (Cambridge: Polity Press, 1998)

Cammalleri, Calogero Massimo, "Social pollution: from flexibility to exploited work (Heretical ideas about flexicurity to tackle undeclared work)," *Annali della Facoltà di Economia area giuridica* anno LXII (Biblioteca della Facoltà di Economia dell’Università di Palermo: 2008): 141-198

Cammalleri, Calogero Massimo, “Flexicurity as a measuring leakage protection of workers: between ‘social pollution’ and ‘total security’” *temilavoro.it*, vol. 4, no. 1 (2012): 1-29

Cammalleri, Calogero Massimo, “Social rights for informal workers – cost-efficiency included. Un[der]-protected workers,” paper presented: 'Social Pillar' – Social Europe? - International Labour Law as a stimulus for better social integration (Hugo Sinzheimer Institute for Labour Law & Institute for Labour Law and Industrial Relations in the European Union (IAAEU): Trier, 22 September 2017, manuscript)

Cammalleri, Calogero Massimo, “From IRAP to SSnWFT (a heretical idea to fix precariat),” *d/SEAS Working Paper,* no. 18-7, (2018), https://papers.ssrn.com/sol3/papers.cfm?abstract_id=3272149

---

organisations, broadly conceived (e.g. either umbrella companies or work cooperatives) can be granted tax exemptions, funded by diverting the SSFT revenue, for having provided labour and social rights to the associated riders, an employer would not have hired the self-employed. In this way, virtual tax exemption is put in place. On the one hand, there is a clear identification of good work and bad work (the phrase, “good employer” (or work) from Crouch 2019, *passim* but mainly pp. 91ff. However, this concept, and the following ones he develops, including the solution proposal, had already been elaborated and delivered since 2008 in all works by this author listed in the bibliography.) The former became cheaper than the latter. In other words, it means that the former does not pay for the surplus-value the latter generated. Correspondingly, the latter does not exploit the surplus-value generated itself, leading to unfair competition at the former's detriment. Consequently, the labour-value labour-price divide will close. On the other hand, both delivery companies and riders keep the surplus value: the former to have not a stiff staffing level without losing deliveries' control; the latter to work when, how much and where they like, without losing labour and social rights.

Cammalleri, Calogero Massimo, "Was not the labour problem the same everywhere. 'Homo ad laborem nascitur et avis ad volatum'!" (Prolegomena per uno studio del diritto del lavoro tra Bibbia e letteratura)," In *Le dimensioni del lavoro al tempo del Jobs Act,* edited by Cammalleri, Calogero Massimo (Roma: Aracne, 2019), pp. 17-75

Cammalleri, Calogero Massimo, "Precarious work and social protection: between flexicurity and social pollution," In *Precarious Work. The Challenge for Labour Law in Europe,* edited by Kenner, Jeff, Otto, Marta, Florczak, Izabela (Cheltenham: Edward Elgar Publishing Limited, 2019), pp. 38-53

Cammalleri, Calogero Massimo, "Before and after the Foodora Italia case. New scenarios for (fake self-employed and) digital workers?" *temilavoro.it,* vol. 11 (2019): pp. 1-20

Cammalleri, Calogero Massimo, "Vecchie risposte a nuovi problemi: l'antropomorfizzazione dei robot e degli algoritmi. Osservazioni critiche e una proposta eterodossa: l'IVISS," In *Il diritto del lavoro e la sua evoluzione. Scritti in onore di Roberto Pessi,* edited by Fabozzi, Raffaele, Massara, Giuseppe Sigillò (Bari: Cacucci. 2021): pp. 417-440

Countouris, Nicola, "Defining and regulating work relations for the future of the work," *GOVERNANCE Working Paper series,* February (Geneva: ILO, 2019): 1-28

Cover, Robert, "Nomos and narrative," *Harvard Law Review*, 97 (1983): 4-68

Crouch, Colin, *Will the gig economy prevail?* (Cambridge: Polity Press, 2019)

Dickens *Hard Times (for this time)* (London: Bradbury and Evans, 1854)

Engels, Friedrich, *Die Lage der arbeitenden Klasse in England* (Leipzig: Otto Wigand, 1845), translated *The Condition of the Working Class in England*, open access at https://www.marxists.org/archive/marx/works/1845/condition-working-class/index.htm accessed March the 19th, 2018

Erasmus of Rotterdam, Desiderium, *Moriae encomium* (Basel: Kupferstichkabinett, 1511), translator unknown, *The Praise of Folly* (New York: P. Eckler, 1922)

Harris, Seth D. and Krueger, Alan B, "A Proposal for Modernising Labor Laws for Twenty-First-Century Work: The 'Independent Worker'," *The Hamilton Project*, Discussion Paper 2015-10, December (2015), at http://www.hamiltonproject.org/assets/files/modernizing_labor_laws_for_twenty_first_century_work_krueger_harris.pdf, accessed 29 April 2018.

Huxely, Aldous, *Brave New World* (London: Chatto & Windus, 1932)

Huxely, Aldous, "Letter to George Orwell, October 1949," In *Letters of Note* (Wrightwood; 1949) at http://www.lettersofnote.com/2012/03/1984-v-brave-new-world.html, accessed April 29, 2018

Kenner, Jeff, "Uber drivers are 'workers': the expanding scope of the 'worker' concept in the UK's gig economy," In *Precarious Work. The Challenge for Labour Law in Europe,* edited by Kenner, Jeff, Otto, Marta, Florczak, Izabela (Cheltenham: Edward Elgar Publishing Limited, 2019), pp. 38-53

Leo the XIII, *Rerum Novarum* (Encyclical of Pope Leo XIII on capital and labour) (Vatican City: 1891).

Mankiw, Gregory N, *Principles of economics* (Fort Worth, Texas: Dreyden Press, 1998), p. 254

Marx, Karl, *Lohnarbeit und Kapital* – (1847-1849), 1891, translated into Italian, *Lavoro salariato e capitale.* (Rome: Ed. Riuniti, 2006)

Massini, Stefano, *Lavoro* (Bologna: Il Mulino, 2016)

Mazzocchio, Fabio, and Notarstefano, Giuseppe, "Lavoro e sviluppo umano nell'orizzonte dell'ecologia integrale," In *Le dimensioni del lavoro al tempo del Jobs Act,* edited by Cammalleri, Calogero Massimo (Roma: Aracne, 2019), pp. 143-158

Mortati, Costantino, "Il lavoro nella Costituizione," *Il diritto del Lavoro* (1954), pp. 149-180

Oropallo, Filippo, and Proto, Gaetano, *L'impatto di alcune misure di riduzione del cuneo fiscale sulle imprese e sulle famiglie* (Roma: Istat, 2005, manuscript)

Oropallo, Filippo, and Proto, Gaetano, *L'impatto sulle imprese della riduzione degli oneri contributivi: una simulazione* (Roma: Istat, 2006, manuscript)

Taylor, Matthew, *Good Work: The Taylor Review of Modern Working Practices* (London: Department for Business, Energy & Industrial Strategy, 2017)

CHAPTER 22

CAPITALISM, DOUGHNUT ECONOMICS, *ELDORICA* AND THE ROLE OF LABOUR LAW

BERYL TER HAAR

1. Introduction

Since the financial and economic crisis in 2008, the call for change in the current economic system has been growing. It is a call that has grown stronger with societal pressure concerning the climate crisis, for example by children's worldwide "climate strikes," but also with judicial cases calling on governments to take more serious actions.[1] The Covid-19 pandemic has further strengthened this call as it has exacerbated pre-existing inequalities in many countries[2] that are contributing to a failing (neo-liberal) growth-based economic system (cf. Busher 2021, among many others). In 2008,

[1] E.g. among others: Urgenda case in the Netherlands, accessed 23 February 2021, https://www.urgenda.nl/en/themas/climate-case/; the Irish citizen case forcing the Irish government to take action on the climate, accessed on 23 February 2021, https://www.euronews.com/green/2020/07/31/irish-citizens-win-case-to-force-government-action-on-climate-change; the case of Portuguese children against 33 states, accessed on 23 February 2021, https://www.theguardian.com/law/2020/sep/03/portuguese-children-sue-33-countries-over-climate-change-at-european-court, and the case against Shell, accessed 28 June 2021, https://www.euronews.com/green/2021/05/26/shell-ordered-to-cut-co2-emissions-by-45-in-landmark-climate-case.

[2] E.g. in relation to health (https://jech.bmj.com/content/74/11/964.full); social position (https://ajph.aphapublications.org/doi/full/10.2105/AJPH.2020.305766); learning opportunities (https://www.sciencedirect.com/science/article/pii/S0276562420300603); and long-term effects (https://onlinelibrary.wiley.com/doi/full/10.1111/1475-5890.12232?casa_token=OVh1qgDkGmwAAAAA%3AWeFh14umCKnafoa3nRqamOH1XpK-PuTPmjP_9JNpi4vZ4oMmvgdlqW03TLxVdvN6_cio2Ov2d2aIiA), all accessed on 28 June 2021.

there was a lack of alternative socio-economic theories,[3] and it was difficult, if not impossible, to determine what direction should be followed for a fundamental change. Following a general call for alternative theories and ideas, many have been developed and presented over the last decade, especially since 2016/17 (cf. e. g. Bregman 2017; Raworth 2017; Fioramonti 2017; Frey 2018). Some are limited to a certain aspect,[4] others are more comprehensive and presented as ready to be put into practice,[5] and some just sketch a trajectory inevitably based on how the author perceives current societal, political and economic developments (e. g. Streeck 2016).

All this together makes it realistic that at a certain moment in a (near) future, a full change will be made from the neoliberal, free-market capitalist growth-based political-economic system into another socio-political-economic system. These new alternative theories and ideas seem to have a strong focus in common to find a new balance between the "three ps" (people, planet, profit), known from sustainability literature and movements. This would mean a paradigm shift from people and planet in service of profit to profit in service of people and planet (e.g. Raworth 2017, although she uses other words for it which I will elaborate on later. More related to work is Suzman 2020, Chapters 14 "The Dead of a Salary Man" and 15 "The New Disease"). Such a paradigm shift will also have an impact on work: how we will work as well as the general perception of the meaning of work in society. The aim of this chapter is to explore the possible change of work to reflect one particular new economic theory, namely Raworth's doughnut economics and one particular utopia, namely Jurriaan Andriessen's *Eldorica*. This utopia is interesting to combine with Raworth's idea for a doughnut economy, because they share similar underlying values, especially a new balance between planet, people and profit. Making use of a utopia for such an exploration is not only interesting but also important, because it enables us to let go of existing ideas, concepts, and conventions. Once such an exercise has been made and a possible future direction is set, considerations could be given to what already existing ideas, concepts, conventions etc. fit

---

[3] Except for (a revival of) Marxist-related ideas that seem to find ground in only a small proportion of the left-wing society in certain countries and a limited academic circle. See versobooks.com for an impression of academic writing within this stream.

[4] Bregman, for example, is limited to the idea of a basic income as a solution to fight inequality.

[5] Raworth's doughnut economics, for example, not only includes existing movements for change, such as the United Nations' Sustainability Development Goals (SDGs), but is also picked up at local and company levels. Cf. for example Bennet 2020, with the city of Amsterdam and the country of New Zealand as examples.

in the (possible) future idea of work and for which aspects new foundations, laws and (contractual) relations should be developed. In other words, it will set a pathway giving direction to change in the field of labour law, employment law, and industrial relations.

The chapter is structured as follows. First, I will elaborate on the crisis of the current neo-liberal free-market capitalist growth-based political-economic system that has resulted in the general call for alternative ideas. Second, I will elaborate on the idea of doughnut economics, followed thirdly by what a shift to this economic model would mean for work, based on Andriessens' *Eldorica*. Finally, I will reflect on these explorations to indicate what role there could or even should be for labour lawyers in these debates.

Before proceeding to the next section a few caveats need to be addressed. It is not my intention to present a new idea or theory myself. It is also not my intention to make normative indications of what I think is a good theory or which economic, political, or sociological views are right or wrong. Such would go far beyond my capabilities. My intention is merely to find ways for how we, labour lawyers, can participate in these debates and searches for new ideas and theories. This is important because work, employment, industrial relations, (collective) labour law, social security law, and social protection are strongly dependent on political-economic models and theories. And *vice versa*, to a large extent, political-economic models and theories aim to address such social issues, of which Marxism probably is one of the most known examples. As labour lawyers, we are pre-eminently the ones capable of understanding the problems of workers and the shortcomings and challenges for labour regulations (in a broad sense). Therefore, we are also pre-eminently the experts to assess what effect new political-economic models and theories are likely to have on labour, especially to what extent alternatives will (also) address a problem of work, or if that is not the case, what the (new) function of labour law should be. Furthermore, getting engaged in these searches and debates could make labour law more prepared to deal with changes rather than always being only responsive and lagging significantly behind those changes.

2. The Crisis

There has always been resistance against the neo-liberal free-market capitalist growth-based economic system. However, after the 2008 financial and subsequent economic crisis, this changed. The huge taxpayer-financed bailouts of banks all over the US and Europe seem to have shaken up the broader public, especially among the many millions of people who lost their jobs, homes, savings, and security (cf. Raworth 2017, 5). Whereas banks are the main institutes that were blamed for the crisis, with hindsight the *Economist* in its *Crash Course* (Schools Brief in the Economist of 7 September 2013)[6] discussing the origins of the financial crisis, indicated that, in fact, there were multiple causes for the crisis. In his book, *Capital in the Twenty-First Century,* Piketty (Piketty 2014) convincingly explains that inequality is a feature of capitalism. Combined with a persistent decline in economic growth in the US and Europe especially, all three assumed prerequisites[7] granting legitimacy to the (neoliberal) capitalist free-market economy are under duress. In other words: capitalism is in crisis. To what extent capitalism is in crisis, what its exact causes are and how it will end is not clear. And while there is substantial disagreement about these three issues, there is agreement about the fact that 'something big looms on the horizon: a structural crisis much bigger than the recent Great Recession [of 2008 – BtH], which might in retrospect seem only a prologue to a period of deeper troubles and transformations' (Wallerstein, Collins, Mann, Derluguian & Calhoun 2013, 1f., as quoted in Streeck 2016, 5).

While some sociologists still see hope in state intervention to counter the negative effects of capitalism or to fix market failure, Streeck is a lot less optimistic when he argues that '[k]eeping labour, land, and money from complete commodification and thereby protecting them against abuse requires the authority of government. That resource, however, has been thoroughly diminished by globalisation' (Streeck 2016, 24f.). What follows after capitalism in its final crisis, which according to Streeck is already under way, is no other defined social order but a lasting *interregnum* (Streeck 2016, 13). Streeck defines *interregnum* as a "breakdown of system integration at the macro level, depriving individuals at the micro level of institutional structuring and collective support, and shifting the burden of ordering social life […] to individuals themselves and such social arrangements as they can create on their own' (Streeck 2016, 14). To explain this, he first turns to the Keynesian setting of capitalism in which 'democracy functioned as an engine for economic and social progress. By redistributing parts of the proceeds of the capitalist market economy downward, through both industrial relations and social policy, democracy provided for rising standards of living among ordinary people and thereby procured legitimacy for a capitalist market economy; at the same time, it stimulated economic growth by securing a sufficient level of aggregate

---

[6] https://www.economist.com/schools-brief/2013/09/07/crash-course, accessed 9 August 2021.

[7] "Steady growth, sound money and a modicum of social equity, spreading some of the benefits of capitalism to those without capital" (Streeck 2016, 47).

demand." The viability of this setting of capitalism was "contingent on labour mobilizing a sufficient amount of political and economic power, which it could do in the more or less closed national economies of the post-war era" (Streeck 2016, 21). With the end of post-war growth, this changed, and the market got extended beyond national borders, also referred to as globalisation, which weakened the power of labour which was locally bound. For the new powers, lower growth rates were acceptable, if that was compensated by higher profit rates, which inherently resulted in an increasingly inegalitarian distribution (Streeck 2016, 22). Being no longer limited to nation states, democracy became redundant for economic growth and therefore had to be decoupled from the political economy (cf. Crouch 2004, as referenced by Streeck 2016, 22). Thus, with globalisation as the dominant political-economic formula, "[n]ow states were located in markets, rather than markets in states' (Streeck 2016, 22). And, while governments "redefined social policy as public provision for private competitiveness, […] capital used its newly gained mobility to push for lower taxes, less regulation, and […] for rigidity being replaced with flexibility" (Streeck 2016, 23). A development that is clearly visible in the policies of the European Union (cf. Copeland 2019).

All this brings Streeck ultimately to describing the *interregnum* as being a *post-social society* governed by "a neoliberal ethos of competitive self-improvement, of untiring cultivation on one's marketable human capital, enthusiastic dedication to work, and cheerfully optimistic, playful acceptance of the risks inherent in a world that has outgrown government" (Streeck 2016, 38). With *disruption* (in a neoliberal version of "creative destruction")[8] and *resilience* (as in voluntary adaptive adjustment)[9] being key concepts, the *interregnum* is doomed to be an era of entropy. The two keep each other alive, as the "de-socialized capitalism of the interregnum hinges on the improvised performances of structurally self-centred, socially disorganized and politically disempowered individuals" (Streeck 2016, 41) which nonetheless are resilient enough to deal with the disruptions caused by de-socialised capitalism.[10]

---

[8] i.e. "more ruthless, more out-of-the-blue, and less willing to take prisoners or accept delay in order to be 'socially compatible'" (Streeck 2016, 39).

[9] Thus, "the more resilience individuals manage to develop at micro-level of everyday life, the less demand will there be for collective action at the macro-level to contain the uncertainties produced by market forces" (Streeck 2016, 40).

[10] "By mastering four broad types of behaviour: coping, hoping, doping and shopping" (Streeck 2016, 41).

For Streeck, this is a path that cannot be averted. When he looks back over the last four decades, he sees a “sustained process of institutional transformation, slow but irresistible and driven, not by democratic politics but by the dynamic logic of capitalist development, that has effectively destroyed most if not all of the political safeguards whose establishment had been the very condition for capitalism being allowed to return after the disasters of the first half of the twentieth century. That logic, and the reorganization – or disorganization – of social life that it dictated, culminates today in the dual crisis of the global financial as well as the national democratic state system” (Streeck 2016, 235).

Not all sociologists have such a strong path-dependent view on the development of capitalism. Block, for example, sees options for reversal of the process by better theories and decisions in the future based on the idea of an “always embedded” capitalism subject to a “primacy of politics” (as such following Polanyi 2001, XIX, “Introduction” by Fred Block; cf. Streeck 2016, 231). Besides sociologists, there are also economists that believe in the possibility of averting the path as seen by Streeck. Some also see a deconstruction of centralised democracy and collective powers but envision more smaller communities. In his idea for *Wellbeing Economy*, Fioramonti provides many examples for moves away from bigger structures and institutions to more localised initiatives (Fioramonti 2017). Most alternatives, though, are less focussed on institutional structures and approach it from societal drivers, especially climate change and the inevitable need to make a paradigm shift to an economic system that is not dependent on growth. One such example is Kate Raworth’s Doughnut Economics.

3. Doughnut Economics

While Streeck tracks powershifts between the state and the market in shaping, correcting and liberalising capitalism, Raworth takes a different approach. She reflects on what capitalism has been doing for humans and the planet. Moreover, she critically reviews how certain core aspects of economic theory have been formed, depicts misunderstandings and representations in these core concepts and transforms this into a new picture and economic theory which presents, very basically, a different balance between people, planet and profit. This results in her introducing seven ways “to think as a Twenty-First Century Economist” (Raworth 2017, 26f.). All of these are supported by pictograms because, as Raworth explains, the history of economic theory has proven that these are important for the tangibility of a theory. By contrasting these to the existing pictograms, these also serve as an illustration of the difference between the current dominant economics of neoliberal free-market capitalism driven by growth (see Figure 1).

With these "seven ways of thinking," Raworth in fact summarises her idea of doughnut economics. Therefore, the simplest way to introduce her idea is by fully quoting these seven ways of thinking (see Figure 1 and textbox 1). After presenting these seven ways of thinking, Raworth stresses that these do not lay out specific policy-prescriptions or institutional fixes. They are fundamental, though, for a radically different way of thinking about economics (Raworth 2017, 30). Furthermore, she adds that rethinking economics is not about finding the correct model (because that does not exist), instead "it is about choosing or creating a model that best serves our purposes – reflecting the context we face, the values we hold, and the aims we have" (Raworth 2017, 22).

Figure 1. Doughnut economics pictograms and key concepts.

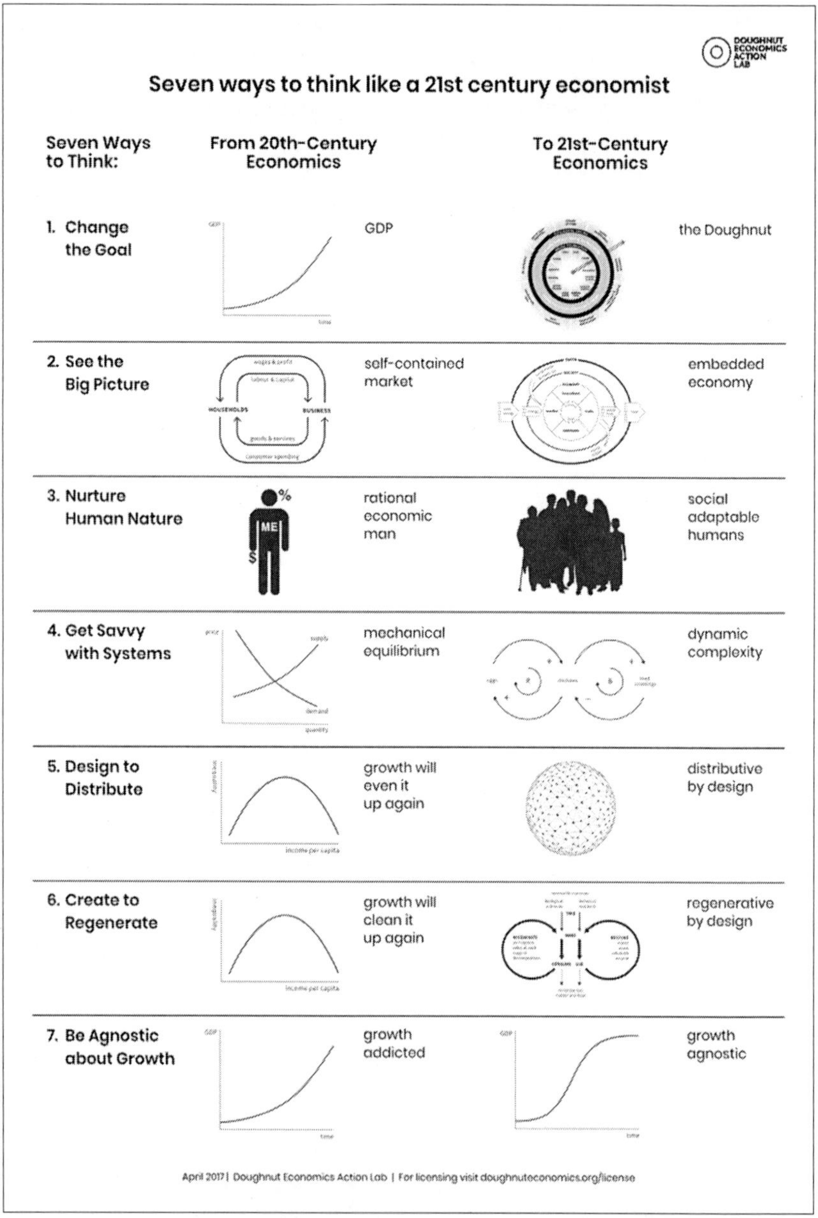

Textbox 1. Seven ways to think like a 21st century economist (Raworth 2017, 25, 28ff.).

1. Change the goal. For over 70 years, economics has been fixed on GDP, or national output, as its primary measure of progress. That fixation has been used to justify extreme inequalities of income and wealth coupled with unprecedented destruction of the living world. For the twenty-first century a far bigger goal is needed: meeting the human rights of every person within the means of our life-giving planet. And that goal is encapsulated in the concept of the Doughnut. The challenge now is to create economies – local to global that help to bring all of humanity into the Doughnut's safe and just space. Instead of pursuing ever-increasing GDP, it is time to discover how to thrive in balance.

2. See the big picture. Mainstream economics depicts the whole economy with just one, extremely limited image, the Circular Flow diagram. Its limitations have, furthermore, been used to reinforce a neoliberal narrative about the efficiency of the market, the incompetence of the state, the domesticity of the household and the tragedy of the commons. It is time to draw the economy anew, embedding it within society and within nature, and powered by the sun. This new depiction invites new narratives—about the power of the market, the partnership of the state, the core role of the household and the creativity of the commons.

3. Nurture human nature. At the heart of 20th-century economics stands the portrait of rational economic man: he has told us that we are self-interested, isolated, calculating, fixed in taste and dominant over nature—and his portrait has shaped who we have become. But human nature is far richer than this, as early sketches of our new self-portrait reveal: we are social, interdependent, approximating, fluid in values and dependent upon the living world. What's more, it is indeed possible to nurture human nature in ways that give us a far greater chance of getting into the Doughnut's safe and just space.

4. Get savvy with systems. The iconic criss-cross of the market's supply and demand curves is the first diagram that every economics student encounters, but it is rooted in misplaced nineteenth-century metaphors of mechanical equilibrium. A far smarter starting point for understanding the economy's dynamism is systems thinking, summed up by a simple pair of feedback loops. Putting such dynamics at the heart of economics opens up many new insights, from the boom and bust of financial markets to the self-reinforcing nature of economic inequality and the tipping points of climate change. It's time to stop searching for the economy's elusive control levers and start stewarding it as an ever-evolving complex system.

__5. Design to distribute.__ In the 20th century, one simple curve—the Kuznets Curve—whispered a powerful message on inequality: It has to get worse before it can get better, and growth will (eventually) even it up. But inequality, it turns out, is not an economic necessity: It is a design failure. 21st-century economists will recognize that there are many ways to design economies to be far more distributive of the value that they generate—an idea best represented as a network of flows. It means going beyond redistributing income to exploring ways of redistributing wealth, particularly the wealth that lies in controlling land, enterprise, technology, knowledge and the power to create money.

__6. Create to regenerate.__ Economic theory has long portrayed a 'clean' environment as a luxury good, affordable only for the well-off. This view was reinforced by the Environmental Kuznets Curve, which once again whispered that pollution has to get worse before it can get better and growth will (eventually) clean it up. But there is no such law: ecological degradation is simply the result of degenerative industrial design. This century needs economic thinking that unleashes regenerative design in order to create a circular—not linear—economy and to restore humans as full participants in Earth's cyclical processes of life.

__7. Be agnostic about growth.__ One diagram in economic theory is so dangerous that it is never actually drawn: the long-term path of GDP growth. Mainstream economics views endless economic growth as a must, but nothing in nature grows forever, and the attempt to buck that trend is raising tough questions in high-income but low-growth countries. It may not be hard to give up having GDP growth as an economic goal, but it is going to be far harder to overcome our addiction to it. Today we have economies that need to grow, whether or not they make us thrive; what we need are economies that make us thrive, whether or not they grow. That radical flip in perspective invites us to become agnostic about growth and to explore how economies that are currently financially, politically and socially addicted to growth could learn to live with or without it.

Raworth's "doughnut economics" proposes many things that the majority of people could probably easily agree with and are also not revolutionary for most economists. As she indicates in the elaborations on the core aspects presented in "the seven ways to think," many thoughts are drawn from other economists like Keynes, Mill, and Rostow. However, they often draw on ideas that have either been ignored or rejected by mainstream economists. One of these ideas that probably is the most difficult one to get accepted, but which is necessary to make a real change in economic thinking, is the idea that we should become agnostic to growth. Letting go of the idea of eternal, indefinite growth is hard to imagine, even when we realise that the planet is, in fact, a closed system and for that reason only indefinite growth cannot exist. We have grown accustomed to it, and it has brought many people a lot of welfare. What will we get in return if we let go of growth? There are of course fears that we have to give up some of the wealth we have gained, but maybe we simply have no choice if we see that the economy does not grow anymore or that it takes more effort to get smaller percentages of growth, as Streeck also indicated in his historical review of capitalism.

Raworth is clearly sensitive to such fears and addresses linked issues all formulated in terms of "addictions" to growth, thus: financial (Raworth 2017, 272ff.), political (ibid., 276ff.), and social (ibid., 280ff.) addiction to growth. Each of these will also have implications for work. The idea of reinventing finance, so that it is in service of the thriving of people and planet rather than (mostly) the economy (or profits) may affect, for example, pension schemes as it may have implications for inflation, exchange rates and interest rates (Raworth 2017, 275). At the political level, it may affect social protection and social security as well as incomes which all have relations to taxation. For example, higher taxation could be presented as tax justice and public investments could have higher returns on the public sector (Raworth 2017, 276, where Raworth refers to Scandinavian countries as an example). Raworth also proposes a shift away from taxation income streams towards taxing accumulated wealth which will diminish the role of growing GDP as well as a means to fight poverty (Raworth 2017, 277, where she indicates that of course pushbacks can be expected on such tax reform by the corporate lobby).[11] Another political addiction is translated by Raworth in "fear of the unemployment line" (Raworth 2017, 277). The option of a shorter working week is mentioned as one way to deal with it. More innovative and integrated in the idea of doughnut economics, is an already

[11] Streeck is even more negative in the feasibility of such a reform due to what he refers to as "oligarchic inequality" or "neo-feudalism" (Streeck 2016, 28). In general, this builds on the idea of Piketty to fight inequality (Piketty 2014).

widely recommended shift from taxing labour to taxing resource use, "which would simultaneously draw human ingenuity away from making more stuff with fewer people towards repairing and remaking more things with less stuff, while employing more people too" (Raworth 2017, 278f., which taps into thinking points 5 (distributive economy) and 6 (regenerative economy)).

The third, social addiction, refers to the culture of consumerism and the tensions created by inequality, which are "rooted in the need for something to aspire to" (Raworth 2017, 280). Reversing consumerism, which is dominated by financial and cultural dominance, is considered an especially big challenge. Not elaborated by Raworth, but in a documentary called *The True Cost*,[12] it is explained how deeply rooted consumerism is in society: we are (subconsciously) indoctrinated by commercials that buying clothes (and broader: goods) will give us a rich and satisfying feeling, even though we do not need those clothes or goods. When we combine this with continuous messages from national governments that we, consumers, have to keep buying things because that is good for GDP, the indoctrination of an over-excessive consumerism is complete. To reverse this, Raworth, but also others, especially anthropologists and psychologists, argue that we need new "aspirations" (among others, Suzman 2020, and Aked et al. 2008). With reference to research by the UK's New Economics Foundation, Raworth mentions five activities that are considered to promote wellbeing: connecting to people around us; being active in our bodies; taking notice of the world; learning new skills; and giving to others (Raworth 2017, 283, with reference to Aked et al. 2008).[13]

To make the image of the "doughnut" more concrete, Raworth fills this in with concrete social and ecological conditions that are assumed to underpin collective human wellbeing (see Figure 2). For social conditions, or foundation, Raworth draws from the Sustainable Development Goals. From an economic point of view this is interesting, since these goals have been operationalised in such a manner that it is possible to measure the extent of humanity's "shortfall." However, it gives little insight into what this may mean for how the world of work will change and what role there will be for labour law under doughnut economics. To understand this, it

---

[12] https://truecostmovie.com/ accessed 2 July 2021.

[13] I will not elaborate on this discussion and here just follow Raworth's argumentation, since the purpose of this part is to present her idea for a doughnut economics. Nonetheless, I would like to mark that this may have been presented somewhat strongly since research also exists stating that the appreciation of these values also depends on to what extent someone is inherently materialistically inclined (cf. Keng, Jung, Jiuan & Wirtz 2000, 317ff.).

would be necessary to create scenarios, or utopias, to make the changes doughnut economics entails more concrete and get an impression of its full impact. To illustrate this, I will discuss in the next section one utopia (*Eldorica* by Jurriaan Andriessen) that already embraces all the ideas of doughnut economics.

Figure 2. The "doughnut" and its social and ecological conditions (Raworth 2017, 44).

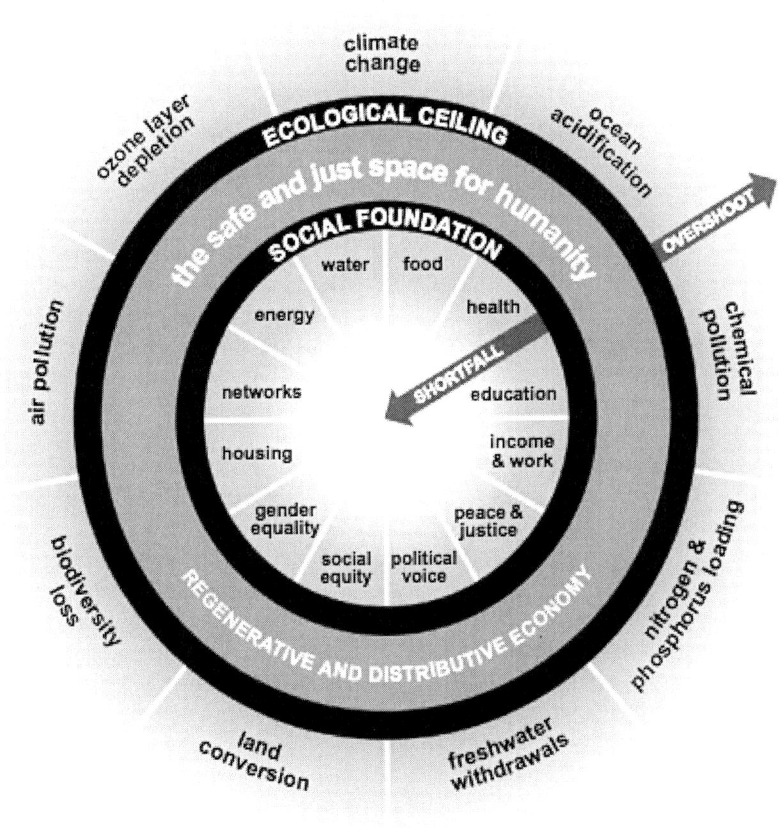

4. *Eldorica*

Eldorica is written by Jurriaan Andriessen, a statistician, composer and lithographer. The first drafts for *Eldorica* were written between 1968 and 1971 (this was thus before the release of the Club of Rome report, *Limits to Growth*) and published in various underground magazines (Andriessen 1990, pre-note to the book). In 1985, he revisited these publications and worked them out into 18 full-colour lithographs, followed by a fully illustrated book in 1989, and a more *au-courant* edition in 1990 (which is the version I own a copy of). This elaboration on the wording of the book *Eldorica* shows that Andriessen was quite a visionary. *Eldorica* is a narrative of a journey the author made to an alternative world. The narrative about the journey is complemented with more technical details about *Eldorica*.

In short, *Eldorica* is Earth's shadow planet. In *Eldorica,* governments and citizens have adjusted their way of living and doing business to the boundaries of the resources of the planet which has resulted in a lifestyle based on renewable energy, sustainability, and a combination of thrift with comfort.[14] The production of single-use or disposable products is banned. The planet is governed by an *eldocraty*, that is a variety on democracy in which decisions are taken based on science and knowledge instead of power relations.[15] In terms of demography, geography, resources (quantity and sorts) and overall welfare, *Eldorica* is virtually identical to Earth (Andriessen 1990, 15).

On the second page, we get a first impression of the role of work in *Eldorica*. In an explanation about the differences between *Earth* and *Eldorica*, guide Henry mentions that what is called work at *Earth*, is called breaking down in *Eldorica* (Andriessen 1990, 8). And Henry´s explanation about how things work at *Eldorica* start with the remark that everyone is unemployed and that everyone loves this. Moreover, work is a form of punishment that is seriously feared by Eldorians (Andriessen 1990, 92, 128). Nevertheless, living standards on *Eldorica* are higher than on Earth and people are happier because they do not work (Andriessen 1990, 15). In a world where no one works and time is no issue, friends can visit whenever it suites them, people sleep and eat whenever they feel like it, and travel whenever they want.[16] Overall, time is spent eating, reading, walking,

[14] This is what makes this an interesting utopia in relation to Raworth's doughnut economics.

[15] My own summary of the main message of the book largely based on the information at www.jurriaan-andriessen.nl/ (accessed 2 July 2021).

[16] Which can be done on a "slow" tempo, which is no problem because time does

discussing, listening to music, playing sports and exercising, writing, making discoveries and coming up with inventions, etc (Andriessen 1990, 16, 58f.). Gaining knew knowledge and insights is a highly attained virtue (ibid., 84), as are genuinity and creativity (ibid., 86f., deduced from the narrative). Competition is considered to be deconstructive and to frustrate progress. The same is thought about economic goals (ibid., 88ff., deduced from the narrative which is constructed around the value of music). Most of the work is performed by robots,[17] which Andriessen explains by example of the construction of houses,[18] and when they travel on a ship.[19]

This is all well and nice as a fantasy, but how can this be realised? Andriessen had some serious thoughts about this but they are too elaborate and complex to be fully explained here. Instead, I will highlight a few ideas that I think are most interesting in light of Raworth's doughnut economics, the position of work, and the role of labour law (see textbox 2).

Textbox 2. Labour-Law-related technical details of *Eldorica's* economy and work, in bullet points.[20]

- Wealth is expressed in terms of free time and talent, not in quantity of goods, value or size of property, etc.
- A working week is in principle, 4 hours, which is possible due to optimised automation of the production of sustainable products, including the use of sustainable packaging materials and a fair distribution of resources;
- Governing by computers (in today's terminology by digitalization and algorithms), care is taken regarding the distribution of individual material needs, so that resources are not wasted, pollution is limited to a minimum, and every individual gets as much free time as possible.

---

not equal money.

[17] In the words of Andriessen *"automaten,"* which is probably best translated as mechanicals (note that he wrote this in the late 1960s and edited it in the 1980s when robotisation was just starting and not a general term as it is nowadays).

[18] Robots build a standard exterior and provide for the connections of utility services, the owner(s) of the house decorate the exterior as they like and take care of the interior of the house. Often they receive the assistance of friends, some with specialities that have been developed as a hobby (not as a profession) (Andriessen 1990, 67).

[19] There is no captain, no sailors, no personnel. Everything is automated, including restaurants, storage, the distribution of energy, and the control of the ship. The passengers' only duty is to keep the ship clean (Andriessen 1990, 82f., 99f.).

[20] Most of it is based on the information provided by Andriessen 1990, 122ff.

- The value of the *Eldorian* currency is coupled to the collective capital, *i.e.* untapped known resources, acquired knowledge, and useful labour.
- In areas that have fully converted to a sustainable and automated economy, people work 4-hours per week, the percentage of "conversion" or "completeness" of an area determines the actual weekly working hours. A reduction of working hours means, therefore, that an area is becoming more sustainable.
- A working week of 2-4 hours is necessary for maintenance activities which is regulated by the law as "necessary labour."
- Working hours are calculated per year (204 hours or 25 8-hour working days). When these hours are to be worked is considered an administrative task performed by computers, taking into account as much as possible the preferences of each individual.
- The *Eldorian* economic system is based on two basic principles: fair distribution of the needs and burdens that are part of living on and managing a planet; and to release the burdens as much as possible for every inhabitant of *Eldorica*.
- At the age of 22, every *Eldorian* gets an entitlement to his/her share of *Eldoria's* resources. Part of this is returned in a house, household equipment, furniture, a car, and a monthly income to cover the costs of living. The rest can freely be spent as the individual sees fit. This can be for an individual's own purpose (e.g. to publish a book), but it can also be spent by making (part of) the resources available for an(other) entrepreneur.
- When the production of a product is scaled up for mass production it needs to be standardised (sustainability requirement) and the production may fall under the law of "necessary labour" (until it is fully automated).
- There are various scales of monthly income depending on the level of entrepreneurship. However, the differences between the scales are not big (they are related to resources and therefore limited per definition).
- Resources are tradeable for other resources. The exchange rate is fixed by the computer (not the market).
- Abuse or fraud of the system (e.g. if someone uses more resources than they are entitled to) is punishable by a financial fine or an extension of the working time.
- Individuals who voluntarily desire to work more hours can request such on the basis of the law on non-necessary labour. Most of the work related to this law deals with research and development and tests.

Andriessen's *Eldorica* is not only interesting because it connects well with Raworth's "7 ways of thinking as a twenty-first-century economist," but also because it brings them more into connection with each other. While Raworth sets out a line of thinking we can follow to make change, Andriessen gives us a possible world if we followed up on it. Moreover, by sketching this alternative world, a number of things become more concrete. For example, going fully sustainable and circular will reduce the production of disposable goods, which will reduce costs (of resources as well as in consumer prices by not having to pay for disposable wrapping materials), which in turn will significantly reduce waste (and therefore the need to collect waste and the consequence of waste pollution, etc.). Something like fast fashion does not exist in *Eldorica* (one of our largest resource absorbers and polluters) (Andriessen 1990, 7, the "journey" to *Eldorica* starts with a comment that shoes produced on Earth tend to last for three months, whereas shoes produced on *Eldorica* last for 50 years). Work that is still needed are jobs that are meaningful for society, and not the kind of jobs that only cost society (in terms of resources as well as time) (Graeber 2019).

Since the value of money is based on the planet's resources and everyone gets an entitlement to an equal share of it, it is possible to provide everyone with an income which is hardly dependent on the hours worked or the kind of job done (all work has equal societal value). Entrepreneurship is stimulated with a higher level of income, provided that the product or service is in the benefit of society.[21] Because every citizen has an entitlement to a share of the planet's resources and working time from the age 22, no special reservations or provisions need to be taken for pensions. Moreover, because of the full turn to sustainable and circular production, the costs of living will be considerably lower, which means that the level of the basic income may also be relatively low, compared to what needs to be provided in our current economic system.

The government of computers (read: artificial intelligence and algorithms in today's language) eradicates power politics. Andriessen presupposes that this will ensure the fair distribution of resources (a computer has no desire for power and is not corrupt, although programmers can be bad) (Andriessen 1990, 68). This was written largely before films like The Lift (directed by Dick Maas and released in 1983), or I Robot (directed by Alex Pyros and released in 2004). He also presumes that this will eradicate war and the need to spend money on weapons, which can therefore be spent making the (economic) transition (Andriessen 166ff.).

[21] Andriessen's idea for a form of basic income is somewhat more nuanced than I presented in Box 2, the main point is though that differences in income levels are not significant which ensures a high level of equality and therewith seems effective in eradicating poverty.

5. Reflections

In the introduction, I have argued that we are on a path that makes a change from the neoliberal, free-market capitalist socio-economic system into another socio-economic system inevitable. To substantiate this argument, I have drawn rather extensively on the work by Wolfgang Streeck. Streeck gives a very realistic image of trends, mostly in the EU, the UK and the USA, that according to him are unavoidable. His main argument is that looking for solutions to the problems caused by neoliberal capitalism is futile because the institutions that need to do this are either no longer in the position to do so (decoupling due to globalisation), or do not exist any longer.

Some of these trends are directly related to the field of work and therefore to labour law (in a broad sense). For example, the deconstruction of collectiveness is visible in the general decline of trade union membership and coverage percentages of collective labour agreements, and a decentralisation of collective bargaining from sectoral level to company level that has taken place under the pressure of financial and economic recovery measures after the 2008 crisis. Although other forms of collectiveness have been developed, such as cooperatives, these lack the powers, rights, and formal institutional positions (especially in tripartite bodies like social-economic councils) that trade unions have. These could therefore be considered as examples of resilience of individuals to creatively deal with the negative impacts of neoliberal free-market capitalism.

Another example is the flexibilisation of the employment relationship which is in an increasing number of ways moving away from the "standard" full-time employment contract for an indefinite term. Thus, since the late 1990s we have seen an increase in the number of fixed-term contracts, part-time contracts, on-call contracts, and more recently a significant increase in civil contracts, either via (false or economic dependent) self-employment or a special contract form acknowledged in contract law (e.g. in Poland). Some employment relationships, for example via platforms like Uber, Deliveroo, or Helpling, are undetermined and therefore present national courts and legislators with huge challenges around how to qualify these employment relationships and how to adjust the law (or not). Consequently, the "standard" employment contract can hardly be called standard any longer and more and more workers fall outside the scope of (parts of) labour law protection.

When we relate these developments to the views of Streeck, we can speak of the erosion of labour law protections due to system failure or system deconstruction. A failure or deconstruction which, according to

Streeck, cannot be restored. To face these challenges, we need to seek, explore, analyse and evaluate alternative systems. Since 2016-17, a number of alternative ideas, theories, systems, and ways of economic thinking have been presented in socio-political-economic literature. Many of these alternatives have in common that they aim for a shift from welfare (based on materialism and economic growth) to wellbeing (based on immaterial values and degrowth or growth agnosticism). To get a more concrete idea of such alternative ideas and what this will mean for work and the role of labour law, I have briefly described one such alternative – Raworth's doughnut economics. Her alternative is mostly a response to the ecological need for change, but also includes aspects that concern work. Her ideas are not revolutionary, new economic theories; indeed, she builds a new economic narrative by reviving economic ideas and theories that in the past have been ignored or pushed aside by mainstream economics as being flawed.

With a reconstructed narrative supported by new pictures for basic aspects of economic theory, Raworth creates a strong, compelling, and comprehensive alternative. An alternative she embeds in existing developments and (global) political agendas, such as the 2030 Sustainable Development Goals of the United Nations. However, no matter how clear, compelling and comprehensive doughnut economics may be, it still makes it difficult to imagine what kind of world we will have when a full shift to doughnut economics is made. For example, when presenting challenges and suggestions on becoming growth agnostic, Raworth mentions a few issues related to work, but it is hard to imagine what the full position of work or the role of labour law will be in a doughnut economy. To get this clearer, I turned to the utopian *Eldorica*, by Jurriaan Andriessen.

Eldorica makes an interesting and suitable utopia because it is based on similar thoughts and ideas as doughnut economics, in particular a distributive and regenerative economy by design and agnosticism about growth. With *Eldorica*, Andriessen has created a world in which work is something negative; to achieve free time as much as possible is what aspires Eldorians. This is something that can be achieved because significantly fewer products are made (because of sustainability) and only meaningful work exists. Eldorians are not dependent on work for their income because they have an entitlement to a percentage of the planet's resources, which includes a basic income that is at more or less the same level for everyone (which ensures equality and eradicates poverty). This puts work in a very different position to how we know it now, or how we've experienced it in the past (cf. Suzman 2020). Moreover, free time is not (only) time to be lazy, rather, it is time to be creative, innovative, socially involved, etc. These are values that are aspired to — values that we currently know as foundations for labour law (social justice, human dignity, capability) to protect workers from the pressures that neoliberal free-market capitalism puts on such values.

For me this illustrates that we, labour lawyers, need to get engaged in debates about alternative ideas, theories, models, etc. for the current, failing economic system. For example, many labour lawyers will applaud a 4-hour working week, but how will this come about in the areas that have not made the full transition yet? What pressures and circumstances exist there and what kind of (protective) regulation will be needed to control negative impacts? In *Eldorica,* work can also be a form of punishment. How will it be guaranteed in such a situation that these workers will be treated the same as any other worker? After all, the punishment is to work more than the obligatory 4-hours per week, not to do this under poorer work conditions. How will it be prevented that such workers do not become modern slaves?

These are just a few examples of the most obvious questions and without doubt there are many more. Besides these rather concrete questions, getting involved in these debates is also interesting for finding solutions to current labour law problems. Understanding what future models and systems of labour law could be can help to design pathways to get there. For example, the idea of a basic income receives mainly resistance. This is partly based on our deep settled aversion to free-riders (basic income is also called free money) (cf. Suzman 2020), but also because is fits poorly with the current growth-based, GDP-measured economy. Having an image of a possibility to grow another sort of society in which free time is valued more than work (paradigm shift of aspirations), makes a basic income much more acceptable, especially when realising that the level of the basic income can become lower, the more progression is made towards a fully sustainable and circular economy in which consumerism is alien.

Another example is our thinking about the development and "invasion" of AI and the digitalization and robotization of the labour market. In the current economic system in which high levels of unemployment will negatively affect GDP (and therewith growth), these developments are seen as only negative. In a world like *Eldorica*, these are fully embraced in order to free society from work. Work that is still necessary is, to a large extent, related to the maintenance of robots and other automated systems (like self-driving cars and ships).

Of course, this way of thinking will not directly resolve the problems we currently have to deal with, but it may point us in directions we may want to take to move towards the solutions. It may also provide us with a frame of reference to evaluate various solutions (which might bring us closer to our new aspirations). At the same time, it will help us take the first steps towards making the necessary changes to realise the paradigm shift that seems to be inevitable: from people and planet in service of profits, to profits in service of people and planet.

Bibliography

Aked, J. et al., *Five Ways to Wellbeing: The Evidence* (London: New Economics Foundation, 2008)

Andriessen, Jurriaan, *Eldorica. Met een reisverslag naar een betere wereld* (Utrecht: Het Spectrum, 1990)

Bennet, Julliet, "Reorienting the post-coronavirus economy for ecological sustainability," *The Journal of Australian Political Economy* 85 (winter 2020): 212-218, https://search.informit.org/doi/abs/10.3316/agispt.20200701032610

Bregman, Rutger, *Utopia for Realists. And how we get there* (London: Bloomsbury, 2017)

Busher, Bram E., "Planning for a world beyond COVID-19: Five pillars post-neoliberal development," *World Development,* issue 105357 (2021): 140

Copeland, Paul, *Governance and the European Social Dimension. Politics, Power and the Social Deficit in a Post-2010 EU* (Oxfordshire: Routledge, 2019)

Crouch, Colin, *Post-Democracy* (Cambridge: Polity Press, 2004)

Fioramonti, Lorenzo, *Wellbeing Economy: Success in a World Without Growth* (South Africa: Pan MacMillan, 2017)

Frey, Bruno, *Economics of Happiness* (New York: Springer, 2018)

Graeber, David, *Bullshit Jobs: The Rise of Pointless Work and What We Can Do About It.* (London: Penguin Books, 2019)

Keng, Kau Ah, Jung, Kwon, Jiuan, Tan Soo and Wirtz, Jochen, "The Influence of Materialistic Inclination on Values, Life Satisfaction and Aspirations: An Empirical Analysis," *Social Indicators Research* Vol. 49 (2000): 317-333

Piketty, Thomas, *Capital in the Twenty-First Century* (Cambridge: Harvard University Press, 2014)

Polanyi, Karl, *The Great Transformation: The Political and Economic Origins of Our Time* (Boston: Beacon, 2001) (first published in 1944)

Raworth, Kate, *Doughnut Economics* (London: Penguin Random House, 2017)

Streeck, Wolfgang, *How will Capitalism End?* (London: Versobooks, 2016)

Suzman, James, *Work. A History of How We Spend Our Time* (London: Bloomsbury Circus, 2020)

Wallerstein, Immanuel, Collins, Randall, Mann, Michael, Derluguian, Georgi and Calhoun, Craig, *Does Capitalism Have a Future?* (Oxford: OUP, 2013)

CONCLUSIONS

Before closing this book, we would like to reflect on the main ideas that have resulted from the different contributions. Concerning our approach, one may note beforehand that the principal characteristic of this book is its interdisciplinarity. Although it was (almost) exclusively written by representatives of the legal discipline, it contains interdisciplinary references to the fields of philosophy, sociology and economics. As the topic deals with labour law in crisis and its possible future developments, these references are not surprising.

The idea of bringing together lawyers from different countries, each of whom questioned themselves on the same topic during a global pandemic that hit all of our legal systems, implied reflections on labour law from a universal point of view. In other words, the approach of this book presupposes that labour law is envisaged as a branch of a discipline that responds to a certain function, without regard to a certain legal system. To justify this approach, one may remind oneself that labour law exists in all legal systems and, as such, responds to the protection of the worker. Nicole Maggi-Germain mentions the universal law approach that would be based on the natural order of the world and the concept of causality, which is being succeeded by laws of society based on the concept of finality. In short, the intercultural approach towards labour law is that it must not be limited to one legal system bound within borders.

Authors take different approaches towards labour law to justify this reading. One of them might be regarded as economic. As Manfred Weiss concludes, the same challenges imposed by the neo-liberal model are present everywhere. Self-regulation by market forces has led to the consequence that labour law focusing on workers' protection has been denounced as an intolerable disturbance of the markets. This makes it necessary to reflect, in particular, on the philosophical foundations of labour law. Recalling the difficulty for early voices from economic science to be heard, who underlined that labour is not a commodity, he reminds us that only in 1944 was there a new focus on human rights with the Philadelphia Declaration. Several contributions to this book insist that "labour is not a commodity." According to Weiss, such a reading would especially imply that one considers human dignity, as it is enshrined in international and regional treaties as well as in the ILO's Decent Work agenda.

The intercultural approach of this book led, at times, to the use of comparative law, with authors evoking legal provisions and court decisions from different countries on similar factual constellations, such as the recurrent questions related to workers of digital platforms. However, some authors limit themselves to the presentation of a country-specific panorama. Their reflections are of utmost importance because they encourage reflections on unique provisions in several legal systems and help us to concentrate on a specific evolution within one legal system. For instance, in Vincenzo Pietrogiovanni's contribution, one finds interesting developments on the concept of sanction in labour law, within the Italian legal system. This does not mean that Pietrogiovanni excludes reflections from other legal systems, though. From a philosophical point of view, he mainly questions the influence that the conception of the law to which one might adhere exercises on this notion in the field of labour law.

The crisis to which we refer was understood in different terms. Although this book started with the incentive of the Covid-19 crisis, only few contributions concentrate solely on this crisis. For Martin Stefko, the Covid-19 crisis was the occasion to reflect on necessary future evolutions in Czech labour law by considering its broader European context. However, crisis is not an unknown phenomenon in labour law. In this regard, experiences from the past, such as the financial crisis of 2008, help us to anticipate the future.

Several authors identify challenges in labour law such as digitalization, which materialised in the form of digital platforms. With this in mind, Jordi Garcia Viña's contribution is to be referenced, as he underlines the difficulties of a legislative approach and quotes contradictory court decisions within different legal systems. A more futuristic, singular text by Mr Damilano & Stürmer refers to artificial intelligence and worries that labour law would not be adapted to the resulting upheaval. Many authors consider globalisation as requiring new adaptations in labour law. Making us aware of the differences in an apparently uniform world, Alfredo Sánchez-Castañeda explains that the emergence of globalised labour relations has provoked a new division of labour on a global scale, the emergence of an unidentifiable or underground economy, and informal workers. Globalisation may also be related to an increasing labour migration, discussed in several contributions. Some authors add the access of certain "minorities" to the labour market as a challenge. In relation to individual labour law, Alexandre Agra Belmonte shows how court decisions can open ways for protection in the most delicate cases. To resume the aforementioned challenges, one might borrow the terms by Leonor Suárez Llanos: "diversity, globalisation and postmodernity."

These and other challenges are mentioned within broader philosophical, sociological and economic reflections on labour law. Before commenting on each of these challenges, one may anticipate reflections on what crisis means to labour law. André Jobim de Azevedo and Vitor Kaiser Jahn discuss the crisis due to Covid within a series of extrajuridical factors that clash with institutes and solutions designed by the traditional dogmatics of labour law. They name these: (i.) the new political, social and economic situation of a post-industrial society; (ii.) the economic crises that have been faced globally in a cyclical way; and (iii.) the Fourth Industrial Revolution and its disruptive technologies. They question whether these factors, along with the Covid-19 pandemic, are not endangering the very sustainability of the labour law system and its protective arrangement in times of crisis.

However, if one goes back to the origins of labour law in the 19th century, one discovers that labour law itself was born out of social unrest that is equivalent to a crisis, as is underlined in Marcel Zernikow's contribution. Before this background, one might add that the characteristic inequality of the contractual relationship made it necessary to adopt protective provisions for the worker. More precisely, it is often observed that labour law emerged as a consequence of industrial revolutions, and nowadays, in the framework of the Fourth Industrial Revolution, it is characterised by the expansion of globalisation and industrialisation. According to Maggi-Germain, other risks associated with industrial activity, or simply with life in society, have emerged due to industrial revolutions, leading to the creation of special regimes of liability.

The reconstitution of the origins of labour law may also influence our approach to new challenges within labour law. In this context, it is quite interesting to discover how authors mobilise philosophy or sociology to reply to universally existing challenges in law. Eduardo von Adamovich suggests not to lose sight of the social significance that norms have to acquire before they are enshrined in ideal reason. It is an unavoidable conclusion to find new forms of collective organisation in social struggles.

Giuseppe Casale presents different branches of jurisprudence that permit a new reading of labour law, that is analytical jurisprudence, normative jurisprudence and critical theories of law. As critical theories of law, he evokes the legal rationality of labour law. This brings him to conclude what labour law systems have in common: a persuasion to comply with the law, seen as necessary to avoid unpleasant consequences, in the sense that compliance is considered just.

Labour law needs to comply with the peculiarities of its object, that is the concept of work. This concept seems to evolve. Suárez Llanos interestingly explores different paths from those established by the simple understanding of work as a mere activity of paid production. She recalls texts, such as those by Bergson, which promote the valorisation of productive work, linking the very dignity of the person to his dimension as a worker, in such a way that *homo faber* is identified with *homo sapiens*. She notably develops reflections on work that allow for the development of expressive and narrative capacities, conceiving of work activities as pleasurable.

These different concepts have been exploited differently by political doctrines. One may also underline that labour law was often associated with democracy. Authors at the beginning of the 20th century, such as Sinzheimer, have already underlined this reading. One author reminds us of Sinzheimer, who considers the democratic workplace as a precondition for labour law in line with human dignity.

This brings us to the question of the main characteristics of labour law. The formula "labour is not a commodity" would have important implications for the recognition of the asymmetric power relationship between the employer and the employee. Weiss quotes Kahn-Freund to underline that the latter would have led to the need to overcome the power inequality by promoting the collectivisation of employees.

Kocher specifies the opposition between the individual and the collective in labour law. Other authors conceive of labour law as an expression of what they call the "socialisation of law." In other words, labour law or social security law would turn its back on the individualist spirit of the French Civil Code of 1804 (*cf.* Maggi-Germain).

Thus, a characteristic feature of labour law is the presence of important collective rights. Nelson Mannrich & Alessandra Barichello Boskovic highlight how trade unions contribute to the achievement and consolidation of social rights, not only because they force public authorities to secure rights, but also because they secure specific guarantees and protections to their leaders through collective labour agreements. This second path has gained even greater relevance in times of economic or social crises.

In this context appears the link between labour law and fundamental rights that help guarantee labour law standards. While describing the difficulties of establishing an effective collective labour law in Poland after 1991, Miroslaw Wlodarczyk reminds us of the importance of the right to freedom of association for an effective trade union law. In their contribution, Monica Uhlerová & Marek Švec insist on the difficult position of trade unions in the Slovak Republic, where they played an important role in the Velvet Revolution of 1989, being part of the social and economic transformation, which also required them to change their organisation and principles. Despite this change, the authors express a certain critique regarding their effective functioning.

That being said, traditional labour law has proven inefficient before these new challenges. In this context, one must add that a sociological reading of labour law underlines the importance of court decisions as a legal source and legal scholars' opinions for the evolution of law itself. From this point of view, one may anticipate different evolutions that are not visible yet in "positive" legislative acts.

Different questions that need to be asked within labour law have been identified throughout the book. The principal one is the scope of labour law (*cf.* Weiss). As has been demonstrated in different contributions, the emergence of the digitalization process blurs the lines between employment and self-employment. This is what Calogero Cammalleri describes by using the metaphor of a fence separating workers from employers who respectively try to push the fence to their side, by either including a personal work relationship in the area of a fully protective labour law (employees' side), or creating more flexible, precarious forms of work. Before the background to the historical foundations of labour law and the interactions with economics, he accuses labour lawyers of having built an epistemic cage which would make it difficult to extend labour law protections nowadays, especially in the context of work through emerging digital platforms.

Recent debates in relation to platform work might be resumed as dealing with reflections on the creation of a specific intermediate category, or on the extension of the scope of labour law to the economically dependent self-employed. Trying to face the challenges resulting from the exclusion of certain workers from the overall benefit of labour law provisions, Weiss suggests a floor of rights that all working people need, independent of their qualification. One could interpret the reflections by the 2019 ILO Commission on the Future of Work in this sense.

Looking closer, labour law shows different "signs of the erosion" (*cf.* Beryl ter Haar), such as the decentralisation of collective bargaining from sectoral level to company level. This is specifically considered as a consequence of the EU measures in response to the financial and economic crisis in 2008. One might learn from negative experiences from the past. Another sign of the erosion, as demonstrated in Polish law, is the end of the "standard" employment contract which is nowadays in competition with several forms of precarious contracts.

One might generalise that labour law does not benefit all workers in the same way. During the recent crisis, this was extremely visible because some workers benefitted from specific protections (e.g. working from home), whereas others were extremely exposed to health and security risks (e.g. frontline workers).

Other labour rights are being challenged by recent technical developments. Namely, the right for humans to strike is diminishing with the emergence of IA. Therefore, Damilano & Stürmer explain the emergence of virtual strikes.

In this context, one has to remind oneself that, in times of crisis, trade unions are even more relevant. However, in recent years, they have experienced a particular crisis of representativeness, which is probably even more visible in developing countries. Therefore, Mannrich & Boskovic are in favour of a reform of the Brazilian trade union system in the light of the effectiveness and the implementation of freedom of association. Other contributions identify similar difficulties concerning collective labour law. Uhlerová and Švec demonstrate what they call "trade union paradoxes" in the Slovak Republic, that is trade unions' failures related to the political, social, societal and economic context, which can be identified as the following: the general decline in trade unionism; the indicated potential stability of collective labour law; the approach by legislators and trade union elites to the quality of legislation in relation to employee representatives.

Considering the erosion of collective labour rights, one might conclude that there is a strong tendency towards loneliness for the worker. Taking the example of telework, Raluca Dimitriu observes that the worker is "going back home," whereas labour law has evolved around the idea that masses of workers work in factories. In this context, specific rights evolve that are characterised by collectivisation and the solidarity of workers as being facilitated by their proximity, and their collective organisation.

This brings us to a broad reflection on whether the goals of labour law are still the same. Weiss responds in the affirmative, admitting however that the reality for which labour law was originally shaped has disappeared.

Does there need to be a paradigm shift? According to Beryl ter Haar, this seems to be inevitable. From people and a planet in service to profits, to profits in service of people and planet, she develops different utopias, settling on Raworth's *Eldorica*, underlining that the planet is a closed system and therefore only provides limited resources, from which one should calculate an equal share. She believes that this idea could be embedded in the 2030 Sustainable Development Goals of the United Nations.

Authors develop different proposals in response to the identified challenges and the fourth part represents a summary. One of these concerns is the concept of a basic income. Would the institution of a basic income be realistic? Several European attempts illustrate interesting paths. Alexander De Becker and Flore Claus found the basic income in several international conventions, examining the different interpretations of the right to work at the moment of the adoption of the Universal Declaration on Human Rights.

They especially explore the Latin American and USSR positions, linking these developments to the evolution of the right to leisure.

Human rights are a key concept in different contributions, interpreted as being a guarantee of essential labour rights. In a globalised world, workers depend on multinational companies that might choose between different legal systems. Human rights also imply due diligence by these companies in favour of workers' protections. In favour of this interpretation, one may quote the Guiding Principles on Business and Human Rights (UNGPs) of 2011. Although Diego Ledesma Iturbide's contribution has already provided an explanation of this new concept, which was conferred in different legal systems (most recently in Germany), it is further developed as one of the major responses to the globalisation of the labour market, in the last part of this book.

CONTRIBUTOR BIOGRAPHIES

Eduardo Henrique Raymundo von Adamovich is Associate Professor in the Faculty of Law at the University of the State of Rio de Janeiro (UERJ) in Brazil. He holds a PhD degree in labour law from the University of São Paulo (USP), which he obtained in 2004. He acts as a judge for the regional labour court of appeal in Rio de Janeiro (*Tribunal Regional do Trabalho da 1ª Região).* He is a member of many Brazilian and foreign institutions dedicated to the study of labour law and the philosophy of law.

Alexandre Agra Belmonte is a judge (*Ministro*) at the Superior Labour Court (*Tribunal Superior do Trabalho*) in Brazil. He holds a PhD degree in the field of *Justiça e Sociedade* and a Master's degree in *Direito das Relações Sociais*. He is a specialist in private law and President of the Brazilian Academy for Labour Law (*Academia Brasileira de Direito do Trabalho*).

Alessandra Barichello Boskovic obtained her Master's and PhD degrees in law from the Pontifical Catholic University of Paraná (PUC-PR) in Brazil. She is a visiting scholar at Fordham University School of Law and a researcher at GETRAB-USP. She is also a member of the Council for Labour Relations of the Trade Association of the State of Paraná (ACP). She has been an invited professor of Labour Law at PUC-PR and *ABDConst*. She is author of several published articles on individual and collective labour rights and a partner lawyer at *Mannrich e Vasconcelos Advogados*.

Calogero Massimo Cammalleri is Associate Professor of Labour and Social Security Law at the University of Palermo (Italy). He is responsible for "The Temilavoro Research Team (TTRT)" and is editor in chief and director of several journals ("temilavoro.it" – internet synopsis of labour law and social security law; "d/SEAS Working Papers"; "AkraJus"). He is director of the monographs series "dif:end". He also acts as a barrister and a judge in the Tax Court of Appeal of Lombardy. He is director of the attorneys at the Law School of Agrigento. He is author of the monograph, *L'inefficacia del licenziamento tutela obbligatoria e diritto comune* and recently edited *Le dimensioni del lavoro al tempo del Jobs Act (dialoghi interdisciplinari)*.

Giuseppe Casale is Deputy Director of the International Training Centre of the International Labour Organisation in Turin (Italy). He is Director of the Turin School of Development and Secretary General of the International Society for Labour and Social Security Law (Geneva). He is Professor of International and Comparative Labour Law at the University of Turin and the Cà Foscari University of Venice. His recent publications are *Reflections on Labour Law at the Time of Covid-19 Crisis – Reflexiones sobre el Derecho del Trabajo en la Epoca de la Crisis de Covid-19* (with G. Arrigo, M. Fasani, H. Villasmil Prieto), Giappichelli, Turin, 2021 and *The Fundamentals of International Labour Law*, 2nd ed., Giappichelli, Turin, 2020.

Flore Claus is an academic assistant in labour law at Ghent University. She obtained her Master's degree in law *magna cum laude* at Ghent University in 2020. Her Master's thesis on the topic of lifelong learning (with a specific view on labour law) received the Award for Best Thesis from the Labour Court of Ghent in 2020. Her academic abilities were underlined in 2021 when she spoke at the global conference of the Labour Law Research Network (LLRN) in Warsaw on the topic *"Utopias: a right to laziness."* She is also a member of the Lab for International and Interdisciplinary Social Affairs (LIISA).

Cláudio Teixeira Damilano is preparing a Master of Law at PUCRS, concentrating on the constitutional foundations of public and private law (CAPES Fellowship). He obtained postgraduate degrees in law and economics from UFRGS, and labour law and labour process from CETRA-CESUSC. He is a lawyer and researcher for the Research Centre CNPQ/PUCRS *Relações de Trabalho e Sindicalismo* (Labour Relations and Unions), coordinated by Prof. Gilberto Stürmer, and *Novas Tecnologias, Processo, e Relações de Trabalho* (New Technology, Process and Labor Relations), coordinated by Prof. Denise Fincato.

Alexander De Becker is Professor of Labour Law at Ghent University and a leading expert in the field of labour law and industrial relations. From 2000 to 2006, he worked as a researcher (with an FWO-grant) and lecturer in labour and public law at the law faculty of *Vrije Universiteit Brussel*. In 2006, he defended his PhD thesis on the "Legal Foundations of the Status of Officials" at the *Vrije Universiteit Brussel*. Between 2008 and 2015 he was visiting researcher at various prestigious universities, including the universities of Copenhagen, Stockholm, Reading, Oxford, Wisconsin-Madison, Florence, the EUI and Turin. Between 2010 and 2017 he held the Chair of "The State as Employer" at the universities of Amsterdam (2010-

2015) and Leiden (2015-2017). Currently, he is the president of the Belgian Society for Labour and Social Security Law and a member of the advisory board of the global Labour Law Research Network (LLRN). He is also the co-founder of the Lab for International and Interdisciplinary Social Affairs (LIISA).

Raluca Dimitriu is Professor in the Faculty of Law at the Bucharest University of Economic Studies, Romania. She published over 100 studies and books in Romania, Austria, France, Belgium, Germany, Portugal and Great Britain. As a member of the European Labour Law Network, she is in charge of national reports on specific areas of labour law and participates in the "Restatement of Labour Law" project, published annually by Hart Publishing. She is also a member of the Central/Eastern European Labour Experts Network and, as an ILO expert, she provides advice on the development of labour legislation in several countries in the region. Furthermore, she is a Eurofound expert, a member of the Scientific Committee of the Legal Research Institute of the Romanian Academy and a board member of the Society of Labour Law and Social Security Law. In the framework of the Academy of European Law (ERA) in Trier, she participates in gender equality events.

Jordi García Viña has been Professor of Labour and Social Security Law at the University of Barcelona (Spain) since 2011. He is the author of several scientific papers in reviews and books as well as in Spanish, European and Latin American journals. He is principal researcher and researcher on several research projects and visiting professor at a number of European and Latin American universities.

Beryl ter Haar is Professor and Director of the Centre for International and European Labour Law Studies (CIELLS) at the University of Warsaw (Poland) and Endowed Professor of European and Comparative Labour Law at the University of Groningen (The Netherlands). She is co-initiator of the Hugo Sinzheimer Moot Court Competition on European and international labour law. Her research is published in many national and international journals. Among her main publications are the *Research Handbook on Labour, Business and Human Rights Law* (Edward Elgar, 2019, co-edited with Prof. Janice Bellace) and the book *EU Collective Labour Law* (part of Edward Elgar's Studies in Labour Law, forthcoming 2021, co-edited with Prof. Attila Kun).

André Jobim de Azevedo is a member of the Brazilian Academy of Labour Law (ABDT) and the *Sul-Rio-Grandense* Academy of Labour Law (ASRDT). He is Adjunct Professor of Law at Pontifical Catholic University of Rio Grande do Sul (PUCRS) in Brazil. He holds a degree in law from the Federal University of Rio Grande do Sul (UFRGS) and a Master's degree in legal and social sciences from the Pontifical Catholic University of Rio Grande do Sul (PUCRS). He is a partner lawyer at Faraco de Azevedo Advogados.

Vitor Kaiser Jahn holds a degree in law from Pontifical Catholic University of Rio Grande do Sul (PUCRS) in Brazil. He obtained a Master's degree in labour law from the Federal University of Rio Grande do Sul (UFRGS). He is also a partner lawyer at Simon, Nadal & Jahn Advocacia.

Eva Kocher is Professor of Civil and Labour Law in the Faculty of Law at the European University Viadrina in Frankfurt (Oder), Germany. She is the director of the Centre for Interdisciplinary Labour Law Research (C*LLaS). Her research focuses on questions of equality, transnational labour law and digitalization. She coedited *Selbstständige Unselbstständigkeit. Crowdworking zwischen Autonomie und Kontrolle* (Nomos 2019). Her most recent publications include "Die Position der Dritten. Objektivität im bürgerlichen Recht," in *Jahrbuch des öffentlichen Rechts der Gegenwart* (2019), and "Arbeit, Kollektivautonomie und Solidarität," in *Autonomie im Recht – Geschlechtertheoretisch vermessen* (Nomos 2018).

Diego Ledesma Iturbide is a Lecturer in the Faculty of Economic Sciences at the University of Buenos Aires, Argentina. He graduated as a Lawyer from the Faculty of Law of the University of Buenos Aires, holds a Master's degree from the University of Palermo, Argentina, and eventually specialised in Labour Law and Social Security Law from Pontifical Catholic University of Argentina.

Nicole Maggi-Germain is a specialist in labour law and Associate Professor and Research Supervisor in Social Law at the University Paris I Panthéon-Sorbonne (France). Between 2018 and 2020 she was part of the Harvard International Advisory Group in charge of providing expertise on the project "*Rebalancing Economic and Political Power: A Clean Slate for the Future of Labor Law*" (https://lwp.law.harvard.edu/clean-slate-international-advisory-group), part of the "Labor and Worklife Program" at Harvard Law School, USA. She is a researcher at the laboratory *Droit et changement social* (http://www.droit.univ-nantes.fr/labos/dcs/) and a member of the Maison des Sciences de l'Homme Ange Guépin, Nantes (http://www.msh.univ-nantes.fr/). Her main fields of research cover vocational training, labour relationships in the public sector and health at work. She is currently working on the legal and anthropological issues surrounding robotics and artificial intelligence. She directed an international scientific book for the centenary of the ILO (*L'impact des normes de l'O.I.T. sur la scène internationale*, Acte du colloque pour le Centenaire de l'Organisation internationale du Travail, Univ. Paris 1 (ISST et IREDIES) 23/24 sept. 2019, éd. Mare & Martin, p. 328).

Nelson Mannrich obtained his Master's and PhD degrees and a postdoctoral researcher award from the University of São Paulo (USP). He is Professor of Labour Law at USP Law School. At USP, he is also coordinator of the research group, GETRAB. He is a member of the Brazilian Academy of Labour Law (chair no. 49) and a member of the Superior Council for Labour Relations of the Federation of Industries of the State of São Paulo (FIESP). He is an invited professor of labour law at PUC-RS and the author of several published articles and books on individual and collective labour rights. He is a named partner at *Mannrich e Vasconcelos Advogados*.

Vincenzo Pietrogiovanni is Associate Professor of Labour Law at the Business Law Department, School of Economic and Management, Lund University (Sweden). He holds a PhD in labour law from the University of Bari (2013), Italy. He was a postdoctoral researcher at Lund University for a project on youth unemployment in Europe. He then served as Senior Lecturer in Labour Law at Lund University and Linnaeus University. He also worked as Adjunct Professor of Industrial Relations at the University of Bologna. He regularly serves as *Professeur Invité* in international labour law at the Université Paris-Nanterre. He has managed a research project on democracy in the workplace and is currently the coordinator of the research unit at Lund University within the Horizon2020 project "WorkYP: Working Yet Poor." He is the co-coordinator of the ARROW Research Group at Aarhus University, where he worked as a postdoctoral fellow. He sits on the organising committees of the Nordic Network of Labour Law Scholars (NNLLS) and the Moving Labour Collective (MLC).

Alfredo Sánchez-Castañeda holds a PhD in labour and social security law from the *Université de Paris 2 Pantheon-Assas* (France). He is a professor and researcher in the Faculty of Law and the Institute of Legal Research at the National Autonomous University of Mexico. He also acts as an external consultant of the ILO for Mexico, Central America and the Caribbean, conducting studies on requested topics, delivering courses in Central

America and the Caribbean, and giving lectures. His principal publications are: *Youth Unemployment and Joblessness: Causes, Consequences, Responses* (editor), Cambridge Scholars Publishing, UK, 2012; *El subappalto: un fenomeno globale. Il caso messicano nel confronto internazionale e comparato*, ADAPT University Press, Italia, 2013; *International Encyclopaedia for Labour Law and Industrial Relations*, Mexico, Kluwer, 2016; "La conciliación laboral en México: Entre nuevas buenas intenciones y viejos errores" in Alternative Labour Dispute Resolutions. A Collection of Comparative Studies (Pio Fuiano, Mario y Olivieri, Antonello, Coordinadores), Cacucci Editore, Bari Italia, 2020, pp. 421-452; Industry 4.0. Labor and Social Security, UNAM, México, 2021; El marco jurídico del trabajo en América Latina (editor), Tirant lo Blanch, Chile, 2021, p. 328.

Martin Štefko is Associate Professor at the Charles University Faculty of Law (Czech Republic) and a correspondent for the Max Planck Institute for Social Policy and Social Security Law in Munich (Germany). In 2009 he was an invited professor at NOVA South Eastern University in Ft. Lauderdale, USA; and at the Catholic University in Leuven, Belgium, in 2016. He holds a degree in law (2003) and a PhD (2005), both from Charles University. He was granted tenure and appointed as an associate professor in the Faculty of Law at Charles University in 2014. He also conducted research in international labour law at the European Research and Studies Centre at the Karol Adamiecki University of Economics in Katowice and has published more than eight books and 300 peer-reviewed articles. He is working as a managing partner of the bestselling legal commentary in the Czech Republic (The Commentary on Labour Code). He edited a book on the divergence of labour law and social security law, for the Faculty of Law, Charles University (Prague) in 2016.

Gilberto Stürmer holds a post-doctoral degree in law from the University of Sevilla (Spain) and a doctoral degree in law from the Universidade Federal de Santa Catarina (UFSC). He is a professor at the Pontifícia Universidade Católica do Rio Grande do Sul and coordinator of the postgraduate degree program in labour law at the Pontifícia Universidade Católica do Rio Grande do Sul. He is also a lawyer and legal advisor.

Leonor Suárez Llanos is Professor of Philosophy of Law and a researcher and lecturer. She has written several monographs, the last one being *El Posmodernismo Jurídico y la Filosofía del Derecho* (Tirant lo Blanch), in which she examines an approach to the theory of the knowledge, creation and application of law. She has also published dozens of articles and book chapters on many different issues within the philosophy of law and bioethics. Currently her research is in the fields of the philosophy of labour law and the philosophy of environmental law. She is also the academic director of the official Master's degree in the legal protection of persons and vulnerable groups, a subject in which she is very active in terms of research and dissemination.

Marek Švec is an associate professor in the Faculty of Law at Matej Bel University in *Banská Bystrica*, and the general secretary and a member of the presidency of the Labour Law Association in Slovakia. He is member of preparatory and expert groups for the preparation of legislative changes in the area of labour law (e.g. Labour Code) and the secretary of the Scientific Council of Wolters Kluwer Publishing for labour law, social security, and personnel management. Since 2012, he has been Vice-President of the advisory Commission of the Secretary of Labour and a member of the tripartite commission for the amendment drafting to the Collective Bargaining Act. He is also listed by the Ministry of Labour, Social Affairs and Family as a mediator and adjudicator for collective bargaining 2019 and 2021. He is the main author of the most extensive commentary on the labour code in the Czech and Slovak Republics.

Monika Uhlerová graduated in political science from the Faculty of Political Sciences and International Relations at Matej Bel University in *Banská Bystrica* (Slovakia). She completed her doctoral studies in the theory of politics at the Department of Political Science in the Faculty of Philosophy at Comenius University in Bratislava (Slovakia). In her research and publication activities she has focused on issues of interest and pressure groups with an emphasis on the trade union movement, social policy, the labour market and social dialogue. She is the author of the monograph Trade Unions in Slovakia after 1989 in the Context of Social Partnership. Until 2018, she was affiliated as an assistant professor in the Faculty of Political Sciences and International Relations at Matej Bel University. She is currently Vice-President of the Confederation of Trade Unions of the Slovak Republic and Vice-Chairwoman of the Economic and Social Council of the Slovak Republic.

Manfred Weiss is Professor in Labour Law and Civil Law at Goethe University in Frankfurt and has been emeritus since 2008. He is visiting professor in many universities all over the world. He was President of ILERA (2000-2003) and Deputy President of the German Lawyers' Association (DJT) (1998-2002). For many years, he served as a consultant to the ILO 1980 and to the European Commission. He received the Bob Hepple Award from the Labour Law Research Network (LLRN) for lifetime achievement (2015) and is also a fellow of the World Academy of Art and Science (WAAS).

Miroslaw Wlodarczyk is a professor and the head of the Department of Labour Law at the University of Łódź (Poland). He is supervising various PhD studies in the Faculty of Law and Administration. He has written more than 100 scientific publications related to the sources of labour law, the subjects and the content of the employment relationship, the employment of young people and children, and the regulation of the labour market.

Marcel Zernikow holds a PhD in law from *Université Paris I Panthéon Sorbonne* (France), specialising in the field of private international law of employment. After concluding his PhD in 2019, he completed a post-doctoral research stay at the University of the State of Rio de Janeiro (UERJ) in Brazil, where he also became a visiting lecturer (*professor visitante*). He is currently lecturing on different topics within the field of private law at the *Université Bretagne Sud*, is a research associate at the *Institut de recherches juridiques de la Sorbonne* (*IRJS*), and is a member of numerous research associations. His principal research activities and publications in the field of labour law include international labour relations, comparative law and interdisciplinary reflections.